ADVANCE PRAISE FOR
THE AMERICAN STORY

"Of all the American History survey texts I have read, this one is the best."

—Charles A. Pilant, Cumberland College

"This text balances the social, political, and economic aspects as well as any text I have read."

—Cherry L. Spruill, Indiana University–Purdue University at Indianapolis

"The writing throughout the text is clear and engaging. Indeed the prose and style are great strengths of the book."

—Kenneth E. Hendrickson, Sam Houston State University

"I do share the goal of a balanced presentation and think that the authors do a good job here. I particularly rely on the text for detailed descriptions of economic issues and cultural history."

—Juli A. Jones, St. Charles County Community College

"The writing is extremely clear and direct, easy to follow."

—William G. Morris, Midland College

"I like the strong, clear writing as well as its attractive appearance and integrated presentation."

—Bruce J. Dierenfield, Canisius College

"The scholarship of the text is both current and varied."

—H. Michael Tarver, McNeese State University

"The writing is the strength of this text. It is the clearest written text available with topic sentences virtually outlining the chapters for students."

—Dr. Peter Murray, Methodist College

ABOUT
THE AUTHORS

ROBERT A. DIVINE

Robert A. Divine, George W. Littlefield Professor Emeritus in American History at the University of Texas at Austin, received his Ph.D. from Yale University in 1954. A specialist in American diplomatic history, he taught from 1954 to 1996 at the University of Texas, where he was honored by both the Student Association and the Graduate School for teaching excellence. His extensive published work includes *The Illusion of Neutrality* (1962); *Second Chance: The Triumphs of Internationalism in America During World War II* (1967); and

Blowing on the Wind (1978). His most recent work is *Perpetual War for Perpetual Peace* (2000), a comparative analysis of twentieth-century American wars. He is also the author of *Eisenhower and the Cold War* (1981) and editor of three volumes of essays on the presidency of Lyndon Johnson. His book, *The Sputnik Challenge* (1992), won the Eugene E. Emme Astronautical Literature Award for 1993. He has been a fellow at the Center for Advanced Study in the Behavioral Sciences and has given the Albert Shaw Lectures in Diplomatic History at Johns Hopkins University.

T. H. BREEN

T. H. Breen, William Smith Mason Professor of American History at Northwestern University, received his Ph.D. from Yale University in 1968. He has taught at Northwestern since 1970. Breen's major books include *The Character of the Good Ruler: A Study of Puritan Political Ideas in New England* (1974); *Puritans and Adventurers: Change and Persistence in Early America* (1980); *Tobacco Culture: The Mentality of the Great Tidewater Planters on the Eve of Revolution* (1985); and, with Stephen Innes of the University of

Virginia, *"Myne Owne Ground": Race and Freedom on Virginia's Eastern Shore* (1980). His *Imagining the Past* (1989) won the 1990 Historic Preservation Book Award. In addition to receiving an award for outstanding teaching at Northwestern, Breen has been the recipient of research grants from the American Council of Learned Societies, the Guggenheim Foundation, the Institute for Advanced Study (Princeton), the National Humanities Center, and the Huntington Library. For his article "Narrative of Commercial Life: Consumption, Ideology, and Community on the Eve of the American Revolution," which appeared in the July 1993 issue of *William and Mary Quarterly*, Breen received an award for best article published in the quarterly in 1993, and the Douglass Adair Memorial

Prize for best article published in the quarterly during the 1988–1993 period. He has served as the Fowler Hamilton Fellow at Christ Church, Oxford University (1987–1988), the Pitt Professor of American History and Institutions, Cambridge University (1990–1991), and the Harmsworth Professor of American History at Oxford University (2000–2001).

GEORGE M. FREDRICKSON

George M. Fredrickson is Edgar E. Robinson Professor of United States History at Stanford University. He is the author or editor of several books, including *The Inner Civil War* (1965), *The Black Image in the White Mind* (1971), and *White Supremacy: A Comparative Study in American and South African History* (1981), which won both the Ralph Waldo Emerson Award from Phi Beta Kappa and the Merle Curti Award from the Organization of American Historians. His most recent books are *Black Liberation: A Comparative History of Black*
Ideologies in the United States and South Africa (1995) and *The Comparative Imagination: Racism, Nationalism, and Social Movements* (1997). He received his A.B. and Ph.D. degrees from Harvard and has been the recipient of a Guggenheim Fellowship, two National Endowment for the Humanities Senior Fellowships, and a Fellowship from the Center for Advanced Studies in the Behavioral Sciences. Before coming to Stanford in 1984, he taught at Northwestern. He has also served as Fulbright lecturer in American History at Moscow University and as the Harmsworth Professor of American History at Oxford. He served as president of the Organization of American Historians in 1997–1998. In 2000 he delivered the University Lectures at Princeton University on the subject of racism in world history.

R. HAL WILLIAMS

R. Hal Williams is Professor of History at Southern Methodist University. He received his A.B. degree from Princeton University (1963) and his Ph.D. degree from Yale University (1968). His books include *The Democratic Party and California Politics, 1880–1896* (1973); *Years of Decision: American Politics in the 1890s* (1978); and *The Manhattan Project: A Documentary Introduction to the Atomic Age* (1990). A specialist in American political history, he taught at Yale University from 1968 to 1975 and came to SMU in 1975 as
chair of the Department of History. From 1980 to 1988, he served as dean of Dedman College, the school of humanities and sciences, at SMU. In 1980, he was a visiting professor at University College, Oxford University. Williams has received grants from the American Philosophical Society and the National Endowment for the Humanities, and he has served on the Texas Committee for the Humanities. He is currently working on a biography of James G. Blaine, the late-nineteenth-century speaker of the House, secretary of state, and Republican presidential candidate.

THE AMERICAN STORY

Penguin Academics

THE AMERICAN STORY

VOLUME TWO: SINCE 1865

ROBERT A. DIVINE
University of Texas

T. H. BREEN
Northwestern University

GEORGE M. FREDRICKSON
Stanford University

R. HAL WILLIAMS
Southern Methodist University

New York   San Francisco   Boston
London   Toronto   Sydney   Tokyo   Singapore   Madrid
Mexico City   Munich   Paris   Cape Town   Hong Kong   Montreal

Vice President and Publisher:	Priscilla McGeehon
Senior Acquisitions Editor:	Jay O'Callaghan
Development Manager:	Betty Slack
Executive Marketing Manager:	Sue Westmoreland
Production Manager:	Donna DeBenedictis
Project Coordination and Electronic Page Makeup:	Elm Street Publishing Services, Inc.
Senior Cover Designer/Manager:	Nancy Danahy
Cover Image:	*Street Carnival* (1948) by Everett Shinn (1876–1953). A. J. Kollar Fine Paintings, Seattle, Washington.
Art Studios:	Maps.com and Burmar Technical Corporation
Photo Researcher:	Photosearch, Inc.
Manufacturing Buyer:	Al Dorsey
Printer and Binder:	Quebecor World/Taunton
Cover Printer:	Phoenix Color Corp.

For permission to use copyrighted material, grateful acknowledgment is made to the copyright holders on pp. C1 – C3, which are hereby made part of this copyright page.

Library of Congress Cataloging-in-Publication Data

The American story / Robert A. Divine ... [et al.].
    p. cm. — (Penguin academics)
  Includes bibliographical reference and index.
  ISBN 0-321-09188-4—ISBN 0-321-09187-6 (P-copy)
  1. United States—History. I. Divine, Robert A. II. Series.

E178.A5545 2002
973—dc21

                                                                    2001041710

Please visit our website at http://www.ablongman.com/divine

For more information about the Penguin Academics series, please contact us by mail at Longman Publishers, attn. Marketing Department, 1185 Avenue of the Americas, 25th Floor, New York, NY 10036, or by e-mail at www.ablongman.com/feedback

ISBN 0-321-09188-4 (Complete Edition)
ISBN 0-321-09196-5 (Volume One)
ISBN 0-321-09189-2 (Volume Two)

1 2 3 4 5 6 7 8 9 10—RNT—04 03 02 01

BRIEF CONTENTS

DETAILED CONTENTS

MAPS

FIGURES

TABLES

PREFACE

For many decades the traditional narratives that framed the story of the United States assumed a unified society in which men and women of various races and backgrounds shared a common culture. In recent years, however, a good many historians have come to believe that traditional narratives stressing the rise of democracy or the advance of free enterprise undervalue the complexity and diversity of the American story. This research makes it hard to sustain a perspective that presumes the inevitability of progress for all men and women and that allows one dominant group to speak for so many others who have struggled over the centuries to make themselves heard. Nevertheless, an awareness that the past is as much about controversy as agreement, as much concerned with diversity as with unity, does not preclude the possibility of a coherent narrative. To create such a narrative while still paying attention to the differences of race and class, ethnicity, and gender is the goal.

The authors of this volume accept the challenge, believing strongly that it is possible to craft a coherent story without silencing difference. We start with the conviction that to tell this story it is essential to listen closely to what people in the past have had to say about their own aspirations, frustrations, and passions. After all, they were the ones who had to figure out how to live with other Americans, many of them totally unsympathetic, even hostile to the demands of others who happened to march to different drummers. Readers of this book will encounter many of these individuals and discover how, in their own terms, they tried to make sense of everyday events connected to family and work, church and community.

We have done our best to avoid the tendency to lump individuals arbitrarily together in groups. It is true, for example, that many early colonists in America were called Puritans, and presumably in their private lives they reflected a bundle of religious values and beliefs known as Puritanism. But we must not conclude that an abstraction—in this case Puritanism—made history. To do so misses the complexity and diversity masked by the abstraction, for at the end of the day, what for the sake of convenience we term Puritanism was in fact a rich, spirited, often truculent conversation among men and women who disagreed to the point of violence on many details of the theology they allegedly shared. The same observation could be made about other movements in American history—unions or civil rights, political parties or antebellum reform, for example. A narrative that sacrifices the rough edges of dissent in the interest of getting on with the story may propel the reader smoothly through the centuries, but a subtler, more complex tale is more honest about how people in the past actually made events.

Even as we stress the significance of human agency, we resist transforming the long history of the peoples of the United States into a form of highbrow antiquarianism. The men and women who appear in this book lived for the most part in small communities. Even in the large cities that drew so many migrants after the Industrial Revolution, individuals defined their daily routines around family, friends, and neighborhoods. But it would be misleading to conclude that these people were effectively cut off from a larger world. However strong and vibrant their local cultures may have been, their social identities were also the product of the experience of accommodation and resistance to external forces, many of them beyond their own control. Industrialization changed the nature of life in the small communities. So too did nationalism, imperialism, global capitalism, and world war. In our accounts of such diverse events as the American Revolution, the Civil War, the New Deal, and the Cold War, we seek the drama of history in the efforts of ordinary people to make sense of the demands imposed upon them by economic and social change.

It was during these confrontations—moments of unexpected opportunity and frightening vulnerability—that ordinary Americans came to understand better those processes of justice and oppression, national security, and distribution of natural resources that we call politics. The outcome of international wars, the policies legislated by Congress, and the decisions handed down by the Supreme Court must be included in a proper narrative history of the peoples of the United States since these occurrences sparked fresh controversies. They were the stuff of expectations as well as disappointments. What one group interpreted as progress, another almost always viewed as a curtailment of rights. For some the conquest of the West, a process that went on for several centuries, opened the door to prosperity; for others it brought degradation and removal. The point is not to turn the history of the United States into a chronicle of broken dreams. Rather, we seek to reconstruct the tensions behind events, demonstrating as best we can why good history can never be written entirely from the perspective of the winners.

From the start of the project, we recognized the risk of treating minorities and women as a kind of afterthought, as if their contributions to the defining events of American history were postscripts, to be taken up only after the reader had learned of important battles and transforming elections. Our treatment of the American Revolution is one example of our balanced and integrated approach to telling the story of the past. Women were not spectators during the war for independence. They understood the language of rights and equality, and while they could not vote for representatives in the colonial assemblies, they made known in other ways their protests against British taxation. They formed the backbone of the boycotts that helped mobilize popular opinion during the prelude to armed confrontation. And they made it clear that they expected liberation from the legal and economic constraints that consigned them to second-class citizenship in the new republic. Their aspirations were woven into every aspect of the American Revolution, and although they were surely disappointed with the male response to their appeals, they deserve—and here receive—attention not as marginal participants in shaping events but as central figures in an ongoing conversation about gender and power in a liberal society.

The story of how African Americans organized after World War II to demand that the nation live up to the promise of the Declaration of Independence offers yet another example of this book's integrated approach. Our account of the civil rights struggle ranges from the eloquent leadership of Martin Luther King, Jr., to the key roles played by unheralded blacks in the ranks at Selma and Birmingham. These brave men, women, and children suffered the blows of local sheriffs and the indignity of being swept off the streets by fire hoses, yet their travails ultimately persuaded white America to enact the landmark civil rights laws of the 1960s. The United States has yet to accord African Americans full equality, but the strides taken after World War II constitute a major step toward racial justice. Similarly, the stories of other grand events integrate the hopes and fears of other groups—Native Americans, new immigrants from Third World nations—into what philosopher Horace Kallen once described as "a multiplicity in a unity, an orchestration of mankind."

An overriding goal in our crafting of this narrative has been to produce a volume that would be enjoyable to read. Striving for this goal, we have sought to avoid the clumsy jargon that can be so irksome to the reader who—like us—believes that good history involves well-told stories. The structure and features of the book are intended to stimulate student interest and reinforce learning. Chapters begin with vignettes or incidents that introduce the specific chapter themes that drive the narrative and preview the topics to be discussed. Our interpretation of the central events of American history is based on the best scholarship of the past as well as the most recent historiography.

Although this book is a joint effort, each author took primary responsibility for a set of chapters. T. H. Breen contributed the first eight chapters, which deal with the long period from the first Indian migrations from Asia some 20,000 years ago to the War of 1812. George M. Fredrickson wrote Chapters 9 through

16, carrying the narrative through the Civil War and Reconstruction. R. Hal Williams was responsible for Chapters 17 through 24, focusing on the industrial transformation and urbanization of the late nineteenth century as well as on the events leading up to America's entry into World War I. Robert A. Divine wrote Chapters 25 through 33, bringing the story through the Great Depression, World War II, and the Cold War, and ending with the most recent national elections. Each author reviewed and revised the work of his colleagues and helped shape the story into its final form.

The Authors

THE AMERICAN STORY

16

THE AGONY OF RECONSTRUCTION

During the Reconstruction period immediately following the Civil War, African Americans struggled to become equal citizens of a democratic republic. They produced a number of remarkable leaders who showed that blacks were as capable as other Americans of voting, holding office, and legislating for a complex and rapidly changing society. Among these leaders was Robert Smalls of South Carolina. Although virtually forgotten by the time of his death in 1915, Smalls was perhaps the most famous and widely respected southern black leader of the Civil War and Reconstruction era. His career reveals some of the main features of the African American experience during that crucial period.

Born a slave in 1839, Smalls had a white father whose identity has never been clearly established. But his white ancestry apparently gained him some advantages, and as a young man he was allowed to live and work independently, hiring his own time from a master who may have been his half brother. Smalls worked as a sailor and trained himself to be a pilot in Charleston Harbor. When the Union navy blockaded Charleston in 1862, Smalls, who was then working on a Confederate steamship called the *Planter,* saw a chance to win his freedom. At three o'clock in the morning on May 13, 1862, when the white officers of the *Planter* were ashore, he took command of the vessel and its slave crew, sailed it out of the heavily fortified harbor, and surrendered it to the Union navy. The *Planter* was turned into a Union army transport, and Smalls was made its captain after being commissioned as an officer. During the remainder of the war, he served as captain and pilot of Union vessels off the coast of South Carolina.

Like a number of other African Americans who had fought valiantly for the Union, Smalls went on to a distinguished political career during Reconstruction, serving in the South Carolina constitutional convention, in the state legislature, and for several terms in the U.S. Congress. He was also a shrewd businessman and became the owner of extensive properties in Beaufort, South Carolina, and its vicinity. The electoral organization that he established was so effective that Smalls was able to control local government and get himself elected to Congress even after the election of 1876 had placed the state under the control of white conservatives bent on depriving blacks of political

With the help of several black crewmen, Robert Smalls—then twenty-three years old—commandeered the Planter, *a Confederate steamship used to transport guns and ammunition, and surrendered it to the Union vessel, U. S. S.* Onward. *Smalls provided distinguished service to the Union during the Civil War and after the war went on to become a successful politician and businessman.*

power. Organized mob violence defeated him in 1878, but he bounced back to win by decision of Congress a contested congressional election in 1880. He did not leave the House of Representatives for good until 1886, when he lost another contested election that had to be decided by Congress.

In their efforts to defeat him, Smalls's white opponents frequently charged that he had a hand in the corruption that was allegedly rampant in South Carolina during Reconstruction. But careful historical investigation shows that he was, by the standards of the time, an honest and responsible public servant. In the South Carolina convention of 1868 and later in the state legislature, he was a conspicuous champion of free and compulsory public education. In Congress, he fought for the enactment and enforcement of federal civil rights laws. Like other middle-class black political leaders in Reconstruction-era South Carolina, he can perhaps be faulted in hindsight for not doing more to help poor blacks gain access to land of their own. But in 1875, he sponsored congressional legislation that opened for purchase at low prices the land in his own district that had been confiscated by the federal government during the war. As a result, blacks were able to buy most of it, and they soon owned three-fourths of the land in Beaufort and its vicinity.

Smalls spent the later years of his life as U.S. collector of customs for the port of Beaufort, a beneficiary of the patronage that the Republican party continued to provide for a few loyal southern blacks. But the loss of real political clout for Smalls and men like him was one of the tragic consequences of the fall of Reconstruction.

THE PRESIDENT VERSUS CONGRESS

The problem of how to reconstruct the Union in the wake of the South's military defeat was one of the most difficult and perplexing challenges American policymakers ever faced. The Constitution provided no firm guidelines, for the framers had not anticipated a division of the country into warring sections. Emancipation compounded the problem with a new issue: how far should the federal government go to secure freedom and civil rights for four million former slaves?

The debate that evolved led to a major political crisis. Advocates of a minimal Reconstruction policy favored quick restoration of the Union with no protection for the freed slaves beyond the prohibition of slavery. Proponents of a more radical policy wanted readmission of the southern states to be dependent on guarantees that "loyal" men would displace the Confederate elite in positions of power and that blacks would acquire basic rights of American citizenship. The White House favored the minimal approach, whereas Congress came to endorse the more radical and thoroughgoing form of Reconstruction. The resulting struggle between Congress and the chief executive was the most serious clash between two branches of government in the nation's history.

WARTIME RECONSTRUCTION

Tension between the president and Congress over how to reconstruct the Union began during the war. Occupied mainly with achieving victory, Lincoln never set forth a final and comprehensive plan for bringing rebellious states back into the fold. But he did take initiatives that indicated he favored a lenient and conciliatory policy toward Southerners who would give up the struggle and repudiate slavery. In December 1863, he issued a proclamation offering a full pardon to all Southerners (with the exception of certain classes of Confederate leaders) who would take an oath of allegiance to the Union and acknowledge the legality of emancipation. Once 10 percent or more of the voting population of any occupied state had taken the oath, they were authorized to set up a loyal government.

Efforts to establish such regimes were quickly undertaken in states that were wholly or partially occupied by Union troops; by 1864, Louisiana and Arkansas had fully functioning Unionist governments.

Lincoln's policy was meant to shorten the war. The president hoped that granting pardons and political recognition to oath-taking minorities would weaken the southern cause by making it easy for disillusioned or lukewarm Confederates to switch sides. He also hoped to strengthen his emancipation policy by insisting that the new governments abolish slavery, an action that might prove crucial if the courts or a future Democratic administration were to disallow or revoke the Emancipation Proclamation. When constitutional conventions operating under the 10 percent plan in Louisiana and Arkansas dutifully abolished slavery in 1864, emancipation came closer to being irreversible.

Displeased with the president's Reconstruction experiments, Congress in 1864 refused to seat the Unionists elected to the House and Senate from Louisiana and Arkansas. A minority of congressional Republicans—the strongly antislavery Radicals—favored protection for black rights and provision for black male enfranchisement as preconditions for the readmission of southern states. But a larger moderate group in Congress also opposed Lincoln's plan, not because they favored civil and political equality for blacks, but because they did not trust the repentant Confederates who would play a major role in the new governments.

Congress also believed the president was exceeding his authority by using executive powers to restore the Union. Lincoln operated on the theory that secession, being illegal, did not place the Confederate states outside the Union in a constitutional sense. Since individuals and not states had defied federal authority, the president could use his pardoning power to certify a loyal electorate, which could then function as the legitimate state government. The dominant view in Congress, on the other hand, was that the southern states had forfeited their place in the Union and that it was up to Congress to decide when and how they would be readmitted.

After refusing to recognize Lincoln's 10 percent governments, Congress passed a Reconstruction bill of its own in July 1864. Known as the Wade-Davis Bill, this legislation required that 50 percent of the voters take an oath of future loyalty before the restoration process could begin. Once this had occurred, those who could swear they had never willingly supported the Confederacy could vote in an election for delegates to a constitutional convention. Lincoln exercised a pocket veto by refusing to sign the bill before Congress adjourned. He justified his action by announcing that he did not want to be committed to any single Reconstruction plan. The sponsors of the bill responded with an angry manifesto, and Lincoln's relations with Congress reached their low.

Congress and the president remained stalemated on the Reconstruction issue for the rest of the war. During his last months in office, however, Lincoln showed some willingness to compromise. However, he died without clarifying his intentions, leaving historians to speculate whether his quarrel with Congress would have worsened or been resolved. Given Lincoln's past record of political flexibility, the best bet is that he would have come to terms with the majority of his party.

ANDREW JOHNSON AT THE HELM

Andrew Johnson, the man suddenly made president by an assassin's bullet, attempted to put the Union back together on his own authority in 1865. But his policies eventually set him at odds with Congress and the Republican party and provoked the most serious crisis in the history of relations between the executive and legislative branches of the federal government.

Johnson's background shaped his approach to Reconstruction. Born in dire poverty in North Carolina, he migrated as a young man to eastern Tennessee, where he made his living as a tailor. Lacking formal schooling, he did not learn to read and write until adult life. Entering politics as a Jacksonian Democrat, he became known as an effective stump speaker. His railing against the planter aristocracy made him the spokesman for Tennessee's nonslaveholding whites. He ad-

Nearly insurmountable problems with a Congress determined to enact its own Reconstruction policy plagued Andrew Johnson throughout his presidency. Impeached in 1868, he escaped conviction by a single vote.

vanced from state legislator to congressman to governor and in 1857 was elected to the U.S. Senate.

When Tennessee seceded in 1861, Johnson was the only senator from a Confederate state who remained loyal to the Union and continued to serve in Washington. But his Unionism did not include antislavery sentiments. While campaigning in Tennessee, he had objected only to the fact that slaveholding was the privilege of a wealthy minority. He revealed his attitude when he wished that "every head of family in the United States had one slave to take the drudgery and menial service off his family."

While acting as military governor of Tennessee during the war, Johnson implemented Lincoln's emancipation policy. But he viewed it primarily as a means of destroying the power of the hated planter class rather than as a recognition of black humanity. He was chosen as Lincoln's running mate in 1864 because it was thought that a proadministration Democrat, who was also a southern Unionist, would strengthen the ticket. No one expected that this fervent white supremacist would ever become president

Some Radical Republicans initially welcomed Johnson's ascent to the nation's highest office. Like the Radicals, he was fiercely loyal to the Union and thought that ex-Confederates should be severely treated. More than Lincoln, who had spoken of "malice toward none and charity for all," Johnson seemed likely to punish southern "traitors" and prevent them from regaining political influence. Only gradually did the deep disagreement between the president and the Republican majority in Congress become evident.

The Reconstruction policy that Johnson initiated on May 29, 1865, disturbed some Radicals, but most Republicans were willing to give it a chance. Johnson placed North Carolina and eventually other states under appointed provisional governors chosen mostly from among prominent southern politicians who had opposed the secession movement and had rendered no conspicuous service to the Confederacy. The governors were responsible for calling constitutional conventions and ensuring that only "loyal" whites were permitted to vote for delegates. Confederate leaders and former officeholders who had participated in the rebellion were excluded. To regain their political and property rights, they had to apply for individual presidential pardons. Johnson made one significant addition to the list of the excluded: all those possessing taxable property exceeding $20,000 in value. In this fashion, he sought to prevent his longtime adversaries—the wealthy planters—from participating in the Reconstruction of southern state governments.

Johnson urged the conventions to do three things: declare the ordinances of secession illegal, repudiate the Confederate debt, and ratify the Thirteenth

Amendment abolishing slavery. After governments had been reestablished under constitutions meeting these conditions, the president assumed that the Reconstruction process would be complete and that the ex-Confederate states could regain their full rights under the Constitution.

The conventions accomplished their tasks in a way satisfactory to the president but troubling to many congressional Republicans. Rather than quickly accepting Johnson's recommendations, delegates in several states approved them begrudgingly or with qualifications. Furthermore, all the resulting constitutions limited suffrage to whites, disappointing the large number of Northerners who hoped that at least some African Americans would be given the vote.

Republican uneasiness turned to disillusionment and anger when the state legislatures elected under the new constitutions proceeded to pass "Black Codes" subjecting former slaves to a variety of special regulations and restrictions on their freedom. Vagrancy and apprenticeship laws forced African Americans to work and denied them a free choice of employers. In some states blacks could not testify in court on the same basis as whites and were subject to a separate penal code. To Radicals, the Black Codes looked suspiciously like slavery under a

"Slavery Is Dead?" asks this 1866 cartoon by Thomas Nast. To the cartoonist, the Emancipation Proclamation of 1863 and the North's victory in the Civil War meant little difference to the treatment of the freed slaves in the South. Freed slaves convicted of crimes often endured the same punishments as had slaves—sale, as depicted in the left panel of the cartoon, or beatings, as shown on the right.

new guise. More upsetting to northern public opinion in general, a number of prominent ex-Confederate leaders were elected to Congress in the fall of 1865.

Johnson himself was partly responsible for this turn of events. Despite his lifelong feud with the planter class, he was generous in granting pardons to members of the old elite who came to him, hat in hand, and asked for them. The growing rift between the president and Congress came into the open in December, when the House and Senate refused to seat the recently elected southern delegation. Instead of recognizing the state governments Johnson had called into being, Congress established a joint committee to review Reconstruction policy and set further conditions for readmission of the seceded states.

CONGRESS TAKES THE INITIATIVE

The struggle over how to reconstruct the Union ended with Congress doing the job of setting policy all over again. The clash between Johnson and Congress was a matter of principle and could not be reconciled. Johnson's stubborn and intolerant nature did not help his political cause. But the root of the problem was that he disagreed with the majority of Congress on what Reconstruction was supposed to accomplish. An heir of the Democratic states' rights tradition, he wanted to restore the prewar federal system as quickly as possible and without change except that states would not have the right to legalize slavery or to secede.

Most Republicans wanted firm guarantees that the old southern ruling class would not regain regional power and national influence by devising new ways to subjugate blacks. Since emancipation had nullified the three-fifths clause of the Constitution by which slaves had been counted as three-fifths of a person, all blacks were now to be counted in determining representation. Consequently, Republicans worried about increased southern strength in Congress and the electoral college. The current Congress favored a Reconstruction policy that would give the federal government authority to limit the political role of ex-Confederates and provide some protection for black citizenship.

Except for a few extreme Radicals, Republican leaders did not believe that blacks were inherently equal to whites. They did agree, however, that in a modern democratic state, all citizens must have the same basic rights and opportunities, regardless of natural abilities. Principle coincided easily with political expediency; southern blacks were likely to be loyal to the Republican party that had emancipated them and thus increase that party's political power in the South.

The disagreement between the president and Congress became irreconcilable in early 1866, when Johnson vetoed two bills that had passed with overwhelming Republican support. The first extended the life of the Freedmen's

Bureau—a temporary agency set up to aid the former slaves by providing relief, education, legal help, and assistance in obtaining land or employment. The second was a civil rights bill meant to nullify the Black Codes and guarantee to freedmen "full and equal benefit of all laws and proceedings for the security of person and property as is enjoyed by white citizens."

Johnson's vetoes shocked moderate Republicans who had expected the president to accept the relatively modest measures. Johnson succeeded in blocking the Freedmen's Bureau bill, although a modified version later passed. But Congress overrode his veto of the Civil Rights Act, signifying that the president was now hopelessly at odds with most of the congressmen from what was supposed to be his own party. Never before had Congress overridden a presidential veto.

Johnson soon revealed that he intended to abandon the Republicans and place himself at the head of a new conservative party uniting the small minority of Republicans who supported him with a reviving Democratic party that was rallying behind his Reconstruction policy. He helped found the National Union movement to promote his plan to readmit the southern states to the Union without further qualifications. A National Union convention meeting in Philadelphia

RECONSTRUCTION AMENDMENTS, 1865–1870

AMENDMENT	MAIN PROVISIONS	CONGRESSIONAL PASSAGE (2/3 MAJORITY IN EACH HOUSE REQUIRED)	RATIFICATION PROCESS (3/4 OF ALL STATES REQUIRED, INCLUDING EX-CONFEDERATE STATES)
13	Slavery prohibited in United States	January 1865	December 1865 (27 states, including 8 southern states)
14	1. National citizenship 2. State representation in Congress reduced proportionally to number of voters disfranchised 3. Former Confederates denied right to hold office 4. Confederate debt repudiated	June 1866	Rejected by 12 southern and border states, February 1867; Radicals make readmission of southern states hinge on ratification; ratified July 1868
15	Denial of franchise because of race, color, or past servitude explicitly prohibited	February 1869	Ratification required for readmission of Virginia, Texas, Mississippi, Georgia; ratified March 1870

in August 1866 called for the election to Congress of men who endorsed the presidential plan for Reconstruction.

Meanwhile, the Republican majority on Capitol Hill, fearing that Johnson would not enforce civil rights legislation or that the courts would declare such federal laws unconstitutional, passed the Fourteenth Amendment. This, perhaps the most important of all our constitutional amendments, gave the federal government responsibility for guaranteeing equal rights under the law to all Americans. Section 1 defined national citizenship for the first time as extending to "all persons born or naturalized in the United States." The states were prohibited from abridging the rights of American citizens and could not "deprive any person of life, liberty, or property, without due process of law; nor deny to any person . . . equal protection of the laws."

The other sections of the amendment were important in the context of the time but had fewer long-term implications. The amendment was sent to the states with the understanding that Southerners would not be readmitted to Congress unless their states ratified it.

The congressional elections of 1866 served as a referendum on the Fourteenth Amendment. Johnson opposed the amendment on the grounds that it created a "centralized" government and denied states the right to manage their own affairs. All the southern states except Tennessee rejected the amendment. But the publicity resulting from bloody race riots in New Orleans and Memphis weakened the president's case for state autonomy. Atrocities against blacks made it clear that the existing southern state governments were failing abysmally to protect the "life, liberty, or property" of the ex-slaves.

Johnson further weakened his cause by taking the stump on behalf of candidates who supported his policies. He toured the nation, slandering his opponents in crude language. Johnson's behavior enraged northern voters who repudiated the administration in the 1866 elections. The Republican majority in Congress increased to a solid two-thirds in both houses, and the Radical wing of the party gained strength at the expense of moderates and conservatives.

CONGRESSIONAL RECONSTRUCTION PLAN ENACTED

Congress was now in a position to implement its own plan of Reconstruction. In 1867 and 1868, it passed a series of acts that reorganized the South on a new basis. Generally referred to as Radical Reconstruction, the measures actually represented a compromise between genuine Radicals and more moderate elements within the party.

Consistent Radicals such as Senator Charles Sumner of Massachusetts and Congressmen Thaddeus Stevens of Pennsylvania and George Julian of Indiana

Among the most influential of the Radical Republicans was Congressman Thaddeus Stevens of Pennsylvania. He advocated seizing land from southern planters and distributing it among the freed slaves.

wanted to reshape southern society before readmitting ex-Confederates to the Union. Their plan required an extended period of military rule, confiscation and redistribution of large landholdings among the freedmen, and federal aid for schools to educate blacks and whites for citizenship. But the majority of Republican congressmen found such a program unacceptable because it broke too sharply with American traditions of federalism and regard for property rights.

The First Reconstruction Act, passed over Johnson's veto on March 2, 1867, reorganized the South into five military districts. But military rule would last for only a short time. Acts in 1867 and 1868 opened the way for the quick readmission of any state that framed and ratified a new constitution providing for black suffrage. Since blacks but not ex-Confederates were permitted to vote for delegates to the constitutional conventions or in the elections to ratify the conventions' work, Republicans thought they had found a way to ensure that "loyal" men would dominate the new governments. Republican leaders anticipated they would need votes from the reconstructed South in order to retain control of Congress and the White House in 1868.

Radical Reconstruction was based on the dubious assumption that once blacks had the vote, they would have the power to protect themselves against white supremacists' efforts to deny them their rights. The Reconstruction Acts thus signaled a retreat from the true Radical position that a sustained use of federal authority was needed to complete the transition from slavery to freedom and prevent the resurgence of the South's old ruling class. An extended period of military rule over civilians went beyond the popular northern consensus on necessary and proper Reconstruction measures. Thus, despite strong reservations, Radicals supported the plan of readmitting the southern states on the basis of

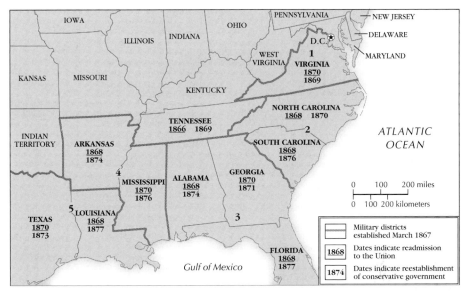

Reconstruction

During the Reconstruction era, the southern state governments passed through three phases: control by white ex-Confederates; domination by Republican legislators, both white and black; and, finally, the regain of control by conservative white Democrats.

black suffrage, recognizing that this was as far as the party and the northern public were willing to go.

Even so, congressional Reconstruction did have a radical aspect. It strongly supported the cause of black male suffrage. The belief that the poor and downtrodden should have access to the ballot box was a bold and innovative application of the principle of government by the consent of the governed. The problem was finding a way to enforce equal suffrage under conditions then existing in the postwar South.

THE IMPEACHMENT CRISIS

The first obstacle to enforcement of congressional Reconstruction was resistance from the White House. Johnson disapproved of the new policy and sought to thwart the will of Congress. He dismissed officeholders who sympathized with Radical Reconstruction, and he countermanded the orders of generals in charge of southern military districts who were zealous in their enforcement of the new legislation. Congress responded by passing laws designed to limit presidential authority over Reconstruction matters. One of the measures was the Tenure of Office Act, requiring Senate approval for the removal of cabinet officers and other officials whose appointment had needed the consent of the

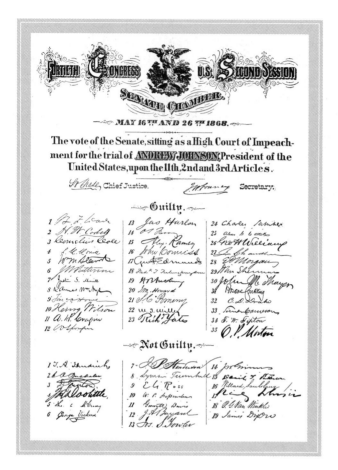

The record of the Senate vote on Andrew Johnson's impeachment trial. Charles Sumner, one of the leaders of the pro-impeachment forces, spoke of the trial as "one of the last great battles with slavery" and urged that "every sentiment, every conviction, every vow against slavery must now be directed against him [Johnson]." James Grimes, who spoke for Johnson's acquittal, argued, "This government can only be preserved and the liberty of the people maintained by preserving intact the coordinate branches of it—legislative, executive, judicial—alike. I am no convert to any doctrine of the omnipotence of Congress."

Senate. Another measure sought to limit Johnson's authority to issue orders to military commanders.

Johnson objected vigorously to the restrictions on the grounds that they violated the constitutional doctrine of the separation of powers. When it became clear that the president would do all in his power to resist the establishment of Radical regimes in the southern states, some congressmen began to call for his impeachment. When Johnson tried to discharge Secretary of War Edwin Stanton, the only Radical in the cabinet, the pro-impeachment forces gained in strength.

In January 1868, Johnson ordered General Grant to replace Stanton as head of the War Department. But Grant had his eye on the Republican presidential nomination and refused to defy Congress. Johnson subsequently appointed General Lorenzo Thomas, who agreed to serve. Faced with this apparent violation of the Tenure of Office Act, the House voted overwhelmingly to impeach the president on February 24, and he was placed on trial before the Senate.

Johnson narrowly avoided conviction and removal from office because seven Republican senators broke with the party leadership and voted for acquittal. The vote thus fell one vote short of the necessary two-thirds. This outcome resulted in part from a skillful defense. Attorneys for the president argued for a narrow interpretation of the constitutional provision that a president could be impeached only for "high crimes and misdemeanors," asserting that this referred only to indictable offenses. Responding to the charge that Johnson had deliberately violated the Tenure of Office Act, the defense contended that the law did not apply to the removal of Stanton because he had been appointed by Lincoln, not Johnson.

The prosecution countered that Johnson had abused the powers of his office in an effort to sabotage the congressional Reconstruction policy. Obstructing the will of the legislative branch, they claimed, was sufficient grounds for conviction even if no crime had been committed. The Republicans who voted for acquittal could not endorse such a broad view of the impeachment power. They feared that removal of a president for essentially political reasons would threaten the constitutional balance of powers and open the way to legislative supremacy over the executive.

Although Johnson's acquittal by the narrowest of margins protected the American presidency from congressional domination, the impeachment episode helped create an impression in the public mind that the Radicals were ready to turn the Constitution to their own use to gain their objectives. But the evidence of congressional ruthlessness and illegality is not as strong as most historians used to think. Modern legal scholars have found merit in the Radicals' claim that their actions did not violate the Constitution.

Failure to remove Johnson from office was an embarrassment to congressional Republicans, but the episode did ensure that Reconstruction in the South would proceed as the majority in Congress intended. During the trial, Johnson helped influence the verdict by pledging to enforce the Reconstruction Acts, and he held to this promise during his remaining months in office. Unable to depose the president, the Radicals had at least succeeded in neutralizing his opposition to their program.

RECONSTRUCTION IN THE SOUTH

The Civil War left the South devastated, demoralized, and destitute. Slavery was dead, but what this meant for future relationships between whites and blacks was still in doubt. Most southern whites wanted to keep blacks adrift between slavery and freedom—without political or civil rights. Blacks sought independence and viewed the acquisition of land, education, and the vote as the best means of achieving this goal. The thousands of Northerners who went south after the war hoped to extend Yankee "civilization" to what they viewed as an unenlightened and barbarous region. For most of them, this reformation required the aid of the freed slaves.

The struggle of these groups to achieve their conflicting goals bred chaos, violence, and instability. The setting was hardly ideal for an experiment in interracial democracy, but one was attempted nonetheless. With massive and sustained support from the federal government, progressive reform could be achieved. When such support faltered, the forces of reaction and white supremacy were unleashed.

SOCIAL AND ECONOMIC ADJUSTMENTS

The Civil War scarred the southern landscape and wrecked its economy. One devastated area—central South Carolina—looked to an 1865 observer "like a broad black streak of ruin and desolation." Several major cities—including Atlanta, Columbia, and Richmond—were gutted by fire. Most factories were dismantled or destroyed, and long stretches of railroad were torn up.

Physical ruin would not have been so disastrous if investment capital had been available for rebuilding. But the substantial wealth represented by Confederate currency and bonds had melted away, and emancipation of the slaves had divested the propertied classes of their most valuable and productive assets. According to some estimates, the South's per capita wealth in 1865 was only about half what it had been in 1860.

Recovery could not even begin until a new labor system replaced slavery. Most Americans assumed that southern prosperity would continue to depend on plantation-grown cotton. Hindering efforts to rebuild the plantation economy were lack of capital, the deep-rooted belief of southern whites that blacks would work only under compulsion, and the freedmen's resistance to labor conditions that recalled slavery.

Blacks strongly preferred to determine their own economic relationships, and they hoped the federal government would support their ambitions. Although they were grateful for the federal aid in ending slavery, freed slaves often had ideas about freedom that contradicted the plans of their northern allies. Many ex-slaves wanted to hold on to the family-based communal work methods that they utilized during slavery rather than adopt the individual piecework system pushed by northern capitalists. Many ex-slaves opposed plans to turn them into

The Civil War brought emancipation to slaves but the sharecropping system kept many of them economically bound to their employers. At the end of a year the sharecropper tenants might owe most—or all—of what they had made to their landlord. Here a sharecropping family poses in front of their cabin. Ex-slaves often built their living quarters near woods in order to have a ready supply of fuel for heating and cooking. The cabin's chimney lists away from the house so that it can be easily pushed away from the living quarters should it catch fire.

wage laborers who produced exclusively for a market. Finally, freed slaves often wanted to stay on the land their families had spent generations farming rather than move elsewhere to assume plots of land as individual farmers.

While not guaranteeing all of the freed slaves' hopes for economic self-determination, the northern military attempted to establish a new economic base for the freed men and women. General Sherman issued an order in January 1865 that set aside the islands and coastal areas of Georgia and South Carolina for exclusive black occupancy on 40-acre plots. The Freedmen's Bureau was given control of hundreds of thousands of acres of abandoned or confiscated land and was authorized to make 40-acre grants to black settlers for three-year periods. By June 1865, forty thousand black farmers were at work on 300,000 acres of what they thought would be their own land.

But for most of them the dream of "forty acres and a mule" was not to be realized. Neither President Johnson nor Congress supported any effective program of land confiscation and redistribution. Consequently, most blacks in physical possession of small farms failed to acquire title, and the mass of freedmen were left with little or no prospect of becoming landowners. Recalling the plight of southern blacks in 1865, an ex-slave later wrote that "they were set free without a dollar, without a foot of land, and without the wherewithal to get the next meal even."

Despite their poverty and landlessness, ex-slaves were reluctant to commit themselves to wage labor for their former masters. Many took to the road, hoping to find something better. Some were still expecting grants of land, but others were simply trying to increase their bargaining power. As the end of 1865 approached, many freedmen had still not signed up for the coming season; anxious planters feared that blacks were plotting to seize land by force. Within a few weeks, however, most holdouts signed for the best terms they could get.

One common form of agricultural employment in 1866 was a contract labor system. Under this system, workers committed themselves for a year in return for fixed wages, a substantial portion of which was withheld until after the harvest. The Freedmen's Bureau assumed responsibility for reviewing the contracts and enforcing them. But bureau officials had differing notions of what it meant to protect African Americans from exploitation. Some stood up strongly for the rights of the freedmen; others served as allies of the planters.

Growing up alongside the contract system and eventually displacing it was an alternative capital-labor relationship—sharecropping. Under this system, blacks worked a piece of land independently for a fixed share of the crop, usually one-half. Credit-starved landlords liked this arrangement because it did not require much expenditure in advance of the harvest and the tenant shared the risks of crop failure or a fall in cotton prices.

African Americans initially viewed sharecropping as a step up from wage labor in the direction of landownership. But during the 1870s, this form of tenancy evolved into a new kind of servitude. Croppers had to live on credit until their cotton was sold, and planters or merchants seized the chance to "provision" them at high prices and exorbitant rates of interest. Creditors were entitled to deduct what was owed to them out of the tenant's share of the crop, and this left most sharecroppers with no net profit at the end of the year—more often than not with a debt that had to be worked off in subsequent years.

African Americans in towns and cities found themselves living in an increasingly segregated society. The Black Codes of 1865 attempted to require separation of the races in public places and facilities; when most of the codes were set aside by federal authorities as violations of the Civil Rights Act of 1866, the same end was often achieved through private initiative and community pressure. Blacks found it almost impossible to gain admittance to most hotels, restaurants, and other privately owned establishments catering to whites. Although separate black, or "Jim Crow," cars were not yet the rule on railroads, African Americans were often denied first-class accommodations. After 1868, black-supported Republican governments passed civil rights acts requiring equal access to public facilities, but little effort was made to enforce the legislation.

A Freedmen's school, one of the more successful endeavors supported by the Freedmen's Bureau. The Bureau, working with teachers from northern abolitionist and missionary societies, founded thousands of schools for freed slaves and poor whites.

Some forms of racial separation were not openly discriminatory, and blacks accepted or even endorsed them. Freedmen who had belonged to white churches as slaves welcomed the chance to join all-black denominations such as the African Methodist Episcopal church. The first schools for ex-slaves were all-black institutions established by the Freedmen's Bureau and various northern missionary societies. Having been denied all education during the antebellum period, most blacks viewed separate schooling as an opportunity rather than as a form of discrimination. When Radical governments set up public school systems, they condoned de facto educational segregation. Only in city schools of New Orleans and at the University of South Carolina were there serious attempts during Reconstruction to bring white and black students together in the same classrooms.

The upshot of all forms of racial separatism was to create a divided society, one in which blacks and whites lived much of the time in separate worlds. There were two exceptions to this pattern: one was at work, where blacks necessarily dealt with white employers; the other was in the political sphere, where blacks sought to exercise their rights as citizens.

POLITICAL RECONSTRUCTION IN THE SOUTH

The state governments that emerged in 1865 had little or no regard for the rights of the freed slaves. Some of their codes made black unemployment a crime, and others limited the rights of African Americans to own property or engage in occupations other than those of servant or laborer. The federal government set aside these codes, but private violence and discrimination against blacks continued on a massive scale unchecked by state authorities. Hundreds, perhaps thousands, of blacks were murdered by whites in 1865–1866, and few of the perpetrators were brought to justice.

The imposition of military rule in 1867 was designed in part to protect former slaves from violence and intimidation, but the task was beyond the capacity of the few thousand troops stationed in the South. When new constitutions were approved and states readmitted to the Union under the congressional plan in 1868, the problem became more severe. White opponents of Radical Reconstruction used systematic terrorism and organized mob violence to keep blacks from voting. The freed slaves tried to protect and defend themselves by organizing their own militia groups. However, these militia groups were not powerful enough to overcome the growing power of the anti-Republican forces. As the military presence was progressively reduced, the new Republican regimes had to fight a losing battle against armed white supremacists.

Hastily organized in 1867, the southern Republican party dominated the constitution making of 1868 and the regimes that came out of it. The party was an attempted coalition of three social groups: newly enfranchised blacks, poor white farmers, and businessmen seeking government aid for private enterprise. Many Republicans in this third group were recent arrivals from the North—the so-called carpetbaggers—but some were "scalawags," former Whig planters or merchants who were born in the South or had immigrated to the region before the war and now saw a chance to realize their dreams for commercial and industrial development.

White owners of small farms expected the Republican party to favor their interests at the expense of the wealthy landowners and to come to their aid with special legislation when they faced the loss of their homesteads to creditors. Blacks formed the vast majority of the Republican rank and file in most states and were concerned mainly with education, civil rights, and landowner-ship.

Under the best of conditions, this coalition would have been difficult to maintain. Each group had its own distinct goals and did not fully support the aims of the other segments. Poor white farmers, for example, had a deeply rooted resistance to black equality. And for how long could one expect essentially conservative businessmen to support costly measures for the elevation or relief of the lower classes of either race? Some Democratic politicians exploited these divisions by appealing to disaffected white Republicans.

But during the relatively brief period when they were in power in the South, the Republicans chalked up some notable achievements. They established (on paper at least) the South's first adequate systems of public education, democratized state and local government, and appropriated funds for an enormous expansion of public services and responsibilities.

Important as these social and political reforms were, they took second place to the Republicans' major effort—to foster economic development and restore southern prosperity by subsidizing the construction of railroads and other internal improvements. But the policy of aiding railroads turned out to be disastrous. Extravagance, corruption, and routes laid out in response to local political pressure rather than on sound economic grounds increased the burden of public debt and taxation. The policy did not produce the promised payoff of efficient, cheap transportation. Subsidized railroads frequently went bankrupt, leaving the taxpayers holding the bag. When the Panic of 1873 brought many southern state governments to the verge of bankruptcy, and railroad building came to an end, it was clear the Republicans' "gospel of prosperity" through state aid to private enterprise had failed miserably. Their political opponents, many of whom had originally favored such policies, now saw an opportunity to take advantage of the situation by charging that Republicans had ruined the southern economy.

In general, the Radical regimes failed to conduct public business honestly and efficiently. Embezzlement of public funds and bribery of state lawmakers or officials were common occurrences. State debts and tax burdens rose enormously, mainly because governments had undertaken heavy new responsibilities, but partly because of waste and graft.

Yet southern corruption was not exceptional, nor was it a special result of the extension of suffrage to uneducated African Americans, as critics of Radical Reconstruction have claimed. It was part of a national pattern during an era when private interests considered buying government favors to be a part of the cost of doing business.

Blacks bore only a limited responsibility for the dishonesty of the Radical governments. Although sixteen African Americans served in Congress—two in the Senate—between 1869 and 1880, only in South Carolina did blacks constitute a majority of even one house of the state legislature. Furthermore, no black governors were elected during Reconstruction (although Pinkney B. S. Pinchback served for a time as acting governor of Louisiana). The biggest grafters were opportunistic whites. Some black legislators went with the tide and accepted "loans" from those railroad lobbyists who would pay most for their votes, but the same men could usually be depended on to vote the will of their constituents on civil rights or educational issues.

If blacks served or supported corrupt and wasteful regimes, it was because they had no alternative. Although the Democrats, or Conservatives as they called themselves in some states, made sporadic efforts to attract African American voters, it was clear that if they won control, they would attempt to strip blacks of their civil and political rights. But opponents of Radical Reconstruction were able to capitalize on racial prejudice and persuade many Americans that "good government" was synonymous with white supremacy.

Contrary to myth, the small number of African Americans elected to state or national office during Reconstruction demonstrated on the average more integrity and competence than their white counterparts. Most were fairly well educated, having been free Negroes or unusually privileged slaves before the war. Among the most capable were Robert Smalls, Senator Blanche K. Bruce of Mississippi, and Congressmen Robert Brown Elliott of South Carolina and James T. Rapier of Alabama.

THE AGE OF GRANT

Ulysses S. Grant was the only president between Jackson and Wilson to serve two full and consecutive terms. But unlike other chief executives so favored by the electorate, Grant is commonly regarded as a failure. His administration was riddled with corruption, and he has also been condemned for the inconsistency and ultimate failure of his southern policy. At times, Grant's highest priority seemed to be loyalty to old friends and to politicians who supported him. But the problems he faced were certainly difficult. A president with a clearer sense of duty might have done little better.

RISE OF THE MONEY QUESTION

The impeachment crisis of 1868 represented the high point of popular interest in Reconstruction issues. Already competing for public attention was the question of how to manage the nation's currency, and more specifically, what to do about greenbacks—paper money issued during the war. Johnson's Sectretary of the Treasury Hugh McCulloch favored a return to "sound" money and in 1866 had initiated a policy of withdrawing greenbacks from circulation. Commercial and financial interests in the East generally endorsed this hard-money policy: they re-

THE ELECTION OF 1868

CANDIDATE	PARTY	POPULAR VOTE	ELECTORAL VOTE
Grant	Republican	3,013,421	214
Seymour	Democratic	2,706,829	80
Not voted*			23

*Unreconstructed states did not participate in the election.

ceived crucial support form intellectuals who regarded government-sponsored inflation as immoral or contrary to the natural laws of classic economics. A number of groups opposed McCulloch's policy; "greenbacks" were the strongest in the West and among expansion-minded manufacturers.

The money question surged to the forefront of national politics in 1868. Faced with a business recession blamed on McCulloch's policy, Congress voted to stop the retirement of greenbacks. The Democratic party, responding to midwestern pressure, included in its platform a plan calling for the redemption of much of the Civil War debt in greenbacks rather than gold. But divisions within the parties prevented the money question from becoming a central issue in the presidential campaign. The Democrats nominated Governor Horatio Seymour of New York, a sound-money supporter, thus nullifying their greenback platform. Republicans based their campaign mainly on a defense of their Reconstruction policy and a celebration of their popular candidate. With the help of votes from the Republican-dominated southern states, Grant won a decisive victory.

In 1869 and 1870, a Republican-controlled Congress passed laws that assured payment in gold to most bondholders but eased the burden of the huge Civil War debt by exchanging bonds soon coming due for those that would not be payable for ten, fifteen, or thirty years. In this way, the public credit was protected.

Still unresolved was the problem of what to do about the $356 million in greenbacks that remained in circulation: retire them quickly as hard-money advocates proposed, or issue more to stimulate the economy, as inflationists argued. The Grant administration decided to allow the greenbacks to float until economic expansion would bring them to a par with gold, thus permitting a painless return to specie payments. But the Panic of 1873, which brought much of the economy to its knees, led to a revival of agitation to inflate the currency. Debt-ridden farmers, who would be the backbone of the greenback movement for years to come, now joined the soft-money clamor for the first time.

Responding to the economic downturn, Congress in 1874 authorized a modest issue of new greenbacks, but Grant, influenced by the opinions of hard-money financiers, vetoed the bill. In 1875 Congress enacted the Specie Resumption Act, which provided for a limited reduction of greenbacks leading to full resumption of specie payments by January 1, 1879. The action was widely interpreted as deflation in the midst of depression, and farmers and workers—who were already suffering acutely from deflation—reacted with dismay and anger.

The Democratic party could not capitalize adequately on these sentiments because of the influence of its own hard-money faction, and in 1876 an independent Greenback party entered the national political arena. The party's nominee for president received an insignificant number of votes, but in 1878 the Greenback Labor party polled more than a million votes and elected fourteen congressmen. The Greenbackers were able to keep the money issue alive into the following decade.

RETREAT FROM RECONSTRUCTION

The Republican effort to make equal rights for blacks the law of the land culminated in the Fifteenth Amendment. Passed by Congress in 1869 and ratified by the states in 1870, the amendment prohibited any state from denying a citizen the right to vote because of race, color, or previous condition of servitude. A more radical version, requiring universal manhood suffrage, was rejected partly because it departed too sharply from traditional views of federal-state relations. States therefore could still limit the suffrage by imposing literacy tests, property qualifications, or poll taxes allegedly applying to all racial groups; such devices would eventually be used to strip southern blacks of the right to vote, though the makers of the amendment did not foresee this result.

Many feminists were bitterly disappointed that the amendment did not extend the vote to women. A militant wing of the women's rights movement, led by Elizabeth Cady Stanton and Susan B. Anthony, was so angered that the Constitution was being amended in a way that, in effect, made gender a qualification for voting that they campaigned against ratification of the Fifteenth Amendment. Another group of feminists led by Lucy Stone supported the amendment on the grounds that this was "the Negro's hour" and that women could afford to wait a few years for the vote. This disagreement divided the women's suffrage movement for a generation to come.

The Grant administration was charged with enforcing the amendment and protecting black men's voting rights in the reconstructed states. Since survival of the Republican regimes depended on African American support, political partisanship dictated federal action, even though the North's emotional and ideological commitment to black citizenship was waning.

Shown seated at the table are feminist leaders Elizabeth Cady Stanton and Susan B. Anthony. They and their adherents split with Lucy Stone (right) and her followers over the Fifteenth Amendment and its failure to extend the vote to women.

Between 1868 and 1872, the main threat to southern Republican regimes came from the Ku Klux Klan and other secret societies bent on restoring white supremacy by intimidating blacks who sought to exercise their political rights. First organized in Tennessee in 1866, the Klan spread rapidly to other states, adopting increasingly lawless and brutal tactics. A grass-roots vigilante movement and not a centralized conspiracy, the Klan thrived on local initiative and gained support from whites of all social classes. Its secrecy, decentralization, popular support, and utter ruthlessness made it very difficult to suppress. As soon as blacks had been granted the right to vote, hooded "night riders" began to visit the cabins of those who were known to be active Republicans; some victims were only threatened, but others were whipped or even murdered.

In the presidential election of 1868, Grant lost in Louisiana and Georgia mainly because the Klan—or the Knights of the White Camelia, as the Louisiana variant was called—launched a reign of terror to prevent prospective black voters from exercising their right. Political violence claimed more than a thousand lives in Louisiana and in Arkansas more than two hundred Republicans, including a congressman, were assassinated.

Thereafter, Klan terrorism was directed mainly at Republican state governments. Virtual insurrections broke out in Arkansas, Tennessee, North Carolina, and parts of South Carolina. Republican governors called out the state militia to

Members of the Ku Klux Klan, a secret white supremacist organization, in typical regalia. Before elections, hooded Klansmen terrorized African Americans to discourage them from voting.

fight the Klan, but only the Arkansas militia succeeded in bringing it to heel. In Tennessee, North Carolina, and Georgia, Klan activities helped undermine Republican control, thus allowing the Democrats to come to power in all of these states by 1870.

In 1870–1871 Congress passed a series of laws designed to enforce the Fifteenth Amendment by providing federal protection for black suffrage and authorizing use of the army against the Klan. The "Ku Klux Klan" or "Force" acts made interference with voting rights a federal crime and established provisions for government supervision of elections. The legislation also empowered the president to call out troops and suspend the writ of habeas corpus to quell insurrection. In 1871–1872, thousands of suspected Klansmen were arrested by the military or U.S. marshals, and the writ was suspended in nine counties of South Carolina that had been virtually taken over by the secret order. Although most of the accused Klansmen were never brought to trial, were acquitted, or received suspended sentences, the enforcement effort was vigorous enough to put a damper on hooded terrorism and ensure relatively fair and peaceful elections in 1872.

A heavy black turnout in these elections enabled the Republicans to hold on to power in most states of the Deep South, despite efforts of the Democratic-Conservative opposition to cut into the Republican vote by taking moderate positions on racial and economic issues. This setback prompted the Democratic-Conservatives to make a significant change in their strategy and ideology. No longer did they try to take votes away from the Republicans by proclaiming support for black suffrage and government aid to business. Instead they began to appeal openly to white supremacy and to the traditional Democratic and agrarian hostility to government promotion of economic development. Consequently, they were able to bring back to the polls a portion of the white electorate, mostly small farmers, who had not been voting because they were alienated by the leadership's apparent concessions to Yankee ideas.

This new and more effective electoral strategy dovetailed with a resurgence of violence meant to reduce Republican, especially black Republican, voting. The new reign of terror differed from the previous Klan episode; its agents no longer wore masks but acted quite openly. They were effective because the northern public was increasingly disenchanted with federal intervention on behalf of what were widely viewed as corrupt and tottering Republican regimes. Grant used force in the South for the last time in 1874 when an overt paramilitary organization in Louisiana tried to overthrow a Republican government accused of stealing an election. When an unofficial militia in Mississippi instigated a series of bloody race riots prior to the state elections of 1875, Grant refused the governor's request for federal troops. Intimidation kept black voters from the polls, and as a result Mississippi fell to the Democratic-Conservatives.

By 1876, Republicans held on to only three southern states: South Carolina, Louisiana, and Florida. Partly because of Grant's hesitant and inconsistent use of presidential power, but mainly because the northern electorate would no longer tolerate military action to sustain Republican governments and black voting rights, Radical Reconstruction was falling into total eclipse.

SPOILSMEN VERSUS REFORMERS

One reason Grant found it increasingly difficult to take strong action to protect southern Republicans was the accusation by reformers that a corrupt national administration was propping up bad governments in the South for personal and partisan advantage. An apparent example was Grant's intervention in Louisiana in 1872 on behalf of an ill-reputed Republican faction headed by his wife's brother-in-law, who controlled federal patronage as collector of customs in New Orleans.

The Republican party in the Grant era was losing the idealism and high purpose associated with the crusade against slavery. By the beginning of the 1870s, the men who had been the conscience of the party were either dead, out of office, or at odds with the administration. New leaders of a different stamp, whom historians have dubbed "spoilsmen" or "politicos," were taking their place. When Grant joined ranks with these new Republicans, such as Senators Roscoe Conkling of New York and James G. Blaine of Maine, he lost credibility with reform-minded members of his party.

During Grant's first administration, an aura of scandal surrounded the White House but did not directly implicate the president. In 1869, the financial buccaneer Jay Gould enlisted the aid of a brother-in-law of Grant to further a fantastic scheme to corner the gold market. Gould failed in the attempt, but he did manage to save himself and come away with a huge profit.

Grant's first-term vice president, Schuyler Colfax of Indiana, was directly involved in the notorious Crédit Mobilier scandal. Crédit Mobilier was a construction company that actually served as a fraudulent device for siphoning off profits that should have gone to the stockholders of the Union Pacific Railroad, which was the beneficiary of massive federal land grants. In order to forestall government inquiry into this arrangement, Crédit Mobilier stock was distributed to influential congressmen, including Colfax (who was speaker of the House before he was elected vice president). The whole business came to light just before the campaign of 1872.

Republicans who could not tolerate such corruption or had other grievances against the administration broke with Grant in 1872 and formed a third party committed to "honest government" and "reconciliation" between the North and the South. These Liberal Republicans endorsed reform of the civil service to curb the corruption-breeding patronage system and advocated a laissez-faire economic policy of low tariffs, an end to government subsidies for railroads, and hard money. Despite their rhetoric of idealism and reform, the Liberal Republicans were extremely conservative in their notions of what government should do to assure justice for blacks and other underprivileged Americans.

The Liberal Republicans' national convention nominated Horace Greeley, editor of the respected New York *Tribune*. This was a curious and divisive choice, since Greeley was at odds with the founders of the movement on the tariff question and was indifferent to civil service reform. The Democrats also nominated

THE ELECTION OF 1872

CANDIDATE	PARTY	POPULAR VOTE	ELECTORAL VOTE*
Grant	Republican	3,598,235	286
Greeley	Democratic and Liberal Republican	2,834,761	Greeley died before the electoral college voted.

*Out of a total of 366 electoral votes. Greeley's votes were divided among the four minor candidates.

Greeley, mainly because he promised to end Radical Reconstruction by restoring "self-government" to the South.

But the journalist turned out to be a poor campaigner who failed to inspire enthusiasm from lifelong supporters of either party. Most Republicans stuck with Grant, and many Democrats, recalling Greeley's previous record as a staunch Republican, simply stayed away from the polls. The result was a decisive victory for Grant.

Grant's second administration seemed to bear out the reformers' worst suspicions about corruption in high places. In 1875, the public learned that federal revenue officials had conspired with distillers to defraud the government of millions of dollars in liquor taxes. Grant's private secretary, Orville E. Babcock, was indicted as a member of the "Whiskey Ring" and was saved from conviction only by the president's personal intercession. The next year, Grant's secretary of war, William E. Belknap, was impeached by the House after an investigation revealed he had taken bribes for the sale of Indian trading posts. He avoided conviction in the Senate only by resigning from office before his trial.

There is no evidence that Grant profited personally from any of the misdeeds of his subordinates. Yet he is not entirely without blame for the corruption in his administration. He failed to take firm action against the malefactors, and, even after their guilt had been clearly established, he sometimes tried to shield them from justice.

REUNION AND THE NEW SOUTH

Congressional Reconstruction prolonged the sense of sectional division and conflict for a dozen years after the guns had fallen silent. Its final liquidation in 1877 opened the way to a reconciliation of North and South. But the costs of reunion were high for less privileged groups in the South. The civil and political rights of African Americans, left unprotected, were progressively and relentlessly stripped away by white supremacist regimes. Lower-class whites saw their interests sacrificed to those of capitalists and landlords. Despite the rhetoric hailing a prosperous "New South," the region remained poor and open to exploitation by northern business interests.

THE COMPROMISE OF 1877

The election of 1876 pitted Republican governor Rutherford B. Hayes of Ohio against Governor Samuel J. Tilden of New York, a Democratic reformer. Honest government was apparently the electorate's highest priority. Tilden won the popular vote and seemed likely to win a narrow victory in the electoral college. But the result was placed in doubt when the returns from the three southern states

THE ELECTION OF 1876

CANDIDATE	PARTY	POPULAR VOTE	UNCONTESTED ELECTORAL VOTE	ELECTORAL TOTAL
Hayes	Republican	4,034,311	165	185
Tilden	Democratic	4,288,546	184	184
Cooper	Greenback	75,973	—	—

still controlled by the Republicans—South Carolina, Florida, and Louisiana— were contested. If Hayes were to be awarded these three states, plus one contested electoral vote in Oregon, Republican strategists realized, he would triumph in the electoral college by a single vote.

The outcome of the election remained undecided for months. To resolve the impasse, Congress appointed a special electoral commission of fifteen members to determine who would receive the votes of the disputed states. Originally composed of seven Democrats, seven Republicans, and an independent, the commission fell under Republican control when the independent member resigned to run for the Senate and a Republican was appointed to take his place. The commission split along party lines and voted 8 to 7 to award Hayes all of the disputed votes. But this decision still had to be ratified by both houses of Congress. The Republican-dominated Senate readily approved it, but the Democrats in the House planned a filibuster to delay the final counting of the electoral votes until after inauguration day. If the filibuster succeeded, neither candidate would have a majority and, as provided in the Constitution, the election would be decided by the House, where the Democrats controlled enough states to elect Tilden.

To ensure Hayes's election, Republican leaders negotiated secretly with conservative southern Democrats, some of whom seemed willing to abandon their opposition if the last troops were withdrawn and "home rule" restored to the South. There were also vague pledges of federal support for southern railroads and internal improvements. Hayes also promised to end federal support for crumbling Radical regimes. Eventually an informal bargain was struck, which historians have dubbed the Compromise of 1877. What precisely was agreed to and by whom remains a matter of dispute; but one thing at least was understood by both sides—Hayes would be president and southern blacks would be abandoned to their fate.

With southern Democratic acquiescence, the filibuster was broken, and Hayes took the oath of office. He immediately ordered the army not to resist a Democratic takeover of state governments in South Carolina and Louisiana. Thus fell the last of the Radical governments, and the entire South was firmly under the control of white Democrats. The trauma of the war and Reconstruction had destroyed the chances for a renewal of two-party competition among white Southerners.

THE NEW SOUTH

The men who came to power after the fall of Radical Reconstruction are usually referred to as the Redeemers. They had differing backgrounds and previous loyalties. Some were members of the Old South's ruling planter class who had warmly supported secession and now sought to reestablish the old order with as few changes as possible. Others, of middle-class origin or outlook, favored commercial and industrial interests over agrarian groups and called for a New South committed to diversified economic development. A third group were professional politicians who shifted positions with the prevailing winds.

The Redeemers subscribed to no single coherent ideology or view of the world but are perhaps best characterized as power brokers mediating among the dominant interest groups of the South in ways that served their own political advantage. In many ways, the "rings" that they established on the state and county level were analogous to the political machines developing at the same time in northern cities.

Redeemers did, however, agree on and endorse two basic principles: laissez-faire and white supremacy. Laissez-faire—the notion that government should be limited and should not intervene openly and directly in the economy—could unite planters, frustrated at seeing direct state support going to businessmen, and capitalist promoters who had come to realize that low taxes and freedom from government regulation were even more advantageous than state subsidies. It soon became clear that the Redeemers responded only to privileged and entrenched interest groups, especially landlords, merchants, and industrialists, and offered little or nothing to tenants, small farmers, and working people. As industrialization began to gather steam in the 1880s, Democratic regimes became increasingly accommodating to manufacturing interests and hospitable to agents of northern capital who were gaining control of the South's transportation system and its extractive industries.

White supremacy was the principal rallying cry that brought the Redeemers to power in the first place. Once in office, they found they could stay there by charging that opponents of ruling Democratic cliques were trying to divide "the white man's party" and open the way for a return to "black domination." Appeals to racism could also deflect attention from the economic grievances of groups without political clout.

The new governments were more economical than those of Reconstruction, mainly because they cut back drastically on appropriations for schools and other needed public services. But they were scarcely more honest—embezzlement of funds and bribery of officials continued to occur to an alarming extent.

The Redeemer regimes of the late 1870s and 1880s badly neglected the interests of small white farmers. Whites, as well as blacks, were suffering from the notorious crop lien system, which gave local merchants who advanced credit at high rates of interest during the growing season the right to take possession of the harvested crop on terms that buried farmers deeper and deeper in debt. As a result, increasing numbers of whites lost title to their homesteads and were reduced to tenancy. When a depression of world cotton prices added to the burden of a ruinous credit system, agrarian protesters began to challenge the ruling elite, first through the Southern Farmers' Alliance of the late 1880s and then by supporting its political descendant—the Populist party of the 1890s.

But African Americans bore the greatest hardships imposed by the new order. The Redeemers had promised, in exchange for the end of federal intervention in 1877, to respect the rights of blacks as set forth in the Fourteenth and Fifteenth Amendments. But when blacks tried to vote Republican in the "redeemed" states, they encountered renewed violence and intimidation. Blacks who withstood the threat of losing their jobs or being evicted from tenant farms if they voted Republican were visited at night and literally whipped into line. The message was clear: vote Democratic, or vote not at all.

Furthermore, white Democrats now controlled the electoral machinery and were able to manipulate the black vote by stuffing ballot boxes, discarding unwanted votes, or reporting fraudulent totals. Some states also imposed complicated new voting requirements to discourage black participation. Full-scale disfranchisement did not occur until literacy tests and other legalized obstacles to voting were imposed in the period from 1890 to 1910, but by that time, less formal and comprehensive methods had already made a mockery of the Fifteenth Amendment.

Nevertheless, blacks continued to vote freely in some localities until the 1890s; a few districts even elected black Republicans to Congress during the immediate post-Reconstruction period. The last of these, Representative George H. White of North Carolina, served until 1901. His farewell address eloquently conveyed the agony of southern blacks in the era of strict segregation:

These parting words are in behalf of an outraged, heart-broken, bruised, and bleeding but God-fearing people, faithful, industrious, loyal people—rising people, full of potential force. . . . The only apology that I have to make for the earnestness with which I have spoken is that I am pleading for the life, the liberty, the future happiness, and manhood suffrage of one-eighth of the entire population of the United States.

The dark night of racism that fell on the South after Reconstruction seemed to unleash all the baser impulses of human nature. Between 1889 and 1899, an average of 187 blacks were lynched every year for alleged offenses against white supremacy. Those convicted of petty crimes against property were often little better off; many were condemned to be leased out to private contractors whose brutality

Perhaps no event better expresses the cruel and barbaric nature of the racism and white supremacy that swept the South after Reconstruction than lynching. Although lynchings were not confined to the South, most occurred there and African American men were the most frequent victims. Here two men lean out of a barn window above a black man who is about to be hanged. Others below prepare to set on fire the pile of hay at the victim's feet. Lynchings were often public events, drawing huge crowds to watch the victim's agonizing death.

SUPREME COURT DECISIONS AFFECTING BLACK CIVIL RIGHTS, 1875–1900

CASE	EFFECTS OF COURT'S DECISIONS
Hall v. *DeCuir* (1878)	Struck down Louisiana law prohibiting racial discrimination by "common carriers" (railroads, steamboats, buses). Declared the law a "burden" on interstate commerce, over which states had no authority.
United States v. *Harris* (1882)	Declared federal laws to punish crimes such as murder and assault unconstitutional. Declared such crimes to be the sole concern of local government. Ignored the frequent racial motivation behind such crimes in the South.
Civil Rights Cases (1883)	Struck down Civil Rights Act of 1875. Declared that Congress may not legislate on civil rights unless a state passes a discriminatory law. Declared the Fourteenth Amendment silent on racial discrimination by private citizens.
Plessy v. *Ferguson* (1896)	Upheld Louisiana statute requiring "separate but equal" accommodations on railroads. Declared that segregation is *not* necessarily discrimination.
Williams v. *Mississippi* (1898)	Upheld state law requiring a literacy test to qualify for voting. Refused to find any implication of racial discrimination in the law, although it permitted illiterate whites to vote if they "understood" the Constitution. Using such laws, southern states rapidly disfranchised blacks.

rivaled that of the most sadistic slaveholders. The convict lease system enabled entrepreneurs, such as mine owners and extractors of forest products, to rent prisoners from the state and treat them as they saw fit. Unlike slaveowners, they suffered no loss when a forced laborer died from overwork. (Annual mortality rates in the convict camps ranged as high as 25 percent.) Finally, the dignity of blacks was cruelly affronted by the wave of segregation laws passed around the turn of the century, which served to remind them constantly that they were deemed unfit to associate with whites on any basis that implied equality. To some extent, the segregation laws were a white reaction to the refusal of many blacks to submit to voluntary segregation of railroads, streetcars, and other public facilities.

The North and the federal government did little or nothing to stem the tide of racial oppression in the South. A series of Supreme Court decisions between 1875 and 1896 gutted the Reconstruction amendments and the legislation passed to enforce them, leaving blacks virtually defenseless against political and social discrimination.

The career of Henry McNeal Turner sums up the bitter side of the black experience in the South during and after Reconstruction. Born free in South Carolina in 1834, Turner became a minister of the African Methodist Episcopal (AME) Church just before the outbreak of the Civil War. During the war, he recruited African Americans for the Union army and later served as chaplain for black troops. After the fighting was over, he went to Georgia to work for the Freedmen's Bureau but encountered racial discrimination from white Bureau officers and left government service for church work and Reconstruction politics. Elected to the 1867 Georgia constitutional convention and to the state legislature in 1868, he was one of a number of black clergymen who assumed leadership roles among the freedmen. But whites won control of the Georgia legislature and expelled all the black members. As the inhabitant of a state in which blacks never gained the degree of power that they achieved in some other parts of the South, Turner was one of the first black leaders to see the failure of Reconstruction as the betrayal of African American hopes for citizenship.

Henry McNeal Turner, who was born in freedom, became a bishop of the African Methodist Episcopal Church and was elected to the Georgia legislature.

Becoming a bishop of the AME Church in 1880, Turner emerged as the late nineteenth century's leading proponent of black emigration to Africa. Because he believed that white Americans were so deeply prejudiced against blacks that they would never grant them equal rights, Turner became an early advocate of black nationalism and a total separation of the races. Emigration became a popular movement among southern blacks, but a majority of blacks in the nation as a whole and even in Turner's own church refused to give up on the hope of eventual equality on American soil. But Bishop Turner's anger and despair were the understandable responses of a proud man to the way that he and his fellow African Americans had been treated in the post–Civil War period.

By the late 1880s, the wounds of the Civil War were healing, and white Americans were celebrating the spirit of sectional reconciliation and their common Americanism. But whites could come back together only because Northerners had tacitly agreed to give Southerners a free hand in their efforts to reduce blacks to a new form of servitude. The "outraged, heart-broken, bruised, and bleeding" African Americans of the South paid the heaviest price for sectional reunion.

17

THE WEST
Exploiting an Empire

In the last three decades of the nineteenth century, a flood of settlers ventured into the vast lands across the Mississippi River. James H. Kyner, a railroad contractor in Oregon, saw in the 1880s "an almost unbroken stream of emigrants from horizon to horizon. . . . Teams and covered wagons, horsemen, little bunches of cows, more wagons, some drawn by cows, men walking, women and children riding—an endless stream of hardy, optimistic folk, going west to seek their fortunes and to settle an empire."

Prospectors poured into unsettled areas in search of "pay dirt," railroads crisscrossed the continent, eastern and foreign capitalists invested in cattle and land bonanzas, and farmers took up the promise of free western lands. In 1867, Horace Greeley, editor of the New York *Tribune,* told New York City's unemployed: "If you strike off into the broad, free West, and make yourself a farm from Uncle Sam's generous domain, you will crowd nobody, starve nobody, and neither you nor your children need evermore beg for something to do."

With the end of the Civil War, white Americans again claimed a special destiny to expand across the continent. In the process, they crushed the culture of the Native Americans and ignored the contributions of people of other races, such as the Chinese miners and laborers and the Mexican herdsmen. As millions moved west, the states of Colorado, Washington, Montana, the Dakotas, Idaho, Wyoming, and Utah were carved out of the lands across the Mississippi. At the turn of the century, only Arizona, New Mexico, and Oklahoma remained as territories.

537

The West became a great colonial empire, harnessed to eastern capital and tied increasingly to national and international markets. Its raw materials, sent east by wagon, train, and ship, helped fuel eastern factories. Western economies relied heavily on the federal government, which subsidized their railroads, distributed their land, and spent millions of dollars for the upkeep of soldiers and Indians. Regional variations persisted; and Westerners remained proud of their individualistic traditions. Yet they imitated the East's social, cultural, and political patterns.

By the 1890s, the West of the lands beyond the Mississippi had undergone substantial change. In place of buffalo and unfenced vistas, there were cities and towns, health resorts, Paris fashions, homesteads, sheep ranches, and, in the arid regions, the beginnings of the irrigated agriculture that would reshape the West in the twentieth century. Ghost towns, abandoned farms, and the scars in the earth left by miners and farmers spoke to the less favorable side of settlement. As the new century dawned, the West had become a place of conquest and exploitation, as well as a mythic land of cowboys and quick fortunes.

BEYOND THE FRONTIER

The line of white settlement had reached the edge of the Missouri timber country by 1840. Beyond lay an enormous land of rolling prairies, parched deserts, and rugged, majestic mountains. Emerging from the timber country, travelers first encountered the Great Plains—treeless, nearly flat, an endless "sea of grassy hillocks." The Prairie Plains, the eastern part of the region, enjoyed rich soil and good rainfall. To the west were the High Plains, rough, semiarid, rising gently to the foothills of the Rocky Mountains.

Running from Alaska to central New Mexico, the Rockies presented a formidable barrier, and most travelers hurried through the northern passes, emerging in the desolate basin of present-day southern Idaho and Utah. On the west, the lofty Coast Ranges—the Cascades and Sierra Nevada—held back rainfall; beyond were the temperate lands of the Pacific Coast.

Early explorers like Zebulon Pike thought the country beyond the Mississippi was uninhabitable, fit only, Pike said, for "wandering and uncivilized aborigines." Mapmakers agreed; between 1825 and 1860, American maps showed this land as "The Great American Desert." As a result, settlement paused on the edge of the Plains, and most early settlers headed directly for California and Oregon.

Few rivers cut through the Plains; those that did raged in the winter and trickled in the summer. Rainfall usually did not reach 15 inches a year, not enough to support extensive agriculture. There was little lumber for homes and fences, and the tools of eastern settlement—the cast-iron plow, the boat, and the ax—were virtually useless on the tough and treeless Plains soil. "East of the Mississippi," historian Walter Prescott Webb noted, "civilization stood on three legs—land, water, and timber; west of the Mississippi not one but two of these legs were withdrawn—water and timber—and civilization was left on one leg—land."

Hot winds seared the Plains in summer, and northers, blizzards, and hail-storms froze them in winter. Wildlife roamed in profusion. The American bison, better known as the buffalo, grazed in enormous herds from Mexico to Canada. In 1865, perhaps fifteen million buffalo lived on the Plains, so many they seemed like "leaves in a forest" to an early observer. A single herd sighted in 1871 had four million head.

CRUSHING THE NATIVE AMERICANS

When Greeley urged New Yorkers to move West and "crowd nobody," he—like almost all white Americans—ignored the fact that large numbers of people al-ready lived there. At the close of the Civil War, Native Americans inhabited nearly half the United States. By 1880, they had been driven onto smaller and smaller reservations and were no longer an independent people. A decade later, even their culture had crumbled under the impact of white domination.

In 1865, nearly a quarter million Native Americans lived in the western half of the country. Tribes such as the Winnebago, Menominee, Cherokee, and Chippewa were resettled there, forced out of their eastern lands by advancing white settlement. Other tribes were native to the region. In the Southwest there were the Pueblo groups, including the Hopi, Zuni, and Rio Grande Pueblos. Peaceful farmers and herders, they had built up complex traditions around a set-tled way of life.

The Pueblo groups were cultivators of corn. They lived on the subdesert plateau of present-day western New Mexico and eastern Arizona. Harassed by powerful neighboring tribes, they built communal houses of adobe brick on high mesas or in cracks in the cliffs. More nomadic were the Camp Dwellers, the Jicarilla Apache and Navajo who roamed eastern New Mexico and western Texas. Blending elements of the Plains and Plateau environments, they lived in tepees or mud huts, grew some crops to supplement their hunting, and moved readily from place to place. The Navajo herded sheep and produced beautiful ornamental silver, baskets, and blankets. Fierce fighters, Apache horsemen were feared by whites and fellow Indians across the southwestern Plains.

Farther west were the tribes that inhabited present-day California. Divided into many small bands, they eked out a difficult existence living on roots, grubs, berries, acorns, and small game. In the Pacific Northwest, where fish and forest animals made life easier, the Klamath, Chinook, Yurok, and Shasta tribes developed a rich civilization. They built plank houses and canoes, worked extensively in wood, and evolved a complex social and political organization. Settled and determined, they resisted the invasion of the whites.

By the 1870s, most of these tribes had been destroyed or beaten into submission. The powerful Ute, crushed in 1855, ceded most of their Utah lands to the United States and settled on a small reservation near Great Salt Lake. The Navajo and Apache fought back fiercely, but between 1865 and 1873 they too were confined to reservations. The Native Americans of California succumbed to the contagious diseases carried by whites during the Gold Rush of 1849. Miners burned their villages, and by 1880, fewer than twenty thousand Indians lived in California.

LIFE OF THE PLAINS INDIANS

In the mid-nineteenth century, nearly two-thirds of the Native Americans lived on the Great Plains. The Plains tribes included the Sioux of present-day Minnesota and the Dakotas; the Blackfoot of Idaho and Montana; the Cheyenne, Crow, and Arapaho of the central Plains; the Pawnee of western Nebraska; and the Kiowa, Apache, and Comanche of present-day Texas and New Mexico.

Nomadic and warlike, the Plains Indians depended on the buffalo and horse. The modern horse, first brought by Spanish explorers in the 1500s, spread north from Mexico onto the Plains, and by the 1700s the Plains Indians' way of life had changed. The Plains tribes gave up farming almost entirely and hunted the buffalo, ranging widely over the rolling plains. The men became superb warriors and horsemen, among the best light cavalry in the world.

Migratory in culture, the Plains Indians formed tribes of several thousand people but lived in smaller bands of three to five hundred. The Comanche, who numbered perhaps seven thousand, had thirteen bands with such names as Burnt Meat, Making Bags While Moving, and Those Who Move Often. Each band was governed by a chief and a council of elder men, and Indians of the same tribe transferred freely from band to band. Bands acted independently, making it difficult for the U.S. government to deal with the fragmented tribes.

The bands followed and lived off the buffalo. Buffalo provided food, clothing, and shelter; the Indians, unlike later white hunters, used every part of the animal. The meat was dried or "jerked" in the hot Plains air. The skins made tepees, blankets, and robes. Buffalo bones became knives; tendons were made into bowstrings; horns and hooves were boiled into glue. Buffalo "chips"—dried manure—were burned as fuel. All in all, the buffalo was "a galloping department store."

Warfare between tribes usually took the form of brief raids and skirmishes. Plains Indians fought few prolonged wars and rarely coveted territory. Most conflicts involved only a few warriors intent on stealing horses or "counting coup"— touching an enemy's body with the hand or a special stick. Tribes developed a fierce and trained warrior class, recognized for achievements in battle. Speaking different languages, Native Americans of various tribes were nevertheless able to communicate with one another through a highly developed sign language.

The Plains tribes divided labor tasks according to gender. Men hunted, traded, supervised ceremonial activities, and cleared ground for planting. They usually held the positions of authority, such as chief or medicine man. Women were responsible for child rearing and artistic activity. They also performed the camp work, grew vegetables, prepared buffalo meat and hides, and gathered berries and roots. In most tribes, women played an important role in political, economic, and religious activities. Among the Navajo and Zuni, kinship descended from the mother's side, and Navajo women were in charge of most of the family's property. In tribes such as the Sioux, there was little difference in status. Men were respected for hunting and war, women for their artistic skills with quill and paint.

"AS LONG AS WATERS RUN": SEARCHING FOR AN INDIAN POLICY

Before the Civil War, Americans used the land west of the Mississippi as "one big reservation." The government named the area "Indian Country," moved eastern tribes there with firm treaty guarantees, and in 1834 passed the Indian Intercourse Act, which prohibited any white person from entering Indian country without a license.

The situation changed in the 1850s. Wagon trains wound their way to California and Oregon, miners pushed into western goldfields, and there was talk of a transcontinental railroad. To clear the way for settlement, the federal government in 1851 abandoned "One Big Reservation" in favor of a new policy of concentration. For the first time, it assigned definite boundaries to each tribe. The Sioux, for example, were given the Dakota country north of the Platte River, the Crows a large area near the Powder River, and the Cheyenne and Arapaho the Colorado foothills between the North Platte and Arkansas rivers for "as long as waters run and the grass shall grow."

The concentration policy lasted only a few years. Accustomed to hunting widely for buffalo, many Native Americans refused to stay within their assigned areas. White settlers poured into Indian lands, then called on the government to protect them. Indians were pushed out of Kansas and Nebraska in the 1850s, even as white reformers fought to hold those territories open for free blacks. In

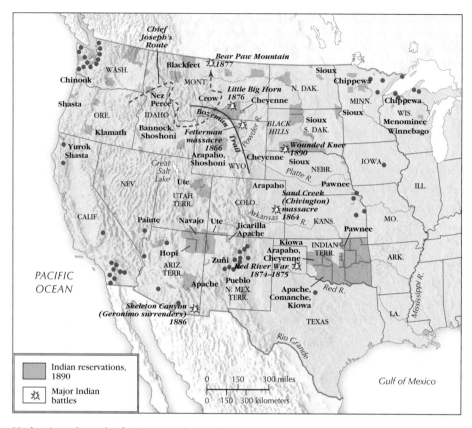

Native Americans in the West: Major Battles and Reservations

"They made us many promises, more than I remember, but they never kept but one; they promised to take our land, and they took it." So said Red Cloud of the Oglala Sioux, summarizing Native American–white relations in the 1870s.

1859, gold miners moved into the Pikes Peak country, touching off warfare with the Cheyenne and Arapaho.

In 1864, tired of the fighting, the two tribes asked for peace. Certain that the war was over, Chief Black Kettle led his seven hundred followers to camp on Sand Creek in southeastern Colorado. Early on the morning of November 29, 1864, a group of Colorado militia led by Colonel John M. Chivington attacked the sleeping group. "Kill and scalp all, big and little," Chivington told his men. "Nits make lice." Black Kettle tried to stop the ambush, raising first an American flag and then a white flag. Neither worked. The Native American men, women, and children were clubbed, stabbed, and scalped.

The Chivington massacre set off angry protests in Colorado and the East. Congress appointed an investigating committee, and the government concluded a treaty with the Cheyenne and Arapaho, condemning "the gross and wanton outrages." Still, the two tribes were forced to surrender their Sand Creek reservation in exchange for lands elsewhere. The Kiowa and Comanche were also ousted from areas they had been granted "forever" only a few years before. As the Sioux chief Spotted Tail said, "Why does not the Great Father put his red children on wheels so that he can move them as he will?"

Before long, the powerful Sioux were on the warpath in the great Sioux War of 1865–1867. Once again, an invasion of gold miners touched off the war, which flared even more intensely when the federal government announced plans to connect the various mining towns by building the Bozeman Trail through the heart of the Sioux hunting grounds in Montana. Red Cloud, the Sioux chief, determined to stop the trail. In December 1866, pursued by an army column under Captain William J. Fetterman, he lured the incautious Fetterman deep into the wilderness, ambushed him, and wiped out all eighty-two soldiers in his command.

The Fetterman massacre, coming so soon after the Chivington massacre, sparked a public debate over the nation's Indian policy. Like the policy itself, the debate reflected differing white views of the Native Americans. In the East, some reform, humanitarian, and church groups wanted a humane peace policy, directed toward educating and "civilizing" the tribes. Many white people, in the East and West, questioned this approach, convinced that Native Americans were savages unfit for civilization. Westerners, of course, had some reason to fear Indian attacks, and the fears often fed on wild rumors of scalped settlers and besieged forts. As a result, Westerners in general favored firm control over the Native Americans, including swift punishment of any who rebelled.

In 1867, the peace advocates won the debate. Halting construction on the Bozeman Trail, Congress created a Peace Commission of four civilians and three generals to end the Sioux War and eliminate permanently the causes of Indian wars. Setting out for the West, the Peace Commissioners agreed that only one policy offered a permanent solution: a policy of "small reservations" to isolate the Native Americans on distant lands, teach them to farm, and gradually "civilize" them.

FINAL BATTLES ON THE PLAINS

Few Native Americans settled peacefully into life on the new reservations. The reservation system not only changed their age-old customs; it chained them in a situation of poverty and isolation. Soon, young warriors and minor chiefs denounced the treaties and drifted back to the open countryside. In late 1868, warfare broke out again, and it took more than a decade of violence to beat the Indians into submission. The Kiowa and Comanche rampaged through the Texas

Panhandle, looting and killing, until the U.S. Army crushed them in the Red River War of 1874–1875 and ended warfare in the Southwest.

On the northern Plains, fighting resulted from the Black Hills Gold Rush of 1875. As prospectors tramped across Native American hunting grounds, the Sioux gathered to stop them. They were led by Rain-in-the-Face, the great war chief Crazy Horse, and the famous medicine man Sitting Bull. The army sent several columns of troops after the Indians, but one, under flamboyant Lieutenant Colonel George Armstrong Custer, pushed recklessly ahead, eager to claim the victory. On the morning of June 25, 1876, thinking he had a small band of Native Americans surrounded in their village on the banks of the Little Bighorn River in Montana, Custer divided his column and took 265 men toward it. Instead of finding a small band, he discovered he had stumbled on the main Sioux camp with 2500 warriors. It was the largest Native American army ever assembled in the United States.

By midafternoon it was over; Custer and his men were dead. Custer was largely responsible for the loss, but "Custer's Last Stand," set in blazing headlines across the country, set off a nationwide demand for revenge. Within a few months, the Sioux were surrounded and beaten, three thousand of them surrendering in October 1876. Sitting Bull and a few followers who had fled to Canada gave up in 1881.

This pictogram by Oglala Sioux Amos Bad Heart Bull is a Native American version of the battle of the Little Bighorn, also known as Custer's Last Stand.

The frozen body of Big Foot, leader of the Sioux band massacred at Wounded Knee, lies covered with snow, awaiting burial by the white burial party shown in the background.

The Sioux War ended the major Indian warfare in the West, but occasional outbreaks occurred for several years thereafter. In 1877, the Nez Percé tribe of Oregon, a people who had warmly welcomed Lewis and Clark in 1805, rebelled against government policy. Hoping to reach Canada, Chief Joseph led the tribe on a courageous flight lasting 75 days and covering 1321 miles. They defeated the pursuing army at every turn but then ran out of food, horses, and ammunition. Surrendering, they were sent to barren lands in the Indian Country of Oklahoma, and there, most of them died from disease.

In 1890, the Teton Sioux of South Dakota, bitter and starving, became restless. Many of them turned to the Ghost Dances, a set of dances and rites that grew from a vision of a Paiute messiah named Wovoka. Performance of the dances, Wovoka said, would bring back Native American lands and would cause the whites to disappear. All Native Americans would reunite, the earth would be covered with dust, and a new earth would come upon the old. The vanished buffalo would return in great herds.

The army intervened to stop the dancing, touching off violence that killed Sitting Bull and a number of other warriors. Frightened Native Americans fled southwest to join other Ghost Dancers under the aging chief Big Foot. Moving quickly, troops of the Seventh Cavalry, Custer's old regiment, caught up with Big Foot's band and took them to the army camp on Wounded Knee Creek in South Dakota. A Native American, it is thought, fired the first shot, returned by the army's new machine guns. Firing a shell a second, they shredded tepees and people. About two hundred men, women, and children were massacred in the snow.

THE END OF TRIBAL LIFE

The final step in Indian policy came in the 1870s and 1880s. Some reformers had long argued against segregating the Native Americans on reservations, urging instead that the nation assimilate them individually into white culture. These "assimilationists" wanted to use education, land policy, and federal law to eradicate tribal society.

Congress began to adopt the policy in 1871 when it ended the practice of treaty making with Native American tribes. Since tribes were no longer separate nations, they lost many of their political and judicial functions, and the power of the chiefs was weakened.

Tom Torlino, a Navajo Indian, photographed before and after his "assimilation." Torlino attended the Carlisle Indian School in Pennsylvania.

While Congress worked to break down the tribes, educators trained young Native Americans to adjust to white culture. In 1879, fifty Pawnee, Kiowa, and Cheyenne youths were brought east to the new Carlisle Indian School in Carlisle, Pennsylvania. Other Native American schools soon opened, including the Haskell Institute in Kansas and numerous day schools on the western reservations. The schools taught students to fix machines and farm; they forced young Indians to trim their long hair and made them speak English, banned the wearing of tribal paint or clothes, and forbade tribal ceremonies and dances. "Kill the Indian and save the man," said Richard H. Pratt, the army officer who founded the Carlisle School.

Land ownership was the final and most important link in the new policy. Native Americans who owned land, it was thought, would become responsible, self-reliant citizens. Deciding to give each Native American a farm, Congress in 1887 passed the Dawes Severalty Act, the most important legal development in Indian-white relations in more than three centuries.

Aiming to end tribal life, the Dawes Act divided tribal lands into small plots for distribution among members of the tribe. Each family head received 160 acres, single adults 80 acres, and children 40 acres.

Through the Dawes Act, 47 million acres of land were distributed to Native Americans and their families. There were another 90 million acres in the reservations, and these lands, often the most fertile, were sold to white settlers. Many Native Americans knew little about farming. Their tools were rudimentary, and in the culture of the Plains Indians, men had not ordinarily participated in farming. In 1934, the government returned to the idea of tribal land ownership, but by then 138 million acres of Indian land had shrunk to 48 million acres, half of which was barren.

The final blow to tribal life came not in the Dawes Act but in the virtual extermination of the buffalo, the Plains Indians' chief resource and the basis for their unique way of life. The killing began in the 1860s as the transcontinental railroads pushed west, and it stepped up as settlers found they could harm the Indians by harming the buffalo. "Kill every buffalo you can," an army officer said. "Every buffalo dead is an Indian gone." Then, in 1871, a Pennsylvania tannery discovered that buffalo hides made valuable leather. Professional hunters such as William F. "Buffalo Bill" Cody swarmed across the Plains, killing millions of the beasts.

Between 1872 and 1874, professional hunters slaughtered three million buffalo a year. In a frontier form of a factory system, riflemen, skinners, and transport wagons pushed through the vast herds, which shrank steadily behind them. A good hunter killed a hundred buffalo a day. Skinners took off the hides, removed the tongue, hump, and tallow, and left the rest.

By 1883, the buffalo were almost gone. When the government set out to produce the famous "buffalo nickel," the designer had to go to the Bronx Zoo in New
York City to find a buffalo.

By 1900, there were only 250,000 Native Americans in the country. (There
were 600,000 within the limits of the present-day United States in 1800, and
more than 5 million in 1492, when Columbus first set foot in the New World.)
Most of the Indians lived on reservations. Many lived in poverty. Alcoholism and
unemployment were growing problems, and Native Americans, no longer able to
live off the buffalo, became wards of the state. They lost their cultural distinctive-
ness. Once possessors of the entire continent, they had been crowded into
smaller and smaller areas, overwhelmed by the demand to become settled, liter-
ate, and English-speaking. "Except for the internment of the West Coast Japanese
during World War II," said historian Roger L. Nichols, "Indian removal is the only
example of large-scale government-enforced migration in American history. For
the Japanese, the move was temporary; for the Indians it was not."

Even as the Native Americans lost their identity, they entered the romantic
folklore of the West. Dime novels, snapped up by readers young and old, told
tales of Indian fighting on the Plains. "Buffalo Bill" Cody turned it all into a profitable business. Beginning in 1883, his Wild West Show ran for more than three
decades, playing to millions of viewers in the United States, Canada, and Europe.
It featured Plains Indians chasing buffalo, performing a war dance, and attacking a
settler's cabin. In 1885, Sitting Bull himself, victor over Custer at the battle of
Little Bighorn, performed in the show.

SETTLEMENT OF THE WEST

Between 1870 and 1900, white—and some African, Hispanic, and Asian—
Americans settled the enormous total of 430 million acres west of the
Mississippi; they took over more land than had been occupied by Americans in all
the years before 1870.

People moved West for many reasons. Some sought adventure; others
wanted to escape the drab routine of factory or city life. Many moved to
California for their health. The Mormons settled Utah to escape religious persecution. Others followed the mining camps, the advancing railroads, and the
farming and cattle frontier.

Whatever the specific reason, most people moved West to better their lot.
On the whole, their timing was good, for as the nation's population grew, so did
demand for the livestock and the agricultural, mineral, and lumber products of
the expanding West. Contrary to older historical views, the West did not act as a
major "safety valve," an outlet for social and economic tensions. The poor and un-

employed did not have the means to move there and establish farms. "Moreover," as Douglass C. North, an economic historian, said, "most people moved West in good times . . . in periods of rising prices, of expanding demand, when the prospects for making money from this new land looked brightest; and this aspect characterized the whole pattern of settlement."

MEN AND WOMEN ON THE OVERLAND TRAIL

The first movement west aimed not for the nearby Plains but for California and Oregon on the continent's far shore. It started in the 1849 Gold Rush to California, and in the next three decades perhaps as many as half a million individuals made the long journey. Some walked; others rode horses alone or in small groups. About half joined great caravans, numbering 150 wagons or more, that inched across the two thousand miles between the Missouri River and the Pacific Coast.

More often than not, men made the decision to make the crossing, but, except for the stampedes to the mines, migration usually turned out to be a family affair. Wives were consulted, though in some cases they had little real choice. They could either go along or live alone at home. While many women regretted leaving family and friends, they agreed to the trip, sometimes as eagerly as the men. The majority of people traveled in family groups, including in-laws, grandchildren, aunts, and uncles. As one historian said, "The quest for something new would take place in the context of the very familiar."

Individuals and wagon trains set out from various points along the Missouri River. Leaving in the spring and traveling through the summer, they hoped to reach their destination before the first snowfall. During April, travelers gradually assembled in spring camp just across the Missouri River, waiting for the new grass to ripen into forage. They packed and repacked the wagons and elected the trains' leaders, who would set the line of march, look for water and campsites, and impose discipline. Some trains adopted detailed rules, fearing a lapse into savagery in the wild lands across the Missouri. "Every man to carry with him a Bible and other religious books, as we hope not to degenerate into a state of barbarism," one agreement said.

Setting out in early May, travelers divided the enormous route into manageable portions. The first leg of the journey followed the Platte River west to Fort Kearney in central Nebraska Territory, a distance of about three hundred miles. The land was even, with good supplies of wood, grass, and water. From a distance, the white-topped wagons seemed driven by a common force, but, in fact, internal discipline broke down almost immediately. Arguments erupted over the pace of the march, the choice of campsites, the number of guards to post, whether to rest or push on. Elected leaders quit; new ones were chosen. Every train was filled with individualists, and as the son of one train captain said, "If you think it's any snap to run a wagon train of 66 wagons with every man in the train having a different idea of what is the best thing to do, all I can say is that some day you ought to try it."

Men, women, and children had different tasks on the trail. Men concerned themselves almost entirely with hunting buffalo and antelope, guard duty, and transportation. They rose at 4 A.M. to hitch the wagons, and after breakfast began the day's march. At noon, they stopped and set the teams to graze. After the midday meal, the march continued until sunset. Then, while the men relaxed, the women fixed dinner and the next day's lunch, and the children kindled the fires, brought water to camp, and searched for wood or other fuel. Walking fifteen miles a day, in searing heat and mountain cold, travelers were exhausted by late afternoon.

For women, the trail was lonely, and they worked to exhaustion. Before long, some adjusted their clothing to the harsh conditions, adopting the new bloomer pants, shortening their skirts, or wearing regular "wash dresses"—so called because they had shorter hemlines that did not drag on the wet ground on washday. Other women continued to wear their long dresses, thinking bloomers "indecent." Both men and women carried firearms in case of Indian attacks, but most emigrants saw few Indians en route.

What they often did see was trash, miles of it, for the wagon trains were an early example of the impact of migration and settlement on the western environment. On the Oregon and other trails, travelers sidestepped mounds of garbage, tin cans, furniture, cooking stoves, kegs, tools, and clothing, all discarded by people who had passed through before. Along a forty-mile trail in the Nevada desert, a migrant tallied two thousand abandoned wagons.

The first stage of the journey was deceptively easy, and travelers usually reached Fort Kearney by late May. The second leg led another 300 miles up the Platte River to Fort Laramie on the eastern edge of Wyoming Territory. The heat of June had dried the grass, and there was no wood. Anxious to beat the early snowfalls, travelers rested a day or two at the fort, then hurried on to South Pass, 280 miles to the west, the best route through the forbidding Rockies. The land was barren. It was now mid-July, but the mountain nights were so cold that ice formed in the water buckets.

Beyond South Pass, some emigrants turned south to the Mormon settlements on the Great Salt Lake, but most headed 340 miles north to Fort Hall on the Snake River in Idaho. It took another three months to cover the remaining 800 miles. California-bound travelers followed the Humboldt River through the summer heat of Nevada. Well into September, they began the final arduous push: first, a 55-mile stretch of desert; then 70 difficult miles up the eastern slopes of

Of the many dangers faced by travelers on the overland trails, among the most severe were prairie blizzards. As temperatures fell to –40 degrees, cattle would inhale particles of snow and sleet and die of suffocation.

the Sierra Nevada, laboriously hoisting wagons over massive outcrops of rock; and finally the last 100 miles down the western slopes to the welcome sight of California's Central Valley in October.

Under the best of conditions the trip took six months, sixteen hours a day, dawn to dusk, of hard, grueling labor. Walking halfway across the continent was no easy task, and it provided a never-to-be-forgotten experience for those who did it. The wagon trains, carrying the dreams of thousands of individuals, reproduced society in small focus: individualistic, hopeful, mobile, divided by age and gender roles, apprehensive, yet willing to strike out for the distant and new.

LAND FOR THE TAKING

As railroads pushed west in the 1870s and 1880s, locomotive trains replaced wagon trains, but the shift was gradual, and until the end of the century, emigrants often combined both modes of travel.

Traffic flowed in all directions, belying the image of a simple "westward" movement. Many people did go west, of course, but others, such as migrants from Mexico, became westerners by moving north, and Asian Americans moved eastward from the Pacific Coast. Whatever their route, they all ended up in the meeting ground of cultures that formed the modern West.

Why did they come? "The motive that induced us to part with the pleasant associations and the dear friends of our childhood days," explained Phoebe Judson, an early emigrant, "was to obtain from the government of the United States a grant of land that 'Uncle Sam' had promised to give to the head of each family who settled in this new country." A popular camp song reflected the same motive:

> Come along, come along—don't be alarmed,
> Uncle Sam is rich enough to give us all a farm.

Uncle Sam owned about 1 billion acres of land in the 1860s, much of it mountain and desert land unsuited for agriculture. By 1900, the various land laws had distributed half of it. Between 1862 and 1890, the government gave away 48 million acres under the Homestead Act of 1862, sold about 100 million acres to private citizens and corporations, granted 128 million acres to railroad companies to tempt them to build across the unsettled West, and sold huge tracts to the states.

The Homestead Act of 1862, a law of great significance, gave 160 acres of land to anyone who would pay a $10 registration fee and pledge to live on it and cultivate it for five years. The offer set off a mass migration of land-hungry Europeans, dazzled by a country that gave its land away. Americans also seized on the act's provisions, and between 1862 and 1900, nearly 600,000 families claimed free homesteads under it.

Yet the Homestead Act did not work as Congress had hoped. Few farmers and laborers had the cash to move to the frontier, buy farm equipment, and wait out the year or two before the farm became self-supporting. Tailored to the timber and water conditions of the East, the act did not work as well in the semiarid West. In the fertile valleys of the Mississippi, 160 acres provided a generous farm. A farmer on the Great Plains needed either a larger farm for dry farming or a smaller one for irrigation.

The Timber Culture Act of 1873 attempted to adjust the Homestead Act to western conditions. It allowed homesteaders to claim an additional 160 acres if they planted trees on a quarter of it within four years. A successful act, it distributed 10 million acres of land, encouraged needed forestation, and enabled homesteaders to expand their farms to a workable size.

Speculators made ingenious use of the land laws. Sending agents in advance of settlement, they moved along choice river bottoms or irrigable areas, accumulating large holdings to be held for high prices. In the arid West, where control of water meant control of the surrounding land, shrewd ranchers plotted their

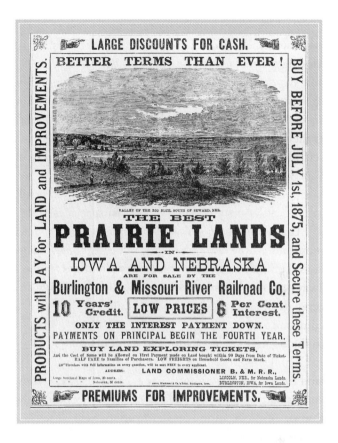

Railroad companies distributed elaborately illustrated brochures and broadsides to lure people to the West, where they could settle on land owned by the railroads.

holdings accordingly. In Colorado, one cattleman, John F. Iliff, owned only 105 small parcels of land, but by placing them around the few water holes, he effectively dominated an empire stretching over 6000 square miles.

Water, in fact, became a dominant western issue, since aside from the Pacific Northwest, northern California, parts of the Rocky Mountain West, and the eastern half of the Great Plains, much of the trans-Mississippi West was arid, receiving less than 20 inches of rainfall annually. People speculated in water as if it were gold and planned great irrigation systems in Utah, eastern Colorado, and California's Central Valley to "make the desert bloom."

Irrigators received a major boost in 1902 when the National Reclamation Act (the Newlands Act) set aside most of the proceeds from the sale of public lands in sixteen western states to finance irrigation projects in the arid states. Over the next decades, dams, canals, and irrigation systems channeled water into dry areas, creating a "hydraulic" society that was rich in crops and cities (such as Los Angeles and Phoenix), but ever thirstier and in danger of outrunning the precious water on which it all depended.

As beneficiaries of the government's policy of land grants for railway construction, the railroad companies were the West's largest landowners. Eager to have immigrants settle on the land they owned near the railroad right-of-way, and eager to boost their freight and passenger business, the companies sent agents to the East and Europe. Attractive brochures touted life in the West. The Union Pacific called the rocky Platte Valley in Nebraska "a flowery meadow of great fertility, clothed in nutritious grasses."

Railroad lines set up land departments and bureaus of immigration. The land departments priced the land, arranged credit terms, and even gave free farming courses to immigrants. The bureaus of immigration employed agents in Europe, met immigrants at eastern seaports, and ran special cars for land seekers heading west.

Half a billion acres of western land were given or sold to speculators and corporations. At the same time, only 600,000 homestead patents were issued, covering 80 million acres. Thus, only one acre in every nine initially went to individual pioneers, the intended beneficiaries of the nation's largesse. Two-thirds of all homestead claimants before 1890 failed in their efforts to farm their new land.

The Spanish-Speaking Southwest

In the nineteenth century, almost all Spanish-speaking people in the United States lived in California, Arizona, New Mexico, Texas, and Colorado. Their numbers were small—California had only 8,086 Mexican residents in 1900—but the influence of their culture and institutions was large. In some respects, the southwestern frontier was more Spanish American than Anglo-American.

Pushing northward from Mexico, the Spanish gradually established the present-day economic structure of the Southwest. They brought with them techniques of mining, stock raising, and irrigated farming. After winning independence in the 1820s, the Mexicans brought new laws and ranching methods as well as chaps and the burro. Both Spanish and Mexicans created the legal framework for distributing land and water, a precious resource in the Southwest.

In Southern California, the Californios, descendants of the original colonizers, began after the 1860s to lose their once vast landholdings to drought and mortgages. But as they died out, Mexican Americans continued the Spanish-Mexican influence. In 1880, one-fourth of the residents of Los Angeles County were Spanish speaking.

In New Mexico, Spanish-speaking citizens remained the majority ethnic group until the 1940s, and the Spanish Mexican culture dominated the territory. Contests over land grants became New Mexico's largest industry; lawyers who dealt in them amassed huge holdings.

Throughout the Southwest, the Spanish Mexican heritage gave a distinctive shape to society. Men headed the families and dominated economic life. Women had substantial economic rights (though few political ones), and they enjoyed a status their English American counterparts did not have. Wives kept full control of property acquired before their marriage; they also held half title to all property in a marriage, which later caused many southwestern states to pass community property laws.

In addition, the Spanish Mexican heritage fostered a modified economic caste system, a strong Roman Catholic influence, and the primary use of the Spanish language. Continuous immigration from Mexico kept language and cultural ties strong. Spanish was the region's first or second language. Confronted by Sheriff Pat Garrett in a darkened room, New Mexico's famous outlaw Billy the Kid died asking, "*Quién es? Quién es?*" ("Who is it? Who is it?").

THE BONANZA WEST

Between 1850 and 1900, wave after wave of newcomers swept across the trans-Mississippi West. There were riches for the taking, hidden in gold-washed streams, spread lushly over grass-covered prairies, or available in the gullible minds of greedy newcomers. The nineteenth-century West took shape in the search for mining, cattle, and land bonanzas that drew eager settlers from the East and around the world.

As with all bonanzas, the consequences in the West were uneven growth, boom-and-bust economic cycles, and wasted resources. Society seemed constantly in the making. People moved here and there, following river bottoms, gold strikes, railroad tracks, and other opportunities. "Instant cities" arose. San Francisco, Salt Lake City, and Denver were the most spectacular examples, but every cow town and mining camp witnessed similar phenomena of growth. Boston needed more than two centuries to attract one-third of a million people; San Francisco did the same in a little more than twenty years.

Many Westerners had left home to get rich quickly, and they adopted institutions that reflected that goal. As a contemporary poem said:

> Love to see the stir an' bustle
> In the busy town,
> Everybody on the hustle
> Saltin' profits down.
> Everybody got a wad a'
> Ready cash laid by;
> Ain't no flies on Colorado—
> Not a cussed fly.

In their lives, the West was an idea as well as a region, and the idea molded them as much as they molded it.

THE MINING BONANZA

Mining was the first important magnet to attract people to the West. Many hoped to "strike it rich" in gold and silver, but at least half the newcomers had no intention of working in the mines. Instead, they provided food, clothing, and services to the thousands of miners.

The California Gold Rush of 1849 began the mining boom and set the pattern for subsequent strikes in other regions. Individual prospectors made the first strikes, discovering pockets of gold along streams flowing westward from the Sierra Nevada. To get the gold, they used a simple process called placer mining, which required little skill, technology, or capital. A placer miner needed only a shovel, a washing pan, and a good claim. As the placers gave out, a great deal of gold remained, but it was locked in quartz or buried deep in the earth. Mining became an expensive business, far beyond the reach of the average miner.

Large corporations moved in to dig the deep shafts and finance costly equipment. Quartz mining required heavy rock crushers, mercury vats to dissolve the gold, and large retorts to recapture it. Eastern and European financiers assumed

Before the California Gold Rush of 1849, San Francisco was a sleepy little Spanish-Mexican village called Yerba Buena. Gold seekers turned it into a boomtown with an international population. Here, Spanish Mexican rancheros, white prospectors, Chinese laborers, and a top-hatted professional gambler mingle in a San Francisco saloon.

control, labor became unionized, and mining towns took on some of the characteristics of the industrial city. Individual prospectors meanwhile dashed on to the next find. Unlike other frontiers, the mining frontier moved from west to east, as the original California miners—the "yonder-siders," they were called—hurried eastward in search of the big strike.

In 1859, fresh strikes were made near Pikes Peak in Colorado and in the Carson River Valley of Nevada. News of both discoveries set off wild migrations—100,000 miners were in Pikes Peak country by June 1859. The gold there quickly played out, but the Nevada find uncovered a thick bluish black ore that was almost pure silver and gold. A quick-witted drifter named Henry T. P. Comstock talked his way into partnership in the claim, and word of the Comstock Lode—with ore worth $3,876 a ton—flashed over the mountains.

Thousands of miners climbed the Sierra Nevada that summer. The biggest strike was yet to come. In 1873, John W. Mackay and three partners formed a company to dig deep into the mountain, and at 1,167 feet they hit the Big Bonanza, a seam of gold and silver more than 54 feet wide. It was the richest discovery in the history of mining. Between 1859 and 1879, the Comstock Lode produced gold and silver worth $306 million.

In the 1860s and 1870s, important strikes were made in Washington, Idaho, Nevada, Colorado, Montana, Arizona, and Dakota. Extremely mobile, miners flocked from strike to strike, and new camps and mining towns sprang up overnight.

The final fling came in the Black Hills rush of 1874 to 1876. The army had tried to keep miners out of the area, the heart of the Sioux hunting grounds, and even sent a scientific party under Colonel George Armstrong Custer to disprove the rumors of gold and stop the miners' invasion. Instead, Custer found gold all over the hills, and the rush was on. Miners, gamblers, desperadoes, and prostitutes flocked to Deadwood, the most lawless of all the mining camps. There, Martha Jane Canary—a crack shot who, as Calamity Jane, won fame as a scout and teamster—fell in love with "Wild Bill" Hickok. Hickok himself—a western legend who had tamed Kansas cow towns, killed an unknown number of men, and toured in Buffalo Bill's Wild West Show—died in Deadwood, shot in the back of the head. Hickok was 39 years old.

Towns such as Deadwood, in the Dakota Territory; Virginia City, Nevada; Leadville, Colorado; and Tombstone, Arizona, demonstrated a new development process in the frontier experience. The farming frontier had developed naturally in a rural setting. On the mining frontier, the germ of a city—the camp—appeared almost simultaneously with the first "strike." Periodicals, the latest fashions, theaters, schools, literary clubs, and lending libraries came quickly to the camps, providing civilized refinements not available on other frontiers.

Urbanization also created the need for municipal government, sanitation, and law enforcement.

Mining camps were governed by a simple democracy. Soon after a strike, the miners in the area met to organize a mining "district" and adopted rules governing behavior in it. Rules regulated the size and boundaries of claims, established procedures for settling disputes, and set penalties for crimes. Petty criminals were banished from the district; serious offenders were hanged. In the case of a major dispute, the whole camp gathered, chose legal counsel for both sides, and heard the evidence. If all else failed, miners formed secret vigilance committees to hang a few offenders as a lesson to the rest. Early visitors to the mining country were struck by the way miners, solitary and competitive, joined together, founded a camp, and created a society.

The camps were mostly male, made up of "men who can rough it" and a few "ladies of spirit and energy." In 1870, men outnumbered women in the mining districts by more than two to one; there were few children.

In most camps, between one-quarter and one-half of the population was foreign born. The lure of gold drew large numbers of Chinese, Chileans, Peruvians, Mexicans, French, Germans, and English. Experienced miners, the Latin Americans brought valuable mining techniques. At least six thousand Mexicans joined the California rush of 1849, and by 1852, there were twenty-five thousand

Leadville, Colorado, in the 1870s. Founded as a gold camp in 1860, by the 1880s Leadville, with thirty thousand residents, was the second largest city in the state, trailing only Denver.

Chinese in California. Painstaking, the Chinese profitably worked claims others had abandoned. In the 1860s, almost one-third of the miners in the West were Chinese.

Hostility often surfaced against foreign miners, particularly the French, Latin Americans, and Chinese. In 1850, California passed a Foreign Miners' Tax that charged foreign miners a $20 monthly licensing fee. As intended, it drove out Mexicans and other foreigners. Riots against Chinese laborers occurred in the 1870s and 1880s in Los Angeles, San Francisco, Seattle, Reno, and Denver. Responding to pressure, Congress passed the Chinese Exclusion Act of 1882, which suspended immigration of Chinese laborers for ten years. The number of Chinese in the United States fell drastically.

By the 1890s, the early mining bonanza was over. All told, the western mines contributed billions of dollars to the economy. They had helped finance the Civil War and provided needed capital for industrialization. The vast boost in silver production from the Comstock Lode changed the relative value of gold and silver, the base of American currency. Bitter disputes over the currency affected politics and led to the famous "battle of the standards" in the presidential election of 1896 (see Chapter 20).

The mining frontier populated portions of the West and sped its process of political organization. Nevada, Idaho, and Montana were granted early statehood because of mining. Merchants, editors, lawyers, and ministers moved with the advancing frontier, establishing permanent settlements. Women in the mining camps helped to foster family life and raised the moral tone by campaigning against drinking, gambling, and prostitution. But not all the effects of the mining boom were positive. The industry also left behind painful scars in the form of invaded Indian reservations, pitted hills, and lonely ghost towns.

GOLD FROM THE ROOTS UP:
THE CATTLE BONANZA

"There's gold from the grass roots down," said California Joe, a guide in the gold districts of Dakota in the 1870s, "but there's more gold from the grass roots up." Ranchers began to recognize the potential of the vast grasslands of the West. The Plains were covered with buffalo or grama grass, a wiry variety with short, hard stems. Cattle thrived on it.

For twenty years after 1865, cattle ranching dominated the "open range," a vast fenceless area extending from the Texas Panhandle north into Canada. The techniques of the business came from Mexico. Long before American cowboys moved herds north, their Mexican counterparts, the *vaqueros,* developed the essential techniques of branding, roundups, and roping. The cattle themselves, the famous Texas longhorns, also came from Mexico. Spreading over the grasslands of southern Texas, the longhorns multiplied rapidly. Although their meat was coarse and stringy, they fed a nation hungry for beef at the end of the Civil War.

The problem was getting the beef to eastern markets, and Joseph G. McCoy, a livestock shipper from Illinois, solved it. Looking for a way to market Texas beef, McCoy conceived the idea of taking the cattle to railheads in Kansas. He talked first with the president of the Missouri Pacific, who ordered him out of his office, and then with the head of the Kansas Pacific, who laughed at the idea. The persistent McCoy finally signed a contract in 1867 with the Hannibal and St. Joseph Railroad. Searching for an appropriate rail junction, he settled on the sleepy Kansas town of Abilene, "a very small, dead place," he remembered, with about a dozen log huts and one nearly bankrupt saloon.

In September 1867, McCoy shipped the first train of twenty cars of longhorn cattle. By the end of the year, a thousand carloads had followed, all headed for Chicago markets. In 1870, 300,000 head of Texas cattle reached Abilene, followed the next year—the peak year—by 700,000 head. The Alamo Saloon, crowded with tired cowboys at the end of the drive, now employed seventy-five bartenders, working three 8-hour shifts.

The profits were enormous. Drivers bought cheap Texas steers for $4 a head and sold them for $30 or $40 a head at the northern railhead. The most famous trail was the Chisholm, running from southern Texas through Oklahoma Territory to Ellsworth and Abilene, Kansas, on the Kansas Pacific Railroad.

Cowboys pushed steers northward in herds of two to three thousand. Novels and films have portrayed the cowboys as white, but at least a quarter of them were black, and possibly another quarter were Mexicans. A typical crew on the trail north might have eight men, half of them black or Mexican. Most of the trail bosses were white; they earned about $125 a month. James "Jim" Perry, a renowned black cowboy who worked for more than twenty years as a rider, roper, and cook for the XIT ranch, said, "If it weren't for my damned old black face, I'd have been a boss long ago."

Like miners, cattlemen lived beyond the formal reach of the law and so established their own. Ranchers adopted rules for cattle ownership, branding, roundups, and drives, and they formed associations to enforce them. The Wyoming Stock Growers' Association, the largest and most formidable, had four hundred members owning two million cattle; its reach extended well beyond Wyoming into Colorado, Nebraska, Montana, and the Dakotas.

Hollywood images to the contrary, there was little violence in the booming cow towns. The number of homicides in a year never topped five in any town, and in many years no one was killed. Doc Holliday and William B. "Bat"

Masterson never killed anyone. John Wesley Hardin, a legendary teenaged gun-man, shot only one man, firing blindly through a hotel room wall to stop him from snoring. Famous western sheriffs had everyday duties. Wild Bill Hickok served as Abilene's street commissioner, and the Wichita city council made its lawmen, including Wyatt Earp, repair streets and sidewalks before each cattle season.

By 1880, more than six million cattle had been driven to northern markets. But the era of the great cattle drive was ending. Farmers were planting wheat on

Cattle Trails
Cattle raised in Texas were driven along the cattle trails to the northern railheads, and trains carried them to market.

the old buffalo ranges; barbed wire, a recent invention, cut across the trails and divided up the big ranches. Mechanical improvements in slaughtering, refrigerated transportation, and cold storage modernized the industry. Ranchers bred the Texas longhorns with heavier Hereford and Angus bulls, and as the new breeds proved profitable, more and more ranches opened on the northern ranges.

By the mid-1880s, some 4.5 million cattle grazed the High Plains, reminding people of the once great herds of buffalo. Stories of vast profits circulated, attracting outside capital. Large investments transformed ranching into big business, often controlled by absentee owners and subject to new problems.

The winter of 1886–1887 was one of the worst in western history. Temperatures dropped to 45 degrees below zero, and cattle that once would have saved themselves by drifting ahead of the storms came up against the new barbed wire fences. Herds jammed together, pawing the frozen ground or stripping bark from trees in search of food. Cattle died by the tens of thousands. In the spring of 1887, when the snows thawed, ranchers found stacks of carcasses piled up against the fences.

The melting snows did, however, produce a lush crop of grass for the survivors. The cattle business recovered, but it took different directions. Outside capital, so plentiful in the boom years, dried up. Ranchers began fencing their lands, reducing their herds, and growing hay for winter food.

The last roundup on the northern ranges took place in 1905. Ranches grew smaller, and some ranchers, at first in the scrub country of the Southwest, then on the Plains themselves, switched to raising sheep. By 1900, there were nearly thirty-eight million sheep west of the Missouri River, far more than there were cattle.

Ranchers and sheepherders fought bitterly to control the grazing lands, but they had one problem in common: the troubles ahead. Homesteaders, armed with barbed wire and new strains of wheat, were pushing onto the Plains, and the day of the open range was over.

SODBUSTERS ON THE PLAINS: THE FARMING BONANZA

Like miners and cattle ranchers, millions of farmers moved into the West in the decades after 1870 to seek crop bonanzas and new ways of life. Some realized their dreams; many fought just to survive.

Between 1870 and 1900, farmers cultivated more land than ever before in American history. They peopled the Plains from Dakota to Texas, pushed the Indians out of their last sanctuary in Oklahoma, and poured into the basins and foothills of the Rockies. By 1900, the western half of the nation contained almost 30 percent of the population, compared to less than 1 percent just a half century earlier.

Unlike mining, farm settlement often followed predictable patterns, taking population from states east of the settlement line and moving gradually westward. Crossing the Mississippi, farmers settled first in western Iowa, Minnesota, Nebraska, Kansas, Texas, and South Dakota. The movement slumped during the depression of the 1870s, but then a new wave of optimism carried thousands more west. Several years of above average rainfall convinced farmers that the Dakotas, western Nebraska and Kansas, and eastern Colorado were the "rain belt of the Plains." Between 1870 and 1900, the population on the Plains tripled.

In some areas, the newcomers were blacks who had fled the South, fed up with beatings and murders, crop liens, and the Black Codes that institutionalized their subordinate status. In 1879, about six thousand African Americans known as the Exodusters left their homes in Louisiana, Mississippi, and Texas to establish new and freer lives in Kansas, the home of John Brown and the Free-Soil campaigns of the 1850s. Once there, they farmed or worked as laborers; women worked in the fields alongside the men or cleaned houses and took in washing to make ends meet. All told, the Exodusters homesteaded 20,000 acres of land, and though they met prejudice, it was not as extreme as they had known at home.

Other African Americans moved to Oklahoma, thinking they might establish the first African American state. Whether headed for Oklahoma or Kansas, they picked up and moved in sizable groups that were based on family units; they took with them the customs they had known, and in their new homes they were able, for the first time, to have some measure of self-government.

For blacks and whites alike, farming on the Plains presented new problems. There was little surface water, and wells ranged between 50 and 500 feet deep. Well drillers charged up to $2 a foot. Taking advantage of the steady Plains winds, windmills brought the water to the surface, but they too were expensive, and until 1900, many farmers could not afford them. Lumber for homes and fences was also scarce.

Unable to afford wood, farmers often started out in dreary sod houses. Cut into 3-foot sections, the thick prairie sod was laid like brick, with space left for two windows and a door. Since glass was scarce, cloth hung over the windows; a blanket was hung from the ceiling to make two rooms. Sod houses were small, provided little light and air, and were impossible to keep clean. When it rained, water seeped through the roof. Yet a sod house cost only $2.78 to build.

Disappointed with the failures of Reconstruction and fearful of the violence that surrounded them, many southern blacks migrated to Kansas in the 1870s and 1880s. Comparing their trek to the biblical story of the Israelites' exodus from Egypt, they became known as "Exodusters."

Outside, the Plains environment sorely tested the men and women who moved there. Neighbors were distant; the land stretched on as far as the eye could see. Always the wind blew.

In the winters, savage storms swept the open grasslands. Summertime temperatures stayed near 110 degrees for weeks at a time. Fearsome rainstorms, building in the summer's heat, beat down the young corn and wheat. The summers also brought grasshoppers, arriving without warning, flying in clouds so huge they shut out the sun. The grasshoppers ate everything in sight: crops, clothing, mosquito netting, tree bark, even plow handles. In the summer of 1874, they devastated the whole Plains from Texas to the Dakotas, eating everything "but the mortgage," as one farmer said.

New Farming Methods

Farmers adopted new techniques to meet conditions on the Plains. For one thing, they needed cheap and effective fencing material, and in 1874, Joseph F. Glidden, a farmer from De Kalb, Illinois, provided it with the invention of barbed wire. By 1883, his factory was turning out 600 miles of barbed wire every day, and farmers were buying it faster than it could be produced.

Dry farming, a new technique, helped compensate for the lack of rainfall. By plowing furrows 12 to 14 inches deep and creating a dust mulch to fill the furrow, farmers loosened the soil and slowed evaporation. Wheat farmers imported European varieties of plants that could withstand the harsh Plains winters.

Farm technology changed long before the Civil War, but later developments improved it. In 1877, James Oliver of Indiana patented a chilled-iron plow with a smooth-surfaced moldboard that did not clog in the thick prairie soils. The spring-tooth harrow (1869) sped soil preparation; the grain drill (1874) opened furrows and scientifically fed seed into the ground. The lister (1880) dug a deep furrow, planted corn at the bottom, and covered the seed—all in one operation.

The first baling press was built in 1866, and the hay loader was patented in 1876. The first successful harvester, the cord binder (1878), cut and tied bundles of grain, enabling two men and a team of horses to harvest 20 acres of wheat a day. Invented earlier, threshers grew larger; employing as many as nine men and ten horses, one machine could thresh 300 bushels of grain a day.

In the late 1870s, huge bonanza farms rose, run by the new machinery and financed with outside capital. Oliver Dalrymple, the most famous of the bonanza farmers, headed an experiment in North Dakota's Red River Valley in 1875, then moved on to manage the Grandin Bonanza of 61,000 acres, five times the size of Manhattan Island. Dalrymple hired armies of workers, bought machinery by the carload, and planted on a scale that dazzled the West.

The bonanza farms—thanks to their size and machinery—captured the country's imagination. Using 200 pairs of harrows, 155 binders, and 16 threshers, Dalrymple produced 600,000 bushels of wheat in 1881. He and other bonanza managers profited from the economies of scale, buying materials at wholesale prices and receiving rebates from the railroads. Then a period of drought began. Rainfall dropped between 1885 and 1890, and the large-scale growers found it hard to compete with smaller farmers who diversified their crops and cultivated more intensively. Many of the large bonanzas slowly disintegrated, and Dalrymple himself went bankrupt in 1896.

DISCONTENT ON THE FARM

Touring the South in the 1860s, Oliver H. Kelley, a clerk in the Department of Agriculture, was struck by the drabness of rural life. In 1867, he founded the National Grange of the Patrons of Husbandry, known simply as the Grange. The Grange provided social, cultural, and educational activities for its members. Its constitution banned involvement in politics, but Grangers often ignored the rules and supported railroad regulation and other measures.

A work crew on the Dalrymple farm in the Red River Valley gathers grain wired into bundles by self-binding harvesters. In 1877, Dalrymple used a hundred workers to harvest his 4000 acres of wheat; by 1884, the number of harvesters employed on the farm had increased to a thousand.

The Grange grew rapidly during the depression of the 1870s, and by 1875, it had more than 800,000 members in 20,000 local Granges. Most were in the Midwest and South. The Granges set up cooperative stores, grain elevators, warehouses, insurance companies, and farm machinery factories. Many failed, but in the meantime the organization made its mark. Picking up where the Grange left off, farm-oriented groups such as the Farmers' Alliance, with branches in both South and West, began to attract followers.

Like the cattle boom, the farming boom ended sharply after 1887. A severe drought that year cut harvests, and other droughts followed in 1889 and 1894. Thousands of new farmers were wiped out on the western Plains. Between 1888 and 1892, more than half the population of western Kansas left. Farmers grew angry and restless. They complained about declining crop prices, rising railroad rates, and heavy mortgages.

Although many farmers were unhappy, the peopling of the West in those years transformed American agriculture. The states beyond the Mississippi became the garden land of the nation. California sent fruit, wine, and wheat to eastern markets. Under the Mormons, Utah flourished with irrigation. Texas beef stocked the country's tables, and vast wheat fields, stretching to the horizon, covered Minnesota, the Dakotas, Montana, and eastern Colorado. All produced more than Americans could consume. By 1890, American farmers were exporting large amounts of wheat and other crops.

Farmers became more commercial and scientific. They needed to know more and work harder. Mail-order houses and rural free delivery diminished their isolation and tied them ever closer to the national future. "This is a new age to the farmer," said a statistician in the Department of Agriculture in 1889. "He is now, more than ever before, a citizen of the world."

THE FINAL FLING

As the West filled in with people, pressure mounted on the president and Congress to open the last Indian territory, Oklahoma, to settlers. In March 1889, Congress acted and forced the Creek and Seminole tribes, who had been moved into Oklahoma in the 1820s, to surrender their rights to the land. With arrangements complete, President Benjamin Harrison announced the opening of the Oklahoma District as of noon, April 22, 1889.

Preparations were feverish all along the frontier. On the morning of April 22, nearly a hundred thousand people lined the Oklahoma borders.

At noon, the starting flag dropped. Bugles and cannon signaled the opening of the "last" territory. Horsemen lunged forward; overloaded wagons collided and overturned.

By sunset that day, settlers claimed twelve thousand homesteads, and the 1.92 million acres of the Oklahoma District were officially settled. Homesteaders threw up shelters for the night. By evening, Oklahoma City, that morning merely a spot on the prairie with cottonwoods and grass, had ten thousand people.

The "Boomers" and "Sooners"—those who had jumped the gun—reflected the speed of western settlement. "Creation!" a character in Edna Ferber's novel *Cimarron* declared. "Hell! That took six days. This was done in one. It was History made in an hour—and I helped make it."

Between the Civil War and 1900, the West witnessed one of the greatest migrations in history. With the Native Americans driven into smaller and smaller areas, farms, ranches, mines, and cities took over the vast lands from the Mississippi to the Pacific. The 1890 census noted that for the first time in the country's history, "there can hardly be said to be a frontier line." Picking up the theme, Frederick Jackson Turner, a young history instructor at the University of Wisconsin, examined its importance in an influential 1893 paper, "The Significance of the Frontier in American History."

"The existence of an area of free land," Turner wrote, "its continuous re-cession, and the advance of American settlement westward, explain American development." It shaped customs and character; gave rise to independence, self-confidence, and individualism; and fostered invention and adaptation. Historians have substantially modified Turner's thesis by pointing to frontier conservatism and imitativeness, the influence of varying racial groups, and the persistence of European ideas and institutions. Most recently, they have shown that family and community loomed as large as individualism on the frontier; men, women, and children played very much the same roles as they had back home.

Rejecting Turner almost completely, a group of "new Western historians" has advanced a different and complex view of the West, and one with few heroes and heroines. Emphasizing the region's racial and ethnic diversity, these historians stress the role of women as well as men, trace struggles between economic inter-ests instead of fights between gunslingers, and question the impact of develop-ment on the environment. White English-speaking Americans, they suggest, could be said to have conquered the West rather than settled it.

The West, in this view, was not settled by a wave of white migrants moving west across the continent (Turner's "frontier") but by a set of waves—Anglo, Mexican American, African American, Asian American, and others—moving in many directions and interacting with each other and with Native American cul-tures to produce the modern West. Nor did western history end in 1890 as Turner would have it. Instead, migration, development, and economic exploita-tion continued into the twentieth century, illustrated in the fact that the number of people who moved to the West after 1900 far exceeded those who had moved there before.

In both the nineteenth and twentieth centuries, there can be no doubt that the image of the frontier and the West influenced American development. Western lands attracted European, Latin American, and Asian immigrants, adding to the society's talent and diversity. The mines, forests, and farms of the West fueled the economy, sent raw materials to eastern factories, and fed the growing cities. Though defeated in warfare, the Native Americans and Mexicans influenced art, architecture, law, and western folklore. The West was the first American empire, and it had a profound impact on the American mind and imagination.

18

THE INDUSTRIAL SOCIETY

I n 1876, Americans celebrated their first century of independence. Survivors of a recent civil war, they observed the centenary proudly and rather self-consciously, in song and speech, and above all in a grand Centennial Exposition held in Philadelphia, Pennsylvania.

Spread over 13 acres, the exposition focused more on the present than the past. Fairgoers strolled through exhibits of life in colonial times, then hurried off to see the main attractions: machines, inventions, and products of the new industrial era. They saw linoleum, a new, easy-to-clean floor covering. For the first time, they tasted root beer, supplied by a young druggist named Charles Hires, and the exotic banana, wrapped in foil and selling for a dime. They saw their first bicycle, an awkward high-wheeled contraption with solid tires.

A Japanese pavilion generated widespread interest in the culture of Japan. There was also a women's building, the first ever in a major exposition. Inside were displayed paintings and sculpture by women artists, along with rows of textile machinery staffed by female operators.

In the entire exposition, machinery was the focus, and Machinery Hall was the most popular building. Here were the products of an ever improving civilization. Long lines of the curious waited to see the telephone, Alexander Graham Bell's new device. ("My God, it talks!" the emperor of Brazil exclaimed.) Thomas A. Edison displayed several recent inventions, while nearby, whirring machines turned out bricks, chewing tobacco, and other products. Fairgoers saw the first public display of the typewriter, Elisha Otis's new elevator, and the Westinghouse railroad air brake.

But above all, they crowded around the mighty Corliss engine, the focal point of the exposition. A giant steam engine, it dwarfed everything else in Machinery Hall, its twin vertical cylinders towering almost four stories in the air. Alone, it supplied power for the eight thousand other machines, large and small, on the exposition grounds. Poorly designed, the Corliss was soon obsolete, but for the moment it captured the nation's imagination. It symbolized swift movement toward an industrial and urban society. John Greenleaf Whittier, the aging rural poet, likened it to the snake in the Garden of Eden and refused to see it.

As Whittier feared, the United States was fast becoming an industrial society. Developments earlier in the century laid the basis, but the most spectacular advances in industrialization came during the three decades after the Civil War. At the start of the war, the country lagged well behind industrializing nations such as Great Britain, France, and Germany. By 1900, it had vaulted far into the lead, with a manufacturing output that exceeded the *combined* output of its three European rivals. Over the same years, cities grew, technology advanced, and farm production rose. Developments in manufacturing, mining, agriculture, transportation, and communications changed society.

Many Americans eagerly sought the change. William Dean Howells, a leading novelist, visited the Centennial Exposition and stood in awe before the Corliss. Comparing it to the paintings and sculpture on display, Howells preferred the machine: "It is in these things of iron and steel," he said, "that the national genius most freely speaks."

INDUSTRIAL DEVELOPMENT

American industry owed its remarkable growth to several considerations. It fed on an abundance of natural resources: coal, iron, timber, petroleum, waterpower. An iron manufacturer likened the nation to "a gigantic bowl filled with treasure." Labor was also abundant, drawn from American farm families and the hosts of European immigrants who flocked to American mines, cities, and factories. Nearly eight million immigrants arrived in the 1870s and 1880s; another fifteen million came between 1890 and 1914—large figures for a nation whose total population in 1900 was about seventy-six million people.

The burgeoning population led to expanded markets, which new devices such as the telegraph and telephone helped to exploit. The swiftly growing urban populations devoured goods, and the railroads, spreading pell-mell across the land, linked the cities together and opened a national market. Within its boundaries, the United States had the largest free-trade market in the world, while tariff barriers partially protected its producers from outside competition.

Expansive market and labor conditions buoyed the confidence of investors, European and American, who provided large amounts of capital. Technological progress, so remarkable in these years, doomed some older industries (tallow, for example) but increased productivity in others, such as the kerosene industry, and created entirely new industries as well. Through inventions such as the harvester and the combine, it also helped foster a firm agricultural base, on which industrialization depended.

Eager to promote economic growth, government at all levels—federal, state, and local—gave manufacturers money, land, and other resources. Other benefits, too, flowed from the American system of government: stability, commitment to the concept of private property, and, initially at least, a reluctance to regulate industrial activity. Unlike their European counterparts, American manufacturers faced few legal or social barriers, and their main domestic rivals, the southern planters, had lost political power in the Civil War.

In this atmosphere, entrepreneurs flourished. Taking steps crucial for industrialization, they organized, managed, and assumed the financial risks of the new enterprises. Admirers called them captains of industry; foes labeled them robber barons. To some degree, they were both—creative *and* acquisitive. If sometimes they seemed larger than life, it was because they dealt in concepts, distances, and quantities often unknown to earlier generations.

Industrial growth, it must be remembered, was neither a simple nor steady nor inevitable process. It involved human decisions and brought with it large social benefits and costs. Growth varied from industry to industry and from year to year. It was concentrated in the Northeast, where in 1890, more than 85 percent of America's manufactured goods originated. The more sparsely settled West provided raw materials, while the South, although making major gains in iron, textiles, and tobacco, had to rebuild after wartime devastation.

Still, industrial development proceeded at an extraordinary pace. Between 1865 and 1914, the real gross national product—the total monetary value of all goods and services produced in a year, with prices held stable—grew at a rate of more than 4 percent a year, increasing about eightfold overall. As Robert Higgs, an economic historian, noted, "Never before had such rapid growth continued for so long."

AN EMPIRE ON RAILS

Genuine revolutions happen rarely, but a major one occurred in the nineteenth century: a revolution in transportation and communications. When the nineteenth century began, people traveled and communicated much as they had for centuries before; when it ended, the railroad, the telegraph, the telephone, and the oceangoing steamship had wrought enormous changes.

The steamship sliced in half the time of the Atlantic crossing and, not dependent on wind and tide, introduced new regularity in the movement of goods and passengers. The telegraph, flashing messages almost instantaneously along miles of wire (400,000 miles of it in the early 1880s), transformed communications, as did the telephone a little later. But the railroad worked the largest changes of all. Along with Bessemer steel, it was the most significant technical innovation of the century.

"EMBLEM OF MOTION AND POWER"

The railroad dramatically affected economic and social life. Economic growth would have occurred without it, of course; canals, inland steamboats, and the country's superb system of interior waterways already provided the outlines of an effective transportation network. But the railroad added significantly to the network and contributed advantages all its own.

Those advantages included more direct routes, greater speed, greater safety and comfort than other modes of land travel, more dependable schedules, a larger volume of traffic, and year-round service. A day's land travel on stagecoach or horseback might cover fifty miles. The railroad covered fifty miles in about an hour, seven hundred miles in a day. It went where canals and rivers did not go—directly to the loading platforms of great factories or across the arid West. As construction crews pushed tracks onward, vast areas of the continent opened for settlement.

Consequently, American railroads differed from European ones. In Europe, railroads were usually built between cities and towns that already existed; they carried mostly the same goods that earlier forms of transportation had. In the United States, they did that and more: They often created the very towns they then served, and they ended up carrying cattle from Texas, fruit from Florida, and other goods that had never been carried before.

Linking widely separated cities and villages, the railroad ended the relative isolation and self-sufficiency of the country's "island communities." It tied people together, brought in outside products, fostered greater interdependence, and encouraged economic specialization. Under its stimulus, Chicago supplied meat to the nation, Minneapolis supplied grain, and Saint Louis, beer. For these and other communities, the railroad made possible a national market and in so doing pointed the way toward mass production and mass consumption, two of the hallmarks of twentieth-century society.

It also pointed the way toward later business development. The railroad, as Alfred D. Chandler, a historian of business, has written, was "the nation's first big business"; it worked out "the modern ways of finance, management, labor relations, competition, and government regulation."

A railroad corporation, far-flung and complex, was a new kind of business. It stretched over thousands of miles, employed thousands of people, dealt with countless customers, and required a scale of organization and decision making unknown in earlier business. Railroad managers never met most customers or even many employees; thus arose new problems in marketing and labor relations. Year by year, railroad companies consumed large quantities of iron, steel, coal, lumber, and glass, stimulating growth and employment in numerous industries.

No wonder, then, that the railroad captured so completely the country's imagination. For nearly a hundred years—the railroad era lasted through the 1940s—children gathered at depots, paused in the fields to wave as the fast express flashed by, listened at night to far-off whistles, and wondered what lay down the tracks. They lived in a world grown smaller.

BUILDING THE EMPIRE

When Lee surrendered at Appomattox in 1865, the country already had 35,000 miles of track, and much of the railroad system east of the Mississippi River was in place. Farther west, the rail network stood poised on the edge of settlement. Although southern railroads were in shambles from the war, the United States had nearly as much railroad track as the rest of the world.

After the Civil War, rail construction increased by leaps and bounds. From 35,000 miles in 1865, the network expanded to 93,000 miles in 1880; 166,000 in 1890; and 193,000 in 1900—more than in all Europe, including Russia. Mileage peaked at 254,037 miles in 1916, just before the industry began its long decline into the mid-twentieth century.

To build such an empire took vast amounts of capital. American and European investors provided some of the money; government supplied the rest. In all, local governments gave railroad companies about $300 million, and state governments added $228 million more. The federal government loaned nearly $65 million to a half dozen western railroads and donated millions of acres of the public domain.

Almost 90 percent of the federal land grants lay in twenty states west of the Mississippi River. Federal land grants helped build 18,738 miles of track, less than 8 percent of the system. The land was frequently distant and difficult to market. Railroad companies sometimes sold it to raise cash, but more often they used it as security for bonds or loans.

Beyond doubt, the grants of cash and land promoted waste and corruption. The companies built fast and wastefully, eager to collect the subsidies that went with each mile of track. The grants also enabled railroads to build into territories

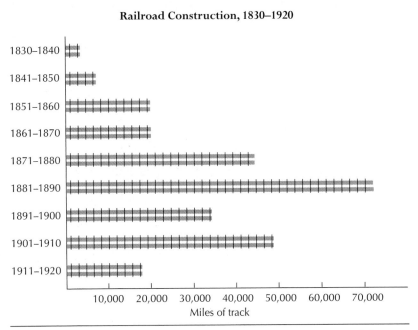

Railroad Construction, 1830–1920

1830–1840	
1841–1850	
1851–1860	
1861–1870	
1871–1880	
1881–1890	
1891–1900	
1901–1910	
1911–1920	

10,000 20,000 30,000 40,000 50,000 60,000 70,000

Miles of track

Source: U.S. Bureau of the Census, *Historical Statistics of the United States, Colonial Times to 1970,* Bicentennial Edition, Washington, DC, 1975.

that were pledged to the Indians, thus contributing to the wanton destruction of Indian life.

Yet, on balance, the grants probably worked more benefits than evils. As Congress had hoped, the grants were the lure for railroad building across the rugged, unsettled West, where it would be years before the railroads' revenues would repay their construction. Farmers, ranchers, and merchants poured into the newly opened areas, settling the country and boosting the value of government and private land nearby. The grants seemed necessary in a nation which, unlike Europe, expected private enterprise to build the railroads. In return for government aid, Congress required the railroads to carry government freight, troops, and mail at substantially reduced rates—resulting in savings to the government of almost $1 billion between 1850 and 1945. In no other cases of federal subsidies to carriers—canals, highways, and airlines—did Congress exact specific benefits in return.

LINKING THE NATION VIA TRUNK LINES

The early railroads may seem to have linked different regions, but in fact they did not. Built with little regard for through traffic, they were designed more to protect local interests than to tap outside markets. Many extended less than fifty miles. To avoid cooperating with other lines, they adopted conflicting schedules, built separate depots, and above all, used different gauges. Gauges, the distance between the rails, ranged from 4 feet 8½ inches, which became the standard gauge, to 6 feet. Without special equipment, trains of one gauge could not run on tracks of another.

The Civil War showed the value of fast long-distance transportation, and after 1865, railroad managers worked to provide it. In a burst of consolidation, the large companies swallowed the small; integrated rail networks became a reality. Railroads also adopted standard schedules, signals, and equipment and finally, in 1886, the standard gauge. In 1866, in a dramatic innovation to speed traffic, railroad companies introduced fast freight lines that pooled cars for service between cities.

In the Northeast, four great trunk lines took shape, all intended to link eastern seaports with the rich traffic of the Great Lakes and western rivers. Like a massive river system, trunk lines drew traffic from dozens of tributaries (feeder lines) and carried it to major markets. The Baltimore and Ohio (B & O), which reached Chicago in 1874, was one; the Erie Railroad, which ran from New York

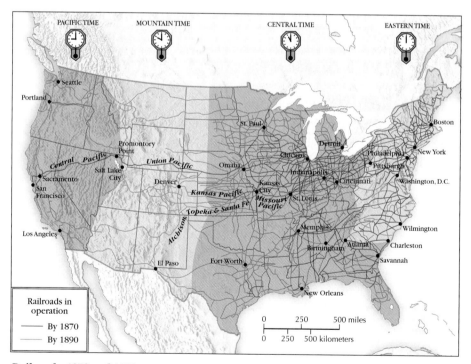

Railroads, 1870 and 1890

In the last quarter of the nineteenth century, railroads expanded into Texas, the far Southwest, and the Northwest, carrying settlers, businesses, and government to the far-flung areas.

to Chicago, was another. The Erie competed bitterly with the New York Central Railroad, the third trunk line, and its owner, Cornelius Vanderbilt—the "Commodore"—a crusty old multimillionaire from the shipping business.

J. Edgar Thomson and Thomas A. Scott built the fourth trunk line, the Pennsylvania Railroad, which initially ran from Philadelphia to Pittsburgh.

In the war-damaged South, consolidation took longer. As Reconstruction waned, northern and European capital rebuilt and integrated the southern lines, especially during the 1880s, when rail construction in the South led the nation. By 1900, the South had five large systems linking its major cities and farming and industrial regions. Four decades after the secession crisis, these systems tied the South into a national transportation network.

Over that rail system, passengers and freight moved in relative speed, comfort, and safety. Automatic couplers (1867), air brakes (1869), refrigerator cars (1867), dining cars, heated cars, electric switches, and stronger locomotives transformed railroad service. George Pullman's lavish sleeping cars became popular. Handsome depots, such as New York's Grand Central and Washington's Union Station, were erected at major terminals.

In November 1883, the railroads even changed time. Ending the crazy quilt jumble of local times that caused scheduling difficulties, the American Railway Association divided the country into four time zones and adopted the modern system of standard time. Congress took thirty-five years longer; it adopted standard time in 1918, in the midst of World War I.

RAILS ACROSS THE CONTINENT

The dream of a transcontinental railroad, linking the Atlantic and Pacific oceans, stretched back many years but had always been lost to sectional quarrels over the route. In 1862 and 1864, with the South out of the picture, Congress moved to build the first transcontinental railroad. It chartered the Union Pacific Railroad Company to build westward from Nebraska and the Central Pacific Railroad Company to build eastward from the Pacific Coast.

Construction began simultaneously at Omaha and Sacramento in 1863, lagged during the war, and moved vigorously ahead after 1865. It became a race, each company vying for land, loans, and potential markets. General Grenville M. Dodge, a tough Union army veteran, served as construction chief for the Union Pacific, while Charles Crocker, a former Sacramento dry goods merchant, led the Central Pacific crews. Dodge organized an army of ten thousand workers, many of them ex-soldiers and Irish immigrants. Pushing rapidly westward, he encountered frequent attacks from Native Americans defending their lands, but he had the advantage of building over flat prairie.

After the last spike was hammered in at Promontory, Utah, the pilots of the two locomotives exchanged champagne toasts. The chief engineers of the two lines are seen shaking hands. Conspicuously absent from the photograph are the Chinese laborers who helped build the railroad.

Crocker faced more trying conditions in the high Sierra Nevada along California's eastern border. After several experiments, he decided that Chinese laborers worked best, and he hired six thousand of them, most brought directly from China. "I built the Central Pacific," Crocker enjoyed boasting, but the Chinese crews in fact did the awesome work. Under the most difficult conditions, they dug, blasted, and pushed their way slowly east.

On May 10, 1869, the two lines met at Promontory, Utah, near the northern tip of the Great Salt Lake. Dodge's crews had built 1086 miles of track, Crocker's 689. The Union Pacific and Central Pacific presidents hammered in a golden spike, and the dreamed-of connection was made. The telegraph flashed the news east and west, setting off wild celebrations. A photograph was taken, but it included none of the Chinese who had worked so hard to build the road; they were all asked to step aside.

The transcontinental railroad symbolized American unity and progress. Along with the Suez Canal, completed the same year, it helped knit the world together. Three more railroads reached the coast in 1883: the Northern Pacific, running from Minnesota to Oregon; the Atchison, Topeka, and Santa Fe, connecting Kansas City and Los Angeles; and the powerful Southern Pacific, running from San Francisco and Los Angeles to New Orleans. Ten years later, James J. Hill's superbly built Great Northern Railway extended from Minneapolis–St. Paul to Seattle, Washington.

By the 1890s, business leaders talked comfortably of railroad systems stretching deep into South America and across the Bering Strait to Asia, Europe, and Africa. In an age of progress, anything seemed possible.

PROBLEMS OF GROWTH

Overbuilding during the 1870s and 1880s caused serious problems for the railroads. Lines paralleled each other, and where they did not, speculators such as Jay Gould often laid one down to force a rival line to buy it at inflated prices. While many managers worked to improve service, Gould and others bought and sold railroads like toys, watered their stock, and milked their assets.

Competition was severe, and managers fought desperately for traffic. They offered special rates and favors: free passes for large shippers; low rates on bulk freight, carload lots, and long hauls; and, above all, rebates—secret, privately negotiated reductions below published rates. Fierce rate wars broke out frequently, convincing managers that ruthless competition helped no one.

Managers such as Albert Fink, the brilliant vice president of the Louisville & Nashville, tried first to arrange pooling agreements, a way to control competition by sharing traffic, but none survived the intense pressures of competition. Legally unenforceable, pools were handshake agreements among individuals who did not always keep their word. Customers grew adept at bargaining for rebates and other privileges, and railroads rarely felt able to refuse them.

Failing to cooperate, railroad owners next tried to consolidate. Through purchase, lease, and merger, they gobbled up competitors and built "self-sustaining systems" that dominated entire regions. But many of the systems, expensive and unwieldy, collapsed in the Panic of 1893. By mid-1894, a quarter of the railroads were bankrupt. The victims of the panic included such legendary names as the Erie, B & O, Santa Fe, Northern Pacific, and Union Pacific.

Needing money, railroads turned naturally to bankers, who finally imposed order on the industry. J. Pierpont Morgan, head of the New York investment house of J. P. Morgan and Company, took the lead. Massively built, with eyes so piercing they seemed like the headlights of an onrushing train, Morgan was the most powerful figure in American finance. He liked efficiency, combination, and order. He disliked "wasteful" competition.

After 1893, Morgan and a few other bankers refinanced ailing railroads, and in the process they took control of the industry. Their methods were direct: fixed costs and debt were ruthlessly cut, new stock was issued to provide capital, rates were stabilized, rebates and competition were eliminated, and control was vested in a "voting trust" of handpicked trustees. Between 1894 and 1898, Morgan reorganized—critics said "Morganized"—the Southern Railway, the Erie, the Northern Pacific, and the B & O. In addition, he took over a half dozen other important railroads. By 1900, he was a dominant figure in American railroading.

As the new century began, the railroads had pioneered the patterns followed by most other industries. Seven giant systems controlled nearly two-thirds of the mileage, and they in turn answered to a few investment banking firms such as the house of Morgan. For good and ill, a national transportation network, centralized and relatively efficient, was now in place.

An Industrial Empire

The new industrial empire was based on steel as well as on railroads. Harder and more durable than other kinds of iron, steel wrought changes in manufacturing, agriculture, transportation, and architecture. It permitted construction of longer bridges, taller buildings, stronger railroad track, deadlier weapons, better plows, heavier machinery, and faster ships. Made in great furnaces by strong men, it symbolized the tough, often brutal nature of industrial society. From the 1870s onward, steel output became the worldwide accepted measure of industrial progress, and nations around the globe vied for leadership.

The Bessemer process, developed in the late 1850s by Henry Bessemer in England and independently by William Kelly in the United States, made increased steel production possible. Both Bessemer and Kelly discovered that a blast of air forced through molten iron burned off carbon and other impurities, resulting in steel of a more uniform and durable quality. The discovery transformed the industry. While earlier methods produced amounts a person could lift, a Bessemer converter handled 5 tons of molten metal at a time. The mass production of steel was now possible.

Carnegie and Steel

Bessemer plants demanded extensive capital investment, abundant raw materials, and sophisticated production techniques. Using chemical and other processes, the plants required research departments, which became critical components of later American industries. Costly to build, they limited entry into the industry to the handful who could afford them.

Great steel districts arose in Pennsylvania, Ohio, and Alabama—in each case around large coal deposits that fueled the huge furnaces. Pittsburgh became the center of the industry, its giant mills employing thousands of workers. Output

International Steel Production, 1880–1914

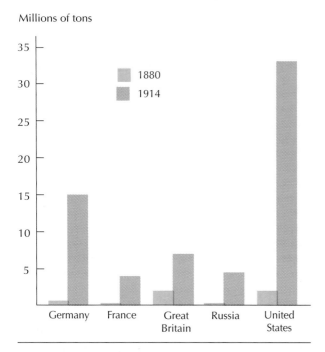

Millions of tons

shot up. In 1874, the United States produced less than half the amount of pig iron produced in Great Britain. By 1890, it took the lead, and in 1900, it produced four times as much as Britain.

Like the railroads, steel companies grew larger and larger. In 1880, only nine companies could produce more than 100,000 tons a year. By the early 1890s, several companies exceeded 250,000 tons, and two—including the great Carnegie Steel Company—produced more than 1 million tons a year. As operations expanded, managers needed more complex skills. Product development, marketing, and consumer preferences became important.

Andrew Carnegie emerged as the undisputed master of the industry. Born in Scotland, he came to the United States in 1848 at the age of 12. Settling near Pittsburgh, he went to work as a bobbin boy in a cotton mill, earning $1.20 a week. He soon took a job in a telegraph office, where in 1852 his hard work and skill caught the eye of Thomas A. Scott of the Pennsylvania Railroad. Starting as Scott's personal telegrapher, Carnegie spent a total of twelve years on the Pennsylvania, a training ground for company managers. By 1859, he had become a divisional superintendent. He was 24 years old.

Soon rich from shrewd investments, Carnegie plunged into the steel industry in 1872. On the Monongahela River south of Pittsburgh, he built the giant

The machinery dwarfs the workers in this engraving of the Bessemer converter in one of Andrew Carnegie's Pittsburgh steel mills. The illustration is from an 1886 issue of Harper's Weekly.

J. Edgar Thomson Steel Works, named after the president of the Pennsylvania Railroad, his biggest customer. With his warmth and salesmanship, he attracted able partners and subordinates such as Henry Clay Frick and Charles M. Schwab, whom he drove hard and paid well. Although he had written magazine articles defending the rights of workers, Carnegie kept the wages of the laborers in his mills low and disliked unions. With the help of Frick, he crushed a violent strike at his Homestead works in 1892 (see p. 600).

In 1878, he won the steel contract for the Brooklyn Bridge. During the next decade, as city building boomed, he converted the huge Homestead works near Pittsburgh to the manufacture of structural beams and angles, which went into the New York City elevated railway, the first skyscrapers, and the Washington Monument. Carnegie profits mounted: from $2 million in 1888 to $40 million in 1900. That year, Carnegie Steel alone produced more steel than Great Britain. Employing twenty thousand people, it was the largest industrial company in the world.

In 1901, Carnegie sold it. Believing that wealth brought social obligations, he wanted to devote his full time to philanthropy. He found a buyer in J. Pierpont Morgan, who in the late 1890s had put together several steel companies, including Federal Steel, Carnegie's chief rival. Carnegie Steel had blocked Morgan's well-known desire for control, and in mid-1900, when a war loomed between the two interests, Morgan decided to buy Carnegie out. In early January 1901, Morgan told Charles M. Schwab: "Go and find his price." Schwab cornered Carnegie on the golf course; Carnegie listened, and the next day he handed Schwab a note, scribbled in blunt pencil, asking almost a half billion dollars. Morgan glanced at it and said, "I accept this price."

Drawing other companies into the combination, Morgan on March 3, 1901, announced the creation of the United States Steel Corporation. The new firm was capitalized at $1.4 billion, the first billion-dollar company. Soon there were other giants, including Bethlehem Steel, Republic Steel, and National Steel. As the nineteenth century ended, steel products—rare just thirty years before—had altered the landscape. Huge firms, investment bankers, and professional managers dominated the industry.

ROCKEFELLER AND OIL

Petroleum worked comparable changes in the economic and social landscape, although mostly after 1900. Distilled into oil, it lubricated the machinery of the industrial age. There seemed little use for gasoline (the internal combustion engine had only just been developed), but kerosene, another major distillate, brought inexpensive illumination into almost every home. Whale oil, cottonseed oil, and even tallow candles were expensive to burn; consequently, many people went to bed at nightfall. Kerosene lamps opened the evenings to activity, altering the patterns of life.

Like other changes in these years, the oil boom happened with surprising speed. In the mid-1850s, petroleum was a bothersome, smelly fluid that occasionally rose to the surface of springs and streams. In 1859, Edwin L. Drake drilled the first oil well near Titusville in northwest Pennsylvania, and the "black gold" fever struck. Chemists soon discovered ways to transform petroleum into lubricating oil, grease, paint, wax, varnish, naphtha, and paraffin. Within a few years, there was a world market in oil.

At first, growth of the oil industry was chaotic. Early drillers and refiners produced for local markets, and since drilling wells and even erecting refineries cost little, competition flourished. Output fluctuated dramatically; prices rose and fell, with devastating effect.

A young merchant from Cleveland named John D. Rockefeller imposed order on the industry. "I had an ambition to build," he later recalled, and beginning in 1863 at the age of 24, he built the Standard Oil Company, soon to become one of the titans of corporate business. Like Morgan, Rockefeller considered competition wasteful, small-scale enterprise inefficient, and consolidation the path of the future.

Methodically, Rockefeller absorbed or destroyed competitors in Cleveland and elsewhere. Like Carnegie, he demanded efficiency, relentless cost cutting, and the latest technology.

Paying careful attention to detail, Rockefeller counted the stoppers in barrels, shortened barrel hoops to save metal, and, in one famous incident, reduced the number of drops of solder on kerosene cans from forty to thirty-nine. In large-scale production, Rockefeller realized, even small reductions meant huge savings. Research uncovered other ways of lowering costs and improving products, and Herman Frasch, a brilliant Standard chemist, solved problem after problem in the refining of oil.

In the end, Rockefeller triumphed over his competitors by marketing products of high quality at the lowest unit cost. But he employed other, less savory methods as well. He threatened rivals and bribed politicians. He employed spies to harass the customers of competing refiners. Above all, he extorted railroad rebates that lowered his transportation costs and undercut competitors. By 1879, he controlled 90 percent of the country's entire oil-refining capacity.

Vertically integrated, Standard Oil owned wells, timberlands, barrel and chemical plants, refineries, warehouses, pipelines, and fleets of tankers and oil cars. Its marketing organization served as the model for the industry. Standard exported oil to Asia, Africa, and South America; its 5-gallon kerosene tin, like Coca-Cola bottles and cans of a later era, was a familiar sight in the most distant parts of the world.

To manage it all, the company developed a new plan of business organization, the trust, which had profound significance for American business. In 1881, Samuel T. C. Dodd, Standard's attorney, set up the Standard Oil Trust, with a board of nine trustees empowered "to hold, control, and manage" all Standard's properties. Stockholders exchanged their stock for trust certificates, on which dividends were paid. On January 2, 1882, the first of the modern trusts was born. As Dodd intended, it immediately centralized control of Standard's far-flung empire.

Competition almost disappeared; profits soared. A trust movement swept the country as industries with similar problems—whiskey, lead, and sugar, among others—followed Standard's example. The word *trust* became synonymous with monopoly, amid vehement protests from the public. *Antitrust* became a watchword for a generation of reformers from the 1880s through the era of

Woodrow Wilson. But Rockefeller's purpose had been *management* of a monopoly, not monopoly itself, which he had already achieved.

Other companies followed suit, including American Sugar Refining, the Northern Securities Company, and the National Biscuit Company. Merger followed merger. By 1900, 1 percent of the nation's companies controlled more than one-third of its industrial production.

In 1897, Rockefeller retired with a fortune of nearly $900 million, but for Standard Oil and petroleum in general, the most expansive period was yet to come. The great oil pools of Texas and Oklahoma had not yet been discovered. Plastics and other oil-based synthetics were several decades in the future. There were only four usable automobiles in the country, and the day of the gasoline engine, automobile, and airplane lay just ahead.

THE BUSINESS OF INVENTION

"America has become known the world around as the home of invention," boasted the commissioner of patents in 1892. It had not always been so; until the last third of the nineteenth century, the country had imported most of its technology. Then an extraordinary group of inventors and tinkerers—"specialists in invention," Thomas A. Edison called them—began to study the world around them. Some of their inventions gave rise to new industries; a few actually changed the quality of life.

The number of patents issued to inventors reflected the trend. During the 1850s, fewer than 2,000 patents were issued each year. By the 1880s and 1890s, the figure reached more than 20,000 a year. Between 1790 and 1860, the U.S. Patent Office issued just 36,000 patents; in the decade of the 1890s alone, it issued more than 200,000.

Some of the inventions transformed communications. In 1866, Cyrus W. Field improved the transatlantic cable linking the telegraph networks of Europe and the United States. By the early 1870s, land and submarine cables ran to Brazil, Japan, and the China coast; in the next two decades, they reached Africa and spread across South America. Diplomats and business leaders could now "talk" to their counterparts in Berlin or Hong Kong. Even before the telephone, the cables quickened the pace of foreign affairs, revolutionized journalism, and allowed businesses to expand and centralize.

The typewriter (1867), stock ticker (1867), cash register (1879), calculating machine (1887), and adding machine (1888) helped business transactions. High-speed spindles, automatic looms, and electric sewing machines transformed the clothing industry, which for the first time in history turned out ready-made clothes for the masses. In 1890, the Census Bureau first used machines to sort

Industrialist George Eastman using his new box camera aboard the S.S. Galia is caught by another photographer using a box camera. The small easy-to-use cameras helped move photography out of the studio and into the realm of everyday activities.

and tabulate data on punched cards, a portent of a new era of information storage and processing.

In 1879, George Eastman patented a process for coating gelatin on photographic dry plates, which led to celluloid film and motion pictures. By 1888, he was marketing the Kodak camera, which weighed 35 ounces, took 100 exposures, and cost $25. Even though early Kodaks had to be returned to the factory, camera and all, for film developing, they revolutionized photography. Now almost anyone could snap a picture.

Other innovations changed the diet. There were new processes for flour, canned meat, vegetables, condensed milk, and even beer (from an offshoot of Louis Pasteur's discoveries about bacteria). Packaged cereals appeared on breakfast tables. Refrigerated railroad cars, ice-cooled, brought fresh fruit from Florida and California to all parts of the country. In the 1870s, Gustavus F. Swift, a Chicago meatpacker, hit on the idea of using the cars to distribute meat nationwide. Setting up "dissembly" factories to butcher meat (Henry Ford later copied them for his famous "assembly" lines), he started an "era of cheap beef," as a newspaper said.

No innovation, however, rivaled the importance of the telephone and the use of electricity for light and power. The telephone was the work of Alexander Graham Bell, a shrewd and genial Scot who settled in Boston in 1871. Interested in the problems of the deaf, Bell experimented with ways to transmit speech electrically, and after several years he had developed electrified metal disks that,

Thomas Edison poses with his favorite invention, the tinfoil phonograph, in Mathew Brady's studio in Washington, DC, in 1878.

much like the human ear, converted sound waves to electrical impulses and back again. On March 10, 1876, he transmitted the first sentence over a telephone: "Mr. Watson, come here; I want you." Later that year, he exhibited the new device to excited crowds at the Centennial Exposition in Philadelphia.

In 1878—the year a telephone was installed in the White House—the first telephone exchange opened in New Haven, Connecticut. Fighting off competitors who challenged the patent, the young Bell Telephone Company dominated the growing industry. By 1895, there were about 310,000 phones; a decade later, there were 10 million—about one for every ten people. American Telephone and Telegraph Company, formed by the Bell interests in 1885, became another of the vast holding companies, consolidating more than a hundred local systems.

If the telephone dissolved communication barriers as old as the human race, Thomas Alva Edison, the "Wizard of Menlo Park," invented processes and products of comparable significance. Born in 1847, Edison had little formal education, although he was an avid reader. Like Carnegie, he went into the new field of telegraphy. Tinkering in his spare time, he made several important improvements, including a telegraph capable of sending four messages over a single wire. Gathering teams of specialists to work on specific problems, Edison built the first modern research laboratory at Menlo Park, New Jersey. It may have been his most important invention.

The laboratory, Edison promised, would turn out "a minor invention every ten days and a big thing every six months or so." In 1877, it turned out a big thing, the phonograph, and in 1879, an even bigger one, the incandescent lamp. Sir Joseph William Swan, an English inventor, had already experimented with the carbon filament, but Edison's task involved more than finding a durable filament. He set out to do nothing less than change light. A trial-and-error inventor, Edison tested sixteen hundred materials before producing, late in 1879, the carbon filament he wanted. Then he had to devise a complex system of conductors, meters, and generators by which electricity could be divided and distributed to homes and businesses.

With the financial backing of J. P. Morgan, he organized the Edison Illuminating Company and built the Pearl Street power station in New York City, the testing ground of the new apparatus. On September 4, 1882, as Morgan and others watched, Edison threw a switch and lit the house of Morgan, the stock exchange, the *New York Times,* and a number of other buildings. Amazed, a *Times* reporter marveled that writing stories in the office at night "seemed almost like writing in daylight." Power stations soon opened in Boston, Philadelphia, and Chicago. By 1900, there were 2774 stations, lighting some 2 million electric lights around the country. In a nation alive with light, the habits of centuries changed. A flick of the switch lit homes and factories at any hour of the day or night.

In a rare blunder, Edison based his system on low-voltage direct current, which could be transmitted only about two miles. George Westinghouse, the inventor of the railroad air brake, demonstrated the advantages of high-voltage alternating current for transmission over great distances. In 1886, he formed the Westinghouse Electric Company and with the inventor Nikola Tesla, a Hungarian immigrant, developed an alternating-current motor that could convert electricity into mechanical power. Electricity could light a lamp or illuminate a skyscraper, pull a streetcar or drive an entire railroad, run a sewing machine or power a mammoth assembly line. Transmitted easily over long distances, it freed factories and cities from location near water or coal. Electricity, in short, brought a revolution.

Taking advantage of the new devices, Frank J. Sprague, a young engineer, electrified the Richmond, Virginia, streetcar system in 1887. Other cities quickly followed. Electric-powered subway systems opened in Boston in 1897 and New York City in 1904. Overhead wires and third rails made urban transportation quieter, faster, and cleaner. Buried under pavement or strung from pole to pole, wires of every description—trolley, telephone, and power—marked the birth of the modern city.

THE SELLERS

The increased output of the industrial age alone was not enough to ensure huge profits. The products still had to be sold, and that gave rise to a new "science" of marketing. Some business leaders—such as Swift in meatpacking, James B. Duke in tobacco, and Rockefeller in oil—built extensive marketing organizations of their own. Others relied on retailers, merchandising techniques, and advertising, developing a host of methods to convince consumers to buy.

In 1867, businesses spent about $50 million on advertising; in 1900, they spent more than $500 million, and the figure was increasing rapidly. The rotary press (1875) churned out newspapers and introduced a new era in newspaper advertising. Brand names became popular, and already Kellogg was promising cornflake eaters "Genuine Joy, Genuine Appetite, Genuine Health and therefore Genuine Complexion."

Bringing producer and consumer together, nationwide advertising was the final link in the national market. From roadside signs to newspaper ads, it pervaded American life.

R. H. Macy in New York, John Wanamaker in Philadelphia, and Marshall Field in Chicago turned the department store into a national institution. There people could browse (a relatively new concept) and buy. Innovations in pricing, display, and advertising helped customers develop wants they did not know they had. In 1870, Wanamaker took out the first full-page newspaper ad, and Macy, an aggressive advertiser, touted "goods suitable for the millionaire at prices in reach of the millions."

The "chain store"—an American term—spread across the country. The A & P grocery stores, begun in 1859, numbered sixty-seven by 1876, all marked by a familiar red-and-gold facade. By 1915, there were a thousand of them. In 1880, F. W. Woolworth, bored with the family farm, opened the first "Five and Ten Cent Store" in Utica, New York. He had fifty-nine stores in 1900, the year he adopted the bright red storefront and heaping counters to lure customers in and persuade them to buy.

In similar fashion, Sears, Roebuck and Montgomery Ward sold to rural customers through mail-order catalogs—a means of selling that depended on effec-

Macy's first store at 6th Avenue and 14th Street in New York City. In addition to the wide variety of household goods and furnishings they offered for sale, the new department stores attempted to attract shoppers with such amenities as tearooms, nurseries, and libraries.

tive transportation and a high level of customer literacy. As a traveler for a dry goods firm, Aaron Montgomery Ward had seen an unfulfilled need of people in the rural West. He started the mail-order trend in 1872, with a one-sheet price list offered from a Chicago loft. By 1884, he offered almost ten thousand items in a catalog of 240 pages.

Richard W. Sears also saw the possibilities in the mail-order business. Starting with watches and jewelry, he gradually expanded his list. In the early 1880s, he moved to Chicago and with Alvah C. Roebuck founded Sears, Roebuck and Company. Sears sold anything and everything, prospering in a business that relied on mutual faith between unseen customers and distant distributors. Sears catalogs, soon more than five hundred pages long, exploited four-color illustration and other new techniques. By the early 1900s, Sears distributed six million catalogs annually.

Advertising, brand names, chain stores, and mail-order houses brought Americans of all varieties into a national market. Even as the country grew, a certain homogeneity of goods bound it together, touching cities and farms, East and West, rich and poor. There was a common language of consumption.

Americans had become a community of consumers, surrounded by goods unavailable just a few decades before, and able to purchase them. They had learned to make, want, and buy. "Because you see the main thing today is—shopping," Arthur Miller, a twentieth-century playwright, said in *The Price*:

> *Years ago a person, he was unhappy, didn't know what to do with himself—he'd go to church, start a revolution—something. Today you're unhappy? Can't figure it out? What is the salvation? Go shopping.*

THE WAGE EARNERS

Although entrepreneurs were important, it was the labor of millions of men and women that built the new industrial society. In their individual stories, nearly all unrecorded, lay much of the achievement, drama, and pain of these years.

In a number of respects, their lot improved during the last quarter of the nineteenth century. Real wages rose, working conditions improved, and the workers' influence in national affairs increased. Between 1880 and 1914, wages of the average worker rose about $7 a year. Like others, workers also benefited from expanding health and educational services.

WORKING MEN, WORKING WOMEN, WORKING CHILDREN

Still, life for workers was not easy. Before 1900, most wage earners worked at least ten hours a day, six days a week. If skilled, they earned about 20 cents an hour; if unskilled, just half that. On average, workers earned between $400 and $500 a year. It took about $600 for a family of four to live decently. Construction workers, machinists, government employees, printers, clerical workers, and western miners made more than the average. Eastern coal miners, agricultural workers, garment workers, and unskilled factory hands made considerably less.

There were few holidays or vacations, and there was little respite from the grueling routine. Skilled workers could turn the system to their own ends— New York City cigar makers, for example, paid someone to read to them while they worked—but the unskilled seldom had such luxury. They were too easily replaced. "A bit of advice to you," said a guidebook for immigrant Jews in the 1890s: "do not take a moment's rest. Run, do, work, and keep your own good in mind."

Work was not only grueling; it was very dangerous. Safety standards were low, and accidents were common, more common in fact than in any other industrial nation in the world at that time. On the railroads, 1 in every 26 workers was

It was not unusual for children in some cities to grow up along with their peers in the factory instead of on the playground, like these girls working in the garment industry.

injured and 1 in every 399 was killed each year. Thousands suffered from chronic illness, unknowing victims of dust, chemicals, and other pollutants. In the early 1900s, physician Alice Hamilton established a link between jobs and disease, but meanwhile, illness weakened or struck down many a breadwinner.

The breadwinner might be a woman or a child; both worked in increasing numbers. In 1870, about 15 percent of women over the age of 16 were employed for wages; in 1900, 20 percent (5.3 million women) were. Of 303 occupations listed in the 1900 census, women were represented in 296. The textile industry was their largest single employer. In 1900, 1 out of every 10 girls and 1 out of every 5 boys between the ages of 10 and 15 held jobs. In Paterson, New Jersey, an important industrial city, about half of all boys and girls aged 11 to 14 had jobs.

There were so many children in the labor force that when people spoke of child labor, they often meant boys and girls under the age of 14. Boys were paid little enough, but girls made even less. Girls, it was argued, were headed for marriage; those who worked were just doing so in order to help out their families. "We try to employ girls who are members of families," a box manufacturer said, "for we don't pay the girls a living wage in this trade."

Most working women were young and single. Many began working at 16 or 17, worked a half dozen years or so, married, and quit. In 1900, only 5 percent of all married women were employed outside the home, although African American women were an important exception. Among them, 25 percent of married women worked in 1900, usually on southern farms or as low-paid laundresses or domestic servants. As clerical work expanded, women learned new skills such as typing and stenography. Moving into formerly male occupations, they became secretaries, bookkeepers, typists, telephone operators, and clerks in the new department stores.

A few women—very few—became ministers, lawyers, and doctors. Arabella Mansfield, admitted to the Iowa bar in 1869, was the first woman lawyer in the country. But change was slow, and in the 1880s, some law schools still were refusing to admit women because they "had not the mentality to study law." Among women entering the professions, the overwhelming majority became nurses, schoolteachers, and librarians. In such professions, a process of "feminization" occurred: women became a majority of the workers, a small number of men took the management roles, and most men left for other jobs, lowering the profession's status.

In most jobs, status and pay were divided unequally between men and women. When employed in factories, women tended to occupy jobs that were viewed as natural extensions of household activity. They made clothes and textiles, processed food, and made cigars, tobacco, and shoes. In the women's garment industry, which employed large numbers of women, they were the sewers and finishers, doing jobs that paid less; men were the higher-paid cutters and pressers.

In general, adults earned more than children, the skilled more than the unskilled, native born more than foreign born, Protestants more than Catholics or Jews, and whites more than blacks and Asians. On average, women made a little more than half as much as men, according to contemporary estimates. In some cases, employers defended the differences—the foreign born, for example, might not speak English—but most simply reflected bias against race, creed, or gender. In the industrial society, white, native-born Protestant men—the bulk of the male population—reaped the greatest rewards.

Blacks labored on the fringes, usually in menial occupations. The last hired and first fired, they earned less than other workers at almost every level of skill. On the Pacific Coast, the Chinese—and later the Japanese—lived in enclaves and suffered periodic attacks of discrimination. In 1879, the Workingmen's party of California got a provision in the state constitution forbidding corporations to employ Chinese, and in 1882, Congress passed the Chinese Exclusion Act, prohibiting the immigration of Chinese workers for ten years.

CULTURE OF WORK

Among almost all groups, industrialization shattered age-old patterns, including work habits and the culture of work, as Herbert G. Gutman, a social historian, noted. It made people adapt "older work routines to new necessities and strained those wedded to premodern patterns of labor." Adaptation was difficult and often demeaning. Virtually everyone went through it, and newcomers repeated the experiences of those who came before.

Men and women fresh from farms were not accustomed to the factory's disciplines. Now they worked indoors rather than out, paced themselves to the clock rather than the movements of the sun, and followed the needs of the market rather than the natural rhythms of the seasons. They had supervisors and hierarchies and strict rules.

As industries grew larger, work became more impersonal. Machines displaced skilled artisans, and the unskilled tended the machines for employers they never saw. Workers picked up and left their jobs with startling frequency, and factories drew on a churning, highly mobile labor supply. Historian Stephan Thernstrom, who carefully studied the census records, found that only about half the people recorded in any census still lived in the same community ten years

A typing pool in the audit division of the Metropolitan Life Insurance Company, 1897. As demand for clerical workers grew, women took over many of the secretarial duties formerly performed by men. Despite their prominence in the workplace, however, the women were usually overseen by male supervisors.

later. "The country had an enormous reservoir of restless and footloose men, who could be lured to new destinations when opportunity beckoned."

Thernstrom and others have also found substantial economic and social mobility. The rags-to-riches stories of Horatio Alger, of course, had always said so, and careers of men such as Andrew Carnegie—the impoverished immigrant boy who made good—seemed to confirm it. The actual record was considerably more limited. Most business leaders in the period came from well-to-do or middle-class families of old American stock. Of 360 iron and steel barons in Pittsburgh, Carnegie's own city, only 5 fit the Carnegie characteristics, and one of those was Carnegie himself. Still, if few workers became steel magnates, many workers made major progress during their lifetimes. Thernstrom discovered that a quarter of the manual laborers rose to middle-class positions, and working-class children were even more likely to move up the ladder.

The chance for advancement played a vital role in American industrial development. It gave workers hope, wedded them to the system, and tempered their response to the appeal of labor unions and working-class agitation. Very few workers rose from rags to riches, but a great many rose to better jobs and higher status.

LABOR UNIONS

Weak throughout the nineteenth century, labor unions never included more than 2 percent of the total labor force or more than 10 percent of industrial workers. To many workers, unions seemed "foreign," radical, and out of step with the American tradition of individual advancement. Craft, ethnic, and other differences fragmented the labor force, and its extraordinary mobility made organization difficult. Employers opposed unions. "I have always had one rule," said an executive of U.S. Steel. "If a worker sticks up his head, hit it."

As the national economy emerged, however, national labor unions gradually took shape. The early unions often represented skilled workers in local areas, but in 1866, William H. Sylvis, a Pennsylvania iron molder, united several unions into a single national organization, the National Labor Union. Like many of the era's labor leaders, Sylvis sought long-range humanitarian reforms, such as the establishment of workers' cooperatives, rather than specific bread-and-butter goals. A talented propagandist, he attracted many members—some 640,000 by 1868—but he died in 1869, and the organization did not long survive him.

The year Sylvis died, Uriah S. Stephens and a group of Philadelphia garment workers founded a far more successful organization, the Noble and Holy Order of the Knights of Labor. A secret fraternal order, it grew slowly through the 1870s, until Terence V. Powderly, the new Grand Master Workman elected in 1879, ended the secrecy and embarked on an aggressive recruitment program.

Women delegates at a national meeting of the Knights of Labor in 1886. Women belonged to separate associations affiliated with local all-male unions.

Wanting to unite all labor, the Knights welcomed everyone who "toiled," regardless of skill, creed, sex, or color. Unlike most unions, it organized women workers, and at its peak, it had 60,000 black members.

Harking back to the Jacksonians, the Knights set the "producers" against monopoly and special privilege. As members they excluded only "nonproducers"—bankers, lawyers, liquor dealers, and gamblers. Since employers were "producers," they could join; and since workers and employers had common interests, the Knights maintained that workers should not strike. The order's platform included the eight-hour day and the abolition of child labor, but more often it focused on uplifting, utopian reform. Powderly, the eloquent and idealistic leader, spun dreams of a new era of harmony and cooperation.

Membership grew steadily—from 42,000 in 1882 to 110,000 in 1885. In March 1885, ignoring Powderly's dislike of strikes, local Knights in St. Louis, Kansas City, and other cities won a victory against Jay Gould's Missouri Pacific Railroad, and membership soared. It soon reached almost 730,000, but neither Powderly nor the union's loose structure could handle the growth. In 1886, the wily Gould struck back, crushing the Knights on the Texas and Pacific Railroad.

The defeat punctured the union's growth and revealed the ineffectiveness of its national leaders. Tens of thousands of unskilled laborers, who had recently rushed to join, deserted the ranks. The Haymarket Riot turned public sympathy against unions like the Knights. By 1890, the order had shrunk to 100,000 members, and a few years later, it was virtually defunct.

Even as the Knights waxed and waned, another organization emerged that was to endure. Founded in 1886, the American Federation of Labor (AFL) was a loose alliance of national craft unions. It organized only skilled workers along craft lines, avoided politics, and worked for specific practical objectives. "I have my own philosophy and my own dreams," said Samuel Gompers, the founder and longtime president, "but first and foremost I want to increase the workingman's welfare year by year."

Born in a London tenement in 1850, Gompers was a child of the union movement. Settling in New York, he worked as a cigar maker, took an active hand in union activities, and experimented for a time with socialism and working-class politics. As leader of the AFL, he adopted a pragmatic approach to labor's needs. Gompers accepted capitalism and did not argue for fundamental changes in it. For labor he wanted simply a recognized place within the system and a greater share of the rewards.

Unlike Powderly, Gompers and the AFL assumed that most workers would remain workers throughout their lives. The task, then, lay in improving lives in "practical" ways: higher wages, shorter hours, and better working conditions. The AFL offered some attractive assurances to employers. As a trade union, the AFL would use the strike and boycott, but only to achieve limited gains; if treated fairly, the organization would provide a stable labor force. The AFL would not oppose monopolies and trusts, as Gompers said, "so long as we obtain fair wages."

By the 1890s, the AFL was the most important labor group in the country, and Gompers, the guiding spirit, was its president, except for one year, until his death in 1924. Membership expanded from 140,000 in 1886, past 250,000 in 1892, to more than 1 million by 1901. The AFL then included almost one-third of the country's skilled workers. By 1914, it had more than 2 million members. The great majority of workers—skilled and unskilled—remained unorganized, but Gompers and the AFL had become a significant force in national life.

The AFL either ignored or opposed women workers. Only two of its national affiliates—the Cigar Makers' Union and the Typographical Union—accepted women as members; others prohibited them outright, and Gompers himself often complained that women workers undercut the pay scales for men. Working conditions improved after 1900, but even then, unions were largely a man's world. In 1910, when there were 6.3 million women at work, only 125,000 of them were in unions.

The AFL did not expressly forbid black workers from joining, but member unions used high initiation fees, technical examinations, and other means to discourage black membership. The AFL's informal exclusion practices were, all in all, a sorry record, but Gompers defended his policy toward blacks, women, and the unskilled by pointing to the dangers that unions faced. Only by restricting membership, he argued, could the union succeed.

LABOR UNREST

Workers used various means to adjust to the factory age. To the dismay of managers and "efficiency" experts, the employees often dictated the pace and quality of their work and set the tone of the workplace. Friends and relatives of newly arrived immigrants found jobs for them, taught them how to deal with factory conditions, and humanized the workplace.

Workers also formed their own institutions to deal with their jobs. Overcoming differences of race or ethnic origin, they often banded together to help each other. They joined social or fraternal organizations, and their unions did more than argue for higher wages. Unions offered companionship, news of job

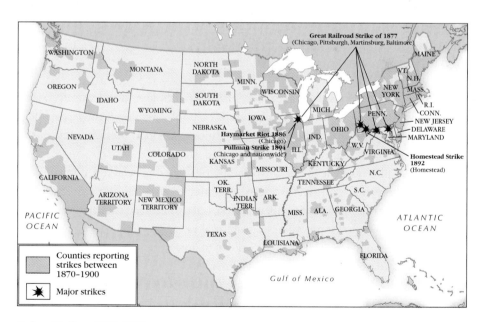

Labor Strikes, 1870–1890
More than 14,000 strikes occurred in the 1880s and early 1890s, involving millions of workers.

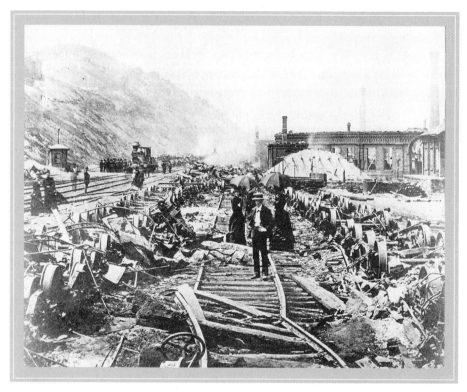

Violence and fires associated with the great railroad strike of 1877 destroyed railyards across the country. By the end of the strike, which lasted about two weeks, $10 million of railroad property had been reduced to rubble, and more than a hundred people had died.

openings, and much needed insurance plans for sickness, accident, or death. Workers went to the union hall to play cards or pool, sing union songs, and hear older workers tell of past labor struggles. Unions provided food for sick members, and there were dances, picnics, and parades.

Many employers believed in an "iron law of wages" in which supply and demand, not the welfare of their workers, dictated wages. Wanting a docile labor force, employers fired union members, hired scabs to replace strikers, and used a new weapon, the court injunction, to quell strikes.

The injunction, which forbade workers to interfere with their employers' business, was used to break the great Pullman strike of 1894, and the Supreme Court upheld use of the injunction in *In re Debs* (1895). Court decisions also affected the legal protection offered to workers. In *Holden* v. *Hardy* (1898), the Court upheld a law limiting working hours for miners because their work was dangerous and long hours might increase injuries. In *Lochner* v. *New York* (1905), however, it struck down a law limiting bakery workers to a sixty-hour week and ten-hour day. Because baking was safer than mining, the Court saw no need to interfere with the right of bakers to sell their labor freely.

As employers' attitudes hardened, strikes and violence broke out. The United States had the greatest number of violent confrontations between capital and labor in the industrial world. Between 1880 and 1900, there were more than 23,000 strikes involving 6.6 million workers. The great railroad strike of 1877 paralyzed railroads from West Virginia to California, resulted in the deaths of more than a hundred workers, and required federal troops to suppress it. Another outburst of labor unrest occurred during the mid-1880s; in 1886, the peak year, 610,000 workers were off the job because of strikes and lockouts.

The worst incident took place at Haymarket Square in Chicago, where workers had been campaigning for an eight-hour workday. In early May 1886, police, intervening in a strike at the McCormick Harvester works, shot and killed two workers. The next evening, May 4, labor leaders called a protest meeting at

In the rioting that followed the bomb explosion in Haymarket Square in Chicago, seven police officers and four workers died and more than seventy officers were wounded, many of them by fellow police. August Spies, one of the anarchists convicted of murder and sent to the gallows, said at his trial, "Let the world know that in A.D. 1886, in the state of Illinois, eight men were sentenced to death because they believed in a better future; because they had not lost their faith in the ultimate victory of liberty and justice!" (Actually, seven of the agitators were sentenced to death, the eighth to imprisonment.)

Haymarket Square near downtown Chicago. The meeting was peaceful, even a bit dull. About three thousand people were there; police ordered them to disperse, and someone threw a dynamite bomb that instantly killed one policeman and fatally wounded six others. Police fired into the crowd and killed four people.

The authorities never discovered who threw the bomb, but many Americans—not just business leaders—demanded action against labor "radicalism." Cities strengthened their police forces and armories. Uncertain who threw the bomb, Chicago police rounded up eight anarchists, who were convicted of murder. Although there was no evidence of their guilt, four were hanged, one committed suicide, and three remained in jail until pardoned by the governor in 1893. Linking labor and anarchism in the public mind, the Haymarket Riot weakened the national labor movement.

Violence again broke out in the unsettled conditions of the 1890s. In 1892, federal troops crushed a strike of silver miners in the Coeur d'Alene district of Idaho. That same year, Carnegie and Henry Clay Frick, Carnegie's partner and manager, cut wages nearly 20 percent at the Homestead steel plant. The Amalgamated Iron and Steel Workers, an AFL affiliate, struck, and Frick responded by locking the workers out of the plant. The workers surrounded it, and Frick, furious, hired a small private army of Pinkerton detectives to drive them off. But alert workers spotted the detectives, pinned them down with gunfire, and forced them to surrender. Three detectives and ten workers died in the battle.

A few days later, the Pennsylvania governor ordered the state militia to impose peace at Homestead. On July 23, an anarchist named Alexander Berkman, who was not one of the strikers, walked into Frick's office and shot him twice, then stabbed him several times. Incredibly, Frick survived, watched the police take Berkman away, called in a doctor to bandage his wounds, and stayed in the office until closing time. In late July, the Homestead works reopened under military guard, and in November the strikers gave up.

Events like those at Homestead troubled many Americans who wondered whether industrialization, for all its benefits, might carry a heavy price in social upheaval, class tensions, and even outright warfare. Most workers did not share in the immense profits of the industrial age, and as the nineteenth century came to a close, there were some who rebelled against the inequity.

In the half century after the Civil War, the United States became an industrial nation—the leading one, in fact, in the world. On one hand, industrialization meant "progress," growth, world power, and in some sense, fulfillment of the American promise of abundance. National wealth grew from $16 billion in 1860 to $88 billion in 1900; wealth per capita more than doubled. For the bulk of the population, the standard of living—a particularly American concept—rose.

But industrialization also meant rapid change, social instability, exploitation of labor, and growing disparity in income between rich and poor. Industry flourished, but control rested in fewer and fewer hands. Maturing quickly, the young system became a new corporate capitalism: giant businesses, interlocking in ownership, managed by a new professional class, and selling an expanding variety of goods in an increasingly controlled market. As goods spread through the society, so did a sharpened, aggressive materialism. Workers felt the strains of the shift to a new social order.

In 1902, a well-to-do New Yorker named Bessie Van Vorst decided to see what it was like to work for a living in a factory. Disguising herself in coarse woolen clothes, she went to Pittsburgh and got a job in a canning factory. She worked ten hours a day, six days a week, including four hours on Saturday afternoons when she and the other women, on their hands and knees, scrubbed the tables, stands, and entire factory floor. For that she earned $4.20 a week, $3 of which went for food alone.

Van Vorst was lucky—when she tired of the life, she could go back to her home in New York. The working men and women around her were not so fortunate. They stayed on the factory floor and, by dint of their labor, created the new industrial society.

19

TOWARD AN URBAN SOCIETY, 1877–1900

One day around 1900, Harriet Vittum, a settlement house worker in Chicago, went to the aid of a young Polish girl who lived in a nearby slum. The girl, aged 15, had discovered she was pregnant and had taken poison. An ambulance was on the way, and Vittum, told of the poisoning, rushed over to do what she could.

Quickly, she raced up the three flights of stairs to the floor where the girl and her family lived. Pushing open the door, she found the father, several male boarders, and two or three small boys asleep on the kitchen floor. In the next room, the mother was on the floor among several women boarders and one or two small children. Glancing out the window, Vittum saw the wall of another building so close she could reach out and touch it.

There was a third room; in it lay the 15-year-old girl, along with two more small children who were asleep. Looking at the scene, Vittum thought about the girl's life in the crowded tenement. Should she try to save her? Vittum asked herself. Should she even try to bring the girl back "to the misery and hopelessness of the life she was living in that awful place"?

The young girl died, and in later years, Vittum often told her story. It was easy to see why. The girl's life in the slum, the children on the floor, the need to take in boarders to make ends meet, the way the mother and father collapsed at the end of a workday that began long before sunup—all reflected the experiences of millions of people living in the nation's cities.

People poured into cities in the last part of the nineteenth century, lured by glitter and excitement, by friends and relatives who were already there, and, above all, by the greater opportunities for jobs and higher wages. Between 1860 and 1910, the rural population of the United States almost doubled; the number of people living in cities increased sevenfold.

Little of the increase came from natural growth, since urban families had high rates of infant mortality, a declining fertility rate, and a high death rate from injury and disease. Many of the newcomers came from rural America, and many more came from Europe, Latin America, and Asia. In one of the most significant migrations in American history, thousands of African Americans began in the 1880s to move from the rural South to northern cities. By 1900, there were large black communities in New York, Baltimore, Chicago, Washington, DC, and other cities. Yet to come was the even greater black migration during World War I.

Two major forces reshaped American society between 1870 and 1920. One was industrialization; the other was urbanization, the headlong rush of people from their rural roots into the modern urban environment. By 1920, the city had become the center of American economic, social, and cultural life.

THE LURE OF THE CITY

Between 1870 and 1900, the city—like the factory—became a symbol of a new America. Drawn from farms, small towns, and foreign lands, newcomers swelled the population of older cities and created new ones almost overnight. At the beginning of the Civil War, only one-sixth of the American people lived in cities of eight thousand people or more. By 1900, one-third did; by 1920, one-half. "We live in the age of great cities," wrote the Reverend Samuel Lane Loomis in 1887. "Each successive year finds a stronger and more irresistible current sweeping in towards the centers of life."

The current brought growth of an explosive sort. Thousands of years of history had produced only a handful of cities with more than a half million in population. In 1900, the United States had six such cities, including three—New York, Chicago, and Philadelphia—with populations greater than one million.

SKYSCRAPERS AND SUBURBS

Like so many things in these years, the city was transformed by a revolution in technology. Beginning in the 1880s, the age of steel and glass produced the skyscraper; the streetcar produced the suburbs and new residential patterns.

On the eve of the change, American cities were a crowded jumble of small buildings. Church steeples stood out on the skyline, clearly visible above the roofs of factories and office buildings. Buildings were usually made of masonry, and since the massive walls had to support their own weight, they could be no taller than a dozen or so stories. Steel frames and girders ended that limitation and allowed buildings to soar higher and higher. "Curtain walls," which concealed the steel framework, were no longer load bearing; they were pierced by many windows that let in fresh air and light. Completed in 1885, the Home Insurance Building in Chicago was the country's first metal-frame structure.

To a group of talented Chicago architects, the new trends served as a springboard for innovative forms. The leaders of the movement were John Root and Louis H. Sullivan, both of whom were attracted by the chance to rebuild Chicago after the great fire of 1871. Noting that the fire had fed on fancy exterior ornamentation, Root developed a plain, stripped-down style, bold in mass and form—the keynotes of modern architecture. He had another important insight, too. In an age of business, Root thought, the office tower, more than a church or a government building, symbolized the society, and he designed office buildings that carried out, as he said, "the ideas of modern business life: simplicity, stability, breadth, dignity."

Sullivan had studied at the Massachusetts Institute of Technology (MIT) and in Paris before settling in Chicago. In 1886, at the age of 30, he began work on the Chicago Auditorium, one of the last great masonry buildings. "Then came the flash of imagination which saw the single thing," he later said. "The trick was turned; and there swiftly came into being something new under the sun." Sullivan's skyscrapers, that "flash of imagination," changed the urban skyline.

In the Wainwright Building in St. Louis (1890), the Schiller Building (1892) and the Carson, Pirie, and Scott department store (1899) in Chicago, and the Prudential Building in Buffalo (1895), Sullivan developed the new forms. Architects must discard "books, rules, precedents," he announced; responding to the new, they should design for a building's function. "Form follows function," Sullivan believed, and he passed the idea on to a talented disciple, Frank Lloyd Wright. The modern city should stretch to the sky. A skyscraper "must be every inch a proud and soaring thing, rising in sheer exaltation . . . from bottom to top."

Electric elevators, first used in 1871, carried passengers upward in the new skyscrapers. During the same years, streetcars, another innovation, carried the people outward to expanded boundaries that transformed urban life.

Cities were no longer largely "walking cities," confined to a radius of two or three miles, the distance an individual might walk. Streetcar systems extended the radius and changed the urban map. Cable lines, electric surface lines, and elevated rapid transit brought shoppers and workers into central business districts and sped them home again. Offering a modest five-cent fare with a free transfer, the mass transit systems fostered commuting and widely separated business and residential districts sprang up. The middle class moved farther and farther out to the leafy greenness of the suburbs.

As the middle class moved out of the cities, the immigrants and working class poured in. They took over the older brownstones, row houses, and workers' cottages, turning them, under the sheer weight of numbers, into the slums of the central city. In the cities of the past, classes and occupations had been thrown together; without streetcars and subways, there was no other choice. The streetcar city, sprawling and specialized, became a more fragmented and stratified society with middle-class residential rings surrounding a business and working-class core.

TENEMENTS AND PRIVIES

In the shadow of the skyscrapers, grimy rows of tenements filled the central city and crowded people into cramped apartments. In the late 1870s, architect James E. Ware won a competition for tenement design with the "dumbbell tenement." Rising seven or eight stories in height, the dumbbell tenement packed about 30 four-room apartments on a lot only 25 by 100 feet. Between four and sixteen families lived on a floor; two toilets in the hall of each floor served their needs. Narrowed at the middle, the tenement resembled a giant dumbbell in shape. The indented middle created an air shaft between adjoining buildings that provided a little light and ventilation. In case of fire, it also carried flames from one story to the next, making the buildings notorious firetraps. In 1890, nearly half the dwellings in New York City were tenements.

That year, more than 1.4 million people lived on Manhattan Island, one of whose wards had a population density of 334,000 people per square mile. Many people lived in alleys and basements so dark they could not be photographed until flashlight photography was invented in 1887. Exploring the city, William Dean Howells, the prominent author, inhaled "the stenches of the neglected street . . . [and] the yet fouler and dreadfuller poverty smell which breathes from the open doorways."

This 1879 dumbbell floor plan was meant to provide four apartments to a floor. However, a whole family might live in each room. Crowded, unsanitary conditions contributed to the spread of tuberculosis, the chief cause of death in the United States until 1909.

The kitchen of a tenement apartment was often a multipurpose room. Here the tenement dwellers prepared and ate their meals; the room might also serve as a workroom, and it might be used as sleeping quarters for one or more members of the family.

Howells smelled more than poverty. In the 1870s and 1880s, cities stank. One problem was horse manure, hundreds of tons of it a day in every city. Another was the privy, "a single one of which," said a leading authority on public health, "may render life in a whole neighborhood almost unendurable in the summer."

Baltimore smelled "like a billion polecats," recalled H. L. Mencken, who grew up there. Said one New York City resident, "The stench is something terrible." Another wrote that "the stink is enough to knock you down." In 1880, the Chicago *Times* said that a "solid stink" pervaded the city. "No other word expresses it so well as stink. A stench means something finite. Stink reaches the infinite and becomes sublime in the magnitude of odiousness."

Cities dumped their wastes into the nearest body of water, then drew drinking water from the same site. Many built modern purified waterworks but could not keep pace with spiraling growth. In 1900, fewer than one in ten city dwellers drank filtered water. Factories, the pride of the era, polluted the urban air. At night, Pittsburgh looked and sounded like "Hell with the lid off," according to contemporary observers. Smoke poured from seventy-three glass factories,

The tenement district of New York City's Lower East Side. As millions emigrated to the United States during the last quarter of the nineteenth century, they crammed into already overpopulated ethnic neighborhoods, seeking others who spoke their language, practiced their religion, and followed their customs.

forty-one iron and steel mills, and twenty-nine oil refineries. The choking air helped prevent lung diseases and malaria—or so the city's advertising claimed.

Crime was another growing problem. The nation's homicide rate nearly tripled in the 1880s, much of the increase coming in the cities. After remaining constant for many decades, the suicide rate rose steadily between 1870 and 1900, according to a study of Philadelphia. Alcoholism also rose, especially among men, though recent studies have shown that for working-class men, the urban saloon was as much a gathering spot as it was a place to drink. Nonetheless, a 1905 survey of Chicago counted as many saloons as grocery stores, meat markets, and dry goods stores combined.

STRANGERS IN A NEW LAND

While some of the new city dwellers came from farms and small towns, many more came from abroad. Most came from Europe, where unemployment, food shortages, and increasing threats of war sent millions fleeing across the Atlantic

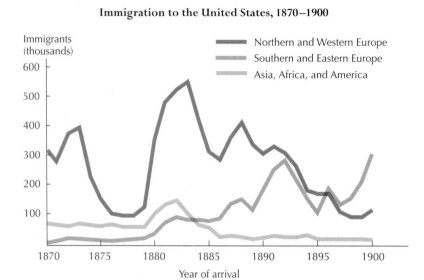

Immigration to the United States, 1870–1900

Immigrants (thousands)

Legend:
- Northern and Western Europe
- Southern and Eastern Europe
- Asia, Africa, and America

Year of arrival

Note: For purposes of classification, "Northern and Western Europe" includes Great Britain, Ireland, Scandinavia, the Netherlands, Belgium, Luxembourg, Switzerland, France, and Germany. "Southern and Eastern Europe" includes Poland, Austria-Hungary, Russia and the Baltic States, Romania, Bulgaria, European Turkey, Italy, Spain, Portugal, and Greece. "Asia, Africa, and America" includes Asian Turkey, China, Japan, India, Canada, the Caribbean, Latin America, and all of Africa.

Source: U.S. Bureau of the Census, *Historical Statistics of the United States, Colonial Times to 1970,* Bicentennial Edition, Washington, DC, 1975.

to make a fresh start. Often they knew someone already in the United States, a friend or relative who had written them about prospects for jobs and freer lives in a new land.

All told, the immigration figures were staggering. Between 1877 and 1890, more than 6.3 million people entered the United States. In one year alone, 1882, almost 789,000 people came. By 1890, about 15 percent of the population, 9 million people, were foreign born.

Most newcomers were job seekers. Nearly two-thirds were males, and the majority were between the ages of 15 and 40. Most were unskilled laborers. Most settled on the eastern seaboard. In 1901, the Industrial Relocation Office was established to relieve overcrowding in the eastern cities; opening Galveston, Texas, as a port of entry, it attracted many Russian Jews to Texas and the Southwest. But most immigrants preferred the shorter, more familiar journey to New York, and they tended to crowd into northern and eastern cities, settling in areas where others of their nationality or religion lived.

They were often dazzled by what they saw. They stared at electric lights, indoor plumbing, soda fountains, streetcars, plush train seats for all classes, ice cream, lemons, and bananas. Relatives whisked them off to buy new "American" clothes and showed them the teeming markets, department stores, and Woolworth's new five-and-ten stores.

Cities had increasingly large foreign-born populations. In 1900, four-fifths of Chicago's population was foreign born or of foreign-born parentage, two-thirds of Boston's, and one-half of Philadelphia's. New York City, where most immigrants arrived and many stayed, had more Italians than lived in Naples, more Germans than lived in Hamburg, and twice as many Irish as lived in Dublin. Four out of five New York City residents in 1890 were of foreign birth or foreign parentage.

Beginning in the 1880s, the sources of immigration shifted dramatically away from northern and western Europe, the chief source of immigration for over two centuries. More and more immigrants came from southern and eastern Europe: Italy, Greece, Austria-Hungary, Poland, and Russia. Between 1880 and 1910, approximately 8.4 million people came from these lands. The "new" immigrants tended to be Catholics or Jews rather than Protestants. Like their predecessors, most were unskilled rather than skilled, and they often spoke "strange" languages. Most were poor and uneducated; sticking together in close-knit communities, they clung to their native customs, languages, and religions.

In a Puck *cartoon titled "Looking Backward," the shadows of their immigrant origins loom over the rich and powerful who wanted to deny the "new" immigrants from central and southern Europe admission to America. The caption on the cartoon reads, "They would close to the newcomer the bridge that carried them and their fathers over."*

More than any previous group, the so-called new immigrants troubled the mainstream society. Could they be assimilated? Did they share "American" values? Such questions preoccupied groups like the American Protective Association, a midwestern anti-Catholic organization that expanded in the 1890s and worked to limit or end immigration.

Anti-Catholicism and anti-Semitism flared up again, as they had in the 1850s. The Immigration Restriction League, founded in 1894, demanded a literacy test for immigrants from southern and eastern Europe. Congress passed such a law in 1896, but President Cleveland vetoed it.

IMMIGRANTS AND THE CITY

Industrial capitalism—the world of factories and foremen and grimy machines— tested the immigrants and placed an enormous strain on their families. Many immigrants came from peasant societies where life proceeded according to outdoor routine and age-old tradition. In their new city homes, they found both new freedoms and new confinements, a different language, and a novel set of customs and expectations. Historians have only recently begun to discover the remarkable ways in which they learned to adjust.

Like native-born families, most immigrant families were nuclear in structure—they consisted of two parents and their children. Though variations occurred from group to group, men and women occupied roles similar to those in native families: men were wage earners, women were housekeepers and mothers. Margaret Byington, who studied steelworkers' homes in Homestead in the early 1900s, learned that the father played a relatively small role in child rearing or managing the family's finances. "His part of the problem is to earn and hers to spend." In Chicago, social reformer Jane Addams discovered that immigrant women made it "a standard of domestic virtue that a man must not touch his pay envelope, but bring it home unopened to his wife."

Although patterns varied among ethnic groups, and between economic classes within ethnic groups, immigrants tended to marry within the group more than did the native born. In one New York community, only 2 percent of French Canadian and 7 percent of Irish workingmen married outside their ethnic group in 1880, compared to almost 40 percent of native-born workingmen. Immigrants also tended to marry at a later age than natives, and they tended to have more children, a fact that worried nativists opposed to immigration.

Immigrants shaped the city as much as it shaped them. Most of them tried to retain their traditional culture for themselves and their children while at the same time adapting to life in their new country. To do this, they spoke their native language, practiced their religious faith, read their own newspapers, and established special parochial or other schools. They observed traditional holidays and formed a myriad of social organizations to maintain ties among members of the group.

Immigrant associations—there were many of them in every city—offered fellowship in a strange land. They helped newcomers find jobs and homes; they provided important services such as unemployment insurance and health insurance. Some groups were no larger than a neighborhood; others spread nationwide. In 1914, the Deutsch-Amerikanischer Nationalbund, the largest of the associations, had more than two million members in dozens of cities and towns. Many women belonged to and participated in the work of the immigrant associations; in addition, there were groups exclusively for women, such as the Polish Women's Alliance, the Jednota Ceskyck Dam (Society of Czech Women), and the National Council of Jewish Women.

Every major city had dozens of foreign language newspapers, with circulations large and small. The first newspaper published in the Lithuanian language appeared in the United States, not in Lithuania. Eagerly read, the papers not only carried news of events in the homeland but also reported on local ethnic leaders, told readers how to vote and become citizens, and gave practical tips on adjusting to life in the United States. The Swedes, Poles, Czechs, and Germans established ethnic theaters that performed national plays and music. The most famous of these, the Yiddish (Jewish) Theater, started in the 1880s in New York City and lasted more than fifty years.

The church and the school were the most important institutions in every immigrant community. Eastern European Jews established synagogues and religious schools wherever they settled; they taught the Hebrew language and raised their children in a heritage they did not want to leave behind. Among such groups as the Irish and the Poles, the Roman Catholic church provided spiritual and educational guidance. In the parish schools, Polish priests and nuns taught Polish American children about Polish as well as American culture in the Polish language.

Church, school, and fraternal societies shaped the way in which immigrants adjusted to life in America. By preserving language, religion, and heritage, they also shaped the country itself.

THE HOUSE THAT TWEED BUILT

Closely connected with explosive urban growth was the emergence of the powerful city political machine. As cities grew, lines of responsibility in city governments became hopelessly confused, increasing the opportunity for corruption and greed. Burgeoning populations required streets, buildings, and public services; immigrants needed even more services. In this situation, political party machines played an important role.

The machines traded services for votes. Loosely knit, they were headed by a strong, influential leader—the "boss"—who tied together a network of ward and precinct captains, each of whom looked after his local constituents. In New York, "Honest" John Kelly, Richard Croker, and Charles F. Murphy led Tammany Hall, the famous Democratic party organization that dominated city politics from the 1850s to the 1930s. Other bosses included "Hinky Dink" Kenna and "Bathhouse John" Coughlin in Chicago, James McManes in Philadelphia, and Christopher A. Buckley—the notorious "Blind Boss," who used an exceptional memory for voices to make up for failing eyesight—in San Francisco.

William M. Tweed, head of the famed Tweed Ring in New York, provided the model for them all. Nearly six feet tall, weighing almost three hundred pounds, Tweed rose through the ranks of Tammany Hall. He served in turn as city alderman, member of Congress, and New York State assemblyman. A man of culture and warmth, he moved easily between the rough back alleys of New York and the parlors and clubs of the city's elite. Behind the scenes, he headed a ring that plundered New York for tens of millions of dollars.

The New York County Courthouse—"the house that Tweed built"—was his masterpiece. Nestled in City Hall Park in downtown Manhattan, the three-story structure was designed to cost $250,000, but the bills ran a bit higher. Furniture, carpets, and window shades alone came to more than $5.5 million. Three tables and forty chairs cost the city $180,000. Tweed's own quarry supplied the marble; the plumber was paid almost $1.5 million for fixtures. Andrew Garvey, the "prince of plasterers," charged $500,000 for plasterwork, and then $1 million to repair the same work. His total bill came to $2,870,464.06. (The *New York Times* suggested that the six cents be donated to charity.) In the end, the building cost more than $13 million—and in 1872, when Tweed fell, it was still not finished.

The role of the political bosses can be overemphasized. Power structures in the turn-of-the-century city were complex, involving a host of people and institutions. Banks, real estate investors, insurance companies, architects, and engineers, among others, played roles in governing the city. Viewed in retrospect, many city governments were remarkably successful. With populations that in some cases doubled every decade, city governments provided water and sewer lines, built parks and playgrounds, and paved streets. When it was over, Boston had the world's largest public library and New York City had the Brooklyn Bridge and Central Park, two of the finest achievements in city planning and architecture of any era. By the 1890s, New York also had 660 miles of water lines, 464 miles of sewers, and 1800 miles of paved streets, far more than comparable cities in Europe.

Bosses, moreover, differed from city to city. Buckley stayed in power in San Francisco by keeping city tax rates low. "Honest" John Kelly earned his nickname serving as a watchdog over the New York City treasury. Tweed was one of the early backers of the Brooklyn Bridge. Some bosses were plainly corrupt; others believed in *honest graft,* a term Tammany's George Washington Plunkitt coined to describe "legitimate" profits made from advance knowledge of city projects.

Why did voters keep the bosses in power? The answers are complex, but two reasons were skillful political organization and the fact that immigrants and others made up the bosses' constituency. Most immigrants had little experience with democratic government and proved easy prey for well-oiled machines. For the most part, however, the bosses stayed in power because they paid attention to the needs of the least privileged city voters. They offered valued services in an era when neither government nor business lent a hand.

If an immigrant, tired and bewildered after the long crossing, came looking for a job, bosses like Tweed, Plunkitt, or Buckley found him one in city offices or local businesses. If a family's breadwinner died or was injured, the bosses donated food and clothing and saw to it that the family made it through the crisis. If the winter was particularly cold, they provided free coal to heat tenement apartments. They ran picnics for slum children on hot summer days and contributed to hospitals, orphanages, and dozens of worthy neighborhood causes.

Most bosses became wealthy; they were not Robin Hoods who took from the rich to give to the poor. They took for themselves as well. Reformers occasionally ousted them. Tweed fell from power in 1872, "Blind Boss" Buckley in 1891, Croker in 1894. But the reformers rarely stayed in power long. Drawn mainly from the middle and upper classes, they had little understanding of the needs of the poor. Before long, they returned to private concerns, and the bosses, who had known that they would all along, cheerily took power again.

"What tells in holdin' your grip on your district," the engaging Plunkitt once said, "is to go right down among the poor families and help them in the different ways they need help. . . . It's philanthropy, but it's politics, too—mighty good politics. . . . The poor are the most grateful people in the world."

SOCIAL AND CULTURAL CHANGE, 1877–1900

The rise of cities and industry between 1877 and the 1890s affected all aspects of American life. Mores changed; family ties loosened. Factories turned out consumer goods, and the newly invented cash register rang up record sales. Public and private educational systems burgeoned, illiteracy declined, life expectancy increased. While many people worked harder and harder just to survive, others found they had a greater amount of leisure time. The roles of women and children changed in a number of ways, and the family took on functions it had not had before. Thanks to advancing technology, news flashed quickly across the oceans, and for the first time in history, people read of the day's events in distant lands when they opened their daily newspapers.

In 1877, the country had 47 million people. In 1900, it had nearly 76 million. Nine-tenths of the population was white; just under one-tenth was black. There were 66,000 Indians, 108,000 Chinese, and 148 Japanese. The bulk of the white population, most of whom were Protestant, came from the so-called Anglo-Saxon countries of northern Europe. WASPs—white Anglo-Saxon Protestants—were the dominant members of American society.

Though the rush to the cities was about to begin, most people of 1877 still lived on farms or in small towns. Their lives revolved around the farm, the church, and the general store. In 1880, nearly 75 percent of the population lived in communities of fewer than 2,500 people. In 1900, in the midst of city growth, 60 percent still did. The average family in 1880 had three children, dramatically fewer than at the beginning of the century, and life expectancy was about 43 years. By 1900, it had risen to 47 years, a result of improved health care. For blacks and other minorities, who often lived in unsanitary rural areas, life expectancy was substantially lower: 33 years in 1900.

Meals tended to be heavy, and so did people. Even breakfast had several courses and could include steak, eggs, fish, potatoes, toast, and coffee. Food prices were low. Families ate fresh homegrown produce in the summer and "put up" their fruits and vegetables for the long winters. Toward the end of the century, eating habits changed. New packaged breakfast cereals became popular; fresh fruit and vegetables came in on fast trains from Florida and California, and commercially canned food became safer and cheaper. The newfangled icebox, cooled by blocks of ice, kept food fresher and added new treats such as ice cream.

Medical science was in the midst of a major revolution. Louis Pasteur's recent discovery that germs cause infection and disease created the new science of microbiology and led the way to the development of vaccines and other preventive measures. But tuberculosis, typhoid, diphtheria, and pneumonia—all now curable—were still the leading causes of death. Infant mortality declined between 1877 and 1900, but the decline was gradual; a great drop did not come until after 1920.

There were few hospitals and no hospital insurance. Most patients stayed at home, although medical practice, especially surgery, expanded rapidly. Once brutal and dangerous, surgery in these years became relatively safe and painless. Anesthetics—ether and chloroform—eliminated pain, and antiseptic practices helped prevent postoperative infections. Antiseptic practices at childbirth also cut down on puerperal fever, an infection that for centuries had killed many women and newborn infants. The new science of psychology began to explore the mind, hitherto uncharted. William James, a leading American psychologist and philosopher, laid the foundations of modern behavioral psychology, which stressed the importance of the environment on human development.

MANNERS AND MORES

The code of Victorian morality, its name derived from the British queen who reigned throughout the period, set the tone for the era. The code prescribed strict standards of dress, manners, and sexual behavior. It was both obeyed and disobeyed, and it reflected the tensions of a generation that was undergoing a change in moral standards.

In 1877, children were to be seen and not heard. They spoke when spoken to, listened rather than chattered—or at least that was the rule. Older boys and girls were often chaperoned, although they could always find moments alone. They played post office and spin the bottle; they puffed cigarettes behind the barn. Journalist William Allen White recalled the high jinks of his boyhood. He and his friends smeared their naked bodies with mud and leaped out in full view of passengers on passing trains. Counterbalancing such youthful exuberance was strong pride in virtue and self-control. "Thank heaven I am absolutely pure," Theodore Roosevelt, the future president, wrote in 1880 after proposing to Alice Lee. "I can tell Alice everything I have ever done."

Gentlemen of the middle class dressed in heavy black suits, derby hats, and white shirts with paper collars. Women wore tight corsets, long dark dresses, and black shoes reaching well above the ankles. As with so many things, styles changed dramatically toward the end of the century, spurred in part by new sporting fads such as golf, tennis, and bicycling, which required looser clothing. By the 1890s, a middle-class woman wore a tailored suit or a dark skirt and a blouse, called a shirtwaist, modeled after men's shirts. Her skirts still draped about the ankles, but more and more she removed or loosened the corset, the dread device that squeezed skin and internal organs into fashionable 18-inch waistlines.

Religious and patriotic values were strong. A center of community life, the church often set the tenor for family and social relationships. In the 1880s, eight out of ten church members were Protestants; most of the rest were Roman Catholics.

With slavery abolished, reformers turned their attention to new moral and political issues. One group, known as the Mugwumps, worked to end corruption in politics. Drawn mostly from the educated and upper class, they included Thomas Nast, the famous political cartoonist, and E. L. Godkin, editor of the influential *Nation*. Other zealous reformers campaigned for prohibition of the sale of intoxicating liquors, hoping to end the social evils that stemmed from drunkenness. In 1874, women who advocated total abstinence from alcoholic beverages formed the Women's Christian Temperance Union (WCTU). Their leader, Frances E. Willard, served as president of the group from 1879 until her death in 1898. By then, the WCTU had 10,000 branches and 500,000 members.

LEISURE AND ENTERTAINMENT

In the 1870s, people tended to rise early. On getting up, they washed from the pitcher and bowl in the bedroom, first breaking the layer of ice if it was winter. After dressing and eating, they went off to work and school. Without large refrigerators, housewives marketed almost daily. In the evening, families gathered in the "second parlor" or living room, where the children did their lessons, played games, sang around the piano, and listened to that day's verse from the Bible.

Popular games included cards, dominoes, backgammon, chess, and checkers. Many homes had a packet of "author cards" that required knowledge of books, authors, and noted quotations. The latest fad was the stereopticon or "magic lantern," which brought three-dimensional life to art, history, and nature. Like author cards and other games, it was instructional as well as entertaining.

The newest outdoor game was croquet, so popular that candles were mounted on the wickets to allow play at night. Croquet was the first outdoor game designed for play by both sexes, and it frequently served as a setting for courtship. Early manuals advised girls how to assume attractive poses while hitting the ball. A popular song of the period told of a pair seated side by side:

> *Mallets and balls unheeded lay . . .*
> *And I thought to myself, is that Croquet?*

Sentimental ballads such as "Silver Threads Among the Gold" (1873) remained the most popular musical form, but the insistent syncopated rhythms of ragtime were being heard, reflecting the influence of the new urban culture. By the time the strains of Scott Joplin's "Maple Leaf Rag" (1899) popularized ragtime, critics complained that "a wave of vulgar, filthy and suggestive music has inundated the land." Classical music flourished. The New England Conservatory (1867), the Cincinnati College of Music (1878), and the Metropolitan Opera (1883) were new sources of civic pride; New York, Boston, and Chicago launched first-rate symphony orchestras between 1878 and 1891.

Fairs, horse races, balloon ascensions, bicycle tournaments, and football and baseball contests attracted avid fans. The years between 1870 and 1900 saw the rise of organized spectator sports, a trend reflecting both the rise of the city and the new uses of leisure. Baseball's first professional team, the Cincinnati Red Stockings, appeared in 1869, and baseball soon became the preeminent national sport. Fans sang songs about it ("Take Me Out to the

Ballgame"), wrote poems about it ("Casey at the Bat"), and made up riddles about it ("What has eighteen feet and catches flies?"). Modern rules were adopted. Umpires were designated to call balls and strikes; catchers wore masks and chest protectors and moved closer to the plate instead of staying back to catch the ball on the bounce. Fielders had to catch the ball on the fly rather than on one bounce in their caps. By 1890, professional baseball teams were drawing crowds of sixty thousand daily. In 1901, the American League was organized, and two years later the Boston Red Sox beat the Pittsburgh Pirates in the first modern World Series.

In 1869, Princeton and Rutgers played the first intercollegiate football game. Soon, other schools picked up the sport, and by the early 1890s, crowds of fifty thousand or more attended the most popular contests. Basketball, invented in 1891, gained a large following. Boxing, a popular topic of conversation in saloons and schoolyards, was outlawed in most states. For a time, championship prize-fights were held in secret, with news of the result spread rapidly by word of mouth. Matches were long and bloody, fought with bare knuckles until the invention in the 1880s of the 5-ounce boxing glove. John L. Sullivan, the "Boston Strong Boy" and the era's most popular champion, won the heavyweight title in 1889 in a brutal 75-round victory over the stubborn Jake Kilrain.

As gas and electric lights brightened the night, and streetcars crisscrossed city streets, leisure habits changed. Delighted with the new technology, people took advantage of an increasing variety of things to do. They stayed home less often. New York City's first electric sign—"Manhattan Beach Swept by Ocean Breezes"—appeared in 1881, and people went out at night, filling the streets on their way to the theater, vaudeville shows, and dance halls or just out for an evening stroll.

CHANGES IN FAMILY LIFE

Under the impact of industrialization and urbanization, family relationships were changing. On the farm, parents and children worked more or less together, and the family was a producing unit. In factories and offices, family members rarely worked together. In working-class families, mothers, fathers, and children separated at dawn and returned, ready for sleep, at dark.

Working-class families of the late nineteenth century, like the family of the young Polish girl that Harriet Vittum saw, often lived in complex household units—taking in relatives and boarders to pay the rent. As many as one-third of all households contained people who were not members of the immediate family. Although driven apart by the daily routine, family ties among the working class tended to remain strong, cemented by the need to join forces in order to survive in the industrial economy.

The middle-class wife and children, however, became increasingly isolated from the world of work. Turning inward, the middle-class family became more self-contained. Older children spent more time in adolescence, and periods of formal schooling were lengthier. Families took in fewer apprentices and boarders. By the end of the century, most middle-class offspring continued to live with their parents into their late teens and their twenties, a larger proportion than today.

Fewer middle-class wives participated directly in their husbands' work. As a result, they and their children occupied what contemporaries called a "separate sphere of domesticity," set apart from the masculine sphere of income-producing work. The family home became a "walled garden," a place to retreat from the crass materialism of the outside world. Middle-class fathers began to move their families out of the city to the suburbs, commuting to work on the new streetcars and leaving wives and children at home and school.

The middle-class family had once functioned in part to transmit a craft or skill, arrange marriages, and offer care for dependent kin. Now, as these functions declined, the family took on new emotional and ideological responsibilities. In a society that worried about the weakening hold of other institutions, the family became more and more important as a means of social control. It also placed new burdens on wives.

"In the old days," said a woman in 1907, "a married woman was supposed to be a frump and a bore and a physical wreck. Now you are supposed to keep up intellectually, to look young and well and be fresh and bright and entertaining." Magazines such as the *Ladies' Home Journal,* which started in 1889, glorified motherhood and the home, but its articles and ads featured women as homebound, child-oriented consumers. While society's leaders spoke fondly of the value of homemaking, the status of housewives declined under the factory system, which emphasized money rewards and devalued household labor.

Underlying all these changes was one of the modern world's most important trends, a major decline in fertility rates that lasted from 1800 to 1939. Though blacks, immigrants, and rural dwellers continued to have more children than white native-born city dwellers, the trend affected all classes and races; among white women, the birthrate fell from 7 in 1800 to just over 4 in 1880 to about 3 in 1900. People everywhere tended to marry later and have fewer children.

Since contraceptive devices were not yet widely used, the decline reflected abstinence and a conscious decision to postpone or limit families. Some women decided to devote greater attention to a smaller number of children, others to pursue their own careers. There was a marked increase in the number of young unmarried women working for wages or attending school, an increase in the number of women delaying marriage or not marrying at all, and a gradual decline in rates of illegitimacy and premarital pregnancy.

In large part, the decline in fertility stemmed from people's responses to the social and economic forces around them, the rise of cities and industry. In a host of individual decisions, they decided to have fewer children, and the result reshaped some of the fundamental attitudes and institutions of American society.

CHANGING VIEWS: A GROWING ASSERTIVENESS AMONG WOMEN

In and out of the family, there was growing recognition of self-sufficient working women, employed in factory, telephone exchange, or business office, who were entering the workforce in increasing numbers. In 1880, 2.6 million women were gainfully employed; in 1890, 4 million. In 1882, the Census Bureau took the first census of working women; most were single and worked out of necessity rather than choice.

Female operators, called "hello girls," were hired to work telephone switchboards after it was discovered that male operators tended to argue too much with subscribers.

Many regarded this "new woman" as a corruption of the ideal vision of the American woman, in which man worshiped "a diviner self than his own," innocent, helpless, and good. Women were to be better than the world around them. They were brought up, said Ida Tarbell, a leading political reformer, "as if wrongdoing were impossible to them."

Views changed, albeit slowly. One important change occurred in the legal codes pertaining to women, particularly in the common law doctrine of *femme couverte*. Under that doctrine, wives were chattel of their husbands; they could not legally control their own earnings, property, or children unless they had drawn up a specific contract before marriage. By 1890, many states had substantially revised the doctrine to allow wives control of their earnings and inherited property. In cases of divorce, the new laws also recognized women's rights to custody or joint custody of their children. Although divorce was still far from being socially acceptable, divorce rates more than doubled during the last third of the century. By 1905, one in twelve marriages was ending in divorce.

In the 1870s and 1880s, a growing number of women were asserting their own humanness. They fought for the vote, lobbied for equal pay, and sought self-fulfillment. The new interest in psychology and medicine strengthened their causes. Charlotte Perkins Gilman, author of *Women and Economics* (1898), joined other women in questioning the ideal of womanly "innocence," which, she argued, actually meant ignorance. In medical and popular literature, menstruation, sexual intercourse, and childbirth were becoming viewed as natural functions instead of taboo topics.

Edward Bliss Foote's *Plain Home Talk of Love, Marriage, and Parentage,* a bestseller that went through many editions between the 1880s and 1900, challenged Victorian notions that sexual intercourse was unhealthy and intended solely to produce children.

Women espoused causes with new fervor. Susan B. Anthony, a veteran of many reform campaigns, tried to vote in the 1872 presidential election and was fined $100, which she refused to pay. In 1890, she helped form the National American Woman Suffrage Association to work for the enfranchisement of women. On New York's Lower East Side, the Ladies Anti–Beef Trust Association, which formed to protest increases in the price of meat, established a boycott of butcher shops. When their demands were ignored, the women invaded the shops, poured kerosene on the meat, and set fire to it. "We don't riot," Rebecca Ablowitz told the judge. "But if all we did was to weep at home, nobody would notice it; so we have to do something to help ourselves."

EDUCATING THE MASSES

Continuing a trend that stretched back a hundred years, childhood was becoming an even more distinct time of life. There was still only a vague concept of adolescence—the special nature of the teenage years—but the role of children was changing. Less and less were children perceived as "little adults," valued for the additional financial gain they might bring into the family. Now children were to grow and learn and be nurtured rather than rushed into adulthood.

As a result, schooling became more important, and American children came closer than ever before to universal education. By 1900, thirty-one states and territories (out of fifty-one) had enacted laws making school attendance compulsory, though most required attendance only until the age of 14. In 1870, there were only 160 public high schools; in 1900, there were 6000. In the same years, illiteracy declined from 20 percent to just over 10 percent of the population. Still, even as late as 1900, the average adult had only five years of schooling.

Educators saw the school as the primary means to train people for life and work in an industrializing society. Hence teachers focused on basic skills—reading and mathematics—and on values—obedience and attentiveness to the clock. Most schools had a highly structured curriculum, built around discipline and rou-

Schools, regarded primarily as training grounds for a life of work, stressed conformity and deportment—feet on the floor, hands folded and resting atop the desk. The teacher was drillmaster and disciplinarian as well as instructor.

tine. In 1892, Joseph Rice, a pediatrician, toured twelve hundred classrooms in thirty-six cities. In a typical classroom, he reported, the atmosphere was "damp and chilly," the teacher strict. "The unkindly spirit of the teacher is strikingly apparent; the pupils being completely subjugated to her will, are silent and motionless." One teacher asked her pupils, "How can you learn anything with your knees and toes out of order?"

School began early; boys attended all day, but girls often stayed home after lunch, since it was thought they needed less in the way of learning. On the teacher's command, students stood and recited from *Webster's Spellers* and *McGuffey's Eclectic Readers,* the period's most popular textbooks. The work of William Holmes McGuffey, a professor of languages at Miami University in Ohio, *McGuffey's Eclectic Readers* had been in use since 1836; 100 million copies were sold in the last half of the nineteenth century. Nearly every child read them; they taught not only reading but also ethics, values, and religion. In the *Readers,* boys grew up to be heroes, girls to be mothers, and hard work always meant success:

> Shall birds, and bees, and ants, be wise,
> While I my moments waste?
> O let me with the morning rise,
> And to my duty haste.

The South lagged far behind in education. The average family size there was about twice as large as in the North, and a greater proportion of the population lived in isolated rural areas. State and local authorities mandated fewer weeks in the average school year, and many southern states refused to adopt compulsory education laws. Most important, Southerners insisted on maintaining separate school systems to segregate the races. Supported by the U.S. Supreme Court decision of 1896 in *Plessy* v. *Ferguson,* segregated schooling added a devastating financial burden to education in the South.

North Carolina and Alabama mandated segregated schools in 1876, South Carolina and Louisiana in 1877, Mississippi in 1878, and Virginia in 1882. A series of Supreme Court decisions in the 1880s and 1890s upheld the concept of segregation. In the *Civil Rights Cases* (1883), the Court ruled that the Fourteenth Amendment barred state governments from discriminating on account of race but did not prevent private individuals or organizations from doing so. *Plessy* v. *Ferguson* (1896) established the doctrine of "separate but equal" and upheld a Louisiana law requiring different railroad cars for whites and blacks. The Court applied the doctrine directly to schools in *Cumming* v. *County Board of Education* (1899), which approved the creation of separate schools for whites, even if there were no comparable schools for blacks.

Southern school laws often implied that the schools would be "separate but equal," and they were often separate but rarely equal. Black schools were usually dilapidated, and black teachers were paid considerably less than white teachers. In 1890, only 35 percent of black children attended school in the South; 55 percent of white children did. That year nearly two-thirds of the country's black population was illiterate.

Educational techniques changed after the 1870s. Educators paid more attention to early elementary education, a trend that placed young children in school and helped the growing number of mothers who worked outside the home. The kindergarten movement, started in St. Louis in 1873, spread across the country. In kindergartens, 4- to 6-year-old children learned by playing, not by keeping their knees and toes in order. For older children, social reformers advocated "practical" courses in manual training and homemaking.

HIGHER EDUCATION

Nearly 150 new colleges and universities opened in the twenty years between 1880 and 1900. The Morrill Land Grant Act of 1862 gave large grants of land to the states for the establishment of colleges to teach "agriculture and the mechanic arts." The act fostered 69 "land-grant" institutions, including the great state universities of Wisconsin, California, Minnesota, and Illinois.

Private philanthropy, born of the large fortunes of the industrial age, also spurred growth in higher education. Leland Stanford gave $24 million to endow Stanford University on his California ranch, and John D. Rockefeller, founder of the Standard Oil Company, gave $34 million to found the University of Chicago. Other industrialists established Cornell (1865), Vanderbilt (1873), and Tulane (1884).

As colleges expanded, their function changed and their curriculum broadened. No longer did they exist primarily to train young men for the ministry. They moved away from the classical curriculum of rhetoric, mathematics, Latin, and Greek toward "reality and practicality," as President David Starr Jordan of Stanford University said. The Massachusetts Institute of Technology (MIT), founded in 1861, focused on science and engineering.

Charles W. Eliot, who became president of Harvard in 1869 at the age of 35, moved to end, as an admirer said, the "old fogyism" that marked the institution. Revising the curriculum, Eliot set up the elective system, in which students chose their own courses rather than following a rigidly prescribed curriculum. Lectures and discussions replaced rote recitation, and courses in the natural and social sciences, fine arts, and modern languages multiplied. In the 1890s, Eliot's Harvard moved to the forefront of educational innovation.

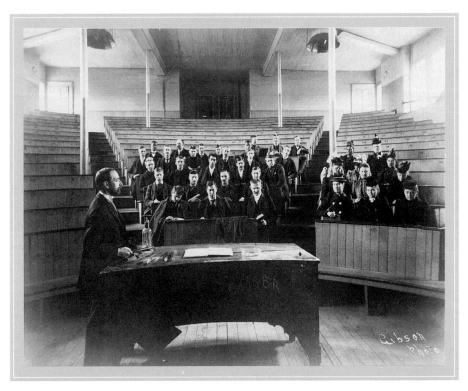

A physics lecture at the University of Michigan in the late 1880s or early 1890s. The land-grant university admitted women, but seating in the lecture hall was segregated by gender—although not by race. Notice that both whites and African Americans are seated in the back rows of the men's section.

Women still had to fight for educational opportunities. Some formed study clubs, an important movement that spread rapidly between 1870 and 1900. Groups such as the Decatur (Illinois) Art Class, the Boston History Class, and the Barnesville (Georgia) Shakespeare Club aimed "to enlarge the mental horizon as well as the knowledge of our members." Club members read Virgil and Chaucer, studied history and architecture, and discussed women's rights. Although they were usually small, study clubs sparked a greater interest in education among women and their daughters and contributed to a rapid rise in the number of women entering college in the early 1900s.

Before the Civil War, only three private colleges admitted women to study with men. After the war, educational opportunities increased for women. A number of women's colleges opened, including Vassar (1865), Wellesley (1875), Smith (1875), Bryn Mawr (1885), Barnard (1889), and Radcliffe (1893). The land-grant colleges of the Midwest, open to women from the outset, spurred a nationwide trend toward coeducation, although some physicians, such as

Harvard Medical School's Dr. Edward H. Clarke in his popular *Sex in Education* (1873), continued to argue that the strain of learning made women sterile. By 1900, women made up about 40 percent of college students, and four out of five colleges admitted them.

Fewer opportunities existed for African Americans and other minorities. Jane Stanford encouraged the Chinese who had worked on her husband's Central Pacific Railroad to apply to Stanford University, but her policy was unusual. Most colleges did not accept minority students, and only a few applied. W. E. B. Du Bois, the brilliant African American sociologist and civil rights leader, attended Harvard in the late 1880s but found the society of Harvard Yard closed against him. Disdained and disdainful, he "asked no fellowship of my fellow students." Chosen as one of the commencement speakers, Du Bois picked as his topic "Jefferson Davis," treating it, said an onlooker, with "an almost contemptuous fairness."

Black students turned to black colleges such as the Hampton Normal and Industrial Institute in Virginia and the Tuskegee Institute in Alabama. These colleges were often supported by whites who favored manual training for blacks. Booker T. Washington, an ex-slave, put into practice his educational ideas at Tuskegee, which opened in 1881. Washington began Tuskegee with limited funds, four run-down buildings, and only thirty students; by 1900, it was a model industrial and agricultural school. Spread over forty-six buildings, it offered instruction in thirty trades to fourteen hundred students.

Washington stressed patience, manual training, and hard work. "The wisest among my race understand," he said in a widely acclaimed speech at the Atlanta Exposition in 1895, "that the agitation of questions of social equality is the extremest folly." Blacks should focus on economic gains; they should go to school, learn skills, and work their way up the ladder. "No race," he said at Atlanta, "can prosper till it learns that there is as much dignity in tilling a field as in writing a poem. It is at the bottom of life we must begin, and not at the top." Southern whites should help out because they would then have "the most patient, faithful, law-abiding, and unresentful people that the world has seen."

Outlined most forcefully in Washington's speech in Atlanta, the philosophy became known as the Atlanta Compromise, and many whites and some blacks welcomed it. Acknowledging white domination, it called for slow progress through self-improvement, not through lawsuits or agitation. Rather than fighting for equal rights, blacks should acquire property and show they were worthy of their rights. But Washington did believe in black equality. Often secretive in his methods, he worked behind the scenes to organize black voters and lobby against harmful laws. In his own way, he bespoke a racial pride that contributed to the rise of black nationalism in the twentieth century.

Booker T. Washington, who served as the first president of Tuskegee Institute, advocated work efficiency and practical skills as keys to advancement for African Americans. Students like these at Tuskegee studied academic subjects and received training in trades and professions.

Du Bois wanted a more aggressive strategy. Born in Massachusetts in 1868, the son of poor parents, he studied at Fisk University in Tennessee and the University of Berlin before he went to Harvard. Unable to find a teaching job in a white college, he took a low-paying research position at the University of Pennsylvania. He had no office but did not need one. Du Bois used the new discipline of sociology, which emphasized factual observation in the field, to study the condition of blacks.

Notebook in hand, he set out to examine crime in Philadelphia's black seventh ward. He interviewed five thousand people, mapped and classified neighborhoods, and produced *The Philadelphia Negro* (1898). The first study of the effect of urban life on blacks, it cited a wealth of statistics, all suggesting that crime in the ward stemmed not from inborn degeneracy but from the environment in which blacks lived. Change the environment, and people would change, too; education was a good way to go about it.

In *The Souls of Black Folk* (1903), Du Bois openly attacked Booker T. Washington and the philosophy of the Atlanta Compromise. He urged African Americans to aspire to professional careers, to fight for the restoration of their civil rights, and, wherever possible, to get a college education. Calling for integrated schools with equal opportunity for all, Du Bois urged blacks to educate their "talented tenth," a highly trained intellectual elite, to lead them.

Du Bois was not alone in promoting careers in the professions. Throughout higher education there was increased emphasis on professional training, particularly in medicine, dentistry, and law. Enrollments swelled, even as standards of admission tightened. The number of medical schools in the country rose from 75 in 1870 to 160 in 1900, and the number of medical students—including more and more women—almost tripled. Schools of nursing grew from only 15 in 1880 to 432 in 1900. Doctors, lawyers, and others became part of a growing middle class that shaped the concerns of the Progressive Era of the early twentieth century.

Although less than 5 percent of the college-age population attended college during the 1877–1890 period, the new trends had great impact. A generation of men and women encountered new ideas that changed their views of themselves and society. Courses never before offered, like Philosophy II at Harvard, "The Ethics of Social Reform," which students called "drainage, drunkenness, and divorce," heightened interest in social problems and the need for reform. Some graduating students burned with a desire to cure society's ills. "My life began . . . at Johns Hopkins University," Frederic C. Howe, an influential reformer, recalled. "I came alive, I felt a sense of responsibility to the world, I wanted to change things."

THE STIRRINGS OF REFORM

When Henry George, one of the era's leading reformers, asked a friend what could be done about the problem of political corruption in American cities, his friend replied: "Nothing! You and I can do nothing at all. . . . We can only wait for evolution. Perhaps in four or five thousand years evolution may have carried men beyond this state of things."

This stress on the slow pace of change reflected the doctrine of social Darwinism, based on the writings of English social philosopher Herbert Spencer. In several influential books, Spencer took the evolutionary theories of Charles Darwin and applied Darwinian principles of natural selection to society, combining biology and sociology in a theory of "social selection" that tried to explain human progress. Like animals, society evolved, slowly, by adapting to the environment. The "survival of the fittest"—a term that Spencer, not Darwin, invented—preserved the strong and weeded out the weak.

Social Darwinism had a number of influential followers in the United States, including William Graham Sumner, a professor of political and social science at

Yale University. One of the country's best known academic figures, Sumner was forceful and eloquent. In writings such as *What Social Classes Owe to Each Other* (1883) and "The Absurd Effort to Make the World Over" (1894), he argued that government action on behalf of the poor or weak interfered with evolution and sapped the species. Reform tampered with the laws of nature.

The influence of social Darwinism on American thinking has been exaggerated, but in the powerful hands of Sumner and others it did influence some journalists, ministers, and policymakers. Between 1877 and the 1890s, however, it came under increasing attack. In fields like religion, economics, politics, literature, and law, thoughtful people raised questions about established conditions and suggested the need for reform.

PROGRESS AND POVERTY

Read and reread, passed from hand to hand, Henry George's nationwide bestseller *Progress and Poverty* (1879) led the way to a more critical appraisal of American society in the 1880s and beyond. The book jolted traditional thought. "It was responsible," one historian has said, "for starting along new lines of thinking an amazing number of the men and women" who became leaders of reform.

Disturbed by the depression of the 1870s and labor upheavals such as the great railroad strikes of 1877, George saw modern society—rich, complex, with material goods hitherto unknown—as sadly flawed.

"The present century," he wrote, "has been marked by a prodigious increase in wealth-producing power. . . . It was natural to expect, and it was expected, that . . . real poverty [would become] a thing of the past." Instead, he argued:

> it becomes no easier for the masses of our people to make a living. On the contrary, it is becoming harder. The wealthy class is becoming more wealthy; but the poorer class is becoming more dependent. The gulf between the employed and the employer is growing wider; social contrasts are becoming sharper; as liveried carriages appear, so do bare-footed children.

George proposed a simple solution. Land, he thought, formed the basis of wealth, and a few people could grow wealthy just because the price of their land rose. Since the rise in price did not result from any effort on their part, it represented an "unearned increment," which, George argued, should be taxed for the good of society. A "single tax" on the increment, replacing all other taxes, would help equalize wealth and raise revenue to aid the poor. "Single-tax" clubs sprang up around the country, but George's solution, simplistic and unappealing, had much less impact than his analysis of the problem itself. He raised questions a generation of readers set out to answer.

NEW CURRENTS IN SOCIAL THOUGHT

George's emphasis on deprivation in the environment excited a young country lawyer in Ashtabula, Ohio—Clarence Darrow. Unlike the social Darwinists, Darrow was sure that criminals were made and not born. They grew out of "the unjust condition of human life." In the mid-1880s, he left for Chicago and a forty-year career working to convince people that poverty lay at the root of crime. "There is no such thing as crime as the word is generally understood," he told a group of startled prisoners in the Cook County jail. "If every man, woman and child in the world had a chance to make a decent, fair, honest living there would be no jails and no lawyers and no courts."

As Darrow rejected the implications of social Darwinism, in similar fashion Richard T. Ely and a group of young economists poked holes in traditional economic thought. Fresh from graduate study in Germany, Ely in 1884 attacked classical economics for its dogmatism, simple faith in laissez-faire, and reliance on self-interest as a guide for human conduct. The "younger" economics, he said, must no longer be "a tool in the hands of the greedy and the avaricious for keeping down and oppressing the laboring classes. It does not acknowledge laissez-faire as an excuse for doing nothing while people starve."

Edward Bellamy dreamed of a cooperative society in which poverty, greed, and crime no longer existed. A lawyer from western Massachusetts, Bellamy published *Looking Backward, 2000–1887,* in 1887 and became a national reform figure virtually overnight. The novel's protagonist, Julian West, falls asleep in 1887 and awakes in the year 2000. Wide-eyed, he finds himself in a socialist utopia: the government owns the means of production, and citizens share the material rewards. Cooperation, rather than competition, is the watchword.

The world of *Looking Backward* had limits; it was regimented, paternalistic, and filled with the gadgets and material concerns of Bellamy's own day. But it had a dramatic effect on many readers. The book sold at the rate of ten thousand copies a week, and its followers formed Nationalist Clubs to work for its objectives.

Some Protestant sects stressed individual salvation and a better life in the next world, not in this one. Poverty was evidence of sinfulness; the poor had only themselves to blame. "God has intended the great to be great and the little to be little," said Henry Ward Beecher, the country's best known pastor. Wealth and destitution, suburbs and slums—all formed part of God's plan.

Challenging those traditional doctrines, a number of churches in the 1880s began establishing missions in the city slums. William Dwight Porter Bliss, an Episcopal clergyman, founded the Church of the Carpenter in a working-class district of Boston. Lewis M. Pease worked in the grim Five Points area of New York; Alexander Irvine, a Jewish missionary, lived in a flophouse in the Bowery.

Irvine walked his skid row neighborhood every afternoon to lend a hand to those in need. Living among the poor and homeless, the urban missionaries grew impatient with religious doctrines that endorsed the status quo.

Many of the new trends were reflected in an emerging religious philosophy known as the Social Gospel. As the name suggests, the Social Gospel focused on society as well as individuals, on improving living conditions as well as saving souls. Sermons in Social Gospel churches called on church members to fulfill their social obligations, and adults met before and after the regular service to discuss social and economic problems. Children were excused from sermons, organized into age groups, and encouraged to make the church a center for social as well as religious activity. Soon churches included dining halls, gymnasiums, and even theaters.

The most active Social Gospel leader was Washington Gladden, a Congregational minister and prolific writer. Linking Christianity to the social and economic environment, Gladden spent a lifetime working for "social salvation." He saw Christianity as a fellowship of love and the church as a social agency. In *Applied Christianity* (1886) and other writings, he denounced competition, urged an "industrial partnership" between employers and employees, and called for efforts to help the poor.

THE SETTLEMENT HOUSES

A growing number of social reformers living in the urban slums shared Gladden's concern. Like Tweed and Plunkitt, they appreciated the dependency of the poor; unlike them, they wanted to eradicate the conditions that underlay it. To do so, they formed settlement houses in the slums and went to live in them to experience the problems they were trying to solve.

Youthful, idealistic, and mostly middle class, these social workers took as their model Toynbee Hall, founded in 1884 in the slums of East London to provide community services. Stanton Coit, a moody and poetic graduate of Amherst College, was the first American to borrow the settlement house idea; in 1886, he opened the Neighborhood Guild on the Lower East Side of New York. The idea spread swiftly. By 1900, there were more than a hundred settlements in the country; five years later, there were more than two hundred, and by 1910, more than four hundred.

The settlements included Jane Addams's famous Hull House in Chicago (1889), Robert A. Woods's South End House in Boston (1892), and Lillian Wald's Henry Street Settlement in New York (1893). The reformers wanted to bridge the socioeconomic gap between rich and poor and to bring education, culture, and hope to the slums. They sought to create in the heart of the city the values and sense of community of small-town America.

Many of the settlement workers were women, some of them college graduates, who found that society had little use for their talents and energy. Jane Addams, a graduate of Rockford College in Illinois, opened Hull House on South Halsted Street in the heart of the Chicago slums. Twenty-nine years old, endowed with a forceful and winning personality, she intended "to share the lives of the poor" and humanize the industrial city. "American ideals," she said, "crumbled under the overpowering poverty of the overcrowded city."

Occupying an old, rundown house, Hull House stressed education, offering classes in elementary English and Shakespeare, lectures on ethics and the history of art, and courses in cooking, sewing, and manual skills. A pragmatist, Addams believed in investigating a problem and then doing something to solve it. Noting the lack of medical care in the area, she established an infant welfare clinic and free medical dispensary. Because the tenements lacked bathtubs, she installed showers in the basement of the house and built a bathhouse for the neighbors. Because there was no local library, she opened a reading room. Gradually, Hull House expanded to occupy a dozen buildings sprawling over more than a city block.

Like settlement workers in other cities, Addams and her colleagues studied the immigrants in nearby tenements. Laboriously, they identified the background of every family in a one-third-square-mile area around Hull House. Finding people of eighteen different nationalities, they taught them American history and the English language, yet Addams also encouraged them—through folk festivals and art—to preserve their own heritage.

Florence Kelley, an energetic graduate of Cornell University, taught night school one winter in Chicago. Watching children break under the burden of poverty, she devoted her life to the problem of child labor. Convinced of the need for political activism, she worked with Addams and others to push through the Illinois Factory Act of 1893, which mandated an eight-hour day for women in factories and for children under the age of 14.

The settlement house movement had its limits. Hull House, one of the best, attracted two thousand visitors a week, still just a fraction of the seventy thousand people who lived within six blocks. Immigrants sometimes resented the middle-class "strangers" who told them how to live. Dressed always in a brown suit and dark stockings, Harriet Vittum, the head resident of Chicago's Northwestern University Settlement (who told the story of the suicide victim at the beginning of this chapter), was known in the neighborhood as "the police lady in brown." She once stopped a dance because it was too wild, and then watched

Jane Addams founded Chicago's Hull House in 1889. The settlement house provided recreational and day-care facilities; offered extension classes in academic, vocational, and artistic subjects; and, above all, sought to bring hope to poverty-stricken slum dwellers.

in disgust as the boys responded by "making vulgar sounds with their lips." Though her attempts to help were sincere, in private Vittum called the people she was trying to help "ignorant foreigners, who live in an atmosphere of low morals . . . surrounded by anarchy and crime."

Although Addams tried to offer a few programs for blacks, most white reformers did not, and after 1900, a number of black reformers opened their own settlements. Like the whites, they offered employment information, medical care, and recreational facilities, along with concerts, lectures, and other educational events. White and black, the settlement workers made important contributions to urban life.

A CRISIS IN SOCIAL WELFARE

The depression of 1893 jarred the young settlement workers, many of whom had just begun their work. Addams and the Hull House workers helped form the Chicago Bureau of Charities to coordinate emergency relief. Kelley, recently appointed the chief factory inspector of Illinois, worked even harder to end child labor, and in 1899, she moved to New York City to head the National Consumers League, which marshaled the buying power of women to encourage employers to provide better working conditions.

In cities and towns across the country, traditional methods of helping the needy foundered in the crisis. Churches, Charity Organization Societies, and Community Chests did what they could, but their resources were limited, and they functioned on traditional lines. Many of them still tried to change rather than aid individual families, and people were often reluctant to call on them for help.

Gradually, a new class of professional social workers arose to fill the need. Unlike the church and charity volunteers, these social workers wanted not only to feed the poor but to study their condition and alleviate it. Revealingly, they called themselves "case workers" and daily collected data on the income, housing, jobs, health, and habits of the poor. Prowling tenement districts, they gathered information about the number of rooms, number of occupants, ventilation, and sanitation of the buildings, putting together a fund of useful data.

Studies of the poor popped up everywhere. W. E. B. Du Bois did his pioneering study of urban blacks; Lillian Pettengill took a job as a domestic servant to see "the ups and downs of this particular dog-life from the dog's end of the chain." Others became street beggars, miners, lumberjacks, and factory laborers.

William T. Stead, a prominent British editor, visited the Chicago World's Fair in 1893 and stayed to examine the city. He roamed the flophouses and tenements and dropped in at Hull House to drink hot chocolate and talk over conditions with Jane Addams. Later he wrote an influential book, *If Christ Came to Chicago* (1894), and in a series of mass meetings during 1893, he called for a civic revival. In response, Chicagoans formed the Civic Federation, a group of forty leaders who aimed to make Chicago "the best governed, the healthiest city in this country." Setting up task forces for philanthropy, moral improvement, and legislation, the new group helped spawn the National Civic Federation (1900), a nationwide organization devoted to reform of urban life.

"The United States was born in the country and moved to the city," historian Richard Hofstadter said. Much of that movement occurred during the nineteenth century when the United States was the most rapidly urbanizing nation in the Western world. American cities bustled with energy; they absorbed millions of migrants who came from Europe and other distant and not-so-distant parts of the world. That migration, and the urban growth that accompanied it, reshaped American politics and culture.

By 1920, the census showed that, for the first time, most Americans lived in cities. By then, too, almost half the population was descended from people who had arrived after the American Revolution. As European, African, and

Asian cultures met in the American city, a culturally pluralistic society emerged. Dozens of nationalities produced a culture whose members considered themselves Polish Americans, African Americans, and Irish Americans. The melting pot sometimes softened distinctions between the various groups, but it only partially blended them into a unified society.

"Ah, Vera," said a character in Israel Zangwill's popular play *The Melting Pot* (1908), "what is the glory of Rome and Jerusalem where all nations and races come to worship and look back, compared with the glory of America, where all races and nations come to labour and look forward!" Critics scorned the play as "romantic claptrap," and indeed it was. But the metaphor of the melting pot clearly depicted a new national image. In the decades after the 1870s a jumble of ethnic and racial groups struggled for a place in society.

That society, it is clear, experienced a crisis between 1870 and 1900. Together, the growth of cities and the rise of industrial capitalism brought jarring change, the exploitation of labor, ethnic and racial tensions, poverty—and, for a few, wealth beyond the imagination. At Homestead, Pullman, and a host of other places, there was open warfare between capital and labor. As reformers struggled to mediate the situation, they turned more and more to state and federal government to look after human welfare, a tendency the Supreme Court stoutly resisted. In the midst of the crisis, the depression of the 1890s struck, adding to the turmoil and straining American institutions. Tracing the changes wrought by waves of urbanization and industrialization, Henry George described the country as "the House of Have and the House of Want," almost in paraphrase of Lincoln's earlier metaphor of the "house divided." The question was, could this house, unlike that one, stand?

20

POLITICAL REALIGNMENTS IN THE 1890s

n June 1894, Susan Orcutt, a young farm woman from western Kansas, sat down to write the governor of her state a letter. She was desperate. The nation was in the midst of a devastating economic depression, and, like thousands of other people, she had no money and nothing to eat. "I take my Pen In hand to let you know that we are Starving to death," she wrote. Hail had ruined the Orcutts' crops, and none of the household could find work. "My Husband went away to find work and came home last night and told me that we would have to Starve. [H]e has bin in ten countys and did not Get no work. . . . I havent had nothing to Eat today and It is three oclock[.]"

As bad as conditions were on the farms, they were no better in the cities. "There are thousands of homeless and starving men in the streets," reported a journalist in Chicago in the winter of 1893. "I have seen more misery in this last week than I ever saw in my life before." Charity societies and churches tried to help, but they could not handle the huge numbers of people who were in need. The records of the Massachusetts state medical examiner told a grim story:

> *K.R., 29*   *Suicide by drowning*
> *Boston*   *October 2, 1896*
> *Out of work and despondent for a long while. Body found floating in the Charles [River].*

> *F.S., 29*   *Suicide by arsenic*
> *Boston*   *January 1, 1896*
> *Much depressed for several weeks. Loss of employment. At 7:50 A.M. Jan. 1, she called her father and told him she had taken poison and wished to die.*

L.M., 38   *Hanging suicide*
E. Boston   *October 15, 1895*
Had been out of work for several weeks and was very despondent. Wife went to market at about 11 A.M. and upon returning at about 12 P.M. found him hanging from bedroom door.... Slipped noose about his neck and [fell] forward upon it.

R.N., 23   *Suicide by bullet wound of brain*
Boston   *June 22, 1896*
Out of work. Mentally depressed. About 3 P.M. June 21 shot himself in right temple.... Left a letter explaining that he killed himself to save others the trouble of caring for him.

Lasting until 1897, the depression was the decisive event of the decade. At its height, three million people were unemployed—fully 20 percent of the workforce. The human costs were enormous, even among the well-to-do. "They were for me years of simple Hell," shattering "my whole scheme of life," said Charles Francis Adams, Jr., the descendant of two American presidents.

Like the Great Depression of the 1930s that gave rise to the New Deal, the depression of the 1890s had profound and lasting effects. Bringing to a head many of the tensions that had been building in the society, it increased rural hostility toward the cities, brought about a bitter fight over the currency, and changed people's thinking about government, unemployment, and reform. There were outbreaks of warfare between capital and labor; farmers demanded a fairer share of economic and social benefits; the "new" immigrants came under fresh attack. The depression of the 1890s changed the course of American history, as did another event of that decade: the war with Spain in 1898.

Under the cruel impact of the depression, ideas changed in many areas, including in politics. A realignment of the American political system, which had been developing since the end of Reconstruction, finally reached its fruition in the 1890s, establishing new patterns that gave rise to the Progressive Era and lasted well into the twentieth century.

POLITICS OF STALEMATE

Politics was a major fascination of the late nineteenth century, its mass entertainment and favorite sport. Political campaigns were events that involved the whole community, even though in most states men were the only ones who could vote. During the weeks leading up to an election, there were rallies, parades, picnics, and torchlight processions. Americans turned out in enormous numbers to vote. In the six presidential elections from 1876 to 1896, an average of almost 79 percent of the electorate voted, a higher percentage than voted before or after.

A delegation of women's rights advocates addressed the judiciary committee of the House of Representatives to present their arguments in favor of woman suffrage. Reading the argument is Victoria Claflin Woodhull, one of the more radical activists in the women's movement.

White males made up the bulk of the electorate; until after the turn of the century, women could vote in national elections only in Wyoming, Utah, Idaho, and Colorado. The National Woman Suffrage Association early sued for the vote, but in 1875, the Supreme Court (*Minor* v. *Happersett*) upheld the power of the states to deny this right to women. On several occasions, Congress refused to pass a constitutional amendment for woman's suffrage, and between 1870 and 1910, nearly a dozen states defeated referenda to grant women the vote.

Black men were another group kept from the polls. In 1877, Georgia adopted the poll tax to make voters pay an annual tax for the right to vote. The technique, aimed at impoverished blacks, was quickly copied across the South.

In 1890, Mississippi required voters to be able to read and interpret the federal Constitution to the satisfaction of registration officials, all of them white. Such literacy tests, which the Supreme Court upheld in the case of *Williams* v. *Mississippi* (1898), excluded poor white voters as well as blacks. In 1898, Louisiana avoided the problem by adopting the famous "grandfather clause," which used a literacy test to disqualify black voters but permitted men who had failed the test to vote anyway if their fathers and grandfathers had voted before 1867—a time, of course, when no blacks could vote. The number of black voters decreased dramatically. In 1896, there were 130,334 registered black voters in Louisiana; in 1904, there were 1,342.

THE PARTY DEADLOCK

The 1870s and 1880s were still dominated by the Civil War generation, the unusual group of people who rose to power in the turbulent 1850s. Five of the six presidents elected between 1865 and 1900 had served in the war, as had many civic, business, and religious leaders. In 1890, well over one million veterans of the Union army were still alive, and Confederate veterans numbered in the hundreds of thousands.

Party loyalties—rooted in Civil War traditions, ethnic and religious differences, and perhaps class distinctions—were remarkably strong. Voters clung to their old parties, shifts were infrequent, and there were relatively few "independent" voters. Although linked to the defeated Confederacy, the Democrats revived quickly after the war. In 1874, they gained control of the House of Representatives, which they maintained for all but four of the succeeding twenty years. The Democrats rested on a less sectional base than the Republicans. Identification with civil rights and military rule cut Republican strength in the South, but the Democratic party's principles of states' rights, decentralization, and limited government won supporters everywhere.

While Democrats wanted to keep government local and small, the Republicans pursued policies for the nation as a whole, in which government was an instrument to promote moral progress and material wealth. The Republicans passed the Homestead Act (1862), granted subsidies to the transcontinental railroads, and pushed other measures to encourage economic growth. They enacted legislation and constitutional amendments to protect civil rights. They advocated a high protective tariff as a tool of economic policy, to keep out foreign products while "infant industries" grew.

In national elections, sixteen states, mostly in New England and the North, consistently voted Republican; fourteen states, mostly in the South, consistently voted Democratic. Elections, therefore, depended on a handful of "doubtful" states, which could swing elections either way. These states—New York, New Jersey, Connecticut, Ohio, Indiana, and Illinois—received special attention at election time. Politicians lavished money and time on them; presidential candidates usually came from them. From 1868 to 1912, eight of the nine Republican presidential candidates and six of the seven Democratic candidates came from the "doubtful" states, especially New York and Ohio.

The two parties were evenly matched, and elections were closely fought. In three of the five presidential elections from 1876 to 1892, the victor won by less than 1 percent of the vote; in 1876 and 1888, the losing candidates actually had more popular votes than the winners but lost in the electoral college. Only twice during these years did one party control both the presidency and the two houses of Congress—the Republicans in 1888 and the Democrats in 1892.

Historians once believed that political leaders accomplished little between 1877 and 1900, but those who saw few achievements were looking in the wrong location. With the impeachment of Andrew Johnson, the authority of the presidency dwindled in relation to congressional strength. For the first time in many years, attention shifted away from Washington itself. North and South, people who were weary of the centralization brought on by war and Reconstruction looked first to state and local governments to deal with the problems of an urban-industrial society.

EXPERIMENTS IN THE STATES

Across the country, state bureaus and commissions were established to regulate the new industrial society. Many of the early commissions were formed to oversee the railroads, at the time the nation's largest businesses. People who shipped goods over the railroads, especially farmers and merchants, wanted to end the policies of rate discrimination and other harmful practices. In 1869, Massachusetts established the first commission to regulate the railroads; by 1900, twenty-eight states had taken such action.

Most of the early commissions were advisory in nature. They collected statistics and published reports on rates and practices—serving, one commissioner said, "as a sort of lens" to focus public attention. Impatient with the results, legislatures in the Midwest and on the Pacific Coast established commissions with greater power to fix rates, outlaw rebates, and investigate rate discrimination. These commissions, experimental in nature, served as models for later policy at the federal level.

Illinois had one of the most thoroughgoing provisions. Responding to local merchants who were upset with existing railroad rate policies, the Illinois state constitution of 1870 declared railroads to be public highways and authorized the legislature to pass laws establishing maximum rates and preventing rate discrimination. In the important case of *Munn v. Illinois* (1877), the Supreme Court upheld the Illinois legislation, declaring that private property "affected with the public interest . . . must submit to being controlled by the public for the common good."

But the Court soon weakened that judgment. In the *Wabash* case of 1886 (*Wabash, St. Louis, & Pacific Railway Co. v. Illinois*), it narrowed the *Munn* ruling and held that states could not regulate commerce extending beyond their borders. Only Congress could. The *Wabash* decision turned people's attention back to the federal government. It spurred Congress to pass the Interstate Commerce Act

(1887), which created the Interstate Commerce Commission (ICC) to investi-gate and oversee railroad activities. The act outlawed rebates and pooling agree-ments, and the ICC became the prototype of the federal commissions that today regulate many parts of the economy.

REESTABLISHING PRESIDENTIAL POWER

Johnson's impeachment, the scandals of the Grant administrations, and the con-troversy surrounding the 1876 election weakened the presidency. During the last two decades of the nineteenth century, presidents fought to reassert their author-ity, and by 1900, under William McKinley, they had succeeded to a remarkable de-gree. The late 1890s, in fact, marked the birth of the modern powerful presidency.

Rutherford B. Hayes entered the White House with his title clouded by the disputed election of 1876. Opponents called him "His Fraudulency" and "Rutherfraud B. Hayes," but soon he began to reassert the authority of the presi-dency. Hayes worked for reform in the civil service, placed well-known reform-ers in high offices, and, ordering the last troops out of South Carolina and Louisiana, ended military Reconstruction. Committed to the gold standard—the only basis, Hayes thought, of a sound currency—in 1878 he vetoed the Bland-Allison Silver Purchase Bill, which called for the partial coinage of silver, but Congress passed it over his veto.

James A. Garfield, a Union army hero and longtime member of Congress, succeeded Hayes. Winning by a handful of votes in 1880, he took office energeti-cally, determined to unite the Republican party (which had been split by person-ality differences and disagreement over policy toward the tariff and the South), lower the tariff to cut taxes, and assert American economic and strategic inter-ests in Latin America. Ambitious and eloquent, Garfield had looked forward to the presidency, yet within a few weeks he said to friends, "My God! What is there in this place that a man should ever want to get into it?"

THE ELECTION OF 1880

CANDIDATE	PARTY	POPULAR VOTE	ELECTORAL VOTE
Garfield	Republican	4,446,158	214
Hancock	Democrat	4,444,260	155
Weaver	Greenback	305,997	0

Office seekers, hordes of them, evoked Garfield's anguish. Each one wanted a government job, and each one thought nothing of cornering the president on every occasion. Garfield planned to leave Washington on July 2, 1881, for a vacation in New England. Walking toward his train, he was shot in the back by Charles J. Guiteau, a deranged lawyer and disappointed office seeker. Suffering through the summer, Garfield died on September 19, 1881, and Vice President Chester A. Arthur—an ally of Senator Conkling—became president.

Arthur was a better president than many had expected. He approved the construction of the modern American navy. Arthur worked to lower the tariff, and in 1883, with his backing, Congress passed the Pendleton Act to reform the civil service. In part a reaction to Garfield's assassination, the act created a bipartisan Civil Service Commission to administer competitive examinations and appoint officeholders on the basis of merit. Initially, the act affected only about 14,000 of some 100,000 government offices, but it laid the basis for the later expansion of the civil service.

In the election of 1884, Grover Cleveland, the Democratic governor of New York, narrowly defeated Republican nominee, James G. Blaine, largely because of the continuing divisions in the Republican party. The first Democratic president since 1861, Cleveland was slow and ponderous, known for his honesty, stubbornness, and hard work. His term in the White House from 1885 to 1889 reflected the Democratic party's desire to curtail federal activities. Cleveland vetoed more than two-thirds of the bills presented to him, more than all his predecessors combined.

Forthright and sincere, he brought a new respectability to a Democratic party still tainted by its link with secession. He continued Arthur's naval construction program. Late in 1887, he devoted his annual message to an attack on the tariff, "the vicious, inequitable, and illogical source of unnecessary taxation," and committed himself and the Democratic party to lowering the tariff.

THE ELECTION OF 1884

CANDIDATE	PARTY	POPULAR VOTE	ELECTORAL VOTE
Cleveland	Democrat	4,874,621	219
Blaine	Republican	4,848,936	182
Butler	Greenback	175,096	0
St. John	Prohibition	147,482	0

THE ELECTION OF 1888

CANDIDATE	PARTY	POPULAR VOTE	ELECTORAL VOTE
Harrison	Republican	5,447,129	233
Cleveland	Democrat	5,537,857	168
	Minor Parties	396,441	0

The Republicans accused him of undermining American industries, and in 1888, they nominated for the presidency Benjamin Harrison, a defender of the tariff. Cleveland garnered ninety thousand more popular votes than Harrison but won the electoral votes of only two northern states and the South. Harrison won the rest of the North, most of the "doubtful" states, and the election.

REPUBLICANS IN POWER: THE BILLION-DOLLAR CONGRESS

Despite Harrison's narrow margin, the election of 1888 was the most sweeping victory for either party in almost twenty years; it gave the Republicans the presidency and both houses of Congress. The Republicans, it seemed, had broken the party stalemate and become the majority party in the country.

TARIFFS, TRUSTS, AND SILVER

As if a dam had burst, law after law poured out of the Republican Congress during 1890. The Republicans passed the McKinley Tariff Act, which raised tariff duties about 4 percent, higher than ever before; it also included a novel reciprocity provision that allowed the president to lower duties if other countries did the same. In addition, the act used duties to promote new industries, such as tinplate for packaging the new "canned" foods appearing on grocery store shelves. A Dependent Pensions Act granted pensions to Union army veterans and their widows and children. The pensions were modest—$6 to $12 a month—but the number of pensioners doubled by 1893, when nearly 1 million individuals received about $160 million in pensions.

With little debate, the Republicans and Democrats joined in passing the Sherman Antitrust Act, the first federal attempt to regulate big business. As the initial attempt to deal with the problem of trusts and industrial growth, the act shaped all later antitrust policy. It declared illegal "every contract, combination in the form of trust or otherwise, or conspiracy, in restraint of trade or commerce." Penalties for violation were stiff, including fines and imprisonment and the dissolution of guilty trusts. Experimental in nature, the act's terms were often vague and left precise interpretation to later experience and the courts.

One of the most important laws Congress passed, the Sherman Antitrust Act made the United States virtually the only industrial nation to regulate business combinations. It tried to harness big business without harming it. Many members of Congress did not expect the new law to have much effect on businesses, and for a decade, in fact, it did not. The Justice Department rarely filed suit under it, and in the *United States* v. *E. C. Knight Co.* decision (1895), the first judicial interpretation of the law, the Supreme Court severely crippled it. Though the E. C. Knight Co. controlled 98 percent of all sugar refining in the country, the Court drew a sharp distinction between commerce and manufacturing, holding that the company, as a manufacturer, was not subject to the law. But judicial interpretations changed after the turn of the century, and the Sherman Antitrust Act gained fresh power.

Another measure, the Sherman Silver Purchase Act, tried to end the troublesome problem presented by silver. As one of the two most commonly used precious metals, silver had once played a large role in currencies around the world, but by the mid-1800s, it had slipped into disuse. With the discovery of the great bonanza mines in Nevada, American silver production quadrupled between 1870 and 1890, glutting the world market, lowering the price of silver, and persuading many European nations to demonetize silver in favor of the scarcer metal, gold. The United States kept a limited form of silver coinage with congressional passage of the Bland-Allison Act in 1878.

Support for silver coinage was especially strong in the South and West, where people thought it might inflate the currency, raise wages and crop prices, and challenge the power of the gold-oriented Northeast. Eager to avert the free coinage of silver, which would require the coinage of all silver presented at the U.S. mints, President Harrison and other Republican leaders pressed for a compromise that took shape in the Sherman Silver Purchase Act of 1890.

The act directed the Treasury to purchase 4.5 million ounces of silver a month and to issue legal tender in the form of Treasury notes in payment for it. The act was a compromise; it satisfied both sides. Opponents of silver were pleased that it did not include free coinage. Silverites, on the other hand, were delighted that the monthly purchases would buy up most of the country's silver production. The Treasury notes, moreover, could be cashed for either gold or silver at the bank, a gesture toward a true bimetallic system based on silver and gold.

*According to the cartoon, a
bimetallic system based on
both silver and gold would
lead to a wobbly economy.*

As a final measure, Republicans in the House courageously passed a federal elections bill to protect the voting rights of blacks in the South. Although restrained in language and intent, it set off a storm of denunciation among the Democrats, who called it a "force bill" that would station army troops in the South. Because of the outcry, the bill failed in the Senate; it was the last major effort until the 1950s to enforce the Fifteenth Amendment to the Constitution.

THE 1890 ELECTIONS

The Republican Congress of 1890 was one of the most important Congresses in American history. It passed a record number of significant laws that helped shape later policy and asserted the authority of the federal government to a degree the country would not then accept. Sensing the public reaction, the Democrats labeled it the "Billion-Dollar Congress" for spending that much in appropriations and grants.

"This is a billion-dollar country," Speaker Reed replied, but the voters disagreed. The 1890 elections crushed the Republicans, who lost an extraordinary seventy-eight seats in the House. Political veterans went down to defeat, and new leaders vaulted into sudden prominence. Nebraska elected a Democratic governor for the first time in its history. The state of Iowa, once so staunchly Republican that a local leader had predicted that "Iowa will go Democratic when Hell goes Methodist," went Democratic in 1890.

THE RISE OF THE POPULIST MOVEMENT

The elections of 1890 drew attention to a fast-growing movement among farmers that soon came to be known far and wide as populism. During the summer of 1890, wagonloads of farm families in the South and West converged on campgrounds and picnic areas to socialize and discuss common problems. They came by the thousands, weary of drought, mortgages, and low crop prices. At the campgrounds, they picnicked, talked, and listened to recruiters from an organization called the National Farmers' Alliance and Industrial Union, which promised unified action to solve agricultural problems.

Farmers were joining the Alliance at the rate of 1,000 a week; the Kansas Alliance alone claimed 130,000 members in 1890. The summer of 1890 became "that wonderful picnicking, speech-making Alliance summer," a time of fellowship and spirit long remembered by farmers.

THE FARM PROBLEM

Farm discontent was a worldwide phenomenon between 1870 and 1900. With the new means of transportation and communication, farmers everywhere were caught up in a complex international market they neither controlled nor entirely understood.

American farmers complained bitterly about declining prices for their products, rising railroad rates for shipping them, and burdensome mortgages. Some of their grievances were valid. Farm profits were certainly low; agriculture in general tends to produce low profits because of the ease of entry into the industry. The prices of farm commodities fell between 1865 and 1890, but they did not fall as low as did other commodity prices. Despite the fact that farmers received less for their crops, their purchasing power actually increased.

Neither was the farmers' second grievance—rising railroad rates—entirely justified. Railroad rates actually fell during these years, benefiting shippers of all products. Farm mortgages, the farmers' third grievance, were common because many farmers mortgaged their property to expand their holdings or buy new farm machinery. While certainly burdensome, most mortgages did not bring hardship. They were often short, with a term of four years or less, after which farmers could renegotiate at new rates, and the new machinery the farmers bought enabled them to triple their output and increase their income.

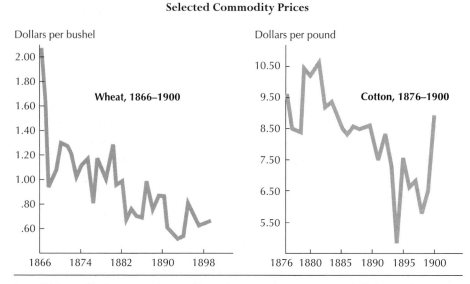

Selected Commodity Prices

Source: U.S. Bureau of the Census, *Historical Statistics of the United States, Colonial Times to 1970,* Bicentennial Edition, Washington, DC, 1975.

The terms of the farm problem varied from area to area and year to year. New England farmers suffered from overworked land; farmers in western Kansas and Nebraska went broke in a severe drought that followed a period of unusual rainfall. Many southern farmers were trapped in the crop lien system that kept them in debt.

Some farmers had valid grievances, though many understandably tended to exaggerate them. More important, many farmers were sure their condition had declined, and this perception—as bitterly real as any actual fact—sparked a growing anger. Equally upsetting, everyone in the 1870s and 1880s seemed excited about factories, not farms. Farmers had become "hayseeds," a word that first appeared in 1889, and they watched their offspring leave for city lights and new careers.

THE FAST-GROWING FARMERS' ALLIANCE

Originally a social organization for farmers, the Grange lost many of its members as it turned more and more toward politics in the late 1870s. In its place, a multitude of farm societies sprang into existence. By the end of the 1880s, they had formed into two major organizations: the National Farmers' Alliance, located on the Plains west of the Mississippi and known as the Northwestern Alliance, and the Farmers' Alliance and Industrial Union, based in the South and known as the Southern Alliance.

The Southern Alliance began in Texas in 1875 but did not assume major proportions until Dr. Charles W. Macune, an energetic and farsighted person, took over the leadership in 1886. Rapidly expanding, the Alliance absorbed other agricultural societies. Its agents spread across the South, where farmers were fed up with crop liens, depleted lands, and sharecropping. In 1890, the Southern Alliance claimed more than a million members. It welcomed to membership the farmers' "natural friends"—country doctors, schoolteachers, preachers, and mechanics. It excluded lawyers, bankers, cotton merchants, and warehouse operators.

An effective organization, the Southern Alliance published a newspaper, and in five years it sent lecturers to forty-three states and territories where they

This advertisement for Farmer's Delight tobacco from the May 21, 1889, issue of the Progressive Farmer *is an example of the type of products sold through Alliance cooperatives. The Alliance organizations formed cooperatives in an effort to guarantee farmers greater profits by negotiating for better prices for farm products sold in bulk. Farmers could also avoid creditors' fees by buying goods through the cooperatives. However, failure to secure the credit necessary to finance the cooperatives and lack of management experience in operating them doomed the cooperative venture to failure.*

spoke to two million farm families. It was "the most massive organizing drive by any citizen institution of nineteenth-century America."

Loosely affiliated with the Southern Alliance, a separate Colored Farmers' National Alliance and Cooperative Union enlisted black farmers in the South. Claiming more than 1 million members, it probably had closer to 250,000, but even that figure was sizable in an era when "uppity" blacks faced not merely defeat, but death. In 1891, black cotton pickers struck for higher wages near Memphis, Tennessee. Led by Ben Patterson, a 30-year-old picker, they walked off several plantations, but a posse hunted them down and, following violence on both sides, lynched fifteen strikers, including Patterson. The abortive strike ended the Colored Farmers' Alliance.

On the Plains, the Northwestern Alliance, a smaller organization, was formed in 1880. Its objectives were similar to those of the Southern Alliance, but it disagreed with the Southerners' emphasis on secrecy, centralized control, and separate organizations for blacks. In 1889, the Southern Alliance changed its name to the National Farmers' Alliance and Industrial Union and persuaded the three strongest state alliances on the Plains—those in North Dakota, South Dakota, and Kansas—to join. Thereafter, the renamed organization dominated the Alliance movement.

The Alliance mainly sponsored social and economic programs, but it turned early to politics. In the West, its leaders rejected both the Republicans and Democrats and organized their own party; in June 1890, Kansas Alliance members formed the first major People's party. The Southern Alliance resisted the idea of a new party for fear it might divide the white vote, thus undercutting white supremacy. The Southerners instead followed leaders such as Benjamin F. Tillman of South Carolina, who wanted to capture control of the dominant Democratic party.

Thomas E. Watson and Leonidas L. Polk, two politically minded Southerners, reflected the high quality of Alliance leadership. Georgia-born, Watson was a talented orator and organizer; he urged Georgia farmers, black and white, to unite against their oppressors. The president of the National Farmers' Alliance, Polk believed in scientific farming and cooperative action. Also from Kansas, Mary E. Lease—Mary Ellen to her friends, "Mary Yellin" to her opponents—helped head a movement remarkably open to female leadership. A captivating speaker, she made 160 speeches during the summer of 1890, calling on farmers to rise against Wall Street and the industrial East.

Meeting in Ocala, Florida, in 1890, the Alliance adopted the Ocala Demands, the platform the organization pushed as long as it existed. First and foremost, the demands called for the creation of a "sub-treasury system," which would allow farmers to store their crops in government warehouses. In return, they could claim Treasury notes for up to 80 percent of the local market value of the crop, a loan to be repaid when the crops were sold. Farmers could thus hold their crops for the best price. The Ocala Demands also urged the free coinage of silver, an end to protective tariffs and national banks, a federal income tax, the direct election of senators by voters instead of state legislatures, and tighter regulation of railroad companies.

The Alliance strategy worked well in the elections of 1890. In Kansas, the Alliance-related People's party, organized just a few months before, elected four congressmen and a U.S. senator. Across the South, the

Populist Mary E. Lease advised farmers to "raise less corn and more hell." She also said, "If one man has not enough to eat three times a day and another man has $25 million, that last man has something that belongs to the first."

Alliance won victories based on the "Alliance yardstick," a demand that Democratic party candidates pledge support for Alliance measures. Alliance leaders claimed thirty-eight Alliance supporters elected to Congress, with at least a dozen more pledged to Alliance principles.

THE PEOPLE'S PARTY

After the 1890 elections, Northern Alliance leaders urged the formation of a national third party to promote reform, although the Southerners remained reluctant, still hopeful of capturing control of the Democratic party. Plans for a new party were discussed at Alliance conventions in 1891 and the following year. In July 1892, a convention in Omaha, Nebraska, formed the new People's (or Populist) party. Southern Alliance leaders joined in, convinced now that there was no reason to cooperate with the Democrats who exploited Alliance popularity but failed to adopt its reforms.

In the South, some Populists had worked to unite black and white farmers. "They are in the ditch just like we are," a white Texas Populist said. Blacks and whites served on Populist election committees; they spoke from the same platforms, and they ran on the same tickets. Populist sheriffs called blacks for jury duty, an unheard-of practice in the close-of-the-century South.

Many of the delegates at the Omaha convention had planned to nominate Leonidas L. Polk for president, but he died suddenly in June, and the convention turned instead to James B. Weaver of Iowa, a former congressman, Union army general, and third-party candidate for president in 1880 (on the Greenback-Labor party ticket). As its platform, the People's party adopted many of the Ocala Demands.

Weaver waged an active campaign but with mixed results. He won 1,029,000 votes, the first third-party presidential candidate ever to attract more than a million. He carried Kansas, Idaho, Nevada, and Colorado, along with portions of North Dakota and Oregon, for a total of twenty-two electoral votes. The Populists elected governors in Kansas and North Dakota, ten congressmen, five senators, and about fifteen hundred members of state legislatures.

Despite the Populists' victories, the election brought disappointment. Southern Democrats used intimidation, fraud, and manipulation to hold down Populist votes. Weaver was held to less than a quarter of the vote in every southern state except Alabama. In most of the country, he lost heavily in urban areas, with the exception of some mining towns in the Far West. He also failed to win over most farmers. In no midwestern state except Kansas and North Dakota did he win as much as 5 percent of the vote.

In the election of 1892, many voters switched parties, but they tended to realign with the Democrats rather than the Populists, whose platform on silver and other issues had relatively little appeal among city dwellers or factory workers. Although the Populists did run candidates in the next three presidential elec-

THE ELECTION OF 1892

CANDIDATE	PARTY	POPULAR VOTE	ELECTORAL VOTE
Cleveland	Democrat	5,555,426	277
Harrison	Republican	5,182,690	145
Weaver	People's (Populist)	1,029,846	22
	Minor Parties	285,297	0

tions, they had reached their peak in 1892. That year, Farmers' Alliance membership dropped for the second year in a row, and the organization, which was once the breeding ground of the People's party, was broken.

While it lived, the Alliance was one of the most powerful protest movements in American history. Catalyzing the feelings of hundreds of thousands of farmers, it attempted to solve specific economic problems while at the same time advancing a larger vision of harmony and community, in which people who cared about each other were rewarded for what they produced.

THE CRISIS OF THE DEPRESSION

It was economic crisis, however, not harmony and community, that dominated the last decade of the century. Responding to the heady forces of industrialization, the American economy had expanded too rapidly in the 1870s and 1880s. Railroads had overbuilt, gambling on future growth. Companies had grown beyond their markets; farms and businesses had borrowed heavily for expansion.

THE PANIC OF 1893

The mood changed early in 1893. In mid-February, panic suddenly hit the New York stock market. In one day, investors dumped one million shares of a leading company, the Philadelphia and Reading Railroad, and it went bankrupt. Business investment dropped sharply in the railroad and construction industries, touching off the worst economic downturn to that point in the country's history.

Frightened, people hurriedly sold stocks and other assets to buy gold. The overwhelming demand depleted the gold reserve of the U.S. Treasury. Eroding almost daily, in March 1893, the Treasury's reserve slumped toward the $100 million mark, an amount that stood for the government's commitment to maintain the gold standard. On April 22, for the first time since the 1870s, the reserve fell below $100 million.

The news shattered business confidence—the stock market broke. On Wednesday, May 3, railroad and industrial stocks plummeted, and the next day, several major firms went bankrupt. When the market opened on Friday, crowds filled its galleries, anticipating a panic. Within minutes, leading stocks plunged to record lows, and there was pandemonium on the floor and in the streets outside.

Afterward, banks cut back on loans. Unable to get capital, businesses failed at an average rate of two dozen a day during the month of May. On July 26, the Erie Railroad, one of the leading names in railroading history, failed. August 1893 was the worst month. Across the country, factories and mines shut down. On August 15, the Northern Pacific Railroad went bankrupt; the Union Pacific and the Santa

The Panic of 1893 touched off a frenzy of activity on the floor of the New York Stock Exchange as investors attempted to unload their stock. Prices on the Exchange fell to a new low on June 27. By the end of 1893, the gold reserve had dipped to $80 million.

Fe soon followed. Some economists estimated unemployment at 2 million people, or nearly 15 percent of the labor force.

The year 1894 was even worse. The gross national product dropped again, and by midyear the number of unemployed stood at 3 million. One out of every five workers was unemployed. In the summer, a heat wave and drought struck the farm belt west of the Mississippi River, creating conditions unmatched until the devastating Dust Bowl of the 1930s. Corn withered in the fields. In the South, the price of cotton fell below five cents a pound, far under the break-even point.

People became restless and angry. As one newspaper said in 1896: "On every corner stands a man whose fortune in these dull times has made him an ugly critic of everything and everybody." There was even talk of revolution and bloodshed. Some of the unemployed wandered across the country—singly, in small groups, and in small armies. In February 1894, police ejected six hundred unemployed men who stormed the State House in Boston demanding relief. During 1894, there were some fourteen hundred strikes involving more than a half million workers.

THE PULLMAN STRIKE

Discontent mounted. The great Pullman strike—one of the largest strikes in the country's history—began when the employees of the Pullman Palace Car Company, living in a company town just outside Chicago (a town in which everything was owned and meted out by the company), struck to protest wage cuts, continuing high rents, and layoffs. On June 26, 1894, the American Railway Union (ARU) under Eugene V. Debs joined the strike by refusing to handle trains that carried Pullman sleeping cars.

Within hours, the strike paralyzed the western half of the nation. Grain and livestock could not reach markets. Factories shut down for lack of coal. The strike extended into twenty-seven states and territories, tying up the economy and renewing talk of class warfare. In Washington, President Grover Cleveland, who had been reelected to the presidency in 1892, decided to break the strike on the grounds that it obstructed delivery of the mail.

On July 2, he secured a court injunction against the ARU, and he ordered troops to Chicago. When they arrived on the morning of Independence Day, the city was peaceful. Before long, however, violence broke out, and mobs, composed mostly of nonstrikers, overturned freight cars, looted, and burned. Restoring order, the army occupied railroad yards in Illinois, California, and other places. By late July, the strike was over; Debs was jailed for violating the injunction.

The Pullman strike had far-reaching consequences for the development of the labor movement. Working people resented Cleveland's actions in the strike, particularly as it became apparent that he sided with the railroads. Upholding Debs's sentence in *In re Debs* (1895), the Supreme Court endorsed the use of the injunction in labor disputes, thus giving business and government an effective antilabor weapon that hindered union growth in the 1890s. The strike's failure catapulted Debs into prominence. During his time in jail, he turned to socialism, and after his release, he worked to build the Socialist party of America, which experienced some success after 1900.

THE MINERS OF THE MIDWEST

The plight of coal miners in the Midwest illustrated the personal and social impact of the depression. Even in the best of times, mining was a dirty and dangerous business. One miner in twelve died underground; one in three suffered injury. Mines routinely closed for as long as six months a year, and wages fell with the depression.

Midwestern mining was often a family occupation, passed down from father to son. It demanded delicate judgments about when to blast, where to follow a seam, and how to avoid rockfalls. Until 1890, English and Irish immigrants dominated the business. They migrated from mine to mine, and they nearly always lived in flimsy shacks owned by the company.

After 1890, immigration from southern and eastern Europe, hitherto a trickle, became a flood. Italians, Lithuanians, Poles, Slovaks, Magyars, Russians, Bohemians, and Croatians came to the mines to find work. In some mining towns, Italian and Polish miners soon made up almost half the population.

As the depression deepened, tensions grew between miners and their employers and between "old" miners and the "new." Many "new" miners spoke no English, and often they were "birds of passage," transients who had come to the United States to make money to take back home. Lacking the skills handed down by the "old" miners, they were often blamed for accidents, and they worked longer hours for less pay. At many a tavern after work, "old" miners grumbled about the different-looking newcomers and considered ways to get rid of them.

In April 1894, a wave of wage reductions sparked an explosion of labor unrest in the mines. The United Mine Workers, a struggling union formed just four years earlier, called for a strike of bituminous coal miners, and on April 21, virtually all midwestern and Pennsylvania miners—some 170,000 in all—quit working. The flow of crucial coal slackened; cities faced blackouts; factories closed.

The violence that soon broke out followed a significant pattern. Over the years, the English and Irish miners had built up a set of unspoken understandings with their employers. The "new" miners had not, and they were more prone to violent action to win a strike. The depression hit them especially hard, frustrating their plans to earn money and return home. In many areas, anger and frustration turned the 1894 strikes into outright war.

For nearly two weeks in June 1894, fighting rocked the Illinois, Ohio, and Indiana coalfields. Mobs ignited mine shafts, dynamited coal trains, and defied state militias. While miners of all backgrounds participated in the violence, it often divided "old" miners and "new." In Spring Valley, Illinois, exiled Italian anarchists took over the strike leadership and incited rioting despite the opposition of the "old" miners. Elsewhere, a mine fired by arsonists burned because the "new" miners prevented the "old" ones from extinguishing the blaze.

Shocked by the violence, public opinion shifted against the strikers. The strike ended in a matter of weeks, but its effects lingered. English and Irish miners moved out into other jobs or up into supervisory positions. Jokes and songs poked cruel fun at the "new" immigrants, and the Pennsylvania and Illinois legislatures adopted laws to keep them out of the mines. Thousands of "old" miners voted Populist in 1894—the Populist platform called for restrictions on immigration—in one of the Populists' few successes that year.

Occurring at the same time, the Pullman strike pulled attention away from the crisis in the coalfields, yet the miners' strike involved three times as many workers and provided a revealing glimpse of the tensions within American society. The miners of the Midwest were the first large group of skilled workers seriously affected by the flood of immigrants from southern and eastern Europe. Buffeted by depression, they reflected the social and economic discord that permeated every industry.

A BELEAGUERED PRESIDENT

Building on the Democratic party's sweeping triumph in the midterm elections of 1890, Grover Cleveland decisively defeated the Populist candidate, James B. Weaver, and the incumbent president, Benjamin Harrison, in 1892. The Democrats increased their strength in the cities and among working-class voters. For the first time since the 1850s, they controlled the White House and both branches of Congress.

The Democrats, it now seemed, had broken the party stalemate, but unfortunately for Cleveland, the Panic of 1893 struck almost as he took office. He was sure that he knew its cause. The Sherman Silver Purchase Act of 1890, he believed, had damaged business confidence, drained the Treasury's gold reserve, and caused the panic. The solution to the depression was equally simple: repeal the act.

In June 1893, Cleveland summoned Congress into special session. The silverites were on the defensive, although they pleaded for a compromise. Rejecting the pleas, Cleveland pushed the repeal bill through Congress, and on November 1, 1893, he signed it into law. Always sure of himself, he had staked everything on a single measure—a winning strategy if he succeeded, a devastating one if he did not.

Repeal of the Sherman Silver Purchase Act was probably a necessary action. It responded to the realities of international finance, reduced the flight of gold out of the country, and, over the long run, boosted business confidence. Unfortunately, it contracted the currency at a time when inflation might have helped. It did not bring economic revival. The stock market remained listless, businesses continued to close, unemployment spread, and farm prices dropped.

The repeal battle of 1893, discrediting the conservative Cleveland Democrats who had dominated the party since the 1860s, reshaped the politics of the country. It confined the Democratic party largely to the South, helped the Republicans become the majority party in 1894, and strengthened the position of the silver Democrats in their bid for the presidency in 1896. It also focused national attention on the silver issue and thus intensified the silver sentiment Cleveland had intended to dampen. In the end, repeal did not even solve the Treasury's gold problem. By January 1894, the reserve had fallen to $65 million. A year later, it fell to $44.5 million.

Still another blow to the morale of the Democrats came in 1894, when they tried to fulfill their long-standing promise to reduce the tariff. Despite all their efforts, the Wilson-Gorman Tariff Act, passed by Congress in August 1894, contained only modest reductions in duties. It reduced the tariff on coal, iron ore, wool, and sugar, ended the McKinley Tariff Act's popular reciprocity agreements with other countries, and moved some duties higher than ever before. It also imposed a small income tax, a provision the Supreme Court overturned in 1895 (*Pollock* v. *Farmer's Loan and Trust Co.*). Very few Democrats, including Cleveland, were pleased with the measure, and the president let it become law without his signature.

BREAKING THE PARTY DEADLOCK

The Democrats were buried in the elections of 1894. Suffering the greatest defeat in congressional history, they lost 113 House seats, while the Republicans gained 117. In twenty-four states, not a single Democrat was elected to Congress. The Democrats even lost some of the "solid South," and in the Midwest, a crucial battleground of the 1890s, the party was virtually destroyed.

Wooing labor and the unemployed, the Populists made striking inroads in parts of the South and West, yet their progress was far from enough. In a year in which thousands of voters switched parties, the People's party elected only four senators and four congressmen. Southern Democrats again used fraud and violence to keep the Populists' totals down. In the Midwest, the Populists won double the number of votes they had received in 1892, yet still attracted less than 7 percent of the vote. Across the country, the discontented tended to vote for the Republicans, not the Populists, a discouraging sign for the Populist party.

The elections of 1894 marked the end of the party deadlock that had existed since the 1870s. The Democrats lost, the Populists gained somewhat, and the Republicans became the majority party in the country. In the midst of the depression, the Republican doctrines of activism and national authority, which voters had repudiated in the elections of 1890, became more attractive. This was a development of great significance, because as Americans became more accepting of the use of government power to regulate the economy and safeguard individual welfare, the way lay open to the reforms of the Progressive Era, the New Deal, and beyond.

CHANGING ATTITUDES

The depression, brutal and far-reaching, did more than shift political alignments. Across the country, it undermined traditional views and caused people to rethink older ideas about government, the economy, and society. As men and women concluded that established ideas had failed to deal with the depression, they looked for new ones.

In prosperous times, Americans had thought of unemployment as the result of personal failure, affecting primarily the lazy and immoral. In the midst of depression, such views were harder to maintain, since everyone knew people who were both worthy and unemployed. Next door, a respected neighbor might be laid off; down the block, an entire factory might be shut down.

People debated issues they had long taken for granted. New and reinvigorated local institutions—discussion clubs, women's clubs, reform societies, university extension centers, church groups, farmers' societies—gave people a place to discuss alternatives to the existing order. Pressures for reform increased, and demand grew for government intervention to help the poor and unemployed.

"EVERYBODY WORKS BUT FATHER"

Women and children had been entering the labor force for years, and the depression accelerated the trend. As husbands and fathers lost their jobs, more and more women and children went to work. Even as late as 1901, well after the depression had ended, a study of working-class families showed that more than half the principal breadwinners were out of work. So many women and children worked that in 1905 there was a popular song titled "Everybody Works But Father."

During the 1890s, the number of working women rose from 4 million to 5.3 million. Trying to make ends meet, they took in boarders and found jobs as laundresses, cleaners, or domestics. Where possible, they worked in offices and factories. Far more black urban women than white worked to supplement their husbands' meager earnings. In New York City in 1900, nearly 60 percent of all black women worked, compared to 27 percent of the foreign-born and 24 percent of native-born white women. Men still dominated business offices, but during the 1890s, more and more employers noted the relative cheapness of female labor. Women telegraph and telephone operators nearly tripled in number during the decade. Women worked as clerks in the new five-and-tens and department stores, and as nurses; in 1900, a half million were teachers. They increasingly entered office work as stenographers and typists.

Tiny children peddling newspapers and women domestics serving the rich—their meager earnings were desperately needed.

The depression also caused an increasing number of children to work. During the 1890s, the number of children employed in southern textile mills jumped more than 160 percent, and boys and girls under 16 years of age made up nearly one-third of the labor force of the mills. Youngsters of 8 and 9 years worked twelve hours a day for pitiful wages. In most cases, however, children worked not in factories but in farming and city street trades such as peddling and shoe shining.

Concerned about child labor, middle-class women in 1896 formed the League for the Protection of the Family, which called for compulsory education to get children out of factories and into classrooms. The Mothers Congress of 1896 gave rise to the National Congress of Parents and Teachers, the spawning ground of thousands of local Parent-Teacher Associations. The National Council of Women and the General Federation of Women's Clubs took up similar issues. By the end of the 1890s, the Federation had 150,000 members who worked for various civic reforms in the fields of child welfare, education, and sanitation.

CHANGING THEMES IN LITERATURE

The depression also gave point to a growing movement in literature toward realism and naturalism. In the years after the Civil War, literature often reflected the mood of romanticism—sentimental and unrealistic.

The novels of Horatio Alger, which provided simple lessons about how to get ahead in business and life, continued to attract large numbers of readers. They told of poor youngsters who made their way to the top through hard work, thrift, honesty, and luck. Louisa May Alcott's *Little Women* (1868–1869) related the daily lives of four girls in a New England family; Anna Sewell's *Black Beauty* (1877) charmed readers with the story of an abused horse that found a happy home.

After the 1870s, however, a number of talented authors began to reject romanticism and escapism, turning instead to realism. Determined to portray life as it was, they studied local dialects, wrote regional stories, and emphasized the "true" relationships between people. In doing so, they reflected broader trends in the society, such as industrialism; evolutionary theory, which emphasized the effect of the environment on humans; and the new philosophy of pragmatism, which stressed the relativity of values.

Regionalist authors such as Joel Chandler Harris and George Washington Cable depicted life in the South. Hamlin Garland described the grimness of life on the Great Plains, and Sarah Orne Jewett wrote about everyday life in rural New England. Another regionalist, Bret Harte, achieved fame with stories that portrayed the local color of the California mining camps, particularly in his popular tale "The Outcasts of Poker Flat."

Harte was joined by a more talented writer, Mark Twain, who became the country's most outstanding realist author. Growing up along the Mississippi River in Hannibal County, Missouri, the young Samuel Langhorne Clemens observed life around him with a humorous and skeptical eye. Adopting a pen name from the river term "mark twain" (two fathoms), he wrote a number of important works that drew on his own experiences. *Life on the Mississippi* (1883) described his career as a steamboat pilot. *The Adventures of Tom Sawyer* (1876) and *The Adventures of Huckleberry Finn* (1884) gained international prominence. In these books, Twain used dialect and common speech instead of literary language, touching off a major change in American prose style.

William Dean Howells—after Twain, the country's most famous author—came more slowly to the realist approach. At first, he wrote about the happier sides of life, but then he grew worried about the impact of industrialization. *A Traveler from Altruria* (1894), a utopian novel, described an industrial society that consumed lives.

Other writers, the naturalists, became impatient even with realism. Pushing Darwinian theory to its limits, they wrote of a world in which a cruel and merciless environment determined human fate. Often focusing on economic hardship, naturalist writers studied the poor, the lower classes, and the criminal mind; they brought to their writing the social worker's passion for direct and honest experience.

A scene from Stephen Crane's novel Maggie: A Girl of the Streets. *Crane's tale painted a grim picture of life in the tenements of New York City's Bowery as it chronicled the story of slum child Maggie Johnson, victimized and trapped in her squalid, violent world.*

Stephen Crane spent a night in a seven-cent lodging house on the Bowery and in "An Experiment in Misery" captured the smells and sounds of the poor. Crane depicted the carnage of war in *The Red Badge of Courage* (1895) and the impact of poverty in *Maggie: A Girl of the Streets* (1893). His poetry suggested the unimportance of the individual in an uncaring world.

Frank Norris assailed the power of big business in two dramatic novels, *The Octopus* (1901) and *The Pit* (1903), both the story of individual futility in the face of the heartless corporations. Norris's *McTeague* (1899) studied the disintegration of character under economic pressure. Jack London, another naturalist author, traced the power of nature over civilized society in novels such as *The Sea Wolf* (1904) and *The Call of the Wild* (1903), his classic tale of a sled dog that preferred the difficult life of the wilderness to the world of human beings.

Theodore Dreiser, the foremost naturalist writer, grimly portrayed a dark world in which human beings were tossed about by forces beyond their understanding or control. In his great novel *Sister Carrie* (1901), he followed a young farm girl who took a job in a Chicago shoe factory. He described the exhausting nature of factory work: "Her hands began to ache at the wrists and then in the fingers, and towards the last she seemed one mass of dull, complaining muscle, fixed in an eternal position, and performing a single mechanical movement."

Like other naturalists, Dreiser focused on environment and character. He thought writers should tell the truth about human affairs, not fabricate romance, and *Sister Carrie,* he said, was "not intended as a piece of literary craftsmanship, but was a picture of conditions."

THE PRESIDENTIAL ELECTION OF 1896

The election of 1896 was known as the "battle of the standards" because it focused primarily on the gold and silver standards of money. As an election, it was exciting and decisive. New voting patterns replaced old, a new majority party confirmed its control of the country, and national policy shifted to suit new realities.

THE MYSTIQUE OF SILVER

Sentiment for free silver coinage grew swiftly after 1894, dominating the South and West, appearing even in the farming regions of New York and New England. Prosilver literature flooded the country.

People wanted quick solutions to the economic crisis. During 1896, unemployment shot up and farm income and prices fell to the lowest point in the decade. "I can remember back as far as 1858," an Iowa hardware dealer said in February 1896, "and I have never seen such hard times as these are." The silverites offered a solution, simple but compelling: the free and independent coinage of silver at the ratio of 16 ounces of silver to every ounce of gold. Free coinage meant that the U.S. mints would coin all the silver offered to them. Independent coinage meant that the country would coin silver regardless of the policies of other nations, nearly all of which were on the gold standard.

It is difficult now to understand the kind of faith the silverites placed in silver as a cure for the depression. But faith it was, and of a sort that some observers compared to religious fervor. Underlying it all was a belief in a quantity theory of money: the silverites believed the amount of money in circulation determined the level of activity in the economy. If money was short, that meant there was a limit on economic activity and ultimately a depression. If the government coined silver as well as gold, that meant more money in circulation, more business for everyone, and thus prosperity. Farm prices would rise; laborers would go back to work.

By 1896, silver was also a symbol. It had moral and patriotic dimensions—by going to a silver standard, the United States could assert its independence in the world—and it stood for a wide range of popular grievances. For many, it reflected rural values rather than urban ones, suggested a shift of power away from the Northeast, and spoke for the downtrodden instead of the well-to-do. Silver represented the common people.

Silver was more than just a political or economic issue. It was a social movement, one of the largest in American history, but its life span turned out to be
brief. As a mass phenomenon, it flourished between 1894 and 1896, then succumbed to electoral defeat, the return of prosperity, and the onset of fresh concerns. But in its time, the silver movement bespoke a national mood and won
millions of followers.

THE REPUBLICANS AND GOLD

Scenting victory over the discredited Democrats, numerous Republicans fought
for the party's presidential nomination, including a Republican favorite, William
McKinley of Ohio.

Able, calm, and affable, McKinley had served in the Union army during the
Civil War. In 1876, he won a seat in Congress, where he became the chief sponsor of the tariff act named for him. In the months before the 1896 national convention, Marcus A. Hanna, his campaign manager and trusted friend, built a powerful national organization that featured McKinley as "the advance agent of

The religious symbolism in
Bryan's "Cross of Gold" speech
is satirized in this cartoon,
but his stirring rhetoric
captivated his audience and
won him the Democratic
presidential nomination for
the election of 1896.

prosperity," an alluring slogan in a country beset with depression. When the convention met in June, McKinley had the nomination in hand, and he backed a platform that favored the gold standard against the free coinage of silver.

Republicans favoring silver proposed a prosilver platform, but the convention overwhelmingly defeated it. Twenty-three silverite Republicans, far fewer than prosilver forces had hoped, marched out of the convention hall. The remaining delegates waved handkerchiefs and flags and shouted "Good-bye" and "Put them out." Hanna stood on a chair screaming "Go! Go! Go!" William Jennings Bryan, who was there as a special correspondent for a Nebraska newspaper, climbed on a desk to get a better view.

THE DEMOCRATS AND SILVER

Silver, meanwhile, had captured large segments of the Democratic party in the South and West. Despite President Cleveland's opposition, more than twenty Democratic state platforms came out for free silver in 1894. Power in the party shifted to the South, where it remained for decades. The party's base narrowed; its outlook increasingly reflected southern views on silver, race, and other issues. In effect, the Democrats became a sectional—no longer a national—party.

The anti-Cleveland Democrats had their issue, but they lacked a leader. Out in Nebraska, Bryan saw the opportunity to take on that role. He was barely 36 years old and had relatively little political experience. But he had spent months wooing support, and he was a captivating public speaker—tall, slender, and handsome, with a resounding voice that, in an era without microphones, projected easily into every corner of an auditorium.

From the outset of the 1896 Democratic convention, the silver Democrats were in charge, and they put together a platform that stunned the Cleveland wing of the party. It demanded the free coinage of silver and attacked Cleveland's actions in the Pullman strike. On July 9, as delegates debated the platform, Bryan's moment came. Striding to the stage, he stood for an instant, a hand raised for silence, waiting for the applause to die down. He would not contend with the previous speakers, he began, for "this is not a contest between persons. The humblest citizen in all the land, when clad in the armor of a righteous cause, is stronger than all the hosts of error. I come to speak to you in defense of a cause as holy as the cause of liberty—the cause of humanity."

The delegates were captivated. Like a trained choir, they rose, cheered each point, and sat back to listen for more. Easterners, Bryan said, liked to praise businessmen but forgot that plain people—laborers, miners, and farmers—were businessmen, too. Shouts rang through the hall, and delegates pounded on chairs. Savoring each cheer, Bryan defended silver. Then came the famous closing:

"Having behind us the producing masses of this nation and the world . . . we will answer their demand for a gold standard by saying to them: 'You shall not press down upon the brow of labor this crown of thorns, you shall not crucify mankind upon a cross of gold.'"

Bryan moved his fingers down his temples, suggesting blood trickling from his wounds. He ended with his arms outstretched as on a cross. Letting the silence hang, he dropped his arms, stepped back, then started to his seat. Suddenly, there was pandemonium. Delegates shouted and cheered. When the tumult subsided, they adopted the anti-Cleveland platform, and the next day, Bryan won the presidential nomination.

CAMPAIGN AND ELECTION

The Democratic convention presented the Populists with a dilemma. The People's party had staked everything on the assumption that neither major party would endorse silver. Now it faced a painful choice: nominate an independent ticket and risk splitting the silverite forces, or nominate Bryan and give up its separate identity as a party.

The choice was unpleasant, and it shattered the People's party. Meeting late in July, the party's national convention nominated Bryan, but rather than accept the Democratic candidate for vice president, it named Tom Watson instead. The Populists' endorsement probably hurt Bryan as much as it helped. It won him relatively few votes, since many Populists would have voted for him anyway. It also identified him as a Populist, which he was not, allowing the Republicans to accuse him of heading a ragtag army of malcontents. The squabble over Watson seemed to prove that the Democratic-Populist alliance could never stay together long enough to govern.

In August 1896, Bryan set off on a campaign that became an American legend. He took his campaign directly to the voters, the first presidential candidate in history to do so in a systematic way. By his own count, Bryan traveled 18,009 miles, visited 27 states, and spoke 600 times to a total of some 3 million people. He built skillfully on a new "merchandising" style of campaign in which he worked to educate and persuade voters.

Bryan summoned voters to an older America: a land where farms were as important as factories, where the virtues of rural and religious life outweighed the doubtful lure of the city, where common people still ruled and opportunity existed for all. He drew on the Jeffersonian tradition of rural virtue, distrust of central authority, and abiding faith in the powers of human reason.

Urged to take the stump against Bryan, McKinley replied, "I might just as well put up a trapeze on my front lawn and compete with some professional ath-

The Election of 1896

CANDIDATE	PARTY	POPULAR VOTE	ELECTORAL VOTE
McKinley	Republican	7,102,246	271
Bryan	Democrat	6,492,559	176
	Minor Parties	315,398	0

lete as go out speaking against Bryan." The Republican candidate let voters come to him. Railroads brought them by the thousands into McKinley's hometown of Canton, Ohio, and he spoke to them from his front porch. Through use of the press, he reached fully as many people as Bryan's more strenuous effort. Appealing to labor, immigrants, well-to-do farmers, businessmen, and the middle class, McKinley defended economic nationalism and the advancing urban-industrial society.

On election day, voter turnout was extraordinarily high, a measure of the intense interest. By nightfall, the outcome was clear: McKinley won 50 percent of the vote to Bryan's 46 percent. He won the Northeast and Midwest and carried four border states. In the cities, McKinley crushed Bryan.

The election struck down the Populists, whose totals sagged nearly everywhere. Many Populist proposals were later adopted under different leadership. The graduated income tax, crop loans to farmers, the secret ballot, and direct election of U.S. senators all were early Populist ideas. But the People's party never could win over a majority of the voters, and failing that, it vanished after 1896.

THE MCKINLEY ADMINISTRATION

The election of 1896 cemented the voter realignment of 1894 and initiated a generation of Republican rule. For more than three decades after 1896, with only a brief Democratic resurgence under Woodrow Wilson, the Republicans remained the country's majority party.

McKinley took office in 1897 under favorable circumstances. To everyone's relief, the economy had begun to revive. The stock market rose, factories once again churned out goods, and farmers prospered. Farm prices climbed sharply during 1897 on bumper crops of wheat, cotton, and corn. Discoveries of gold in Australia and Alaska—together with the development of a new cyanide process for extracting gold from ore—enlarged the world's gold supply, decreased its price, and inflated the currency as the silverites had hoped. For the first time since 1890, the 1897 Treasury statements showed a comfortable gold reserve.

McKinley and the Republicans basked in the glow. They became the party of progress and prosperity, an image that helped them win victories until another depression hit in the 1930s. McKinley's popularity soared. An activist president, he set the policies of the administration. Conscious of the limits of power, he maintained close ties with Congress and worked hard to educate the public on national choices and priorities. McKinley struck new relations with the press and traveled far more than previous presidents. In some ways, he began the modern presidency.

Shortly after taking office, he summoned Congress into special session to revise the tariff. In July 1897, the Dingley Tariff passed the House and Senate. It raised average tariff duties to a record level, and as the final burst of nineteenth-century protectionism, it caused trouble for the Republican party. By the end of the 1890s, consumers, critics, and the Republicans themselves were wondering if the tariff had outlived its usefulness in the maturing American economy.

From the 1860s to the 1890s, the Republicans had built their party on a pledge to *promote* economic growth through the use of state and national power. By 1900, with the industrial system firmly in place, the focus had shifted. The need to *regulate,* to control the effects of industrialism, became a central public concern of the new century. McKinley prodded the Republicans to meet that shift, but he died before his plans matured.

McKinley toyed with the idea of lowering the tariff, but one obstacle always stood in the way: the government needed revenue, and tariff duties were one of the few taxes the public would support. The Spanish-American War of 1898 persuaded people to accept greater federal power and, with it, new forms of taxation. In 1899, McKinley spoke of lowering tariff barriers in a world that technology had made smaller. "God and man have linked the nations together," he said in his last speech at Buffalo, New York, in 1901. "Isolation is no longer possible or desirable."

In 1898 and 1899, the McKinley administration focused on the war with Spain, the peace treaty that followed, and the dawning realization that the war had thrust the United States into a position of world power. In March 1900, Congress passed the Gold Standard Act, which declared gold the standard of currency and ended the silver controversy that had dominated the 1890s.

The presidential campaign of 1900 was a replay of the McKinley-Bryan fight of 1896. McKinley's running mate was Theodore Roosevelt, hero of the Spanish-American War and former governor of New York, who was nominated for vice president to capitalize on his popularity and, his enemies hoped, to sidetrack his

THE ELECTION OF 1900

CANDIDATE	PARTY	POPULAR VOTE	ELECTORAL VOTE
McKinley	Republican	7,218,039	292
Bryan	Democrat	6,358,345	155
Woolley	Prohibition	209,004	0
Debs	Socialist	86,935	0

political career into oblivion. Bryan stressed the issues of imperialism and the trusts; McKinley stressed his record at home and abroad. The result in 1900 was a landslide.

On September 6, 1901, a few months after his second inauguration, McKinley stood in a receiving line at the Pan-American Exposition in Buffalo. Leon Czolgosz, a 28-year-old unemployed laborer and anarchist, moved through the line and, reaching the president, shot him. Surgeons probed the wound but could find nothing. A recent discovery called the X ray was on display at the exposition, but it was not used. On September 14, McKinley died, and Vice President Theodore Roosevelt became president. A new century had begun.

As the funeral train carried McKinley's body back to Ohio, Mark Hanna, McKinley's old friend and ally, sat slumped in his parlor car. "I told William McKinley it was a mistake to nominate that wild man at Philadelphia," he mourned. "I asked him if he realized what would happen if he should die. Now look, that damned cowboy is president of the United States!"

Hanna's world had changed, and so had the nation's—not so much because "that damned cowboy" was suddenly president, but because events of the 1890s had had powerful effects. In the course of that decade, political patterns shifted, the presidency acquired fresh power, and massive unrest prompted social change. The war with Spain brought a new empire and worldwide responsibilities. Economic hardship posed questions of the most difficult sort about industrialization, urbanization, and the quality of American life. Worried, people embraced new ideas and causes. Reform movements begun in the 1890s flowered in the Progressive Era after 1900.

Technology continued to alter the way Americans lived. In 1896, Henry Ford produced a two-cylinder, four-horsepower car, the first of the famous line that bore his name. In 1899, the first automobile salesroom opened in New York, and some innovative thinkers were already imagining a network of service stations to keep the new cars running. At Kitty Hawk, North Carolina, Wilbur and Orville Wright, two bicycle manufacturers, neared the birth of powered flight.

The realignments that reached their peak in the 1890s seem distant, yet they are not. Important decisions in those years shaped nearly everything that came after them. In character and influence, the 1890s were as much a part of the twentieth century as of the nineteenth and continue to have repercussions into the twenty-first century.

21

TOWARD EMPIRE

Many Americans regretted the start of the war with Spain that began in April 1898, but many others welcomed it. War was different then, shorter and more personal than the all-encompassing, lengthy, and mechanistic wars of the twentieth century. Many highly respected people believed that nations must fight every now and then to prove their power and test the national spirit.

Theodore Roosevelt, 39 years old in 1898, was one of them. Nations needed to fight in order to survive, he thought. For months, Roosevelt argued strenuously for war with Spain for three reasons: first, on grounds of freeing Cuba and expelling Spain from the hemisphere; second, because of "the benefit done to our people by giving them something to think of which isn't material gain"; and third, because the army and navy needed the practice.

In April 1898, Roosevelt was serving in the important post of assistant secretary of the navy. When war broke out, he quickly resigned to join the army, rejecting the advice of the secretary of the navy, who warned he would only "ride a horse and brush mosquitoes from his neck in the Florida sands." The secretary was wrong—dead wrong—and later had the grace to admit it. "Roosevelt was right," he said. "His going into the Army led straight to the Presidency."

Joining a friend, Roosevelt chose to enlist his own regiment, and after a few telephone calls to friends, and telegrams to the governors of Arizona, New Mexico, and Oklahoma asking for "good shots and good riders," he had more than enough men. The First United States Volunteer Cavalry, an intriguing mixture of Ivy League athletes and western frontiersmen, was born.

Known as the Rough Riders, it included men from the Harvard, Yale, and Princeton clubs of New York City; the Somerset Club of Boston; and New York's

Colonel Theodore Roosevelt poses in his custom-designed uniform. With surgeon Leonard Wood, Roosevelt organized the First U.S. Volunteer Cavalry—the Rough Riders—for service in the Spanish-American War.

exclusive Knickerbocker Club. Former college athletes—football players, tennis players, and track stars—enlisted. Woodbury Kane, a wealthy yachtsman, signed up and promptly volunteered for kitchen duty.

Other volunteers came from the West—natural soldiers, Roosevelt called them, "tall and sinewy, with resolute, weather-beaten faces, and eyes that looked a man straight in the face without flinching." Among the cowboys, hunters, and prospectors, there were Bucky O'Neill, a legendary Arizona sheriff and Indian fighter; a half dozen other sheriffs and Texas Rangers; a large number of Indians; a famous broncobuster; and an ex-marshal of Dodge City, Kansas.

Eager for war, the men trained hard, played harder, and rarely passed up a chance for an intellectual discussion—if Roosevelt's memoir of the war is to be believed. Once, he overheard Bucky O'Neill and a Princeton graduate "discussing Aryan word-roots together, and then sliding off into a review of the novels of Balzac, and a discussion as to how far Balzac could be said to be the founder of the modern realistic school of fiction." In such a camp, discipline was lax, and enlisted men got on easily with the officers.

The troops howled with joy when orders came to join the invasion army for Cuba. They set sail on June 14, 1898, and Lieutenant Colonel Roosevelt, who had performed a war dance for the troops the night before, caught their mood: "We knew not whither we were bound, nor what we were to do; but we believed that the nearing future held for us many chances of death and hardship, of honor and renown. If we failed, we would share the fate of all who fail; but we were sure that we would win, that we should score the first great triumph in a mighty world-movement."

AMERICA LOOKS OUTWARD

The overseas expansion of the 1890s differed in several important respects from earlier expansionist moves of the United States. From its beginning, the American republic had been expanding. After the first landings in Jamestown and Plymouth, settlers pushed westward: into the trans-Appalachian region, the Louisiana Territory, Florida, Texas, California, Arizona, and New Mexico. Most of these lands were contiguous with existing territories of the United States, and most were intended for settlement, usually agricultural.

The expansion of the 1890s was different. It sought to gain island possessions, the bulk of them already thickly populated. The new territories were intended less for settlement than for use as naval bases, trading outposts, or commercial centers on major trade routes. More often than not, they were viewed as colonies, not as states-in-the-making.

Historian Samuel F. Bemis described the overseas expansion of the 1890s as "the great aberration," a time when the country adopted expansionist policies that did not fit with prior experience. Other historians, pointing to expansionist tendencies in thought and foreign policy that surfaced during the last half of the nineteenth century, have found a developing pattern that led naturally to the overseas adventures of the 1890s. In the view of Walter LaFeber, "the United States did not set out on an expansionist path in the late 1890s in a sudden, spur-of-the-moment fashion. The overseas empire that Americans controlled in 1900 was not a break in their history, but a natural culmination."

CATCHING THE SPIRIT OF EMPIRE

Most people in most times in history tend to look inward, and Americans in the years following the Civil War were no exception. Among other things, they focused on Reconstruction, the movement westward, and simply making a living.

Throughout the nineteenth century, Americans enjoyed "free security" without fully appreciating it. Sheltered by two oceans and the British navy, they could enunciate bold policies such as the Monroe Doctrine, which instructed European nations to stay out of the affairs of the Western Hemisphere, while remaining virtually impregnable to foreign attack.

In the 1870s and after, however, Americans began to take an increasing interest in events abroad. There was a growing sense of internationalism, which stemmed in part from the telegraphs, telephones, and undersea cables that kept people better informed about political and economic developments in distant lands. Many Americans continued to be interested in expansion of the country's borders; relatively few were interested in imperialism. Expansion meant the kind of growth that had brought California and Oregon into the American system. Imperialism meant the imposition of control over other peoples through annexation, military conquest, or economic domination.

Several developments in these years combined to shift attention outward across the seas. The end of the frontier, announced officially in the census report of 1890, sparked fears about diminishing opportunities at home. Further growth, it seemed to some, must take place abroad. Factories and farms multiplied, producing more goods than the domestic market could consume. Both farmers and

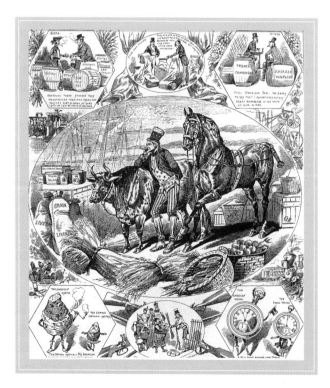

Titled "The World Is My Market, My Customers Are All Mankind," this 1877 cartoon reflects America's interest in foreign markets. With its emphasis on agricultural produce and light industry, the cartoon understates America's role in foreign commerce.

industrialists looked for new overseas markets, and the growing volume of exports—including more and more manufactured goods—changed the nature of American trade relations with the world.

Political leaders such as James G. Blaine began to argue for the vital importance of foreign markets to continued economic growth. Blaine, secretary of state under Garfield and again under Harrison, aggressively sought wider markets in Latin America, Asia, and Africa, using tariff reciprocity agreements and other measures. To some extent, he and others were also caught up in a worldwide scramble for empire. In the last third of the century, Great Britain, France, and Germany divided up Africa and looked covetously at Asia. The idea of imperialistic expansion was in the air, and the great powers measured their greatness by the colonies they acquired.

Intellectual currents that supported expansion drew on Charles Darwin's theories of evolution. Adherents pointed, for example, to *The Origin of Species*, which mentioned in its subtitle *The Preservation of Favoured Races in the Struggle for Life*. Applied to human and social development, biological concepts seemed to call for the triumph of the fit and the elimination of the unfit. "In this world," said Theodore Roosevelt, who thought of himself as one of the fit, "the nation that has trained itself to a career of unwarlike and isolated ease is bound, in the end, to go down before other nations which have not lost the manly and adventurous qualities."

John Fiske, a popular writer and lecturer, argued for Anglo-Saxon racial superiority, a result of the process of natural selection. The English and Americans, Fiske said, would occupy every land on the globe that was not already "civilized," bringing the advances of commerce and democratic institutions. Eminent scholars such as John W. Burgess, a professor of political science at Columbia University, argued that people of English origin were destined to impose their political institutions on the world.

The career of Josiah Strong, a Congregational minister and fervent expansionist, suggested the strength of the developing ideas. A champion of overseas missionary work, Strong traveled extensively through the West for the Home Missionary Society, and in 1885, drawing on his experiences, he published a book titled *Our Country: Its Possible Future and Its Present Crisis*. An immediate best-seller, the book called on foreign missions to civilize the world under the Anglo-Saxon races. Strong became a national celebrity.

Our Country argued for expanding American trade and dominion. Trade was important, it said, because the desire for material things was one of the hallmarks of civilized people. So was the Christian religion, and by exporting both trade and religion, Americans could civilize and Christianize "inferior" races around the world. Anglo-Saxons already owned one-third of the earth, Strong said, and in a famous passage he concluded that they would take more. In "the final competition of races," they would win and "move down upon Mexico, down upon Central and South America, out upon the islands of the sea, over upon Africa and beyond."

Taken together, these developments in social, political, and economic thought prepared Americans for a larger role in the world. The change was gradual, and there was never a day when people awoke with a sudden realization of their interests overseas. But change there was, and by the 1890s, Americans were ready to reach out into the world in a more determined and deliberate fashion than ever before. For almost the first time, they felt the need for a foreign "policy."

FOREIGN POLICY APPROACHES, 1867–1900

Rarely consistent, American foreign policy in the last half of the nineteenth century took different approaches to different areas of the world. In relation to Europe, seat of the dominant world powers, policymakers promoted trade and tried to avoid diplomatic entanglements. In North and South America, they based policy on the Monroe Doctrine, a recurrent dream of annexing Canada or Mexico, a hope for extensive trade, and Pan-American unity against the nations of the Old World. In the Pacific, they coveted Hawaii and other outposts on the sea-lanes to China.

Secretary of State William Henry Seward, who served from 1861 to 1869, aggressively pushed an expansive foreign policy. Seward developed a vision of an American empire stretching south into Latin America and west to the shores of Asia. His vision included Canada and Mexico; islands in the Caribbean as strategic bases to protect a canal across the isthmus; and Hawaii and other islands as stepping-stones to Asia, which Seward and many others considered a virtually bottomless outlet for farm and manufactured goods.

Seward tried unsuccessfully to negotiate a commercial treaty with Hawaii in 1867, and the same year he annexed the Midway Islands, a small atoll group twelve hundred miles northwest of Hawaii. In 1867, he concluded a treaty with Russia for the purchase of Alaska (which was promptly labeled "Seward's Folly") partly to sandwich western Canada between American territory and lead to its annexation. As the American empire spread, Seward thought, Mexico City would become its capital.

Secretary of State Hamilton Fish, an urbane New Yorker, followed Seward in 1869, serving under President Ulysses S. Grant. An avid expansionist, Grant wanted to extend American influence in the Caribbean and Pacific, though the more conservative Fish often restrained him. They moved first to repair relations with Great Britain. The first business was settlement of the *Alabama* claims—demands that Britain pay the United States for damages to Union ships caused by

Confederate vessels which, like the *Alabama,* had been built and outfitted in British shipyards. Negotiating patiently, Fish signed the Treaty of Washington in 1871, providing for arbitration of the *Alabama* issue and other nettlesome controversies. The treaty, one of the landmarks in the peaceful settlement of international disputes, marked a significant step in cementing Anglo-American relations.

Grant and Fish looked most eagerly to Latin America. In 1870, Grant became the first president to proclaim the nontransfer principle—"hereafter no territory on this continent shall be regarded as subject to transfer to a European power." Fish also promoted the independence of Cuba, restive under Spanish rule, while holding off the annexation desired by the more eager Grant.

James G. Blaine served briefly as secretary of state under President James Garfield and laid extensive plans to establish closer commercial relations with Latin America. Blaine's successor, Frederick T. Frelinghuysen, changed Blaine's approach but not his strategy. Like Blaine, Frelinghuysen wanted to find Caribbean markets for American goods; he negotiated separate reciprocity treaties with Mexico, Cuba and Puerto Rico, the British West Indies, Santo Domingo, and Colombia. Using these treaties, Frelinghuysen hoped not only to obtain markets for American goods but to bind these countries to American interests.

When Blaine returned to the State Department in 1889 under President Benjamin Harrison, he moved again to expand markets in Latin America. Drawing on earlier ideas, he envisaged a hemispheric system of peaceful intercourse, arbitration of disputes, and expanded trade. He also wanted to annex Hawaii.

Harrison and Blaine toyed with naval acquisitions in the Caribbean and elsewhere, but in general they focused on Pan-Americanism and tariff reciprocity. Blaine presided over the first Inter-American Conference in Washington on October 2, 1889, where delegates from nineteen American nations were present. They negotiated several agreements to promote trade and created the International Bureau of the American Republics, later renamed the Pan-American Union, for the exchange of general information, including political, scientific, and cultural knowledge. The conference, a major step in hemispheric relations, led to later meetings promoting trade and other agreements.

Grover Cleveland, Harrison's successor, also pursued an aggressive policy toward Latin America. In 1895, he brought the United States precariously close to war with Great Britain over a boundary dispute between Venezuela and British Guiana. Cleveland sympathized with Venezuela, and he and Secretary of State Richard Olney urged Britain to arbitrate the dispute. When Britain failed to act, Olney drafted a stiff diplomatic note affirming the Monroe Doctrine and denying European nations the right to meddle in Western Hemisphere affairs.

Four months passed before Lord Salisbury, the British foreign secretary, replied. Rejecting Olney's arguments, he sent two letters, the first bluntly repudiating the Monroe Doctrine as international law. The second letter, carefully reasoned and sometimes sarcastic, rejected Olney's arguments for the Venezuelan boundary. Enraged, Cleveland defended the Monroe Doctrine, and he asked Congress for authority to appoint a commission to decide the boundary and enforce its decision. "I am fully alive to the responsibility incurred and keenly realize all the consequences that may follow," he told Congress, plainly implying war.

Preoccupied with larger diplomatic problems in Africa and Europe, Britain changed its position. In November 1896, the two countries signed a treaty of arbitration, under which Great Britain and Venezuela divided the disputed territory. Though Cleveland's approach was clumsy—throughout the crisis, for example, he rarely consulted Venezuela—the Venezuelan incident demonstrated a growing determination to exert American power in the Western Hemisphere. Cleveland and Olney had persuaded Great Britain to recognize the United States' dominance, and they had increased American influence in Latin America. The Monroe Doctrine assumed new importance. In averting war, an era of Anglo-American friendship was begun.

THE LURE OF HAWAII AND SAMOA

The islands of Hawaii offered a tempting way station to Asian markets. In the early 1800s, they were already called the "Crossroads of the Pacific," and trading ships of many nations stopped there. In 1820, the first American missionaries arrived to convert the islanders to Christianity. Like missionaries elsewhere, they advertised Hawaii's economic and other benefits and attracted new settlers.

After the Civil War, the United States tightened its connections with the islands. The reciprocity treaty of 1875 allowed Hawaiian sugar to enter the United States free of duty and bound the Hawaiian monarchy to make no territorial or economic concessions to other powers. The treaty increased Hawaiian economic dependence on the United States; its political clauses effectively made Hawaii an American protectorate. In 1887, a new treaty reaffirmed these arrangements and granted the United States exclusive use of Pearl Harbor, a magnificent harbor that had early caught the eye of naval strategists.

Following the 1875 treaty, white Hawaiians became more and more influential in the islands' political life. The McKinley Tariff Act of 1890 ended the special status given Hawaiian sugar and at the same time awarded American producers a bounty of two cents a pound. Hawaiian sugar production dropped dramatically, unemployment rose, and property values fell. The following year, the weak King Kalakaua died, bringing to power a strong-willed nationalist, Queen Liliuokalani.

Resentful of white minority rule, she decreed a new constitution that gave greater power to native Hawaiians.

Unhappy, the American residents revolted in early 1893 and called on the United States for help. John L. Stevens, the American minister in Honolulu, sent 150 marines ashore from the cruiser *Boston,* and within three days, the bloodless revolution was over. Queen Liliuokalani surrendered "to the superior force of the United States," and the victorious rebels set up a provisional government. On February 14, 1893, Harrison's secretary of state, John W. Foster, and delegates of the new government signed a treaty annexing Hawaii to the United States.

But only two weeks remained in Harrison's term, and the Senate refused to ratify the agreement. Five days after taking office, Cleveland withdrew the treaty; he then sent a representative to investigate the cause of the rebellion. The investigation revealed that the Americans' role in it had been improper, and

The first step toward American annexation of Hawaii came in 1893 when Queen Liliuokalani was removed from the throne. Hawaii was annexed to the United States as a possession in 1898 and became a U.S. territory in 1900.

Cleveland decided to restore the queen to her throne. He made the demand, but the provisional government in Hawaii politely refused and instead established the Republic of Hawaii, which the embarrassed Cleveland, unable to do otherwise, recognized.

The debate over Hawaiian annexation, continuing through the 1890s, foreshadowed the later debate over the treaty to end the Spanish-American War. People in favor of annexation pointed to Hawaii's strategic location, argued that Japan or other powers might seize the islands if the United States did not, and suggested that Americans had a responsibility to civilize and Christianize the native Hawaiians. Opponents warned that annexation might lead to a colonial army and colonial problems, the inclusion of a "mongrel" population in the United States, and rule over an area not destined for statehood.

Annexation came swiftly in July 1898 in the midst of excitement over victories in the Spanish-American War. The year before, President William McKinley had sent a treaty of annexation to the Senate, but opposition quickly arose, and the treaty stalled.

In 1898, annexationists redoubled arguments about Hawaii's commercial and military importance. McKinley and congressional leaders switched strategies to seek a joint resolution, rather than a treaty, for annexation. A joint resolution required only a majority of both houses, while a treaty needed a two-thirds vote in the Senate. Bolstered by the new strategy, the annexation measure moved quickly through Congress, and McKinley signed it on July 7, 1898.

While annexation of Hawaii represented a step toward China, the Samoan Islands, three thousand miles to the south, offered a strategic location astride the sea-lanes of the South Pacific. Americans showed early interest in Samoa, and in 1872, a naval officer negotiated a treaty granting the United States the use of Pago Pago, a splendid harbor on one of its islands. The Senate rejected the treaty, but six years later approved a similar agreement providing for a naval station there. Great Britain and Germany also secured treaty rights in Samoa, and thereafter the three nations jockeyed for position.

The situation grew tense in 1889, when warships from all three countries gathered in a Samoan harbor. But a sudden typhoon damaged the fleets, and tensions eased. A month later, delegates from Britain, Germany, and the United States met in Berlin to negotiate the problem. Britain and Germany wanted to divide up the islands; Secretary of State Blaine held out for some degree of authority by the indigenous population, with American control over Pago Pago.

The agreement, an uneasy one, ended in 1899 when the United States and Germany divided Samoa and compensated Britain with lands elsewhere in the Pacific. Germany claimed the two larger islands in the chain; the United States kept the harbor at Pago Pago.

THE NEW NAVY

Large navies were vital in the scramble for colonies, and in the 1870s the United States had almost no naval power. One of the most powerful fleets in the world during the Civil War, the American navy had fallen into rapid decline. By 1880, there were fewer than two thousand vessels, only forty-eight of which could fire a gun. Ships rotted, and many officers left the service.

Conditions changed during the 1880s. A group of rising young officers, steeped in a new naval philosophy, argued for an expanded navy equipped with fast, aggressive fleets capable of fighting battles across the seas. Big-navy proponents pointed to the growing fleets of Great Britain, France, and Germany, arguing that the United States needed greater fleet strength to protect its economic and other interests in the Caribbean and Pacific.

In 1883, Congress authorized construction of four steel ships, marking the beginning of the new navy. Between 1885 and 1889, Congress budgeted funds for thirty additional ships. The initial building program focused on lightly armored fast cruisers for raiding enemy merchant ships and protecting American shores, but after 1890, the program shifted to the construction of a seagoing offensive battleship navy capable of challenging the strongest fleets of Europe.

Alfred Thayer Mahan and Benjamin F. Tracy were two of the main forces behind the new navy. Austere and scholarly, Mahan was the era's most influential naval strategist. After graduating from the Naval Academy in 1859, he devoted a lifetime to studying the influence of sea power in history; for more than two decades, he headed the Newport Naval War College, where officers imbibed the latest in strategic thinking. A clear, logical writer, Mahan summarized his beliefs in several major books, including *The Influence of Sea Power upon History, 1660–1783* (1890), and *The Interest of America in Sea Power* (1897).

Mahan's reasoning was simple and, to that generation, persuasive. Industrialism, he argued, produced vast surpluses of agricultural and manufactured goods, for which markets must be found. Markets involved distant ports; reaching them required a large merchant marine and a powerful navy to protect it. Navies, in turn, needed coaling stations and repair yards. Coaling stations meant colonies, and colonies became strategic bases, the foundation of a nation's wealth and power. The bases might serve as markets themselves, but they were more important as stepping-stones to other objectives, such as the markets of Latin America and Asia.

Mahan called attention to the worldwide race for power, a race, he warned, the United States could not afford to lose. To compete in the race, Mahan argued, the United States must expand. It needed strategic bases, a powerful oceangoing navy, a canal across the isthmus to link the East Coast with the Pacific, and Hawaii as a way station on the route to Asia.

Mahan influenced a generation of policymakers in the United States and Europe; one of them, Benjamin F. Tracy, became Harrison's secretary of the navy in 1889. Tracy organized the Bureau of Construction and Repair to design and build new ships, established the Naval Reserve in 1891, and ordered construction of the first American submarine in 1893. He also adopted the first heavy rapid-fire guns, smokeless powder, torpedoes, and heavy armor. Above all, Tracy joined with big-navy advocates in Congress to push for a far-ranging battleship fleet capable of attacking distant enemies. He wanted two fleets of battleships, eight ships in the Pacific and twelve in the Atlantic. He got four first-class battleships.

In 1889, when Tracy entered office, the United States ranked twelfth among world navies; in 1893, when he left, it ranked seventh and was climbing rapidly. "The sea," he predicted in 1891, "will be the future seat of empires. And we shall rule it as certainly as the sun doth rise." By the end of the decade, the navy had seventeen steel battleships, six armored cruisers, and many smaller craft. It ranked third in the world.

WAR WITH SPAIN

The war with Spain in 1898 built a mood of national confidence, altered older, more insular patterns of thought, and reshaped the way Americans saw themselves and the world. Its outcome pleased some people but troubled others, who raised questions about war itself, colonies, and subject peoples. The war left a lingering strain of isolationism and antiwar feeling that affected later policy. It also left an American empire, small by European standards, but quite new to the American experience by virtue of its overseas location. When the war ended, American possessions stretched into the Caribbean and deep into the Pacific. American influence went further still, and the United States was recognized as a "world power."

The Spanish-American War established the United States as a dominant force for the twentieth century. It brought America colonies and millions of colonial subjects; it brought the responsibilities of governing an empire and protecting it. For better or worse, it involved the country in other nations' arguments and affairs. The war strengthened the office of the presidency, swept the nation together in a tide of emotion, and confirmed the long-standing belief in the superiority of the New World over the Old. When it was over, Americans looked outward as never before, touched, they were sure, with a special destiny.

A WAR FOR PRINCIPLE

By the 1890s, Cuba and the nearby island of Puerto Rico comprised nearly all that remained of Spain's once vast empire in the New World. Several times,

Cuban insurgents had rebelled against Spanish rule, including a decade-long rebellion from 1868 to 1878 that failed to settle the conflict. The depression of
1893 damaged the Cuban economy, and the Wilson-Gorman Tariff of 1894 pros-
trated it. Duties on sugar, Cuba's lifeblood, were raised 40 percent. With the island's sugar market in ruins, discontent with Spanish rule heightened, and in late
February 1895, revolt again broke out.

Recognizing the importance of the nearby United States, Cuban insurgents
established a junta in New York City to raise money, buy weapons, and wage a
propaganda war to sway American public opinion. Conditions in Cuba were
grim. Spain in January 1896 sent a new commander, General Valeriano Weyler y
Nicolau. Relentless and brutal, Weyler gave the rebels ten days to lay down their
arms. He then put into effect a "reconcentration" policy designed to move the native population into camps and destroy the rebellion's popular base. Herded into
fortified areas, Cubans died by the thousands, victims of unsanitary conditions,
overcrowding, and disease.

There was a wave of sympathy for the insurgents, stimulated by the newspapers, but so-called yellow or sensationalist journalism did not cause the war. The
conflict stemmed from larger disputes in policies and perceptions between Spain
and the United States. Grover Cleveland, under whose administration the rebellion began, preferred Spanish rule to the kind of turmoil that might invite foreign

This illustration appeared in Harper's Weekly. *Titled "Starvation by Proclamation," it shows Cubans being
marched into one of General Weyler's "reconcentration" camps.*

intervention. Opposed to the annexation of Cuba, he issued a proclamation of neutrality and tried to restrain public opinion.

Taking office in March 1897, President McKinley also urged neutrality but leaned slightly toward the insurgents. He immediately sent a trusted aide on a fact-finding mission to Cuba; the aide reported in mid-1897 that Weyler's policy had wrapped Cuba "in the stillness of death and the silence of desolation." The report in hand, McKinley offered to mediate the struggle, but, concerned over the suffering, he protested against Spain's "uncivilized and inhuman" conduct. The United States, he made clear, did not contest Spain's right to fight the rebellion but insisted it be done within humane limits.

Late in 1897, a change in government in Madrid brought a temporary lull in the crisis. The new government recalled Weyler and agreed to offer the Cubans some form of autonomy. It also declared an amnesty for political prisoners and released Americans from Cuban jails. The new initiatives pleased McKinley, though he again warned Spain that it must find a humane end to the rebellion. Then, in January 1898, Spanish army officers led riots in Havana against the new autonomy policy, shaking the president's confidence in Madrid's control over conditions in Cuba.

McKinley ordered the battleship *Maine* to Havana to demonstrate strength and protect American citizens if necessary. On February 9, 1898, the *New York Journal,* a leader of the yellow press, published a letter stolen from Enrique Dupuy de Lôme, the Spanish ambassador in Washington. In the letter, which was private correspondence to a friend, de Lôme called McKinley "weak," "a would-be politician," and "a bidder for the admiration of the crowd." Many Americans were angered by the insult; McKinley himself was more worried about other sections of the letter that revealed Spanish insincerity in the negotiations. De Lôme immediately resigned and went home, but the damage was done.

A few days later, at 9:40 in the evening of February 15, an explosion tore through the hull of the *Maine,* riding at anchor in Havana harbor. The ship, a trim symbol of the new steel navy, sank quickly; 266 lives were lost. McKinley cautioned patience and promised an immediate investigation. Crowds gathered quietly on Capitol Hill and outside the White House, mourning the lost men. Soon there was a new slogan: "Remember the *Maine* and to Hell with Spain!"

The most recent study of the *Maine* incident blames the sinking on an accidental internal explosion, caused perhaps by spontaneous combustion in poorly ventilated coal bunkers. In 1898, Americans blamed it on Spain. Roosevelt, William Jennings Bryan, and others urged war, but McKinley delayed, hopeful that Spain might yet agree to an armistice and perhaps Cuban independence.

In early March 1898, wanting to be ready for war if it came, McKinley asked Congress for $50 million in emergency defense appropriations, a request

Headlines like these in
William Randolph Hearst's
New York Journal *left little
doubt among his readers that
Spain had sunk the* Maine.

Congress promptly approved. The unanimous vote stunned Spain; allowing the
president a latitude that was highly unusual for the era, it appropriated the money
"for the National defense and for each and every purpose connected therewith to
be expended at the discretion of the President." In late March, the report of the
investigating board blamed the sinking of the *Maine* on an external (and thus presumably Spanish) explosion. Pressures for war increased.

On March 27, McKinley cabled Spain his final terms. He asked Spain to declare an armistice, end the reconcentration policy, and—implicitly—move toward Cuban independence. When the Spanish answer came, it conceded some
things, but not, in McKinley's judgment, the important ones. Spain offered a suspension of hostilities (but not an armistice) and left the Spanish commander in
Cuba to set the length and terms of the suspension. It also revoked the reconcentration policy. But the Spanish response made no mention of a true armistice,
McKinley's offer to mediate, or Cuba's independence.

Reluctantly McKinley prepared his war message, and Congress heard it on
April 11, 1898. On April 19, Congress passed a joint resolution declaring Cuba
independent and authorizing the president to use the army and navy to expel the

Spanish from it. An amendment by Colorado senator Henry M. Teller pledged that the United States had no intention of annexing the island.

On April 21, Spain severed diplomatic relations. The following day, McKinley proclaimed a blockade of Cuba and called for 125,000 volunteers. On Monday, April 25, Congress passed a declaration of war. Late that afternoon, McKinley signed it.

Some historians have suggested that in leading the country toward war, McKinley was weak and indecisive, a victim of war hysteria in the Congress and the country; others have called him a wily manipulator for war and imperial gains. In truth, he was neither. Throughout the Spanish crisis, McKinley pursued a moderate middle course that sought to end the suffering in Cuba, promote Cuba's independence, and allow Spain time to adjust to the loss of the remnant of empire. He also wanted peace, as did Spain, but in the end, the conflicting national interests of the two countries brought them to war.

"A SPLENDID LITTLE WAR"

Ten weeks after the declaration of war, the fighting was over. For Americans, they were ten glorious, dizzying weeks, with victories to fill every headline and slogans to suit every taste. No war can be a happy occasion for those who fight it, but the Spanish-American War came closer than most. Declared in April, it ended in August. Relatively few Americans died, and the quick victory seemed to verify burgeoning American power. John Hay, soon to be McKinley's secretary of state, called it "a splendid little war."

At the outset, the United States was militarily unprepared. The regular army consisted of only 28,000 officers and men, most of them more experienced in quelling Indian uprisings than fighting large-scale battles. The Indian wars did produce effective small-scale forces, well trained and tightly disciplined, but the army was unquestionably too small for war against Spain.

When McKinley called for 125,000 volunteers, as many as 1 million young Americans responded. Ohio alone had 100,000 volunteers. Keeping the regular army units intact, War Department officials enlisted the volunteers in National Guard units that were then integrated into the national army. Men clamored to join. William Jennings Bryan, a pacifist by temperament, took command of a regiment of Nebraska volunteers; Roosevelt chafed to get to the front. The secretary of war feared "there is going to be more trouble to satisfy those who are not going than to find those who are willing to go."

In an army inundated with men, problems of equipment and supply quickly appeared. The regulars had the new .30-caliber Krag-Jorgensen rifles, but National Guard units carried Civil War Springfield rifles that used old black-powder cartridges. The cartridges gave off a puff of smoke when fired, neatly marking the troops' position. Spanish troops were better equipped; they had modern Mausers with smokeless powder, which they used to devastating effect. Food was also a problem, as was sickness. Tropical disease felled many soldiers. Scores took ill after landing in Cuba and the Philippines, and it was not uncommon for half a regiment to be unable to answer the bugle call.

Americans then believed that "a foreign war should be fought by the hometown military unit acting as an extension of their community." Soldiers identified with their hometowns, dressed in the local fashion, and thought of themselves as members of a town unit in a national army.

Not surprisingly, then, National Guard units mirrored the social patterns of their communities. Since everyone knew each other, there was an easygoing familiarity, tempered by the deference that went with hometown wealth, occupation, education, and length of residence. Enlisted men resented officers who grabbed too much authority, and they expected officers and men to call each other by their first names. "Officers and men of the Guard mingle on a plane of beautiful equality," said a visitor to one volunteer camp. "Privates invade the tents of their officers at will, and yell at them half the length of the street."

Each community thought of the hometown unit as its own unit, an extension of itself. In later wars, the government censored news and dominated press relations; there was little censorship in the war with Spain, and the freshest news arrived in the latest letter home. Small-town newspapers printed news of the men; towns sent food, clothing, and occasionally even local doctors to the front.

"SMOKED YANKEES"

When the invasion force sailed for Cuba, nearly one-fourth of it was African American. In 1898, the regular army included four regiments of African American soldiers, the Twenty-fourth and Twenty-fifth Infantry and the Ninth and Tenth Cavalry. Black regiments had served with distinction in campaigns against the Indians in the West. Most African American troops in fact were posted in the West; no eastern community would accept them. A troop of the Ninth Cavalry was stationed in Virginia in 1891, but whites protested and the troop was ordered back to the West.

When the war broke out, the War Department called for five black volunteer regiments. The army needed men, and military authorities were sure that black men had a natural immunity to the climate and diseases of the tropics. But most state governors refused to accept black volunteers. African American leaders protested the discrimination. The McKinley administration intervened, and in the end, the volunteer army included more than ten thousand black troops.

Orders quickly went out to the four black regular army regiments in the West to move to camps in the South to prepare for the invasion of Cuba. Crowds

Charge of the 24th and 25th Colored Infantry and Rescue of the Rough Riders at San Juan Hill, July 2, 1898, *colored lithograph by Kurz and Allison, 1899. The 24th and 25th Colored Infantry regiments served with exceptional gallantry in the Spanish-American War.*

Charles Young, an 1889 graduate of West Point, was the only African American officer in the army during the Spanish-American War except for a few chaplains.

and cheers followed the troop trains across the Plains, but as they crossed into Kentucky and Tennessee, the cheering stopped. Welcoming crowds were kept away from the trains, and the troops were hustled onward. Station restaurants refused to serve them; all waiting rooms were segregated. "It mattered not if we were soldiers of the United States, and going to fight for the honor of our country," Sergeant Frank W. Pullen of the Twenty-fourth Infantry wrote; "we were 'niggers' as they called us and treated us with contempt."

Many soldiers were not prepared to put up with the treatment. Those stationed near Chickamauga Park, Tennessee, shot "at some whites who insulted them" and forcibly desegregated the railroad cars on the line into Chattanooga. Troops training near Macon, Georgia, refused to ride in the segregated "trailers" attached to the trolleys, and fights broke out.

More than four thousand black troops training near Tampa and Lakeland, Florida, found segregated saloons, cafes, and drugstores. "Here the Negro is not allowed to purchase over the same counter in some stores as the white man purchases over," Chaplain George W. Prioleau charged. "Why sir, the Negro of this country is a freeman and yet a slave. Talk about fighting and freeing poor Cuba and of Spain's brutality; of Cuba's murdered thousands, and starving reconcentrados. Is America any better than Spain?"

When the invasion force sailed a few days later, segregation continued on some of the troopships. Blacks were assigned to the lowest decks, or whites and blacks were placed on different sides of the ship. But the confusion of war often ended the problem, if only temporarily. Blacks took command as white officers died, and Spanish troops soon came to fear the "smoked Yankees," as they called them. Black soldiers played a major role in the Cuban campaign and probably staved off defeat for the Rough Riders at San Juan Hill. In Cuba, they won twenty-six Certificates of Merit and five Congressional Medals of Honor.

THE COURSE OF THE WAR

Mahan's Naval War College had begun studying strategy for a war with Spain in 1895. By 1898, it had a detailed plan for operations in the Caribbean and Pacific. Naval strategy was simple: destroy the Spanish fleet, damage Spain's merchant marine, and harry the colonies or the coast of Spain. Planners were excited; two steam-powered armored fleets had yet to meet in battle anywhere in the world. The army's task was more difficult. It must defend the United States, invade Cuba and probably Puerto Rico, and undertake possible action in far-flung places such as the Philippines or Spain.

Even before war was declared, the secretary of war arranged joint planning between the army and navy. Military intelligence was plentiful, and planners knew the numbers and locations of the Spanish troops. Earlier they had rejected a proposal to send an officer in disguise to map Cuban harbors; such things, they said, were simply not done in peacetime. Still, the War Department's new Military Information Division, a sign of the increasing professionalization of the army, had detailed diagrams of Spanish fortifications in Havana and other points. On the afternoon of April 20, 1898, McKinley summoned the strategists to the White House; to the dismay of those who wanted a more aggressive policy, they decided on the limited strategy of blockading Cuba, sending arms to the insurgents, and annoying the Spanish with small thrusts by the army.

Victories soon changed the strategy. In case of war, long-standing naval plans had called for a holding action against the Spanish base in the Philippines. On May 1, 1898, with the war barely a week old, Commodore George Dewey, commander of the Asiatic Squadron located at Hong Kong, crushed the Spanish fleet in Manila Bay. Suddenly, Manila and the Philippines lay within American grasp. At home, Dewey portraits, songs, and poems blossomed everywhere, and his calm order to the flagship's captain—"You may fire when ready, Gridley"—hung on every tongue. Dewey had two modern cruisers, a gunboat, and a Civil War paddle steamer. He sank eight Spanish warships. Dewey had no troops to attack the Spanish army in Manila, but the War Department, stunned by the speed and size of the victory, quickly raised an expeditionary force. On August 13, 1898, the troops accepted the surrender of Manila, and with it, the Philippines.

McKinley and his aides were worried about Admiral Pascual Cervera's main Spanish fleet, thought to be headed across the Atlantic for an attack on Florida. On May 13, the navy found Cervera's ships near Martinique in the Caribbean but then lost them again. A few days later, Cervera slipped secretly into the harbor of Santiago de Cuba, a city on the island's southern coast. But a spy in the Havana telegraph office alerted the Americans, and on May 28, a superior American force under Admiral William T. Sampson bottled Cervera up.

In early June, a small force of Marines seized Guantánamo Bay, the great harbor on the south of the island. They established depots for the navy to refuel and pinned down Spanish troops in the area. On June 14, an invasion force of about seventeen thousand men set sail from Tampa. Seven days later, they landed at Daiquiri on Cuba's southeastern coast. All was confusion, but the Spanish offered no resistance. Helped by Cuban insurgents, the Americans immediately pushed west toward Santiago, which they hoped to surround and capture. At first, the advance through the lush tropical countryside was peaceful.

The first battle broke out at Las Guasimas, a crossroads on the Santiago road. After a sharp fight, the Spanish fell back. On July 1, the Rough Riders, troops from the four black regiments, and the other regulars reached the strong fortifications at El Caney and San Juan Hill. Black soldiers of the Twenty-fifth Infantry charged the El Caney blockhouses, surprising the Spanish defenders with Comanche yells. For the better part of a day, the defenders fought stubbornly and held back the army's elite corps. In the confusion of battle, Roosevelt rallied an assortment of infantry and cavalry to take Kettle Hill, adjacent to San Juan Hill.

They charged directly into the Spanish guns, Roosevelt at their head, mounted on a horse, a blue polka-dot handkerchief floating from the brim of his sombrero. "I waved my hat and we went up the hill with a rush," he recalled in his autobiography. Actually, it was not quite so easy. Losses were heavy; eighty-nine Rough Riders were killed or wounded in the attack. Dense foliage concealed the enemy; smokeless powder gave no clue to their position. At nightfall, the surviving Spanish defenders withdrew, and the Americans prepared for the counterattack.

American troops now occupied the ridges overlooking Santiago. They were weakened by sickness, a fact unknown to the Spanish, who decided the city was lost. The Spanish command in Havana ordered Cervera to run for the open sea, although he knew the attempt to escape was hopeless. On the morning of July 3, Cervera's squadron steamed down the bay and out through the harbor's narrow channel, but the waiting American fleet closed in, and in a few hours every Spanish vessel was destroyed. Two weeks later, Santiago surrendered.

Soon thereafter, army troops, meeting little resistance, occupied Puerto Rico. Cervera had commanded Spain's only battle fleet, and when it sank, Spain was helpless against attacks on the colonies or even its own shores. The war was over. Lasting 113 days, it took relatively few lives, most of them the result of accident, yellow fever, malaria, and typhoid in Cuba. Of the 5,500 Americans who died in the war, only 379 were killed in battle. The navy lost one man in the battle at Santiago Bay, and only one to heatstroke in the stunning victory in Manila Bay.

DEBATE OVER EMPIRE

Late in the afternoon of August 12, 1898, representatives of Spain and the United States met in McKinley's White House office to sign the preliminary instrument of peace. Secretary of State William R. Day beckoned a presidential aide over to a large globe, remarking, "Let's see what we get by this."

What the United States got was an expansion of its territory and an even larger expansion of its responsibilities. According to the preliminary agreement, Spain granted independence to Cuba, ceded Puerto Rico and the Pacific island of Guam to the United States, and allowed Americans to occupy Manila until the two countries reached final agreement on the Philippines. To McKinley, the Philippines were the problem. Puerto Rico was close to the mainland, and it appealed even to many of the opponents of expansion. Guam was small and unknown; it escaped attention. The Philippines, on the other hand, were huge, sprawling, and thousands of miles from America.

McKinley weighed a number of alternatives for the Philippines, but he liked none of them. He believed he could not give the islands back to Spain; public opinion would not allow it. He might turn them over to another nation, but then they would fall, as he later said, "a golden apple of discord, among the rival powers." Germany, Japan, Great Britain, and Russia had all expressed interest in ac-

A Puck *cartoon titled "School Begins" satirizes Uncle Sam's course in civilization, in which he tells his students that they will soon be glad for all they will learn.*

quiring them. Germany even sent a large fleet to Manila and laid plans to take the Philippines if the United States let them go.

Rejecting those alternatives, McKinley considered independence for the islands but was soon talked out of it. People who had been there, reflecting the era's racism, told him the Filipinos were not ready for independence. He thought of establishing an American protectorate but discarded the idea, convinced it would bring American responsibilities without full American control. Sifting the alternatives, McKinley decided there was only one practical policy: annex the Philippines, with an eye to future independence after a period of tutelage.

At first hesitant, American opinion was swinging to the same conclusion. Religious and missionary organizations appealed to McKinley to hold on to the Philippines in order to "Christianize" them. Some merchants and industrialists saw them as the key to the China market and the wealth of Asia. Many Americans simply regarded them as the legitimate fruits of war. In October 1898, representatives of the United States and Spain met in Paris to discuss a peace treaty. Spain agreed to recognize Cuba's independence, assume the Cuban debt, and cede Puerto Rico and Guam to the United States.

Acting on instructions from McKinley, the American representatives demanded the cession of the Philippines. In return, the United States offered a payment of $20 million. Spain resisted but had little choice, and on December 10, 1898, the American and Spanish representatives signed the Treaty of Paris.

Submitted to the Senate for ratification, the treaty set off a storm of debate throughout the country. Industrialist Andrew Carnegie, reformer Jane Addams, labor leader Samuel Gompers, Mark Twain, and a host of others argued forcefully against annexing the Philippines. Annexation of the Philippines, the anti-imperialists protested over and over again, violated the very principles of independence and self-determination on which the United States was founded.

Some labor leaders feared the importation of cheap labor from new Pacific colonies. Gompers warned about the "half-breeds and semi-barbaric people" who might undercut wages and the union movement. Other anti-imperialists argued against assimilation of different races. Such racial views were also common among those favoring expansion, and the anti-imperialists usually focused on different arguments. If the United States established a tyranny abroad, they were sure, there would soon be tyranny at home. "This nation," declared William Jennings Bryan, "cannot endure half republic and half colony—half free and half vassal."

Charles Francis Adams, Jr., warned that the possession of colonies meant big armies, government, and debts ("an income tax looms up in the largest possible proportions," he said). Bryan scoffed at the argument that colonies were good for trade, pointing out, "It is not necessary to own people to trade with them." Many others thought there was no way to reconcile the country's republican ideals with the practice of keeping people under heel abroad. To Booker T. Washington, the country had more important things to think about at home, including its treatment of Indians and blacks.

In November 1898, opponents of expansion formed the Anti-Imperialist League to fight against the peace treaty. Membership centered in New England; the cause was less popular in the West and South. It enlisted more Democrats than Republicans, though never a majority of either. The anti-imperialists were weakened by the fact that they lacked a coherent program. Some favored keeping naval bases in the conquered areas. Some wanted Hawaii and Puerto Rico but not the Philippines. Others wanted nothing at all to do with any colonies.

The treaty debate in the Senate lasted a month. Pressing hard for ratification, McKinley earlier toured the South to rally support and consulted closely with senators. Though opposed to taking the Philippines, Bryan supported ratification in order to end the war; his support influenced some Democratic votes. Still, on the final weekend before the vote, the treaty was two votes short. That Saturday night, news reached Washington that fighting had broken out between American troops and Filipino insurgents who demanded immediate independence. The news increased pressure to ratify the treaty, which the Senate did on February 6, 1899, with two votes to spare. An amendment promising independence as soon as the Filipinos established a stable government lost by one vote. The United States had a colonial empire.

GUERRILLA WARFARE IN THE PHILIPPINES

Historians rarely write of the Philippine-American War, but it was an important event in American history. The war with Spain was over a few months after it began, but war with the Filipinos lasted more than three years. Four times as many American soldiers fought in the Philippines as in Cuba. For the first time, Americans fought men of a different color in an Asian guerrilla war. The Philippine-American War of 1898–1902 took a heavy toll: 4,300 American lives and untold thousands of Filipino lives (estimates range from 50,000 to 200,000).

Emilio Aguinaldo, the Filipino leader, was 29 years old in 1898. An early organizer of the anti-Spanish resistance, he had gone into exile in Hong Kong, from where he welcomed the outbreak of the Spanish-American War. Certain the United States would grant independence, he worked for an American victory. Filipino insurgents helped guide Dewey into Manila Bay, and Dewey himself sent a ship to Hong Kong to bring back Aguinaldo to lead a native uprising against the Spanish. On June 12, 1898, the insurgents proclaimed their independence.

Cooperating with the Americans, they drove the Spanish out of many areas of the islands. In the liberated regions, Aguinaldo established local governments

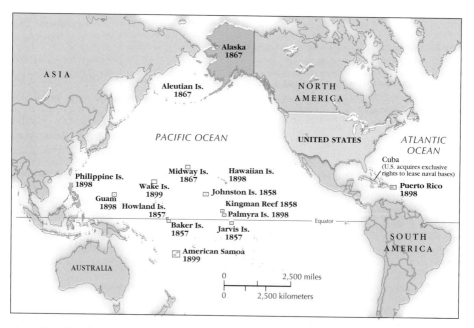

American Empire, 1900

With the Treaty of Paris, the United States gained an expanded colonial empire stretching from the Caribbean to the far Pacific. It embraced Puerto Rico, Alaska, Hawaii, part of Samoa, Guam, the Philippines, and a chain of Pacific islands. The dates on the map refer to the date of U.S. acquisition.

with appointed provincial governors. He waited impatiently for American recognition, but McKinley and others had concluded that the Filipinos were not ready. Soon, warfare broke out between the Filipinos and Americans over the question of Filipino independence.

By late 1899, the American army had defeated and dispersed the organized Filipino army, but claims of victory proved premature. Aguinaldo and his advisers shifted to guerrilla tactics, striking suddenly and then melting into the jungle or friendly native villages. There were terrible atrocities on both sides. The Americans found themselves using brutal, Weyler-like tactics. After any attack on an American patrol, the Americans burned all the houses in the nearest district. They tortured people and executed prisoners. They established protected "zones" and herded Filipinos into them. Seizing or destroying all food outside the zones, they starved many guerrillas into submission.

Emilio Aguinaldo (seated, in vest) and his advisors in the Philippines, 1896. Aguinaldo's forces helped the Americans drive Spain out of the Philippines, expecting that the United States would recognize Filipino independence. When the United States failed to do so, Aguinaldo led his forces in warfare against the Americans.

Bryan tried to turn the election of 1900 into a debate over imperialism, but the attempt failed. For one thing, he himself refused to give up the silver issue, which cost him some support among anti-imperialists in the Northeast who were for gold. McKinley, moreover, was able to take advantage of the surging economy, and he could defend expansion as an accomplished fact. Riding a wave of patriotism and prosperity, McKinley won the election handily—by an even larger margin than he had in 1896.

In 1900, McKinley sent a special Philippine Commission to the islands under William Howard Taft, a prominent Ohio judge. Directed to establish a civil government, the commission organized municipal administrations and, in stages, created a government for the Philippines. In March 1901, five American soldiers tricked their way into Aguinaldo's camp deep in the mountains and took him prisoner. Back in Manila, he signed a proclamation urging his people to end the fighting. Some guerrillas held out for another year, but to no avail. On July 4, 1901, authority was transferred from the army to Taft, who was named civilian governor of the islands, and his civilian commission. McKinley reaffirmed his purpose to grant the Filipinos self-government as soon as they were deemed ready for it.

Given broad powers, the Taft Commission introduced many changes. New schools provided education and vocational training for Filipinos of all social classes. The Americans built roads and bridges, reformed the judiciary, restructured the tax system, and introduced sanitation and vaccination programs. They established local governments built on Filipino traditions and hierarchies. Taft encouraged Filipino participation in government. During the following decades, other measures broadened Filipino rights. Independence finally came on July 4, 1946, nearly fifty years after Aguinaldo proclaimed it.

GOVERNING THE EMPIRE

Ruling the colonies raised new and perplexing questions. How could—and how should—the distant dependencies be governed? Did their inhabitants have the rights of American citizens? Some people contended that acquisition did not automatically incorporate the new possessions into the United States and endow them with constitutional privileges. Others argued that "the Constitution followed the flag," meaning that acquisition made the possessions part of the nation and thus entitled them to all constitutional guarantees. A third group suggested that only "fundamental" constitutional guarantees—citizenship, the right to vote, and the right to trial by jury—not "formal" privileges—the right to use American currency, the right to be taxed, and the right to run for the presidency—were applicable to the new empire.

In a series of cases between 1901 and 1904 (*De Lima* v. *Bidwell, Dooley* v. *U.S., and Downes* v. *Bidwell*), the Supreme Court asserted the principle that the Constitution did not automatically and immediately apply to the people of an annexed territory and did not confer upon them all the privileges of U.S. citizenship. Instead, Congress could specifically extend such constitutional provisions as it saw fit. "Ye-es," the secretary of war said of the Court's ambiguous rulings, "as near as I can make out the Constitution follows the flag—but doesn't quite catch up with it."

Four dependencies—Hawaii, Alaska, Guam, and Puerto Rico—were organized quickly. In 1900, Congress granted territorial status to Hawaii, gave American citizenship to all citizens of the Hawaiian republic, authorized an elective legislature, and provided for a governor appointed from Washington. A similar measure made Alaska a territory in 1912. Guam and American Samoa were simply placed under the control of naval officers.

Unlike the Filipinos, Puerto Ricans readily accepted the war's outcome, and McKinley early withdrew troops from the island. The Foraker Act of 1900 established civil government in Puerto Rico. It organized the island as a territory, made its residents citizens of Puerto Rico (U.S. citizenship was extended to them in 1917), and empowered the president to appoint a governor general and a council to serve as the upper house of the legislature. A lower house of delegates was to be elected.

Cuba proved a trickier matter. McKinley asserted the authority of the United States over conquered territory and promised to govern the island until the Cubans had established a firm and stable government of their own. "I want you to go down there to get the people ready for a republican form of government," he instructed General Leonard Wood, commander of the army in Cuba until 1902. "I leave the details of procedure to you. Give them a good school system, try to straighten out their ports, and put them on their feet as best you can. We want to do all we can for them and to get out of the island as soon as we safely can."

Wood moved quickly to implement the instructions. Early in 1900, he completed a census of the Cuban population, conducted municipal elections, and arranged the election of delegates to a constitutional convention. The convention adopted a constitution modeled on the U.S. Constitution and, at Wood's prodding, included provisions for future relations with the United States. Known as the Platt Amendment to the new Cuban Constitution, the provisions stipulated that Cuba should make no treaties with other powers that might impair its independence, acquire no debts it could not pay, and lease naval bases such as Guantánamo Bay to the United States. Most important, the amendment empowered the United States to intervene in Cuba to maintain orderly government.

Between 1898 and 1902, the American military government worked hard for the economic and political revival of the island, though it often demonstrated a paternalistic attitude toward the Cubans themselves. It repaired the damage of the civil war, built roads and schools, and established order in rural areas. A public health campaign headed by Dr. Walter Reed, an army surgeon, wiped out yellow fever. Most troops withdrew at the end of 1899, but a small American occupation force remained until May 1902. When it sailed for home, the Cubans at last had a form of independence, but they were still under the clear domination of their neighbor to the north.

THE OPEN DOOR

Poised in the Philippines, the United States had become an Asian power on the doorstep of China. Weakened by years of warfare, China in 1898 and 1899 was unable to resist foreign influence. Japan, England, France, Germany, and Russia eyed it covetously, dividing parts of the country into "spheres of influence." They forced China to grant "concessions" that allowed them exclusive rights to develop particular areas and threatened American hopes for extensive trade with the country.

McKinley first outlined a new China policy in September 1898 when he said that Americans sought more trade, "but we seek no advantages in the Orient which are not common to all. Asking only the open door for ourselves, we are ready to accord the open door to others." In September 1899, Secretary of State John Hay addressed identical diplomatic notes to England, Germany, and Russia, and later to France, Japan, and Italy, asking them to join the United States in establishing the "Open Door." The policy urged three agreements: nations possessing a sphere of influence would respect the rights and privileges of other nations in that sphere; the Chinese government would continue to collect tariff duties in all spheres; and nations would not discriminate against other nations in levying port dues and railroad rates within their respective spheres of influence.

Under the Open Door policy, the United States would retain many commercial advantages it might lose if China was partitioned into spheres of influence. McKinley and Hay also attempted to preserve for the Chinese some semblance of national authority. Great Britain most nearly accepted the principle of the Open Door. Russia declined to approve it, and the other powers, sending evasive replies, stated they would agree only if all the other nations did. Hay turned the situation to American advantage by boldly announcing in March 1900 that all the powers had accepted the Open Door policy.

The policy's first test came just three months later with the outbreak of the Boxer Rebellion in Peking (now Beijing). In June 1900, a secret, intensely nationalistic Chinese society called the Boxers tried to oust all foreigners from their

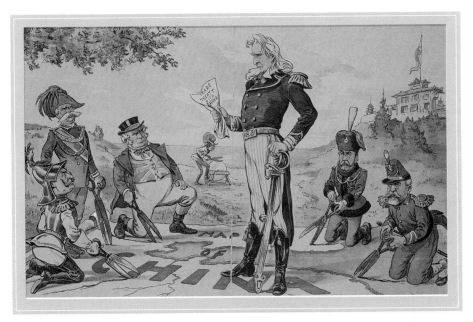

In this 1899 cartoon, "Putting His Foot Down" from Puck, *the nations of Europe are getting ready to cut up China to expand their spheres of influence, but Uncle Sam stands firm on American commitments to preserve China's sovereignty.*

country. Overrunning Peking, they drove foreigners into their legations and penned them up for nearly two months. In the end, the United States joined Britain, Germany, and other powers in sending troops to lift the siege.

Fearing that the rebellion gave some nations, especially Germany and Russia, an excuse to expand their spheres of influence, Hay took quick action to emphasize American policy. In July, he sent off another round of Open Door notes affirming U.S. commitment to equal commercial opportunity and respect for China's independence. While the first Open Door notes had implied recognition of China's continued independence, the second notes explicitly stated the need to preserve it. Together, the two notes comprised the Open Door policy, which became a central element in American policy in the Far East.

To some degree, the policy tried to help China, but it also led to further American meddling in the affairs of another country. Moreover, by committing itself to a policy that Americans were not prepared to defend militarily, the McKinley administration left the opportunity for later controversy with Japan and other expansion-minded powers in the Pacific.

The war with Spain over, Roosevelt and the Rough Riders sailed for home in mid-August 1898. They sauntered through the streets of New York, the heroes of the city. A few weeks later, Roosevelt bade them farewell. Close to tears, he told them, "I am proud of this regiment beyond measure." Soon, Roosevelt was governor of New York and on his way to the White House.

Other soldiers were also glad to be home, although they were sometimes resentful of the reception they found. "The war is over now," said Winslow Hobson, a black trooper from the Ninth Ohio, "and Roosevelt . . . and others (white of course) have all there is to be gotten out of it." Bravery in Cuba and the Philippines won some recognition for black soldiers, but the war itself set back the cause of civil rights. It spurred talk about "inferior" races, at home and abroad, and united whites in the North and South. "The Negro might as well know it now as later," a black editor said, "the closer the North and South get together by this war, the harder he will have to fight to maintain a footing." A fresh outburst of segregation and lynching occurred during the decade after the war.

McKinley and the Republican party soared to new heights of popularity. Firmly established, the Republican majority dominated politics until 1932. Scandals arose about the food and the conduct of the War Department, but there was none of the sharp sense of deception and betrayal that was to mark the years after World War I. In a little more than a century, the United States had grown from thirteen states stretched along a thin Atlantic coastline into a world power that reached from the Caribbean to the Pacific. As Seward and others had hoped, the nation now dominated its own hemisphere, dealt with European powers on more equal terms, and was a major power in Asia.

22

THE PROGRESSIVE ERA

n 1902, Samuel S. McClure, the shrewd owner of *McClure's Magazine,* sensed something astir in the country that his reporters were not covering. Like *Life, Munsey's,* the *Ladies' Home Journal,* and *Cosmopolitan, McClure's* was reaching more and more people—more than a quarter million readers a month. Americans were snapping up the new popular magazines filled with eye-catching illustrations and up-to-date fiction. Advances in photoengraving during the 1890s dramatically reduced the cost of illustrations; at the same time, income from advertisements rose sharply. By the turn of the century, some magazines earned as much as $60,000 an issue from advertising alone, and publishers could price them as low as 10 cents a copy.

McClure was always chasing new ideas and readers, and in 1902, certain that something was happening in the public mood, he told one of his editors, 36-year-old Lincoln Steffens, a former Wall Street reporter, to find out what it was. "Get out of here, travel, go—somewhere," he said to Steffens. "Buy a railroad ticket, get on a train, and there, where it lands you, there you will learn to edit a magazine."

Steffens traveled west. In St. Louis, he came across a young district attorney named Joseph W. Folk who had found a trail of corruption linking politics and some of the city's respected business leaders. Eager for help, Folk did not mind naming names to the visiting editor from New York. "It is good business men that are corrupting our bad politicians," he stressed again and again. Steffens's story, "Tweed Days in St. Louis," appeared in the October 1902 issue of *McClure's.*

The November *McClure's* carried the first installment of Ida Tarbell's scathing "History of the Standard Oil Company," and in January 1903, Steffens was back

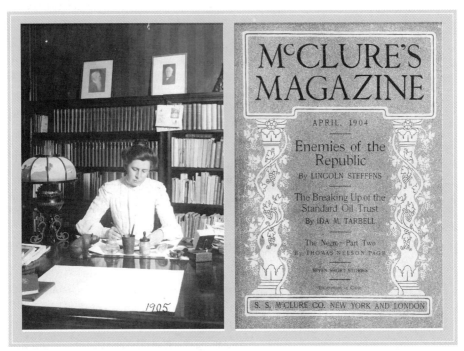

During the Progressive Era, McClure's Magazine *was at the forefront of the journalistic crusade for reform, which took the form of muckraking articles by such writers as Ida Tarbell (left). Her exposé of the Standard Oil Company ran side by side with Lincoln Steffens's article on the alliances between businesses and corrupt political machines in several cities.*

with "The Shame of Minneapolis," another tale of corrupt partnership between business and politics. McClure had what he wanted, and in the January issue he printed an editorial, "Concerning Three Articles in This Number of *McClure's,* and a Coincidence That May Set Us Thinking." Steffens on Minneapolis, Tarbell on Standard Oil, and an article on abuses in labor unions—all, McClure said, on different topics but actually on the same theme: corruption in American life. "Capitalists, workingmen, politicians, citizens—all breaking the law, or letting it be broken."

Readers were enthralled, and articles and books by other muckrakers—Theodore Roosevelt coined the unflattering term in 1906 to describe the practice of exposing the corruption of public and prominent figures—spread swiftly. *Collier's* had articles on questionable stock market practices, patent medicines, and the beef trust. Novelist Upton Sinclair tackled the meatpackers in *The Jungle* (1906). In 1904, Steffens collected his *McClure's* articles in *The Shame of the Cities,* with an introduction expressing confidence that reform was possible, "that our shamelessness is superficial, that beneath it lies a pride which, being real, may save us yet."

Muckraking flourished from 1903 to 1909, and while it did, good writers and bad investigated almost every corner of American life: government, labor unions, big business, Wall Street, health care, the food industry, child labor, women's rights, prostitution, ghetto living, and life insurance.

The muckrakers were a journalistic voice of a larger movement in American society. Called *progressivism,* it lasted from the mid-1890s through World War I. Like muckraking itself, progressivism reflected worry about the state of society, the effects of industrialization and urbanization, social disorder, political corruption, and a host of other issues. With concerns so large, progressivism often had a sense of crisis and urgency, although it was rooted in a spirit of hopefulness and confidence in human progress. For varying reasons, thousands of people became concerned about their society, and, separately and together, they set out to cure some of the ills they saw around them. The efforts of the so-called progressives changed the nation and gave the era its name.

As McClure had hoped, Steffens *had* found something astir in the country, something so important and pervasive that it altered the course of American history in the twentieth century. This chapter examines in detail the economic, social, and intellectual conditions that gave rise to progressivism. Chapter 23 examines progressivism itself, in the cities, states, and nation.

THE CHANGING FACE OF INDUSTRIALISM

As the new century turned, conditions in America were better than just a few years before. Farms and factories were once again prosperous; in 1901, for the first time in years, the economy reached full capacity. Farm prices rose almost 50 percent between 1900 and 1910. Unemployment dropped. Not everyone was progressing. Many of the problems that had angered people in the 1890s continued into the new century, and millions of Americans still suffered from poverty and disease. Racism sat even more heavily on African Americans in both South and North, and there was increasing hostility against immigrants from southern and eastern Europe and from Mexico and Asia. Yet economic conditions were better for many people, and as a result, prosperity became one of the keys to understanding the era and the nature of progressive reform.

The start of the new century was another key as well, for it influenced people to take a fresh look at themselves and their times. Excited about beginning the twentieth century, people believed technology and enterprise would shape a better life. Savoring the word *new,* they talked of the new poetry, new cinema, new history, new democracy, new woman, new art, new immigration, new morality, and new city. Presidents Theodore Roosevelt and Woodrow Wilson called their political programs the New Nationalism and the New Freedom.

The word *mass* also cropped up frequently. Victors in the recent war with Spain, Americans took pride in teeming cities, burgeoning corporations, and other marks of the mass society. They enjoyed the fruits of mass production, read mass circulation newspapers and magazines, and took mass transit from the growing spiral of suburbs into the central cities.

Behind mass production lay significant changes in the nation's industrial system. Businesses grew at a rapid rate. They were large in the three decades after the Civil War, but in the years between 1895 and 1915, industries became mammoth, employing thousands of workers and equipped with assembly lines to turn out huge quantities of the company's product. Inevitably, changes in management attitudes, business organization, and worker roles influenced the entire society. Inevitably, too, the growth of giant businesses gave rise to a widespread fear of "trusts" and a desire among many progressive reformers to break them up or regulate them.

THE INNOVATIVE MODEL T

In the movement toward large-scale business and mass production, the automobile industry was one of those that led the way. In 1895, there were only four cars on the nation's roads; in 1917, there were nearly five million, and the automobile had already helped work a small revolution in industrial methods and social mores.

In 1903, Henry Ford and a small group of associates formed the Ford Motor Company, the firm that transformed the business. Ford was 40 years old. He had tried farming and hated it. During the 1890s, he worked as an engineer, but spent his spare time designing internal combustion engines and automobiles. At first, like many others in the industry, he concentrated on building luxury and racing cars.

In 1903, Ford sold the first Ford car. The price was high, and in 1905, Ford raised prices still higher. Sales plummeted. In 1907, he lowered the price; sales and revenues rose. Ford learned an important lesson of the modern economy: a smaller unit profit on a large number of sales meant enormous revenues. Early in 1908, he introduced the Model T, a four-cylinder, 20-horsepower "Tin Lizzie," costing $850, and available only in black. Eleven thousand were sold the first year.

"I am going to democratize the automobile," Ford proclaimed. "When I'm through everybody will be able to afford one, and about everyone will have one." The key was mass production, and after many experiments, Ford copied the techniques of meatpackers who moved animal carcasses along overhead trolleys from station to station. Adapting the process to automobile assembly, Ford in 1913 set up moving assembly lines in his plant in Highland Park, Michigan, that

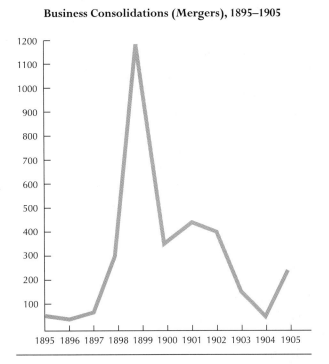

Business Consolidations (Mergers), 1895–1905

dramatically reduced the time and cost of producing cars. Emphasizing continuous movement, he strove for a nonstop flow from raw material to finished product. In 1914, he sold 248,000 Model T cars.

That year, Ford workers assembled a car in 93 minutes, one-tenth the time it had taken just eight months before. By 1925, the Ford plant turned out 9,109 Model T's, a new car for every ten seconds of the workday.

While Ford was putting more and more cars on the road, the 1916 Federal Aid Roads Act, a little noticed measure, set the framework for road building in the twentieth century. Removing control from county governments, it required every state desiring federal funds to establish a highway department to plan routes, oversee construction, and maintain roads. In states that had such departments, the federal government paid half the cost of building the roads. Providing for a planned highway system, the act produced a national network of two-lane all-weather intercity roads.

THE BURGEONING TRUSTS

As businesses like Ford's grew, capital and organization became increasingly important, and the result was the formation of a growing number of trusts. Between 1898 and 1903, a series of mergers and consolidations swept the economy. Many smaller firms disappeared, swallowed up in giant corporations. By 1904, large-scale combinations of one form or another controlled nearly two-fifths of the capital in manufacturing in the country.

The result was not monopoly but oligopoly—control of a commodity or service by a small number of large, powerful companies. Six great financial groups dominated the railroad industry; a handful of holding companies controlled utilities and steel. Rockefeller's Standard Oil owned about 85 percent of the oil business. After 1898, financiers and industrialists formed the Amalgamated Copper Company, Consolidated Tobacco, U.S. Rubber, and a host of others.

By 1909, just 1 percent of the industrial firms were producing nearly half of all manufactured goods. Giant businesses reached abroad for raw materials and new markets. United Fruit, an empire of plantations and steamships in the

As early as 1886, cartoonist Thomas Nast attacked trusts. Here the people's welfare is sinking as the Statue of Liberty is defaced.

THE RISING OF THE USURPERS.

And the sinking of the liberties of the people.

Caribbean, exploited opportunities created by victory in the war with Spain. U.S. Steel worked with overseas companies to fix the price of steel rails, an unattainable dream just a few years before.

Though the trend has been overstated, finance capitalists such as J. P. Morgan tended to replace the industrial capitalists of an earlier era. Able to finance the mergers and reorganizations, investment bankers played a greater and greater role in the economy. A multibillion-dollar financial house, J. P. Morgan and Company operated a network of control that ran from New York City to every industrial and financial center in the nation. Like other investment firms, it held directorships in many corporations, creating "interlocking directorates" that allowed it to control many businesses.

Massive business growth set off a decade-long debate over what government should do about the trusts. Some critics who believed that the giant companies were responsible for stifling individual opportunity and raising prices wanted to break them up into small competitive units. Others argued that large-scale business was a mark of the times, and that it produced more goods and better lives.

The debate over the trusts was one of the issues that shaped the Progressive Era, but it was never a simple contest between high-minded reformers and greedy business titans. Some progressives favored big business; others wanted it broken up. Business leaders themselves were divided in their viewpoints, and some welcomed reform-led assaults on giant competitors. As a rule, both progressives and business leaders drew on similar visions of the country: complex, expansive, hopeful, managerially minded, and oriented toward results and efficiency. They both believed in private property and the importance of economic progress. In fact, in working for reform, the progressives often drew on the managerial methods of a business world they sought to regulate.

MANAGING THE MACHINES

Mass production changed the direction of American industry. Size, system, organization, and marketing became increasingly important. Management focused on speed and product, not on workers. Assembly-line technology changed tasks and, to some extent, values. The goal was no longer to make a unique product that would be better than the one before. "The way to make automobiles," Ford said as early as 1903, "is to make one automobile like another automobile, to make them all alike, to make them come through the factory just alike."

In a development that rivaled assembly lines in importance, businesses established industrial research laboratories where scientists and engineers developed new products. General Electric founded the first one in 1900, housed in a barn. It soon attracted experts who designed improvements in light bulbs, invented the cathode-ray tube, worked on early radio, and even tinkered with atomic theory.

Du Pont opened its labs in 1911, Eastman Kodak in 1912, and Standard Oil in 1919. As the source of new ideas and technology, the labs altered life in the twentieth century.

Through all this, business became large-scale, mechanized, and managed. While many shops still employed fewer than a dozen workers, the proportion of such shops shrank. By 1920, close to one-half of all industrial workers toiled in factories employing more than 250 people. More than one-third worked in factories that were part of multiplant companies.

Industries that processed materials—iron and steel, paper, cement, and chemicals—were increasingly automated and operated continuously. Workers in those industries could not fall behind. Foremen still managed the laborers on the factory floor, but more and more, the rules came down from a central office where trained professional managers supervised production flow. Systematic record keeping, cost accounting, and inventory and production controls became widespread. In the automobile industry, output per worker-hour multiplied an extraordinary four times between 1909 and 1919.

Folkways of the workplace—workers passing job-related knowledge to each other, performing their tasks with little supervision, setting their own pace, and in effect running the shop—began to give way to "scientific" labor management. More than anyone else, Frederick Winslow Taylor, an inventive mechanical engineer, strove to extract maximum efficiency from each worker. "In the past," he believed, "the man has been first; in the future the system must be first."

In his book *The Principles of Scientific Management* (1911), Taylor proposed two major reforms. First, management must take responsibility for job-related knowledge and classify it into "rules, laws, and formulae." Second, management should control the workplace "through *enforced* standardization of methods, *enforced* adoption of the best implements and working conditions, and *enforced* cooperation."

Workers caught up in the changing industrial system experienced the benefits of efficiency and productivity; in some industries, they earned more. But they suffered important losses as well. Performing repetitive tasks, they seemed part of the machinery, moving to the pace and needs of their mechanical pacesetters. Bored, they might easily lose pride of workmanship, though many workers, it is clear, did not. Efficiency engineers experimented with tools and methods, a process many workers found unsettling. Yet the goal was to establish routine—to work out, as someone said of a garment worker, "one single precise motion each second, 3,600 in one hour, and all exactly the same." Praising that worker, the manager said, "She is a sure machine."

Fire nets were of no avail to the workers at the Triangle Shirtwaist Company who jumped from the upper stories to escape the flames. Speaking to a mass meeting after the fire, labor organizer Rose Schneiderman (right) inveighed against a system that treated human beings as expendable commodities.

Jobs became not only monotonous but dangerous. As machines and assembly lines sped up, boredom or miscalculation could bring disaster. In March 1911, a fire at the Triangle Shirtwaist Company in New York focused nationwide attention on unsafe working conditions. When the fire started, five hundred men and women, mostly Italians and Jews from eastern Europe, were just finishing their workday. Firefighters arrived within minutes, but they were already too late. Terrified seamstresses raced to the exits to try to escape the flames, but most exit doors were closed, locked by the company to prevent theft and shut out union organizers. Many died in the stampede down the narrow stairways or the single fire escape. Still others, trapped on the building's top stories far above the reach of the fire department's ladders, jumped to their deaths on the street below. One hundred forty-six people died.

A few days later, eighty thousand people marched silently in the rain in a funeral procession up Fifth Avenue. A quarter million people watched. At a mass meeting held to protest factory working conditions, Rose Schneiderman, a dynamic 29-year-old organizer for the Women's Trade Union League, told New York City's civic and religious leaders that they had not done enough, they had not cared. "Every week I must learn of the untimely death of one of my sister workers. Every year thousands of us are maimed. The life of men and women is so cheap and property is so sacred."

The outcry impelled New York's governor to appoint a State Factory Investigating Commission that recommended laws to shorten the workweek and improve safety in factories and stores.

SOCIETY'S MASSES

Spreading consumer goods through society, mass production not only improved people's lives but sometimes cost lives, too. Tending the machines took hard, painful labor, often under dangerous conditions. As businesses expanded, they required more and more people, and the labor force increased tremendously to keep up with the demand for workers in the factories, mines, and forest. Women, African Americans, Asian Americans, and Mexican Americans played larger and larger roles. Immigration soared. Between 1901 and 1910, nearly 8.8 million immigrants entered the United States; between 1911 and 1920, another 5.7 million came.

For many of these people, life was harsh, spent in crowded slums and long hours on the job. Fortunately, the massive unemployment of the 1890s was over, and in many skilled trades, such as cigar making, there was plenty of work to go around. Though the economic recovery helped nearly everyone, the less skilled continued to be the less fortunate. Migrant workers, lumberjacks, ore shovelers, and others struggled to find jobs that paid decently.

Under such circumstances, many people fought to make a living, and many, too, fought to improve their lot. Their efforts, along with the efforts of the reform-minded people who came to their aid, became another important hallmark of the Progressive Era.

BETTER TIMES ON THE FARM

While people continued to flee the farms—by 1920, fewer than one-third of all Americans lived on farms, and fewer than one-half lived in rural areas—farmers themselves prospered, the beneficiaries of greater production and expanding urban markets. Rural free delivery, begun in 1893, helped diminish the farmers' sense of isolation and changed farm life. The delivery of mail to the farm door opened that door to a wider world; it exposed farmers to urban thinking, national advertising, and political events. In 1911, more than one billion newspapers and magazines were delivered over RFD routes.

Parcel post (1913) permitted the sending of packages through the U.S. mail. Mail-order houses flourished; rural merchants suffered. Within a year, 300 million packages were being mailed annually. While telephones and electricity did not reach most rural areas for decades, better roads, mail-order catalogs, and other innovations knit farmers into the larger society. Early in the new century, Mary E. Lease—who in her Populist days had urged Kansas farmers to raise less corn and more Hell—moved to Brooklyn.

Farmers still had problems. Land prices rose with crop prices, and farm tenancy increased, especially in the South. Tenancy grew from one-quarter of all farms in 1880 to more than one-third in 1910. Many southern tenant farmers were African Americans, and they suffered from farm-bred diseases. In one of the reforms of the Progressive Era, in 1909, the Rockefeller Sanitary Commission, acting on recent scientific discoveries, began a sanitation campaign that eventually wiped out the hookworm disease.

In the arid West, irrigation transformed the land as the federal government and private landholders joined to import water from mountain watersheds. The dry lands bloomed, and so did a rural class structure that sharply separated owners from workers. Under the Newlands Act of 1902, the secretary of the interior formed the U.S. Reclamation Service, which gathered a staff of thousands of engineers and technicians, "the largest bureaucracy ever assembled in irrigation history."

Dams and canals channeled water into places such as California's Imperial Valley, and as the water streamed in, cotton, cantaloupes, oranges, tomatoes, lettuce, and a host of other crops streamed out to national markets. By 1920, Idaho, Montana, Utah, Wyoming, Colorado, and Oregon had extensive irrigation systems, all drawing on scarce water supplies; California, the foremost importer of water, had 4.2 million acres under irrigation, many of them picked by migrant workers from Mexico, China, and Japan.

WOMEN AT WORK

Women worked in larger and larger numbers. In 1900, more than five million worked—one-fifth of all adult women—and among those aged 14 to 24, the employment rate was almost one-third. Of those employed, single women outnumbered married women by seven to one, yet more than one-third of married women worked. Most women held service jobs. Only a small number held higher-paying jobs as professionals or managers.

In the 1890s, women made up more than one-quarter of medical school graduates. Using a variety of techniques, men gradually squeezed them out, and by the 1920s, only about 5 percent of the graduates were women. Few women taught in colleges and universities, and those who did were expected to resign if they married.

More women than men graduated from high school, and with professions like medicine and science largely closed to them, they often turned to the new "business schools" that offered training in stenography, typing, and bookkeeping. In 1920, more than one-quarter of all employed women held clerical jobs. Many others taught school.

Black women had always worked, and in far larger numbers than their white counterparts. The reason was usually economic; an African American man or

LAD FELL TO DEATH IN BIG COAL CHUTE

Dennis McKee Dead and Arthur Allbecker Had Leg Burned In the Lee Mines.

Falling into a chute at the Chauncey colliery of the George S. Lee Coal Company at Avondale, this afternoon, Dennis McKee, aged 6, of West Nanticoke, was smothered to death and Arthur Allbecker, aged 15, had both of his legs burned and injured. Dr. Biel, of Plymouth, was summoned and

He was removed to his home at Avondale.

Both boys were employed as breaker boys, and going too close to the chutes fell in. Fellow workmen rushed to their assistance and soon had them out of the chutes. When taken out McKee was found to be dead. His remains were removed to his home at West Nanticoke. All-

Breaker boys, who picked out pieces of slate from the coal as it rushed past, often became bent-backed after years of working fourteen hours a day in the coal mines. Accidents—and deaths—were common in the mines.

woman alone could rarely earn enough to support a family. Unlike many white women, black women tended to remain in the labor force after marriage or the start of a family. They also had less opportunity for job advancement, and in 1920, between one-third and one-half of all African American women who were working were restricted to personal and domestic service jobs.

Critics charged that women's employment endangered the home, threatened their reproductive functions, and even, as one man said, stripped them of "that modest demeanor that lends a charm to their kind." Adding to these fears, the birthrate continued to drop between 1900 and 1920, and the divorce rate soared, in part because working-class men took advantage of the newer moral freedom and deserted their families in growing numbers. By 1916, there was one divorce for every nine marriages as compared to one for twenty-one in 1880.

Many children worked. In 1900, about three million children—nearly 20 percent of those between the ages of 5 and 15—held full-time or almost full-time jobs. Twenty-five thousand boys under 16 worked in mining; twenty thousand children under 12, mainly girls, worked in southern cotton mills. Gradually, as public indignation grew, the use of child labor shrank.

Determined to do something about the situation, the Women's Trade Union League lobbied the federal Bureau of Labor to investigate the conditions under which women and children worked. Begun in 1907, the investigation took four years and produced nineteen volumes of data, some of it shocking, all of it factual. In 1911, spurred by the data, the Children's Bureau was formed within the

Margaret Higgins Sanger with her son Stuart in 1904. In 1921, Sanger organized the American Birth Control League, which later became the Planned Parenthood Federation of America.

U.S. Bureau of Labor, with Grace Abbott, a social worker, at its head. It immediately began its own investigations, showing among other things the need for greater protection of maternal and infant health. In 1921, Congress passed the Sheppard-Towner Maternity and Infancy Protection Act, which helped fund maternity and pediatric clinics. Providing a precedent for the Social Security Act of 1935, it demonstrated the increasing effectiveness of women reformers in the Progressive Era.

Numerous middle-class women became involved in the fight for reform, while many others, reflecting the ongoing changes in the family, took increasing pride in homemaking and motherhood. Mother's Day, the national holiday, was formally established in 1913. With families preferring smaller numbers of children, birth control became a more acceptable practice. Margaret Sanger, a nurse and outspoken social reformer, led a campaign to give physicians broad discretion in prescribing contraceptives.

THE NIAGARA MOVEMENT AND THE NAACP

At the turn of the century eight of every ten African Americans still lived in rural areas, mainly in the South. Most were poor sharecroppers. Jim Crow laws segregated many schools, railroad cars, hotels, and hospitals. Poll taxes and other devices disfranchised blacks and many poor whites. Violence was common; from 1900 to 1914, white mobs murdered more than a thousand black people.

Many African Americans labored on the cotton farms and in the railroad camps, sawmills, and mines of the South under conditions of peonage. Peons traded their lives and labor for food and shelter. Often illiterate, they were forced to sign contracts allowing the planter "to use such force as he or his agents may deem necessary to require me to remain on his farm and perform good and satisfactory services." Armed guards patrolled the camps and whipped those trying to escape.

Few blacks belonged to labor unions, and blacks almost always earned less than whites in the same job. Black songs such as "I've Got a White Man Workin' for Me" (1901) voiced more hope than reality. The illiteracy rate among African Americans dropped from 45 percent in 1900 to 30 percent in 1910, but nowhere

The wish to have "our children . . . enjoy fairer conditions than have fallen to our lot" was the impetus behind the NAACP, which sponsored this parade in New York City.

were they given equal school facilities, teachers' salaries, or educational materials. In 1910, scarcely eight thousand African American youths were attending high schools in all the states of the Southeast.

African American leaders grew increasingly impatient with this kind of treatment, and in 1905 a group of them, led by sociologist W. E. B. Du Bois, met near Niagara Falls, New York (they met on the Canadian side of the Falls, since no hotel on the American side would take them). There they pledged action in the matters of voting, equal access to economic opportunity, integration, and equality before the law. Rejecting Booker T. Washington's gradualist approach, the Niagara Movement claimed for African Americans "every single right that belongs to a freeborn American, political, civil and social; and until we get these rights we will never cease to protest."

The Niagara Movement focused on equal rights and the education of African American youth. Keeping alive a program of militant action, it spawned later civil rights movements. Du Bois was its inspiration. In *The Souls of Black Folk* (1903) and other works, he called eloquently for justice and equality.

Still, race riots broke out in Atlanta, Georgia, in 1906 and in Springfield, Illinois, in 1908, the latter the home of Abraham Lincoln. Unlike the riots of the 1960s, white mobs invaded black neighborhoods, burning, looting, and killing. They lynched two blacks—one 84 years old—in Springfield.

Outrage was voiced by William E. Walling, a wealthy southerner and settlement house worker; Mary Ovington, a white anthropology student; and Oswald Garrison Villard, grandson of the famous abolitionist William Lloyd Garrison. Along with other reformers, white and black (among them Jane Addams and John Dewey), they issued a call for the conference that organized the National Association for the Advancement of Colored People, which swiftly became the most important civil rights organization in the country. Created in 1910, within four years the NAACP grew to fifty branches and more than six thousand members. Walling headed it, and Du Bois, the only African American among the top officers, directed publicity and edited *The Crisis,* the voice of the organization.

Joined by the National Urban League, which was created in 1911, the NAACP pressured employers, labor unions, and the government on behalf of African Americans. It had some victories. In 1918, in the midst of World War I, the NAACP and the National Urban League persuaded the federal government to form a special Bureau of Negro Economics within the Labor Department to look after the interests of African American wage earners.

Despite these gains, African Americans continued to experience disfranchisement, poor job opportunities, and segregation. As Booker T. Washington said in 1913, "I have never seen the colored people so discouraged and so bitter as they are at the present time."

"I Hear the Whistle":
Immigrants in the Labor Force

While women and African Americans worked in growing numbers, much of the huge increase in the labor force in these years came from outside the country, particularly from Europe and Mexico. Between 1901 and 1920, the extraordinarily high total of 14.5 million immigrants entered the country, more than in any previous twenty-year period. Continuing the trend begun in the 1880s, many came from southern and eastern Europe. Still called the "new" immigrants, they met hostility from "older" immigrants of northern European stock who questioned their values, religion (often Catholic or Jewish), traditions, and appearance.

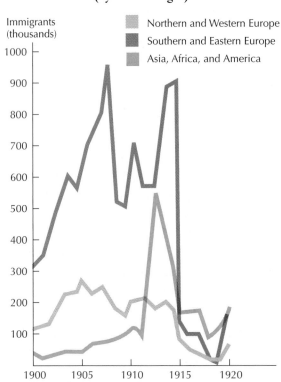

**Immigration to the United States, 1900–1920
(by area of origin)**

Immigrants (thousands)

- Northern and Western Europe
- Southern and Eastern Europe
- Asia, Africa, and America

Note: For purposes of classification, "Northern and Western Europe" includes Great Britain, Ireland, Scandinavia, the Netherlands, Belgium, Luxembourg, Switzerland, France, and Germany. "Southern and Eastern Europe" includes Poland, Austria-Hungary, Russia and the Baltic States, Romania, Bulgaria, European Turkey, Italy, Spain, Portugal, and Greece. "Asia, Africa, and America" includes Asian Turkey, China, Japan, India, Canada, the Caribbean, Latin America, and all of Africa.

Source: U.S. Bureau of the Census, *Historical Statistics of the United States, Colonial Times to 1970,* Bicentennial Edition, Washington, DC, 1975.

Immigrant patterns often departed from traditional stereotypes. Immigrants, for example, moved both to and from their homelands. Fifty percent or more of the members of some groups returned home, although the proportion varied. Jews and Czechs often brought their families to resettle in America; Serbs and Poles tended to come singly, intent on earning enough money to make a fresh start at home. Many Italian men virtually commuted, "birds of passage" who returned home every slack season.

Older residents lumped the newcomers together, ignoring geographic, religious, and other differences. Preserving important regional distinctions, Italians tended to settle as Calabreses, Venetians, Abruzzis, and Sicilians. Old-stock Americans viewed them all simply as Italians. Henry Ford and other employers tried to erase the differences through English classes and deliberate "Americanization" programs. The Ford Motor Company ran a school where immigrant employees were first taught to say, "I am a good American." At the graduation ceremony, the pupils acted out a gigantic pantomime in which, clad in their old-country dress, they filed into a large "melting pot." When they emerged, they were wearing identical American-made clothes, and each was waving a little American flag.

In similar fashion, the International Harvester Corporation taught Polish laborers to speak English, but it had other lessons in view as well. According to Lesson One, drilled into the Polish "pupils":

> *I hear the whistle. I must hurry.*
> *I hear the five minute whistle.*
> *It is time to go into the shop.*
> *I take my check from the gate board and hang it on the department board.*
> *I change my clothes and get ready to work.*
> *The starting whistle blows.*
> *I eat my lunch.*
> *It is forbidden to eat until then.*
> *The whistle blows at five minutes of starting time.*
> *I get ready to go to work.*
> *I work until the whistle blows to quit.*
> *I leave my place nice and clean.*
> *I put all my clothes in the locker.*
> *I must go home.*

Labor groups soon learned to counter these techniques. The Women's Trade Union League (WTUL) urged workers to ignore business-sponsored English lessons because they did not "tell the girl worker the things she really wants to know. They do not suggest that $5 a week is not a living wage. They tell her to be respectful to her employer." Designing its own educational program, the WTUL in 1912 published "New World Lessons for Old World Peoples," which provided quite a different kind of English lesson:

> *A Union girl takes me into the Union.*
> *The Union girls are glad to see me.*
> *They call me sister.*
> *I will work hard for our Union.*
> *I will come to all the Union meetings.*

In another significant development at the beginning of the twentieth century, Mexicans for the first time immigrated in large numbers, especially after a revolution in Mexico in 1910 forced many to flee across the northern border into Texas, New Mexico, Arizona, and California. Their exact numbers were unknown. American officials did not count border crossings until 1907, and even then, many migrants avoided the official immigration stations. Almost all came from the Mexican lower class, eager to escape peonage and violence in their native land. Labor agents called *coyotes*—usually in the employ of large corporations or working for ranchers—recruited Mexican workers.

Between 1900 and 1910, the Mexican population of Texas and New Mexico nearly doubled; in Arizona, it more than doubled; in California, it quadrupled. In all four states, it doubled again between 1910 and 1920. After the turn of the century, almost 10 percent of the total population of Mexico moved to the American Southwest.

In time, these Mexican Americans and their children transformed the Southwest. They built most of the early highways in Texas, New Mexico, and Arizona; dug the irrigation ditches that watered crops throughout the area; laid railroad track; and picked the cotton and vegetables that clothed and fed millions of Americans. Many lived in shacks and shanties along the railroad tracks, isolated in a separate Spanish-speaking world. Like other immigrant groups, they also formed enclaves in the cities; these *barrios* became cultural islands of family life, foods, church, and festivals.

Fewer people immigrated from China in these years, deterred in part by anti-Chinese laws and hostility. Like many other immigrants, most Chinese who came did not intend to remain. Wanting to make money and return home, they mined, farmed, and worked as common laborers. In their willingness to work hard for low wages, their desire to preserve clan and family associations from China, and their maintenance of strong ties with their home villages, Chinese Americans resembled other immigrant groups, but they differed in two important respects. As late as 1920, men outnumbered women by ten to one in the Chinese American population, and with a male median age of 42, their communities were generally dominated by the elderly.

The Chinese American population differed in another respect as well. Unlike other immigrant groups, whose numbers tended to grow, the number of Chinese Americans shrank in these years—from about 125,000 in the early 1880s to just over 60,000 in 1920. After 1910, the U.S. government set up a special immigration facility at Angel Island in San Francisco Bay, but unlike European immigrants who landed at Ellis Island in New York and were quickly sent on, Chinese immigrants were kept for weeks and months, examined and reexamined, before being

Immigrants from Asia arrive at the quarantine station at Angel Island, near San Francisco. Quota systems and exclusionary laws severely limited Asian immigration, while other laws placed restrictions on the immigrants, curtailing their right to own or even rent agricultural land. Some Asian immigrants, after months of detention at Angel Island, were refused permission to enter the United States and were forced to return to their homelands.

allowed to cross the narrow band of water to San Francisco. Angel Island remained open until 1940.

Many Japanese also arrived at Angel Island, and though at first fewer in numbers than the Chinese, they developed communities along the Pacific Coast, where they settled mainly on farms. The number of Japanese Americans grew. In 1907, the heaviest year of immigration from Japan, nearly 31,000 Japanese entered the United States; by 1920, there were 111,000 Japanese in the country, nearly three-quarters of them in California.

As the newcomers arrived from Asia, Europe, and Mexico, nativist sentiment, which had criticized earlier waves of immigrants, intensified. Old-stock Americans sneered at their dress and language. Racial theories emphasized the superiority of northern Europeans, and the new "science" of eugenics suggested the need to control the population growth of "inferior" peoples. Hostility toward Catholics and Jews was common but touched other groups as well.

In 1902, Congress enacted a law prohibiting immigration from China. Statutes requiring literacy tests designed to curtail immigration from southern and eastern Europe were vetoed by William Howard Taft in 1913 and by Woodrow Wilson in 1915 and 1917. In 1917, such a measure passed despite Wilson's veto. Other measures tried to limit immigration from Mexico and Japan.

CONFLICT IN THE WORKPLACE

Assembly lines, speedups, long hours, and low pay produced a dramatic increase in American industrial output (and profits) after 1900; they also gave rise to numerous strikes and other kinds of labor unrest. Sometimes strikes took place through the action of unions; sometimes workers just decided they had had enough and walked off the job. Whatever the cause, strikes were frequent. In one industry, in one city—the meatpacking industry in Chicago—there were 251 strikes in 1903 alone.

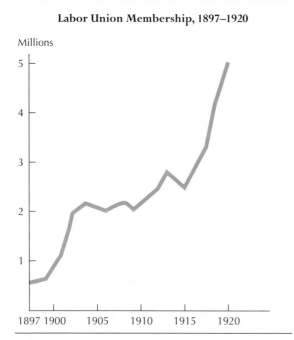

Labor Union Membership, 1897–1920

Millions

Source: U.S. Bureau of the Census, *Statistical Abstract of the United States: 1982–83* (103rd edition), Washington, DC, 1982.

Strikes and absenteeism increased after 1910; labor productivity dropped 10 percent between 1915 and 1918, the first such decline in memory. In many industries, labor turnover became a serious problem; workers changed jobs in droves. Union membership grew. In 1900, only about a million workers—less than 4 percent of the workforce—belonged to unions. By 1920, five million workers belonged, increasing the unionized portion of the workforce to about 13 percent.

As tensions grew between capital and labor, some people in the middle class became fearful that, unless something was done to improve the workers' situation, there might be violence or even revolution. This fear motivated some of the labor-oriented reforms of the Progressive Era. While some reform supporters genuinely wanted to improve labor's lot, others embraced reform because they were afraid of something else.

ORGANIZING LABOR

Samuel Gompers's American Federation of Labor increased from 250,000 members in 1897 to 1.7 million in 1904. By far the largest union organization, it remained devoted to the interests of skilled craftspeople. While it aimed partly at better wages and working conditions, it also sought to limit entry into the crafts and protect worker prerogatives. Within limits, the AFL found acceptance among giant business corporations eager for conservative policies and labor stability.

Of the 8 million female workers in 1910, only 125,000 belonged to unions. Gompers continued to resist organizing them, saying they were too emotional and, as union organizers, "had a way of making serious mistakes." Margaret Dreier Robins, an organizer of proven skill, scoffed at that. "These men died twenty years ago and are just walking around dead!" she protested.

Robins helped found the Women's Trade Union League in 1903. The WTUL led the effort to organize women into trade unions, to lobby for legislation protecting female workers, and to educate the public on the problems and needs of working women. It took in all working women who would join, regardless of skill (although not, at first, African American women), and it won crucial financial support from well-to-do women such as Anne Morgan, daughter of the feared financier J. P. Morgan. Robins's close friend Jane Addams belonged, as did Dr. Alice Hamilton, a pioneer in American research on the causes of industrial disease.

The WTUL never had many members—a few thousand at most—but its influence extended far beyond its membership. In 1909, it supported the "Uprising of the 20,000," a strike of shirtwaist workers in New York City. When female employees of the Triangle Shirtwaist Company tried to form a union, the company fired them, and they walked out; 20,000 men and women in 500 other shops followed. Strike meetings were conducted in three languages—English, Yiddish, and Italian—and before being forced to go back to work, the strikers won a shorter workweek and a few other gains. Sadly, the Triangle women lost out on another important demand—for unlocked shop doors and safe fire escapes. Their loss proved lethal in the famous Triangle Shirtwaist Company fire of 1911.

The WTUL also backed a strike in 1910 against Hart, Schaffner and Marx, Chicago's largest manufacturer of men's clothing. One day, Annie Shapiro, the 18-year-old daughter of Russian immigrants, was told her wages were being cut from $7 a week to $6.20. That was a large cut, and along with sixteen other young women, Shapiro refused to accept it and walked out. "We had to be recognized as people," she said later. Soon other women walked out, and the revolt spread.

In a matter of days, some forty thousand garment workers were on strike, about half of them women. Manufacturers hurried to negotiate, and the result was the important Hart, Schaffner agreement, which created an arbitration committee composed of management and labor to handle grievances and settle disputes. The first successful experiment in collective bargaining, the Hart, Schaffner agreement became the model for the kind of agreements that govern industrial relations today.

Another union, the Industrial Workers of the World (IWW), attracted by far the greatest attention (and the most fears) in these years. Unlike the WTUL, it welcomed everyone regardless of gender or race. Unlike the AFL, it tried to organize the unskilled and foreign-born laborers who worked in the mass production industries. Founded in Chicago in 1905, it aimed to unite the American working class into a mammoth union to promote labor's interests. Its motto—"An injury to one is an injury to all"—stressed labor solidarity, as had the earlier Knights of Labor. But unlike the Knights, the IWW, or Wobblies as they were often known, urged social revolution.

"It is our purpose to overthrow the capitalist system by forcible means if necessary," William D. "Big Bill" Haywood, one of its founders, said; and he went on in his speeches to say he knew of nothing a worker could do that "will bring as much anguish to the boss as a little sabotage in the right place."

IWW leaders included Mary Harris ("Mother") Jones, a famous veteran of battles in the Illinois coalfields; Elizabeth Gurley Flynn, a fiery young radical who joined as a teenager; and Big Bill Haywood himself, the strapping one-eyed founder of the Western Federation of Miners.

The IWW led a number of major strikes. Strikes in Lawrence, Massachusetts (1912), and Paterson, New Jersey (1912), attracted national attention: in Lawrence when the strikers sent their children, ill-clad and hungry, out of the city to stay with sympathetic families; in Paterson when they rented New York's Madison Square Garden for a massive labor pageant. IWW leaders welcomed the revolutionary tumult sweeping Russia and other countries. In the United States, they thought, a series of local strikes would bring about capitalist repression, then a general strike, and eventually a workers' commonwealth.

Elizabeth Gurley Flynn, labor's "Joan of Arc," addresses textile workers on strike at Paterson, New Jersey.

The IWW fell short of these objectives, but during its lifetime—from 1905 to the mid-1920s—it made major gains among immigrant workers in the Northeast, migrant farm laborers on the Plains, and loggers and miners in the South and Far West. In factories like Ford's, it recruited workers resentful of the speedups on the assembly lines. Although IWW membership probably amounted to no more than 100,000 at any one time, workers came and left so often that its total membership may have reached as high as 1 million.

WORKING WITH WORKERS

Concerned about labor unrest, some business leaders used violence and police action to keep workers in line, but others turned to the new fields of applied psychology and personnel management. A school of industrial psychology emerged. As had Taylor, industrial psychologists studied workers' routines, and, further, they showed that output was also affected by job satisfaction. While most businesses pushed ahead with efficiency campaigns, a few did establish industrial relations departments, hire public relations firms to improve their corporate image, and link productivity to job safety and worker happiness.

Ivy L. Lee, a pioneer in the field of corporate public relations, advised clients such as the Pennsylvania Railroad and Standard Oil on how to improve relations with labor and the public. Calling himself a "physician to corporate bodies," Lee urged complete openness on the company's part. To please employees, companies printed newsletters and organized softball teams; they awarded prizes and celebrated retirements. Ford created a "sociology department" staffed by 150 experts who showed workers how to budget their incomes and care for their health. They even taught them how to shop for meat.

On January 5, 1914, Ford took another significant step. He announced the five-dollar day, "the greatest revolution," he said, "in the matter of rewards for workers ever known to the industrial world." With a stroke, he doubled the wage rate for common labor, reduced the working day from nine hours to eight, and established a personnel department to place workers in appropriate jobs. The next day, ten thousand applicants stood outside the gates.

As a result, Ford had the pick of the labor force. Turnover declined; absenteeism, previously as much as one-tenth of all Ford workers every day, fell to 0.3 percent. Output increased; the IWW at Ford collapsed. The plan increased wages, but it also gave the company greater control over a more stable labor force. Workers had to meet a behavior code in order to qualify for the five-dollar day. At first scornful of the "utopian" plan, business leaders across the country soon copied it, and on January 2, 1919, Ford announced the six-dollar day.

AMOSKEAG

In size, system, and worker relations, the record of the Amoskeag Company textile mills was revealing. Located beside the Merrimack River in Manchester, New Hampshire, the mills—an enormous complex of factories, warehouses, canals, and machinery—had been built in the 1830s. By the turn of the century, they were producing nearly 50 miles of cloth an hour, more cloth each day than any other mills in the entire world.

The face of the mills, an almost solid wall of red brick, stretched nearly a mile. Archways and bridges pierced the facade. Amoskeag resembled a walled medieval city within which workers found "a total institution, a closed and almost self-contained world." At first the mills employed young women for labor, but by 1900, more and more immigrant males staffed the machines. French

The playground at Amoskeag, provided for the children of the company's workers. The Amoskeag Textile Club, part of the employer-sponsored employee welfare program, had reading rooms, card tables, billiard and pool tables, a golf course, and a baseball field for the use of the workers. All was demolished when the mill closed in 1935. Many firms between 1910 and 1917 established employee programs similar to those introduced at Amoskeag.

Canadians, Irish, Poles, and Greeks—seventeen thousand in all—worked there, and their experiences revealed a great deal about factory work and life at the turn of the century.

The company hired and fired at will, and it demanded relentless output from the spindles and spinning frames. Yet it also viewed employees as its "children" and looked for total loyalty in return, an expectation often realized. Workers identified with Amoskeag and, decades later, still called themselves Amoskeag men and women. "We were all like a family," one said.

Most Amoskeag workers preferred the industrial world of the mills to the farms they had left behind. They did not feel displaced; they knew the pains of industrial life; and they adapted in ways that fit their own needs and traditions. Families played a large role. They neither disintegrated nor lost their relationships.

French Canadians and others often came in family units. One or two family members left the farm for the mills, maintained close ties with those back home, and then sent for others, creating a form of "chain migration."

Once in Manchester, families often toiled in the same workrooms. Looking after each other, they asked for transfers and promotions for relatives; they taught their children technical skills and how to get along with bosses and fellow workers. Although low paid, Amoskeag employees took pride in their work, and for many of them, a well-turned-out product provided dignity and self-esteem.

As part of its paternal interest in employee welfare, in 1910 the company inaugurated a welfare and efficiency program, which aimed to increase productivity, accustom immigrants to industrial work, instill company loyalty, and curb labor unrest. Playgrounds and visiting nurses, home-buying plans, a cooking school, and dental service were part of the plan. The Amoskeag Textile Club held employee dinners and picnics, organized shooting clubs and a baseball team, sponsored Christmas parties for the children, and put out the *Amoskeag Bulletin,* a monthly magazine of employee news.

From 1885 to 1919, no strike touched the mills. Thereafter, however, labor unrest increased. Overproduction and foreign competition took their toll, and Amoskeag closed in 1935.

A NEW URBAN CULTURE

For many Americans, the quality of life improved significantly between 1900 and 1920. Jobs were relatively plentiful, and, in a development of great importance, more and more people were entering the professions as doctors, lawyers, teachers, and engineers. With comfortable incomes, a growing middle class could take advantage of new lifestyles, inventions, and forms of entertainment. Mass production could not have worked without mass consumption, and Americans in these years increasingly became a nation of consumers.

PRODUCTION AND CONSUMPTION

In 1900, business firms spent about $95 million on advertising; twenty years later, they spent more than $500 million. Ads and billboards touted cigarettes, cars, perfumes, and cosmetics. Advertising agencies boomed. Using new sampling techniques, they developed modern concepts of market testing and research. Sampling customer preferences affected business indirectly as well, making it more responsive to public opinion on social and political issues.

Mass production swept the clothing industry and dressed more Americans better than any people ever before. Using lessons learned in making uniforms during the Civil War, manufacturers for the first time developed standard clothing and shoe sizes that fit most bodies. Clothing prices dropped; the availability of inexpensive "off-the-rack" clothes lessened distinctions between rich and poor. By 1900, nine of every ten men and boys wore the new "ready-to-wear" clothes.

In 1900, people employed in manufacturing earned on average $418 a year. Two decades later, they earned $1342 a year, though inflation took much of the increase. While the middle class expanded, the rich also grew richer. In 1920, the new income tax showed the first accurate tabulation of income, and it confirmed what many had suspected all along. Five percent of the population received almost one-fourth of all income.

LIVING AND DYING IN AN URBAN NATION

In 1920, the median age of the population was only 25. (It is now 30.) Immigration accounted for part of the population's youthfulness, since most immigrants were young. Thanks to medical advances and better living conditions, the death rate dropped in the early years of the century; the average life span increased. Between 1900 and 1920, life expectancy rose from 49 to 56 years for white women and from 47 to 54 years for white men. It rose from 33 to 45 years for blacks and other racial minorities.

Despite the increase in life expectancy, infant mortality remained high; nearly 10 percent of white babies and 20 percent of minority babies died in the first year of life. In comparison to today, fewer babies on average survived to adolescence, and fewer people survived beyond middle age. In 1900, the death rate among people between 45 and 65 was more than twice the modern rate. As a result, there were relatively fewer older people—in 1900, only 4 percent of the population was older than 65 compared to nearly 13 percent today. Fewer children than today knew their grandparents. Still, improvements in health care helped people live longer, and as a result, the incidence of cancer and heart disease increased.

Cities grew, and by any earlier standards, they grew on a colossal scale. Downtowns became a central hive of skyscrapers, department stores, warehouses, and hotels. Strips of factories radiated from the center. As street railways spread, cities took on a systematic pattern of socioeconomic segregation, usually in rings. The innermost ring filled with immigrants, circled by a belt of working-class housing. The remaining rings marked areas of rising affluence outward toward wealthy suburbs, which themselves formed around shopping strips and grid patterns of streets that restricted social interaction.

The giants were New York, Chicago, and Philadelphia, industrial cities that turned out every kind of product from textiles to structural steel. Smaller cities such as Rochester, New York, or Cleveland, Ohio, specialized in manufacturing a specific line of goods or processing regional products for the national market. Railroads instead of highways tied things together; in 1916, the rail network, the largest in the world, reached its peak—254,000 miles of track that carried more than three-fourths of all intercity freight tonnage.

Step by step, cities adopted their twentieth-century forms. Between 1909 and 1915, Los Angeles, a city of 300,000 people, passed a series of ordinances that gave rise to modern urban zoning. For the first time, the ordinances divided a city into three districts of specified use: a residential area, an industrial area, and an area open to residence and a limited list of industries. Other cities followed. Combining several features, the New York zoning law of 1916 became the model for the nation; within a decade, 591 cities copied it.

Zoning ordered city development, keeping skyscrapers out of factory districts, factories out of the suburbs. It also had powerful social repercussions. In the South, zoning became a tool to extend racial segregation; in northern cities, it acted against ethnic minorities. Jews in New York, Italians in Boston, Poles in Detroit, African Americans in Chicago—zoning laws held them all at arm's length. Like other migrants, African Americans often preferred to settle together, but zoning also helped put them there. By 1920, ten districts in Chicago were more than three-quarters black. In Los Angeles, Cleveland, Detroit, and Washington, D.C., most blacks lived in only two or three wards.

POPULAR PASTIMES

Thanks to changing work rules and mechanization, many Americans enjoyed more leisure time. The average workweek for manufacturing laborers fell from 60 hours in 1890 to 51 in 1920. By the early 1900s, white-collar workers might spend only 8 to 10 hours a day at work and a half day on weekends. Greater leisure time gave more people more opportunity for play and people flocked to places of entertainment. Baseball entrenched itself as the national pastime. Automobiles and streetcars carried growing numbers of fans to ballparks; attendance at major league games doubled between 1903 and 1920. Football also drew fans, although critics attacked the sport's violence and the use of "tramp athletes," nonstudents whom colleges paid to play. In 1905, the worst year, 18 players were killed and 150 seriously injured.

Alarmed, President Theodore Roosevelt—who had once said, "I am the father of three boys [and] if I thought any one of them would weigh a possible broken bone against the glory of being chosen to play on Harvard's football team I would disinherit him"—called a White House conference to clean up college sports. The conference founded the Intercollegiate Athletic Association, which in 1910 became the National Collegiate Athletic Association (NCAA).

Movie theaters opened everywhere. By 1910, there were 10,000 of them, drawing a weekly audience of 10 million people. Admission was usually 5 cents, and movies stressing laughter and pathos appealed to a mass market. In 1915, D. W. Griffith, a talented and creative director—as well as a racist—produced the first movie spectacular: *Birth of a Nation*. Griffith adopted new film techniques, including close-ups, fade-outs, and artistic camera angles.

Phonographs brought ready-made entertainment into the home. By 1901, phonograph and record companies included the Victor Talking Machine Company, the Edison Speaking Machine Company, and Columbia Records. Ornate mahogany Victrolas became standard fixtures in middle-class parlors. In 1919, 2.25 million phonographs were produced; two years later, more than 100 million records were sold.

As record sales grew, families sang less and listened more. Music became a business. In 1909, Congress enacted a copyright law that provided a two-cent royalty on each piece of music on phonograph records or piano rolls. The royalty, small as it was, offered welcome income to composers and publishers, and in 1914, composer Victor Herbert and others formed the American Society of Composers, Authors, and Publishers (ASCAP) to protect musical rights and royalties.

The faster rhythms of syncopated ragtime became the rage, especially after 1911, when Irving Berlin, a Russian immigrant, wrote "Alexander's Ragtime Band." Ragtime set off a nationwide dance craze. Secretaries danced on their lunch hour, the first nightclubs opened, and restaurants and hotels introduced dance floors. Waltzes and polkas gave way to a host of new dances, many with animal names: the fox-trot, bunny hop, turkey trot, snake, and kangaroo dip. Partners were not permitted to dance too close; bouncers tapped them on the shoulder if they got closer than 9 inches.

Vaudeville, increasingly popular after 1900, reached maturity around 1915. Drawing on the immigrant experience, it voiced the variety of city life and included skits, songs, comics, acrobats, and magicians. Dances and jokes showed an earthiness new to mass audiences. By 1914, stage runways extended into the crowd; women performers had bared their legs and were beginning to show glimpses of the midriff. Fanny Brice; Ann Pennington, the "shimmy" queen; and

Eva Tanguay, who sang "It's All Been Done Before But Not the Way I Do It," starred in Florenz Ziegfeld's Follies, the peak of vaudeville.

In songs like "St. Louis Blues" (1914), W. C. Handy took the black southern folk music of the blues to northern cities. Gertrude "Ma" Rainey, the daughter of minstrels, sang in black vaudeville for nearly thirty-five years. Performing in Chattanooga, Tennessee, about 1910, she came across a 12-year-old orphan, Bessie Smith, who became the "Empress of the Blues." Smith's voice was huge and sweeping. Recording for the Race division of Columbia Records, she made more than eighty records that together sold nearly ten million copies.

Another musical innovation came north from New Orleans. Charles (Buddy) Bolden, a cornetist; Ferdinand "Jelly Roll" Morton, a pianist; and a youngster named Louis Armstrong played an improvisational music that had no formal name. Reaching Chicago, it became "jas," then "jass," and finally "jazz." Jazz jumped, and jazz musicians relied on feeling and mood.

Popular fiction reflected changing interests. Kate Douglas Wiggins's *Rebecca of Sunnybrook Farm* (1903) and Lucy M. Montgomery's *Anne of Green Gables* (1908) showed the continuing popularity of rural themes. Westerns also sold well, but readers turned more and more to detective thrillers with hard-bitten city detectives and science fiction featuring the latest dream in technology. The Tom Swift series, begun in 1910, looked ahead to spaceships, ray guns, and gravity nullifiers.

Edward L. Stratemeyer, the mind behind Tom Swift, brought the techniques of mass production to book writing. In 1906, he formed the Stratemeyer Literary Syndicate, which employed a stable of writers to turn out hundreds of Tom Swift, Rover Boys, and Bobbsey Twins stories for young readers. Burt Standish, another prolific author, took the pen name Gilbert Patten and created the character of Frank Merriwell, wholesome college athlete. As Patten said, "I took the three qualities I most wanted him to represent—frank and merry in nature, well in body and mind—and made the name Frank Merriwell." The Merriwell books sold twenty-five million copies.

EXPERIMENTATION IN THE ARTS

"There is a state of unrest all over the world in art as in all other things," the director of New York's Metropolitan Museum said in 1908. "It is the same in literature, as in music, in painting, and in sculpture."

Isadora Duncan and Ruth St. Denis transformed the dance. Departing from traditional ballet steps, both women stressed improvisation, emotion, and the human form. "Listen to the music with your soul," Duncan told her students. "Unless your dancing springs from an inner emotion and expresses an idea, it will be meaningless." Draped in flowing robes, she revealed more of her legs than some thought tasteful, and she proclaimed that the "noblest art is the nude." Duncan died tragically in 1927, her neck broken when her long red scarf caught in the wheel of a racing car.

The lofts and apartments of New York's Greenwich Village attracted artists, writers, and poets interested in experimentation and change. To these artists, the city was the focus of national life and the sign of a new culture. Robert Henri and the realist painters—known to their critics as the Ashcan School—relished the city's excitement. They wanted, a friend said, "to paint truth and to paint it with strength and fearlessness and individuality."

To the realists, a painting carried into the future the look of life as it happened. Their paintings depicted street scenes, colorful crowds, and slum children swimming in the river. In paintings such as the *Cliff Dwellers,* George W. Bellows captured the color and excitement of the tenements; John Sloan, one of Henri's most talented students, painted the vitality of ordinary people and familiar scenes.

In 1913, a show at the New York Armory presented sixteen hundred modernist paintings, prints, and sculptures. The work of Picasso, Cézanne, Matisse, Brancusi, Van Gogh, and Gauguin dazed and dazzled American observers. Critics attacked the show as worthless and depraved; a Chicago official wanted it banned from the city because the "idea that people can gaze at this sort of thing without [it] hurting them is all bosh."

The postimpressionists changed the direction of twentieth-century art and influenced adventuresome American painters. John Marin, Max Weber, Georgia O'Keeffe, Arthur Dove, and other modernists experimented in ways foreign to Henri's realists. Defiantly avant-garde, they shook off convention and experimented with new forms. Using bold colors and abstract patterns, they worked to capture the energy of urban life.

There was an extraordinary outburst of poetry. In 1912, Harriet Monroe started the magazine *Poetry* in Chicago, the hotbed of the new poetry; Ezra Pound and Vachel Lindsay, both daring experimenters with ideas and verse, published in the first issue. T. S. Eliot published the classic "Love Song of J. Alfred Prufrock" in *Poetry* in 1915. Attacked bitterly by conservative critics, the poem established Eliot's leadership among a group of poets, many of them living and writing in London, who rejected traditional meter and rhyme as artificial constraints. Eliot, Pound, and Amy Lowell, among others, believed the poet's task was to capture fleeting images in verse.

Others experimenting with new techniques in poetry included Robert Frost (*North of Boston*, 1915), Edgar Lee Masters (*Spoon River Anthology*, 1915), and Carl Sandburg (*Chicago Poems*, 1916). Sandburg's poem "Chicago" celebrated the vitality of the city:

> *Come and show me another city with lifted head*
> > *singing so proud to be*
> > > *alive and coarse and strong and cunning*
>
> . . . .
>
> *Fierce as a dog with tongue lapping for action,*
> > *cunning as a savage*
> > > *pitted against the wilderness,*
> > > > *Bareheaded,*
> > > > *Shoveling,*
> > > > *Wrecking,*
> > > > *Planning,*
> > > > *Building, breaking, rebuilding,*
>
> . . . .
>
> *Bragging and laughing that under his wrist is the*
> > *pulse, and under his*
> > > *ribs the heart of the people,*
> > > > > *Laughing!*
> *Laughing the stormy, husky, brawling laughter of*
> > *Youth, half-naked,*
> > > *sweating, proud to be Hog Butcher, Tool*
> > > > *Maker, Stacker of Wheat,*
> > > *Player with Railroads and Freight Handler to*
> > > > *the Nation.*

Manners and morals change slowly, and many Americans overlooked the importance of the first two decades of the twentieth century. Yet sweeping change was under way; anyone who doubted it could visit a gallery, see a film, listen to music, or read one of the new literary magazines. Garrets and galleries were filled with a breathtaking sense of change. "There was life in all these new things," Marsden Hartley, a modernist painter, recalled. "There was excitement, there was healthy revolt, investigation, discovery, and an utterly new world out of it all."

The ferment of progressivism in city, state, and nation reshaped the country. In a burst of reform, people built playgrounds, restructured taxes, regulated business, won the vote for women, shortened working hours, altered political systems, opened kindergartens, and improved factory safety. They tried to fulfill the national promise of dignity and liberty.

Marsden Hartley, it turned out, had voiced a mood that went well beyond painters and poets. Across society, people in many walks of life were experiencing a similar sense of excitement and discovery. Racism, repression, and labor conflict were present, to be sure, but there was also talk of hope, progress, and change. In politics, science, journalism, education, and a host of other fields, people believed for a time that they could make a difference, and in trying to do so, they became part of the progressive generation.

23

$$\rightarrow\!\!\!\rightarrow \cdot\!\!-\!\!-\!\!-\!\!\cdot \leftarrow\!\!\!\leftarrow$$

FROM ROOSEVELT TO WILSON IN THE AGE OF PROGRESSIVISM

O n a sunny spring morning in 1909, Theodore Roosevelt, wearing the greatcoat of a colonel of the Rough Riders, left New York for a safari in Africa. An ex-president at the age of 50, he had turned over the White House to his chosen successor, William Howard Taft, and was now off for "the joy of wandering through lonely lands, the joy of hunting the mighty and terrible lords" of Africa, "where death broods in the dark and silent depths."

Some of Roosevelt's enemies hoped he would not return. "I trust some lion will do its duty," Wall Street magnate J. P. Morgan said. Always prepared, Roosevelt took nine extra pairs of eyeglasses, and, just in case, several expert hunters accompanied him. When the nearsighted Roosevelt took aim, three others aimed at the same moment. "Mr. Roosevelt had a fairly good idea of the general direction," the safari leader said, "but we couldn't take chances with the life of a former president."

It was all good fun, and afterward Roosevelt set off on a tour of Europe. He attended the funeral of the king of England, dined with the king and queen of Italy, and happily spent five hours reviewing troops of the German empire. Less happily, he followed events back home where, in the judgment of many friends, Taft was not working out as president. At almost every stop there were letters waiting for him from disappointed Republicans.

For his part, Taft was puzzled by it all. Honest and warmhearted, he had intended to continue Roosevelt's policies, even writing Roosevelt that he would "see to it that your judgment in selecting me as your successor and bringing about that succession shall be vindicated." But events turned out differently. The conservative and progressive wings of the Republican party split, and Taft often sided with the conservatives. Among progressive Republicans, Taft's troubles stirred talk of a Roosevelt "back from Elba" movement, akin to Napoleon's return from exile.

Thousands gathered to greet Roosevelt on his return from Europe. He sailed into New York harbor on June 18, 1910, to the sound of naval guns and loud cheers. In characteristic fashion, he had helped make the arrangements: "If there is to be a great crowd, do arrange it so that the whole crowd has a chance to see me and that there is as little disappointment as possible."

Roosevelt carried with him a touching letter from Taft, received just before he left Europe. "I have had a hard time—I do not know that I have had harder luck than other Presidents, but I do know that thus far I have succeeded far less than have others. I have been conscientiously trying to carry out your policies but my method of doing so has not worked smoothly." Taft invited Teddy to spend a

Teddy Roosevelt, with his hunting party in Africa, poses with one of the more than 300 animals he and his group took down. As president, Roosevelt had supported measures protecting wildlife in the United States, including designating Pelican Island, Florida, as the nation's first wildlife refuge.

night or two at the White House, but Roosevelt declined, saying that ex-presidents should not visit Washington. Relations between the two friends cooled.

A year later, there was a desperate fight between Taft and Roosevelt for the Republican presidential nomination. Taft won the nomination, but, angry and ambitious, Roosevelt bolted and helped form a new party, the Progressive (or "Bull Moose") party, to unseat Taft and capture the White House. With Taft, Roosevelt, Woodrow Wilson (the Democratic party's candidate), and Socialist party candidate Eugene V. Debs all in the race, the election of 1912 became one of the most exciting in American history.

It was also one of the most important. People were worried about the social and economic effects of urban-industrial growth. The election of 1912 provided a forum for those worries, and, to a degree unusual in American politics, it pitted deeply opposed candidates against one another and outlined differing views of the nation's future. In the spirited battle between Roosevelt and Wilson, it also brought to the forefront some of the currents of progressive reform.

THE SPIRIT OF PROGRESSIVISM

In one way or another, progressivism touched all aspects of society. Politically, it fostered a reform movement that sought cures for the problems of city, state, and nation. Intellectually, it drew on the expertise of the new social sciences and reflected a shift from older absolutes of class and religion to newer schools of thought that emphasized the role of the environment in human development and the relative nature of truth. Culturally, it inspired fresh modes of expression in dance, film, painting, literature, and architecture. Touching individuals in different ways, progressivism became a set of attitudes as well as a definable movement.

Though broad and diverse, progressivism as a whole had a half dozen characteristics that gave it definition. First, the progressives acted out of concern about the effects of industrialization and the conditions of industrial life. While their viewpoints varied, they did not, as a rule, set out to harm big business, but instead sought to humanize and regulate it.

In pursuing these objectives, the progressives displayed a second characteristic: a fundamental optimism about human nature, the possibilities of progress, and the capacity of people to recognize problems and take action to solve them. Progressives believed they could "investigate, educate, and legislate"—learn about a problem, inform people about it, and, with the help of an informed public, find and enforce a solution.

Third, more than many earlier reformers, the progressives were willing to intervene in people's lives, confident that it was their right to do so. They knew best, some of them thought, and as a result, there was an element of coercion in a number of their ideas. Fourth, while progressives preferred if possible to use voluntary means to achieve reform, they tended to turn more and more to the authority of the state and government at all levels in order to put into effect the reforms they wanted.

As a fifth characteristic, many progressives drew on a combination of evangelical Protestantism (which gave them the desire—and, they thought, the duty—to purge the world of sins such as prostitution and drunkenness) and the natural and social sciences (whose theories made them confident that they could understand and control the environment in which people lived). Progressives tended to view the environment as a key to reform, thinking—in the way some economists, sociologists, and other social scientists were suggesting—that if they could change the environment, they could change the individual.

Finally, progressivism was distinctive because it touched virtually the whole nation. Not everyone, of course, was a progressive, and there were many who opposed or ignored the ideas of the movement. There were also those who were untouched by progressive reforms and those whom the movement overlooked. But in one way or another, a remarkable number of people were caught up in it, giving progressivism a national reach and a mass base.

That was one of the features, in fact, that set it off from populism, which had grown mostly in the rural South and West. Progressivism drew support from across society. "The thing that constantly amazed me," said William Allen White, a leading progressive journalist, "was how many people were with us." Progressivism appealed to the expanding middle class, prosperous farmers, and skilled laborers; it also attracted significant support in the business community.

The progressives believed in progress and disliked waste. No single issue or concern united them all. Some progressives wanted to clean up city governments, others to clean up city streets. Some wanted to purify politics or control corporate abuses, others to eradicate poverty or prostitution. Some demanded social justice in the form of women's rights, child labor laws, temperance, and factory safety. They were Democrats, Republicans, Socialists, and independents.

Progressives believed in a better world and in the ability of people to achieve it. Progress depended on knowledge. The progressives stressed individual morality and collective action, the scientific method, and the value of expert opinion. Like contemporary business leaders, they valued system, planning, management, and predictability. They wanted not only reform but efficiency.

Historians once viewed progressivism as the triumph of one group in society over another. In this view, farmers took on the hated and powerful railroads; upstart reformers challenged the city bosses; business interests fought for favorable legislation; youthful professionals carved out their place in society. Now, historians stress the way progressivism brought people together rather than drove them apart. Disparate groups united in an effort to improve the well-being of many groups in society.

THE RISE OF THE PROFESSIONS

Progressivism fed on an organizational impulse that encouraged people to join forces, share information, and solve problems. Between 1890 and 1920, a host of national societies and associations took shape—nearly four hundred of them in just three decades. Groups such as the National Child Labor Committee, which lobbied for legislation to regulate the employment and working conditions of children, were formed to attack specific issues. Other groups reflected one of the most significant developments in American society at the turn of the century— the rise of the professions.

Growing rapidly in these years, the professions—law, medicine, religion, business, teaching, and social work—were the source of much of the leadership of the progressive movement. The professions attracted young, educated men and women, who in turn were part of a larger trend: a dramatic increase in the number of individuals working in administrative and professional jobs. In businesses, these people were managers, architects, technicians, and accountants. In city governments, they were experts in everything from education to sanitation. They organized and ran the urban-industrial society.

Together these professionals formed part of a new middle class whose members did not derive their status from birth or inherited wealth, as had many members of the older middle class. Instead, they moved ahead through education and personal accomplishment. They had worked to become doctors, lawyers, ministers, and teachers. Proud of their skills, they were ambitious and self-confident, and they thought of themselves as experts who could use their knowledge for the benefit of society.

As a way of asserting their status, they formed professional societies to look after their interests and govern entry into their professions. Just a few years before, for example, a doctor had become a doctor simply by stocking up on patent medicines and hanging out a sign. Now doctors began to insist they were part of a medical profession, and they wanted to set educational requirements and minimum standards for practice. In 1901, they reorganized the American Medical Association (AMA) and made it into a modern national professional society.

Other groups and professions showed the same pattern. Lawyers formed bar associations, created examining boards, and lobbied for regulations restricting entry into the profession. Teachers organized the National Education

Association (1905) and pressed for teacher certification and compulsory education laws. Social workers formed the National Federation of Settlements (1911); business leaders created the National Association of Manufacturers (1895) and the U.S. Chamber of Commerce (1912); and farmers joined the National Farm Bureau Federation to spread information about farming and to try to improve their lot.

Working both as individuals and groups, members of the professions had a major impact on the era, as the career of one of them, Dr. Alice Hamilton, illustrated. Hamilton early decided to devote her life to helping the less fortunate. Choosing medicine, she went to the University of Michigan Medical School, one of a shrinking number of medical schools that admitted women, and then settled in Chicago, where she met Jane Addams and took a room in Hull House. Soon thereafter, she traced a local typhoid epidemic to flies carrying germs from open privies.

Combining field study with meticulous laboratory techniques, she pioneered research into the causes of lead poisoning and other industrial disease. In 1908, the governor of Illinois appointed her to a commission on occupational diseases; two years later, she headed a statewide survey of industrial poisons. Thanks to her work, in 1911, Illinois passed the first state law providing compensation for industrial disease caused by poisonous fumes and dust. By the end of the 1930s, all the major industrial states had such laws.

One of the new professionals, Hamilton had used her education and skill to broaden knowledge of her subject, change industrial practices, and improve the lives of countless workers. "For me," she said later in a comment characteristic of the progressives, "the satisfaction is that things are better now, and I had some part in it."

THE SOCIAL-JUSTICE MOVEMENT

As Alice Hamilton's career exemplified, progressivism began in the cities during the 1890s. It first took form around settlement workers and others interested in freeing individuals from the crushing impact of cities and factories.

Ministers, intellectuals, social workers, and lawyers joined in a social-justice movement that focused national attention on the need for tenement house laws, more stringent child labor legislation, and better working conditions for women. They brought pressure on municipal agencies for more and better parks, playgrounds, day nurseries, schools, and community services. Blending private and public action, settlement leaders turned increasingly to government aid.

Social-justice reformers were more interested in social cures than individual charity. Unlike earlier reformers, they saw problems as endless and interrelated;

individuals became part of a city's larger patterns. With that insight, social-service casework shifted from a focus on an individual's well-being to a scientific analysis of neighborhoods, occupations, and classes.

Social-justice reformers, banding together to work for change, formed the National Conference of Charities and Corrections, which in 1915 became the National Conference of Social Work. Controlled by social workers, the conference reflected the growing professionalization of reform. Through it, social workers discovered each other's efforts, shared methodology, and tried to establish themselves as a separate field within the social sciences. Once content with informal training sessions in a settlement house living room, they now founded complete professional schools at Chicago, Harvard, and other universities. Instead of piecemeal reforms, they aimed at a comprehensive program of minimum wages, maximum hours, workers' compensation, and widows' pensions.

THE PURITY CRUSADE

Working in city neighborhoods, social-justice reformers were often struck by the degree to which alcohol affected the lives of the people they were trying to help. Workers drank away their wages; some men spent more time at the saloon than at home. Drunkenness caused violence, and it angered employers who did not want intoxicated workers on the job. In countless ways, alcohol wasted human resources, the reformers believed, and they launched a crusade to remove the evils of drink from American life.

At the head of the crusade was the Women's Christian Temperance Union (WCTU), which had continued to grow since it was founded in the 1870s. By 1911, the WCTU had nearly a quarter of a million members; it was the largest organization of women in American history to that time. In 1893, it was joined by the Anti-Saloon League, and together the groups pressed to abolish alcohol and the places where it was consumed. By 1916, they had succeeded in nineteen states, but as drinking continued elsewhere, they pushed for a nationwide law. In the midst of the moral fervor of World War I, they succeeded, and the Eighteenth Amendment to the Constitution, prohibiting the manufacture, sale, and transportation of intoxicating liquors, took effect in January 1920.

The amendment encountered troubles later in the 1920s as the social atmosphere changed, but at the time it passed, progressives thought Prohibition was a major step toward eliminating social instability and moral wrong. In a similar fashion, some progressive reformers also worked to get rid of prostitution, convinced that poverty and ignorance drove women to the trade. By 1915, nearly every state had banned brothels, and in 1910, Congress passed the Mann Act, which prohibited the interstate transportation of women for immoral purposes.

WOMAN SUFFRAGE, WOMEN'S RIGHTS

Women played a large role in the social-justice movement. Feminists were particularly active, especially in the political sphere, between 1890 and 1914—feminists were more active then, in fact, than at any other time until the 1960s. Some working-class women pushed for higher wages and better working conditions. College-educated women—five thousand a year graduated after 1900—took up careers in the professions, from which some of them supported reform. From 1890 to 1910, the work of a number of national women's organizations, including the National Council of Jewish Women, the National Congress of Mothers, and the Women's Trade Union League, furthered the aims of the progressive movement.

Excluded from most of these organizations, African American women formed their own groups. The National Association of Colored Women was founded in 1895, fifteen years before the better known male-oriented National Association for the Advancement of Colored People (NAACP). Aimed at social

Woman suffrage was a key element in the social-justice movement. Without the right to vote, women working actively for reform had little real power to influence elected officials to support their endeavors.

welfare, the women's organization was the first African American social-service agency in the country.

From 200,000 members in 1900, the General Federation of Women's Clubs grew to more than 1 million by 1912. The clubs met, as they had before, for coffee and literary conversation, but they also began to look closely at conditions around them.

Forming an Industrial Section and a Committee on Legislation for Women and Children, the federation supported reforms to safeguard child and women workers, improve schools, ensure pure food, and beautify the community. Reluctant at first, the federation finally lent support in 1914 to woman suffrage, a cause that dated back to the first women's rights convention in Seneca Falls, New York, in 1848. Divided over tactics since the Civil War, the suffrage movement suffered from disunity, male opposition, indecision over whether to seek action at the state or at the national level, resistance from the Catholic Church, and opposition from liquor interests, who linked the cause to Prohibition.

Because politics was an avenue for reform, growing numbers of women activists became involved in the suffrage movement. After years of disagreement, the two major suffrage organizations, the National Woman Suffrage Association and the American Woman Suffrage Association, merged in 1890 to form the National American Woman Suffrage Association. The merger opened a new phase of the suffrage movement, characterized by unity and a tightly controlled national organization.

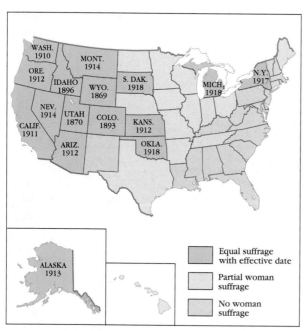

Woman Suffrage Before 1920

State-by-state gains in woman suffrage were limited to the Far West and were agonizingly slow in the early years of the twentieth century.

In 1900, Carrie Chapman Catt, a superb organizer, became

president of the National American Woman Suffrage Association, which by 1920 had nearly two million members. Catt and Anna Howard Shaw, who became the association's head in 1904, believed in organization and peaceful lobbying to win the vote. Alice Paul and Lucy Burns, founders of the Congressional Union, were more militant; they interrupted public meetings, focused on Congress rather than the states, and in 1917 picketed the White House.

Significantly, Catt, Paul, and others made a major change in the argument for woman suffrage. When the campaign began in the nineteenth century, suffragists had claimed the vote as a natural right, owed to women as much as men. Now, they stressed a pragmatic argument: since women were more sensitive to moral issues than men, they would use their votes to help create a better society. They would support temperance, clean government, laws to protect workers, and other reforms. In 1918, the House passed a constitutional amendment stating simply that the right to vote shall not be denied "on account of sex." The Senate and enough states followed, and, after three generations of suffragist efforts, the Nineteenth Amendment took effect in 1920.

The social-justice movement had the most success in passing state laws limiting the working hours of women. By 1913, thirty-nine states set maximum working hours for women or banned the employment of women at night. As early as 1900, thanks to groups such as the National Child Labor Committee, twenty-eight states had laws regulating child labor. But the courts often ruled against such laws, and families—needing extra income—sometimes ignored them. Parents sent children off to jobs with orders to lie about their ages.

A FERMENT OF IDEAS: CHALLENGING THE STATUS QUO

A dramatic shift in ideas became one of the most important forces behind progressive reform. Most of the ideas focused on the role of the environment in shaping human behavior. Progressive reformers accepted society's growing complexity, called for factual treatment of piecemeal problems, allowed room for new theories, and, above all, rejected age-encrusted divine or natural "laws" in favor of thoughts and actions that worked.

A new doctrine called pragmatism emerged in this ferment of ideas. It came from William James, a brilliant Harvard psychologist who became the key figure in American thought from the 1890s to World War I. A warm, tolerant person, James was impatient with theories that regarded truth as abstract. Truth, he believed, should work for the individual, and it worked best not in abstraction, but in action.

People, James thought, not only were shaped by their environment; they shaped it. In *Pragmatism* (1907), he praised "tough-minded" individuals who could live effectively in a world with no easy answers. The tough-minded accepted change; they knew how to pick manageable problems, gather facts, discard ideas that did not work, and act on those that did. Ideas that worked became truth.

The most influential educator of the Progressive Era, John Dewey, applied pragmatism to educational reform. A friend and disciple of William James, he argued that thought evolves in relation to the environment and that education is directly related to experience. In 1896, Dewey founded a separate School of Pedagogy at the University of Chicago, with a laboratory in which educational theory based on the newer philosophical and psychological studies could be tested and practiced.

Dewey introduced an educational revolution that stressed children's needs and capabilities. He opposed memorization, rote learning, and dogmatic, authoritarian teaching methods; he emphasized personal growth, free inquiry, and creativity.

Rejecting the older view of the law as universal and unchanging, lawyers and legal theorists instead viewed it as a reflection of the environment—an instrument for social change. Law reflected the environment that shaped it. A movement grew among judges for "sociological jurisprudence" that related the law to social reform.

In Denver, Colorado, after Judge Ben Lindsey sentenced a boy to reform school for stealing coal, the boy's mother rushed forward and, grief-stricken, beat her head against the wall. Lindsey investigated the case and found that the father was a smelting worker dying of lead poisoning; the family needed coal for heat. From such experiences, Lindsey concluded that children were not born with a genetic tendency to crime; they were made good or bad by the environment in which they grew. Lindsey "sentenced" youthful offenders to education and good care. He worked for playgrounds, slum clearance, public baths, and technical schools.

Socialism, a reformist political philosophy, grew dramatically before World War I. Eugene V. Debs, president of the American Railway Union, in 1896 formed the Social Democratic party. Gentle and reflective, not at all the popular image of the wild-eyed radical, Debs was thrust into prominence by the Pullman strike. In 1901, he formed the important Socialist party of America. Neither Debs nor the party ever developed a cohesive platform, nor was Debs an effective organizer. But he was eloquent, passionate, and visionary. An excellent speaker, he captivated audiences, attacking the injustices of capitalism and urging a workers' republic.

Some of Eugene Debs's supporters surround the "Red Special," the train Debs used in his 1908 presidential campaign. To attract voters to his socialist message, Debs traveled over 9000 miles in less than four weeks. A Detroit newspaper, trying to discredit the socialist candidate, criticized Debs's use of a "magnificent parlor car."

The Socialist party of America enlisted some intellectuals, factory workers, disillusioned Populists, tenant farmers, miners, and lumberjacks. By 1911, there were Socialist mayors in thirty-two cities. Although its doctrines were aimed at an urban proletariat, the Socialist party drew support in rural Texas, Missouri, Arkansas, Idaho, and Washington. In Oklahoma, it attracted as much as one-third of the vote. Most Socialists who won promised progressive reform rather than threatening to overthrow capitalists.

Although torn by factions, the Socialist party doubled in membership between 1904 and 1908, then tripled in the four years after that. Running for president, Debs garnered 100,000 votes in 1900; 400,000 in 1904; and 900,000 in 1912, the party's peak year.

REFORM IN THE CITIES AND STATES

Progressive reformers realized government could be a crucial agent in accomplishing their goals. They wanted to curb the influence of "special interests" and, through such measures of political reform as the direct primary and the direct election of senators, make government follow the public will. Once it did, they welcomed government action at whatever level was appropriate.

As a result of this thinking, the use of federal power increased, as did the power and prestige of the presidency. Progressives not only lobbied for government-sponsored reform but also worked actively in their home neighborhoods, cities, and states; much of the significant change occurred in local settings, outside the national limelight. Most important, the progressives believed in the ability of experts to solve problems. At every level—local, state, and federal—thousands of commissions and agencies took form. Staffed by trained experts, they oversaw a multitude of matters ranging from railroad rates to public health.

INTEREST GROUPS AND THE DECLINE OF POPULAR POLITICS

Placing government in the hands of experts was one way to get it out of the hands of politicians and political parties. The direct primary was another way. These initiatives and others like them were part of a fundamental change in the way Americans viewed their political system.

As one sign of the change, fewer and fewer people were going to the polls. Voter turnout dropped dramatically after 1900, when the intense partisanship of the decades after the Civil War gave way to media-oriented political campaigns based largely on the personalities of the candidates. From 1876 to 1900, the average turnout in presidential elections was 77 percent. From 1900 to 1916, it was 65 percent, and in the 1920s, it dropped to 52 percent, close to the average today. Turnout was lowest among young people, immigrants, the poor, and, ironically, the newly enfranchised women.

There were numerous causes for the falloff, but among the most important was the fact that people had found another way to achieve some of the objectives they had once assigned to political parties. They had found the "interest group," a means of action that assumed importance in this era and became a major feature of politics ever after. Professional societies, trade associations, labor organizations, farm lobbies, and scores of other interest groups worked outside the party system to pressure government for things their members wanted. Social workers, women's clubs, reform groups, and others learned to apply pressure in similar ways, and the result was much significant legislation of the Progressive Era.

Reform in the Cities

During the early years of the twentieth century, urban reform movements, many of them born in the depression of the 1890s, spread across the nation. In 1894, the National Municipal League was organized, and it became the forum for debate over civic reform, changes in the tax laws, and municipal ownership of public utilities. Within a few years, nearly every city had a variety of clubs and organizations directed at improving the quality of city life.

In city after city, reformers reordered municipal government. Tightening controls on corporate activities, they broadened the scope of utility regulation and restricted city franchises. They updated tax assessments, often skewed in favor of corporations, and tried to clean up the electoral machinery. Devoted to efficiency, they developed a trained civil service to oversee planning and operations. The generation of the 1880s also had believed in civil service, but the goal then was mostly negative: to get spoilsmen out and "good" people in. Now the goal was efficiency and, above all, results.

In constructing their model governments, urban reformers often turned to recent advances in business management and organization. They stressed continuity and expertise, a system in which professional experts staffed a government overseen by elected officials. At the top, the elected leader surveyed the breadth of city, state, or national affairs and defined directions. Below, a corps of experts—trained in the various disciplines of the new society—funneled the definition into specific scientifically based policies.

Reformers created a growing number of regulatory commissions and municipal departments. They hired engineers to oversee utility and water systems, physicians and nurses to improve municipal health, and city planners to oversee park and highway development.

In the race for reform, a number of city mayors won national reputations—among them Seth Low in New York City and Hazen S. Pingree in Detroit—working to modernize taxes, clean up politics, lower utility rates, and control the awarding of valuable city franchises.

In Cleveland, Ohio, Tom L. Johnson demonstrated an innovative approach to city government. A millionaire who had made his fortune manipulating city franchises, Johnson one day read Henry George's *Progress and Poverty* and turned to reform. Elected mayor of Cleveland, he served from 1901 to 1909. Believing in an informed citizenry, he held outdoor meetings in huge tents. He used colorful charts to give Cleveland residents a course in utilities and taxation. He cut down on corruption, cut off special privilege, updated taxes, and gave Cleveland a reputation as the country's best governed city.

Tom L. Johnson (in derby hat) and companions in a car known as the "Red Devil," the first automobile used in a political campaign. Johnson, who made his fortune in the streetcar business, served as mayor of Cleveland from 1901 to 1909. His administration, noted for its efficiency and many municipal reforms, also waged a long and bitter fight with streetcar business interests opposed to Johnson's efforts to lower streetcar fares to make them affordable for working-class people. Muckraking journalist Lincoln Steffens praised Johnson's Cleveland as "the best-governed city in America."

ACTION IN THE STATES

Reformers soon discovered, however, that many problems lay beyond a city's boundaries, and they turned for action to the state governments. From the 1890s to 1920, reformers worked to stiffen state laws regulating the labor of women and children, to create and strengthen commissions to regulate railroads and utilities, to impose corporate and inheritance taxes, to improve mental and penal institutions, and to allocate more funds for state universities, which were viewed as the training ground for the experts and educated citizenry needed for the new society.

New York was one of the states that led the way in adopting significant reforms. Around 1905, a series of dramatic investigations in the state revealed a systematic and corrupt alliance between politicians and business leaders in the gas, electricity, and insurance industries—all of which directly touched the general public. An angry public responded immediately, supporting greater state regulation and management by independent expert commissions. In 1905 and

1906, the state established regulatory boards to oversee utilities and insurance; it also outlawed corporate contributions to political campaigns and restricted business lobbying in the state legislature.

To regulate business, virtually every state created regulatory commissions empowered to examine corporate books and hold public hearings. Building on earlier experience, state commissions after 1900 were given new power to initiate actions, rather than await complaints, and in some cases to set maximum prices and rates. Dictating company practices, they pioneered regulatory methods later adopted in federal legislation of 1906 and 1910.

Historians have long praised the regulation movement, but the commissions did not always act wisely or even in the public interest. Elective commissions often produced commissioners who had little knowledge of corporate affairs. In addition, to win election, some promised specific rates or reforms, obligations that might bias the commission's investigative functions. Appointive commissions sometimes fared better, but they too had to oversee extraordinarily complex businesses such as the railroads.

To the progressives, commissions offered a way to end the corrupt alliance between business and politics. There was another way, too, and that was to "democratize" government by reducing the power of politicians and increasing the influence of the electorate. To do that, progressives backed three measures to make officeholders responsive to popular will: the initiative, which allowed voters to propose new laws; the referendum, which allowed them to accept or reject a law at the ballot box; and the recall, which gave them a way to remove an elected official from office.

Oregon adopted the initiative and referendum in 1902; by 1912, twelve states had them. That year Congress added the Seventeenth Amendment to the Constitution to provide for the direct election of U.S. senators. By 1916, all but three states had direct primaries, which allowed the people, rather than nominating conventions, to choose candidates for office.

Robert M. La Follette became the most famous reform governor. In 1901, he became governor of Wisconsin, and in the following six years, he put together the "Wisconsin Idea," one of the most important reform programs in the history of state government. He established an industrial commission, the first in the country, to regulate factory safety and sanitation. He improved education, workers' compensation, public utility controls, and resource conservation. He lowered railroad rates and raised railroad taxes. Under La Follette's prodding, Wisconsin became the first state to adopt a direct primary for all political nominations. It also became the first to adopt a state income tax. Theodore Roosevelt called La Follette's Wisconsin "the laboratory of democracy," and the Wisconsin Idea soon spread to many other states.

The most famous of the reform leaders in the states was Wisconsin's Robert M. "Fighting Bob" La Follette, pictured here campaigning in Cumberland, Wisconsin, in 1897.

After 1905, the progressives looked more and more to Washington. For one thing, Teddy Roosevelt was there, with his zest for publicity and his alluring grin. But progressives also had a growing sense that many concerns—corporations and conservation, factory safety and child labor—crossed state lines. Federal action seemed desirable; specific reforms fit into a larger plan perhaps best seen from the nation's center. Within a few years, the focus of progressivism shifted to Washington.

THE REPUBLICAN ROOSEVELT

When President William McKinley died of gunshot wounds in September 1901, Vice President Theodore Roosevelt succeeded him in the White House. The new president initially vowed to carry on McKinley's policies. He continued some, developed others of his own, and in the end brought to them all the particular exuberance of his own personality.

At age 42, Roosevelt was then the youngest president in American history. In contrast to the dignified McKinley, he was open, aggressive, and high-spirited. At his desk by 8:30 every morning, he worked through the day, usually with visitors for breakfast, lunch, and dinner. Politicians, labor leaders, industrialists, poets, artists, and writers paraded through the White House.

If McKinley cut down on presidential isolation, Roosevelt virtually ended it. The presidency, he thought, was the "bully pulpit," a forum of ideas and leadership for the nation. The president was "a steward of the people bound actively and affirmatively to do all he could for the people." Self-confident, Roosevelt enlisted talented associates, including Elihu Root, secretary of war and later secretary of state; William Howard Taft, secretary of war; Gifford Pinchot, the nation's chief forester and leading conservationist; and Oliver Wendell Holmes, Jr., whom he named to the Supreme Court.

In 1901, Roosevelt invited Booker T. Washington, the prominent African American educator, to dinner at the White House. Many Southerners protested—"a crime equal to treason," a newspaper said—and they protested again when Roosevelt appointed several African Americans to important federal offices in South Carolina and Mississippi. At first, Roosevelt considered building a biracial "black-and-tan" southern Republican party, thinking it would foster racial progress and his own renomination in 1904.

But Roosevelt soon retreated. In some areas of the South, he supported "lily-white" Republican organizations, and his policies often reflected his own belief in African American inferiority. He said nothing when a race riot broke out in Atlanta in 1906, although twelve persons died. He joined others in blaming African American soldiers stationed near Brownsville, Texas, after a night of violence there in August 1906. Acting quickly and on little evidence, he discharged "without honor" three companies of African American troops. Six of the soldiers who were discharged held the Congressional Medal of Honor.

BUSTING THE TRUSTS

"There is a widespread conviction in the minds of the American people that the great corporations known as trusts are in certain of their features and tendencies hurtful to the general welfare," Roosevelt reported to Congress in 1901. Like most people, however, the president wavered on the trusts. Large-scale production and industrial growth, he believed, were natural and beneficial; they needed only to be controlled. Still he distrusted the trusts' impact on local enterprise and individual opportunity. Distinguishing between "good" and "bad" trusts, he pledged to protect the former while controlling the latter.

In 1903, Roosevelt asked Congress to create a Department of Commerce and Labor, with a Bureau of Corporations empowered to investigate corporations engaged in interstate commerce. Congress balked; Roosevelt called in reporters and, in an off-the-record interview, charged that John D. Rockefeller had organized the opposition to the measure. The press spread the word, and in the outcry that followed, the proposal passed easily in a matter of weeks. Roosevelt was delighted. With the new Bureau of Corporations publicizing its findings, he thought, the glare of publicity would eliminate most corporate abuses.

Roosevelt also undertook direct legal action. On February 18, 1902, he instructed the Justice Department to bring suit against the Northern Securities Company for violation of the Sherman Antitrust Act. It was a shrewd move. A mammoth holding company, Northern Securities controlled the massive rail networks of the Northern Pacific, Great Northern, and Chicago, Burlington & Quincy railroads.

In 1904, the Supreme Court, in a 5 to 4 decision, upheld the suit against Northern Securities and ordered the company dissolved. Roosevelt was jubilant, and he followed up the victory with several other antitrust suits. In 1902, he had moved against the beef trust, an action applauded by western farmers and urban consumers alike. After a lull, he initiated suits in 1906 and 1907 against the American Tobacco Company, the Du Pont Corporation, the New Haven Railroad, and Standard Oil.

But Roosevelt's policies were not always clear, nor his actions always consistent. He asked for (and received) business support in his bid for reelection in 1904. Large donations came in from industrial leaders, and J. P. Morgan himself later testified that he gave $150,000 to Roosevelt's campaign. In 1907, acting in part to avert a threatened financial panic, the president permitted Morgan's U.S. Steel to absorb the Tennessee Coal and Iron Company, an important competitor.

Roosevelt, in truth, was not a trustbuster, although he was frequently called that. William Howard Taft, his successor in the White House, initiated forty-three antitrust indictments in four years—nearly twice as many as the twenty-five Roosevelt initiated in the seven years of his presidency. Instead, Roosevelt used antitrust threats to keep businesses within bounds. Regulation, he believed, was a better way to control large-scale enterprise.

"SQUARE DEAL" IN THE COALFIELDS

A few months after announcing the Northern Securities suit, Roosevelt intervened in a major labor dispute involving the anthracite coal miners of northeastern Pennsylvania. Led by John Mitchell, a moderate labor leader, the United Mine Workers demanded wage increases, an eight-hour workday, and company recognition of the union. The coal companies refused, and in May 1902, 140,000 miners walked off the job. The mines closed.

As the months passed and the strike continued, coal prices rose. With winter coming on, schools, hospitals, and factories ran short of coal. Public opinion turned against the companies. Morgan and other industrial leaders privately urged them to settle, but George F. Baer, head of one of the largest companies, refused.

Roosevelt was furious. Complaining of the companies' arrogance, he invited both sides in the dispute to an October 1902 conference at the White House. There, Mitchell took a moderate tone and offered to submit the issues to arbitration, but the companies again refused to budge. Roosevelt ordered the army to prepare to seize the mines and then leaked word of his intent to Wall Street leaders.

Alarmed, Morgan and others again urged settlement of the dispute, and at last the companies retreated. They agreed to accept the recommendations of an independent commission the president would appoint. In late October, the strikers returned to work, and in March 1903, the commission awarded them a 10 percent wage increase and a cut in working hours. It recommended, however, against union recognition. The coal companies, in turn, were encouraged to raise prices to offset the wage increase.

More and more, Roosevelt saw the federal government as an honest and impartial "broker" between powerful elements in society. Rather than leaning toward labor, he pursued a middle way to curb corporate and labor abuses, abolish privilege, and enlarge individual opportunity. Conservative by temperament, he sometimes backed reforms in part to head off more radical measures.

During the 1904 campaign, Roosevelt called his actions in the coal miners' strike a "square deal" for both labor and capital, a term that stuck to his administration. Roosevelt was not the first president to take a stand for labor, but he was the first to bring opposing sides in a labor dispute to the White House to settle it.

ROOSEVELT PROGRESSIVISM AT ITS HEIGHT

In the election of 1904, the popular Roosevelt soundly drubbed his Democratic opponent, Alton B. Parker of New York, and the Socialist party candidate, Eugene V. Debs of Indiana. Roosevelt attracted a large campaign chest and won votes everywhere. After a landslide victory, he pledged that "under no circumstances will I be a candidate for or accept another nomination," a statement he later regretted.

THE ELECTION OF 1904

CANDIDATE	PARTY	POPULAR VOTE	ELECTORAL VOTE
T. Roosevelt	Republican	7,626,593	336
Parker	Democrat	5,082,898	140
Debs	Socialist	402,489	0
Swallow	Prohibition	258,596	0

REGULATING THE RAILROADS

Following his election, Roosevelt in late 1904 laid out a reform program that included railroad regulation, employers' liability for federal employees, greater federal control over corporations, and laws regulating child labor, factory inspection, and slum clearance in the District of Columbia. He turned first to railroad regulation. In 1903, he had worked with Congress to pass the Elkins Act to prohibit railroad rebates and increase the powers of the Interstate Commerce Commission (ICC). The Elkins Act, a moderate law, was framed with the consent of railroad leaders. In 1904 and 1905, the president wanted much more, and he urged Congress to empower the ICC to set reasonable and nondiscriminatory rates and prevent inequitable practices.

Widespread demand for railroad regulation strengthened Roosevelt's hand. In the Midwest and Far West, the issue was a popular one, and reform governors La Follette in Wisconsin and Albert B. Cummins in Iowa urged federal action. Roosevelt maneuvered cannily. As the legislative battle opened, he released figures showing that Standard Oil had reaped $750,000 a year from railroad rebates. He also skillfully traded congressional support for a strong railroad measure in return for his promise to postpone a reduction of the tariff, a stratagem that came back to plague President Taft.

Triumph came with passage of the Hepburn Act of 1906. A significant achievement, the act strengthened the rate-making power of the Interstate Commerce Commission. It increased membership on the ICC from five to seven, empowered it to fix reasonable maximum railroad rates, and broadened its jurisdiction to include oil pipeline, express, and sleeping car companies. ICC orders were binding, pending any court appeals, thus placing the burden of proof of injustice on the companies. Delighted, Roosevelt viewed the Hepburn Act as a major step in his plan for continuous expert federal control over industry.

CLEANING UP FOOD AND DRUGS

Soon Roosevelt was dealing with two other important bills, these aimed at regulating the food and drug industries. Muckraking articles had touched frequently on filthy conditions in meatpacking houses, but Upton Sinclair's *The Jungle* (1906) set off a storm of indignation. Ironically, Sinclair had set out to write a novel about the packinghouse workers, the "wage slaves of the Beef Trust," hoping to do for wage slavery what Harriet Beecher Stowe had done for chattel slavery. But readers largely ignored his story of the workers and seized instead on the graphic descriptions of the things that went into their meat.

Sinclair was disappointed at the reaction. "I aimed at the public's heart," he later said, "and by accident I hit it in the stomach." He had, indeed. After reading *The Jungle,* Roosevelt ordered an investigation. The result, he said, was "hideous,"

A poster for the movie version of Upton Sinclair's The Jungle *promises a "wonderful story of the beef packing industry." The conditions that Sinclair described in the book brought to public attention the scandals of the meatpacking industry knowingly selling diseased meat and the filthy, disease-ridden, dangerous conditions in which the workers toiled for their subsistence wages.*

The Pure Food and Drug Act, passed in 1906, did not ban the sale of patent medicines, nor did it curb the exaggerated claims of some of the manufacturers. Reid's Cough and Kidney Remedy, for example, promised relief within 20 minutes from colds, coughs, bronchitis, hoarseness, whooping cough, asthma, and kidney disease. The makers of the drug complied with the Pure Food and Drug Act by noting on the bottle's label that the remedy contained 30 percent grain alcohol.

and he threatened to publish the entire "sickening report" if Congress did not act. Meat sales plummeted in the United States and Europe. Demand for reform grew. Alarmed, the meatpackers themselves supported a reform law, which they hoped would be just strong enough to still the clamor. The Meat Inspection Act of 1906, stronger than the packers wanted, set rules for sanitary meatpacking and government inspection of meat products.

A second measure, the Pure Food and Drug Act, passed more easily. Samuel Hopkins Adams, a muckraker, exposed the dangers of patent medicines in several sensational articles in *Collier's*. Patent medicines, Adams pointed out, contained mostly alcohol, drugs, and "undiluted fraud." Dr. Harvey W. Wiley, the chief chemist in the Department of Agriculture, led a "poison squad" of young assistants who experimented with the medicines. With evidence in hand, Wiley pushed for regulation; Roosevelt and the recently reorganized American Medical Association joined the fight, and the act passed on June 30, 1906. Requiring manufacturers to list certain ingredients on the label, it represented a pioneering effort to ban the manufacture and sale of adulterated, misbranded, or unsanitary food or drugs.

CONSERVING THE LAND

An expert on birds, Roosevelt loved nature and the wilderness, and some of his most enduring accomplishments came in the field of conservation. Working closely with Gifford Pinchot, chief of the Forest Service, he established the first comprehensive national conservation policy. To Roosevelt, conservation meant the wise use of natural resources, not locking them away, so those who thought the wilderness should be preserved rather than developed generally opposed his policies.

Using experts in the federal government, Roosevelt undertook a major reclamation program, created the federal Reclamation Service, and strengthened

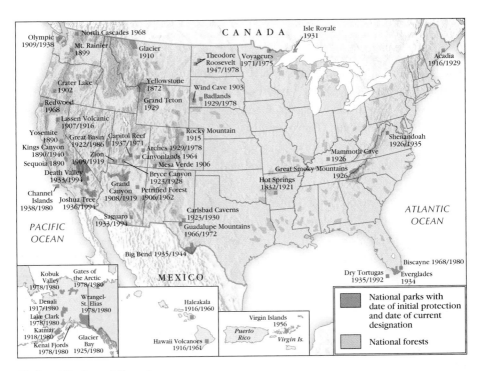

National Parks and Forests
During the presidency of Theodore Roosevelt, who considered conservation his most important domestic achievement, millions of acres of land were set aside for national parks and forests.

the forest preserve program in the Department of Agriculture. Broadening the concept of conservation, he placed power sites, coal lands, and oil reserves as well as national forest in the public domain.

When Roosevelt took office in 1901, there were 45 million acres in government preserves. In 1908, there were almost 195 million.

As 1908 approached, Roosevelt became increasingly strident in his demand for sweeping reforms. He attacked "malefactors of great wealth," urged greater federal regulatory powers, criticized the conservatism of the federal courts, and called for laws protecting factory workers. Many business leaders blamed him for a severe financial panic in the autumn of 1907, and conservatives in Congress stiffened their opposition. Divisions between Republican conservatives and progressives grew.

Immensely popular, Roosevelt prepared in 1908 to turn over the White House to William Howard Taft, his close friend and colleague. As expected, Taft soundly defeated the Democratic standard-bearer William Jennings Bryan, who was making his third try for the presidency. The Republicans retained control of Congress. Taft prepared to move into the White House, ready and willing to carry on the Roosevelt legacy.

THE ORDEAL OF WILLIAM HOWARD TAFT

The Republican national convention that nominated Taft had not satisfied either Roosevelt or Taft. True, Taft won the presidential nomination as planned, but conservative Republicans beat back the attempts of progressive Republicans to influence the convention. They named a conservative, James S. Sherman, for vice president and built a platform that reflected conservative views on labor, the courts, and other issues. Taft wanted a pledge to lower the tariff but got only a promise of revision, which might lower—or raise—it. La Follette, Cummins, Jonathan P. Dolliver of Iowa, Albert J. Beveridge of Indiana, and other progressive Republicans were openly disappointed.

Taking office in 1909, Taft felt "just a bit like a fish out of water." The son of a distinguished Ohio family and a graduate of Yale Law School, he became an Ohio judge, solicitor general of the United States, and a judge of the federal circuit court. In 1900, McKinley asked him to head the Philippine Commission, charged with the difficult and challenging task of forming a civil government in the Philippines. Later Taft was named the first governor general of the Philippines. In 1904, Roosevelt appointed him secretary of war. In all these positions, Taft made his mark as a skillful administrator. He worked quietly behind the scenes, avoided controversy, and shared none of Roosevelt's zest for politics. A good-natured man, Taft had personal charm and infectious humor. He fled from fights rather

THE ELECTION OF 1908

CANDIDATE	PARTY	POPULAR VOTE	ELECTORAL VOTE
Taft	Republican	7,676,258	321
Bryan	Democrat	6,406,801	162
Debs	Socialist	420,380	0
Chafin	Prohibition	252,821	0

than seeking them out, and he disliked political maneuvering, preferring instead quiet solitude. "I don't like politics," he said. "I don't like the limelight."

Weighing close to 300 pounds, Taft enjoyed conversation, golf and bridge, good food, and plenty of rest. Compared to the hardworking Roosevelt and Wilson, he was lazy. He was also honest, kindly, and amiable, and in his own way he knew how to get things done.

Taft's years as president were not happy. As it turned out, he presided over a Republican party torn with tensions that Roosevelt had either brushed aside or concealed. The tariff, business regulation, and other issues split conservatives and progressives, and Taft often wavered or sided with the conservatives. Taft revered the past and distrusted change; although an ardent supporter of Roosevelt, he never had Roosevelt's faith in the ability of government to impose reform and alter individual behavior. He named five corporation attorneys to his cabinet, leaned more to business than to labor, and spoke of a desire to "clean out the unions."

At that time and later, Taft's reputation suffered by comparison to the flair of Roosevelt and the moral majesty of Woodrow Wilson. He deserved better. Taft was an honest and sincere president, who—sometimes firm, sometimes befuddled—faced a series of important and troublesome problems during his term of office.

PARTY INSURGENCY

Taft started his term with an attempt to curb the powerful Republican speaker of the House, Joseph "Uncle Joe" Cannon of Illinois. Using the powers of his position, Cannon had been setting House procedures, appointing committees, and virtually dictating legislation. Straightforward and crusty, he often opposed reform. In March 1909, thirty Republican congressmen joined Taft's effort to curb Cannon's power, and the president sensed success. But Cannon retaliated and, threatening to block all tariff bills, forced a compromise. Taft stopped the anti-Cannon campaign in return for Cannon's pledge to help with tariff cuts.

Republicans were divided over the tariff, and there was a growing party insurgency against high rates. The House quickly passed a bill providing for lower rates, but in the Senate, protectionists raised them. Senate leader Nelson W. Aldrich of Rhode Island introduced a revised bill that added more than eight hundred amendments to the rates approved in the House.

Angry, La Follette and other Republicans attacked the bill as the child of special interests. In speeches on the Senate floor they called themselves "progressives," invoked Roosevelt's name, and urged Taft to defeat the high-tariff proposal. Caught between protectionists and progressives, Taft wavered, then tried to compromise. In the end, he backed Aldrich. The Payne-Aldrich Act, passed in November 1909, called for higher rates than the original House bill, though it lowered them from the Dingley Tariff of 1897. An unpopular law, Payne-Aldrich helped discredit Taft and revealed the tensions in the Republican party.

Republican progressives and conservatives drifted apart. Thin-skinned, Taft resented the persistent pinpricks of the progressives who criticized him for virtually everything he did. He tried to find middle ground but leaned more and more toward the conservatives. During a nationwide speaking tour in the autumn of 1909, he praised Aldrich, scolded the low-tariff insurgents, and called the Payne-Aldrich Act "the best bill that the Republican party ever passed."

By early 1910, progressive Republicans in Congress no longer looked to Taft for leadership. As before, they challenged Cannon's power, and Taft wavered. In an outcome embarrassing to the president, the progressives won, managing to curtail Cannon's authority to dictate committee assignments and schedule debate. In progressive circles there was growing talk of a Roosevelt return to the White House.

THE BALLINGER-PINCHOT AFFAIR

The conservation issue dealt another blow to relations between Roosevelt and President Taft. In 1909, Richard A. Ballinger, Taft's secretary of the interior, offered for sale a million acres of public land that Pinchot, who had stayed on as Taft's chief forester, had withdrawn from sale. Pinchot, fearing that Ballinger would hurt conservation programs, protested and, seizing on a report that Ballinger had helped sell valuable Alaskan coal lands to a syndicate that included J. P. Morgan, asked Taft to intervene. After investigating, Taft supported Ballinger on every count, although he asked Pinchot to remain in office.

Pinchot refused to drop the matter. Behind the scenes, he provided material for two anti-Ballinger magazine articles. Taft had had enough. He fired the insubordinate Pinchot, an action which, though appropriate, again lost support for

Taft. Newspapers followed the controversy for months, and muckrakers assailed the administration's "surrender" to Morgan and other "despoilers of the national heritage."

The Ballinger-Pinchot controversy obscured Taft's important contributions to conservation. He won from Congress the power to remove lands from sale, and he used it to conserve more land than Roosevelt did. Still, the controversy tarred Taft, and it upset his old friend Roosevelt.

TAFT ALIENATES THE PROGRESSIVES

Interested in railroad regulation, Taft backed a bill in 1910 to empower the ICC to fix maximum railroad rates. Progressive Republicans favored that plan but attacked Taft's suggestion of a special Commerce Court to hear appeals from ICC decisions because most judges were traditionally conservative in outlook and usually rejected attempts to regulate railroad rates. They also thought the railroads had been consulted too closely in drawing up the bill. Democratic and Republican progressives tried to amend the bill to strengthen it; Taft made support of it a test of party loyalty.

The Mann-Elkins Act of 1910 gave something to everyone. It gave the ICC power to set rates, stiffened long- and short-haul regulations, and placed telephone and telegraph companies under ICC jurisdiction. These provisions delighted progressives. The act also created a Commerce Court, pleasing conservatives. In a trade-off, conservative Republican Senate leaders pledged their support for a statehood bill for Arizona and New Mexico, which were both predicted to be Democratic. In return, enough Democratic senators promised to vote for the Commerce Court provision to pass the bill. While pleased with the act, Taft and the Republican party lost further ground. In votes on key provisions of the Mann-Elkins Act, Taft raised the issue of party regularity, and progressive Republicans defied him.

Taft attempted to defeat the progressive Republicans in the 1910 elections. He helped form antiprogressive organizations, and he campaigned against progressive Republican candidates for the Senate. Progressive Republicans retaliated by organizing a nationwide network of anti-Taft Progressive Republican Clubs.

The 1910 election results were a major setback for Taft and the Republicans—especially conservative Republicans. A key issue in the election, the high cost of living, gave an edge to the progressive wings in both major parties, lending support to their attack on the tariff and the trusts. In party primaries, progressive Republicans overwhelmed most Taft candidates, and in the general election, they tended to fare better than the conservatives, which increased progressive influence in the Republican party.

For Republicans of all persuasions, however, it was a difficult election. The Democrats swept the urban-industrial states from New York to Illinois. New York, New Jersey, Indiana, and even Taft's Ohio elected Democratic governors. For the first time since 1894, Republicans lost control of both the House and the Senate. Disappointed, Taft called it "not only a landslide, but a tidal wave and holocaust all rolled into one general cataclysm."

Despite the defeat, Taft pushed through several important measures before his term ended. With the help of the new Democratic House, he backed laws to regulate safety in mines and on railroads, create a Children's Bureau in the federal government, establish employers' liability for all work done on government contracts, and mandate an eight-hour workday for government workers.

In 1909, Congress initiated a constitutional amendment authorizing an income tax, which, along with woman suffrage, was one of the most significant legislative measures of the twentieth century. The Sixteenth Amendment took effect early in 1913. A few months later, an important progressive goal was realized when the direct election of senators was ratified as the Seventeenth Amendment to the Constitution.

An ardent supporter of competition, Taft relentlessly pressed a campaign against trusts. The Sherman Antitrust Act, he said in 1911, "is a good law that ought to be enforced, and I propose to enforce it." That year, the Supreme Court in cases against Standard Oil and American Tobacco established the "rule of reason," which allowed the Court to determine whether a business presented "reasonable" restraint on trade. Taft thought the decisions gave the Court too much discretion, and he pushed ahead with the antitrust effort.

In October 1911, he sued U.S. Steel for its acquisition of the Tennessee Coal and Iron Company in 1907. Roosevelt had approved the acquisition, and the suit seemed designed to impugn his action. Enraged, he attacked Taft, and Taft, for once, fought back. He accused Roosevelt of undermining the conservative tradition in the country and began working to undercut the influence of the progressive Republicans. Increasingly now, Roosevelt listened to anti-Taft Republicans who urged him to run for president in 1912. In February 1912, he announced, "My hat is in the ring."

DIFFERING PHILOSOPHIES IN THE ELECTION OF 1912

Delighted Democrats looked on as Taft and Roosevelt fought for the Republican nomination. As the incumbent president, Taft controlled the party machinery, and when the Republican convention met in June 1912, he took the nomination. In early July, the Democrats met in Baltimore and, confident of victory for the first time in two decades, struggled through forty-six ballots before finally nominating Woodrow Wilson, the reform-minded governor of New Jersey.

A month later, some of the anti-Taft and progressive Republicans—now calling themselves the Progressive party—whooped it up in Chicago. Roosevelt was there to give a stirring "Confession of Faith." Naming Roosevelt for president at its convention, the Progressive party—soon known as the Bull Moose party—set the stage for the first important three-cornered presidential contest since 1860.

Taft was out of the running before the campaign even began. "I think I might as well give up so far as being a candidate is concerned," he said in July. "There are so many people in the country who don't like me." Taft stayed at home and made no speeches before the election. Roosevelt campaigned strenuously, even completing one speech after being shot in the chest by an anti-third-term fanatic. "I have a message to deliver," he said, "and will deliver it as long as there is life in my body."

Roosevelt's message involved a program he called the New Nationalism. An important phase in the shaping of twentieth-century American political thought, it demanded a national approach to the country's affairs and a strong president to deal with them. The New Nationalism called for efficiency in government and society. It exalted the executive and the expert; urged social-justice reforms to protect workers, women, and children; and accepted "good" trusts. The New Nationalism encouraged large concentrations of labor and capital, serving the nation's interests under a forceful federal executive.

For the first time in the history of a major political party, the Progressive campaign enlisted women in its organization. Jane Addams, the well-known settlement worker, seconded Roosevelt's nomination at Chicago, and she and other women played a leading role in his campaign. Some labor leaders, who saw potential for union growth, and some business leaders, who saw relief from destructive competition and labor strife, supported the new party.

Wilson, in contrast, set forth a program called the New Freedom that emphasized business competition and small government. A states' rights Democrat, he wanted to rein in federal authority, using it only to sweep away special privilege, release individual energies, and restore competition. Drawing on the thinking of Louis D. Brandeis, the brilliant shaper of reform-minded law, he echoed the Progressive party's social-justice objectives, while continuing to attack Roosevelt's planned state. For Wilson, the vital issue was not a planned economy but a free one. "The history of liberty is the history of the limitation of governmental power," he said in October 1912. "If America is not to have free enterprise, then she can have freedom of no sort whatever."

In the New Nationalism and New Freedom, the election of 1912 offered competing philosophies of government. Both Roosevelt and Wilson saw the central problem of the American nation as economic growth and its effect on individuals and society. Both focused on the government's relation to business, both

THE ELECTION OF 1912

CANDIDATE	PARTY	POPULAR VOTE	ELECTORAL VOTE
Wison	Democrat	6,296,547	435
Roosevelt	Progressive (Bull Moose)	4,118,571	88
Taft	Republican	3,486,720	8
	Minor Parties	1,135,697	0

believed in bureaucratic reform, and both wanted to use government to protect the ordinary citizen. But Roosevelt welcomed federal power, national planning, and business growth; Wilson distrusted them all.

On election day, Wilson won 6.3 million votes to 4.1 million for Roosevelt (who had recovered quickly from his wound) and 900,000 for Eugene V. Debs, the Socialist party candidate. Taft, the incumbent president, finished third with 3.5 million votes; he carried only Vermont and Utah for 8 electoral votes. The Democrats also won outright control of both houses.

WOODROW WILSON'S NEW FREEDOM

If under Roosevelt social reform took on the excitement of a circus, "under Wilson it acquired the dedication of a sunrise service." Born in Virginia in 1856 and raised in the South, Wilson was the son of a Presbyterian minister. As a young man, he wanted a career in public service, and he trained himself carefully in history and oratory. A moralist, he reached judgments easily. Once reached, almost nothing shook them. Opponents called him stubborn and smug.

After graduating from Princeton University and the University of Virginia Law School, Wilson found that practicing law bored him. Shifting to history, from 1890 to 1902 he served as professor of jurisprudence and political economy at Princeton. In 1902, he became president of the university. Eight years later, he was governor of New Jersey, where he led a campaign to reform election procedures, abolish corrupt practices, and strengthen railroad regulation.

Wilson's rise was rapid, and he knew relatively little about national issues and personalities. But he learned fast, and in some ways the lack of experience served him well. He had few political debts to repay, and he brought fresh perspectives to older issues. Ideas intrigued Wilson; details bored him. Although he

Woodrow Wilson and outgoing President William Taft share a carriage ride en route to Wilson's inauguration following his victory in the election of 1912. The Republican Party split over the election with the Progressives supporting Theodore Roosevelt and his Bull Moose ticket and the party machine supporting Taft. Even though the Republican split encouraged the Democrats to hope for victory, it still took forty-six ballots before they could agree on Wilson as their candidate.

was outgoing at times, he could also be cold and aloof, and aides soon learned that he preferred loyalty and flattery to candid criticism.

Prone to self-righteousness, Wilson often turned differences of opinion into bitter personal quarrels. Like Roosevelt, he believed in strong presidential leadership. A scholar of the party system, he cooperated closely with Democrats in Congress, and his legislative record placed him among the most effective presidents in terms of passing bills that he supported. Forbidding in individual conversation, Wilson could move crowds with graceful oratory. Unlike Taft, and to a greater degree than Roosevelt, he could inspire.

His inaugural address was eloquent. "The Nation," he said, "has been deeply stirred, stirred by a solemn passion, stirred by the knowledge of wrong, of ideals lost, of government too often debauched and made an instrument of evil. The feelings with which we face this new age of right and opportunity sweep across our heartstrings like some air out of God's own presence."

THE NEW FREEDOM IN ACTION

On the day of his inauguration, Wilson called Congress into special session to lower the tariff. When the session opened on April 8, 1913, Wilson himself was there, the first president since John Adams in 1801 to appear personally before Congress. In forceful language, he urged Congress to reduce tariff rates.

As the bill moved through Congress, Wilson showed exceptional skill. He worked closely with congressional leaders, and when lobbyists threatened the bill in the Senate, he appealed for popular support. The result was a triumph for Wilson and the Democratic party. The Underwood Tariff Act passed in 1913. The first tariff cut in nineteen years, it lowered rates about 15 percent and removed duties from sugar, wool, and several other consumer goods.

To make up for lost revenue, the act also levied a modest graduated income tax, authorized under the just ratified Sixteenth Amendment. Marking a significant shift in the American tax structure, it imposed a 1 percent tax on individuals and corporations earning more than $4,000 annually and an additional 1 percent tax on incomes more than $20,000. Above all, the act reflected a new unity within the Democratic party, which had worked together to pass a difficult tariff law.

Wilson himself emerged as an able leader. "At a single stage," a foreign editor said, "[he went] from the man of promise to the man of achievement." Encouraged by his success, Wilson decided to keep Congress in session through the hot Washington summer. Now he focused on banking reform, and the result in December 1913 was the Federal Reserve Act, the most important domestic law of his administration.

Meant to provide the United States with a sound yet flexible currency, the act established the country's first efficient banking system since Andrew Jackson killed the second Bank of the United States in 1832. It created twelve regional banks, each to serve the banks of its district. The regional banks answered to a Federal Reserve Board, appointed by the president, which governed the nationwide system.

A compromise law, the act blended public and private control of the banking system. Private bankers owned the federal reserve banks but answered to the presidentially appointed Federal Reserve Board. The reserve banks were authorized to issue currency, and through the discount rate—the interest rate at which they loaned money to member banks—they could raise or lower the amount of money in circulation. Monetary affairs no longer depended solely on the price of gold. Within a year, nearly half the nation's banking resources were in the Federal Reserve System.

The Clayton Antitrust Act (1914) completed Wilson's initial legislative program. Like previous antitrust measures, it reflected confusion over how to disci-

pline a growing economy without putting a brake on output. In part it was a response to the revelations of the Pujo Committee of the House, publicized by
Brandeis in a disquieting series of articles, "Other People's Money." In its investigation of Wall Street, the committee discovered a pyramid of money and power
capped by the Morgan-Rockefeller empire that, through "interlocking directorates," controlled companies worth $22 billion, more than one-tenth of the na-
tional wealth.

The Clayton Act outlawed such directorates and prohibited unfair trade practices. It forbade pricing policies that created monopoly, and it made corporate officers personally responsible for antitrust violations. Delighting Samuel Gompers
and the labor movement, the act declared that unions were not conspiracies in
restraint of trade, outlawed the use of injunctions in labor disputes unless necessary to protect property, and approved lawful strikes and picketing. To Gompers's
dismay, the courts continued to rule against union activity.

A related law established a powerful Federal Trade Commission to oversee
business methods. Composed of five members, the commission could demand
special and annual reports, investigate complaints, and order corporate compliance, subject to court review. At first, Wilson opposed the commission concept,
which was an approach more suitable to Roosevelt's New Nationalism, but he
changed his mind and, along with Brandeis, called it the cornerstone of his antitrust plan. To reassure business leaders, he appointed a number of conservatives
to the new commission and to the Federal Reserve Board.

In November 1914, Wilson proudly announced the completion of his New
Freedom program. Tariff, banking, and antitrust laws promised a brighter future,
he said, and it was now "a time of healing because a time of just dealing." Many
progressives were aghast. That Wilson could think society's ills were so easily
cured, the *New Republic* said, "casts suspicion either upon his own sincerity or
upon his grasp of the realities of modern social and industrial life."

WILSON MOVES TOWARD THE NEW NATIONALISM

Distracted by the start of war in Europe, Wilson gave less attention to domestic
issues for more than a year. When he returned to concern with reform, he
adopted more and more of Roosevelt's New Nationalism and blended it with the
New Freedom to set it off from his earlier policies.

One of Wilson's problems was the Congress. To his dismay, the Republicans
gained substantially in the 1914 elections. Reducing the Democratic majority in
the House, they swept key industrial and farm states. At the same time, a recession struck the economy, which had been hurt by the outbreak of the European
war in August 1914. Some business leaders blamed the tariff and other New

Freedom laws. On the defensive, Wilson soothed business sentiment and invited bankers and industrialists to the White House. He allowed companies fearful of antitrust actions to seek advice from the Justice Department.

Preoccupied with such problems, Wilson blocked significant action in Congress through most of 1915. He refused to support a bill providing minimum wages for women workers, sidetracked a child labor bill on the ground that it was unconstitutional, and opposed a bill to establish long-term credits for farmers. He also refused to endorse woman suffrage, arguing that the right to vote was a state matter, not a federal one.

Wilson's record on race disappointed African Americans and many progressives. He had appealed to African American voters during the 1912 election, and a number of African American leaders campaigned for him. Soon after the inauguration, Oswald Garrison Villard, a leader of the NAACP, proposed a National Race Commission to study the problem of race relations. Initially sympathetic, Wilson rejected the idea because he feared he might lose southern Democratic votes in Congress. A Virginian himself, he appointed many Southerners to high office, and for the first time since the Civil War, southern views on race dominated the nation's capital.

At one of Wilson's first cabinet meetings, the postmaster general proposed the segregation of all African Americans in the federal service. No one dissented, including Wilson. Several government bureaus promptly began to segregate workers in offices, shops, rest rooms, and restaurants. Employees who objected were fired. African American leaders protested, and they were joined by progressive leaders and clergymen. Surprised at the protest, Wilson backed quietly away from the policy, although he continued to insist that segregation benefited African Americans.

As the year 1916 began, Wilson made a dramatic switch in focus and again pushed for substantial reforms. The result was a virtual river of reform laws, which was significant because it began the second, more national-minded phase of the New Freedom. With scarcely a glance over his shoulder, Wilson embraced important portions of Roosevelt's New Nationalism campaign.

In part, he was motivated by the approaching presidential election. A minority president, Wilson owed his victory in 1912 to the split in the Republican party, now almost healed. Roosevelt was moving back into Republican ranks, and there were issues connected with the war in Europe that he might use against Wilson. Moreover, many progressives were voicing disappointment with Wilson's limited reforms and his failure to support more advanced reform legislation on matters such as farm credits, child labor, and woman suffrage.

Moving quickly to patch up the problem, Wilson named Brandeis to the Supreme Court in January 1916. Popular among progressives, Brandeis was also the first person of Jewish faith to serve on the Court. When conservatives in the Senate tried to defeat the nomination, Wilson stood firm and won, earning further praise from progressives, Jews, and others. In May, he reversed his stand on farm loans and accepted a rural credits bill to establish farm-loan banks backed by federal funds. The Federal Farm Loan Act of 1916 created a Federal Farm Loan Board to give farmers credit similar to the Federal Reserve's benefits for trade and industry.

Wilson was already popular within the labor movement. Going beyond Roosevelt's policies, which had sought a balance between business and labor, he defended union recognition and collective bargaining. In 1913, he appointed William B. Wilson, a respected leader of the United Mine Workers, as the first head of the Labor Department, and he strengthened the department's Division of Conciliation. In 1914, in Ludlow, Colorado, state militia and mine guards fired machine guns into a tent colony of coal strikers, killing twenty-one men,

Miners in Ludlow, Colorado, went on strike in September 1913 for better working conditions and union recognition. Expecting eviction from company housing, they built a tent colony near the company town. The company, John D. Rockefeller's Colorado Fuel and Iron Company, hired guards to break the strike. On April 20, 1914, state troops and guards sprayed the tents with gunfire, then soaked the tents with kerosene and set the colony afire. Twenty-one of the colonists died, including eleven children.

women, and children. Outraged, Wilson stepped in and used federal troops to end the violence while negotiations to end the strike went on.

In August 1916, a threatened railroad strike again revealed Wilson's sympathies with labor. Like Roosevelt, he invited the two sides to the White House, where he urged the railroad companies to grant an eight-hour day and labor leaders to abandon the demand for overtime pay. Labor leaders accepted the proposal; railroad leaders did not. "I pray God to forgive you, I never can," Wilson said as he left the room. Soon he signed the Adamson Act (1916) that imposed the eight-hour day on interstate railways and established a federal commission to study the railroad problem. Ending the threat of a strike, the act marked a milestone in the expansion of the federal government's authority to regulate industry.

With Wilson leading the way, the flow of reform legislation continued until the election. The Federal Workmen's Compensation Act established workers' compensation for government employees. The Keating-Owen Act, the first federal child labor law, prohibited the shipment in interstate commerce of products manufactured by children under the age of 14. It too expanded the authority of the federal government, though it was soon struck down by the Supreme Court. The Warehouse Act authorized licensed warehouses to issue negotiable receipts for farm products deposited with them.

In September, Wilson signed the Tariff Commission Act creating an expert commission to recommend tariff rates. The same month, the Revenue Act of 1916 boosted income taxes and furthered tax reform. Four thousand members of the National American Woman Suffrage Association cheered when Wilson finally came out in support of woman suffrage. Two weeks later he endorsed the eight-hour day for all the nation's workers.

The 1916 presidential election was close, but Wilson won it on the issues of peace and progressivism. By the end of 1916, he and the Democratic party had enacted most of the important parts of Roosevelt's Progressive party platform of 1912. To do it, Wilson abandoned portions of the New Freedom and accepted much of the New Nationalism, including greater federal power and commissions governing trade and tariffs. In mixing the two programs, he blended some of the competing doctrines of the Progressive Era, established the primacy of the federal government, and foreshadowed the pragmatic outlook of Franklin D. Roosevelt's New Deal of the 1930s.

The election of 1916 showed how deeply progressivism had reached into American society. "We have in four years," Wilson said that fall, "come very near to carrying out the platform of the Progressive party as well as our own; for we are also progressives."

In retrospect, however, 1916 also marked the beginning of progressivism's decline. At most, the years of progressive reform lasted from the 1890s to

1921, and in large measure they were compressed into a single decade between 1906 and American entry into World War I in 1917. Many problems the progressives addressed but did not solve; and some important ones, such as race, they did not even tackle. Yet their regulatory commissions, direct primaries, city improvements, and child labor laws marked an era of important and measured reform.

The institution of the presidency expanded. From the White House radiated executive departments that guided a host of activities. Independent commissions, operating within flexible laws, supplemented executive authority.

These developments owed a great deal to both Roosevelt and Wilson. To manage a complex society, TR developed a simple formula: expert advice; growth-minded policies; a balancing of business, labor, and other interests; the use of publicity to gather support; and stern but often permissive oversight of the economy. TR strengthened the executive office, and he called on the newer group of professional, educated, public-minded citizens to help him. "I believe in a strong executive," he said; "I believe in power."

At first, Wilson had different ideas, wanting to dismantle much of Roosevelt's governing apparatus. But driven by outside forces and changes in his own thinking, Wilson soon moved in directions similar to those Roosevelt had championed. Starting out to disperse power, he eventually consolidated it.

Through such movements, government at all levels accepted responsibility for the welfare of various elements in the social order. A reform-minded and bureaucratic society took shape, in which men and women, labor and capital, political parties and social classes competed for shares in the expansive framework of twentieth-century life. But there were limits to reform. As both TR and Wilson found, the new government agencies, understaffed and underfinanced, depended on the responsiveness of those they sought to regulate.

Soon there was a far darker cloud on the horizon. The spirit of progressivism rested on a belief in human potential, peace, and progress. After Napoleon's defeat in 1815, a century of peace began in western Europe, and as the decades passed, war seemed a dying institution. "It looks as though this were going to be the age of treaties rather than the age of wars," an American said in 1912, "the century of reason rather than the century of force." It was not to be. Two years later, the most devastating of wars broke out in Europe, and in 1917, Americans were fighting on the battlefields of France.

24

THE NATION AT WAR

O n the morning of May 1, 1915, the German government took out an advertisement in the *New York World* warning Americans and other voyagers against setting sail for England: "Travellers intending to embark on the Atlantic voyage are reminded that a state of war exists between Germany and her allies and Great Britain and her allies"; anyone sailing "in the war zone on ships of Great Britain or her allies do so at their own risk." At 12:30 that afternoon, the British steamship *Lusitania* set sail from New York to Liverpool. Secretly, it carried a load of ammunition as well as passengers.

The steamer was two hours late in leaving, but it held several speed records and could easily make up the time. Six days later, back on schedule, it reached the coast of Ireland. German U-boats were known to patrol the dangerous waters. When the war began in 1914, Great Britain imposed a naval blockade of Germany. In return, Germany in February 1915 declared the area around the British Isles a war zone; all enemy vessels, armed or unarmed, were at risk. Germany had only a handful of U-boats, but the submarines were a new and frightening weapon. On behalf of the United States, President Woodrow Wilson protested the German action, and on February 10, he warned Germany of its "strict accountability" for any American losses resulting from U-boat attacks.

Off Ireland, the passengers lounged on the deck of the *Lusitania*. As if it were peacetime, the ship sailed straight ahead, with no zigzag maneuvers to throw off pursuit. But the submarine U-20 was there, and its commander, seeing a large ship, fired a single torpedo. Seconds after it hit, a boiler exploded and blew a hole in the *Lusitania*'s side. The ship listed immediately, hindering the launching of lifeboats, and in eighteen minutes it sank. Nearly 1200 people died, including 128 Americans. As the ship's bow lifted and went under, the U-20 commander for the first time read the name: *Lusitania.*

The sinking, the worst since the *Titanic* went down with 1500 people in 1912, horrified Americans. Theodore Roosevelt called it "an act of piracy" and demanded war. Most Americans, however, wanted to stay out of war; like Wilson, they hoped negotiations could solve the problem. "There is such a thing," Wilson said a few days after the sinking, "as a man being too proud to fight. There is such a thing as a nation being so right that it does not need to convince others by force."

In a series of diplomatic notes, Wilson demanded a change in German policy. The first *Lusitania* note (May 13, 1915) called on Germany to abandon unrestricted submarine warfare, disavow the sinking, and compensate for lost American lives. Germany sent an evasive reply, and Wilson drafted a second *Lusitania* note (June 9) insisting on specific pledges. Fearful the demand would

With the sinking of the Lusitania, *the American people learned firsthand of the horrors of total war. President Wilson's decision to protest the incident through diplomacy kept the United States out of the war—but only temporarily.*

lead to war, Secretary of State William Jennings Bryan resigned rather than sign the note. Wilson sent it anyway and followed with a third note (July 21)—almost an ultimatum—warning Germany that the United States would view similar sinkings as "deliberately unfriendly."

Unbeknownst to Wilson, Germany had already ordered U-boat commanders not to sink passenger liners without warning. In August 1915, a U-boat mistakenly torpedoed the British liner *Arabic,* killing two Americans. Wilson protested, and Germany, eager to keep the United States out of the war, backed down. The *Arabic* pledge (September 1) promised that U-boats would stop and warn liners, unless they tried to resist or escape. Germany also apologized for American deaths on the *Arabic,* and for the rest of 1915, U-boats hunted freighters, not passenger liners.

Although Wilson's diplomacy had achieved his immediate goal, the *Lusitania* and *Arabic* crises contained the elements that led to war. Trade and travel tied the world together, and Americans no longer hid behind safe ocean barriers. New weapons, such as the submarine, strained old rules of international law. But while Americans sifted the conflicting claims of Great Britain and Germany, they hoped for peace. A generation of progressives, inspired with confidence in human progress, did not easily accept war.

Wilson also hated war, but he found himself caught up in a worldwide crisis that demanded the best in American will and diplomacy. In the end, diplomacy failed, and in April 1917, the United States entered a war that changed the nation's history.

A NEW WORLD POWER

As they had in the late nineteenth century, Americans after 1900 continued to pay relatively little attention to foreign affairs. Newspapers and magazines ran stories every day about events abroad, but people paid closer attention to what was going on at home.

For Americans at the time, foreign policy was something to be left to the president in office, an attitude the presidents themselves favored. Foreign affairs became an arena in which they could exert a free hand largely unchallenged by Congress or the courts, and Roosevelt, Taft, and Wilson all took advantage of the opportunity to do so.

The foreign policy they pursued from 1901 to 1920 was aggressive and nationalistic. During these years, the United States intervened in Europe, the Far East, and Latin America. It dominated the Caribbean.

In 1898, the United States left the peace table possessing the Philippines, Puerto Rico, and Guam. Holding distant possessions required a colonial policy; it also required a change in foreign policy, reflecting an outward approach. From the Caribbean to the Pacific, policymakers paid attention to issues and countries they had earlier ignored. Like other nations in these years, the United States built a large navy, protected its colonial empire, and became increasingly involved in international affairs.

The nation also became more and more involved in economic ventures abroad. Turning out goods from textiles to steel, mass production industries sold products overseas, and financiers invested in Asia, Africa, Latin America, and Europe. During the years between the Spanish-American War and World War I, investments abroad rose from $445 million to $2.5 billion. While investments and trade never wholly dictated American foreign policy, they fostered greater involvement in foreign lands.

"I TOOK THE CANAL ZONE"

Convinced the United States should take a more active international role, Theodore Roosevelt spent his presidency preparing the nation for world power. Working with Secretary of War Elihu Root, he modernized the army, using lessons learned from the war with Spain. Determined to end dependence on the British fleet, Roosevelt doubled the strength of the navy during his term in office.

Stretching his authority to the limits, Roosevelt took steps to consolidate the country's new position in the Caribbean and Central America. European powers, which had long resisted American initiatives there, now accepted American supremacy. Preoccupied with problems in Europe and Africa, Great Britain agreed to U.S. plans for an Isthmian canal in Central America and withdrew much of its military force from the area.

Roosevelt wanted a canal to link the Atlantic and Pacific oceans across the isthmus connecting North and South America. Secretary of State John Hay negotiated with Britain the Hay-Pauncefote Treaty of 1901 that permitted the United States to construct and control an Isthmian canal, providing it would be free and open to ships of all nations.

Delighted, Roosevelt began selecting the route. One route, fifty miles long, wandered through the rough, swampy terrain of the Panama region of Colombia. A French company had recently tried and failed to dig a canal there. To the northwest, another route ran through mountainous Nicaragua. Although two hundred miles in length, it followed natural waterways, a factor that would make construction easier.

An Isthmian Canal Commission investigated both routes in 1899 and recommended the shorter route through Panama. Roosevelt backed the idea, and he authorized Hay to negotiate an agreement with the Colombian chargé d'affaires, Thomas Herrán. The Hay-Herrán Convention (1903) gave the United States a

99-year lease, with option for renewal, on a canal zone 6 miles in width. In exchange, the United States agreed to pay Colombia a onetime fee of $10 million and an annual rental of $250,000.

To Roosevelt's dismay, the Colombian Senate rejected the treaty, in part because it infringed on Colombian sovereignty. The Colombians also wanted more money. Roosevelt considered seizing Panama, then hinted he would welcome a Panamanian revolt from Colombia. In November 1903, the Panamanians took the hint, and Roosevelt moved quickly to support them. Sending the cruiser *Nashville* to prevent Colombian troops from putting down the revolt, he promptly recognized the new Republic of Panama.

Two weeks later, the Hay-Bunau-Varilla Treaty with Panama granted the United States control of a canal zone 10 miles wide across the Isthmus of Panama. In return, the United States guaranteed the independence of Panama and agreed to pay the same fees offered Colombia. On August 15, 1914, the first ocean steamer sailed through the completed canal, which had cost $375 million to build.

Roosevelt's actions angered many Latin Americans. Trying to soothe feelings, Wilson agreed in 1914 to pay Colombia $25 million in cash, give it preferential treatment in using the canal, and express "sincere regret" over American actions. Roosevelt was furious, and his friends in the Senate blocked the agreement. Colombian-American relations remained strained until 1921, when the two countries signed a treaty that included Wilson's first two provisions but omitted the apology.

For his part, Roosevelt took great pride in the canal, calling it "by far the most important action in foreign affairs." Defending his methods, he said in 1911, "If I had followed traditional conservative methods, I would have submitted a dignified state paper of 200 pages to Congress and the debate on it would have been going on yet; but I took the Canal Zone and let Congress debate; and while the debate goes on the Canal does also."

THE ROOSEVELT COROLLARY

With interests in Puerto Rico, Cuba, and the canal, the United States developed a Caribbean policy to ensure its dominance in the region. It established protectorates over some countries and subsidized others to keep them dependent.

From 1903 to 1920, the United States intervened often in Latin America to protect the canal, promote regional stability, and exclude foreign influence. One problem worrying American policymakers was the scale of Latin American debts to European powers. Many countries in the Western Hemisphere owed money to European governments and banks, and often these nations were poor, prone to revolution, and unable to pay. The situation invited European intervention. In

1902, Venezuela defaulted on debts; England, Germany, and Italy sent Venezuela an ultimatum and blockaded its ports. American pressure forced a settlement of the issue, but the general problem remained.

Roosevelt was concerned about it, and in 1904, when the Dominican Republic defaulted on its debts, he was ready with a major announcement. Known as the Roosevelt Corollary of the Monroe Doctrine, the policy warned Latin American nations to keep their affairs in order or face American intervention.

Applying the new policy immediately, Roosevelt in 1905 took charge of the Dominican Republic's revenue system. American officials collected customs and saw to the payment of debt. Within two years, Roosevelt also established protectorates in Cuba and Panama. Continued by Taft, Wilson, and other presidents, the Roosevelt Corollary guided American policy in Latin America until the 1930s, when Franklin D. Roosevelt's Good Neighbor policy replaced it.

VENTURES IN THE FAR EAST

The Open Door policy toward China and possession of the Philippine Islands shaped American actions in the Far East. Roosevelt wanted to balance Russian and Japanese power, and he was not unhappy at first when war broke out between them in 1904. As Japan won victory after victory, however, Roosevelt grew worried. Acting on a request from Japan, he offered to mediate the conflict, and both Russia and Japan accepted: Russia because it was losing, and Japan because it was financially drained.

In August 1905, Roosevelt convened a peace conference at Portsmouth, New Hampshire. The conference ended the war, but Japan emerged as the dominant force in the Far East. Adjusting policy, Roosevelt sent Secretary of War Taft to Tokyo to negotiate the Taft-Katsura Agreement (1905), which recognized Japan's dominance over Korea in return for its promise not to invade the Philippines. Giving Japan a free hand in Korea violated the Open Door policy, but Roosevelt argued that he had little choice.

Relations between Japan and the United States were again strained in 1907 when the California legislature considered a bill limiting the immigration of Japanese laborers into the state. As resentment mounted in Japan, Roosevelt obtained from Japan the "Gentlemen's Agreement" (1907) promising to stop the flow of Japanese agricultural laborers into the United States.

In case Japan viewed his policy as a sign of weakness, Roosevelt sent sixteen battleships of the new American fleet around the world, including a stop in Tokyo in October 1908. European naval experts felt certain Japan would attack the fleet, but the Japanese welcomed it. For the moment, Japanese-American relations improved, and in 1908 the two nations, in an exchange of diplomatic notes, reached the comprehensive Root-Takahira Agreement in which they promised to maintain the status quo in the Pacific, uphold the Open Door, and support Chinese independence.

TAFT AND DOLLAR DIPLOMACY

In foreign as well as domestic affairs, President Taft tried to continue Roosevelt's policies. For secretary of state he chose Philander C. Knox, Roosevelt's attorney general, and together they pursued a policy of "dollar diplomacy" to promote American financial and business interests abroad. The policy had profit-seeking motives, but it also aimed to substitute economic ties for military alliances with the idea of increasing American influence and bringing lasting peace.

Intent, like Roosevelt, on supremacy in the Caribbean, Taft worked to replace European loans with American ones, thereby reducing the danger of outside meddling. In 1909, he asked American bankers to assume the Honduran debt in order to fend off English bondholders, and in 1911 he helped Nicaragua secure a large loan in return for American control of Nicaragua's National Bank. When Nicaraguans revolted against the agreement, Taft sent marines to put them down.

In the Far East, Knox worked closely with Willard Straight, an agent of American bankers, who argued that dollar diplomacy was the financial arm of the Open Door. Straight had close ties to Edward H. Harriman, the railroad magnate, who wanted to build railroads in Manchuria in northern China. Roosevelt had tacitly promised Japan he would keep American investors out of the area, and Knox's plan reversed the policy. Trying to organize an international syndicate to loan China money to purchase the Manchurian railroads, Knox approached England, Japan, and Russia. In January 1910, all three turned him down.

The outcome was a blow to American policy and prestige in Asia. Russia and Japan found reasons to cooperate with each other and staked out spheres of influence in violation of the Open Door. Japan resented Taft's initiatives in Manchuria, and China's distrust of the United States deepened. Instead of cultivating friendship, as Roosevelt had envisioned, Taft had started an intense rivalry with Japan for commercial advantage in China.

FOREIGN POLICY UNDER WILSON

When he took office in 1913, Woodrow Wilson knew little about foreign policy. During the 1912 campaign he mentioned foreign policy only when it affected domestic concerns. "It would be the irony of fate if my administration had to deal chiefly with foreign affairs," he said to a friend before becoming president. And so it was. During his two terms, Wilson faced crisis after crisis in foreign affairs, including the outbreak of World War I.

The idealistic Wilson believed in a principled, ethical world in which militarism, colonialism, and war were brought under control. He stressed moral purposes over material interests and said during one crisis, "The force of America is the force of moral principle." Rejecting the policy of dollar diplomacy, Wilson initially chose a course of moral diplomacy, designed to bring right to the world, preserve peace, and extend to other peoples the blessings of democracy.

CONDUCTING MORAL DIPLOMACY

William Jennings Bryan, whom Wilson appointed as secretary of state, was also an amateur in foreign relations. He was a fervent pacifist, and like Wilson, he believed in the American duty to "help" less favored nations.

In 1913 and 1914, he embarked on an idealistic campaign to negotiate treaties of arbitration throughout the world. Known as "cooling-off" treaties, they provided for submitting all international disputes to permanent commissions of investigation. Neither party could declare war or increase armaments until the investigation ended, usually within one year. The idea drew on the era's confidence in commissions and the sense that human reason, given time for emotions to fade, could settle problems without war. Bryan negotiated cooling-off treaties with thirty nations, including Great Britain, France, and Italy. Germany refused to sign one. Based on a generous idea, the treaties were naive, and they did not work.

Wilson and Bryan promised a dramatic new approach in Latin America, concerned not with the "pursuit of material interest" but with "human rights" and "national integrity." Signaling the change, in 1913 they negotiated the treaty with Colombia apologizing for Roosevelt's Panamanian policy. Yet in the end, Wilson, distracted by other problems and impatient with the results of his idealistic approach, continued the Roosevelt-Taft policies. He defended the Monroe Doctrine, gave unspoken support to the Roosevelt Corollary, and intervened in Latin America more than had either Roosevelt or Taft.

In 1914, Wilson negotiated a treaty with Nicaragua to grant the United States exclusive rights to build a canal and lease sites for naval bases. This treaty made Nicaragua an American satellite. In 1915, he sent marines into Haiti to quell a revolution; they stayed until 1934. In 1916, he occupied the Dominican Republic, establishing a protectorate that lasted until 1924. By 1917, American troops "protected" Nicaragua, Haiti, the Dominican Republic, and Cuba—four nations that were U.S. dependencies in all but name.

TROUBLES ACROSS THE BORDER

Wilson's moral diplomacy encountered one of its greatest challenges across the border in Mexico. Porfirio Díaz, president of Mexico for thirty-seven years, was overthrown in 1911, and a liberal reformer, Francisco I. Madero, succeeded him. But Madero could not keep order in the troubled country, and opponents of his reforms undermined him. With support from wealthy landowners, the army, and the Catholic Church, General Victoriano Huerta ousted Madero in 1913, threw him in jail, and arranged his murder. Most European nations immediately recognized Huerta, but Wilson, calling him a "butcher," refused to do so. Instead, he announced a new policy toward revolutionary regimes in Latin America. To win American recognition, they must not only exercise power but reflect "a just government based upon law, not upon arbitrary or irregular force."

On that basis, Wilson withheld recognition from Huerta and maneuvered to oust him. Early in 1914, he stationed naval units off Mexico's ports to cut off arms shipments to the Huerta regime. The action produced trouble. On April 9, 1914, several American sailors, who had gone ashore in Tampico to purchase supplies, were arrested. They were promptly released, but the American admiral demanded an apology and a 21-gun salute to the American flag. Huerta agreed—if the Americans also saluted the Mexican flag.

Wilson asked Congress for authority to use military force if needed; then, just as Congress acted, he learned that a German ship was landing arms at Veracruz on Mexico's eastern coast. With Wilson's approval, American warships shelled the harbor, and marines went ashore. Against heavy resistance, they took the city. Outraged, Mexicans of all factions denounced the invasion, and for a time the two countries hovered on the edge of war.

Retreating hastily, Wilson explained that he desired only to help Mexico. Argentina, Brazil, and Chile came to his aid with an offer to mediate the dispute, and tensions eased. In July 1914, weakened by an armed rebellion, Huerta resigned. Wilson recognized the new government, headed by Venustiano Carranza, an associate of Madero. Early in 1916, Francisco ("Pancho") Villa, one of Carranza's generals, revolted. Hoping to goad the United States into an action that would help him seize power, he raided border towns, injuring American civilians.

Stationing militia along the border, Wilson ordered General John J. Pershing on a punitive expedition to seize Villa in Mexico. Pershing led six thousand troops deep into Mexican territory. At first, Carranza agreed to the drive, but as the Americans pushed farther and farther into his country, he changed his mind. As the wily Villa eluded Pershing, Carranza protested bitterly, and Wilson, worried about events in Europe, ordered Pershing home.

Wilson's policy had laudable goals; he wanted to help the Mexicans achieve political and agrarian reform. But his motives and methods were condescending. Wilson tried to impose gradual progressive reform on a society sharply divided along class and other lines. With little forethought, he interfered in the affairs of another country, and in doing so he revealed the themes—moralism, combined with pragmatic self-interest and a desire for peace—that also shaped his policies in Europe.

TOWARD WAR

In May 1914, Colonel Edward M. House, Wilson's close friend and adviser, sailed to Europe on a fact-finding mission. Tensions there were rising. "The situation is extraordinary," he reported to Wilson. ". . . There is too much hatred, too many jealousies."

In Germany, the ambitious Kaiser Wilhelm II coveted a world empire to match those of Britain and France. Germany had military treaties with Turkey and Austria-Hungary, a sprawling central European country of many nationalities. Linked in another alliance, England, France, and Russia agreed to aid each other in case of attack.

On June 28, 1914, a Bosnian assassin linked to Serbia murdered Archduke Franz Ferdinand, heir to the Austro-Hungarian throne. Within weeks, Germany, Turkey, and Austria-Hungary (the Central Powers) were at war with England, France, and Russia (the Allied Powers). Americans were shocked at the events. Wilson immediately proclaimed neutrality and asked Americans to remain "impartial in thought as well as in action."

The war, he said, was one "with which we have nothing to do, whose causes cannot touch us." In private, Wilson was stunned. A man who loved peace, he had long admired the British parliamentary system, and he respected the leaders of the British Liberal party, who supported social programs akin to his own. "Everything I love most in the world," he said, "is at stake."

THE NEUTRALITY POLICY

In general, Americans accepted neutrality. They saw no need to enter the conflict, especially after the Allies in September 1914 halted the first German drive toward Paris. America resisted involvement in other countries' problems, with the notable exception of Latin America, and had a tradition of freedom from foreign entanglements.

Many of the nation's large number of progressives saw additional reasons to resist. War, they thought, violated the very spirit of progressive reform. Why demand safer factories in which people could work and then kill them by the millions in war? To many progressives, moreover, England represented international finance, an institution they detested. Germany, on the other hand, had pioneered some of their favorite social reforms. Above all, progressives were sure that war would end reform. It consumed money and attention; it inflamed emotions.

As a result, Jane Addams, Florence Kelley, Frederic C. Howe, Lillian Wald, and other progressives fought to keep the United States out of war. In late 1915, they formed the American Union Against Militarism, to throw, they said, "a monkey wrench into the machinery" of war. In 1915, Addams and Wald helped organize the League to Limit Armament, and shortly thereafter, Addams and Carrie Chapman Catt formed the Woman's Peace Party to organize women against the war.

The war's outbreak also tugged at the emotions of millions of immigrant Americans. At the deepest level, a majority in the country, bound by common language and institutions, sympathized with the Allies and blamed Germany for the war. Like Wilson, many Americans admired English literature, customs, and law; they remembered Lafayette and the times when France had helped the United States in its early years. Germany, on the other hand, seemed arrogant and militaristic. When the war began, it invaded Belgium to strike at France and violated a treaty which the German chancellor called "just a scrap of paper."

Both sides sought to sway American opinion, and fierce propaganda campaigns flourished. German propaganda tended to stress strength and will; Allied propaganda called on historical ties and took advantage of German atrocities, both real and alleged. In the end, the propaganda probably made little difference. Ties of heritage and the course of the war, not propaganda, decided the American position. At the outset, no matter which side they cheered for, Americans of all persuasions preferred simply to remain at peace.

FREEDOM OF THE SEAS

The demands of trade tested American neutrality and confronted Wilson with difficult choices. Under international law, neutral countries were permitted to trade in nonmilitary goods with all belligerent countries. But Great Britain controlled the seas, and it intended to cut off shipments of war materials to the Central Powers.

As soon as war broke out, Britain blockaded German ports and limited the goods Americans could sell to Germany. American ships had to carry cargoes to neutral ports from which, after examination, they could be carried to Germany. As time passed, Britain stepped up the economic sanctions by forbidding the shipment to Germany of all foodstuffs and most raw materials, seizing and censoring mail, and "blacklisting" American firms that dealt directly with the Central Powers.

Again and again, Wilson protested against such infringements on neutral rights. Sometimes Britain complied, sometimes not, and Wilson often grew angry. But needing American support and supplies, Britain pursued a careful strategy to disrupt German-American trade without disrupting Anglo-American relations. When necessary, it promised to reimburse American businesses after the war's end.

Other than the German U-boats, there were no constraints on trade with the Allies, and a flood of Allied war orders fueled the American economy. To finance the purchases, the Allies turned to American bankers for loans. By 1917, loans to Allied governments exceeded $2 billion; loans to Germany came to only $27 million.

In a development that influenced Wilson's policy, the war produced the greatest economic boom in the nation's history. Loans and trade drew the United States ever closer to the Allied cause. And even though Wilson often protested English maritime policy, the protests involved American goods and money, whereas Germany's submarine policy threatened American lives.

THE U-BOAT THREAT

A relatively new weapon, the *Unterseeboot,* or submarine, strained the guidelines of international law. Traditional law required a submarine to surface, warn the target to stop, send a boarding party to check papers and cargo, then allow time for passengers and crew to board lifeboats before sinking the vessel. Flimsy and slow, submarines could ill afford to surface while the prey radioed for help. If they did surface, they might be rammed or blown up by deck guns.

When Germany announced the submarine campaign in February 1915, Wilson protested sharply, calling the sinking of merchant ships without checking cargo "a wanton act." The Germans promised not to sink American ships—an agreement that lasted until 1917—and thereafter the issue became the right of Americans to sail on the ships of belligerent nations. In March, an American citizen aboard the British liner *Falaba* perished when the ship was torpedoed off the Irish coast. Bryan urged Wilson to forbid Americans to travel in the war zones, but the president, determined to stand by the principles of international law, refused.

Wilson reacted more harshly in May and August of 1915 when U-boats sank the *Lusitania* and the *Arabic*. He demanded that the Germans protect passenger vessels and pay for American losses. At odds with Wilson's understanding of neutrality, Bryan resigned as secretary of state and was replaced by Robert Lansing, a lawyer and counselor in the State Department. Lansing brought a very different spirit to the job. He favored the Allies and believed that democracy was threat-

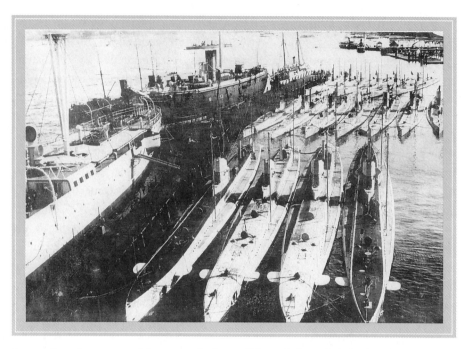

A new and terrifying weapon of the war was the German U-boat, which attacked silently and without warning.

ened in a world dominated by Germany. He urged strong stands against German violations of American neutrality.

In February 1916, Germany declared unrestricted submarine warfare against all armed ships. Lansing protested and told Germany it would be held strictly accountable for American losses. A month later, a U-boat torpedoed the unarmed French channel steamer *Sussex* without warning, injuring several Americans. Arguing that the sinking violated the *Arabic* pledge, Lansing urged Wilson to break relations with Germany. Wilson rejected the advice, but on April 18 he sent an ultimatum to Germany, stating that unless the Germans immediately called off attacks on cargo and passenger ships, the United States would sever relations.

The Kaiser, convinced he did not yet have enough submarines to risk war, yielded. In the *Sussex* pledge of May 4, 1916, he agreed to Wilson's demands and promised to shoot on sight only ships of the enemy's navy.

The *Sussex* pledge marked the beginning of a short period of friendly relations between Germany and the United States. The agreement applied not only to passenger liners but to all merchant ships, belligerent or not. There was one problem: Wilson had taken such a strong position that if Germany renewed submarine warfare on merchant shipping, war was likely. Most Americans, however, viewed the agreement as a diplomatic stroke for peace by Wilson, and the issues of peace and preparedness dominated the presidential election of 1916.

"He Kept Us Out of War"

The "preparedness" issue pitted antiwar groups against those who wanted to prepare for war. Bellicose as always, Teddy Roosevelt led the preparedness campaign. He called Wilson "yellow" for not pressing Germany harder and scoffed at the popular song "I Didn't Raise My Boy to Be a Soldier," which he compared to singing "I Didn't Raise My Girl to Be a Mother." Defending the military's state of readiness, Wilson refused to be stampeded just because "some amongst us are nervous and excited."

Roosevelt's campaign for preparedness became a personal attack on Wilson, whom TR called a coward and a weakling.

Wilson's position was attacked from both sides as preparedness advocates charged cowardice, while pacifists denounced any attempt at military readiness. The difficulty of his situation, plus the growing U-boat crisis, soon changed Wilson's mind. In mid-1915, he asked the War Department to increase military planning, and he quietly notified congressional leaders of a switch in policy. Later that year, Wilson approved large increases in the army and navy, a move that upset many peace-minded progressives.

For their standard-bearer in the presidential election of 1916, the Republicans nominated Charles Evans Hughes, a moderate justice of the Supreme Court. Hughes seemed to have all the qualifications for victory. A former reform governor of New York, he could lure back the Roosevelt progressives while at the same time appealing to the Republican conservatives. To woo the Roosevelt wing, Hughes called for a tougher line against Germany, thus allowing the Democrats to label him the "war" candidate.

The Democrats renominated Wilson in a convention marked by spontaneous demonstrations for peace. Determined to outdo Republican patriotism, Wilson himself had ordered the convention's theme to be "Americanism." The delegates were to sing "America" and "The Star-Spangled Banner" and to cheer any mention of America and the flag. They did it all dutifully but then broke into spontaneous applause at the mention of Wilson's careful diplomatic moves. As the keynote speaker reviewed them, the delegates shouted, "What did we do? What did we do?" The speaker shouted back, "We didn't go to war! We didn't go to war!"

Picking up the theme, perhaps with reservations, Wilson said in October, "I am not expecting this country to get into war." The campaign slogan "He kept us out of war" was repeated again and again, and just before the election, the Democrats took full-page ads in leading newspapers:

You Are Working—Not Fighting!
   Alive and Happy—Not Cannon Fodder!
   Wilson and Peace with Honor?
        or
   Hughes with Roosevelt and War?

On election night, Hughes had swept most of the East, and Wilson retired at 10 P.M. thinking he had lost. During the night, the results came in from California, New Mexico, and North Dakota; all supported Wilson—California by a mere 3773 votes. Wilson won with 9.1 million votes against 8.5 million for Hughes. Holding the Democratic South, he carried key states in the Midwest and West and took large portions of the labor and progressive vote. Women—who

THE ELECTION OF 1916

CANDIDATE	PARTY	POPULAR VOTE	ELECTORAL VOTE
Wilson	Democrat	9,127,695	277
Hughes	Republican	8,533,507	254
	Minor Parties	819,022	0

were then allowed to vote in presidential elections in twelve states—also voted heavily for Wilson.

THE FINAL MONTHS OF PEACE

Just before election day, Great Britain further limited neutral trade, and there were reports from Germany of a renewal of unrestricted submarine warfare. Fresh from his victory, Wilson redoubled his efforts for peace. Aware that time was running out, he hoped to start negotiations to end the bloodshed and create a peaceful postwar world.

In December 1916, he sent messages to both sides asking them to state their war aims. Should they do so, he pledged the "whole force" of the United States to end the war. The Allies refused, although they promised privately to negotiate if the German terms were reasonable. The Germans replied evasively and in January 1917 revealed their real objectives. Close to forcing Russia out of the war, Germany sensed victory and wanted territory in eastern Europe, Africa, Belgium, and France.

On January 22, in an eloquent speech before the Senate, Wilson called for a "peace without victory." Outlining his own ambitious aims, he urged respect for all nations, freedom of the seas, arms limitations, and a League of Nations to keep the peace. The speech made a great impression on many Europeans, but it was too late. The Germans had decided a few weeks before to unleash the submarines and gamble on a quick end to the war. Even as Wilson spoke, U-boats were in the Atlantic west of Ireland, preparing to attack.

On January 31, the German ambassador in Washington informed Lansing that beginning February 1, U-boats would sink on sight all ships—passenger or merchant, neutral or belligerent, armed or unarmed—in the waters around England and France. Staking everything on a last effort, the Germans calculated that if they could sink 600,000 tons of shipping a month, they could defeat

U.S. Losses to the German Submarine Campaign, 1916–1918

Tonnage of vessels sunk
(thousands)

England in six months. As he had pledged in 1916, Wilson broke off relations with Germany, although he still hoped for peace.

On February 25, the British government privately gave Wilson a telegram intercepted from Arthur Zimmermann, the German foreign minister, to the German ambassador in Mexico. A day later, Wilson asked Congress for authority to arm merchant ships to deter U-boat attacks. When La Follette and a handful of others threatened to filibuster, Wilson divulged the contents of the Zimmermann telegram. It proposed an alliance with Mexico in case of war with the United States, offering financial support and recovery of Mexico's "lost territory" in New Mexico, Texas, and Arizona.

Spurred by a wave of public indignation toward the Germans, the House passed Wilson's measure, but La Follette and others still blocked action in the Senate. On March 9, 1917, Wilson ordered merchant ships armed on his own authority. Three days later, he announced the arming, and on March 13, the navy instructed all vessels to fire on submarines. Between March 12 and March 21, U-boats sank five American ships, and Wilson decided to wait no longer.

He called Congress into special session and at 8:30 in the evening on April 2, 1917, asked for a declaration of war. "It is a fearful thing to lead this great peaceful people into war, into the most terrible and disastrous of all wars, civilization itself seeming to be in the balance. But the right is more precious than peace, and we shall fight for the things which we have always carried nearest our hearts,—

for democracy, . . . for the rights and liberties of small nations, for a universal dominion of right by such a concert of free peoples as shall bring peace and safety to all nations and make the world itself at last free."

Congressmen broke into applause and crowded the aisles to congratulate Wilson. "My message today was a message of death for our young men," he said afterward. "How strange it seems to applaud that."

Pacifists in Congress continued to hold out, and for four days they managed to postpone action. Finally, on April 6, the declaration of war passed, with fifty members of the House and six senators voting against it. Even then, the country was divided over entry into the war.

OVER THERE

With a burst of patriotism, the United States entered a war its new allies were in danger of losing. That same month, the Germans sank 881,000 tons of Allied shipping, the highest amount for any one month during the war. There were mutinies in the French army; a costly British drive in Flanders stalled. In November, the Bolsheviks seized power in Russia, and, led by V. I. Lenin, they soon signed a

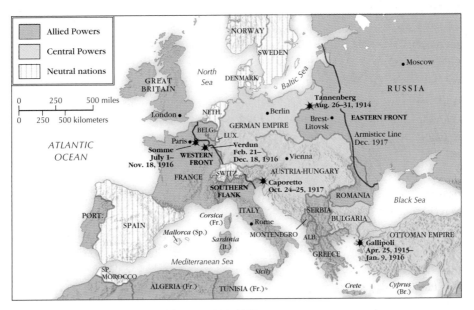

European Alliances and Battlefronts, 1914–1917
Allied forces suffered early defeats on the eastern front (Tannenberg) and in the Dardanelles (Gallipoli). In 1917, the Allies were routed on the southern flank (Caporetto); the western front then became the critical theater of the war.

Administered to soldiers in groups, the IQ test was used in World War I to classify recruits and determine which of them were "officer material." The results of the tests raised questions not only about the mental abilities and backgrounds of the men but also about possible biases in the tests themselves.

separate peace treaty with Germany, freeing German troops to fight in the West. German and Austrian forces routed the Italian army on the southern flank, and the Allies braced for a spring 1918 offensive.

MOBILIZATION

The United States was not prepared for war. Some Americans hoped the declaration of war itself might daunt the Germans; there were those who thought that naval escorts of Allied shipping would be enough. Others hoped money and arms supplied to the Allies would be sufficient to produce victory without sending troops.

Bypassing older generals, Wilson named John J. ("Black Jack") Pershing, leader of the Mexican campaign, to head the American Expeditionary Force (AEF). Pershing inherited an army unready for war. In April 1917, it had 200,000 officers and men, equipped with 300,000 old rifles, 1,500 machine guns, 55 out-of-date airplanes, and 2 field radio sets. Its most recent battle experience had been chasing Pancho Villa around northern Mexico. It had not caught him.

Although some in Congress preferred a voluntary army of the kind that had fought in the Spanish-American War, Wilson turned to conscription, which he believed was both efficient and democratic. In May 1917, Congress passed the Selective Service Act, providing for the registration of all men between the ages of 21 and 30 (later changed to 18 and 45). Early in June, 9.5 million men registered for the draft. By the end of the war, the act had registered 24.2 million men, about 2.8 million of whom were inducted into the army.

The draft included black men as well as white, and four African American regiments were among the first sent into action. Despite their contributions, however, no black soldiers were allowed to march in the victory celebrations that eventually took place in Paris. Nor were they included in a French mural of the different races in the war, even though black servicemen from English and French colonies were represented.

WAR IN THE TRENCHES

World War I may have been the most terrible war of all time, more terrible even than World War II and its vast devastation. After the early offensives, the European armies dug themselves into trenches only hundreds of yards apart in places. Artillery, poison gas, hand grenades, and a new weapon—rapid-fire machine guns—kept them pinned down.

Even in moments of respite, the mud, rats, cold, fear, and disease took a heavy toll. Deafening bombardments shook the earth, and there was a high incidence of shell shock. From time to time, troops went "over the top" of the trenches in an effort to break through the enemy's lines, but the costs were enormous. The German offensive at Verdun in 1916 killed 600,000 men; the British lost 20,000 on the first day of an offensive on the Somme.

The first American soldiers reached France in June 1917. By March of the following year, 300,000 Americans were there, and by war's end, 2 million men had crossed the Atlantic. No troop ships were sunk, a credit to the British and American navies. In the summer of 1917, Admiral William S. Sims, a brilliant American strategist, pushed through a convoy plan that used Allied destroyers to escort merchant vessels across the ocean. At first resisted by English captains who liked to sail alone, the plan soon cut shipping losses in half.

As expected, on March 21, 1918, the Germans launched a massive assault in western Europe. Troops from the Russian front added to the force, and by May they had driven Allied forces back to the Marne River, just 50 miles from Paris.

There, the Americans saw their first action. The American forces blocked the Germans at the town of Château-Thierry and four weeks later forced them out of Belleau Wood, a crucial stronghold. On July 15, the Germans threw everything into a last drive for Paris, but they were halted at the Marne, and in three days of battle they were finished.

With the German drive stalled, the Allies counterattacked along the entire front. On September 12, 1918, a half million Americans and a smaller contingent of French drove the Germans from the St. Mihiel salient, 12 miles south of Verdun. Two weeks later, 896,000 American soldiers attacked between the Meuse River and the Argonne Forest. Focusing their efforts on a main railroad supply line for the German army in the West, American troops broke through in early November, cut the line, and drove the Germans back along the whole front.

The German high command knew that the war was lost. On October 6, 1918, Germany appealed to Wilson for an armistice, and by the end of the month, Turkey, Bulgaria, and Austria-Hungary were out of the war. At 4 A.M. on November 11, Germany signed the armistice. The AEF lost 48,909 dead and 230,000 wounded; losses to disease brought the total of dead to over 112,000.

The American contribution, although small in comparison to the enormous costs to European nations, was vital. Fresh, enthusiastic American troops raised Allied morale; they helped turn the tide at a crucial point in the war.

OVER HERE

Victory at the front depended on economic and emotional mobilization at home. Consolidating federal authority, Wilson moved quickly in 1917 and 1918 to organize war production and distribution. An idealist who knew how to sway public opinion, he also recognized the need to enlist American emotions. To him, the war for people's minds, the "conquest of their convictions," was as vital as events on the battlefield.

THE CONQUEST OF CONVICTIONS

A week after war was declared, Wilson formed the Committee on Public Information (CPI) and asked George Creel, an outspoken progressive journalist, to head it. Creel hired progressives such as Ida Tarbell and Ray Stannard Baker and recruited thousands of people in the arts, advertising, and film industries to publicize the war. He worked out a system of voluntary censorship with the press, plastered walls with colorful posters, and issued more than 75 million pamphlets.

Creel also enlisted 75,000 "four-minute men" to give quick speeches at public gatherings and places of entertainment on "Why We Are Fighting" and "The Meaning of America." At first, they were instructed to stress facts and stay away from emotions, particularly hatred, but by the beginning of 1918, the instructions shifted; the Germans were to be depicted as bloodthirsty Huns bent on world conquest.

Helped along by the propaganda campaign, anti-German sentiment spread rapidly. Many schools stopped offering instruction in the German language—California's state education board called it a language "of autocracy, brutality, and hatred." Sauerkraut became "liberty cabbage"; saloonkeepers removed pretzels from the bar. Orchestral works by Bach, Beethoven, and Brahms vanished from some symphonic programs, and the New York Philharmonic agreed not to perform the music of living German composers.

Rather than curbing the repression, Wilson encouraged it. "Woe be to the man or group of men that seeks to stand in our way," he told peace advocates soon after the war began. At his request, Congress passed the Espionage Act of 1917, which imposed sentences of up to twenty years in prison for persons found guilty of aiding the enemy, obstructing recruitment of soldiers, or encouraging disloyalty. It allowed the postmaster general to remove from the mails materials that incited treason or insurrection. The Trading-with-the-Enemy Act of 1917 authorized the government to censor the foreign language press.

In 1918, Congress passed the Sedition Act, imposing harsh penalties on anyone using "disloyal, profane, scurrilous, or abusive language" about the government, flag, or armed forces uniforms. In all, more than fifteen hundred persons were arrested under the new laws. People indicted or imprisoned included a Californian who laughed at rookies drilling at an army camp, a woman who greeted a Red Cross solicitor in a "hostile" way, and an editor who printed this sentence: "We must make the world safe for democracy even if we have to 'bean' the Goddess of Liberty to do it."

The sedition laws clearly went beyond any clear or present danger. There were, to be sure, German spies in the country, Germans who wanted to encourage strikes in American arms factories. Moreover, the U.S. government and other national leaders were painfully aware of how divided Americans had been about entering the war. They set out to promote unity—by force, if necessary—in order to convince Germany that the nation was united behind the war.

But none of these matters warranted a nationwide program of repression. Conservatives took advantage of wartime feelings to try to stamp out American socialists, who in fact were vulnerable because, unlike their European counterparts, they continued to oppose the war even after their country had entered it.

Eugene V. Debs, serving time in an Atlanta penitentiary for speaking out against the war, is shown here after receiving word of his nomination for the presidency. Debs campaigned in 1920 from behind bars.

Using the sedition laws, conservatives harried the Socialist party and another favorite target, the Industrial Workers of the World.

Wilson's postmaster general banned from the mails more than a dozen socialist publications, including the *Appeal to Reason,* which went to more than half a million people weekly. In 1918, Eugene V. Debs, the Socialist party leader, delivered a speech denouncing capitalism and the war. He was convicted for violation of the Espionage Act and spent the war in a penitentiary in Atlanta. Nominated as the Socialist party candidate in the presidential election of 1920, Debs—prisoner 9653—won nearly a million votes, but the Socialist movement never fully recovered from the repression of the war.

In fostering hostility toward anything that smacked of dissent, the war also gave rise to the great "Red Scare" that began in 1919. Pleased at first with the Russian revolution, Americans in general turned quickly against it, especially after Lenin and the Bolsheviks seized control late in 1917. The Americans feared

Lenin's anticapitalist program, and they denounced his decision in early 1918 to make peace with Germany because it freed German troops to fight in France.

Once again, Wilson himself played a prominent role in the development of anti-Bolshevik sentiment. In the summer of 1918, he sent fifteen thousand American troops into the Soviet Union, where they joined other Allied soldiers. Ostensibly, the troops were there to protect Allied supplies from the Germans and to rescue a large number of Czechs who wanted to return home to fight Germany. But the underlying reason for their presence was that Wilson and others hoped to bring down the fledgling Bolshevik government, fearful it would spread revolution around the world. American troops remained in Russia until April 1920, and on the whole, American willingness to interfere soured Russian-American relations for decades to come.

A BUREAUCRATIC WAR

Quick, effective action was needed to win the war. To meet the need, Wilson and Congress set up an array of new federal agencies, nearly five thousand in all. Staffed largely by businessmen, the agencies drew on funds and powers of a hitherto unknown scope.

By the time the war was over, it had cost $32 billion in direct war expense—in an era when the entire federal budget rarely exceeded $1 billion. To raise the money, the administration sold about $23 billion in "Liberty Bonds," and, using the new Sixteenth Amendment, boosted taxes on corporations and personal incomes. The taxes brought in another $10 billion to help pay for the war.

At first, Wilson tried to organize the wartime economy along decentralized lines, almost in the fashion of his early New Freedom thinking. But that proved unworkable, and he moved instead to a series of highly centralized planning boards, each with broad authority over a specific area of the economy. There were boards to control virtually every aspect of transportation, agriculture, and manufacturing. Though only a few of them were as effective as Wilson had hoped, they did coordinate the war effort to some degree.

The War Industries Board (WIB), one of the most powerful of the new agencies, oversaw the production of all American factories. Headed by millionaire Bernard M. Baruch, a Wall Street broker and speculator, it determined priorities, allocated raw materials, and fixed prices. It told manufacturers what they could and could not make. Working closely with business, Baruch for a time acted as the dictator of the American economy.

Herbert Hoover, the hero of a campaign to feed starving Belgians, headed a new Food Administration, and he set out with customary energy to supply food to the armies overseas. Appealing to the "spirit of self-sacrifice," Hoover convinced people to save food by observing "meatless" and "wheatless" days. He fixed prices to boost production, bought and distributed wheat, and encouraged people to plant "victory gardens" behind homes, churches, and schools. One householder—Wilson—set an example by grazing sheep on the White House lawn.

At another new agency, the Fuel Administration, Harry A. Garfield, the president of Williams College, introduced daylight saving time, rationed coal and oil, and imposed gasless days when motorists could not drive. To save coal, he shut down nonessential factories one day a week, and in January 1918, he closed all factories east of the Mississippi for four days to divert coal to munitions ships stranded in New York harbor. A fourth agency, the Railroad Administration, dictated rail traffic over nearly 400,000 miles of track—standardizing rates, limiting passenger travel, and speeding arms shipments. The War Shipping Board coordinated shipping, the Emergency Fleet Corporation supervised shipbuilding, and the War Trade Board oversaw foreign trade.

As never before, the government intervened in American life. When strikes threatened the telephone and telegraph companies, the government simply seized and ran them. Businessmen, paid a nominal dollar a year, flocked to Washington to run the new agencies, and the partnership between government and business grew closer. As government expanded, business expanded as well, responding to wartime contracts. Industries such as steel, aluminum, and cigarettes boomed, and corporate profits increased threefold between 1914 and 1919.

LABOR IN THE WAR

The war also brought organized labor into the partnership with government, although the results were more limited than in the business-government alliance. Samuel Gompers, president of the AFL, served on Wilson's Council of National Defense, an advisory group formed to unify business, labor, and government. Gompers hoped to trade labor peace for labor advances, and he formed a War Committee on Labor to enlist workers' support for the war. With the blessing of the Wilson administration, membership in the AFL and other unions grew from about 2.7 million in 1916 to more than 4 million in 1919.

Hoping to encourage production and avoid strikes, Wilson adopted many of the objectives of the social-justice reformers. He supported an eight-hour day in war-related industries and improved wages and working conditions. In May 1918, he named Felix Frankfurter, a brilliant young law professor, to head a new War Labor Board (WLB). The agency standardized wages and hours, and at Wilson's direction, it protected the right of labor to organize and bargain collectively. Although it did not forbid strikes, it used various tactics to discourage them.

Housewives did not leave home for the factory en masse in 1917 as they later did during World War II, but many women already employed outside the home found new, well-paying opportunities in jobs previously held by men.

The WLB also ordered that women be paid equal wages for equal work in war industries. In 1914, the flow of European immigrants suddenly stopped because of the war, and in 1917, the draft began to take large numbers of American men. The result was a labor shortage, filled by women, African Americans, and Mexican Americans. One million women worked in war industries. Some of them took jobs previously held by men, but for the most part, they moved from one set of "women's jobs" into another. From the beginning of the war to the end, the number of women in the workforce held steady at about eight million, and unlike the experience in World War II, large numbers of housewives did not leave the home for machine shops and arms plants.

Still, there were some new opportunities and in some cases higher pay. In food, airplane, and electrical plants, women made up one-fifth or more of the workforce. As their wages increased, so did their expectations; some became more militant, and conflict grew between them and male coworkers. To set standards for female employment, a Women's Bureau was established in the Department of Labor, but the government's influence varied. In the federally run railroad industry, women often made wages equal to those of men; in the federally run telephone industry, they did not.

Looking for more people to fill wartime jobs, corporations found another major source among southern blacks. Beginning in 1916, northern labor agents traveled across the South, promising jobs, high wages, and free transportation. Soon the word spread, and the movement northward became a flood. Between 1916 and 1918, more than 450,000 African Americans left the Old South for the booming industrial cities of Saint Louis, Chicago, Detroit, and Cleveland. In the decade before 1920, Detroit's black population grew by more than 600 percent, Cleveland's by more than 300 percent, and Chicago's by 150 percent.

Most of the newcomers were young, unmarried, and skilled or semiskilled. The men found jobs in factories, railroad yards, steel mills, packinghouses, and coal mines; black women worked in textile factories, department stores, and restaurants. In their new homes, African Americans found greater racial freedom but also different living conditions. If the South was often hostile, the North could be impersonal and lonely. Accustomed to the pace of the farm—ruled by the seasons and the sun—those blacks who were able to enter the industrial sector now worked for hourly wages in mass production industries, where time clocks and line supervisors dictated the daily routine.

Racial tensions increased, resulting in part from growing competition for housing and jobs. In mid-1917, a race war in East St. Louis, Illinois, killed nine whites and about forty blacks. In July 1919, the month President Wilson returned from the peace conference in Paris, a race riot in Washington, DC, killed six people. Riots in Chicago that month killed thirty-eight—fifteen whites and twenty-three blacks—and there were later outbreaks in New York City and Omaha. Lynch mobs killed forty-eight blacks in 1917, sixty-three in 1918, and seventy-eight in 1919. Ten of the victims in 1919 were war veterans, several still in uniform.

Blacks were more and more inclined to fight back. Two hundred thousand blacks served in France—forty-two thousand as combat troops. Returning home, they expected better treatment. "I'm glad I went," a black veteran said. "I done my part and I'm going to fight right here till Uncle Sam does his." Roscoe Jameson, Claude McKay, and other black poets wrote biting poetry, some of it—such as Fenton Johnson's "The New Day"—drawn from the war experience:

> For we have been with thee in No Man's Land,
> Through lake of fire and down to Hell itself;
> And now we ask of thee our liberty,
> Our freedom in the land of Stars and Stripes.

The 369th infantry regiment returning from the war on the Stockholm *in February 1919. They were awarded the Croix de Guerre for bravery in the Meuse-Argonne.*

"Lift Ev'ry Voice and Sing," composed in 1900, became known as the "Negro National Anthem." Parents bought black dolls for their children, and W. E. B. Du Bois spoke of a "New Negro," proud and more militant: "We return. We return from fighting. We return fighting."

Eager for cheap labor, farmers and ranchers in the Southwest persuaded the federal government to relax immigration restrictions, and between 1917 and 1920, more than 100,000 Mexicans migrated into Texas, Arizona, New Mexico, and California. The Mexican American population grew from 385,000 in 1910 to 740,000 in 1920. Tens of thousands of Mexican Americans moved to Chicago, St. Louis, Omaha, and other northern cities to take wartime jobs. Often scorned and insecure, they created urban barrios similar to the Chinatowns and Little Italys around them.

Like most wars, World War I affected patterns at home as much as abroad. Business profits grew, factories expanded, and industries turned out huge amounts of war goods. Government authority swelled, and people came to expect different things of their government. Labor made some gains, as did women and blacks. Society assimilated some of the shifts, but social and economic tensions grew, and when the war ended, they spilled over in the strikes and violence of the Red Scare that followed.

The United States emerged from the war the strongest economic power in the world. In 1914, it was a debtor nation, and American citizens owed foreign investors about $3 billion. Five years later, the United States had become a creditor nation. Foreign governments owed more than $10 billion, and foreign citizens owed American investors nearly $3 billion. The war marked a shift in economic power rarely equaled in history.

THE TREATY OF VERSAILLES

Long before the fighting ended, Wilson began to formulate plans for the peace. Like many others, he was disconcerted when the new Bolshevik government in Russia began revealing the terms of secret agreements among Britain, France, and czarist Russia to divide up Germany's colonies. To try to place the war on a higher plane, he appeared before Congress on January 8, 1918, and outlined terms for a far-reaching, nonpunitive settlement. Wilson's Fourteen Points were

WOODROW WILSON'S FOURTEEN POINTS, 1918: SUCCESS AND FAILURE IN IMPLEMENTATION

1. Open covenants of peace openly arrived at	Not fulfilled
2. Absolute freedom of navigation on the seas in peace and war	Not fulfilled
3. Removal of all economic barriers to the equality of trade among nations	Not fulfilled
4. Reduction of armaments to the level needed only for domestic safety	Not fulfilled
5. Impartial adjustments of colonial claims	Not fulfilled
6. Evacuation of all Russian territory; Russia to be welcomed into the society of free nations	Not fulfilled
7. Evacuation and restoration of Belgium	**Fulfilled**
8. Evacuation and restoration of all French lands; return of Alsace-Lorraine to France	**Fulfilled**
9. Readjustment of Italy's frontiers along lines of Italian nationality	Compromised
10. Self-determination for the former subjects of the Austro-Hungarian Empire	Compromised
11. Evacuation of Rumania, Serbia, and Montenegro; free access to the sea for Serbia	Compromised
12. Self-determination for the former subjects of the Ottoman Empire; secure sovereignty for Turkish portion	Compromised
13. Establishment of an independent Poland, with free and secure access to the sea	**Fulfilled**
14. Establishment of a League of Nations affording mutual guarantees of independence and territorial integrity	Not fulfilled

Sources: Data from G. M. Gathorne-Hardy, *The Fourteen Points and the Treaty of Versailles* (Oxford Pamphlets on World Affairs, no. 6, 1939), pp. 8–34; Thomas G. Paterson et al., *American Foreign Policy: A History Since 1900*, 2nd ed., vol. 2, pp. 282–93.

generous and farsighted, but they failed to satisfy wartime emotions that sought vindication.

England and France distrusted Wilsonian idealism as the basis for peace. They wanted Germany disarmed and crippled; they wanted its colonies; and they were skeptical of the principle of self-determination. As the end of the war neared, the Allies, who had in fact made secret commitments with one another, balked at making the Fourteen Points the basis of peace. When Wilson threatened to negotiate a separate treaty with Germany, however, they accepted.

Wilson had won an important victory, but difficulties lay ahead. As Georges Clemenceau, the 78-year-old French premier, said, "God gave us the Ten Commandments, and we broke them. Wilson gives us the Fourteen Points. We shall see."

A PEACE AT PARIS

Unfortunately, Wilson made a grave error just before the peace conference began. He appealed to voters to elect a Democratic Congress in the November 1918 elections, saying that any other result would be "interpreted on the other side of the water as a repudiation of my leadership." Many Republicans were furious, especially those who had supported the Fourteen Points; Wilson's problems deepened when the Democrats went on to lose both the House and Senate.

Two weeks after the elections, Wilson announced he would attend the peace conference. This was a dramatic break from tradition, and his personal involvement drew attacks from Republicans. They renewed criticism when he named the rest of the delegation: Secretary of State Lansing; Colonel House; General Tasker H. Bliss, a military expert; and Henry White, a career diplomat. Wilson named no member of the Senate, and the only Republican in the group was White.

In selecting the delegation, Wilson passed over Henry Cabot Lodge, the powerful Republican senator from Massachusetts who opposed the Fourteen Points and would soon head the Senate Foreign Relations Committee. He also decided not to appoint Elihu Root or ex-President Taft, both of them enthusiastic internationalists. Never good at accepting criticism or delegating authority, Wilson wanted a delegation he could control—an advantage at the peace table but not in any battle over the treaty at home.

Upon his arrival, Wilson received a tumultuous welcome in England, France, and Italy. Never before had such crowds acclaimed a democratic political figure. In Paris, two million people lined the Champs-Elysées, threw flowers at him, and shouted, "Wilson le Juste [the just]" as his carriage drove by. Overwhelmed, Wilson was sure that the people of Europe shared his goals and would force their leaders to accept his peace. He was wrong. Like their leaders, many people on the Allied side hated Germany and wanted victory unmistakably reflected in the peace.

Opening in January 1919, the Peace Conference at Paris continued until May. Although twenty-seven nations were represented, the "Big Four" dominated it: Wilson; Clemenceau of France, tired and stubborn, determined to end the German threat forever; David Lloyd George, the crafty British prime minister who had pledged to squeeze Germany "until the pips squeak"; and the Italian prime minister, Vittorio Orlando. A clever negotiator, Wilson traded various "small" concessions for his major goals—national self-determination, a reduction in tensions, and a League of Nations to enforce the peace.

Wilson had to surrender some important principles. Departing from the Fourteen Points by violating the principle of self-determination, the treaty created two new independent nations—Poland and Czechoslovakia—with large German-speaking populations. It divided up the German colonies in Asia and Africa.

Instead of a peace without victory, it made Germany accept responsibility for the war and demanded enormous reparations—which eventually totaled $33 billion. It made no mention of disarmament, free trade, or freedom of the seas. Instead of an open covenant openly arrived at, the treaty was drafted behind closed doors.

But Wilson deflected some of the most extreme Allied demands, and he won his coveted Point 14, a League of Nations, designed "to achieve international peace and security." The League

Europe After the Treaty of Versailles, 1919
The treaty changed the map of Europe, creating a number of new and reconstituted nations. (Note the boundary changes from the war map on p. 787.)

included a general assembly; a smaller council composed of the United States, Great Britain, France, Italy, Japan, and four nations to be elected by the assembly; and a court of international justice. League members pledged to submit to arbitration every dispute threatening peace and to enjoin military and economic sanctions against nations resorting to war. Article X, for Wilson the heart of the League, obliged members to look out for one another's independence and territorial integrity.

The draft treaty in hand, Wilson returned home in February 1919 to discuss it with Congress and the people. Most Americans, the polls showed, favored the League. But over dinner with the Senate and House Foreign Relations Committees, Wilson learned of the strength of congressional opposition to it. On March 3, Senator Lodge produced a "round robin" signed by thirty-seven senators declaring they would not vote for the treaty without amendment. Should the numbers hold, Lodge had enough votes to defeat it.

Returning to Paris, Wilson attacked his critics, while he worked privately for changes to improve the chances of Senate approval. In return for major concessions, the Allies amended the League draft treaty, agreeing that domestic affairs remained outside League jurisdiction (exempting the Monroe Doctrine) and allowing nations to withdraw after two years' notice. On June 28, 1919, they signed the treaty in the Hall of Mirrors at Versailles, and Wilson started home for his most difficult fight.

REJECTION IN THE SENATE

There were ninety-six senators in 1919, forty-nine of them Republicans. Fourteen Republicans, led by William E. Borah of Idaho, were the "irreconcilables" who opposed the League on any grounds. Frank B. Kellogg of Minnesota led a group of twelve "mild reservationists" who accepted the treaty but wanted to insert several reservations that would not greatly weaken it. Finally, there were the Lodge-led "strong reservationists," twenty-three of them in all, who wanted major changes that the Allies would have to approve.

With only four Democratic senators opposed to the treaty, the Democrats and Republicans willing to compromise had enough votes to ratify it, once a few reservations were inserted. Democratic leaders urged Wilson to appeal to the Republican "mild reservationists," but he refused: "Anyone who opposes me in that I'll crush!"

Fed up with Lodge's tactics, Wilson set out in early September to take the case directly to the people. Crossing the Midwest, his speeches aroused little emotion, but on the Pacific Coast he won ovations, which heartened him. On his way back to Washington, he stopped in Pueblo, Colorado, where he delivered one of the most eloquent speeches of his career. People wept as he talked of Americans who died in battle and the hope that they would never fight again in foreign lands. That night Wilson felt ill. He returned to Washington, and on October 2, Mrs. Wilson found him lying unconscious on the floor of the White House, the victim of a stroke that paralyzed his left side.

After the stroke, Wilson could not work more than an hour or two at a time. No one was allowed to see him except family members, his secretary, and his physician. For more than seven months, he did not meet with the cabinet. Focusing his remaining energy on the fight over the treaty, Wilson lost touch with other issues, and critics charged that his wife, Edith Bolling Wilson, ran the government.

On November 6, 1919, while Wilson convalesced, Lodge finally reported the treaty out of committee, along with "Fourteen Reservations," one for each of Wilson's points. The most important reservation stipulated that implementation

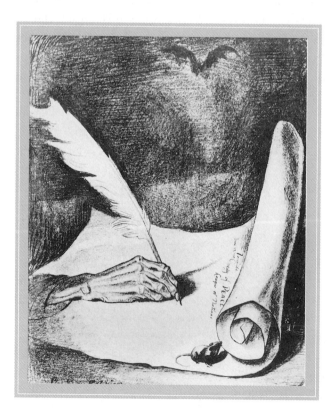

The skeletal hand signing the Treaty of Versailles in this cartoon reflects the disillusionment many Americans felt with the treaty's emphasis on extracting revenge from Germany. Even though the treaty departed from Wilson's idealistic plan for peace based on his Fourteen Points, he supported it in exchange for endorsement of his plan for a League of Nations. The treaty faced more obstacles in the United States from isolationists who wanted to keep the country out of European affairs and opposed U.S. membership in any League of Nations.

THE ELECTION OF 1920

CANDIDATE	PARTY	POPULAR VOTE	ELECTORAL VOTE
Harding	Republican	16,133,314	404
Cox	Democrat	9,140,884	127
Debs	Socialist	913,664	0

of Article X, Wilson's key article, required the action of Congress before any American intervention abroad.

On November 19, the treaty—with the Lodge reservations—failed, 39 to 55. Following Wilson's instructions, the Democrats voted against it. A motion to approve without the reservations lost 38 to 53, with only one Republican voting in favor. The defeat brought pleas for compromise, but neither Wilson nor Lodge would back down. When the treaty with reservations again came up for vote on March 19, 1920, Wilson ordered the Democrats to hold firm against it. Although twenty-one of them defied him, enough obeyed his orders to defeat it, 49 to 35, seven votes short of the necessary two-thirds majority.

To Wilson, walking now with the help of a cane, one chance remained: the presidential election of 1920. For a time, he thought of running for a third term himself, but his party shunted him aside. The Democrats nominated Governor James M. Cox of Ohio, along with the young and popular Franklin D. Roosevelt, assistant secretary of the navy, for vice president. Wilson called for "a great and solemn referendum" on the treaty. The Democratic platform endorsed the treaty but agreed to accept reservations that clarified the American role in the League.

On the Republican side, Senator Warren G. Harding of Ohio, who had nominated Taft in 1912, won the presidential nomination. Harding waffled on the treaty, but that issue made little difference. Voters wanted a change. Harding won in a landslide, taking 61 percent of the vote and beating Cox by seven million votes. Without a peace treaty, the United States remained technically at war, and it was not until July 1921, almost three years after the last shot was fired, that Congress passed a joint resolution ending the war.

After 1919, there was disillusionment. World War I was feared before it started, popular while it lasted, and hated when it ended. To a whole generation that followed, it appeared futile, killing without cause, sacrificing without benefit.

Books, plays, and movies—Hemingway's *A Farewell to Arms* (1929), John Dos Passos's *Three Soldiers* (1921), Laurence Stallings and Maxwell Anderson's *What Price Glory?* (1924), among others—showed it as waste, horror, and death.

The war and its aftermath damaged the humanitarian, progressive spirit of the early years of the century. It killed "something precious and perhaps irretrievable in the hearts of thinking men and women." Progressivism survived well into the 1920s and the New Deal, but it no longer had the old conviction and broad popular support. Bruising fights over the war and the League drained people's energy and enthusiasm.

Confined to bed, Woodrow Wilson died in Washington in 1924, three years after Harding, the new president, promised "not heroics but healing; not nostrums but normalcy; not revolution but restoration." Nonetheless, the "war to end all wars" and the spirit of Woodrow Wilson left an indelible imprint on the country.

25

TRANSITION TO MODERN AMERICA

The moving assembly line that Henry Ford perfected in 1913 for manufacture of the Model T marked only the first step toward full mass production and the beginning of America's worldwide industrial supremacy. A year later, Ford began buying large plots of land along the Rouge River southeast of Detroit, Michigan. He already had a vision of a vast industrial tract where machines, moving through a sequence of carefully arranged manufacturing operations, would transform raw materials into finished cars, trucks, and tractors. The key would be control over the flow of goods at each step along the way—from lake steamers and railroad cars bringing in the coal and iron ore, to overhead conveyor belts and huge turning tables carrying the moving parts past the stationary workers on the assembly line. "Everything must move," Ford commanded, and by the mid-1920s at River Rouge, as the plant became known, it did.

Ford began fulfilling his industrial dream in 1919 when he built a blast furnace and foundry to make engine blocks for both the Model T and his tractors. By 1924, more than forty thousand workers were turning out nearly all the metal parts used in making Ford vehicles. One tractor factory was so efficient that it took just over twenty-eight hours to convert raw ore into a new farm implement.

Visitors from all over the world came to marvel at River Rouge. Some were disturbed by the jumble of machines (by 1926, there were forty-three thousand in operation) and the apparent congestion on the plant floor, but industrial experts recognized that the arrangement led to incredible productivity because "the work moves and the men stand still."

In May 1927, after producing more than fifteen million Model Ts, Ford closed the assembly line at Highland Park. For the next six months, his engineers worked on designing a more compact and efficient assembly line at River Rouge for the Model A, which went into production in November. By then, River Rouge had more than justified Ford's vision. "Ford had brought together everything at a single site and on a scale no one else had ever attempted," concluded historian Geoffrey Perrett. "The Rouge plant became to a generation of engineers far more than a factory. It was a monument."

Mass production, born in Highland Park in 1913 and perfected at River Rouge in the 1920s, became the hallmark of American industry. Other carmakers copied Ford's methods, and soon his emphasis on the flow of parts moving past stationary workers became the standard in nearly every American factory. The moving assembly line—with its emphasis on uniformity, speed, precision, and coordination—took away the last vestiges of craftsmanship and turned workers into near robots. It led to amazing efficiency that produced both high profits for manufacturers and low prices for buyers. By the mid-1920s, the cost of the Model T had dropped from $950 to $290.

Most important, mass production led to a consumer goods revolution. American factories turned out a flood of automobiles and electrical appliances that made life easier and more pleasant for the vast majority of the American people. The result was the creation of a new America, one in which individualism was sacrificed to conformity as part of the price to be paid for a new era of abundance.

The 1920s, often seen as a time of escape and frivolity before the onset of the Depression, actually marked a beginning, a time when the American people learned to adapt to life in the city, when they decided (wisely or not) to center their existence on the automobile, and when they rejected their rural past while still longing for the old values it had created. It is in the 1920s that we can find the roots of modern America—the America we know today.

THE SECOND INDUSTRIAL REVOLUTION

The first Industrial Revolution in the late nineteenth century had catapulted the United States into the forefront among the world's richest and most highly developed nations. With the advent of the new consumer goods industries, the American people by the 1920s enjoyed the highest standard of living of any nation on earth. After a brief postwar depression, 1922 saw the beginning of a great

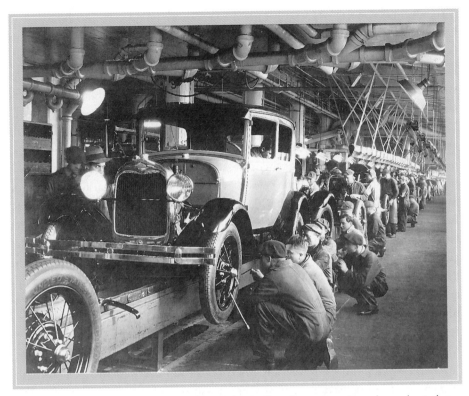

On the assembly line at Ford's River Rouge plant, workers performed repetitive tasks on the car chassis that rushed by at a rate of 6 feet per minute.

boom that peaked in 1927 and lasted until 1929. In this brief period, American industrial output nearly doubled, and the gross national product rose by 40 percent. Most of this explosive growth took place in industries producing consumer goods—automobiles, appliances, furniture, and clothing. Equally important, the national per capita income increased by 30 percent to $681 in 1929. American workers became the highest paid in history and thus were able to buy the flood of new goods they were turning out on the assembly lines.

The key to the new affluence lay in technology. The moving assembly line pioneered by Ford became a standard feature in nearly all American plants. Electric motors replaced steam engines as the basic source of energy in factories; by 1929, 70 percent of all industrial power came from electricity. Efficiency experts broke down the industrial process into minute parts, using time and motion studies, and then showed managers and workers how to maximize the output of their labor. Production per worker-hour increased an amazing 75 percent over the decade; in 1929, a workforce no larger than that of 1919 was producing almost twice as many goods.

THE AUTOMOBILE INDUSTRY

The nature of the consumer goods revolution can best be seen in the automobile industry, which became the nation's largest in the 1920s. Rapid growth was its hallmark. In 1920, there were ten million cars in the nation; by the end of the decade, twenty-six million were on the road. Production jumped from fewer than two million units a year to more than five million by 1929.

The automobile boom, at its peak from 1922 to 1927, depended on the apparently insatiable appetite of the American people for cars. But as the decade continued, the market became saturated as more and more of those who could afford the new luxury had become car owners. Marketing became as crucial as production. Automobile makers began to rely heavily on advertising and annual model changes, seeking to make customers dissatisfied with their old vehicles and eager to order new ones. Despite these efforts, sales slumped in 1927 when Ford stopped making the Model T, picked up again the next year with the new Model A, but began to slide again in 1929. The new industry revealed a basic weakness in the consumer goods economy; once people had bought an item with a long life, they would be out of the market for a few years.

In the affluent 1920s, few noticed the emerging economic instability. Instead, contemporary observers focused on the stimulating effect the automobile had on the rest of the economy. The mass production of cars required huge quantities of steel; entire new rolling mills had to be built to supply sheet steel for car bodies. Rubber factories boomed with the demand for tires, and paint and glass suppliers had more business than ever before. The auto changed the pattern of city life, leading to a suburban explosion. Real estate developers, no longer dependent on streetcars and railway lines, could now build houses in ever wider concentric circles around the central cities.

Even in smaller communities, the car ruled. In Muncie, Indiana, site of a famous sociological survey in the 1920s, one elder replied when asked what was taking place, "I can tell you what's happening in just four letters: A-U-T-O!" A nation that had always revered symbols of movement, from the *Mayflower* to the covered wagon, now had a new icon to worship.

PATTERNS OF ECONOMIC GROWTH

Automobiles were the most conspicuous of the consumer products that flourished in the 1920s, but certainly not the only ones. The electrical industry grew almost as quickly. Central power stations, where massive steam generators converted coal into electricity, brought current into the homes of city and town dwellers. Two-thirds of all American families enjoyed electricity by the end of the decade, and they spent vast sums on washing machines, vacuum cleaners, refrigerators, and ranges. The new appliances eased the burdens of housework and ushered in an age of leisure.

Radio broadcasting and motion picture production also boomed in the 1920s. The early success of KDKA in Pittsburgh stimulated the growth of more than eight hundred independent radio stations, and by 1929, NBC had formed the first successful radio network. Five nights a week, *Amos 'n Andy*, a comic serial featuring two "blackface" vaudevillians, held the attention of millions of Americans. The film industry thrived in Hollywood, reaching its maturity in the mid-1920s when in every large city there were huge theaters seating as many as four thousand people. With the advent of the "talkies" by 1929, average weekly movie attendance climbed to nearly 100 million.

The corporation continued to be the dominant economic unit in the 1920s. Growing corporations now had hundreds of thousands of stockholders, and one individual or family rarely held more than 5 percent of the stock. The enormous profits generated by the corporations enabled their managers to finance growth and expansion internally, thus freeing companies from their earlier dependence on investment bankers like J. P. Morgan. Voicing a belief in social responsibility and enlightened capitalism, the new professional class operated independently, free from outside restraint. In the final analysis, the corporate managers were accountable only to other managers.

Another wave of mergers accompanied the growth of corporations during the 1920s. From 1920 to 1928, some eight thousand mergers took place as more and more small firms proved unable to compete effectively with the new giants. By the end of the decade, the two hundred largest nonfinancial corporations owned almost half of the country's corporate wealth.

The most distinctive feature of the new consumer-oriented economy was the emphasis on marketing. Advertising earnings rose from $1.3 billion in 1915 to $3.4 billion in 1926. Skillful practitioners such as Edward Bernays and Bruce Barton sought to control public taste and consumer spending by identifying the good life with the possession of the latest product of American industry, whether it be a car, a refrigerator, or a brand of cigarettes.

Uniformity and standardization, the characteristics of mass production, now prevailed. The farmer in Kansas bought the same kind of car, the same groceries, and the same pills as the factory worker in Pennsylvania. Sectional differences in dress, food, and furniture began to disappear. Even the regional accents that distinguished Americans in different parts of the country were threatened with extinction by the advent of radio and films, which promoted a standard national dialect devoid of any local flavor.

ECONOMIC WEAKNESSES

The New Era, as business leaders labeled the decade, was not as prosperous as it first appeared. The revolution in consumer goods disguised the decline of many traditional industries in the 1920s. Railroads, overcapitalized and poorly managed, suffered from internal woes and from competition with the growing trucking industry. The coal industry was also troubled, with petroleum and natural gas beginning to replace coal as a fuel. The use of cotton textiles declined with the development of rayon and other synthetic fibers. The New England mills moved south in search of cheap labor, leaving behind thousands of unemployed workers and virtual ghost towns in the nation's oldest industrial center.

Hardest hit of all was agriculture. American farmers had expanded production to meet the demands of World War I, when they fed their own nation and most of Europe as well. A sharp cutback of exports in 1919 caused a rapid decline in prices. By 1921, farm exports had fallen by more than $2 billion. Throughout the 1920s, the farmers' share of the national income dropped, until by 1929, the per capita farm income was only $273, compared to the national average of $681.

Workers were better off than farmers in the 1920s, but they did not share fully in the decade's affluence. The industrial labor force remained remarkably steady during this period of economic growth; technical innovations meant the same number of workers could produce far more than before. Most new jobs appeared in the lower-paying service industry. During the decade, factory wage rates rose only a modest 11 percent; by 1929, nearly half of all American families had an income of less than $1500. At the same time, however, conditions of life improved. Prices remained stable, even dropping somewhat in the early 1920s, so workers enjoyed a gain in real wages.

Organized labor proved unable to advance the interests of workers in the 1920s. Conservative leadership in the AFL neglected the task of organizing the vast number of unskilled laborers in the mass production industries. Aggressive management weakened the appeal of unions by portraying them as radical organizations after a series of strikes in 1919. The net result was a decline in union membership from a postwar high of five million to less than three million by 1929.

Black workers remained on the bottom, both economically and socially. Nearly half a million African Americans had migrated northward from the rural South during World War I. Some found jobs in northern industries, but many more worked in menial service areas, collecting garbage, washing dishes, and sweeping floors. Yet even these jobs offered them a better life than they found on the depressed southern farms, where millions of African Americans still lived in poverty, and so the migration continued. The black ghettos in northern cities grew rapidly in the 1920s; Chicago's African American population doubled during the decade, while New York's rose from 152,467 to 327,706, with most African Americans living in Harlem.

Middle- and upper-class Americans were the groups who thrived in the 1920s. The rewards of this second Industrial Revolution went to the managers—the engineers, bankers, and executives—who directed the new industrial economy. Corporate profits nearly doubled in ten years, and income from dividends rose 65 percent, nearly six times the rate of increase in workers' wages. Bank accounts, reflecting the accumulated savings of the upper-middle and wealthy classes, rose from $41.1 billion to $57.9 billion. These were the people who bought the fine new houses in the suburbs and who could afford more than one car.

The economic trends of the decade had both positive and negative implications for the future. On the one hand, there was the solid growth of new consumer-based industries. Automobiles and appliances were not passing fancies; their production and use became a part of the modern American way of life, creating a high standard of living that roused the envy of the rest of the world. The future pattern of American culture—cars and suburbs, shopping centers and skyscrapers—was determined by the end of the 1920s.

But at the same time, there were ominous signs of danger. The unequal distribution of wealth, the saturation of the market for consumer goods, and the growing speculation all created economic instability. The boom of the 1920s would end in a great crash; yet the achievements of the decade would survive even that dire experience to shape the future of American life.

THE NEW URBAN CULTURE

The city replaced the countryside as the focal point of American life in the 1920s. The 1920 census revealed that for the first time, slightly more than half of the population lived in cities (defined broadly to include all places of more than 2,500 people). During the decade, the metropolitan areas grew rapidly as both whites and blacks from rural areas came seeking jobs in the new consumer industries. Between 1920 and 1930, cities with populations of 250,000 or more had added some 8 million people to their ranks. New York City grew by nearly 25 percent, while Detroit more than doubled its population during the decade.

The skyscraper soon became the most visible feature of the city. Faced with inflated land prices, builders turned upward—developing a distinctively American architectural style in the process. New York led the way with the ornate Woolworth Building in 1913. The sleek 102-story Empire State Building, completed in 1930, was for years the tallest building in the world. Other cities

Its 102 stories rising 1,250 feet into the sky (222 feet were added in 1950), the Empire State Building had space for 25,000 workers.

erected their own jagged skylines. By 1929, there were 377 buildings more than 20 stories tall across the nation. Most significantly, the skyscraper came to symbolize the new mass culture. "The New York skyscrapers are the most striking manifestation of the triumph of numbers," wrote one French observer. "One cannot understand or like them without first having tasted and enjoyed the thrill of counting or adding up enormous totals and of living in a gigantic, compact and brilliant world."

In the metropolis, life was different. The old community ties of home, church, and school were absent, but there were important gains to replace them—new ideas, new creativity, new perspectives. Some city dwellers became lost and lonely without the old institutions; others thrived in the urban environment.

WOMEN AND THE FAMILY

The urban culture of the 1920s witnessed important changes in the American family. This vital institution began to break down under the impact of economic and social change. A new freedom for women and children seemed to be emerging in its wake.

Women had already begun to leave the home in the early twentieth century as the second Industrial Revolution opened up new jobs for them. World War I sped up the process, but in the 1920s there was no great permanent gain in the number of working women. Although two million more women were employed in 1930 than in 1920, this represented an increase of only 1 percent. Most women workers, moreover, had low-paying jobs, ranging from stenographers to maids. For the most part, the professions were reserved for men, with women relegated to such fields as teaching and nursing.

Women had won the right to vote in 1920, but the Nineteenth Amendment proved to have less impact than its proponents had hoped. Adoption of the amendment robbed women of a unifying cause, and the exercise of the franchise itself did little to change prevailing sex roles. Men remained the principal breadwinners in the family; women cooked, cleaned, and reared the children. "The creation and fulfillment of a successful home," a

Women finally realized the hard-won right to vote. The cover of Leslie's Illustrated Newspaper *for September 11, 1920, celebrates the fact.*

Ladies Home Journal writer advised women, "is a bit of craftsmanship that compares favorably with building a beautiful cathedral."

The feminist movement, however, still showed signs of vitality in the 1920s. Social feminists pushing for humanitarian reform won enactment of the Sheppard-Towner Act of 1921, which provided for federal aid to establish state programs for maternal and infant health care. Although the failure to enact the child labor amendment in 1925 marked the beginning of a decline in humanitarian reform, for the rest of the decade, women's groups continued to work for good-government measures, for the inclusion of women on juries, and for consumer legislation.

One group of activists, led by Alice Paul's National Woman's Party (NWP), lobbied for full equality for women under the law. In 1923, the NWP succeeded in having an Equal Rights Amendment introduced in Congress. The amendment stated simply, "Men and women shall have equal rights throughout the United States and every place subject to its jurisdiction." Most other women's organizations, notably the League of Women Voters, opposed the amendment because it threatened gender-specific legislation such as the Sheppard-Towner Act that women had fought so hard to enact. The drive for the ERA in the 1920s failed.

Growing assertiveness had a profound impact on feminism in the 1920s. Instead of crusading for social progress, young women concentrated on individual self-expression by rebelling against Victorian restraints. In the larger cities, some quickly adopted what critic H. L. Mencken called the flapper image, portrayed most strikingly by artist John Held, Jr. Cutting their hair short, raising their skirts above the knee, and binding their breasts, "flappers" set out to compete on equal terms with men on the golf course and in the speakeasy. The flappers assaulted the traditional double standard in sex, demanding that equality with men should include sexual fulfillment before and during marriage. New and more liberal laws led to a sharp rise in the divorce rate; by 1928, there were 166 divorces for every 1,000 marriages, compared to only 81 in 1900.

The sense of woman's emancipation was heightened by a continuing drop in the birthrate and by the abundance of consumer goods. With fewer children to care for and with washing machines and vacuum cleaners to ease their household labor, it seemed that women of the 1920s would have more leisure time. Yet appearances were deceptive. Advertisers eagerly sought out women as buyers of laborsaving consumer products, but wives exercised purchasing power only as delegated by their husbands. In addition, many women were not in the position to put the new devices to use—one-fourth of the homes in Cleveland lacked running water in the 1920s, and three-quarters of the nation's families did not have washing machines.

The family, however, did change. It became smaller as new techniques of birth control enabled couples to limit the number of their offspring. More and more married women took jobs outside the home, bringing in an income and gaining a measure of independence (although their rate of pay was always lower than that for men). Young people, who had once joined the labor force when they entered their teens, now discovered adolescence as a stage of life. A high school education was no longer uncommon, and college attendance increased.

Prolonged adolescence led to new strains on the family in the form of youthful revolt. Freed of the traditional burden of earning a living at an early age, youths in the 1920s went on a great spree. Heavy drinking, casual sexual encounters, and a constant search for excitement became the hallmarks of the upper-class youth immortalized by F. Scott Fitzgerald. "I have been kissed by dozens of men," one of his characters commented. "I suppose I'll kiss dozens more." The theme of rebellion against parental authority, which runs through all aspects of the 1920s, was at the heart of the youth movement.

THE ROARING TWENTIES

Frivolity and excitement ran high in the cities as both crime waves and highly publicized sports events flourished. Prohibition ushered in such distinctive features of the decade as speakeasies, bootleggers, and bathtub gin. Crime rose sharply as middle- and upper-class Americans willingly broke the law to gain access to alcoholic beverages. City streets became the scene of violent shoot-outs between rival bootleggers; by 1929, Chicago had witnessed more than five hundred gangland murders.

Sports became a national mania in the 1920s as people found more leisure time. Golf boomed, with some two million men and women playing on nearly five thousand courses across the country. Spectator sports attracted even more attention. Boxing drew huge crowds to see fighters such as Jack Dempsey and Gene Tunney. Baseball attendance soared. More than twenty million fans attended games in 1927, the year Babe Ruth became a national idol by hitting sixty home runs.

In what Frederick Lewis Allen called "the ballyhoo years," the popular yearning for excitement led people to seek vicarious thrills in all kinds of ways—applauding Charles Lindbergh's solo flight across the Atlantic, cheering Gertrude Ederle's swim across the English Channel, and flocking to such bizarre events as six-day bicycle races, dance marathons, and flagpole sittings.

Sex became another popular topic in the 1920s as Victorian standards began to crumble. Sophisticated city dwellers seemed to be intent on exploring a new freedom in sexual expression. Plays and novels focused on adultery, and the new urban tabloids—led by the *New York Daily News*—delighted in telling their readers about love nests and kept women. The popular songs of the decade, such as "Hot Lips" and "Burning Kisses," were less romantic and more explicit than those of years before. Hollywood exploited the obsession with sex by producing movies with such provocative titles as *Up in Mabel's Room, A Shocking Night,* and *Women and Lovers.* Young people embraced the new permissiveness joyfully, with the automobile giving couples an easy way to escape parental supervision.

There is considerable debate, however, over the extent of the sexual revolution in the 1920s. Later studies by Dr. Alfred C. Kinsey showed that premarital intercourse was twice as common among women born after 1900 than for those born before the turn of the century. But a contemporary survey of more than two thousand middle-class women by Katherine B. Davis found that only 7 percent of those who were married had had sexual relations before marriage and that only 14 percent of the single women had engaged in intercourse. Actual changes in sexual behavior are beyond the historian's reach, hidden in the privacy of the bedroom, but the old Victorian prudishness was a clear casualty of the 1920s. Sex was no longer a taboo subject, at least in urban areas; men and women now could discuss it openly, and many of them did.

THE LITERARY FLOWERING

The greatest cultural advance of the 1920s was visible in the outpouring of literature. The city gave rise to a new class of intellectuals—writers who commented on the new industrial society. Many had been uprooted by World War I. They were bewildered by the rapidly changing social patterns of the 1920s and appalled by the materialism of American culture. Some fled to Europe to live as expatriates, congregating in Paris cafés to bemoan the loss of American innocence and purity. Others stayed at home, observing and condemning the excesses of a business civilization. All shared a sense of disillusionment and wrote pessimistically of the flawed promise of American life. Yet, ironically, their body of writing revealed a profound creativity that suggested America was coming of age intellectually.

The exiles included the poets T. S. Eliot and Ezra Pound and the novelist Ernest Hemingway. Pound discarded rhyme and meter in a search for clear, cold images that conveyed reality. Like many of the writers of the 1920s, he reacted against World War I, expressing a deep regret for the tragic waste of a whole generation in defense of a "botched civilization."

Eliot, who was born in Missouri but became a British citizen, displayed even more profound despair. In *The Waste Land,* which appeared in 1922, he evoked images of fragmentation and sterility that had a powerful impact on the other disillusioned writers of the decade. He reached the depths in *The Hollow Men* (1925), a biting description of the emptiness of modern man.

Ernest Hemingway sought redemption from the modern plight in the romantic individualism of his heroes. Preoccupied with violence, he wrote of men alienated from society who found a sense of identity in their own courage and quest for personal honor. His own experiences, ranging from driving an ambulance in the war to stalking lions in Africa, made him a legendary figure; his greatest impact on other writers, however, came from his sparse, direct, and clean prose style.

The writers who stayed home were equally disdainful of contemporary American life. F. Scott Fitzgerald chronicled American youth in *This Side of Paradise* (1920) and *The Great Gatsby* (1925), writing in bittersweet prose about "the beautiful and the damned." Amid the glitter of life among the wealthy on Long Island's North Shore came the haunting realization of emptiness and lack of human concern.

Most savage of all was H. L. Mencken, the Baltimore newspaperman and literary critic who founded *American Mercury* magazine in 1923. Declaring war on "Homo boobiens," Mencken mocked everything he found distasteful in America, from the Rotary Club to the Ku Klux Klan. "From Boy Scouts, and from Home Cooking, from Odd Fellows' funerals, from Socialists, from Christians—Good Lord, deliver us," he pleaded. It was not difficult to discover what Mencken disliked (including Jews, as his published diary makes clear); the hard part was finding out what he affirmed, other than wit and a clever turn of phrase.

The cultural explosion of the 1920s was surprisingly broad. It included novelists such as Sherwood Anderson and John Dos Passos, who described the way the new machine age undermined such traditional American values as craftsmanship and a sense of community, and playwrights such as Eugene O'Neill, Maxwell Anderson, and Elmer Rice, who added greatly to the stature of American theater. Women writers were particularly effective in dealing with regional themes. Edith Wharton continued to write penetratingly about eastern aristocrats in books such as *The House of Mirth* (1905) and *The Age of Innocence* (1921); Willa Cather and Ellen Glasgow focused on the plight of women in the Midwest and the South, respectively, in their short stories and novels. These writers portrayed their heroines in the traditional roles of wives and mothers; playwright Zona Gale, on the other hand (who won the Pulitzer Prize for drama in 1920 for *Miss Lulu Bett*), used her title character to depict the dilemmas facing an unmarried woman in American society.

Art and music lagged behind literature but still made significant advances. Edward Hopper and Charles Burchfield captured the ugliness of city life and the

W. E. B. Du Bois (top left), editor of The Crisis, *was one of the intellectual and political leaders of the Harlem Renaissance, which fostered the rise of literary figures such as Zora Neale Hurston (top right) and Langston Hughes (left). Hurston wrote four novels and two books of black folklore that "helped to remind the Renaissance . . . of the richness in racial heritage." Hughes wrote sensitively and eloquently of the world of common black people.*

loneliness of its inhabitants in their realistic paintings. Aaron Copland and George Gershwin added a new vitality to American music. But African Americans migrating northward brought the most significant contribution: the spread of jazz—first to St. Louis, Kansas City, and Chicago, and finally to New York. The form of jazz known as the blues, so expressive of the suffering of African

Americans, became an authentic national folk music, and performers such as Louis Armstrong enjoyed popularity around the world.

The cultural growth of the 1920s was the work of blacks as well as whites. W. E. B. Du Bois, the editor of the newspaper *Crisis,* became the intellectual voice of the black community developing in New York City's Harlem. In 1917, James Weldon Johnson, who had been a professor of literature at Fisk University, published *Fifty Years and Other Poems,* in which the title poem commented on the half century of suffering that had followed the Emancipation Proclamation. As other African American writers gathered around them, Du Bois and Johnson became the leaders of the Harlem Renaissance. The NAACP moved its headquarters to Harlem, and in 1923, the Urban League began publishing *Opportunity,* a magazine devoted to scholarly studies of racial issues.

Art and music also flourished during Harlem's golden age. Plays and concerts at the 135th Street YMCA; floor shows at Happy Rhone's nightclub (attended by many white celebrities); rent parties where jazz musicians played to raise money to help writers, artists, and neighbors pay their bills—all were part of the ferment that made Harlem "the Negro Capital of the World" in the 1920s. "Almost everything seemed possible above 125th Street in the early twenties for these Americans who were determined to thrive separately to better proclaim the ideals of integration," comments historian David Lewis. "You could be black and proud, politically assertive and economically independent, creative and disciplined—or so it seemed."

Although its most famous writers were identified with New York's Harlem, the new African American cultural awareness spread to other cities in the form of poetry circles and theater groups. The number of African Americans graduating from college rose from 391 in 1920 to 1,903 by 1929. Although blacks were still an oppressed minority in the America of the 1920s, they had taken major strides toward achieving cultural and intellectual fulfillment.

In retrospect, there is a striking paradox about the literary flowering of the 1920s. Nearly all the writers, black as well as white, cried out against the conformity and materialism of the contemporary scene. They were critical of mass production and reliance on the machine; they wrote wistfully of the disappearance of the artisan and of a more relaxed way of life. Few took any interest in politics or in social reform. They retreated instead into individualism, seeking an escape into their art from the prevailing business civilization. Whether they went abroad or stayed home, the writers of the 1920s turned inward to avoid being swept up in the consumer goods revolution. Yet despite their withdrawal, and perhaps because of it, they produced an astonishingly rich and varied body of work. American writing had a greater intensity and depth than in the past; American writers, despite their alienation, had placed their country in the forefront of world literature.

THE RURAL COUNTERATTACK

The shift of population from the countryside to the city led to heightened social tensions in the 1920s. Intent on preserving traditional social values, rural Americans saw in the city all that was evil in contemporary life. Saloons, whore-houses, little Italys and little Polands, communist cells, free love, and atheism—all were identified with the city. Accordingly, the countryside struck back at the newly dominant urban areas, aiming to restore the primacy of the Anglo-Saxon and predominantly Protestant culture they revered. This counterattack won con-siderable support in the cities from those so recently uprooted from their rural backgrounds.

Other factors contributed to the intensity of the counterattack. The war had unleashed a nationalistic spirit that craved unity and conformity. In a nation where one-third of the people were foreign born, the attack on immigrants and the call for 100 percent Americanism took on a frightening zeal. When the war was over, groups such as the American Legion tried to root out "un-American" behavior and insisted on cultural as well as political conformity. The prewar pro-gressive reform spirit added to the social tension. Stripped of much of its former idealism, progressivism focused on such social problems as drinking and illiteracy to justify repressive measures like Prohibition and immigration restriction. The result was tragic. Amid the emergence of a new urban culture, the movements aimed at preserving the values of an earlier America succeeded only in complicat-ing life in an already difficult period of cultural transition.

THE "RED SCARE"

The first and most intense outbreak of national alarm came in 1919. The height-ened nationalism of World War I, aimed at achieving unity at the expense of eth-nic diversity, found a new target in bolshevism. The Russian Revolution and the triumph of Marxism frightened many Americans. A growing turn to communism among American radicals (especially the foreign born) accelerated these fears. Although the numbers involved were tiny—at most there were sixty thousand communists in the United States in 1919—they were highly visible. Located in the cities, their influence appeared to be magnified with the outbreak of wide-spread labor unrest.

A general strike in Seattle, a police strike in Boston, and a violent strike in the iron and steel industry thoroughly alarmed the American people in the spring and summer of 1919. A series of bombings led to panic. First the mayor of strikebound Seattle received a small brown package containing a homemade bomb; then an alert New York postal employee detected sixteen bombs addressed to a variety of famous citizens (including John D. Rockefeller); and finally, on June 2, a bomb shattered the front of Attorney General A. Mitchell Palmer's home. Although the man who delivered it was blown to pieces, authorities quickly identified him as an Italian anarchist from Philadelphia.

In the ensuing public outcry, Attorney General Palmer led the attack on the alien threat. A Quaker and progressive, Palmer abandoned his earlier liberalism to launch a massive roundup of foreign-born radicals. In a series of raids that began on November 7, federal agents seized suspected anarchists and communists and held them for deportation with no regard for due process of law. In December, 249 aliens—including such well-known radical leaders as Emma Goldman and Alexander Berkman—were sent to Russia aboard the *Buford,* dubbed the "Soviet Ark" by the press. Nearly all were innocent of the charges against them.

For a time, it seemed that the Red Scare reflected the prevailing views of the American people. Instead of condemning their government's action, citizens voiced their approval and even urged more drastic steps. One patriot said his solution to the alien problem was simple: "S.O.S.—ship or shoot." General Leonard Wood, the former army chief of staff, favored placing Bolsheviks on "ships of stone with sails of lead," while evangelist Billy Sunday preferred to take "these ornery, wild-eyed Socialists" and "stand them up before a firing squad and save space on our ships."

The very extremism of the Red Scare led to its rapid demise. In early 1920, courageous government officials from the Department of Labor insisted on due process and full hearings before anyone else was deported. Prominent public leaders began to speak out against the acts of terror. Finally, Palmer himself, with evident presidential ambition, went too far. In April 1920, he warned of a vast revolution to occur on May 1; the entire New York City police force, some eleven thousand strong, was placed on duty to prepare for imminent disaster. When no bombings or violence took place on May Day, the public began to react against Palmer's hysteria. Despite a violent explosion on Wall Street in September that killed thirty-three people, the Red Scare died out by the end of 1920. Palmer passed into obscurity, the tiny Communist party became torn with factionalism, and the American people tried hard to forget their loss of balance.

Yet the Red Scare exerted a continuing influence on American society in the 1920s. The foreign born lived in the uneasy realization that they were viewed with hostility and suspicion. Two Italian aliens in Massachusetts, Nicola Sacco and Bartolomeo Vanzetti, were arrested in May 1920 for a payroll robbery and murder. They faced a prosecutor and jury who condemned them more for their ideas

The explosion in Wall Street on September 16, 1920, left thirty-three dead and nearly two hundred wounded. Attorney General Palmer saw the blast as the work of a communist conspiracy, but relatively few Americans subscribed to his view.

than for any evidence of criminal conduct and a judge who referred to them as "those anarchist bastards." Despite a worldwide effort that became the chief liberal cause of the 1920s, the courts rejected all appeals. Sacco, a shoemaker, and Vanzetti, a fish peddler, died in the electric chair on August 23, 1927. Their fate symbolized the bigotry and intolerance that lasted through the 1920s and made that decade one of the least attractive in American history.

PROHIBITION

In December 1917, Congress adopted the Eighteenth Amendment, prohibiting the manufacture and sale of alcoholic beverages. A little over a year later, Nebraska was the necessary thirty-sixth state to ratify, and Prohibition became the law of the land.

As implemented under the Volstead Act, beginning January 16, 1920, it was illegal for anyone to make, sell, or transport any drink that contained more than one-half of 1 percent alcohol by volume. Prohibition was the result of both a rural effort of the Anti-Saloon League, backed by Methodist and Baptist clergymen, and the urban progressive concern over the social disease of drunkenness, especially among industrial workers. The moral issue had already led to the enactment of Prohibition laws in twenty-six states by 1920; the real tragedy would occur in the effort to extend this "noble experiment" to the growing cities, where it was deeply resented by ethnic groups such as the Germans and the Irish and was almost totally disregarded by the well-to-do and the sophisticated.

Prohibition did in fact lead to a decline in drinking. Americans consumed much less alcohol in the 1920s than in the prewar years. Rural areas became totally dry, and in the cities, the consumption of alcoholic beverages dropped sharply among the lower classes, who could not afford the high prices for bootleg liquor. Among the middle class and the wealthy, however, drinking became fashionable; Americans consumed some 150 million quarts of liquor a year in the 1920s. Bootleggers took in nearly $2 billion annually, about 2 percent of the gross national product.

Urban resistance to Prohibition finally led to its repeal in 1933. But in the intervening years, it damaged American society by breeding a profound disrespect for the law. The flamboyant excesses of bootleggers were only the more obvious evils spawned by Prohibition. In city after city, police openly tolerated the traffic in liquor, and judges and prosecutors agreed to let bootleggers pay merely token fines, creating almost a system of licenses. Prohibition satisfied the countryside's desire for vindication, yet rural and urban America alike suffered from this overzealous attempt to legislate morals.

THE KU KLUX KLAN

The most ominous expression of protest against the new urban culture was the rebirth of the Ku Klux Klan. On Thanksgiving night in 1915, on Stone Mountain in Georgia, Colonel William J. Simmons and thirty-four followers founded the modern Klan. Only "native born, white, gentile Americans" were permitted to join "the Invisible Empire, Knights of the Ku Klux Klan." Membership grew slowly during World War I, but after 1920, fueled by postwar fears and shrewd promotional techniques, the Klan mushroomed. In villages, towns, and small cities across the nation, Anglo-Saxon Protestant men flocked into the newly formed chapters, seeking to relieve their anxiety over a changing society by embracing the Klan's unusual rituals and by demonstrating their hatred against blacks, aliens, Jews, and Catholics.

The Klan of the 1920s, unlike the night riders of the post–Civil War era, was not just antiblack; the threat to American culture, as Klansmen perceived it, came from aliens—Italians and Russians, Jews and Catholics. They attributed much of the tension and conflict in society to the prewar flood of immigrants, foreigners who spoke different languages, worshiped in strange churches, and

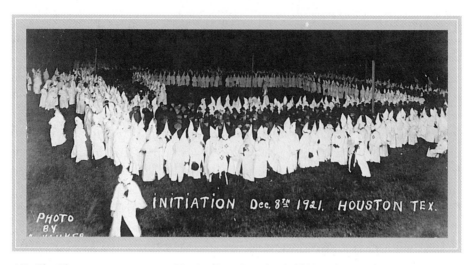

A Ku Klux Klan initiation ceremony in Houston, Texas, December 8, 1921. Only native-born, white Americans "who believe in the tenets of the Christian religion" were admitted into the Klan. The original Ku Klux Klan, formed during the Reconstruction era to terrorize and intimidate former slaves, disbanded in 1869. The Klan that formed in 1915 declined through the 1920s but did not officially disband until 1944. Two years later a third Klan emerged, focusing on the civil rights movement and communism as its enemies.

lived in distant, threatening cities. The Klansmen struck back by coming together and enforcing their own values. They punished blacks who did not know their place, women who practiced the new morality, and aliens who refused to conform. Beating, flogging, burning with acid—even murder—were condoned. They also tried more peaceful methods of coercion, formulating codes of behavior and seeking communitywide support.

The Klan entered politics, at first hesitantly, then with growing confidence. The KKK gained control of the legislatures in Texas, Oklahoma, Oregon, and Indiana; in 1924, it blocked a resolution of censure at the Democratic national convention. With an estimated five million members by the mid-1920s, the Klan seemed to be fully established.

Its appeal lay in the sanctuary it offered to insecure and anxious people. Each Klan had its own Klalendar, held its weekly Klonklave in the local Klavern, and followed the rules set forth in the Kloran. Protestant to the core, the members found in the local Klavern a reassurance missing in their churches. The poor and ignorant became enchanted with the titles, ranging from Imperial Wizard to Grand Dragon. Members found a sense of identity in the group activities, whether they were peaceful picnics, ominous parades in white robes, or fiery cross burnings at night.

The Klan fell even more quickly than it rose. Its more violent activities—which included kidnapping, lynching, setting fire to synagogues and Catholic churches, and, in one case, murdering a priest—began to offend the nation's conscience. Misuse of funds and sexual scandals among Klan leaders, notably in Indiana, repelled many of the rank and file; effective counterattacks by traditional politicians ousted the KKK from control in Texas and Oklahoma. Membership declined sharply after 1925; by the end of the decade, the Klan had virtually disappeared. But its spirit lived on, testimony to the recurring demons of nativism and hatred that have surfaced periodically throughout the American experience.

IMMIGRATION RESTRICTION

The nativism that permeated the Klan found its most successful outlet in the immigration legislation of the 1920s. The sharp increase in immigration in the late nineteenth century had led to a broad-based movement, spearheaded by organized labor and by New England aristocrats such as Henry Cabot Lodge, to restrict the flow of people from Europe. In 1917, over Wilson's veto, Congress enacted a literacy test that reduced the number of immigrants allowed into the country. The war caused a much more drastic decline—from an average of 1 million a year between 1900 and 1914 to only 110,000 in 1918.

After the armistice, however, rumors began to spread of an impending flood of people seeking to escape war-ravaged Europe. Kenneth Roberts, a popular historical novelist, warned that all Europe was on the move, with only the limits of available steamship space likely to stem the flow. Even though the actual number of immigrants, 810,000 in 1920 (fewer than the prewar yearly average), did not match these projections, Congress in 1921 passed an emergency immigration act. The new quota system restricted immigration from Europe to 3 percent of the number of nationals from each country living in the United States in 1910.

The 1921 act failed to satisfy the nativists. The quotas still permitted more than 500,000 Europeans to come to the United States in 1923, nearly half of them from southern and eastern Europe. The declining percentage of Nordic immigrants alarmed writers such as Madison Grant, who warned the American people the Anglo-Saxon stock that had founded the nation was about to be overwhelmed by lesser breeds with inferior genes. "These immigrants adopt the language of the native American, they wear his clothes and are beginning to take his women, but they seldom adopt his religion or understand his ideals," Grant wrote.

In 1924, Congress adopted the National Origins Quota Act, which limited immigration from Europe to 150,000 a year; allocated most of the available slots to immigrants from Great Britain, Ireland, Germany, and Scandinavia; and banned all Asian immigrants. The measure passed Congress with overwhelming rural support.

The new restrictive legislation marked the most enduring achievement of the rural counterattack. Unlike the Red Scare, Prohibition, and the Klan, the quota system would survive until the 1960s, enforcing a racist bias that excluded Asians and limited the immigration of Italians, Greeks, and Poles to a few thousand a year while permitting a steady stream of Irish, English, and Scandinavian immigrants. The large corporations, no longer dependent on armies of unskilled immigrant workers, did not object to the 1924 law; the machine had replaced the immigrant on the assembly line. Yet even here the victory was not complete. A growing tide of Mexican laborers, exempt from the quota act, flowed northward across the Rio Grande to fill the continuing need for unskilled workers on the farms and in the service trades. The Mexican immigrants, as many as 100,000 a year, marked the strengthening of an element in the national ethnic mosaic that would grow in size and influence until it became a major force in modern American society.

The Fundamentalist Controversy

The most famous of all attacks on the new urban culture was the Scopes trial held in Dayton, Tennessee. There, in 1925, William Jennings Bryan, who had unsuccessfully run for president several times in previous decades, engaged in a crusade against the theory of evolution, appearing as a chief witness against John Scopes. Scopes, a high school biology teacher, had initiated the case by deliberately violating a new Tennessee law that forbade the teaching of Darwin's theory.

In the trial, Bryan testified under oath that he believed Jonah had been swallowed by a big fish and declared, "It is better to trust in the Rock of Ages than in the age of rocks." Chicago defense attorney Clarence Darrow succeeded in making Bryan look ridiculous. The court found Scopes guilty but let him off with a token fine; Bryan, exhausted by his efforts, died a few days later. H. L. Mencken, who covered the trial in person, rejoiced in the belief that fundamentalism was dead.

In reality, however, traditional rural religious beliefs were stronger than ever. As middle- and upper-class Americans drifted into a genteel Christianity that stressed good works and respectability, the Baptist and Methodist churches continued to hold on to the old faith. In addition, aggressive fundamentalist sects such as the Churches of Christ, the Pentecostals, and Jehovah's Witnesses grew

Crowds of spectators throng the courtroom during the Scopes trial as defense attorney Clarence Darrow rests on the table during the proceedings. Scopes is seated to Darrow's right with his arms interlocked, staring straight ahead.

rapidly. While church membership increased from 41.9 million in 1916 to 54.5 million in 1926, the number of churches actually declined during the decade. More and more rural dwellers drove their cars into town instead of going to the local crossroads chapel.

POLITICS OF THE 1920s

The tensions between the city and the countryside also shaped the course of politics in the 1920s. On the surface, it was a Republican decade. The GOP ("Grand Old Party") controlled the White House from 1921 to 1933 and had majorities in both houses of Congress from 1918 to 1930. The Republicans used their return to power after World War I to halt further reform legislation and to establish a friendly relationship between government and business. Important shifts were taking place, however, in the American electorate. The Democrats, although divided into competing urban and rural wings, were laying the groundwork for the future by winning over millions of new voters, especially among the ethnic groups in the cities. The rising tide of urban voters indicated a fundamental shift away from the Republicans toward a new Democratic majority.

HARDING, COOLIDGE, AND HOOVER

The Republicans regained the White House in 1920 with the election of Warren G. Harding of Ohio. A dark-horse contender, Harding won the GOP nomination when the convention deadlocked and he became the compromise choice. Handsome and dignified, Harding reflected both the virtues and blemishes of small-town America. Conventional in outlook, Harding was a genial man who lacked the capacity to govern and who, as president, broadly delegated power.

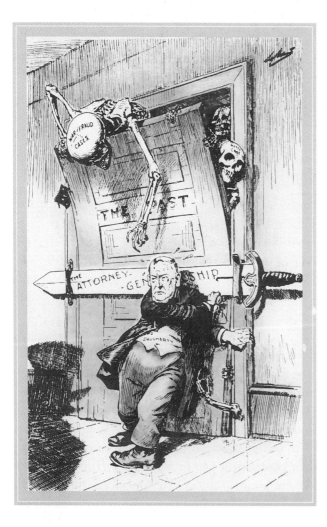

Attorney General Daugherty struggles to keep the scandals of the Harding administration hidden in the closet.

He made some good cabinet choices, notably Charles Evans Hughes as secretary of state and Herbert C. Hoover as secretary of commerce, but two corrupt officials—Attorney General Harry Daugherty and Secretary of the Interior Albert Fall—sabotaged his administration. Daugherty became involved in a series of questionable deals that led ultimately to his forced resignation; Fall was the chief figure in the Teapot Dome scandal. Two oil promoters gave Fall nearly $400,000 in loans and bribes; in return, he helped them secure leases on naval oil reserves in Elk Hills, California, and Teapot Dome, Wyoming. The scandal came to light after Harding's death from a heart attack in 1923. Fall eventually served a year in jail, and the reputation of the Harding administration never recovered.

Vice President Calvin Coolidge assumed the presidency upon Harding's death, and his honesty and integrity quickly reassured the nation. Coolidge, born in Vermont of old Yankee stock, had first gained national attention in 1919 as governor of Massachusetts when he had dealt firmly with a Boston police strike by declaring, "There is no right to strike against the public safety by anybody, anywhere, any time." A reserved, reticent man, Coolidge became famous for his epigrams, which contemporaries mistook for wisdom. "The business of America is business," he proclaimed. "The man who builds a factory builds a temple; the man who works there worships there." Consistent with this philosophy, he believed his duty was simply to preside benignly, not govern the nation. Satisfied with the prosperity of the mid-1920s, the people responded favorably. Coolidge was elected to a full term by a wide margin in 1924.

When Coolidge announced in 1927 that he did not "choose to run," Herbert Hoover became the Republican choice to succeed him. By far the ablest GOP leader of the decade, Hoover epitomized the American myth of the self-made man. Orphaned as a boy, he had worked his way through Stanford University and had gained both wealth and fame as a mining engineer. During World War I, he had displayed admirable administrative skills in directing Wilson's food program at home and relief activities abroad. Sober, intelligent, and immensely hardworking, Hoover embodied the nation's faith in individualism and free enterprise.

As secretary of commerce under Harding and Coolidge, he had sought cooperation between government and business. Instead of viewing business and government as antagonists, he saw them as partners, working together to achieve efficiency and affluence for all Americans. His optimistic view of the future led him to declare in his speech accepting the Republican presidential nomination in 1928 that "we in America today are nearer to the final triumph over poverty than ever before in the history of any land."

REPUBLICAN POLICIES

During the 1920 campaign, Warren Harding urged a return to "not heroism, but healing, not nostrums, but normalcy." Misreading his speechwriter's "normality," he coined a new word that became the theme for the Republican administrations of the 1920s. Aware that the public was tired of zealous reform-minded presidents such as Teddy Roosevelt and Woodrow Wilson, Harding and his successors sought a return to traditional Republican policies. In some areas they were successful, but in others the Republican leaders were forced to adjust to the new realities of a mass production society. The result was a mixture of traditional and innovative measures that was neither wholly reactionary nor entirely progressive.

The most obvious attempt to go back to the Republicanism of William McKinley came in tariff and tax policy. Fearful of a flood of postwar European imports, Congress passed an emergency tariff act in 1921 and followed it a year later with the protectionist Fordney-McCumber Tariff Act. The net effect was to raise the basic rates substantially over the moderate Underwood Tariff schedules of the Wilson period.

Secretary of the Treasury Andrew Mellon, a wealthy Pittsburgh banker and industrialist, worked hard to achieve a similar return to normalcy in taxation. Using the new budget system adopted by Congress in 1921, he reduced government spending from its World War I peak of $18 billion to just over $3 billion by 1925, thereby creating a slight surplus. Congress responded in 1926 by cutting the highest income tax bracket to a modest 20 percent.

The revenue acts of the 1920s greatly reduced the burden of taxation; by the end of the decade, the government was collecting one-third less than it had in 1921, and the number of people paying income taxes dropped from more than 6.5 million to 4 million. Yet the greatest relief went to the wealthy. The public was shocked to learn in the 1930s that J. P. Morgan and his nineteen partners had paid no income tax at all during the depths of the Depression.

The growing crisis in American farming during the decade forced the Republican administrations to seek new solutions. The end of the European war led to a sharp decline in farm prices and a return to the problem of overproduction. Southern and western lawmakers formed a farm bloc in Congress to press for special legislation for American agriculture. The farm bloc supported the higher tariffs, which included protection for constituents' crops, and helped secure passage of legislation to create federal supervision over stockyards, packinghouses, and grain trading.

Despite Republican rhetoric, the government's role in the economy increased rather than lessened in the 1920s. Herbert Hoover led the way in the Commerce Department, establishing new bureaus to help make American industry more efficient in housing, transportation, and mining. Under his leadership, the government encouraged corporations to develop welfare programs that undercut trade unions, and he tried to minimize labor disturbances by devising new federal machinery to mediate disputes. Instead of going back to the laissez-faire tradition of the nineteenth century, the Republican administrations of the 1920s were pioneering a close relationship between government and private business.

THE DIVIDED DEMOCRATS

While the Republicans ruled in the 1920s, the Democrats seemed bent on self-destruction. The Wilson coalition fell apart in 1920 as pent-up dissatisfaction stemming from the war enabled Harding to win by a landslide. The pace of the second Industrial Revolution and the growing urbanization split the party in two. One faction was centered in the rural South and West. Traditional Democrats who had supported Wilson stood for Prohibition, fundamentalism, the Klan, and other facets of the rural counterattack against the city. In contrast, a new breed of Democrat was emerging in the metropolitan areas of the North and Midwest. Immigrants and their descendants began to become active in the Democratic party. Catholic or Jewish in religion and strongly opposed to Prohibition, they had little in common with their rural counterparts.

The split within the party surfaced dramatically at the national convention in New York in 1924. Held in Madison Square Garden, a hall built in the 1890s and too small and cramped for the more than one thousand delegates, the convention soon degenerated into what one observer described as a "snarling, cursing, tenuous, suicidal, homicidal roughhouse." An urban resolution to condemn the Ku Klux Klan led to a spirited response from the rural faction and its defeat by a single vote. Then for nine days, in the midst of a stifling heat wave, the delegates divided between Alfred E. Smith, the governor of New York, and William G. McAdoo of California, Wilson's secretary of the treasury. When it became clear that neither the city nor the rural candidate could win a majority, both men withdrew; on the 103rd ballot, the weary Democrats finally chose John W. Davis, a former West Virginia congressman and New York corporation lawyer, as their compromise nominee.

In the ensuing election, the conservative Davis had difficulty setting his views apart from those of Republican president Calvin Coolidge. For the discontented, Senator Robert La Follette of Wisconsin offered an alternative by running on an independent Progressive party ticket. Coolidge won easily, receiving 15 million votes to 8 million for Davis and nearly 5 million for La Follette. Davis had made the poorest showing of any Democratic candidate in the twentieth century.

Yet the Democrats were in far better shape than this setback indicated. Beginning in 1922, the party had made heavy inroads into the GOP majority in Congress. The Democrats took seventy-eight seats away from Republicans in that

THE ELECTION OF 1924

CANDIDATE	PARTY	POPULAR VOTE	ELECTORAL VOTE
Coolidge	Republican	15,717,553	382
Davis	Democrat	8,386,169	136
La Follette	Progressive	4,814,050	13

election, many of them in the cities of the East and Midwest. In New York alone, they gained thirteen new congressmen, all but one in districts with heavy immigrant populations. By 1926, the Democrats were within one vote of controlling the Senate and had picked up nine more seats in the House in metropolitan areas. The large cities were swinging clearly into the Democratic column; all the party needed was a charismatic leader who could fuse the older rural elements with the new urban voters.

THE ELECTION OF 1928

The selection of Governor Al Smith of New York as the Democratic candidate in 1928 indicated the growing power of the city. Born on the Lower East Side of Manhattan of mixed Irish-German ancestry, Smith was the prototype of the urban Democrat. He was Catholic; he was associated with a big-city machine; he was a "wet" who wanted to end Prohibition. Rejected by rural Democrats in 1924, he still had to prove he could unite the South and West behind his leadership. His lack of education, poor grammar, and distinctive New York accent all hurt him, as did his eastern provincialism. When reporters asked him about his appeal in the states west of the Mississippi, he replied, "What states are west of the Mississippi?"

The choice facing the American voter in 1928 seemed unusually clear-cut. Herbert Hoover was a Protestant, a dry, and an old-stock American, who stood for efficiency and individualism; Smith was a Catholic, a wet, and a descendant of immigrants, who was closely associated with big-city politics. Just as Smith appealed to new voters in the cities, so Hoover won the support of many old-line Democrats who feared the city, Tammany Hall, and the pope.

Yet beneath the surface, as Allan J. Lichtman points out, there were "striking similarities between Smith and Hoover." Both were self-made men who embodied the American belief in freedom of opportunity and upward mobility. Neither advocated any significant degree of economic change nor any redistri-

THE ELECTION OF 1928

CANDIDATE	PARTY	POPULAR VOTE	ELECTORAL VOTE
Hoover	Republican	21,391,993	444
Smith	Democrat	15,016,169	87
	Minor Parties	330,725	–

bution of national wealth or power. Though religion proved to be the most important issue in the minds of the voters, hurting Smith far more than Prohibition or his identification with the city, the Democratic candidate's failure to spotlight the growing cracks in prosperity or to offer alternative economic policies ensured his defeat.

The 1928 election was a dubious victory for the Republicans. Hoover won easily, defeating Smith by more than six million votes and carrying such traditionally Democratic states as Oklahoma, Texas, and Florida. But Smith succeeded for the first time in winning a majority of votes for the Democrats in the nation's twelve largest cities. A new Democratic electorate was emerging, consisting of Catholics and Jews, Irish and Italians, Poles and Greeks. Now the task was to unite the traditional Democrats of the South and West with the urban voters of the Northeast and Midwest.

The growing influence of the city on politics of the 1920s reflected the sweeping changes taking place throughout the decade in American social and economic development. Al Smith, despite his defeat in 1928, symbolized the emergence of the city as the center of twentieth-century American life. An older nation founded on rural values had given way to a new urban society in which the production and use of consumer goods led to a very different lifestyle. Just as nineteenth-century American culture had revolved around the farm and the railroad, modern America focused on the automobile and the city. Yet despite the genuine economic progress achieved in the 1920s, the decade ended in a severe depression that lasted all through the 1930s. Only after World War II would the American people finally enjoy an abundance and prosperity rooted in the urban transformation that began in the 1920s.

26

FRANKLIN D. ROOSEVELT AND THE NEW DEAL

The prosperity of the 1920s came to an abrupt halt in October 1929. The stock market, which had boomed during the decade, suddenly faltered. Investors who had borrowed heavily to take part in the speculative mania that had swept Wall Street suddenly were forced to sell their securities to cover their loans. The wave of selling triggered an avalanche. On October 24, later known as Black Thursday, nearly thirteen million shares were traded as highfliers such as RCA and Westinghouse lost nearly half their value. The stock market rallied for the next two days, but on Tuesday, October 29, the downslide resumed. Frightened sellers dumped more than sixteen million shares and the industrial average fell by 43 points. The panic ended in November, with stocks at 1927 levels. For the next four years, there was a steady drift downward, until by 1932, prices were 80 percent below their 1929 highs.

The Great Depression that followed the crash of 1929 was the most devastating economic blow ever suffered by the nation. It lasted for more than ten years, dominating every aspect of American life during the 1930s. Unemployment rose to twelve million by 1932, and though it dipped midway through the decade, it still stood at ten million by 1939. Children grew up thinking that economic deprivation was the norm rather than the exception in America. Year after year, people kept looking for a return to prosperity, but the outlook remained dismal. Intractable and all-encompassing, the Depression loosened its grip on the nation only after the outbreak of World War II. Even then, it left enduring psychological scars—never again would the Americans who lived through it be quite so optimistic about their economic future.

The Depression led to a profound shift in American political loyalties. The Republicans, dominant since the 1890s, gave way to a new Democratic majority. The millions of immigrants who had come to the United States before World War I became more active politically, as did their children who were beginning to reach voting age. The result was the election of Franklin D. Roosevelt to the presidency and the development of the New Deal, a broad program of relief, recovery, and reform that greatly increased the role of government in American life.

THE GREAT DEPRESSION

The economic collapse altered American attitudes. In the 1920s, optimism had prevailed as people looked forward to an ever increasing flow of consumer goods and a better way of life. But after 1929, despair set in. Factories closed, machines fell silent, and millions upon millions of people walked the streets, looking for jobs that did not exist.

THE GREAT BULL MARKET

The consumer goods revolution contained the seeds of its own collapse. The steady expansion of the automobile and appliance industries had led gradually to a saturation of the market. Each year after 1924, the rate of increase in the sale of cars and refrigerators and ranges slowed, a natural consequence as more and more people already owned these durable goods. Production began to falter, and in 1927, the nation underwent a mild recession. The sale of durable goods de-

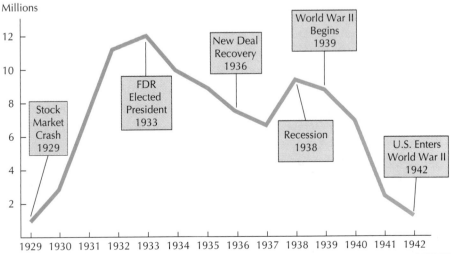

Unemployment, 1929–1942

Millions

Stock Market Crash 1929

FDR Elected President 1933

New Deal Recovery 1936

World War II Begins 1939

Recession 1938

U.S. Enters World War II 1942

1929 1930 1931 1932 1933 1934 1935 1936 1937 1938 1939 1940 1941 1942

clined, and construction of houses and buildings fell slightly. If corporate leaders had heeded these warning signs, they might have responded by raising wages or lowering prices, both effective ways to stimulate purchasing power and sustain the consumer goods revolution. Or if government officials had recognized the danger signals and forced a halt in installment buying and slowed bank loans, the nation might have experienced a sharp but brief depression.

Neither government nor business leaders were so farsighted. The Federal Reserve Board lowered the discount rate, charging banks less for loans in an attempt to stimulate the economy. Much of this additional credit, however, went not into solid investment in factories and machinery but instead into the stock market, touching off a new wave of speculation that obscured the growing economic slowdown and ensured a far greater crash to come.

Individuals with excess cash began to invest heavily in the stock market, betting the already impressive rise in security prices would bring them even greater windfall profits. The market had advanced in spurts during the decade; the value of all stocks listed on the New York Stock Exchange rose from $27 billion in 1925 to $67 billion in early 1929. People bet their savings on speculative stocks. Corporations used their large cash reserves to supply money to brokers who in turn loaned it to investors on margin; in 1929, for example, the Standard Oil Company of New Jersey loaned out $69 million a day in this fashion.

Investors could now play the market on credit, buying stock listed at $100 a share with $10 down and $90 on margin, the broker's loan for the balance. If the stock advanced to $150, the investor could sell and reap a gain of 500 percent on the $10 investment. And in the bull market climate of the 1920s, everyone was sure the market would go up.

By 1929, it seemed the whole nation was engaged in speculation. In city after city, brokers opened branch offices, each complete with a stock ticker and a huge board covered with the latest Wall Street quotations. In reality, though, more people were spectators than speculators; fewer than three million Americans owned stocks in 1929, and only about a half million were active buyers and sellers. But the bull market became a national obsession, assuring everyone that the economy was healthy and preventing any serious analysis of its underlying flaws.

The great crash in October 1929 put a sudden and tragic end to the speculative mania. The false confidence that had kept the economy from collapsing in 1927 evaporated overnight. Suddenly, corporations and financial institutions were no longer willing to provide capital for stock market purchases. More important, investors and bankers cut off consumer credit as well, drying up buying power and leading to a sharp decline in the sales of consumer goods. Factories began to cut back production, laying off some workers and reducing hours for others. The layoffs and cutbacks lowered purchasing power even further, so fewer people bought cars and appliances. More factory layoffs resulted, and some plants closed entirely, leading to the availability of even less money for the purchase of consumer goods.

This downward economic spiral continued for four years. By 1932, unemployment had swelled to 25 percent of the workforce, while the gross national product fell to 67 percent of the 1929 level. The bright promise of mass production had ended in a nightmare.

The basic explanation for the Great Depression lies in the fact that U.S. factories produced more goods than the American people could consume. The problem was not that the market for such products was fully saturated. In 1929, there were still millions of Americans who did not own cars or radios or refrigerators, but many of them could not afford the new products. There were other contributing causes—unstable economic conditions in Europe, the agricultural decline since 1919, corporate mismanagement, and excessive speculation—but it all came down to the fact that people did not have enough money to buy the consumer products coming off the assembly lines. Installment sales helped bridge the gap, but by 1929 the burden of debt was just too great.

The new economic system had failed to distribute wealth more broadly. Too much money had gone into profits, dividends, and industrial expansion, and not enough had gone into the hands of the workers, who were also consumers. If the billions that went into stock market speculation had been used instead to increase wages—which would then have increased consumer purchasing power—production and consumption could have been brought into balance. Yet it is too much to expect that the prophets of the new era could have foreseen this flaw and corrected it. They were pioneering a new industrial system, and only out of the bitter experience of the Depression would they discover the full dynamics of the consumer goods economy.

EFFECT OF THE DEPRESSION

It is difficult to measure the human cost of the Great Depression. The material hardships were bad enough. Men and women lived in lean-tos made of scrap wood and metal, and families went without meat and fresh vegetables for months, existing on a diet of soup and beans. The psychological burden was even greater: Americans suffered through year after year of grinding poverty with no letup in sight. The unemployed stood in line for hours waiting for relief checks; veterans sold apples or pencils on street corners, their manhood—once prized so highly by the nation—now in question.

Few escaped the suffering. African Americans who had left the poverty of the rural South for factory jobs in the North were among the first to be laid off. Mexican immigrants, who had flowed in to replace European immigrants, met

Unemployment devastated thousands, who sought any way to earn a few pennies—such as selling apples from a makeshift sidewalk stand.

with competition from angry citizens now willing to do stoop labor in the fields and work as track layers on the railroads. Immigration officials used technicalities to halt the flow across the Rio Grande and even to reverse it; nearly a half million Mexicans were deported in the 1930s, including families with children born in the United States.

The poor—black, brown, and white—survived because they knew better than most Americans how to exist in poverty. They stayed in bed in cold weather, both to keep warm and to avoid unnecessary burning up of calories; they patched their shoes with pieces of rubber from discarded tires, heated only the kitchens of their homes, and ate scraps of food that others would reject.

The suddenly homeless gathered in hobo camps and shantytowns, seeking shelter in flimsy shacks made of corrugated metal or cardboard. The camps were nicknamed "Hoovervilles," for the president who believed that relief for the poor, hungry, and unemployed was the responsibility of local governments and private charities—not the federal government.

The middle class, which had always lived with high expectations, was hit hard. Professionals and white-collar workers refused to ask for charity even while their families went without food; one New York dentist and his wife turned on the gas and left a note saying, "We want to get out of the way before we are forced to accept relief money." People who fell behind in their mortgage payments lost their homes and then faced eviction when they could not pay the rent.

Even the well-to-do were affected, giving up many of their former luxuries and weighed down with guilt as they watched former friends and business associates join the ranks of the impoverished. "My father lost everything in the Depression" became an all-too-familiar refrain among young people who dropped out of college.

Many Americans sought escape in movement. Men, boys, and some women rode the rails in search of jobs, hopping freights to move south in the winter or west in the summer. One town in the Southwest hired special police to keep vagrants from leaving the boxcars. Those who became tramps had to keep on the move, but they did find a sense of community in the hobo jungles that sprang up along the major railroad routes. Here the unfortunate could find a place to eat and sleep, and people with whom to share their misery. Louis Banks, a black veteran, told interviewer Studs Terkel what the informal camps were like:

> Black and white, it didn't make any difference who you were, 'cause everybody was poor. All friendly, sleep in a jungle. We used to take a big pot and cook food, cabbage, meat and beans all together. We all set together, we made a tent. Twenty-five or thirty would be out on the side of the rail, white and colored: They didn't have no mothers or sisters, they didn't have no home, they were dirty, they had overalls on, they didn't have no food, they didn't have anything.

FIGHTING THE DEPRESSION

The Great Depression presented an enormous challenge for American political leadership. The inability of the Republicans to overcome the economic catastrophe provided the Democrats with the chance to regain power. Although they failed to achieve full recovery before the outbreak of World War II, the Democrats did succeed in alleviating some of the suffering and establishing political dominance.

HOOVER AND VOLUNTARISM

Herbert Hoover was the Depression's most prominent victim. When the economic downturn began in late 1929, he tried to rally the nation with bold forecasts of better days ahead. His repeated assertion that prosperity was just around the corner bred cynicism and mistrust. Expressing complete faith in the American economic system, Hoover blamed the Depression on foreign causes, especially unstable European banks. The president rejected proposals for bold government action and relied instead on voluntary cooperation within business to halt the slide.

Hoover also believed in voluntary efforts to relieve the human suffering brought about by the Depression. He called on private charities and local governments to help feed and clothe those in need. But when these sources were exhausted, he rejected all requests for direct federal relief, asserting that such handouts would undermine the character of proud American citizens.

As the Depression deepened, Hoover reluctantly began to move beyond voluntarism to undertake more sweeping government measures. A new Federal Farm Board loaned money to aid cooperatives and bought up surplus crops in the open market in a vain effort to raise farm prices. At Hoover's request, Congress cut taxes in an attempt to restore public confidence and adopted a few federal public works projects, such as Boulder (Hoover) Dam, to provide jobs for idle men.

To help imperiled banks and insurance companies, Hoover proposed the Reconstruction Finance Corporation (RFC), which Congress established in early 1932. The RFC loaned government money to financial institutions to save them from bankruptcy. Hoover's critics, however, pointed out that while he favored aid to business, he still opposed measures such as direct relief and massive public works that would help the millions of unemployed.

By 1932, Hoover's efforts to overcome the Depression had clearly failed. The Democrats had gained control of the House of Representatives in the 1930 elections and were pressing the president to take bolder action, but Hoover stubbornly resisted. His public image suffered its sharpest blow in the summer of 1932 when he ordered General Douglas MacArthur to clear out the "bonus army." This ragged group of some twenty-two thousand World War I veterans had come to Washington in the summer of 1932 to lobby Congress to pay immediately a bonus for military service that was due them in 1945.

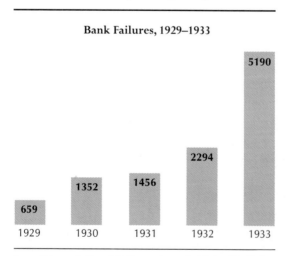

Bank Failures, 1929–1933

Year	Bank Failures
1929	659
1930	1352
1931	1456
1932	2294
1933	5190

Source: Data compiled from C. D. Bremer, *American Bank Failures* (New York: Columbia University Press, 1935), p. 42.

Meanwhile, the nation's banking structure approached collapse. Bank failures rose steadily in 1931 and 1932 as customers responded to rumors of bankruptcy by rushing in to withdraw their deposits. The banking crisis completed the nation's disenchantment with Hoover; people were ready for a new leader in the White House.

THE EMERGENCE OF ROOSEVELT

The man who stepped forward to meet this national need was Franklin D. Roosevelt. Born into the old Dutch colonial aristocracy of New York, FDR was a distant cousin of the Republican Teddy. He grew up with all the advantages of wealth—private tutors, his own sailboat and pony, frequent trips to Europe, and education at Groton and Harvard. After graduation from Harvard, he briefly attended law school but left to plunge into politics. He served in the New York legislature and then went to Washington as assistant secretary of the navy under Wilson, a post he filled capably during World War I. Defeated as the Democratic vice presidential candidate in 1920, Roosevelt had just begun a banking career when he suffered an attack of polio in the summer of 1921. Refusing to give in, he fought back bravely, and though he never again walked unaided, he reentered politics in the mid-1920s and was elected governor of New York in 1928.

Roosevelt's dominant trait was his ability to persuade and convince other people. He possessed a marvelous voice, deep and rich; a winning smile; and a buoyant confidence he could easily transmit to others. Some believed he was too vain and superficial as a young man, but his bout with polio gave him both an understanding of human suffering and a broad political appeal as a man who had faced heavy odds and overcome them. He understood the give-and-take of politics, knew how to use flattery to win over doubters, and was especially effective in exploiting the media. Although his mind was quick and agile, he had little patience with philosophical nuances; he dealt with the appearance of issues, not their deeper substance, and he displayed a flexibility toward political principles that often dismayed even his warmest admirers.

Roosevelt took advantage of the opportunity offered by the Depression. With the Republicans discredited, he cultivated the two wings of the divided Democrats, appealing to both the traditionalists from the South and West and the new urban elements in the North. After winning the party's nomination in 1932, he broke with tradition by flying to Chicago and accepting in person, telling the cheering delegates, "I pledge you—I pledge myself to a new deal for the American people."

In the fall, he defeated Herbert Hoover in a near landslide for the Democrats. Roosevelt tallied 472 electoral votes as he swept the South and West and carried nearly all the large industrial states as well. Farmers and workers, Protestants and Catholics, immigrants and native born rallied behind the new

The Election of 1932

CANDIDATE	PARTY	POPULAR VOTE	ELECTORAL VOTE
Roosevelt	Democratic	22,809,638	472
Hoover	Republican	15,758,901	59
	Minor Parties	1,153,306	—

leader who promised to restore prosperity. Roosevelt not only met the challenge of the Depression but also solidified the shift to the Democratic party and created an enduring coalition that would dominate American politics for a half century.

THE HUNDRED DAYS

When Franklin Roosevelt took the oath of office on March 4, 1933, the nation's economy was on the brink of collapse. Unemployment stood at nearly thirteen million, one-fourth of the labor force; banks were closed in thirty-eight states. Speaking from the steps of the Capitol, FDR declared boldly, "First of all, let me assert my firm belief that the only thing we have to fear is fear itself—nameless, unreasoning, unjustified terror." Then he announced he would call Congress into special session and request "broad executive power to wage a war against the emergency, as great as the power that would be given to me if we were in fact invaded by a foreign foe."

Within the next ten days, Roosevelt won his first great New Deal victory by saving the nation's banks. On March 5, he issued a decree closing the banks and called Congress back into session. His aides drafted new banking legislation and presented it to Congress on March 9; a few hours later, both houses passed it, and FDR signed the new legislation that evening. The measure provided for government supervision and aid to the banks. Strong ones would be reopened with federal support, weak ones closed, and those in difficulty bolstered by government loans.

On March 12, FDR addressed the nation by radio in the first of his fireside chats. In conversational tones, he told the public what he had done. Some banks would begin to reopen the next day, with the government standing behind them. Other banks, once they became solvent, would open later, and the American people could safely put their money back into these institutions. The next day, March 13, the nation's largest and strongest banks opened their doors; at the end of the day, customers had deposited more cash than they withdrew. The crisis was over; gradually, other banks opened, and the runs and failures ceased.

"Capitalism was saved in eight days," boasted one of Roosevelt's advisers. Most surprising was the conservative nature of FDR's action. Instead of nationalizing the banks, he had simply thrown the government's resources behind them and preserved private ownership. Though some other New Deal measures would be more radical, Roosevelt set a tone in the banking crisis. He was out to reform and restore the American economic system, not change it drastically.

For the next three months, until it adjourned in June, Congress responded to a series of presidential initiatives. During these "Hundred Days," Roosevelt sent fifteen major requests to Congress and received back fifteen pieces of legislation. A few created permanent agencies that have become a part of American life: the Tennessee Valley Authority (TVA) proved to be the most successful and enduring of all Roosevelt's New Deal measures. This innovative effort at regional planning resulted in the building of a series of dams in seven states along the Tennessee River to control floods, ease navigation, and produce electricity.

With his fireside chats, FDR became the first president to use radio to reach and reassure the American people.

Other New Deal agencies were temporary in nature, designed to meet the specific economic problems of the Depression. None were completely successful; the Depression would continue for another six years, immune even to Roosevelt's magic. But psychologically, the nation turned the corner in the spring of 1933. Under FDR, the government seemed to be responding to the economic crisis, enabling people for the first time since 1929 to look to the future with hope.

ROOSEVELT AND RECOVERY

Two major New Deal programs launched during the Hundred Days were aimed at industrial and agricultural recovery. The first was the National Recovery Administration (NRA), FDR's attempt to achieve economic advance through planning and cooperation among government, business, and labor. In the midst of the Depression, businessowners were intent on stabilizing production and raising prices for their goods. Labor leaders were equally determined to spread work through maximum hours and to put a floor under workers' income with minimum wages.

The NRA hoped to achieve both goals by permitting companies in each major industry to cooperate in writing codes of fair competition that would set realistic limits on production, allocate percentages to individual producers, and set firm guidelines for prices. Section 7a of the enabling act mandated protection for labor in all the codes by establishing maximum hours, minimum wage, and the guarantee of collective bargaining by unions. No company could be compelled to join, but the New Deal sought complete participation by appealing to patriotism. Each firm that took part could display a blue eagle and stamp the symbol on its products. By the summer of 1933, more than five hundred industries had adopted codes that covered 2.5 million workers.

The NRA quickly bogged down in a huge bureaucratic morass. The codes proved to be too detailed to enforce easily. Written by the largest companies, the rules favored big business at the expense of smaller competitors. Labor quickly became disenchanted with Section 7a. The minimum wages were often near starvation level, while business avoided the requirement for collective bargaining by creating company unions that did not represent the real needs of workers. After a brief upsurge in the spring of 1933, industrial production began to sag as disillusionment with the NRA grew. When the Supreme Court finally invalidated the NRA in 1935 on constitutional grounds, few mourned its demise. The idea of trying to overcome the Depression by relying on voluntary cooperation between competing businesses and labor leaders had collapsed in the face of individual self-interest and greed.

The New Deal's attempt at farm recovery fared a little better. Henry A. Wallace, FDR's secretary of agriculture, came up with an answer to the farmers' old dilemma of overproduction. The government would act as a clearinghouse for producers of major crops, arranging for them to set production limits for wheat, cotton, corn, and other leading crops. The Agricultural Adjustment Administration (AAA) created by Congress in May 1933 would allocate acreage among individual farmers, encouraging them to take land out of production by paying them subsidies (raised by a tax on food processors). Unfortunately, Wallace preferred not to wait until the 1934 planting season to implement this program, and so farmers were paid in 1933 to plow under crops they had already planted and to kill livestock they were raising. Faced with the problem of hunger in the midst of plenty, the New Deal seemed to respond by destroying the plenty.

The AAA program worked better in 1934 and 1935 as land removed from production led to smaller harvests and rising farm prices. Farm income rose for the first time since World War I, increasing from $2 billion in 1933 to $5 billion by 1935. Severe weather, especially Dust Bowl conditions on the Great Plains, contributed to the crop-limitation program, but most of the gain in farm income came from the subsidy payments themselves rather than from higher market prices.

On the whole, large farmers benefited most from the program. Possessing the capital to buy machinery and fertilizer, they were able to farm more efficiently than before on fewer acres of land. Small farmers, tenants, and sharecroppers did not fare as well, receiving very little of the government payments and often being driven off the land as owners took the acreage previously cultivated by tenants and sharecroppers out of production.

The Supreme Court eventually found the AAA unconstitutional in 1936, but Congress reenacted it in modified form that year and again in 1938. The system of allotments, now financed directly by the government, became a standard feature of the farm economy. The result of the New Deal for American farming was to hasten its transformation into a business in which only the efficient and well capitalized would thrive.

ROOSEVELT AND RELIEF

The New Deal was far more successful in meeting the most immediate problem of the 1930s—relief for the millions of unemployed and destitute citizens. Roosevelt never shared Hoover's distaste for direct federal support; on May 12, 1933, in response to FDR's March request, Congress authorized the RFC to distribute $500 million to the states to help individuals and families in need.

Drought and soil erosion brought on by overfarming turned the agricultural land of the Great Plains into a giant dust bowl during the 1930s. Especially hard hit were western Kansas and Oklahoma, eastern Colorado, and the Texas Panhandle. In May 1934 a dust storm blew across Montana and Wyoming. Picking up as much as 350 million tons of dirt, it blew eastward spreading dust over Chicago, Buffalo, New York, and Boston. Even ships at sea in the Atlantic found dust on their decks.

Roosevelt brought in Harry Hopkins to direct the relief program. A former social worker who seemed to live on black coffee and cigarettes, Hopkins set up a desk in the hallway of the RFC building and proceeded to spend more than $5 million in less than two hours. The relief payments were modest in size, but they enabled millions to avoid starvation and stay out of humiliating breadlines.

Another, more imaginative early effort was the Civilian Conservation Corps (CCC), which was Roosevelt's own idea. The CCC enrolled youth from city families on relief and sent them to the nation's parks and recreational areas to build trails and improve public facilities. Ultimately, more than two million young people served in the CCC, contributing both to their families' incomes and to the nation's welfare.

Hopkins realized the need to do more than just keep people alive, and he soon became an advocate of work relief. Hopkins argued that the government should put the jobless to work, not just to encourage self-respect, but also to enable them to earn enough to purchase consumer goods and thus stimulate the entire economy. In the fall of 1933, Roosevelt created the Civil Works Administration (CWA) and charged Hopkins with getting people off the unemployment lines and relief rolls and back to work. Hopkins had more than four

Federal work relief programs helped millions maintain their self-respect. Workers in the CCC received $30 a month for planting trees and digging drainage ditches.

million men and women at work by January 1934, building roads, schools, playgrounds, and athletic fields. Many of the workers were unskilled, and some of the projects were shoddy, but the CWA at least enabled people to work and earn enough money to survive the winter. Roosevelt, appalled at the huge expenditures involved, shut down the CWA in 1934.

The final commitment to the idea of work relief came in 1935 when Roosevelt established the Works Progress Administration (WPA) to spend nearly $5 billion authorized by Congress for emergency relief. The WPA, under Hopkins, put the unemployed on the federal payroll so they could earn enough to meet their basic needs and help stimulate the stagnant economy. Conservatives complained that the WPA amounted to nothing more than hiring the jobless to do make-work tasks with no real value. But Hopkins cared less about what was accomplished than about helping those who had been unemployed for years to get off the dole and gain self-respect by working again.

In addition to funding the usual construction and conservation projects, the WPA tried to preserve the skills of American artists, actors, and writers. The Federal Theatre Project produced plays, circuses, and puppet shows that enabled

The WPA program employed artists like Jackson Pollock, Willem de Kooning, and Ben Shahn to decorate public buildings with murals that celebrated American culture.

entertainers to practice their crafts and to perform before people who often had never seen a professional production before. Similar projects for writers and artists led to a series of valuable state guidebooks and to murals that adorned public buildings across the land.

The WPA helped ease the burden for the unemployed, but it failed to overcome the Depression. Rather than spending too much, as his critics charged, Roosevelt's greatest failure was not spending enough. The WPA never employed at any one time more than three million of the ten million jobless. The wages, although larger than relief payments, were still pitifully low, averaging only $52 a month. Thus the WPA failed to prime the American economy by increasing consumer purchasing power. Factories remained closed and machinery idle because the American people still did not have the money, either from relief or the WPA, to buy cars, radios, appliances, and the other consumer goods that had been the basis for the prosperity of the 1920s. By responding to basic human needs, Roosevelt had made the Depression bearable. The New Deal's failure, however, to go beyond relief to achieve prosperity led to a growing frustration and the appearance of more radical alternatives that challenged the conservative nature of the New Deal and forced FDR to shift to the left.

ROOSEVELT AND REFORM

In 1935, the focus of the New Deal shifted from relief and recovery to reform. During his first two years in office, FDR had concentrated on fighting the Depression by shoring up the sagging American economy. Roosevelt was developing a "broker-state" concept of government, responding to pressures from organized elements such as corporations, labor unions, and farm groups while ignoring the needs and wants of the dispossessed who had no clear political voice. The early New Deal tried to assist bankers and industrialists, large farmers, and members of the labor unions, but it did little to help unskilled workers and sharecroppers.

As head of the Federal Emergency Relief Administration and later the Works Progress Administration, Harry Hopkins oversaw the distribution of $8.5 billion for unemployment relief. Here he observes a potter working at his wheel at an exhibit entitled "Skills of the Unemployed" held in St. Louis, Missouri, in 1938.

The continuing Depression and high unemployment began to build pressure for more sweeping changes. Roosevelt faced the choice of either providing more radical programs, ones designed to end historical inequities in American life, or deferring to others who put forth solutions to the nation's ills. Bolstered by an impressive Democratic victory in the 1934 congressional elections, Roosevelt responded by embracing a reform program that marked the climax of the New Deal.

ANGRY VOICES

The signs of discontent were visible everywhere by 1935. In the upper Midwest, progressives and agrarian radicals were calling for government action to raise farm and labor income. Upton Sinclair, the muckraking novelist, nearly won the governorship of California in 1934 running on the slogan "End poverty in California," while in the East a violent strike in the textile industry shut down plants in twenty states. The most serious challenge to Roosevelt's leadership, however, came from three demagogues who captured national attention in the mid-1930s.

The first was Father Charles Coughlin, a Roman Catholic priest from Detroit, who had originally supported FDR. Speaking to a rapt nationwide radio audience in his rich, melodious voice, Coughlin appealed to the discontented with a strange mixture of crank monetary schemes and anti-Semitism. He broke with the New Deal in late 1934, denouncing it as the "Pagan Deal," and founded his own National Union for Social Justice.

A more benign but equally threatening figure appeared in California. Francis Townsend, a 67-year-old physician, came forward in 1934 with a scheme to assist the elderly, who were suffering greatly during the Depression. The Townsend Plan proposed giving everyone over the age of 60 a monthly pension of $200 with the proviso that it must be spent within thirty days. Although designed less as an old-age pension plan than as a way to stimulate the economy, the proposal understandably had its greatest appeal among the elderly. Despite the criticism from economists that the plan would transfer more than half the national income to less than 10 percent of the population, more than ten million people signed petitions endorsing the Townsend Plan, and few politicians dared oppose it.

The third new voice of protest was that of Huey Long, the flamboyant senator from Louisiana. Like Coughlin, an original supporter of the New Deal, Long turned against FDR and by 1935 had become a major political threat to the president. A shrewd, ruthless, yet witty man, Long had a remarkable ability to mock those in power. The Kingfish (a nickname he borrowed from *Amos 'n Andy*) announced a nationwide "Share the Wealth" movement in 1934. He spoke grandly of taking from the rich to make "every man a king," guaranteeing each American a home worth $5000 and an annual income of $2500. To finance the plan, Long advocated seizing all fortunes of more than $5 million and levying a tax of 100 percent on incomes greater than $1 million. By 1935, Long claimed to have founded twenty-seven thousand Share the Wealth clubs. Threatening to run as a third-party candidate in 1936, Long generated fear among Democratic leaders that he might attract three to four million votes, possibly enough to swing the election to the Republicans. Although an assassin killed Huey Long in Louisiana in late 1935, his popularity showed the need for the New Deal to do more to help those still in distress.

SOCIAL SECURITY

When the new Congress met in January 1935, Roosevelt was ready to support a series of reform measures designed to take the edge off national dissent. The recent elections had increased Democratic congressional strength significantly, with the Republicans losing thirteen seats in the House and retaining less than one-third of the Senate. Many of the Democrats were to the left of Roosevelt, favoring increased spending and more sweeping federal programs. "Boys—this is our hour," exulted Harry Hopkins. "We've got to get everything we want . . . now or never."

The most significant reform enacted in 1935 was the Social Security Act. The Townsend movement had reminded Americans that the United States, alone among modern industrial nations, had never developed a welfare system to aid the aged, the disabled, and the unemployed. A cabinet committee began studying the problem in 1934, and President Roosevelt sent its recommendations to Congress the following January.

The proposed legislation had three major parts. First, it provided for old-age pensions financed equally by a tax on employers and workers, without government contributions. In addition, it gave states federal matching funds to provide modest pensions for the destitute elderly. Second, it set up a system of unemployment compensation on a federal-state basis, with employers paying a payroll tax and with each state setting benefit levels and administering the program locally. Finally, it provided for direct federal grants to the states, on a matching basis, for welfare payments to the blind, handicapped, needy elderly, and dependent children.

Although there was criticism from conservatives who mourned the passing of traditional American reliance on self-help and individualism, the chief objections came from those who argued that the administration's measure did not go far enough. Democratic leaders, however, defeated efforts to incorporate Townsend's proposal for $200 monthly pensions and increases in unemployment benefits. Congress then passed the Social Security Act by overwhelming margins.

Despite the administration's boosterism, many felt that Social Security could not fulfill its promises.

Critics began to point out its shortcomings, as they have ever since. The old-age pensions were paltry. Designed to begin in 1942, they ranged from $10 to $85 a month. Not everyone was covered; those who most needed protection in their old age, such as farmers and domestic servants, were not included. The regressive feature of the act was even worse. All participants, regardless of income or economic status, paid in at the same rate, with no supplement from the general revenue.

Other portions of the act were equally open to question. The cumbersome unemployment system offered no aid to those currently out of work, only to people who would lose their jobs in the future. The outright grants to the handicapped and dependent children were minute in terms of the need; in New York City, for example, a blind person received only $5 a week in 1937.

The conservative nature of the legislation reflected Roosevelt's own fiscal orthodoxy, but even more it was a product of his political realism. Despite the severity of the Depression, he realized that establishing a system of federal welfare went against deeply rooted American convictions. He insisted on a tax on participants to give those involved in the pension plan a vested interest in Social Security. He wanted them to feel they had earned their pensions and that in the future no one would dare take them away. "With those taxes in there," he explained privately, "no damned politician can ever scrap my social security program." Above all, FDR had succeeded in establishing the principle of government responsibility for the aged, the handicapped, and the unemployed. Whatever the defects of the legislation, Social Security stood as a landmark of the New Deal, creating a system to provide for the welfare of individuals in a complex industrial society.

LABOR LEGISLATION

The other major reform achievement in 1935 was passage of the National Labor Relations Act. Senator Robert Wagner of New York introduced legislation in 1934 to outlaw company unions and other unfair labor practices in order to ensure collective bargaining for unions. FDR, who had little knowledge of labor-management relations and apparently little interest in them, opposed the bill. In 1935, however, Wagner began to gather broad support for his measure, which passed the Senate in May with only twelve opposing votes, and the president, seeing passage as likely, gave it his approval. The bill moved quickly through the House, and Roosevelt signed it into law in July.

The Wagner Act, as it became known, created a National Labor Relations Board to preside over labor-management relations and enable unions to engage in collective bargaining with federal support. The act outlawed a variety of union-busting tactics and in its key provision decreed that whenever the majority of a company's workers voted for a union to represent them, management would be compelled to negotiate with the union on all matters of wages, hours, and working conditions. With this unprecedented government sanction, labor unions could now recruit the large number of unorganized workers throughout the country. The Wagner Act, the most far-reaching of all New Deal measures, led to the revitalization of the American labor movement and a permanent change in labor-management relations.

Three years later, Congress passed a second law that had a lasting impact on American workers—the Fair Labor Standards Act. A long-sought goal of the New Deal, this measure aimed to establish both minimum wages and maximum hours of work per week. Since labor unions usually were able to negotiate adequate levels of pay and work for their members, the act was aimed at unorganized workers and met with only grudging support from unions.

The Fair Labor Standards Act provided for a minimum wage of 40 cents an hour by 1940 and a standard workweek of forty hours, with time and a half for overtime. Despite its loopholes, the legislation did lead to pay raises for the twelve million workers earning less than 40 cents an hour. More important, like Social Security it set up a system—however inadequate—that Congress could build on in the future to reach more generous and humane levels.

All in all, Roosevelt's record in reform was similar to that in relief and recovery—modest success but no sweeping victory. A cautious and pragmatic leader, FDR moved far enough to the left to overcome the challenges of Coughlin, Townsend, and Long without venturing too far from the mainstream. His reforms improved the quality of life in America significantly, but he made no effort to correct all the nation's social and economic wrongs.

IMPACT OF THE NEW DEAL

The New Deal had a broad influence on the quality of life in the United States in the 1930s. Government programs reached into areas hitherto untouched. Many of them brought about long-overdue improvements, but others failed to make any significant dent in historic inequities. The most important advances came with the dramatic growth of labor unions; the conditions for working women and minorities in nonunionized industries showed no comparable advance.

RISE OF ORGANIZED LABOR

Trade unions were weak at the onset of the Depression, with a membership of fewer than three million workers. Most were in the American Federation of Labor (AFL), composed of craft unions that served the needs of skilled workers. The nation's basic industries, such as steel and automobiles, were unorganized; the great mass of unskilled workers thus fared poorly in terms of wages and working conditions.

John L. Lewis, head of the United Mine Workers, took the lead in forming the Committee on Industrial Organization (CIO) in 1935. The son of a Welsh coal miner, Lewis was a dynamic and ruthless man. He had led the mine workers since 1919 and was determined to spread the benefits of unions throughout industry. Lewis first battled with the leadership of the AFL, and then—after being expelled—he renamed his group the Congress of Industrial Organizations and announced in 1936 that he would use the Wagner Act to extend collective bargaining to the nation's auto and steel industries.

Within five years, Lewis had scored a remarkable series of victories. Some came easily. The big steel companies, led by U.S. Steel, surrendered without a fight in 1937; management realized that federal support put the unions in a strong position. There was greater resistance in the automobile industry. When General Motors, the first target, resisted, the newly created United Automobile

Workers (UAW) developed an effective strike technique. In late December 1936, GM workers in Flint, Michigan, simply sat down in the factory, refusing to leave until the company recognized their union, and threatening to destroy the valuable tools and machines if they were removed forcibly. When the Michigan governor refused to call out the national guard to break the strike, General Motors conceded defeat and signed a contract with the UAW. Chrysler quickly followed suit, but Henry Ford refused to give in and fought the UAW, hiring strikebreakers and beating up organizers. In 1941, however, Ford finally recognized the UAW.

By the end of the 1930s, the CIO had some five million members, slightly more than the AFL. The successes were remarkable—in addition to the automaking and steel unions, organizers for the CIO and the AFL had been successful in the textile, rubber, electrical, and metal industries. For the first time, unskilled as well as skilled were unionized. Women and African Americans benefited from the creation of the CIO, not because the union followed enlightened policies, but simply because they made up a substantial proportion of the unskilled workforce that the CIO organized.

Yet despite these impressive gains, only 28 percent of all Americans (excluding farmworkers) belonged to unions by 1940. Millions in the restaurant, retail, and service trades remained unorganized, working long hours for very low wages. Employer resistance and traditional hostility to unions blocked further progress, as did the aloof attitude of President Roosevelt, who commented to labor and management, "A plague on both your houses" during the steel strike. The Wagner Act had helped open the way, but labor leaders such as Lewis, Philip Murray of the Steel Workers Organizing Committee, and Walter Reuther of the United Automobile Workers deserved most of the credit for union achievements.

THE NEW DEAL RECORD ON HELP TO MINORITIES

The Roosevelt administration's attempts to aid the downtrodden were least effective with African Americans and other racial minorities. The Depression had hit blacks with special force. Sharecroppers and tenant farmers had seen the price of cotton drop from 18 to 6 cents a pound, far below the level to sustain a family on the land. In the cities, the saying "Last hired, First fired" proved all too true; by 1933, more than 50 percent of urban blacks were unemployed. Hard times sharpened racial prejudice. "No jobs for niggers until every white man has a job" became a rallying cry for many whites in Atlanta.

The New Deal helped African Americans survive the Depression, but it never tried to confront squarely the racial injustice built into the federal relief programs. Although the programs served blacks as well as whites, in the South the weekly payments blacks received were much smaller. Nor did later reform

African American contralto Marian Anderson sang on the steps of the Lincoln Memorial in a concert given April 9, 1939.

measures help very much. Neither the minimum wage nor Social Security covered those working as farmers or domestic servants, categories that comprised 65 percent of all African American workers. Thus an NAACP official commented that Social Security "looks like a sieve with the holes just large enough for the majority of Negroes to fall through."

Despite this bleak record, African Americans rallied behind Roosevelt's leadership, abandoning their historic ties to the Republican party. In 1936, more than 75 percent of those African Americans who voted supported FDR. In part, this switch came in response to Roosevelt's appointment of a number of prominent African Americans to high-ranking government positions. Eleanor Roosevelt spoke out eloquently throughout the decade against racial discrimination, most notably in 1939 when the Daughters of the American Revolution refused to let African American contralto Marian Anderson sing in Constitution Hall. The First Lady and Interior Secretary Harold Ickes arranged for the singer to perform at the Lincoln Memorial, where 75,000 people gathered to hear her on Easter Sunday.

Perhaps the most influential factor in the African Americans' political switch was the color-blind policy of Harry Hopkins. He had more than one million blacks working for the WPA by 1939, many of them in teaching and artistic positions as well as in construction jobs. Overall, the New Deal provided assistance to 40 percent of the nation's blacks during the Depression. Uneven as his record was, Roosevelt had still done more to aid this oppressed minority than any previous president since Lincoln. One African American newspaper commented that while "relief and WPA are not ideal, they are better than the Hoover bread lines and they'll have to do until the real thing comes along."

The New Deal did far less for Mexican Americans. Engaged primarily in agricultural labor, these people found their wages in California fields dropping from 35 to 14 cents an hour by 1933. The pool of unemployed migrant labor expanded rapidly with Dust Bowl conditions in the Great Plains and the subsequent flight of "Okies" and "Arkies" to the cotton fields of Arizona and the truck farms of California. The Roosevelt administration cut off any further influx from Mexico by barring entry of any immigrant "likely to become a public charge"; local authorities rounded up migrants and shipped them back to Mexico to reduce the welfare rolls.

Native Americans, after decades of neglect, fared slightly better under the New Deal. Roosevelt appointed John Collier, a social worker who championed Indian rights, to serve as commissioner of Indian affairs. In 1934, Congress passed the Indian Reorganization Act, a reform measure designed to stress tribal unity and autonomy instead of attempting (as previous policy had done) to transform Indians into self-sufficient farmers by granting them small plots of land.

Roosevelt appointed John Collier as commissioner of Indian affairs to bring the New Deal to Native Americans. Under the Indian Reorganization Act of 1934, more than 7 million acres of land were restored to Native American control. Still, many Indians continued to distrust the government and its New Deal programs. Collier is shown here with a group of Flathead Indian chiefs standing behind Secretary of the Interior Harold L. Ickes on October 28, 1935, as Ickes signs the first constitution providing for Indian self-rule. Previously, the Bureau of Indian Affairs had directed the government of the Indians.

Despite modest gains, however, the nation's one-third million Indians remained the most impoverished citizens in America.

WOMEN AT WORK

The decade witnessed no significant gain in the status of American women. In the midst of the Depression, there was little concern expressed for protecting or extending their rights. The popular idea that women worked for "pin money" while men were the breadwinners for their families led employers to discriminate in favor of men when cutting the workforce. Working women "are holding jobs that rightfully belong to the God-intended providers of the household," declared a Chicago civic group. More than three-fourths of the nation's school boards refused to hire married women, and more than half of them fired women teachers who married. Federal regulations prohibited more than one member of a family from working in the civil service, and almost always it was the wife who had to defer to her husband.

Many of the working women in the 1930s were either single or the sole supporters of an entire family. Yet their wages remained lower than those for men, and their unemployment rate ran higher than 20 percent throughout the decade. The New Deal offered little encouragement. NRA codes sanctioned lower wages for women, permitting laundries, for example, to pay them as little as 14 cents an hour. The minimum wage did help those women employed in industry, but too many worked as maids and waitresses—jobs not covered by the law—for the new law to have much overall effect on women's income.

The one area of advance in the 1930s came in government. Eleanor Roosevelt set an example that encouraged millions of American women. Instead of presiding sedately over the White House, she traveled continually around the country, always eager to uncover wrongs and bring them to the president's attention. Frances Perkins, the secretary of labor, became the first woman cabinet member, and FDR appointed women as ambassadors and federal judges for the first time.

Women also were elected to office in larger numbers in the 1930s. Hattie W. Caraway of Arkansas succeeded her husband in the Senate, winning a full term in 1934. That same year, voters elected six women to the House of Representatives. Public service, however, was one of the few professions open to women. The nation's leading medical and law schools discouraged women from applying, and the percentage of female faculty members in colleges and universities continued to decline in the 1930s. In sum, a decade that was grim for most Americans was especially hard on American women.

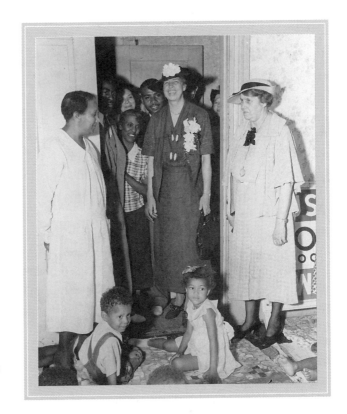

Eleanor Roosevelt visited many sites in her efforts to bring the New Deal to the forgotten and the dispossessed. She is shown here visiting an African American nursery school run by the WPA in Des Moines, Iowa.

END OF THE NEW DEAL

The New Deal reached its high point in 1936, when Roosevelt was overwhelmingly reelected and the Democratic party strengthened its hold on Congress. This political triumph was deceptive. In the next two years, Roosevelt met with a series of defeats in Congress. Yet despite the setbacks, he remained a popular political leader who had restored American self-confidence as he strove to meet the challenges of the Depression.

THE ELECTION OF 1936

Franklin Roosevelt enjoyed his finest political hour in 1936. A man who loved the give-and-take of politics, FDR faced challenges from both the left and the right as he sought reelection. Father Coughlin helped organize a Union party, with North Dakota Progressive Congressman William Lemke heading the ticket. At the other extreme, a group of wealthy industrialists formed the Liberty League to fight what they saw as the New Deal's assault on property rights. The Liberty League

THE ELECTION OF 1936

CANDIDATE	PARTY	POPULAR VOTE	ELECTORAL VOTE
Roosevelt	Democratic	27,752,869	523
Landon	Republican	16,674,665	8

endorsed the Republican presidential candidate, Governor Alfred M. Landon of Kansas. A moderate, colorless figure, Landon disappointed his backers by refusing to campaign for repeal of the popular New Deal reforms.

Roosevelt ignored Lemke and the Union party, focusing attention instead on the assault from the right. In his speeches, FDR condemned the "economic royalists" who were "unanimous in their hatred for me." "I welcome their hatred," he declared, and promised that in his second term, these forces would meet "their master."

This frank appeal to class sympathies proved enormously successful. Roosevelt won easily, receiving five million more votes than he had in 1932 and outscoring Landon in the electoral college by 523 to 8. The Democrats did almost as well in Congress, piling up margins of 331 to 89 in the House and 76 to 16 in the Senate (with 4 not aligned with either major party).

Equally important, the election marked the stunning success of a new political coalition that would dominate American politics for the next three decades. FDR, building on the inroads into the Republican majority that Al Smith had begun in 1928, carried urban areas by impressive margins, winning 3.6 million more votes than his opponents in the nation's twelve largest cities. He held on to the traditional Democratic votes in the South and West and added to them by appealing strongly to the diverse religious and ethnic groups in the northern cities—Catholics and Jews, Italians and Poles, Irish and Slavs. The strong support of labor, together with three-quarters of the black vote, indicated that the nation's new alignment followed economic as well as cultural lines. The poor and the oppressed, who in the Depression years included many middle-class Americans, became attached to the Democratic party, leaving the GOP in a minority position, limited to the well-to-do and to rural and small-town Americans of native stock.

THE SUPREME COURT FIGHT

FDR proved to be far more adept at winning electoral victories than in achieving his goals in Congress. In 1937, he attempted to use his recent success to overcome the one obstacle remaining in his path—the Supreme Court. During his first term, the Court had ruled several New Deal programs unconstitutional, most notably the NRA and the AAA. Only three of the nine justices were sympathetic to the need for emergency measures in the midst of the Depression. Two others were unpredictable, sometimes approving New Deal measures and sometimes opposing them. Four justices were bent on using the Constitution to block Roosevelt's proposals.

When Congress convened in 1937, the president offered a startling proposal to overcome the Court's threat to the New Deal. Instead of seeking a constitutional amendment either to limit the Court's power or to clarify the constitutional issues, FDR chose an oblique attack. Declaring the Court was falling behind schedule because of the age of its members, he asked Congress to appoint a new justice for each member of the Court over the age of 70, up to a maximum of six.

Although this "court-packing" scheme, as critics quickly dubbed it, was perfectly legal, it outraged not only conservatives but liberals as well, who realized it could set a dangerous precedent for the future. Republicans wisely kept silent, letting prominent Democrats lead the fight against Roosevelt's plan. Despite all-out pressure from the White House, resistance in the Senate blocked early action on the proposal.

The Court defended itself well. Chief Justice Charles Evans Hughes testified tellingly to the Senate Judiciary Committee, pointing out that in fact the Court was up to date and not behind schedule as Roosevelt charged. The Court then surprised observers with a series of rulings approving such controversial New Deal measures as the Wagner Act and Social Security. Believing he had proved his point, the president allowed his court-packing plan to die in the Senate.

During the next few years, Roosevelt was able to appoint such distinguished jurists as Hugo Black, William O. Douglas, and Felix Frankfurter to the Supreme Court. Yet the price was high. The court fight had badly weakened the president's relations with Congress, opening deep rifts with members of his own party. Many senators and representatives who had voted reluctantly for Roosevelt's measures during the depths of the Depression now felt free to oppose any further New Deal reforms.

THE NEW DEAL IN DECLINE

The legislative record during Roosevelt's second term was meager. Aside from the minimum wage and maximum-hour law passed in 1938, Congress did not extend the New Deal into any new areas. Disturbed by the growing congressional resistance, Roosevelt set out in the spring of 1938 to defeat a number of conservative Democratic congressmen and senators, primarily in the South. His

Major New Deal Legislation and Agencies

YEAR CREATED	ACT OR AGENCY	PROVISIONS
1933	Agricultural Adjustment Administration (AAA)	Attempted to regulate agricultural production through farm subsidies; reworked after the Supreme Court ruled its key regulatory provisions unconstitutional in 1936; coordinated agricultural production during World War II, after which it was disbanded.
	Banking Act of 1933 (Glass-Steagall Act)	Prohibited commercial banks from selling stock or financing corporations; created FDIC.
	Civilian Conservation Corps (CCC)	Young men between the ages of 18 and 25 volunteered to be placed in camps to work on regional environmental projects, mainly west of the Mississippi; they received $30 a month, of which $25 was sent home; disbanded during World War II.
	Civil Works Administration (CWA)	Emergency work relief program put more than four million people to work during the extremely cold winter of 1933–1934, after which it was disbanded.
	Federal Deposit Insurance Corporation (FDIC)	A federal guarantee of savings bank deposits initially of up to $2,500, raised to $5,000 in 1934, and frequently thereafter; continues today with a limit of $100,000.
	Federal Emergency Relief Administration (FERA)	Combined cash relief to needy families with work relief; superseded in early 1935 by the extensive work relief projects of the WPA and unemployment insurance established by Social Security.
	National Recovery Administration (NRA)	Attempted to combat the Depression through national economic planning by establishing and administering a system of industrial codes to control production, prices, labor relations, and trade practices among leading business interests; ruled unconstitutional by the Supreme Court in 1935.
	Public Works Administration (PWA)	Financed more than 34,000 federal and nonfederal construction projects at a cost of more than $6 billion; initiated the first federal public housing program, made the federal government the nation's leading producer of power, and advanced conservation of the nation's natural resources; discontinued in 1939 due to its effectiveness at reducing unemployment and promoting private investment.
	Tennessee Valley Authority (TVA)	An attempt at regional planning. Included provisions for environment and recreational design; architectural, educational, and health projects; and controversial public power projects; continues today to meet the Tennessee Valley's energy and flood-control needs.
1934	Federal Communications Commission (FCC)	Regulatory agency with wide discretionary powers established to oversee wired and wireless communication; reflected growing importance of radio in everyday lives of Americans during the Depression; continues to regulate television as well as radio.

YEAR CREATED	ACT OR AGENCY	PROVISIONS
	Federal Housing Administration (FHA)	Expanded private home ownership among moderate-income families through federal guarantees of private mortgages, the reduction of down payments from 30 to 10 percent, and the extension of repayment from 20 to 30 years; continues to function today.
	Securities and Exchange Commission (SEC)	Continues today to regulate trading practices in stocks and bonds according to federal laws.
1935	National Labor Relations Board (NLRB); established by Wagner Act	Greatly enhanced power of American labor by overseeing collective bargaining; continues to arbitrate labor-management disputes today.
	National Youth Administration (NYA)	Established by the WPA to reduce competition for jobs by supporting education and training of youth; paid grants to more than 2 million high school and college students in return for work performed in their schools; also trained another 2.6 million out-of-school youths as skilled labor to prepare them for later employment in the private sector; disbanded during World War II.
	Rural Electrification Administration (REA)	Transformed American rural life by making electricity available at low rates to American farm families in areas that private power companies refused to service; closed the cultural gap between rural and urban everyday life by making modern amenities, such as radio, available in rural areas.
	Social Security Act	Guaranteed retirement payments for enrolled workers beginning at age 65; set up federal-state system of unemployment insurance and care for dependent mothers and children, the handicapped, and public health; continues today.
	Works Progress Administration (WPA)	Massive work relief program funded projects ranging from construction to acting; disbanded by FDR during World War II.
1937	Farm Security Administration (FSA)	Granted loans to small farmers and tenants for rehabilitation and purchase of small-sized farms; Congress slashed its appropriations during World War II when many poor farmers entered the armed forces or migrated to urban areas.
1938	Fair Labor Standards Act	Established a minimum wage of 40 cents an hour and a maximum workweek of 40 hours for businesses engaged in interstate commerce.

targets gleefully charged the president with interference in local politics; only one of the men he sought to defeat lost in the primaries. The failure of this attempted purge further undermined Roosevelt's strained relations with Congress.

The worst blow came in the economic sector. The slow but steady improvement in the economy suddenly gave way to a sharp recession in the late summer of 1937. In the following ten months, industrial production fell by one-third, and nearly four million workers lost their jobs. Critics of the New Deal quickly labeled the downturn "the Roosevelt recession," and business executives claimed that it reflected a lack of confidence in FDR's leadership.

Actually, Roosevelt was at fault. In an effort to reduce expanding budget deficits, he had cut back sharply on WPA and other government programs after the election. For several months, Roosevelt refused to heed calls from economists to renew heavy government spending. Finally, in April 1938, Roosevelt asked Congress for a $3.75 billion relief appropriation, and the economy began to revive. But FDR's premature attempt to balance the budget had meant two more years of hard times and had marred his reputation as the energetic foe of the Depression.

The political result of the attempted purge and the recession was a strong Republican upsurge in the elections of 1938. The GOP won an impressive 81 seats in the House and 8 more in the Senate, as well as 13 governorships. The Democrats still held a sizable majority in Congress, but their margin in the House was particularly deceptive. There were 262 Democratic representatives to 169 Republicans, but 93 southern Democrats held the balance of power. More and more often after 1938, anti–New Deal Southerners voted with Republican conservatives to block social and economic reform measures. Thus not only was the New Deal over by the end of 1938, but a new bipartisan conservative coalition that would prevail for a quarter century had formed in Congress.

EVALUATION OF THE NEW DEAL

The New Deal lasted a brief five years, and most of its measures came in two legislative bursts in the spring of 1933 and the summer of 1935. Yet its impact on American life was enduring. Nearly every aspect of economic, social, and political development in the decades that followed bore the imprint of Roosevelt's leadership.

The least impressive achievement of the New Deal came in the economic realm. Whatever credit Roosevelt is given for relieving human suffering in the depths of the Depression must be balanced against his failure to achieve recovery in the 1930s. The moderate nature of his programs, especially the unwieldy NRA, led to slow and halting industrial recovery. Although much of the improvement that was made came as a result of government spending, FDR never embraced the concept of planned deficits, striving instead for a balanced budget. As a result, the nation had barely reached the 1929 level of production a decade later, and there were still nearly ten million men and women unemployed.

Equally important, Roosevelt refused to make any sweeping changes in the American economic system. Aside from the TVA, there were no broad experiments in regional planning and no attempt to alter free enterprise beyond imposing some limited forms of government regulation. The New Deal did nothing to alter the basic distribution of wealth and power in the nation. The outcome was the preservation of the traditional capitalist system with a thin overlay of federal control.

More significant change occurred in American society. With the adoption of Social Security, the government acknowledged for the first time its responsibility to provide for the welfare of those unable to care for themselves in an industrial society. The Wagner Act helped stimulate the growth of labor unions to balance corporate power, and the minimum wage law provided a much needed floor for many workers.

Yet the New Deal tended to help only the more vocal and organized groups, such as union members and commercial farmers. Those without effective voices or political clout—African Americans, Mexican Americans, women, sharecroppers, restaurant and laundry workers—received little help from the New Deal. For all the appealing rhetoric about the "forgotten man," Roosevelt did little more than Hoover in responding to the long-term needs of the dispossessed.

The most lasting impact of the Roosevelt leadership came in politics. Taking advantage of the emerging power of ethnic voters and capitalizing on the frustration growing out of the Depression, FDR proved to be a genius at forging a new coalition. Overcoming the friction between rural and urban Democrats that had prolonged Republican supremacy in the 1920s, he attracted new groups to the Democratic party, principally African Americans and organized labor. His political success led to a major realignment that lasted long after he left the scene.

His political achievement also reveals the true nature of Roosevelt's success. He was a brilliant politician who recognized the essence of leadership in a democracy—appealing directly to the people and giving them a sense of purpose. He succeeded in infusing them with the same indomitable courage and jaunty optimism that had marked his own battle with polio. Thus, despite his limitations as a reformer, Roosevelt proved to be the leader the American people needed in the 1930s—a president who provided the psychological lift that helped them endure and survive the Great Depression.

27

AMERICA AND THE WORLD, 1921–1945

On August 27, 1928, U.S. Secretary of State Frank B. Kellogg, French Foreign Minister Aristide Briand, and representatives of twelve other nations met in Paris to sign a treaty outlawing war. Several hundred spectators crowded into the ornate clock room of the Quai d'Orsay to watch the historic ceremony. Six huge klieg lights illuminated the scene so photographers could record the moment for a world eager for peace. Briand opened the ceremony with a speech in which he declared, "Peace is proclaimed," and then Kellogg signed the document with a foot-long gold pen given to him by the citizens of Le Havre as a token of Franco-American friendship. In the United States, a senator called the Kellogg-Briand Pact "the most telling action ever taken in human history to abolish war."

In reality, the Pact of Paris was the result of a determined American effort to avoid involvement in the European alliance system. In June 1927, Briand had sent a message to the American people inviting the United States to join with France in signing a treaty to outlaw war between the two nations. The invitation struck a sympathetic response, especially among pacifists who had advocated the outlawing of war throughout the 1920s, but the State Department feared correctly that Briand's true intention was to establish a close tie between France and the United States. The French had already created a network of alliances with the smaller countries of eastern Europe; an antiwar treaty with the United States would at least ensure American sympathy, if not involvement, in case of another European war. Kellogg delayed several months and then outmaneuvered Briand by propos-

Secretary of State Frank Kellogg signs the Kellogg-Briand Pact renouncing war. A grand document, the treaty included no method to enforce its provisions. The agreement was formally broken when Japan invaded Manchuria in 1931.

ing the pledge against war not be confined just to France and the United States, but instead be extended to all nations.

Eventually the signers of the Kellogg-Briand Pact included nearly every nation in the world, but the effect was negligible. All promised to renounce war as an instrument of national policy, except of course, as the British made clear in a reservation, in matters of self-defense. Enforcement of the treaty relied solely on the moral force of world opinion. The Pact of Paris was, as one senator shrewdly commented, only "an international kiss."

Unfortunately, the Kellogg-Briand Pact was symbolic of American foreign policy in the years after World War I. Instead of asserting the role of leadership its resources and power commanded, the United States kept aloof from other nations. America went its own way, extending trade and economic dominance but refusing to take the lead in maintaining world order. This retreat from responsibility seemed unimportant in the 1920s when exhaustion from World War I ensured relative peace and tranquility. But in the 1930s, when threats to world order arose in Europe and Asia, the American people retreated even deeper, searching for an isolationist policy that would spare them the agony of another great war.

There was no place to hide in the modern world. The Nazi onslaught in Europe and the Japanese expansion in Asia finally led to American entry into World War II in late 1941, at a time when the chances for an Allied victory seemed most remote. With incredible swiftness, the nation mobilized its military and industrial strength. American armies were soon fighting on three continents, the U.S. Navy controlled the world's oceans, and the nation's factories were sending a vast stream of war supplies to more than twenty Allied countries.

When victory came in 1945, the United States was by far the most powerful nation in the world. But instead of the enduring peace that might have permitted a return to a less active foreign policy, the onset of the Cold War with the Soviet Union brought on a new era of tension and conflict. This time the United States could not retreat from responsibility. World War II was a coming of age for American foreign policy.

RETREAT, REVERSAL, AND RIVALRY

"The day of the armistice America stood on the hilltops of glory, proud in her strength, invincible in her ideals, acclaimed and loved by a world free of an ancient fear at last," wrote journalist George Creel in 1920. "Today we writhe in a pit of our own digging; despising ourselves and despised by the betrayed peoples of earth." The bitter disillusionment Creel described ran through every aspect of American foreign policy in the 1920s. In contrast to diplomatic actions under Wilsonian idealism, American diplomats in the 1920s made loans, negotiated treaties and agreements, and pledged the nation's good faith, but they were careful not to make any binding commitments on behalf of world order. The result was neither isolation nor involvement but rather a cautious middle course that managed to alienate friends and encourage foes.

RETREAT IN EUROPE

The United States emerged from World War I as the richest nation on earth, displacing England from its prewar position of economic primacy. The Allied governments owed the United States a staggering $10 billion in war debts, money they had borrowed during and immediately after the conflict. Each year of the 1920s saw the nation increase its economic lead as the balance of trade tipped heavily in America's favor. By 1929, American exports totaled more than $7 billion a year, three times the prewar level, and American overseas investment had risen to $17.2 billion.

The European nations could no longer compete on equal terms. The high American tariff, first imposed in 1922 and then raised again in 1930, frustrated attempts by England, France, and a defeated Germany to earn the dollars necessary to meet their American financial obligations. The Allied partners in World War I asked Washington to cancel the $10 billion in war debts, particularly after they were forced to scale down their demands for German reparations payments. American leaders from Wilson to Hoover indignantly refused the request, claiming the ungrateful Allies were trying to repudiate their sacred obligations.

Only a continuing flow of private American capital to Germany allowed the payment of reparations to the Allies and the partial repayment of the Allies' war debts in the 1920s. The financial crash of 1929 halted the flow of American dollars across the Atlantic and led to subsequent default on the debt payments, with accompanying bitterness on both sides of the ocean.

Political relations fared little better. The United States never joined the League of Nations, nor did it take part in the attempts by England and France to negotiate European security treaties. The Republican administrations of the 1920s refused to compromise American freedom of action by embracing collective security, the principle on which the League was founded. And FDR, always realistic, made no effort to renew Wilson's futile quest. Thus the United States remained aloof from the European balance of power and refused to stand behind the increasingly shaky Versailles settlement.

The U.S. government ignored the Soviet Union throughout the 1920s. In 1933, Franklin Roosevelt finally ended the long estrangement by signing an agreement opening up diplomatic relations between the two countries. The Soviets soon went back on promises to stop all subversive activity in the United States and to settle prerevolutionary debts, but even if they rarely understood one another, at least the two nations had opened a channel of communication.

COOPERATION IN LATIN AMERICA

U.S. policy was both more active and more enlightened in the Western Hemisphere than in Europe. The State Department sought new ways in the 1920s to pursue traditional goals of political dominance and economic advantage in Latin America. The outcome of World War I lessened any fears of European threats to the area and thus enabled the United States to dismantle the interventions in the Caribbean carried out by Roosevelt, Taft, and Wilson. At the same time, both Republican and Democratic administrations worked hard to extend American trade and investment in the nations to the south.

Under Harding, Coolidge, and Hoover, American marines were withdrawn from Haiti and the Dominican Republic, and in 1924 the last detachment left

Nicaragua, ending a twelve-year occupation. Renewed unrest there the next year, however, led to a second intervention in Nicaragua, which did not end until the early 1930s.

When FDR took office in 1933, relations with Latin America were far better than they had been under Wilson, but American trade in the hemisphere had fallen drastically as the Depression worsened. Roosevelt moved quickly to solidify the improved relations and gain economic benefits. With his usual flair for the dramatic, he proclaimed a policy of the "good neighbor" and then proceeded to win goodwill by renouncing the imperialism of the past.

In 1933, Secretary of State Cordell Hull signed a conditional pledge of nonintervention at a Pan-American conference in Montevideo, Uruguay. A year later, the United States renounced the right to intervene in Cuban affairs it had asserted under the Platt Amendment and loosened its grip on Panama. By 1936, American troops were no longer occupying any Latin American nation.

The United States had not changed its basic goal of political and economic dominance in the hemisphere; rather, the new policy of benevolence reflected Roosevelt's belief that cooperation and friendship were more effective tactics than threats and armed intervention. Mexico tried his patience in 1938 by nationalizing its oil resources; with admirable restraint, the president finally negotiated a settlement in 1941 on terms favorable to Mexico. Yet this economic loss was more than offset by the new trade opportunities opened up by the Good Neighbor policy. American commerce with Latin America increased fourfold in the 1930s, and investment rose substantially from its Depression low. Most important, FDR succeeded in forging a new policy of regional collective security. As the ominous events leading to World War II unfolded in Europe and Asia, the nations of the Western Hemisphere looked to the United States for protection against external danger.

RIVALRY IN ASIA

In the years following World War I, the United States and Japan were on a collision course in the Pacific. The Japanese, lacking the raw materials to sustain their developing industrial economy, were determined to expand onto the Asian mainland. They had taken Korea by 1905 and during World War I had extended their control over the mines, harbors, and railroads of Manchuria, the industrial region of northeast China. The American Open Door policy remained the primary obstacle to complete Japanese dominion over China. The United States thus faced the clear-cut choice of either abandoning China or forcefully opposing Japan's expansion. American efforts to avoid making this painful decision postponed the eventual showdown but not the growing rivalry.

The first attempt at a solution came in 1921 when the United States convened the Washington Conference, which included delegates from the United States, Japan, Great Britain, and six other nations. The major objective was a political settlement of the tense Asian situation, but the most pressing issue was a dangerous naval race between Japan and the United States. Both nations were engaged in extensive shipbuilding programs begun during the war; Great Britain was forced to compete in order to preserve its traditional control of the sea.

In his welcoming address at the Washington Conference, Secretary of State Charles Evans Hughes outlined a specific plan for naval disarmament, calling for the scrapping of sixty-six battleships—thirty American, nineteen British, and seventeen Japanese. Three months later, delegates signed a Five Power Treaty embodying the main elements of Hughes's proposal: limitation of capital ships (battleships and aircraft carriers) in a ratio of 5:5:3 for the United States, Britain, and Japan, respectively, and 1.67:1.67 for France and Italy. England reluctantly accepted equality with the United States, while Japan agreed to the lower ratio only in return for an American pledge not to fortify Pacific bases such as the Philippines and Guam. The treaty cooled off the naval race even though it did not include cruisers, destroyers, or submarines.

The Washington Conference produced two other major agreements: the Nine Power Treaty and the Four Power Treaty. The first simply pledged all the countries involved to uphold the Open Door policy, while the other compact replaced the old Anglo-Japanese alliance with a new Pacific security pact signed by the United States, Great Britain, Japan, and France. Neither document contained any enforcement provision beyond a promise to consult in case of a violation. In essence, the Washington treaties formed a parchment peace, a pious set of pledges that attempted to freeze the status quo in the Pacific.

This compromise lasted less than a decade. In September 1931, Japanese forces violated the Nine Power Treaty and the Kellogg-Briand Pact by overrunning Manchuria in a brutal act of aggression. The United States, paralyzed by the Depression, responded feebly. Secretary of State Henry L. Stimson issued notes in January 1932 vowing the United States would not recognize the legality of the Japanese seizure of Manchuria. Despite concurrence by the League on nonrecognition, the Japanese ignored the American moral sanction and incorporated the former Chinese province, now renamed Manchukuo, into their rapidly expanding empire.

Aside from the Good Neighbor approach in the Western Hemisphere, American foreign policy faithfully reflected the prevailing disillusionment with world power that gripped the country after World War I. The United States avoided taking any constructive steps toward preserving world order, preferring instead the empty symbolism of the Washington treaties and the Kellogg-Briand Pact.

ISOLATIONISM

The retreat from an active world policy in the 1920s turned into a headlong flight back to isolationism in the 1930s. Two factors were responsible. First, the Depression made foreign policy seem remote and unimportant to most Americans. As unemployment increased and the economic crisis intensified after 1929, many people grew apathetic about events abroad. Second, the danger of war abroad, when it did finally penetrate the American consciousness, served only to strengthen the desire to escape involvement.

Three powerful and discontented nations were on the march in the 1930s—Germany, Italy, and Japan. In Germany, Adolf Hitler came to power in 1933 as the head of a National Socialist, or Nazi, movement. A shrewd and charismatic leader, Hitler capitalized on both domestic discontent and bitterness over World War I. Blaming the Jews for all of Germany's ills and asserting the supremacy of the "Aryan" race of blond, blue-eyed Germans, he quickly imposed a totalitarian dictatorship in which the Nazi party ruled and the *Führer* was supreme. Hitler took Germany out of the League of Nations, reoccupied the Rhineland, and formally denounced the Treaty of Versailles. His boasts of uniting all Germans into a Greater Third Reich that would last a thousand years filled his European opponents with terror, blocking any effective challenge to his regime.

In Italy, another dictator, Benito Mussolini, had come to power in 1922. Emboldened by Hitler's success, he embarked on an aggressive foreign policy in 1935. His invasion of the independent African nation of Ethiopia led its emperor, Haile Selassie, to call on the League of Nations for support. With England and France far more concerned about Hitler, the League's halfhearted measures utterly failed to halt Mussolini's conquest. "Fifty-two nations had combined to resist aggression," commented historian A. J. P. Taylor; "all they accomplished was that Haile Selassie lost all his country instead of only half." Collective security had failed its most important test.

Japan formed the third element in the threat to world peace. Militarists began to dominate the government in Tokyo by the mid-1930s, using tactics of fear and even assassination against their liberal opponents. By 1936, Japan had left the League of Nations and had repudiated the Washington treaties. A year later, its armies began an invasion of China that marked the beginning of the Pacific phase of World War II.

The resurgence of militarism in Germany, Italy, and Japan undermined the Versailles settlement and threatened to destroy the existing balance of power. In 1937, the three totalitarian nations signed an anti-Comintern pact completing a Berlin-Rome-Tokyo axis. Their alliance ostensibly was aimed at the Soviet Union, but in fact it threatened the entire world. Only a determined American response could unite the other nations against the Axis threat. Unfortunately, the United States deliberately abstained from assuming the role of leadership until it was nearly too late.

THE LURE OF PACIFISM AND NEUTRALITY

The growing danger of war abroad led to a rising American desire for peace and noninvolvement. Memories of World War I contributed heavily. Erich Maria Remarque's novel *All Quiet on the Western Front,* as well as the movie based on it, reminded people of the brutality of war. Historians began to treat the Great War as a mistake, criticizing Wilson for failing to preserve American neutrality and claiming the clever British had duped the United States into entering the war. Walter Millis advanced this thesis in *America's Road to War, 1914–1917,* published in 1935. It was hailed as a vivid description of the process by which "a peace-loving democracy, muddled but excited, misinformed and whipped to a frenzy, embarked upon its greatest foreign war."

The pacifism that swept college campuses in the 1930s touched students at the University of Chicago. The university undergraduates shown here hold placards bearing antiwar slogans as they wait to join a parade as part of a nationwide demonstration against war.

American youth made clear their determination not to repeat the mistakes of their elders. Pacifism swept across college campuses. A Brown University poll indicated 72 percent of the students opposed military service in wartime. At Princeton, undergraduates formed the Veterans of Future Wars, a parody on veterans' groups, to demand a bonus of $1000 apiece before they marched off to a foreign war.

The pacifist movement found a scapegoat in the munitions industry. The publication of several books exposing the unsavory business tactics of large arms dealers such as Krupp in Germany and Vickers in Britain led to a demand to curb these "merchants of death." Senator Gerald Nye of North Dakota headed a special Senate committee that spent two years investigating American munitions dealers. The committee revealed the enormous profits firms such as Du Pont reaped from World War I, but Nye went further, charging that bankers and munitions makers were responsible for American intervention in 1917. No proof was forthcoming, but the public—prepared to believe the worst of businessmen during the Depression—accepted the "merchants of death" thesis.

The Nye Committee's revelations culminated in neutrality legislation. In 1935, Senator Nye and another Senate colleague introduced measures to ban arms sales and loans to belligerents and to prevent Americans from traveling on belligerent ships. By outlawing the activities that led to World War I, they hoped, the United States could avoid involvement in the new conflict. This "never again" philosophy proved irresistible. In August 1935, Congress passed the first of three neutrality acts. The 1935 law banned the sale of arms to nations at war and warned American citizens not to sail on belligerent ships. In 1936, a second act added a ban on loans, and in 1937, a third neutrality act made these prohibitions permanent and required, on a two-year trial basis, that all trade other than munitions be conducted on a cash-and-carry basis.

President Roosevelt played a passive role in the adoption of the neutrality legislation. At first opposed to the arms embargo, he finally approved it for six months in 1935 in a compromise designed to save important New Deal legislation in Congress. Others in the administration criticized the mandatory nature of the new law, pointing out that it prevented the United States from distinguishing between aggressors and their victims. Privately, Roosevelt expressed some of the same reservations, but publicly he bowed to the prevailing isolationism. He signed the subsequent neutrality acts without protest, and during the 1936 election, he delivered an impassioned denunciation of war.

Yet FDR did take a few steps to try to limit the nation's retreat into isolationism. His failure to invoke the neutrality act after the Japanese invasion of China in 1937 enabled the hard-pressed Chinese to continue buying arms from the United States. FDR's strongest public statement came in Chicago in October 1937, when he denounced "the epidemic of world lawlessness" and called for an international effort to "quarantine" the disease. When reporters asked him if his call for "positive efforts to preserve peace" signaled a repeal of the neutrality acts, however, Roosevelt quickly reaffirmed this isolationist legislation. Whatever his private yearning for cooperation against aggressors, the president had no intention of challenging the prevailing public mood of the 1930s.

WAR IN EUROPE

The neutrality legislation played directly into the hands of Adolf Hitler. Bent on the conquest of Europe, he could now proceed without worrying about American interference. In March 1938, he seized Austria in a bloodless coup. Six months later, he was demanding the Sudetenland, a province of Czechoslovakia with a large German population. When the British and French leaders agreed to meet with Hitler at Munich, FDR voiced his approval. Roosevelt carefully kept the United States aloof from the subsequent surrender of the Sudetenland. At the same time, he gave his tacit approval of the Munich agreement.

Six months after the meeting at Munich, Hitler violated his promises by seizing nearly all of Czechoslovakia. In the United States, Roosevelt permitted the State Department to press for neutrality revision. The administration proposal to repeal the arms embargo and place *all* trade with belligerents, including munitions, on a cash-and-carry basis soon met stubborn resistance from isolationists. They argued that cash-and-carry would favor England and France, who controlled the sea. The House rejected the measure by a narrow margin, and the Senate's Foreign Relations Committee voted 12 to 11 to postpone any action on neutrality revision.

On September 1, 1939, Hitler began World War II by invading Poland. England and France responded two days later by declaring war, although there was no way they could prevent the German conquest of Poland. Russia had played a key role, refusing Western overtures for a common front against Germany and finally signing a nonaggression treaty with Hitler in late August. The Nazi-Soviet Pact enabled Germany to avoid a two-front war; the Russians were rewarded with a generous slice of eastern Poland.

President Roosevelt reacted to the outbreak of war by proclaiming American neutrality, but the successful aggression by Nazi Germany brought into question the isolationist assumption that American well-being did not depend on the European balance of power. Strategic as well as ideological considerations began to undermine the earlier belief that the United States could safely pursue a policy of neutrality and noninvolvement. The long retreat from responsibility was about to end as Americans came to realize that their own democracy and security were at stake in the European war.

Hitler sent his armies into Poland with tremendous force and firepower, devastating the country. When Jews, such as these residents of the Warsaw Ghetto, fell into the hands of the Nazi occupiers, they were deported to slave labor camps that soon became the sites of mass extermination.

The Road to War

For two years, the United States tried to remain at peace while war raged in Europe and Asia. In contrast to the climate of the country while Wilson attempted to be impartial during most of World War I, however, the American people displayed an overwhelming sympathy for the Allies and total distaste for Germany and Japan. Roosevelt made no secret of his preference for an Allied victory, but a fear of isolationist criticism compelled him to move slowly, and often deviously, in adopting a policy of aid for England and France.

From Neutrality to Undeclared War

Two weeks after the outbreak of war in Europe, Roosevelt called Congress into special session to revise the neutrality legislation. He wanted to repeal the arms embargo in order to supply weapons to England and France, but he refused to state this aim openly. Instead he asked Congress to replace the arms embargo with cash-and-carry regulations. Belligerents would be able to purchase war supplies in the United States, but they would have to pay cash and transport the goods in their own ships. Public opinion strongly supported the president, and

Congress passed the revised neutrality policy by heavy margins in early November 1939.

A series of dramatic German victories had a profound impact on American opinion. Quiet during the winter of 1939–1940, the Germans struck with lightning speed and devastating effect in the spring. In April, they seized Denmark and Norway, and on May 10, 1940, they unleashed the *blitzkrieg* (lightning war) on the western front. Within three weeks, the British were driven off the Continent. In another three weeks, France fell to Hitler's victorious armies.

Americans were stunned. Hitler had taken only six weeks to achieve what Germany had failed to do in four years of fighting in World War I. Suddenly they realized they did have a stake in the outcome; if England fell, Hitler might well gain control of the British navy. The Atlantic would no longer be a barrier; instead, it would be a highway for German penetration of the New World.

Roosevelt responded by invoking a policy of all-out aid to the Allies, short of war. In a speech at Charlottesville, Virginia, in June (just after Italy entered the war by invading France), he denounced Germany and Italy as representing "the gods of force and hate" and vowed, "The whole of our sympathies lies with those nations that are giving their life blood in combat against these forces." It was too late to help France, but in early September, FDR announced the transfer of fifty old destroyers to England in exchange for rights to build air and naval bases on eight British possessions in the Western Hemisphere.

Isolationists cried out against this departure from neutrality. A bold headline in the *St. Louis Post-Dispatch* read, "Dictator Roosevelt Commits Act of War." A group of Roosevelt's opponents in the Midwest formed the America First Committee to protest the drift toward war. Voicing belief in a "Fortress America," they denied that Hitler threatened American security and claimed that the nation had the strength to defend itself regardless of what happened in Europe.

To support the administration's policies, opponents of the isolationists organized the Committee to Defend America by Aiding the Allies. Eastern Anglophiles, moderate New Dealers, and liberal Republicans made up the bulk of the membership, with Kansas newspaper editor William Allen White serving as chairman. The White Committee, as it became known, advocated unlimited assistance to England short of war. Above all, the interventionists challenged the isolationist premise that events in Europe did not affect American security. "The future of western civilization is being decided upon the battlefield of Europe," White declared.

In the ensuing debate, the American people gradually came to agree with the interventionists. The battle of Britain helped. "Every time Hitler bombed London, we got a couple of votes," noted one interventionist. Frightened by the

THE ELECTION OF 1940

CANDIDATE	PARTY	POPULAR VOTE	ELECTORAL VOTE
Roosevelt	Democratic	27,263,448	449
Willkie	Republican	22,336,260	82

events in Europe, Congress approved large sums for preparedness, increasing the defense budget from $2 billion to $10 billion during 1940. Roosevelt courageously asked for a peacetime draft, the first in American history, to build up the army; in September, Congress agreed.

The sense of crisis affected domestic politics. Roosevelt ran for an unprecedented third term in 1940 because of the European war; the Republicans nominated Wendell Willkie, a former Democratic businessman who shared FDR's commitment to aid for England. Both candidates made appeals to peace sentiment during the campaign, but Roosevelt's decisive victory made it clear that the nation supported his increasing departure from neutrality.

After the election, FDR took his boldest step. Responding to British Prime Minister Winston Churchill's warning that England was running out of money, the president asked Congress to approve a new program to lend and lease goods and weapons to countries fighting against aggressors.

Isolationists angrily denounced Lend-Lease as both unnecessary and untruthful. "Lending war equipment is a good deal like lending chewing gum," commented Senator Taft. "You don't want it back." In March 1941, however, Congress voted by substantial margins to authorize the president to "sell, transfer title to, exchange, lease, lend, or otherwise dispose of" war supplies to "any country the President deems vital to the defense of the United States." The accompanying $7 billion appropriation ended the "cash" part of cash-and-carry and ensured Britain full access to American war supplies.

The "carry" problem still remained. German submarines were sinking more than 500,000 tons of shipping a month. England desperately needed the help of the American navy in escorting convoys across the U-boat–infested waters of the North Atlantic. Roosevelt, fearful of isolationist reaction, responded with naval patrols in the western half of the ocean. Hitler placed his submarine commanders under strict restraints to avoid drawing America into the European war.

Nevertheless, incidents were bound to occur. On October 17, 1941, a German submarine damaged the U.S. destroyer *Kearney;* ten days later, another U-boat sank the *Reuben James,* killing more than one hundred American sailors.

FDR issued orders for the destroyers to shoot U-boats on sight. He also asked Congress to repeal the "carry" section of the neutrality laws and permit American ships to deliver supplies to England. In mid-November, Congress approved these moves by slim margins. Now American merchant ships as well as destroyers would become targets for German attacks. By December, it seemed only a matter of weeks—or months at most—until repeated sinkings would lead to a formal declaration of war against Germany.

In leading the nation to the brink of war in Europe, Roosevelt opened himself to criticism from both sides in the domestic debate. Interventionists believed he had been too cautious in dealing with the danger to the nation from Nazi Germany. Isolationists were equally critical of the president, claiming he had misled the American people by professing peace while plotting for war. Roosevelt was certainly less than candid, relying on executive discretion to engage in highly provocative acts in the North Atlantic. He agreed with the interventionists that in the long run a German victory in Europe would threaten American security. But he also was aware that a poll taken in September 1941 showed nearly 80 percent of the American people wanted to stay out of World War II. Realizing that leading a divided nation into war would be disastrous, FDR played for time, inching the country toward war while waiting for the Axis nations to make the ultimate move. Japan finally obliged at Pearl Harbor.

SHOWDOWN IN THE PACIFIC

Japan had taken advantage of the war in Europe to expand farther in Asia. Although successful after 1937 in conquering the populous coastal areas of China, the Japanese had been unable to defeat Chiang Kai-shek, whose forces retreated into the vast interior of the country. The German defeat of France and the Netherlands in 1940, however, left their colonial possessions in the East Indies and Indochina vulnerable and defenseless. Japan now set out to incorporate these territories—rich in oil, tin, and rubber—into a Greater East Asia Co-Prosperity Sphere.

The Roosevelt administration countered with economic pressure. Japan depended heavily on the United States for petroleum and scrap metal. In July 1940, President Roosevelt signed an order setting up a licensing and quota system for the export of these crucial materials to Japan and banned the sale of aviation gasoline altogether.

Tokyo appeared to be unimpressed. In early September, Japanese troops occupied strategic bases in the northern part of French Indochina. Later in the month, Japan signed the Tripartite Pact with Germany and Italy, a defensive treaty that confronted the United States with a possible two-ocean war. The new Axis alignment confirmed American suspicions that Japan was part of a worldwide totalitarian threat. Roosevelt and his advisers, however, saw Germany as the primary danger; thus they pursued a policy of all-out aid to England while hoping that economic measures alone would deter Japan.

The embargo on aviation gasoline, extended to include scrap iron and steel in late September 1940, was a burden Japan could bear, but a possible ban on all oil shipments was a different matter. Japan lacked petroleum reserves of its own and was entirely dependent on imports from the United States and the Dutch East Indies. In an attempt to ease the economic pressure through negotiation, Japan sent a new envoy to Washington in the spring of 1941.

In July 1941, Japan invaded southern Indochina, beginning the chain of events that led to war. Washington knew of this aggression before it occurred. Naval intelligence experts had broken the Japanese diplomatic code and were intercepting and reading all messages between Tokyo and the Japanese embassy in Washington. President Roosevelt responded on July 25, 1941, with an order freezing all Japanese assets in the United States. Trade with Japan, including the vital oil shipments, came to a complete halt. When the Dutch government in exile took similar action, Japan faced a dilemma: in order to have oil shipments resumed, Tokyo would have to end its aggression; the alternative would be to seize the needed petroleum supplies in the Dutch East Indies, an action that would mean war.

After one final diplomatic effort failed, General Hideki Tojo, an army militant, became the new premier of Japan. To mask its war preparations, Tokyo sent yet another envoy to Washington with new peace proposals. Army and navy leaders urged President Roosevelt to seek at least a temporary settlement with Japan to give them time to prepare American defenses in the Pacific. Secretary of State Cordell Hull, however, refused to allow any concession; on November 26, he sent a stiff ten-point reply to Tokyo that included a demand for Japanese withdrawal from China.

The Japanese response came two weeks later. On the evening of December 6, 1941, the first thirteen parts of the reply to Hull's note arrived in Washington, with the fourteenth part to follow the next morning. Naval intelligence actually decoded the message faster than the Japanese embassy clerks. A messenger delivered the text to President Roosevelt late that night; after glancing at it, he commented, "This means war." The next day, December 7, the fourteenth part arrived, revealing that Japan totally rejected the American position.

Officials in Washington immediately sent warning messages to American bases in the Pacific, but they failed to arrive in time. At 7:55 in the morning, just before 1 P.M. in Washington, squadrons of Japanese carrier-based planes caught the American fleet at Pearl Harbor totally by surprise. In little more than an hour,

American ships were destroyed in the surprise attack on Pearl Harbor, December 7, 1941. Caught completely off guard, U.S. forces still managed to shoot down twenty-nine enemy planes.

they crippled the American Pacific fleet and its major base, sinking eight battle-ships and killing more than twenty-four hundred American sailors.

Speaking before Congress the next day, President Roosevelt termed December 7 "a date which will live in infamy" and asked for a declaration of war on Japan. With only one dissenting vote, both branches passed the measure. On December 11, Germany and Italy declared war against the United States; the nation was now fully involved in World War II.

The whole country united behind Roosevelt's leadership to seek revenge for Pearl Harbor and to defeat the Axis threat to American security. After the war, however, critics charged that FDR had entered the conflict by a back door, claiming the president had deliberately exposed the Pacific fleet to attack. Subsequent investigations uncovered negligence in both Hawaii and Washington but no evidence to support the conspiracy charge. Commanders in Hawaii, like most military experts, believed the Japanese would not launch an attack on a base four thousand miles from Japan. FDR, like too many Americans, had badly underestimated the daring and skill of the Japanese; he and the nation alike paid a heavy price for this cultural and racial prejudice. But there was no plot. Roosevelt could not have known that Hitler, so restrained in the Atlantic, would reverse his policy and foolishly declare war against the United States after Pearl Harbor. Perhaps the most frightening aspect of the whole episode is that it took the shock of the Japanese sneak attack to make the American people aware of the extent of the Axis threat to their well-being and lead them to end the long American retreat from responsibility.

TURNING THE TIDE AGAINST THE AXIS

In the first few months after the United States entered the war, the outlook for victory was bleak. In Europe, Hitler's armies controlled virtually the entire continent, from Norway in the north to Greece in the south. Despite the nonaggression pact, German armies had penetrated deep into Russia after an initial invasion in June 1941. Although they had failed to capture either Moscow or Leningrad, the Nazi forces had conquered the Ukraine and by the spring of 1942 were threatening to sweep across the Volga River and seize vital oil fields in the Caucasus. In North Africa, General Erwin Rommel's Afrika Korps had pushed the British back into Egypt and threatened the Suez Canal (see the map on p. 896).

The situation was no better in Asia. The Pearl Harbor attack had enabled the Japanese to move unopposed across Southeast Asia. Within three months, they had conquered Malaya and the Dutch East Indies, with its valuable oil fields, and were pressing the British back both in Burma and New Guinea. American forces under General Douglas MacArthur had tried vainly to block the Japanese conquest of the Philippines. MacArthur finally escaped by torpedo boat to Australia; the American garrison at Corregidor surrendered after a long siege, the survivors then enduring the cruel death march across the Bataan peninsula. With the American navy still recovering from the devastation at Pearl Harbor, Japan controlled the western half of the Pacific (see the map on p. 885).

Over the next two years, the United States and its allies would finally halt the German and Japanese offensives in Europe and Asia. But then they faced the difficult process of driving back the enemy, freeing the vast conquered areas, and finally defeating the Axis powers on their home territory. It would be a difficult and costly struggle that would require great sacrifice and heavy losses; World War II would test American will and resourcefulness to the utmost.

WARTIME PARTNERSHIPS

The greatest single advantage that the United States and its partners possessed was their willingness to form a genuine coalition to bring about the defeat of the Axis powers. Although there were many strains within the wartime alliance, it did permit a high degree of coordination. In striking contrast was the behavior of Germany and Japan, each fighting a separate war without any attempt at cooperation.

The United States and Britain achieved a complete wartime partnership. The close cooperation between President Roosevelt and Prime Minister Churchill ensured a common strategy. The leaders decided at the outset that a German victory posed the greater danger and thus gave priority to the European theater in the conduct of the war. In a series of meetings in December 1941, Roosevelt and Churchill signed a Declaration of the United Nations, eventually subscribed to by twenty-six countries, that pledged them to fight together until the Axis powers were defeated.

Relations with the other members of the United Nations coalition in World War II were not quite so harmonious. The decision to defeat Germany first displeased the Chinese, who had been at war with Japan since 1937. France posed a more delicate problem. FDR virtually ignored the Free French government in exile under General Charles de Gaulle; Roosevelt preferred to deal with the Vichy regime.

The greatest strain of all within the wartime coalition was with the Soviet Union. Although Roosevelt had ended the long period of nonrecognition in 1933, close ties had failed to develop. The great Russian purge trials and the temporary Nazi-Soviet alliance from 1939 to 1941, along with deep-seated cultural and ideological differences, made wartime cooperation difficult.

Ever the pragmatist, Roosevelt tried hard to break down the old hostility and establish a more cordial relationship with Russia during the war. Even before Pearl Harbor, he extended Lend-Lease aid to Russia, and after American entry into the war, this economic assistance grew rapidly, limited only by the difficulty of delivering the supplies. Eager to keep Russia in the war, the president promised a visiting Russian diplomat in May 1942 that the United States would create a second front in Europe by the end of that year—a pledge he could not fulfill. In January 1943, Roosevelt and Churchill met in Casablanca, Morocco, where they declared a policy of unconditional surrender, vowing that the Allies would fight until the Axis nations were completely defeated.

Despite these promises, the Soviet Union bore the brunt of battle against Hitler in the early years of the war, fighting alone against more than two hundred German divisions. The United States and England, grateful for the respite to build up their forces, could do little more than offer promises of future help and send Lend-Lease supplies. The result was a rift that never fully healed—one that did not prevent the defeat of Germany but did ensure future tensions and uncertainties between the Soviet Union and the Western nations.

HALTING THE GERMAN BLITZ

From the outset, the United States favored an invasion across the English Channel. Army planners, led by Chief of Staff George C. Marshall and his protégé, Dwight D. Eisenhower, were convinced such a frontal assault would be the quickest way to win the war. Roosevelt concurred, in part because it fulfilled his second-front commitment to the Soviets.

The initial plan, drawn up by Eisenhower, called for a full-scale invasion of Europe in the spring of 1943. Marshall surprised everyone by placing Eisenhower, until then a relatively junior general, in charge of implementing the plan.

But the British, remembering the heavy casualties of trench warfare in World War I, preferred a perimeter approach, with air and naval attacks around the edge of the Continent until Germany was softened up for the final invasion. British strategists assented to the basic plan but strongly urged a preliminary invasion of North Africa in the fall of 1942. Roosevelt agreed and American and British troops landed on the Atlantic and Mediterranean coasts of Morocco and Algeria in November 1942.

The British launched an attack against Rommel at El Alamein in Egypt and soon forced the Afrika Korps to retreat across Libya to Tunisia. Eisenhower, despite initial setbacks, advanced from Algeria, and by May 1943, Germany had been driven from Africa, leaving behind nearly 300,000 troops.

During these same months, the Soviet Union's Red Army had broken the back of German military power in the battle of Stalingrad. Turned back at the critical bend in the Volga, Hitler had poured in division after division in what was ultimately a losing cause; never again would Germany be able to take the offensive in Europe.

At Churchill's insistence, FDR agreed to follow up the North African victory with the invasion first of Sicily and then Italy in the summer of 1943. Italy dropped out of the war when Mussolini fled to Germany, but the Italian campaign proved to be a strategic dead end.

More important, these Mediterranean operations delayed the second front, postponing it eventually to the spring of 1944. Meanwhile, the Soviets began to push the Germans out of Russia and looked forward to the liberation of Poland, Hungary, and Romania, where they could establish "friendly" communist regimes. Having borne the brunt of the fighting against Nazi Germany, Russia was ready to claim its reward—the postwar domination of eastern Europe.

CHECKING JAPAN IN THE PACIFIC

Both the decision to defeat Germany first and the vast expanses of the Pacific dictated the nature of the war against Japan. The United States conducted amphibious island-hopping campaigns rather than attempting to reconquer the Dutch East Indies, Southeast Asia, and China. There would be two separate American operations. One, led by Douglas MacArthur based in Australia, would move from New Guinea back to the Philippines, while the other, commanded by Admiral Chester Nimitz from Hawaii, was directed at key Japanese islands in the Central Pacific.

World War II in the Pacific

The tide of battle turned in the Pacific the same year as in Europe. The balance of sea power shifted back to the United States from Japan after the naval victories of 1942.

Success in the Pacific depended above all else on control of the sea. The devastation at Pearl Harbor gave Japan the initial edge, but fortunately, the United States had not lost any of its four aircraft carriers. The turning point came in June 1942 at Midway. A powerful Japanese task force threatened to seize this remote American outpost more than a thousand miles west of Pearl Harbor; Japan's real objective was the destruction of what remained of the American Pacific fleet. Superior American airpower enabled Nimitz's forces to engage the enemy at long range. The battle of Midway ended with the loss of four Japanese aircraft carriers compared to just one American carrier. It was the first defeat the modern Japanese navy had ever suffered, and it left the United States in control of the Central Pacific.

Encouraged by the victory, American forces launched their first Pacific offensive in the Solomon Islands, east of New Guinea, in August 1942. Both sides suffered heavy losses, but six months later the last Japanese were driven from the key island of Guadalcanal. At the same time, MacArthur began the long, slow, and bloody job of driving the Japanese back along the north coast of New Guinea.

By early 1943, the defensive phase of the war with Japan was over. The enemy surge had been halted in both the central and the southwestern Pacific, and the United States was preparing to penetrate the Gilbert, Marshall, and Caroline Islands and recapture the Philippines. Just as Russia had broken German power in Europe, so the United States, fighting alone except for Australia and New Zealand, had halted the Japanese. And, like the USSR with its plans for eastern Europe, America expected to reap the rewards of victory by dominating the Pacific in the future.

THE HOME FRONT

World War II had a greater impact than the Depression on the future of American life. While American soldiers and sailors fought abroad, the nation underwent sweeping social and economic changes at home.

American industry made the nation's single most important contribution to victory. Even though more than fifteen million Americans served in the armed forces, it was the nearly sixty million who worked on farms and factories who achieved the miracle of production that ensured the defeat of Germany and Japan. The manufacturing plants that had run at half capacity through the 1930s now hummed with activity. In Detroit, automobile assembly lines were converted to produce tanks and airplanes. Henry J. Kaiser, a California industrialist, constructed huge West Coast shipyards to meet the demand for cargo vessels and

American war production was twice that of all the Axis countries. Here, Boeing aircraft workers celebrate the completion of their five thousandth bomber.

landing craft. His plant in Richmond, California, reduced the time to build a merchant ship from 105 to 14 days. In part, America won the battle of the Atlantic by building ships faster than German U-boats could sink them.

This vast industrial expansion, however, created many problems. In 1942, President Roosevelt appointed Donald Nelson, a Sears, Roebuck executive, to head a War Production Board (WPB). A jovial, easygoing man, Nelson soon was outmaneuvered by the army and the navy, which preferred to negotiate directly with large corporations. Shortages of critical materials such as steel, aluminum, and copper led to an allocation system based on military priorities. Rubber, cut off by the Japanese conquest of Southeast Asia, was particularly scarce; the administration finally began gasoline rationing in 1943 to curb pleasure driving and prolong tire life.

Roosevelt revealed the same tendency toward compromise in directing the economic mobilization as he did in shaping the New Deal. When the Office of Price Administration—which tried to curb inflation by controlling prices and rationing scarce goods such as sugar, canned food, and shoes—clashed with the

WPB, FDR appointed James Byrnes to head an Office of Economic Stabilization. Byrnes, a former South Carolina senator and Supreme Court justice, used political judgment to settle disputes between agencies and keep all groups happy.

A result of the wartime economic explosion was a growing affluence. Despite the federal incentives to business, heavy excess-profit taxes and a 94 percent tax rate for the very rich kept the wealthy from benefiting unduly. The huge increase in federal spending, from $9 billion in 1940 to $98 billion in 1944, spread through American society. A government agreement with labor unions in 1943 held wage rates to a 15 percent increase, but the long hours of overtime resulted in doubling and sometimes tripling the weekly paychecks of factory workers. Farmers shared in the new prosperity as their incomes quadrupled between 1940 and 1945. For the first time in the twentieth century, the lowest fifth of wage earners increased their share of the national income in relation to the more affluent; their income rose by 68 percent between 1941 and 1945, compared to a 20 percent increase for the well-to-do. Most important, this rising income ensured postwar prosperity. Workers and farmers saved their money, channeling much of it into government war bonds, waiting for the day when they could buy the cars and home appliances they had done without during the long years of depression and war.

A NATION ON THE MOVE

The war led to a vast migration of the American population. Young men left their homes for training camps and then for service overseas. Defense workers and their families, some nine million people in all, moved to work in the new booming shipyards, munitions factories, and aircraft plants. Rural areas lost population while coastal regions, especially along the Pacific and the Gulf of Mexico, drew millions of people. The location of army camps in the South and West created boom conditions in the future Sunbelt, as did the concentration of aircraft factories and shipyards in this region. California had the greatest gains, adding nearly two million to its population in less than five years.

This movement of people caused severe social problems. Housing was in short supply. Migrating workers crowded into house trailers and boardinghouses, bringing unexpected windfalls to landlords. In one boomtown, a reporter described an old Victorian house that had five bedrooms on the second floor. "Three of them," he wrote, "held two cots apiece, the two others held three cots." But the owner revealed that "the third floor is where we pick up the velvet. . . . We rent to workers in different shifts . . . three shifts a day . . . seven bucks a week apiece."

Family life suffered under these crowded living conditions. An increase in the number of marriages, as young people searched for something to hang on to in the midst of wartime turmoil, was offset by a rising divorce rate. The baby boom

As men left for military service in World War II and U.S. industry expanded to keep up with defense needs, millions of women joined the paid labor force. By 1944, the peak year for female wartime employment, women made up 36 percent of the American workforce. Women took jobs that before the war had been done by men, such as riveting, welding, and operating heavy equipment. "Rosie the Riveter," a popular song of the era, celebrated women's new role in the labor force.

that would peak in the 1950s began during the war and brought its own set of problems. Only a few publicly funded day-care centers were available, and working mothers worried about their "latchkey children."

Despite these problems, women found the war a time of economic opportunity. The demand for workers led to a dramatic rise in women's employment, from fourteen million working women in 1940 to nineteen million by 1945. Most of the new women workers were married and many were middle-aged, thus broadening the composition of the female workforce, which in the past had been composed primarily of young single women. Women entered industries once viewed as exclusively male; by the end of the war, they worked alongside men tending blast furnaces in steel mills and welding hulls in shipyards. Women enjoyed the hefty weekly paychecks, which rose by 50 percent from 1941 to 1943, and they took pride in their contributions to the war effort. "To hell with the life I have had," commented a former fashion designer. "This war is too damn serious, and it is too damn important to win it."

African Americans shared in the wartime migration, but racial prejudice limited their social and economic gains. Nearly one million served in the armed forces, but relatively few saw combat. The army placed black soldiers in segregated units, usually led by white officers, and used them for service and construction tasks. The navy was even worse, relegating them to menial jobs until late in the war. African Americans were denied the chance to become petty officers, Secretary of the Navy Frank Knox explained, because experience had shown that "men of the colored race . . . cannot maintain discipline among men of the white race."

African American civilians fared a little better. In 1941, black labor leader A. Philip Randolph threatened a massive march on Washington to force President Roosevelt to end racial discrimination in defense industries and government employment and to integrate the armed forces. FDR compromised, persuading Randolph to call off the march and drop his integration demand in return for an executive order creating a Fair Employment Practices Committee (FEPC) to ban racial discrimination in war industries. As a result, African American employment by the federal government rose from 60,000 in 1941 to 200,000 by the end of the war. The FEPC proved less successful in the private sector. The nationwide shortage of labor was more influential than the FEPC in accounting for the rise in black employment during wartime. African Americans moved from the rural South to northern and western cities, finding jobs in the automobile, aircraft, and shipbuilding industries.

The movement of an estimated 700,000 people helped transform black-white relations from a regional issue into a national concern that could no longer be ignored. The limited housing and recreational facilities for both black and white war workers created tensions that led to race riots in Detroit and New York City.

These outbursts of racial violence fueled the resentments that would grow into the postwar civil rights movement. For most African Americans, despite economic gains, World War II was a reminder of the inequality of American life. "Just carve on my tombstone," remarked one black soldier in the Pacific, "'Here lies a black man killed fighting a yellow man for the protection of a white man.'"

One-third of a million Mexican Americans served in the armed forces and shared some of the same experiences as African Americans. Although they were not as completely segregated, many served in the 88th Division, made up largely of Mexican American officers and troops, which earned the nickname "Blue Devils" in the Italian campaign. At home, Spanish-speaking people left the rural areas of Texas, New Mexico, and California for jobs in the cities, especially in aircraft plants and petroleum refineries. Despite low wages and union resistance, they improved their economic position substantially. But they still faced discrimination based both on skin color and language. The racial prejudice heightened feelings of ethnic identity and led returning Mexican American veterans to form organizations such as the American G.I. Forum to press for equal rights in the future.

A tragic counterpoint to the voluntary movement of American workers in search of jobs was the forced relocation of 120,000 Japanese Americans from the

A mother and son, interned at a temporary relocation camp, pose with a picture of her older son wearing his U.S. Army uniform. Japanese Americans living on the West Coast were first ordered to large assembly centers such as the racetrack at Santa Anita, California. There whole families were assigned to individual horse stalls while they awaited relocation to one of the internment camps located in isolated areas of California, Arizona, Idaho, Utah, Colorado, Wyoming, and Arkansas. Conditions in the camps were equally dismal. Whole families lived in a single room furnished with little more than a few cots, some blankets, and a single light bulb.

West Coast. Responding to racial fears in California after Pearl Harbor, President Roosevelt approved an army order in February 1942 to move all Japanese Americans on the West Coast to concentration camps in the interior. More than two-thirds of those detained were *Nisei,* native-born Americans whose only crime was their Japanese ancestry. Forced to sell their farms and businesses at distress prices, the Japanese Americans lost not only their liberty but also most of their worldly goods. Herded into ten hastily built detention centers in seven western and southern states, they lived as prisoners in tar-papered barracks behind barbed wire, guarded by armed troops.

Appeals to the Supreme Court proved fruitless; in 1944, six justices upheld relocation on grounds of national security in wartime. Beginning in 1943, individual Nisei could win release by pledging their loyalty and finding a job away from the West Coast. Some thirty-five thousand left the camps during the next two years, including more than thirteen thousand who joined the armed forces. The all-Nisei 442nd Combat Team served gallantly in the European theater, losing more than five hundred men in battle and winning more than a thousand citations for bravery.

For other Nisei, the experience was bitter. More than five thousand renounced their American citizenship and chose to live in Japan at the war's end. Japanese Americans never experienced the torture and mass death of the German concentration camps, but their treatment was a disgrace to a nation fighting for freedom and democracy. Finally, in 1988, Congress voted an indemnity of $1.2 billion for the estimated sixty thousand surviving Japanese Americans detained during World War II. Susumi Emori, who had been moved with his wife and four children from his farm in Stockton, California, to a camp in Arkansas, felt vindicated. "It was terrible," he said, with tears in his eyes, "but it was a time of war. Anything can happen. I didn't blame the United States for that."

WIN-THE-WAR POLITICS

Franklin Roosevelt used World War II to strengthen his leadership and maintain Democratic political dominance. As war brought about prosperity and removed the economic discontent that had sustained the New Deal, FDR announced that "Dr. New Deal" had given way to "Dr. Win-the-War." Congress, already controlled by a conservative coalition of southern Democrats and northern Republicans, had almost slipped into GOP hands in 1942. With a very low voter turnout, the Republicans won forty-four new seats in the House and nine in the Senate and elected governors in New York and California as well.

In 1944, Roosevelt responded to the Democratic slippage by dropping Henry Wallace, his liberal and visionary vice president, for Harry Truman, a moderate and down-to-earth Missouri senator who was acceptable to all factions of the Democratic party. Equally important, FDR received increased political support from organized labor, which had grown in membership during the war from ten to fifteen million.

The Republicans nominated Thomas E. Dewey, who had been elected governor of New York after gaining fame as a prosecutor of organized crime. Dewey, moderate in his views, played down opposition to the New Deal and instead tried to make Roosevelt's age and health the primary issues, along with the charge that the Democrats were soft on communism.

Despite his abrasive campaign style, Dewey did not advocate a return to isolationism. The Republican party was trying hard to shake the obstructionist image it had gained during the League of Nations fight in 1919; it went on record in 1943 as favoring American postwar cooperation for world peace. Indeed, Dewey pioneered a bipartisan approach to foreign policy. He accepted wartime planning for the future United Nations and kept the issue of an international organization out of the campaign.

THE ELECTION OF 1944

CANDIDATE	PARTY	POPULAR VOTE	ELECTORAL VOTE
Roosevelt	Democrat	25,611,936	432
Dewey	Republican	22,013,372	99

Reacting to the issues of his age and health, especially after a long bout with influenza in the spring, FDR took a five-hour drive in an open car through the rain-soaked streets of New York City just before the election. His vitality impressed the voters, and in November 1944 he swept back into office for a fourth term, although the margin of 3.6 million votes was his smallest yet. The campaign, however, had taken its toll. The president, suffering from high blood pressure and congestive heart failure, had only a few months left to lead the nation.

VICTORY

World War II ended with surprising swiftness. By 1943, the Axis tide had been turned in Europe and Asia, and it did not take long for Russia, the United States, and England to mount the offensives that drove Germany and Japan back across the vast areas they had conquered and set the stage for their final defeat.

The long-awaited second front finally came on June 6, 1944. For two years, the United States and England concentrated on building up an invasion force of nearly three million troops and a vast armada of ships and landing craft to carry them across the English Channel. In hopes of catching Hitler by surprise, Eisenhower chose the Normandy peninsula, where the absence of good harbors had led to lighter German fortifications.

D-Day was originally set for June 5, but bad weather forced a delay. Relying on a forecasted break in the storm, Eisenhower gambled on going ahead on June 6. During the night, three divisions parachuted down behind the German defenses; at dawn, the British and American troops fought their way ashore at five points along a sixty-mile stretch of beach, encountering stiff German resistance at several points. By the end of the day, however, Eisenhower had won his beachhead; a week later, more than one-third of a million men were slowly pushing back the German forces through the hedgerows of Normandy. The breakthrough came on July 25 when General Omar Bradley decimated the enemy with a massive artillery and aerial bombardment at Saint-Lô, opening a gap for General George Patton's Third Army. American tanks raced across the French countryside, trapping thousands of Germans and liberating Paris by August 25. Allied troops reached the Rhine River by September, but a shortage of supplies, especially gasoline, forced a three-month halt.

Hitler took advantage of this breathing spell to deliver a daring counterattack. In mid-December, the remaining German armored divisions burst through a weak point in the Allied lines in the Ardennes Forest, planning a breakout to the coast that would have cut off nearly one-third of Eisenhower's forces. But an airborne division dug in at the key crossroads of Bastogne, in Belgium, and held off a much larger German force. Allied reinforcements and clearing weather then combined to end the attack. By committing nearly all his reserves to the Battle of the Bulge, Hitler had delayed Eisenhower's advance into Germany, but he also had fatally weakened German resistance in the west.

The end came quickly. A massive Russian offensive began in mid-January and swept across the Oder River toward Berlin. General Bradley's troops, finding a bridge left virtually intact by the retreating Germans, crossed the Rhine on March 7. The Allied forces advanced on a broad front, capturing the industrial Ruhr basin and meeting the Russians at the Elbe by the last week in April. With the Red Army already in the suburbs of Berlin, Adolf Hitler committed suicide on April 30. A week later, on May 7, 1945, Eisenhower accepted the unconditional surrender of all German forces. Just eleven months and a day after the landings in Normandy, the Allied forces had brought the war in Europe to a successful conclusion.

After they entered Germany, American troops found horrifying evidence of the holocaust—Hitler's eradication of six million European Jews. American soldiers were shocked at the conditions within the German concentration camps—lethal gas chambers, huge ovens for cremation, bodies stacked like cords of wood, and most vivid of all, the emaciated, skeleton-like survivors with their blank stares. One battle-hardened veteran commented on the scene at Nordhausen, where his unit had found 3,000 dead and only 700 survivors:

> *The odors, well there is no way to describe the odors . . . . Many of the boys I am talking about now—these were tough soldiers, there were combat men who had been all the way through the invasion—were ill and vomiting, throwing up, just at the sight of this.*

These awful discoveries removed any doubt in the minds of the American people about the evil nature of the Nazi regime they had just helped to destroy.

Victims at the Bergen-Belsen concentration camp were buried in a mass grave. The camp was liberated by the Allies on April 14, 1945, less than a month before Germany's surrender.

WAR AIMS AND WARTIME DIPLOMACY

The American contribution to Hitler's defeat was relatively minor compared to the damage inflicted by the Soviet Union. At the height of the German invasion of Russia, more than 300 Soviet divisions had been locked in battle with 250 German ones, a striking contrast to the 58 divisions the United States and Britain used in the Normandy invasion. As his armies overran Poland and the Balkan countries, Joseph Stalin was determined to retain control over this region, which had been the historic pathway for Western invasion into Russia. Delay in opening the second front and an innate distrust of the West convinced the Soviets that they should maximize their territorial gains by imposing communist regimes on eastern Europe.

American postwar goals were quite different. Now believing the failure to join the League of Nations in 1919 had led to the coming of World War II, the American people and their leaders vowed to put their faith in a new attempt at collective security. At Moscow in 1943, Secretary of State Cordell Hull had won Russian agreement to participate in a future world organization at the war's end.

World War II in Europe and North Africa

The tide of battle shifted in this theater during the winter of 1942–1943. The massive German assault on the eastern front was turned back by the Russians at Stalingrad, and the Allied forces recaptured North Africa.

The first wartime Big Three conference brought together Roosevelt, Churchill, and Stalin at Teheran, Iran, in late 1943. Stalin reaffirmed this commitment and also indicated to President Roosevelt that Russia would enter the war against Japan once Germany was defeated.

By the time the Big Three met again at Yalta, in February 1945, the military situation favored the Russians. Stalin drove a series of hard bargains. He refused to give up his plans for communist domination of Poland and the Balkans, although he did agree to Roosevelt's request for a Declaration of Liberated Europe, which called for free elections without providing for any method of enforcement or supervision. More important for the United States, Stalin promised to enter the Pacific war three months after Germany surrendered. In return,

The nation's grief at FDR's death is mirrored in the face of this serviceman as the president's funeral cortege passes.

Roosevelt offered extensive concessions in Asia, including Russian control over Manchuria. While neither a sellout nor a betrayal, as some critics have charged, Yalta was a significant diplomatic victory for the Soviets—one that reflected Russia's major contribution to a victory in Europe.

For the president, the long journey to Yalta proved to be too much. His health continued to fail after his return to Washington. In early April, FDR left the capital for Warm Springs, Georgia, where he had always been able to relax. He was sitting for his portrait at midday on April 12, 1945, when he suddenly complained of a "terrific headache," then slumped forward and died.

The nation mourned a man who had gallantly met the challenge of depression and global war. Unfortunately, FDR had taken no steps to prepare his successor for the difficult problems that lay ahead. The defeat of Nazi Germany dissolved the one strong bond between the United States and the Soviet Union. With very different histories, cultures, and ideologies, the two nations were bound to drift apart. It was now up to the inexperienced Harry Truman to manage the growing rivalry that was destined to develop into the future Cold War.

TRIUMPH AND TRAGEDY IN THE PACIFIC

The total defeat of Germany in May 1945 turned all eyes toward Japan. Although the combined chiefs of staff had originally estimated it would take eighteen months after Germany's surrender to conquer Japan, American forces moved with surprising speed. Admiral Nimitz swept through the Gilbert, Caroline, and Marshall Islands in 1944, while General MacArthur cleared New Guinea of the last Japanese defender and began planning his long-heralded return to the Philippines. American troops landed on the island of Leyte on October 20, 1944, and Manila fell in early February 1945. The Japanese navy launched a daring three-pronged attack on the American invasion fleet in Leyte Gulf. The U.S. Navy rallied to blunt all three Japanese thrusts, sinking four carriers and ending any further Japanese naval threat.

The defeat of Japan was now only a matter of time. The United States had three possible ways to proceed. The military favored a full-scale invasion, beginning on the southernmost island of Kyushu in November 1945 and culminating with an assault on Honshu (the main island of Japan) and a climatic battle for Tokyo in 1946; casualties were expected to run into the hundreds of thousands. Diplomats suggested a negotiated peace, urging the United States to modify the unconditional surrender formula to permit Japan to retain the institution of the emperor.

The third possibility involved the highly secret Manhattan Project. Since 1939, the United States had spent $2 billion to develop an atomic bomb based on the fission of radioactive uranium and plutonium. Scientists, many of them refugees from Europe, worked to perfect this deadly new weapon at the University of Chicago; Oak Ridge, Tennessee; Hanford, Washington; and a remote laboratory in Los Alamos, New Mexico. In the New Mexico desert on July 16, 1945, they successfully tested the first atomic bomb.

Truman had been unaware of the existence of the Manhattan Project before he became president on April 12. Now he simply followed the recommendation of a committee headed by Secretary of War Henry L. Stimson to drop the bomb on a Japanese city. Neither Truman nor Stimson had any qualms about the decision to drop the bomb without warning. They viewed it as a legitimate wartime measure, one designed to save the lives of hundreds of thousands of Americans— and Japanese—that would be lost in a full-scale invasion.

Weather conditions on the morning of August 6 dictated the choice of Hiroshima as the bomb's target. The explosion incinerated 4 square miles of the city, instantly killing more than sixty thousand. Two days later, Russia entered the war against Japan, and the next day, August 9, the United States dropped a second bomb on Nagasaki. The emperor personally broke a deadlock in the Japanese cabinet and persuaded his ministers to surrender unconditionally on August 14, 1945. Three weeks later, Japan signed a formal capitulation agreement on the decks of the battleship *Missouri* in Tokyo Bay to bring World War II to its official close.

The atomic bomb dropped on Nagasaki, a provincial capital and naval base in southern Japan, on August 9, 1945, virtually obliterated the city and killed about 40,000 people. Only buildings made with reinforced concrete remained standing after the blast.

Many years later, scholars charged that Truman had more in mind than defeating Japan when he decided to use the atomic bomb. Citing air force and naval officers who claimed Japan could be defeated by a blockade or by conventional air attacks, these revisionists suggested the real reason for dropping the bomb was to impress the Soviet Union with the fact that the United States had exclusive possession of the ultimate weapon. The available evidence indicates that while Truman and his associates were aware of the possible effect on the Soviet Union, their primary motive was to end World War II as quickly and effortlessly as possible. The saving of American lives, along with a desire for revenge for Pearl Harbor, were uppermost in the decision to bomb Hiroshima and Nagasaki. Yet in using the atomic bomb to defeat Japan, the United States virtually guaranteed a postwar arms race with the Soviet Union.

The second great war of the twentieth century has had a lasting impact on American life. For the first time, the nation's military potential had been reached. In 1945, the United States was unquestionably the strongest country on the earth, with eleven million men and women in uniform; a vast array of shipyards, aircraft plants, and munitions factories in full production; and a monopoly over the atomic bomb. For better or worse, the nation was now launched on a global career. In the future, the United States would be involved in all parts of the world, from western Europe to remote jungles in Asia, from the nearby Caribbean to the distant Persian Gulf. And despite its enormous strength in 1945, the nation's new world role would encompass failure and frustration as well as power and dominion.

The legacy of war was equally strong at home. Four years of fighting brought about industrial recovery and unparalleled prosperity. The old pattern of unregulated free enterprise was as much a victim of the war as of the New Deal; big government and huge deficits had now become the norm as economic control passed from New York and Wall Street to Washington and Pennsylvania Avenue. The war led to far-reaching changes in American society that would become apparent only decades later. Such distinctive patterns of recent American life as the baby boom and the growth of the Sunbelt can be traced back to wartime origins. World War II was a watershed in twentieth-century America, ushering in a new age of global concerns and domestic upheaval.

28

THE ONSET OF THE COLD WAR

"I am getting ready to go see Stalin and Churchill," President Truman wrote to his mother in July 1945, "and it is a chore." On board the cruiser *Augusta,* the new president continued to complain about the up-coming Potsdam conference in his diary. "How I hate this trip!" he confided. "But I have to make it win, lose, or draw and we must win. I am giving nothing away except to save starving people and even then I hope we can only help them to help themselves."

Halfway around the world, Joseph Stalin left Moscow a day late because of a slight heart attack. The Russian leader hated to fly, so he traveled by rail. Moreover, he ordered the heavily guarded train to detour around Poland for fear of an ambush, further delaying his arrival. When he made his entrance into Potsdam, a suburb of Berlin miraculously spared the total destruction that his forces had created in the German capital, he was ready to claim the spoils of war.

These two men, one the veteran revolutionary who had been in power for two decades, the other an untested leader in office for barely three months, symbolized the enormous differences that now separated the wartime allies. Stalin was above all a realist. Brutal in securing total control at home, he was more flexible in his foreign policy, bent on exploiting Russia's victory in World War II rather than aiming at world domination. Cunning and caution were the hallmarks of his diplomatic style. Small in stature, ungainly in build, he radiated a catlike quality as he waited behind his unassuming facade, ready to dazzle an opponent with his "brilliant, terrifying tactical mastery." Truman, in contrast, personified traditional Wilsonian idealism. Lacking Roosevelt's guile, the new president placed his faith in international cooperation. Like many Americans, he believed implicitly in his country's innate goodness. Self-assured to the point of cockiness, he came to Potsdam clothed in the armor of self-righteousness.

Truman and Stalin met for the first time on July 17, 1945. "I told Stalin that I am no diplomat," the president recorded in his diary, "but usually said yes and no to questions after hearing all the argument." The Russian dictator's reaction to Truman remains a mystery, but Truman believed the first encounter went well. "I can deal with Stalin," he wrote. "He is honest—but smart as hell."

Together with Winston Churchill and his replacement, Clement Attlee, whose Labour party had just triumphed in British elections, Truman and Stalin clashed for the next ten days over such difficult issues as reparations, the Polish border, and the fate of eastern Europe. Truman presented the ideas and proposals formulated by his advisers; he saw his task as essentially procedural, and when he presided, he moved the agenda along in brisk fashion. In an indirect, roundabout way, he informed Stalin of the existence of the atomic bomb, tested successfully in the New Mexico desert just before the conference began. Truman offered no details, and the impassive Stalin asked for none, commenting only that he hoped the United States would make "good use of it against the Japanese."

Reparations proved to be the crucial issue at Potsdam. The Russians wanted to rebuild their war-ravaged economy with German industry; the United States feared it would be saddled with the entire cost of caring for the defeated Germans. A compromise was finally reached. Each side would take reparations primarily from its own occupation zone, a solution that foreshadowed the future division of Germany. "Because they could not agree on how to govern Europe," wrote historian Daniel Yergin, "Truman and Stalin began to divide it." The other issues were referred to the newly created Council of Foreign Ministers, which would meet in the fall in London.

The conference thus ended on an apparent note of harmony; beneath the surface, however, the bitter antagonism of the Cold War was festering. America and Russia, each distrustful of the other, were preparing for a long and bitter confrontation. A dozen years later, Truman reminisced to an old associate about Potsdam. "What a show that was!" Describing himself as "an innocent idealist" surrounded by wolves, he claimed that all the agreements reached there were "broken as soon as the unconscionable Russian Dictator returned to Moscow!" He added ruefully, "And I liked the little son of a bitch."

THE COLD WAR BEGINS

The conflict between the United States and the Soviet Union began gradually. For two years, the nations tried to adjust their differences over the division of

Europe, postwar economic aid, and the atomic bomb through discussion and negotiation. The Council of Foreign Ministers provided the forum. Beginning in London during the fall of 1945 and meeting with their Russian counterparts in Paris, New York, and Moscow, American diplomats searched for a way to live in peace with a suspicious Soviet Union.

THE DIVISION OF EUROPE

The fundamental disagreement was over who would control postwar Europe. In the east, the Red Army had swept over Poland and the Balkans, laying the basis for Soviet domination there. American and British forces had liberated western Europe from Scandinavia to Italy. The Russians, mindful of past invasions from the west across the plains of Poland, were intent on imposing communist governments loyal to Moscow in the Soviet sphere. The United States, on the other hand, upheld the principle of national self-determination, insisting the people in each country should freely choose their postwar rulers. The Soviets saw the demand for free elections as subversive, since they knew that popularly chosen regimes would be unfriendly to Russia. Suspecting American duplicity, Stalin brought down an "Iron Curtain" (Churchill's phrase) from the Baltic to the Adriatic as he created a series of satellite governments.

Germany was the key. The temporary zones of occupation gradually hardened into permanent lines of division. Ignoring the Potsdam Conference agreement that the country be treated as an economic unit, the United States and Great Britain were by 1946 refusing to permit the Russians to take reparations from the industrial western zones. The initial harsh occupation policy gave way to more humane treatment of the German people and a slow but steady economic recovery. The United States and England merged their zones and championed the idea of the unification of all Germany. Russia, fearing a resurgence of German military power, responded by intensifying the communization of its zone, which included the jointly occupied city of Berlin.

The Soviet Union consolidated its grip on eastern Europe in 1946 and 1947. One by one, communist regimes replaced coalition governments in Poland, Hungary, Romania, and Bulgaria. Moving cautiously to avoid provoking the West, Stalin used communism as a means to dominate half of Europe, both to protect the security of the Soviet state and to advance its international power. The climax came in March 1948 when a coup in Czechoslovakia overthrew a democratic government and gave the Soviets a strategic foothold in central Europe.

The division of Europe was an inevitable aftereffect of World War II. Both sides were intent on imposing their values in the areas liberated by their troops. A frank recognition of competing spheres of influence might have avoided further escalation of tension. But the Western nations, remembering Hitler's aggression

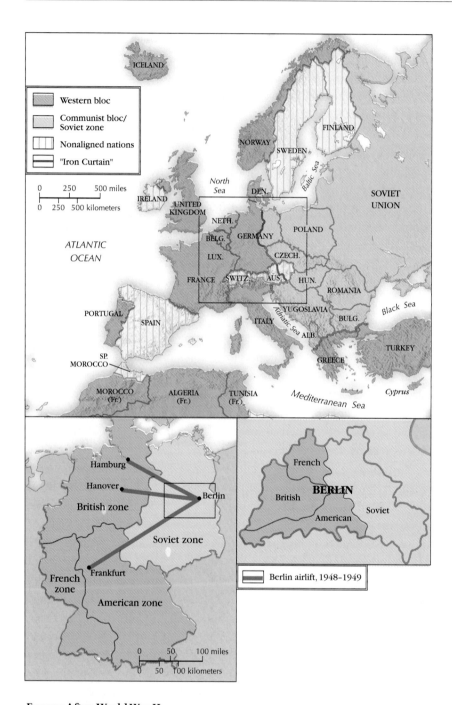

Legend:
- Western bloc
- Communist bloc/ Soviet zone
- Nonaligned nations
- "Iron Curtain"

0   250   500 miles
0   250   500 kilometers

ICELAND

NORWAY
SWEDEN
FINLAND

North Sea
Baltic Sea
DEN.
SOVIET UNION

IRELAND
UNITED KINGDOM
NETH.
BELG.
GERMANY
POLAND
LUX.
CZECH.
FRANCE
SWITZ.
AUS.
HUN.
ROMANIA

ATLANTIC OCEAN

PORTUGAL
SPAIN
ITALY
Adriatic Sea
YUGOSLAVIA
BULG.
Black Sea

ALB.
TURKEY

SP. MOROCCO
GREECE
Cyprus

MOROCCO (Fr.)
ALGERIA (Fr.)
TUNISIA (Fr.)
Mediterranean Sea

Hamburg
Hanover
Berlin
British zone
Soviet zone
French zone
Frankfurt
American zone

French
BERLIN
British
Soviet
American

Berlin airlift, 1948–1949

0   50   100 miles
0   50   100 kilometers

Europe After World War II

The heavy line splitting Germany shows in graphic form the division of Europe between the Western and Soviet spheres of influence. "From Stettin in the Baltic to Trieste in the Adriatic," said Churchill in a speech at Fulton, Missouri, in 1946, "an iron curtain has descended across the Continent."

in the 1930s, began to see Stalin as an equally dangerous threat to their well-being. Instead of accepting him as a cautious leader bent on protecting Russian security, they perceived him as an aggressive dictator leading a communist drive for world domination.

WITHHOLDING ECONOMIC AID

World War II had inflicted enormous damage on Russia. The brutal fighting had taken between fifteen and twenty million Russian lives, destroyed more than thirty thousand factories, and torn up forty thousand miles of railroad track. The industrialization that Stalin had achieved at such great sacrifice in the 1930s had been badly set back; even agricultural production had fallen by half during the war. Outside aid and assistance were vital for the reconstruction of the Soviet Union.

American leaders knew of Russia's plight and hoped to use it to good advantage. President Truman was convinced that economically "we held all the cards and the Russians had to come to us."

There were two possible forms of postwar assistance: loans and Lend-Lease. In January 1945, the Soviets requested a $6 billion loan to finance postwar reconstruction. Despite initial American encouragement, President Roosevelt deferred action on this request; as relations with Russia cooled, the chances for action dimmed. By the war's end, the loan request, though never formally turned down, was dead.

Lend-Lease proved no more successful. In the spring of 1945, Congress instructed the administration not to use Lend-Lease for postwar reconstruction. President Truman went further, however, by signing an order on May 11, 1945, terminating all shipments to Russia, including those already at sea. Heeding Russian protests, Truman resumed Lend-Lease shipments, but only until the war was over in August. After that, all Lend-Lease ended.

Deprived of American assistance, the Russians were forced to rebuild their economy through reparations. The Soviets systematically removed factories and plants from areas they controlled, including their zone of Germany, eastern Europe, and Manchuria. Slowly, the Russian economy recovered from the war, but the bitterness over the American refusal to extend aid convinced Stalin of Western hostility and thus deepened the growing antagonism between the Soviet Union and the United States.

THE ATOMIC DILEMMA

Overshadowing all else was the atomic bomb. Used by the United States with deadly success at Hiroshima and Nagasaki, the new weapon raised problems that would have been difficult for even friendly nations to resolve. Given the uneasy state of Soviet-American relations, the effect was disastrous.

The wartime policy followed by Roosevelt and Churchill ensured a postwar nuclear arms race. Instead of informing their major ally of the developing atomic bomb, they kept it a closely guarded secret. Stalin learned of the Manhattan Project through espionage and responded by starting a Soviet atomic program in 1943. By the time Truman informed Stalin of the weapon's existence at Potsdam, the Russians, aided by a steady stream of information from spies in the United States, were well on the way to making their own bomb.

After the war, the United States developed a disarmament plan that would turn control of fissionable material, then the processing plants, and ultimately the American stockpile of bombs over to an international agency. When President Truman appointed financier Bernard Baruch to present this proposal to the United Nations, Baruch insisted on changing it in several important ways, adding sanctions against violators and exempting the international agency from the UN veto. Ignoring scientists who pleaded for a more cooperative position, Baruch argued that "we cannot at this time limit our capability to produce or use this weapon." In effect, the Baruch Plan, with its multiple stages and emphasis on inspection, would preserve the American atomic monopoly for the indefinite future.

The Soviets responded predictably. Diplomat Andrei Gromyko presented a simple plan calling for a total ban on the production and use of the new weapon as well as the destruction of all existing bombs. The Russian proposal was founded on the same perception of national self-interest as the Baruch Plan. Russia still had nearly three million men under arms in 1947 and wanted to use its conventional strength to the utmost by outlawing the atomic bomb.

No agreement was possible. Neither the United States nor the Soviet Union could abandon its position without surrendering a vital national interest. Wanting to preserve its monopoly, America stressed inspection and control; hoping to neutralize the U.S. advantage, Russia advocated immediate disarmament. The nuclear dilemma, inherent in the Soviet-American rivalry, blocked any national settlement. Instead, the two superpowers agreed to disagree. Trusting neither each other nor any form of international cooperation, each concentrated on taking maximum advantage of its wartime gains. Thus the Russians exploited the territory they had conquered in Europe while the United States retained its economic and strategic advantages over the Soviet Union. The result was the Cold War.

CONTAINMENT

A major departure in American foreign policy occurred in January 1947, when General George C. Marshall, the wartime army chief of staff, became secretary of state. Calm, mature, and orderly of mind, Marshall had the capability—honed in World War II—to think in broad strategic terms. An extraordinarily good judge of ability, he relied on gifted subordinates to handle the day-to-day implementation of his policies. In the months after taking office, he came to rely on two men in particular: Dean Acheson and George Kennan.

Acheson, an experienced Washington lawyer and bureaucrat, was appointed undersecretary of state and given free rein by Marshall to conduct American diplomacy. A man of keen intelligence, he had a carefully cultivated reputation for arrogance and a low tolerance for mediocrity. As an ardent Anglophile, he wanted to see the United States take over a faltering Britain's role as the supreme arbiter of world affairs. Recalling the lesson of Munich, he opposed appeasement and advocated a policy of negotiating only from strength.

George Kennan, Marshall's other mainstay, headed the newly created Policy Planning Staff. A career foreign service officer, Kennan had become a Soviet expert, mastering Russian history and culture as well as speaking the language fluently. He served in Moscow after U.S. recognition in 1933 and again during World War II, developing there a profound distrust for the Soviet regime. In a crucial telegram in 1946, he advocated a policy of containment, arguing that only strong and sustained resistance could halt the outward flow of Russian power. As self-assured as Acheson, Kennan believed that neither Congress nor public opinion should interfere with the conduct of foreign policy by the experts.

In the spring of 1947, a sense of crisis impelled Marshall, Acheson, and Kennan to set out on a new course in American diplomacy. Dubbed "containment," after an article by Kennan in *Foreign Affairs,* the new policy both consolidated the evolving postwar anticommunism and established guidelines that would shape America's role in the world for more than two decades. What Kennan proposed was "a long-term, patient but firm, and vigilant containment of Russian expansive tendencies." Such a policy of halting Soviet aggression would not lead to any immediate victory, Kennan warned. In the long run, however, he believed that the United States could force the Soviet Union to adopt more reasonable policies and live in peace with the West.

THE TRUMAN DOCTRINE

The initial step toward containment came in response to an urgent British request. Since March 1946, England had been supporting the Greek government in a bitter civil war against communist guerrillas. On February 21, 1947, the British informed the United States that they could no longer afford to aid Greece or Turkey, the latter under heavy pressure from the Soviets for access to the Mediterranean. Believing the Russians responsible for the strife in Greece (in fact, they were not), Marshall, Acheson, and Kennan quickly decided the United States would have to assume Britain's role in the eastern Mediterranean.

Worried about congressional support, especially since the Republicans had gained control of Congress in 1946, Marshall called a meeting with the legislative leadership in late February. He outlined the problem; then Acheson took over to warn that "a highly possible Soviet breakthrough might open three continents to Soviet penetration." Claiming that the Soviets were "playing one of the greatest gambles in history," Acheson concluded that "we and we alone were in a position to break up the play."

The bipartisan group of congressional leaders was deeply impressed. Finally, Republican Senator Arthur M. Vandenberg spoke up, saying he would support the president, but adding that to ensure public backing, Truman would have to "scare hell" out of the American people.

The president followed the senator's advice. On March 12, 1947, he asked Congress for $400 million for military and economic assistance to Greece and Turkey. In stating what would become known as the Truman Doctrine, he made clear that more was involved than just these two countries—the stakes in fact were far higher. "It must be the policy of the United States," Truman told the Congress, "to support free peoples who are resisting attempted subjugation by armed minorities or by outside pressure." After a brief debate, both the House and the Senate approved the program by margins of better than three to one.

The Truman Doctrine marked an informal declaration of cold war against the Soviet Union. Truman used the crisis in Greece to secure congressional approval and build a national consensus for the policy of containment. In less than two years, the civil war in Greece ended, but the American commitment to oppose communist expansion, whether by internal subversion or external aggression, placed the United States on a collision course with the Soviet Union around the globe.

THE MARSHALL PLAN

Despite American interest in controlling Soviet expansion into Greece, western Europe was far more vital to U.S. interests than was the eastern Mediterranean. Yet by 1947, many Americans believed that western Europe was open to Soviet penetration. The problem was economic in nature. Despite $9 billion in piecemeal American loans, England, France, Italy, and the other European countries had great difficulty in recovering from World War II. Food was scarce, with millions existing on less than fifteen hundred calories a day; industrial machinery was broken down and obsolete; and workers were demoralized by years of depression and war. Resentment and discontent led to growing communist voting strength, especially in Italy and France. If the United States could not reverse the process, it seemed as though all Europe might drift into the communist orbit.

In the weeks following proclamation of the Truman Doctrine, American officials dealt with this problem. Secretary of State Marshall, returning from a frustrating Council of Foreign Ministers meeting in Moscow, warned that "the patient is sinking while the doctors deliberate." The experts drew up a plan for the massive infusion of American capital to finance the economic recovery of Europe. Speaking at a Harvard commencement on June 5, 1947, Marshall presented the broad outline. He offered extensive economic aid to all the nations of Europe if they could reach agreement on ways to achieve "the revival of a working economy in the world so as to permit the emergence of political and social conditions in which free institutions can exist."

The fate of the Marshall Plan depended on the reaction of the Soviet Union and the U.S. Congress. Marshall had taken, in the words of one American diplomat, "a hell of a gamble" by including Russia in his offer of aid. At a meeting of the European nations in Paris in July 1947, the Soviet foreign minister ended the suspense by abruptly withdrawing. Neither the Soviet Union nor its satellites would take part. The other European countries then made a formal request for $17 billion in assistance over the next four years.

Congress responded cautiously to the proposal, appointing a special joint committee to investigate. The administration lobbied vigorously, pointing out that the Marshall Plan would help the United States by stimulating trade with Europe as well as checking Soviet expansion. It was the latter argument, however, that proved decisive. When the Czech coup touched off a war scare in March 1948, Congress quickly approved the Marshall Plan by heavy majorities. Over the next four years, the huge American investment paid rich dividends, generating a broad industrial revival in western Europe that became self-sustaining by the 1950s. The threat of communist domination faded, and a prosperous Europe proved to be a bonanza for American farmers, miners, and manufacturers.

THE WESTERN MILITARY ALLIANCE

The third and final phase of containment came in 1949 with the establishment of the North Atlantic Treaty Organization (NATO). NATO grew out of European fears of Russian military aggression. Recalling Hitler's tactics in the 1930s, the people of western Europe wanted assurance that the United States would protect them from attack as they began to achieve economic recovery.

England, France, and the Low Countries (Belgium, the Netherlands, and Luxembourg) began the process in March 1948 when they signed the Brussels Treaty, providing for collective self-defense. In January 1949, President Truman

The Soviet view of the Cold War, as depicted in this Soviet cartoon, shows the United States stretching out long arms to take hold of Korea, Iran, Turkey, Taiwan, and Vietnam.

called for a broader defense pact including the United States; ten European nations, from Norway in the north to Italy in the south, joined the United States and Canada in signing the North Atlantic Treaty in Washington on April 4, 1949. This historic departure from the traditional policy of isolation caused extensive debate, but the Senate ratified it in July by a vote of 82 to 13.

There were two main features of NATO. First, the United States committed itself to the defense of Europe in the key clause, which stated that "an armed attack against one or more shall be considered an attack against them all." In effect, the United States was extending its atomic shield over Europe. The second feature was designed to reassure worried Europeans that the United States would honor this commitment. In late 1950, President Truman authorized the stationing of four American divisions in Europe to serve as the nucleus of the NATO army. It was believed that the threat of American troop involvement in any Russian assault would deter the Soviet Union from making such an attack.

The Western military alliance escalated the developing Cold War. Whatever its advantage in building a sense of security among worried Europeans, it represented an overreaction to the Soviet danger. Americans and Europeans alike were attempting to apply the lesson of Munich to the Cold War. But Stalin was not Hitler, and the Soviets were not the Nazis. There was no evidence of any Russian plan to invade western Europe, and in the face of the American atomic bomb, none was likely. NATO only intensified Russian fears of the West and thus increased the level of international tension.

THE BERLIN BLOCKADE

The main Russian response to containment came in 1948 at the West's most vulnerable point. American, British, French, and Soviet troops each occupied a sector of Berlin, but the city was located more than a hundred miles within the Russian zone of Germany (see the map of postwar Europe on p. 904). Stalin decided to test his opponents' resolve by cutting off all rail and highway traffic to Berlin on June 20, 1948.

The timing was very awkward for Harry Truman. He had his hands full resisting efforts to force him off the Democratic ticket, and he faced a difficult reelection effort against a strong Republican candidate, Governor Thomas E. Dewey of New York. Immersed in election-year politics, Truman was caught unprepared by the Berlin blockade. The alternatives were not very appealing. The United States could withdraw its forces and lose not just a city, but the confidence of all Europe; it could try to send in reinforcements and fight for Berlin; or it could sit tight and attempt to find a diplomatic solution. Truman made the basic decision in characteristic fashion, telling the military that there would be no thought of pulling out. "We were going to stay, period," an aide reported Truman as saying.

In the next few weeks, the president and his advisers adopted a two-phase policy. The first part was a massive airlift of food, fuel, and supplies for the ten thousand troops and the two million civilians in Berlin. A fleet of fifty-two C-54s and eighty C-47s began making two daily round-trip flights to Berlin, carrying 2500 tons every twenty-four hours. Then, to guard against Soviet interruption of the airlift, Truman transferred sixty American B-29s, planes capable of delivering atomic bombs, to bases in England. The president was bluffing; the B-29s were not equipped with atomic bombs, but at the time, the threat was effective.

For a few weeks, the world teetered on the edge of war. Stalin did not attempt to disrupt the flights to Berlin, but he rejected all American diplomatic initiatives. Although at any time the Russians could have halted it by jamming

The Berlin airlift of 1948–1949 broke the Soviet blockade. Called Operation Vittles, it provided food and fuel for West Berliners. Here children wait for the candy that American pilots dropped in tiny handkerchief parachutes.

radar or shooting down the defenseless cargo planes, the airlift gradually increased to more than 4000 tons a day. Governor Dewey patriotically supported the president's policy, thus removing foreign policy from the presidential campaign.

Slowly, the tension eased. The Russians did not shoot down any planes, and the daily airlift climbed to nearly 7000 tons. Truman, a decided underdog, won a surprising second term in November over a complacent Dewey, in part because the Berlin crisis had rallied the nation behind his leadership. In early 1949, the Soviets gave in, ending the blockade in return for another meeting of the Council of Foreign Ministers on Germany—a conclave that proved as unproductive as all the earlier ones.

The Berlin crisis marked the end of the initial phase of the Cold War. The airlift had given the United States a striking political victory, showing the world the triumph of American ingenuity over Russian stubbornness. Yet it could not disguise the fact that the Cold War had cut Europe in two. Behind the Iron Curtain, the Russians had consolidated control over the areas won by their troops in the war, while the United States had used the Marshall Plan to revitalize western Europe. But a divided continent was a far cry from the wartime hopes for a peaceful world. And the rivalry that began in Europe would soon spread into a worldwide contest between the superpowers.

THE COLD WAR EXPANDS

The rivalry between the United States and the Soviet Union grew in the late 1940s and early 1950s. Both sides began to rebuild their military forces with new methods and new weapons. Equally significant, the diplomatic competition spread from Europe to Asia as each of the superpowers sought to enhance its influence in the Far East. By the time Truman left office in early 1953, the Cold War had taken on global proportions.

THE MILITARY DIMENSION

After World War II, American leaders were intent on reforming the nation's military system in light of their wartime experience. Two goals were uppermost. First, nearly everyone agreed in the aftermath of Pearl Harbor that the U.S. armed services should be unified into an integrated military system. The developing Cold War reinforced this decision. Equally important, planners realized, was the need for new institutions to coordinate military and diplomatic strategy so the nation could cope effectively with threats to its security.

In 1947, Congress passed the National Security Act. It established a Department of Defense, headed by a civilian secretary of cabinet rank presiding over three separate services—the army, the navy, and the new air force. In addition, the act created the Central Intelligence Agency (CIA) to coordinate the intelligence-gathering activities of various government agencies. Finally, the act provided for a National Security Council (NSC)—composed of the service secretaries, the secretary of defense, and the secretary of state—to advise the president on all matters regarding the nation's security.

Despite the appearance of equality among the services, the air force quickly emerged as the dominant power in the atomic age, based on its capability both to deter an enemy from attacking and to wage war if deterrence failed. President Truman, intent on cutting back defense expenditures, favored the air force in his 1949 military budget, allotting this branch more than one-half the total sum. After the Czech coup and the resulting war scare, Congress granted an additional $3 billion to the military.

American military planners received even greater support in the fall of 1949 when the Soviet Union exploded its first atomic bomb. President Truman appointed a high-level committee to explore mounting an all-out effort to build a hydrogen bomb to maintain American nuclear supremacy.

Some scientists had technical objections to the H-bomb, which was still far from being perfected, while others opposed the new weapon on moral grounds, claiming that its enormous destructive power (intended to be one thousand times greater than the atomic bomb) made it unthinkable. Dean Acheson—who succeeded Marshall as secretary of state in early 1949—believed it was imperative that the United States develop the hydrogen bomb before the Soviet Union. When Acheson presented the committee's favorable report to the president in January 1950, Truman took only seven minutes to decide to go ahead with the awesome new weapon.

At the same time, Acheson ordered the Policy Planning Staff to draw up a new statement of national defense policy. NSC-68, as the document eventually became known, was based on the premise that the Soviet Union sought "to impose its absolute authority over the rest of the world." Rejecting such options as appeasement or a return to isolation, NSC-68 called for a massive expansion of American military power so the United States could halt and overcome the Soviet threat and proposed an increase in defense spending from $13 to $45 billion annually. Approved in principle by the National Security Council in April 1950, NSC-68 stood as a symbol of the Truman administration's determination to win the Cold War regardless of cost.

THE COLD WAR IN ASIA

The Soviet-American conflict developed more slowly in Asia. At Yalta, the two superpowers had agreed to a Far Eastern balance of power, with the Russians dominating Northeast Asia and the Americans in control of the Pacific, including both Japan and its former island empire.

The United States moved quickly to consolidate its sphere of influence. General Douglas MacArthur, in charge of Japanese occupation, denied the Soviet Union any role in the reconstruction of Japan. Instead, he supervised the transition of the Japanese government into a constitutional democracy, shaped along Western lines, in which communists were barred from all government posts. The Japanese willingly renounced war in their new constitution, relying instead on American forces to protect their security. American policy was equally nationalistic in the Pacific. A trusteeship arrangement with the United Nations merely disguised the fact that the United States held full control over the Marshall, Mariana, and Caroline Islands.

As defined at Yalta, China lay between the Soviet and American spheres. When World War II ended, the country was torn between Chiang Kai-shek's Nationalists in the South and Mao Tse-tung's Communists in the North. Chiang had many advantages, including American political and economic backing and official Soviet recognition. But corruption was widespread among the Nationalist leaders, and a raging inflation that soon reached 100 percent a year devastated the Chinese middle classes and thus eroded Chiang's base of power. Mao used tight discipline and patriotic appeals to strengthen his hold on the peasantry and extend his influence. When the Soviets abruptly vacated Manchuria in 1946, after stripping it of virtually all the industrial machinery Japan had installed, Mao inherited control of this rich northern province. Ignoring American advice, Chiang rushed north to occupy Manchurian cities, overextending his supply lines and exposing his forces to Communist counterattack.

American policy sought to prevent a Chinese civil war. Before he became secretary of state, George Marshall undertook the difficult task of forming a coalition government between Chiang and Mao. There was no basis for compromise. Chiang insisted he "was going to liquidate Communists," while Mao was trying to play the United States against Russia in his bid for power. By 1947, as China plunged into full-scale civil war, the Truman administration had given up any meaningful effort to influence the outcome. Political mediation had failed, military intervention was out of the question so soon after World War II, and a policy of continued American economic aid served only to appease domestic supporters of Chiang Kai-shek; 80 percent of the military supplies ended up in Communist hands.

The Chinese conflict climaxed at the end of the decade. Mao's forces drove the Nationalists out of Manchuria in late 1948 and advanced across the Yangtze by mid-1949. Acheson released a lengthy report justifying American policy in China on the grounds that the civil war there "was beyond the control of the government of the United States." Republican senators, however, disagreed, blaming American diplomats for sabotaging the Nationalists and terming Acheson's report "a 1054-page white-wash of a wishful, do-nothing policy." While the domestic debate raged over responsibility for the loss of China, Chiang's forces fled the mainland for sanctuary on Formosa (Taiwan) in December 1949. Two months later, Mao and Stalin signed a Sino-Soviet treaty of mutual assistance that clearly placed China in the Russian orbit.

The American response to the Communist triumph in China was twofold. First, the State Department refused to recognize the legitimacy of the new regime in Peking, maintaining instead formal diplomatic relations with the Nationalists on Formosa. Citing the Sino-Soviet alliance, Assistant Secretary of State Dean Rusk called the Peking regime "a colonial Russian government." Then, to compensate for the loss of China, the United States focused on Japan as its main ally in Asia. The State Department encouraged the buildup of Japanese industry, and the Pentagon expanded American bases on the Japanese home islands and Okinawa. A Japanese-American security pact led to the end of American occupation by 1952. The Cold War had now split Asia in two.

THE KOREAN WAR

The showdown between the United States and the Soviet Union in Asia came in Korea. Traditionally the cockpit of international rivalry in Northeast Asia, Korea had been divided at the 38th parallel in 1945. The Russians occupied the industrial North, installing a communist government under the leadership of Kim Il-Sung. In the agrarian South, Syngman Rhee, a conservative nationalist, emerged as the American-sponsored ruler. Neither regime heeded a UN call for elections to unify the country. The two superpowers pulled out most of their occupation forces by 1949. The Russians, however, helped train a well-equipped army in the North, while the United States—fearful Rhee would seek unification through armed conquest—gave much more limited military assistance to South Korea.

On June 25, 1950, the North Korean army suddenly crossed the 38th parallel in great strength. We now know that Stalin had approved this act of aggression in advance. In January 1950, the Soviet leader had told Mao Tse-tung that he was ready to overthrow the Yalta settlement in the Far East ("and to hell with it," he exclaimed to Mao). In April, when Kim Il-Sung came to Moscow to gain approval for the assault on South Korea, Stalin gave it willingly, apparently in the belief that the United States was ready to abandon Syngman Rhee. Despite expressing some reservations, Mao also approved the planned North Korean aggression.

Both Stalin and Mao had badly miscalculated the American response. President Truman saw the invasion as a clear-cut case of Soviet aggression reminiscent of the 1930s. "Communism was acting in Korea just as Hitler, Mussolini,

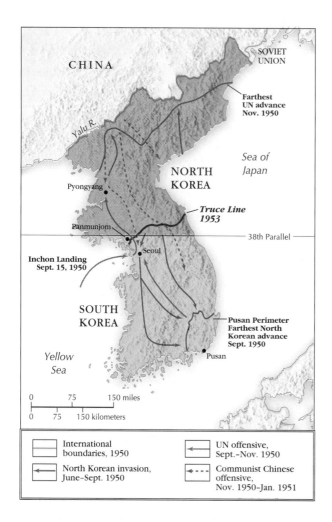

CHINA

SOVIET
UNION

Farthest
UN advance
Nov. 1950

Yalu R.

NORTH
KOREA

Sea of
Japan

Pyongyang

Truce Line
1953

Panmunjom

38th Parallel

Inchon Landing
Sept. 15, 1950

Seoul

SOUTH
KOREA

Pusan Perimeter
Farthest North
Korean advance
Sept. 1950

Yellow
Sea

Pusan

| 0 | 75 | 150 miles |
| 0 | 75 | 150 kilometers |

| International boundaries, 1950 | UN offensive, Sept.–Nov. 1950 |
| North Korean invasion, June–Sept. 1950 | Communist Chinese offensive, Nov. 1950–Jan. 1951 |

The Korean War, 1950–1953

After a year of rapid movement up and down the Korean peninsula, the fighting stalled just north of the 38th parallel. The resulting truce line has divided North and South Korea since the July 1953 armistice.

and the Japanese had acted ten, fifteen, and twenty years earlier," he commented in his memoirs. Following Acheson's advice, the president convened the UN Security Council and, taking advantage of a temporary Soviet boycott, secured a resolution condemning North Korea as an aggressor and calling on the member nations to engage in a collective security action. Within a few days, American troops from Japan were in combat in South Korea. The conflict, which would last for more than three years, was technically a police action fought under UN auspices; in reality, the United States was at war with a Soviet satellite in Asia.

In the beginning, the fighting went badly as the North Koreans continued to drive down the peninsula. But by August, American forces had halted the communist advance near Pusan. In September, General MacArthur changed the whole complexion of the war by carrying out a brilliant amphibious assault at

Douglas MacArthur, supreme commander of UN forces in Korea, launched the invasion at Inchon in September 1950 and within a few days recaptured Seoul, the South Korean capital.

Inchon, on the waist of Korea, cutting off and destroying most of the North Korean army in the South. Encouraged by this victory, Truman began to shift from his original goal of restoring the 38th parallel to a new one: the unification of Korea by military force.

The administration ignored warnings from Peking against an American invasion of North Korea. "I should think it would be sheer madness for the Chinese to intervene," commented Acheson. MacArthur was even more confident. "We are no longer fearful of their intervention," he told Truman at a Wake Island conference in mid-October.

Rarely has an American president received worse advice than Truman did from Acheson and MacArthur. The UN forces crossed the 38th parallel in October, advanced confidently to the Yalu in November, and then were completely routed by a massive Chinese counterattack that drove them out of all North Korea by December. MacArthur finally stabilized the fighting near the

38th parallel, but when Truman decided to give up his attempt to unify Korea, the general protested to Congress, calling for a renewed offensive and proclaiming, "There is no substitute for victory."

Truman courageously relieved the popular hero of the Pacific of his command on April 11, 1951. At first, MacArthur seemed likely to force the president to back down. Huge crowds came forward to welcome him home and hear him call for victory over the communists in Asia. At a special congressional hearing, the administration struck back effectively by warning that MacArthur's strategy would expose all Europe to Soviet attack. General Omar Bradley, Truman's chief military adviser, succinctly pointed out that a "showdown" with communism in Asia would be "the wrong war, at the wrong place, at the wrong time, and with the wrong enemy."

Congress and the American people came to accept MacArthur's recall. The Korean War settled into a stalemate near the 38th parallel as truce talks with the communists bogged down for the rest of Truman's term in office. The president could take heart from the fact that he had achieved his primary goal, defense of South Korea and the principle of collective security. Yet by taking the gamble to unify Korea by force, he had confused the American people and humiliated the United States in the eyes of the world.

In the last analysis, the most significant result of the Korean conflict was the massive American rearmament it brought about. The army expanded to 3.5 million troops, the defense budget increased to $50 billion a year by 1952, and the United States acquired distant military bases from Saudi Arabia to Morocco. America was now committed to waging a global contest against the Soviet Union with arms as well as words.

THE COLD WAR AT HOME

The Cold War cast a long shadow over American life in the late 1940s and early 1950s. Truman tried to carry on the New Deal reform tradition he had inherited from FDR, but the American people were more concerned about events abroad. The Republican party used both growing dissatisfaction with postwar economic adjustment and fears of communist penetration of the United States to revive its sagging fortunes and regain control of the White House in 1952 for the first time in twenty years.

TRUMAN'S TROUBLES

Matching his foreign policy successes with equal achievements at home was not easy for Harry S Truman. As a loyal supporter of Franklin D. Roosevelt's

New Deal programs during his Senate career, Truman had earned a reputation for being a hardworking, reliable, and intensely partisan legislator. But he was relatively unknown to the general public, and his background as a Missouri county official associated with Kansas City machine politics did little to inspire confidence in his ability to lead the nation. Surprisingly well-read—especially in history and biography—Truman possessed sound judgment, the ability to reach decisions quickly, and a fierce and uncompromising sense of right and wrong.

Two weaknesses marred his performance in the White House. One was a fondness for old friends, which resulted in the appointment of many Missouri and Senate cronies to high office. The president's other serious limitation was his lack of political vision. Failing to pursue a coherent legislative program of his own, he tried to perpetuate FDR's New Deal and, as a result, engaged in a running battle with Congress.

The postwar mood was not conducive to an extension of New Deal reforms. Americans were weary of shortages and sacrifices; they wanted the chance to buy the consumer goods denied them under wartime conditions. But in the rush to convert industry from producing planes and tanks to cars and appliances, problems soon emerged. Prices and wages rose quickly as Congress voted to end wartime controls. With prices going up 25 percent in two years, workers demanded higher wages to offset the loss of overtime pay. A wave of labor unrest swept over the country in the spring of 1946.

President Truman was caught in the middle. Sensitive to union demands, he permitted businesses to negotiate large pay increases for their workers and then pass on the cost to consumers in the form of higher prices. He criticized Congress for weakening wartime price controls, but he failed to offer anything else to curb inflation.

In the face of rising discontent, Truman's efforts to extend the New Deal met with little success. The only measure Congress passed was the Employment Act of 1946. This legislation created the Council of Economic Advisers to assist the president and asserted the principle that the government was responsible for the state of the economy, but it failed to address Truman's original goal of mandatory federal planning to achieve full employment.

The Republicans took advantage of increasing public dissatisfaction with postwar economic woes to attack the Democrats. "To err is Truman," the GOP proclaimed and then adopted a very effective two-word slogan for the 1946 congressional elections: "Had enough?" The American people, weary of inflation and labor unrest, responded by electing Republican majorities in both the House and Senate for the first time since 1930.

THE ELECTION OF 1948

CANDIDATE	PARTY	POPULAR VOTE	ELECTORAL VOTE
Truman	Democratic	24,105,182	303
Dewey	Republican	21,970,065	189
Thurmond	States' Rights	1,169,063	39
	Minor Parties	442,667	—

TRUMAN VINDICATED

The president's relations with Congress became even stormier after the 1946 election. Truman successfully vetoed two GOP measures to give large tax cuts to the wealthy, but Congress overrode his veto of the Taft-Hartley Act in 1947. Designed to correct the imbalance in labor-management relations created by the Wagner Act, the Taft-Hartley Act outlawed specific labor union activities—including the closed shop and secondary boycotts. Despite Truman's claim that it was a "slave-labor" bill, unions were able to survive its provisions.

President Truman's political fortunes reached their lowest ebb in early 1948. Former vice president Henry A. Wallace, claiming to represent the New Deal, announced his third-party (Progressive) candidacy in the presidential contest that year. The Democrats reluctantly nominated Truman. His prospects for victory in the fall, however, looked very dim—especially after disgruntled Southerners bolted the Democratic party in protest over a progressive civil rights platform. The Dixiecrats, as they became known, nominated Strom Thurmond, the governor of South Carolina, on a States' Rights party ticket.

The defection of the Dixiecrats in the South and Wallace's liberal followers in the North led political experts to predict an almost certain Republican victory. Governor Thomas E. Dewey of New York, the GOP candidate, was so certain of winning that he waged a cautious and bland campaign designed to give him a free hand once he was in the White House. With nothing to lose, Truman barnstormed around the country denouncing the "do-nothing" Republican Eightieth Congress. To the amazement of the pollsters, Truman won a narrow but decisive victory in November. The old Roosevelt coalition—farmers, organized labor, urban ethnic groups, and blacks—had held together, enabling Truman to remain in the White House and the Democrats to regain control of Congress.

A jubilant Harry Truman, on the morning after his 1948 election win, displays the headline blazoned on the front page of the Chicago Daily Tribune—*a newspaper that believed the pollsters.*

There was one more reason for Truman's win in 1948. During this election, held at the height of the Berlin crisis, the GOP failed to challenge Truman's conduct of the Cold War. Locked in a tense rivalry with the Soviet Union, the American people saw no reason to reject a president who had countered aggression overseas with the Truman Doctrine and the Marshall Plan. The Republicans, committed to support the bipartisan policy of containment, had allowed the Democrats to preempt the foreign policy issue. Until they found a way to challenge Truman's Cold War policies, GOP leaders had little chance to regain the White House.

THE LOYALTY ISSUE

Despite Truman's surprising victory in 1948, there was one area on which the Democrats were vulnerable. The fear of communism abroad that had led to the bipartisan containment policy could be used against them at home by politicians who were more willing to exploit the public's deep-seated anxiety.

Fear of radicalism had been a recurrent feature of American life since the early days of the republic. The Cold War heightened the traditional belief that subversion from abroad endangered the republic. Bold rhetoric from members of the Truman administration, portraying the men in the Kremlin as inspired revolutionaries bent on world conquest, frightened the American people. They viewed the Soviet Union as a successor to Nazi Germany—a totalitarian police state that threatened the basic liberties of a free people.

A series of revelations of communist espionage activities reinforced these fears. Canadian officials uncovered a Soviet spy ring in 1946, and the House Un-American Activities Committee held hearings indicating that communist agents had flourished in the Agriculture and Treasury departments in the 1930s.

Although Truman tried to dismiss the loyalty issue as a "red herring," he felt compelled to take protective measures, thus lending substance to the charges of subversion. In March 1947, he had initiated a loyalty program, ordering security checks of government employees in order to root out communists. Originally intended to remove subversives for whom "reasonable grounds exist for belief that the person involved is disloyal," within four years the Loyalty Review Board was dismissing workers as security risks if there was "reasonable doubt" of their loyalty. Thousands of government workers lost their jobs, charged with guilt by association with radicals or with membership in left-wing organizations. Often those who were charged had no chance to face their accusers.

The most famous disclosure came in August 1948, when Whittaker Chambers, a repentant communist, accused Alger Hiss of having been a Soviet spy in the 1930s. When Hiss, who had been a prominent State Department official, denied the charges, Chambers led investigators to a hollowed-out pumpkin on his Maryland farm. Inside the pumpkin were microfilms of confidential government documents. Chambers claimed that Hiss had passed the State Department materials to him in the late 1930s. Although the statute of limitations prevented a charge of treason against Hiss, he was convicted of perjury in January 1950 and sentenced to a five-year prison term.

Events abroad intensified the sense of danger. The communist triumph in China in the fall of 1949 came as a shock; soon there were charges that "fellow travelers" in the State Department were responsible for "the loss of China." In September 1949, when the Truman administration announced that the Russians had detonated their first atomic bomb, the end of America's nuclear monopoly was blamed on Soviet espionage. In early 1950, Klaus Fuchs—a British scientist who had worked on the wartime Manhattan Project—admitted giving the Russians vital information about the A-bomb.

A few months later, the government charged American communists Ethel and Julius Rosenberg with conspiracy to transmit atomic secrets to the Soviet

Three days before Julius and Ethel Rosenberg were executed for treason, their two young sons, 10 and 6 years old, marched to the White House to plead executive clemency for their parents.

Union. In 1951, a jury found the Rosenbergs guilty of treason, and Judge Irving Kaufman sentenced them to die for what he termed their "loathsome offense." Despite their insistent claims of innocence and worldwide appeals on their behalf, the Rosenbergs were electrocuted on June 19, 1953. Thus by the early 1950s, nearly all the ingredients were at hand for a new outburst of hysteria— fear of Russia, evidence of espionage, and a belief in a vast unseen conspiracy. The only element missing was a leader to release the new outburst of intolerance.

MCCARTHYISM IN ACTION

On February 12, 1950, Senator Joseph R. McCarthy of Wisconsin delivered a routine Lincoln's Birthday speech in Wheeling, West Virginia. This little known Republican suddenly attracted national attention when he declared, "I have here in my hand a list of 205—a list of names that were made known to the secretary of state as being members of the communist party and who nevertheless are still working and shaping policy in the State Department." The charge that there were communists in the State Department was never substantiated. But McCarthy's Wheeling speech triggered a four-and-a-half-year crusade to hunt down alleged

Senator Joseph McCarthy maintained a steady stream of unsubstantiated charges, always ready to make new accusations of communist infiltration before the preceding ones could be proven untrue. McCarthy's ruthless, vicious attacks cost hundreds of people their jobs and careers.

communists in government. The stridency and sensationalism of the senator's accusations soon won the name "McCarthyism."

McCarthy's basic technique was the multiple untruth. He leveled a bevy of charges of treasonable activities in government. While officials were refuting his initial accusations, he brought forth a steady stream of new ones, so the corrections never caught up with the latest blast. He failed to unearth a single confirmed communist in government, but he kept the Truman administration in turmoil. Drawing on an army of informers, primarily disgruntled federal workers with grievances against their colleagues and superiors, McCarthy charged government agencies with harboring and protecting communist agents and accused the State Department of deliberately losing the Cold War.

The secret of McCarthy's power was the fear he engendered among his Senate colleagues. In 1950, Maryland Senator Millard Tydings, who headed a committee critical of McCarthy's activities, failed to win reelection when

McCarthy opposed him; after that, other senators ran scared. McCarthy delighted in making sweeping, startling charges of communist sympathies against prominent public figures. A favorite target was patrician Secretary of State Dean Acheson; he even went after General George Marshall, claiming that the wartime army chief of staff was an agent of the communist conspiracy. Nor were fellow Republicans immune. One GOP senator was described as "a living miracle in that he is without question the only man who has lived so long with neither brains nor guts."

The attacks on the wealthy, famous, and privileged won McCarthy a devoted national following, though at the height of his influence in early 1954, he gained the approval of only 50 percent of the respondents in a Gallup poll. He offered a simple solution to the complicated Cold War: defeat the enemy at home rather than continue to engage in costly foreign aid programs and entangling alliances abroad. Above all, McCarthy appealed to conservative Republicans in the Midwest who shared his right-wing views and felt cheated by Truman's upset victory in 1948. Even GOP leaders who viewed McCarthy's tactics with distaste, such as Robert A. Taft of Ohio, quietly encouraged him to attack the vulnerable Democrats.

THE REPUBLICANS IN POWER

In 1952, the GOP capitalized on a growing sense of national frustration to capture the presidency. The stalemate in Korea and the fear of communism created a desire for political change; revelations of scandals by several individuals close to Truman intensified the feeling that someone needed to clean up "the mess in Washington." In Dwight D. Eisenhower, the Republican party found the perfect candidate to explore what one senator called K_1C_2—Korea, communism, and corruption.

Immensely popular because of his amiable manner, winning smile, and heroic stature, Eisenhower alone appeared to have the ability to unite a divided nation. In the 1952 campaign, Ike displayed hidden gifts as a politician in running against Adlai Stevenson, the eloquent Illinois governor whose appeal was limited to diehard Democrats and liberal intellectuals. Eisenhower delivered the most telling blow of all on the Korean War. Speaking in Detroit in late October, just after the fighting had intensified again in Korea, Ike promised if elected he would go personally to the battlefield in an attempt "to bring the Korean War to an early and honorable end."

"That does it—Ike is in," several reporters exclaimed after they heard this pledge. The hero of World War II had clinched his election by committing himself to end an unpopular war. Ten days later, he won the presidency handily, carrying thirty-nine states, including four in the formerly solid Democratic South. The

THE ELECTION OF 1952

CANDIDATE	PARTY	POPULAR VOTE	ELECTORAL VOTE
Eisenhower	Republican	33,936,137	442
Stevenson	Democratic	27,314,649	89

Republican party, however, did not fare as well in Congress; it gained just a slight edge in the House and controlled the Senate by only one seat.

Once elected, Eisenhower moved quickly to fulfill his campaign pledge. He spent three days in early December touring the battlefront in Korea, quickly ruling out the new offensive the military favored. "Small attacks on small hills," he later wrote, "would not end the war." Instead he turned to diplomacy, relying on subtle hints to China on the possible use of nuclear weapons to break the stalemated peace talks. These tactics, together with the death of Joseph Stalin in early March, finally led to the signing of an armistice on July 27, 1953, which ended the fighting but left Korea divided—as it had been before the war—near the 38th parallel.

The new president was less effective in dealing with the problem raised by Senator McCarthy's continuing witch-hunt. Instead of toning down his anticommunist crusade after the Republican victory in 1952, McCarthy used his new position as chairman of the Senate Committee on Government Operations as a base for ferreting out communists on the federal payroll. Eisenhower's advisers urged the president to use his own great prestige to stop McCarthy. But Ike refused such a confrontation, saying, "I will not get into a pissing contest with a skunk." Eisenhower preferred to play for time, hoping the American people would eventually come to their senses.

The Wisconsin senator finally overreached himself. In early 1954, he uncovered an army dentist suspected of disloyalty and proceeded to attack the upper echelons of the U.S. Army, telling one much decorated general that he was "not fit to wear the uniform." The controversy culminated in the televised Army-McCarthy hearings. For six weeks, the senator revealed his crude, bullying behavior to the American people. Viewers were repelled by his frequent outbursts that began with the insistent cry, "Point of order, Mr. Chairman, point of order," and by his attempt to slur the reputation of a young lawyer associated with army counsel Joseph Welch.

Courageous Republicans, led by Senators Ralph Flanders of Vermont and Margaret Chase Smith of Maine, joined with Democrats to bring about the Senate's censure of McCarthy in December 1954, by a vote of 67 to 22. Once rebuked, McCarthy fell quickly from prominence. He died three years later virtually unnoticed and unmourned.

Yet his influence was profound. Not only did he paralyze national life with what a Senate subcommittee described as "the most nefarious campaign of half-truth and untruth in the history of the Republic," but he also helped impose a political and cultural conformity that froze dissent for the rest of the 1950s. Long after McCarthy's passing, the nation tolerated loyalty oaths for teachers, the banning of left-wing books in public libraries, and the blacklisting of entertainers in radio, television, and films. Freedom of expression was inhibited, and the opportunity to try out new ideas and approaches was lost as the United States settled into a sterile Cold War consensus.

While Dwight Eisenhower could claim that his policy of giving McCarthy enough rope to hang himself had worked, it is possible that a bolder and more forthright presidential attack on the senator might have spared the nation some of the excesses of the anti-communist crusade.

EISENHOWER WAGES THE COLD WAR

Dwight D. Eisenhower came into the presidency in 1952 unusually well prepared to lead the nation at the height of the Cold War. His long years of military service had exposed him to a wide variety of international issues, both in Asia and in Europe, and to an even broader array of world leaders, such as Winston Churchill and Charles de Gaulle. He was not only an experienced military strategist but a gifted politician and diplomat as well. He was blessed with a sharp, pragmatic mind and organizational genius that enabled him to plan and carry out large enterprises, grasping the precise relationship between the parts and the whole. Above all, he had a serene confidence in his own ability. At the end of his first day in the White House, he confided in his diary: "Plenty of worries and difficult problems. But such has been my portion for a long time—the result is that this just seems like a continuation of all I've been doing since July 1941."

Eisenhower chose John Foster Dulles as his secretary of state. The myth soon developed that Ike had given Dulles free rein to conduct American diplomacy. Appearances were deceptive. Eisenhower preferred to work behind the scenes. He let Dulles make the public speeches and appearances before congressional committees, where the secretary's hard-line views placated GOP extremists. But Dulles carefully consulted with the president before every appearance, meeting

"Don't be afraid—I can always pull you back"

Cartoonist Herblock, a sharp critic of Dulles's hard line, depicts him in a Superman suit pushing Uncle Sam to the brink of nuclear war. (From Herblock's Special for Today *(Simon & Schuster, 1958).)*

frequently with Eisenhower at the White House and telephoning him several times a day. Ike respected his secretary of state's broad knowledge of foreign policy and skill in conducting American diplomacy, but he made all the major decisions himself.

From the outset, Eisenhower was determined to bring the Cold War under control. Ideally, he wanted to end it, but as a realist, he would settle for a relaxation of tensions with the Soviet Union. In part, he was motivated by a deeply held concern about the budget. Defense spending had increased from $13 billion to $50 billion under Truman; Ike was convinced the nation was in danger of going bankrupt unless military spending was reduced. As president, he inaugurated a "new look" for American defense, cutting back on the army and navy and relying even more heavily than Truman had on the air force and its nuclear striking power. As a result, the defense budget dropped below $40 billion annually. In 1954, Dulles announced reliance on massive retaliation—in fact a continuance of Truman's policy of deterrence. Rather than becoming involved in limited wars such as Korea, the United States would consider the possibility of using nuclear weapons to halt any communist aggression that threatened vital U.S. interests anywhere in the world.

While he permitted Dulles to make his veiled nuclear threats, Eisenhower's fondest dream was to end the arms race. Sobered by the development of the hydrogen bomb, successfully tested by the United States in November 1952 and by the Soviet Union in August 1953, the president began a new effort at disarmament with the Russians. Yet before this initiative could take effect, Ike had to weather a series of crises around the world that tested his skill and patience to the utmost.

ENTANGLEMENT IN INDOCHINA

The first crisis facing the new president came in Indochina. Since 1950, the United States had been giving France military and economic aid in a war in Indochina against communist guerrillas led by Ho Chi Minh. The Chinese increased their support to Ho's forces, known as the Vietminh, after the Korean War ended; by the spring of 1954, the French were on the brink of defeat. The Vietminh had surrounded nearly ten thousand French troops at Dien Bien Phu deep in the interior of northern Indochina; in desperation, France turned to the United States for help. Admiral Arthur Radford, chairman of the Joint Chiefs of Staff, proposed an American air strike to lift the siege. Although the other Joint Chiefs had strong objections to involving American forces in another Asian war so soon after Korea, hawkish Republican senators were clamoring for action.

Eisenhower decided against Radford's bold proposal, but he killed it in his typically indirect fashion. Fearful that an air attack would lead inevitably to the use of ground troops, Ike insisted that both Congress and American allies in Europe approve the strike in advance. Congressional leaders, recalling the recent

A French soldier stands guard over a truckload of Vietnamese nationalists captured in the fighting in Indochina. French efforts to quash the rebellion in Vietnam ended on May 7, 1954, when the Vietminh took the French stronghold at Dien Bien Phu.

Korean debacle, were reluctant to agree; the British were appalled and ruled out any joint action. The president used these objections to reject intervention in Indochina in 1954.

Dien Bien Phu fell to the Vietminh in May 1954. At an international conference held in Geneva a few weeks later, Indochina was divided at the 17th parallel. Ho gained control of North Vietnam, while the French continued to rule in the South. The United States gradually took over from the French in South Vietnam, sponsoring a new government in Saigon headed by Ngo Dinh Diem, a Vietnamese nationalist from a northern Catholic family. While Eisenhower can be given credit for refusing to engage American forces on behalf of French colonialism in Indochina, his determination to resist communist expansion had committed the United States to a long and eventually futile struggle to prevent Ho Chi Minh from achieving his long-sought goal of a unified, independent Vietnam.

CONTAINING CHINA

The communist government in Peking posed a serious challenge for the Eisenhower administration. Senate Republicans, led by William Knowland of California, blamed the Democrats for the "loss" of China. They viewed Mao as a puppet of the Soviet Union and insisted the United States recognize the Nationalists on Formosa as the only legitimate government of China. While State Department experts realized there were underlying tensions between China and Russia, Mao's intervention in the Korean War had convinced most Americans that the Chinese communists were an integral part of a larger communist effort at world domination. Thus Truman and Acheson had abandoned any hope of trying to exploit differences between Mao and Stalin by wooing China away from the Soviet Union.

Eisenhower and Dulles chose to accentuate the potential conflict between Russia and China. By taking a strong line against China, the United States could make the Chinese realize that Russia was unable to protect their interests; at the same time, such a hawkish policy would please congressional conservatives such as Knowland. Ultimately, Eisenhower and Dulles hoped that a policy of firmness would not only contain communist Chinese expansion in Asia but also drive a wedge between Moscow and Peking.

A crisis in the Formosa Straits provided the first test of the new policy. In the fall of 1954, communist China threatened to seize coastal islands, notably Quemoy and Matsu, occupied by the Nationalists. Fearful that seizure of these offshore islands would be the first step toward an invasion of Formosa, Eisenhower permitted Dulles to sign a security treaty with Chiang Kai-shek committing the United States to defend Formosa. When the communists began shelling the offshore islands, Eisenhower persuaded Congress to pass a resolution authorizing him to use force to defend Formosa and "closely related localities."

Despite repeated requests, however, the president refused to say whether he would use force to repel a Chinese attack on Quemoy or Matsu. Instead he and Dulles hinted at the use of nuclear weapons. The Chinese leaders, unsure whether Eisenhower was bluffing, decided not to test American resolve. The shelling ended in 1955, and when the communists resumed it again in 1958, another firm but equally ambiguous American response forced them to desist. The apparent refusal of the Soviet Union to come to China's aid in these crises with the United States contributed to a growing rift between the two communist nations by the end of the 1950s. Unfortunately, the Eisenhower administration failed to take full advantage of the opportunity that it had helped to create.

TURMOIL IN THE MIDDLE EAST

The gravest crisis for Eisenhower came in the Middle East when Egyptian leader Gamal Nasser seized the Suez Canal in July 1956. England and France were ready to use force immediately; their citizens owned the canal company, and their economies were dependent on the canal for the flow of oil from the Persian Gulf. President Eisenhower, however, was staunchly opposed to intervention, preferring to seek a diplomatic solution with Nasser, who kept the canal running smoothly. For three months, Dulles did everything possible to restrain the European allies, but finally they decided to take a desperate gamble—they invaded Egypt and seized the canal, relying on the United States to prevent any Russian interference.

Eisenhower was furious when England and France launched their attack in early November. Campaigning for reelection against Adlai Stevenson on the slogan of keeping the peace, Ike had to abandon domestic politics to deal with the threat of war. Unhesitatingly, he instructed Dulles to sponsor a UN resolution calling for British and French withdrawal from Egypt. Yet when the Russians supported the American proposal and went further, threatening rocket attacks on British and French cities and even offering to send "volunteers" to fight in Egypt, Eisenhower made it clear he would not tolerate Soviet interference. He put the Strategic Air Command on alert and said of the Russians, "If those fellows start something, we may have to hit 'em—and, if necessary, with everything in the bucket."

Just after noon on election day, November 6, 1956, British Prime Minister Anthony Eden called the president to inform him that England and France were ending their invasion. Eisenhower breathed a sigh of relief. American voters rallied behind Ike, electing him to a second term by a near landslide. As a result of the Suez crisis, the United States replaced England and France as the main Western influence in the Middle East. With Russia strongly backing Egypt and Syria, the Cold War had found yet another battleground.

Two years later, Eisenhower found it necessary to intervene in the strategic Middle Eastern country of Lebanon. Political power in this neutral nation was divided between Christian and Muslim elements. When the outgoing Christian president, Camille Chamoun, broke with tradition by seeking a second term, Muslim groups (aided by Egypt and Syria) threatened to launch a rebellion. After initial hesitation, Ike decided to act in order to uphold the U.S. commitment to political stability in the Middle East.

American marines from the Sixth Fleet moved swiftly ashore on July 15, 1958, securing the Beirut airport and preparing the way for a force of some fourteen thousand troops airlifted from bases in Germany. The military wanted to occupy the entire country, but Eisenhower insisted on limiting American forces to the area of Beirut. Lebanese political leaders quickly agreed on a successor to Chamoun, and American soldiers left the country before the end of October. The restrained use of force achieved Eisenhower's primary goal of quieting the explosive Middle East. It also served, as Secretary of State Dulles pointed out, "to reassure many small nations that they could call on us in a time of crisis."

COVERT ACTIONS

Amid these dangerous crises, the Eisenhower administration worked behind the scenes in the 1950s to expand the nation's global influence. In 1953, the CIA was instrumental in overthrowing a popularly elected government in Iran and placing the shah in full control of that country. American oil companies were rewarded with lucrative concessions, and Eisenhower believed he had gained a valuable ally on the Russian border. But these short-run gains created a deep-seated animosity among Iranians that would haunt the United States in the future.

Closer to home, in Latin America, Eisenhower once again relied on covert action. In 1954, the CIA masterminded the overthrow of a leftist regime in Guatemala. The immediate advantage was in denying the Soviets a possible foothold in the Western Hemisphere, but Latin Americans resented the thinly disguised interference of the United States in their internal affairs. More important, when Fidel Castro came to power in Cuba in 1959, the Eisenhower administration—after a brief effort at conciliation—adopted a hard line that helped drive Cuba into the Soviet orbit and led to new attempts at covert action.

Eisenhower's record as a cold warrior was thus mixed. His successful ending of the Korean War and his peacekeeping efforts in Indochina and Formosa and in the Suez crisis are all to his credit. Yet his reliance on coups and subversion di-

The first wave of U.S. Marines splashed ashore on the beach near Beirut, Lebanon, in July 1958. Sent to avert a Christian-Muslim civil war, they stayed only one hundred days.

rected by the CIA in Iran and Guatemala reveal Ike's corrupting belief that the ends justified the means.

Nevertheless, Eisenhower did display an admirable ability to stay calm and unruffled in moments of great tension, reassuring the nation and the world. And above all, he could boast, as he did in 1962, of his ability to keep the peace. "In those eight years," he reminded the nation, "we lost no inch of ground to tyranny. One war was ended and incipient wars were blocked."

WAGING PEACE

Eisenhower hoped to ease Cold War tensions by ending the nuclear arms race. The advent of the hydrogen bomb intensified his concern over nuclear warfare; by 1955, both the United States and the Soviet Union had added this dread new weapon to their arsenals. With new long-range ballistic missiles being perfected, it was only a matter of time before Russia and the United States would be capable of destroying each other completely. Peace, as Winston Churchill noted, now depended on a balance of terror.

Throughout the 1950s, Eisenhower sought a way out of the nuclear dilemma. In April 1953, shortly after Stalin's death, he gave a speech in which he called on the Russians to join him in a new effort at disarmament, pointing out that "every warship launched, every rocket fired signifies, in the final sense, a theft from those who hunger and are not fed, those who are cold and are not clothed." When the Soviets ignored this appeal, Eisenhower tried again. At a summit conference in Geneva, Switzerland, in 1955, Ike proposed to Nikita Khrushchev, just emerging as Stalin's successor after a two-year struggle for power, a way to break the disarmament deadlock. "Open skies," as reporters dubbed the plan, would overcome the traditional Russian objection to on-site inspection by having both superpowers open their territory to mutual aerial surveillance. Unfortunately, Khrushchev dismissed open skies as "a very transparent espionage device," and the conference ended without any significant breakthrough in the Cold War.

After his reelection in 1956, the president renewed his efforts toward nuclear arms control. Concern over atmospheric fallout from nuclear testing had led presidential candidate Adlai Stevenson to propose a mutual ban on such experiments. At first, Eisenhower rejected the test ban idea, but in 1958 the president changed his mind after American and Soviet scientists developed a system to detect nuclear testing in the atmosphere. In October 1958, Eisenhower and Khrushchev each voluntarily suspended further weapons tests pending the outcome of a conference held at Geneva to work out a test ban treaty. Although the Geneva Conference failed to make progress, neither the United States nor the Soviet Union resumed testing for the remainder of Ike's term in office.

The suspension of testing halted the pollution of the world's atmosphere, but it did not lead to the improvement in Soviet-American relations that Eisenhower sought. Instead, the Soviet feat in launching *Sputnik,* the first artificial satellite to orbit the earth, intensified the Cold War. Fearful that the Russians were several years ahead of the United States in the development of intercontinental ballistic missiles (ICBMs), Democrats criticized Eisenhower for not spending enough on defense and warned that a dangerous missile gap would open up by the early 1960s—a time when the Russians might have such a commanding lead in ICBMs that they could launch a first strike and destroy America. Despite the president's belief that the American missile program was in good shape, he allowed increased defense spending to speed up the building of American ICBMs and the new Polaris submarine–launched intermediate range missile (IRBM).

The most serious threat came in November 1958, when the Russian leader declared that within six months he would sign a separate peace treaty with East

"Handshake" is the title of this cartoon depicting a British view of relations between Soviet Premier Khrushchev and U.S. President Eisenhower during the Cold War. But the "handshake" between the two superpowers is more a contest of strength than a gesture of cooperation.

Germany, calling for an end to American, British, and French occupation rights in Berlin.

Eisenhower met the second Berlin crisis as firmly as Truman had the first. He refused to abandon the city but also tried to avoid a military showdown. Prudent diplomacy forced Khrushchev to extend his deadline indefinitely. After a trip to the United States, culminating in a personal meeting with Eisenhower at Camp David, the Russian leader agreed to attend a summit conference in Paris in May 1960.

This much heralded meeting never took place. On May 1, two weeks before the leaders were to convene in Paris, the Soviets shot down an American U-2 plane piloted by Francis Gary Powers. The United States had been overflying Russia since 1956 in the high-altitude spy planes, gaining vital information about the Soviet missile program which showed there was little basis for the public's fear that the Russians had opened up a dangerous missile gap. After initially denying any knowledge, Eisenhower took full responsibility for Powers's overflight, and Khrushchev responded with a scathing personal denunciation and a refusal to meet with the American president.

Russians view the wreckage of the U-2 reconnaissance plane piloted by Francis Powers that was shot down over Soviet territory on May 1, 1960. Although Eisenhower originally disavowed any knowledge of Powers's mission, Khrushchev produced photographs of Soviet military and industrial sites, which he said had been taken by the U-2 pilot. Powers was held in a Soviet prison for two years before he was released in exchange for a Russian spy.

Eisenhower deeply regretted the breakup of the Paris summit, telling an aide that "the stupid U-2 mess" had destroyed all his efforts for peace. Khrushchev marked time for the next nine months, waiting for the American people to choose a new president. Eisenhower did make a final effort at peace, however. Three days before leaving office, he delivered a farewell address in which he gave a somber warning about the danger of massive military spending. "In the councils of government," he declared, "we must guard against the acquisition of unwarranted influence, whether sought or unsought, by the military-industrial complex.

Rarely has an American president been more prophetic. In the next few years, the level of defense spending would skyrocket as the Cold War escalated. The military-industrial complex reached its acme of power in the 1960s when the United States realized the full implications of Truman's doctrine of containment. Eisenhower had succeeded in keeping the peace for eight years, but he had failed to halt the momentum of the Cold War he had inherited from Harry Truman. Ike's efforts to ease tension with the Soviet Union were dashed by his own distrust of communism and by Khrushchev's belligerent rhetoric and behavior. Still, he had begun to relax tensions, a process that would survive the troubled 1960s and, after several false starts, would finally begin to erode the Cold War by the end of the 1980s.

29

AFFLUENCE AND ANXIETY

O n May 7, 1947, William Levitt announced plans to build two thousand
rental houses in a former potato field on Long Island, thirty miles from
Midtown Manhattan. Using mass production techniques he had learned
while erecting navy housing during the war, Levitt quickly built four thousand
homes and rented them to young veterans eager to leave crowded city apartments or their parents' homes to begin raising families. A change in government
financing regulations led him to begin offering his houses for sale in 1948 for a
small amount down and a low monthly payment. Young couples, many of them
the original renters, quickly bought the first four thousand; by the time
Levittown—as he called the new community—was completed in 1951, it contained more than seventeen thousand homes. So many babies were born in
Levittown that it soon became known as "Fertility Valley" and "the Rabbit Hutch."

Levitt eventually built two more Levittowns, one in Pennsylvania and one in
New Jersey; each contained the same curving streets, neighborhood parks and
playgrounds, and community swimming pools characteristic of the first development. The secret of Levittown's appeal was the basic house, a 720-square-foot
Cape Cod design built on a concrete slab. It had a kitchen, two bedrooms and
bath, a living room complete with a fireplace and 16-foot picture window, and an
expansion attic with room for two more bedrooms. Levitt built only one interior,
but there were four different facades to break the monotony. The original house
sold for $6,990 in 1948; even the improved model, a ranch-style house, sold for
less than $10,000 in 1951.

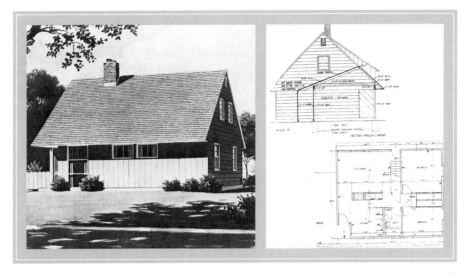

A photograph, floor plan, and elevation for a Levittown house. The Levittown builders applied the principles of mass production used in auto manufacturing to house construction. One important difference was the fact that the product stood stationary while workers came to the site to perform their specialized tasks. Construction was broken down into twenty-seven separate tasks, and a house could be assembled in fifteen minutes.

Levitt's houses were ideal for young people just starting out in life. They were cheap, comfortable, and efficient, and each home came with a refrigerator, cooking range, and washing machine. Despite the conformity of the houses, the three Levittowns were surprisingly diverse communities; residents had a wide variety of religious, ethnic, and occupational backgrounds. African Americans, however, were rigidly excluded. In time, as the more successful families moved on to larger homes in more expensive neighborhoods, the Levittowns became enclaves for lower-middle-class families.

Levittown symbolized the most significant social trend of the postwar era in the United States—the flight to the suburbs. The residential areas surrounding cities such as New York and Chicago nearly doubled in the 1950s. While central cities remained relatively stagnant during the decade, suburbs grew by 46 percent; by 1960, some sixty million people, one-third of the nation, lived in suburban rings around the cities. This massive shift in population from the central city was accompanied by a baby boom that started during World War II. Young married couples began to have three, four, or even five children (compared with only one or two children in American families during the 1930s). These larger families led to a 19 percent growth in the nation's population between 1950 and 1960, the highest growth rate since 1910.

The economy boomed as residential construction soared. By 1960, one-fourth of all existing homes were less than ten years old, and factories were turning out large quantities of appliances and television sets for the new households. A multitude of new consumer products—ranging from frozen foods to cars equipped with automatic transmissions and tubeless tires—appeared in stores and showrooms. In the suburbs, the corner grocery gave way to the supermarket carrying a vast array of items that enabled homemakers to provide their families with a more varied diet.

A new affluence replaced the poverty and hunger of the Great Depression for most Americans, but many had haunting memories of the 1930s. The obsession with material goods took on an almost desperate quality, as if a profusion of houses, cars, and home appliances could guarantee that the nightmare of depression would never return. Critics were quick to disparage the quality of life in suburban society. They condemned the conformity, charging the newly affluent with forsaking traditional American individualism to live in identical houses, drive look-alike cars, and accumulate the same material possessions. Folksinger Malvina Reynolds caught the essence of postwar suburbia in a 1963 song:

Little boxes on the hillside,
Little boxes made of ticky tacky
Little boxes on the hillside,
Little boxes all the same.
There's a green one and a pink one
And a blue one and a yellow one
And they're all made out of ticky tacky
*And they all look just the same.**

Events abroad added to the feeling of anxiety in the postwar years. Nuclear war became a frighteningly real possibility. The rivalry with the Soviet Union had led to the second Red Scare, with charges of treason and disloyalty being leveled at loyal Americans. Many Americans joined Senator Joseph McCarthy in searching for the communist enemy at home rather than abroad. Loyalty oaths and book burning revealed how insecure Americans had become in the era of the Cold War. Thus beneath the bland surface of suburban affluence, a dark current of distrust and insecurity marred the picture of a nation fulfilling its economic destiny.

THE POSTWAR BOOM

For fifteen years following World War II, the nation witnessed a period of unparalleled economic growth. A pent-up demand for consumer goods fueled a steady industrial expansion. Heavy government spending during the Cold War added an extra stimulus to the economy, offsetting brief recessions in 1949 and 1953 and moderating a steeper one in 1957–1958. By the end of the 1950s, the American people had achieved an affluence that finally erased the lingering fears of the Great Depression.

POSTWAR PROSPERITY

The economy began its upward surge as the result of two long-term factors. First, American consumers—after being held in check by depression and then by wartime scarcities—finally had a chance to indulge their suppressed appetites for material goods. At the war's end, personal savings in the United States stood at more than $37 billion, providing a powerful stimulus to consumption. Initially, American factories could not turn out enough automobiles and appliances to satisfy the horde of buyers. By 1950, however, production lines had finally caught up with the demand.

The Cold War provided the additional stimulus the economy needed when postwar expansion slowed. The Marshall Plan and other foreign aid programs financed a heavy export trade. The Korean War helped overturn a brief recession and ensured continued prosperity as the government spent massive amounts on guns, planes, and munitions. In 1952, the nation spent $44 billion, two-thirds of the federal budget, on national defense. Although Eisenhower managed to bring about some modest reductions, defense spending continued at a level of $40 billion throughout the decade.

The nation achieved an affluence in the 1950s that made the persisting fear of another Great Depression seem irrational. The baby boom and the spectacular growth of suburbia served as great stimulants to the consumer goods industries. Manufacturers turned out an ever increasing number of refrigerators, washing machines, and dishwashers to equip the kitchens of Levittown and its many imitators across the country. The automobile industry thrived with suburban expansion as two-car families became more and more common. In 1955, in an era when oil was abundant and gasoline sold for less than 30 cents a gallon, Detroit sold a record eight million cars.

Commercial enterprises snapped up office machines and the first generation of computers; industry installed electronic sensors and processors as it underwent extensive automation; and the military displayed an insatiable appetite for electronic devices for its planes and ships. As a result, American industry averaged more than $10 billion a year in capital investment, and the number of persons employed rose above the long-sought goal of sixty million nationwide.

Yet the economic abundance of the 1950s was not without its problems. While some sections of the nation (notably the emerging Sunbelt areas of the South and West) benefited enormously from the growth of the aircraft and electronics industries, older manufacturing regions, such as New England, did not fare as well. The steel industry increased its capacity during the decade, but it began to fall behind the rate of national growth. Agriculture continued to experience bumper crops and low prices, so rural regions failed to share in the general affluence. Unemployment persisted despite the boom, rising to more than 7 percent in a sharp recession that hit the country in the fall of 1957 and lasted through the summer of 1958.

None of these flaws, however, could disguise the fact that the nation was prospering to an extent no one dreamed possible in the 1930s. The GNP grew to $440 billion by 1960, more than double the 1940 level. By the mid-1950s, the average American family had twice as much real income to spend as its counterpart had possessed in the boom years of the 1920s. From 1945 to 1960, per capita disposable income rose by $500—to $1845—for every man, woman, and child in the country. The American people, in one generation, had moved from poverty and depression to the highest standard of living the world had ever known.

LIFE IN THE SUBURBS

Sociologists had difficulty describing the nature of suburban society in the 1950s. Some saw it as classless, while others noted the absence of both the very rich and the very poor and consequently labeled it "middle class." Rather than forming a homogeneous social group, though, the suburbs contained a surprising variety of people, whether classified as "upper lower," "lower middle," and "upper middle" or simply as blue collar, white collar, and professional. Doctors and lawyers often lived in the same developments as salesclerks and master plumbers. The traditional distinctions of ancestry, education, and size of residence no longer differentiated people as easily as they had in the past.

Yet suburbs could vary widely, from working-class communities clustered near factories built in the countryside to old, elitist areas such as Scarsdale, New York, and Shaker Heights, Ohio. Most were almost exclusively white and Christian, but suburbs such as Great Neck on Long Island and Richmond Heights outside Miami enabled Jews and blacks to take part in the flight from the inner city.

Life in all the suburban communities depended on the automobile. Highways and expressways allowed fathers to commute to jobs in the cities, often an hour or more away. Children might ride buses to and from school, but mothers had to drive them to piano lessons and Little League ballgames. Two cars became a necessity for almost every suburban family, thus helping spur the boom in automobile production.

In the new drive-in culture, people shopped at the stores that grew up first in "miracle miles" along the highways and later at the shopping centers that began to dot the countryside by the mid-1950s. There were only eight shopping centers in the entire country in 1946; hundreds appeared over the next fifteen years, including Poplar Plaza in Memphis, with one large department store, thirty retail shops, and parking for more than five hundred cars.

Despite the increased mobility provided by the car, the home became the focus for activities and aspirations. The postwar shortage of housing that often forced young couples to live with their parents or in-laws created an intense demand for new homes in the suburbs. When questioned, prospective buyers expressed a desire for "more space," for "comfort and roominess," and for "privacy and freedom of action" in their new residences. "Togetherness" became the code word of the 1950s. Families did things together, whether gathering around the TV sets that dominated living rooms, attending community activities, or taking vacations in the huge station wagons of the era.

But there were some less attractive consequences of the new suburban lifestyle. The extended family, in which several generations had lived in close proximity, was a casualty of the boom in small detached homes. As historian Kenneth Jackson has noted, suburban life "ordained that most children would grow up in intimate contact only with their parents and siblings." Grandparents, aunts and uncles, cousins, and more distant relatives would become remote figures, seen only on special occasions.

The nuclear family, typical of the suburb, did nothing to encourage the development of feminism. The end of the war saw many women who had entered the workforce return to the home, where the role of wife and mother continued to be viewed as the ideal for women in the 1950s. Trends toward getting married earlier and having larger families reinforced the pattern of women devoting all their efforts to housework and child raising rather than acquiring professional skills and pursuing careers outside the home. Adlai Stevenson, extolling "the humble role of housewife," told Smith College graduates that there was much they could do "in the living room with a baby in your lap or in the kitchen with a can opener in your hand."

Nonetheless, the number of working wives doubled between 1940 and 1960. By the end of the 1950s, 40 percent of American women, and nearly one-third of all married women, had jobs outside the home. The heavy expenses involved in rearing and educating children led wives and mothers to seek ways to augment the family income, inadvertently preparing the way for a new demand for equality in the 1960s.

THE GOOD LIFE?

Consumerism became the dominant social theme of the 1950s. Yet even with an abundance of creature comforts and added hours of leisure time, the quality of life left many Americans anxious and dissatisfied.

AREAS OF GREATEST GROWTH

Organized religion flourished in the climate of the 1950s. Ministers, priests, and rabbis all commented on the rise in church and synagogue attendance in the new communities. Will Herberg claimed that religious affiliation had become the primary identifying feature of modern American life, dividing the nation into three separate segments—Protestant, Catholic, and Jewish.

Some observers condemned the bland, secular nature of suburban churches, which seemed to be an integral part of the consumer society. "On weekdays one shops for food," wrote one critic, "on Saturdays one shops for recreation, and on Sundays one shops for the Holy Ghost." But the popularity of religious writer Norman Vincent Peale, with his positive gospel that urged people to "start thinking faith, enthusiasm and joy," suggested that the new churches filled a genuine if shallow human need.

Schools provided an immediate problem for the growing new suburban communities. The increase in the number of school-age children, from twenty to thirty million in the first eight grades, overwhelmed the resources of many local districts, leading to demands for federal aid. Congress granted limited help for areas affected by defense plants and military bases, but Eisenhower's reluctance to unbalance the budget blocked further federal assistance prior to 1957, when the government reacted to *Sputnik*.

Equally important, a controversy arose over the nature of education in the 1950s. Critics of "progressive" education called for sweeping educational reforms and a new stress on traditional academic subjects. The one thing all seemed to agree on was the desirability of a college education. The number of young people attending colleges increased from 1.5 million in 1940 to 3.6 million in 1960.

The largest advances were made in the exciting new medium of television. From a shaky start just after the war, TV boomed in the 1950s, pushing radio aside and undermining many of the nation's magazines. By 1957, three networks controlled the airwaves, reaching forty million sets over nearly five hundred stations.

Entertainment for all age levels was the focus of television in the 1950s. Then, as now, shows were targeted for specific age groups, such as these children watching intently the antics of the puppets and live actors on the "Howdy Doody Show." The television became the focal center of rooms where families gathered to spend their leisure time.

At first, the insatiable demand for programs encouraged a burst of creativity. Playwrights such as Reginald Rose, Rod Serling, and Paddy Chayefsky wrote a series of notable dramas for *Playhouse 90, Studio One,* and the *Goodyear Television Playhouse*. Broadcast live from cramped studios, these productions thrived on tight dramatic structures, movable scenery, and frequent close-ups of the actors.

Advertisers, however, quickly became disillusioned with the live anthology programs, which usually dealt with controversial subjects or focused on ordinary people and events. In contrast, sponsors wanted shows that stressed excitement, glamour, and instant success. Aware that audiences were fascinated by contestants with unusual expertise (a shoemaker answering tough questions on operas, a grandmother stumping experts on baseball), producers began giving away huge cash prizes on *The $64,000 Question* and *Twenty-one*. In 1959, the nation was shocked when Charles Van Doren, a Columbia University professor, confessed he had been given the answers in advance to win $129,000 on *Twenty-one*. The three networks quickly dropped all the big-prize quiz programs, replacing them with comedy, action, and adventure shows such as *The Untouchables* and *Bonanza*. Despite its early promise of artistic innovation, television had become a technologically sophisticated but safe conveyor of the consumer culture.

CRITICS OF THE CONSUMER SOCIETY

One striking feature of the 1950s was the abundance of self-criticism. A number of widely read books explored the flaws in the new suburbia. John Keats's *The Crack in the Picture Window* described the endless rows of tract houses "vomited up" by developers as "identical boxes spreading like gangrene." Their occupants lost any sense of individuality in their obsession with material goods.

Richard Gordon, Katherine Gordon, and Max Gunther were more concerned about the psychological toll of suburban life in their 1960 book *The Split-Level Trap*. They labeled the new lifestyle "Disturbia" and bemoaned the "haggard" men, the "tense and anxious" women, and the "gimme" kids it produced. The most sweeping indictment came in William H. Whyte's *The Organization Man* (1956), based on a study of the Chicago suburb of Park Forest. Whyte perceived a change from the old Protestant ethic, with its emphasis on hard work and personal responsibility, to a new social ethic centered on "the team" with the ultimate goal of "belongingness." The result was a stifling conformity and the loss of personal identity.

The most influential social critic of the 1950s was Harvard sociologist David Riesman. His book *The Lonely Crowd* appeared in 1950 and set the tone for intellectual commentary about suburbia for the rest of the decade. Riesman described the shift from the "inner-directed" Americans of the past who had relied on such traditional values as self-denial and frugality to the "other-directed" Americans of the consumer society who constantly adapted their behavior to conform to social pressures. The resulting decline in individualism produced a bland and tolerant society of consumers lacking creativity and a sense of adventure.

C. Wright Mills was a far more caustic commentator on American society in the 1950s. Anticipating government statistics that revealed white-collar workers (salesclerks, office workers, bank tellers) now outnumbered blue-collar workers (miners, factory workers, millhands), Mills described the new middle class in ominous terms in his books *White Collar* (1951) and *Power Elite* (1956). The industrial assembly line had given way to an even more dehumanizing workplace, the modern office. "At rows of blank-looking counters sat rows of blank-looking girls with blank, white folders in their blank hands, all blankly folding blank papers."

This disenchantment with the consumer culture reached its most eloquent expression with the "beats," literary groups that rebelled against the materialistic society of the 1950s. Jack Kerouac's novel *On the Road*, published in 1957, set the

Novelist Jack Kerouac and his fellow "beat" writers bemoaned the moral bankruptcy of popular culture. They sought not to improve conditions but to find release from the moral and social confines contricting their lives and the literary convention circumscribing their writing.

tone for the new movement. The name came from the quest for beatitude, a state of inner grace sought in Zen Buddhism. Flouting the respectability of suburbia, the "beatniks"—as middle America termed them—were easily identified by their long hair and bizarre clothing; they also had a penchant for sexual promiscuity and drug experimentation. They were conspicuous dropouts from a society they found senseless.

Despite the disapproval they evoked from mainstream Americans, the beat generation had only compassion for their detractors. "We love everything," Kerouac proclaimed, "Billy Graham, the Big Ten, Rock and Roll, Zen, apple pie, Eisenhower—we dig it all." Yet as highly visible nonconformists in an era of stifling conformity, the beats demonstrated a style of social protest that would flower into the counterculture of the 1960s.

THE REACTION TO *SPUTNIK*

The profound insecurity that underlay American life throughout the 1950s burst into view in October 1957, when the Soviets sent the 184-pound satellite *Sputnik* into orbit. People around the world applauded the scientific feat, but in the United States the reaction was one of dismay at being bested by a communist rival.

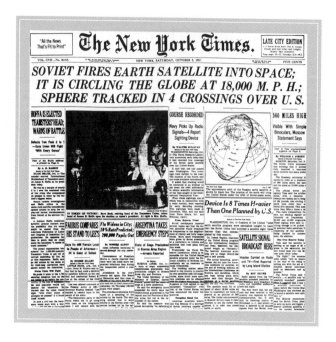

The Soviet's successful launching of Sputnik *shook American confidence and triggered new interest and activity in the "space race." Both houses of Congress established space committees, and President Eisenhower created the National Aeronautics and Space Administration (NASA).*

Americans became afraid that their nation had somehow lost its previously unquestioned primacy in the eyes of the world.

The national sense of humiliation only deepened in December, when TV cameras showed the rocket bearing the first American satellite exploding only a few feet after liftoff. Finally, on January 31, 1958, the United States launched its first orbiting satellite. Although the *Explorer,* only 6 inches wide and weighing just over 30 pounds, was tiny compared to *Sputnik,* it carried a much more sophisticated set of scientific instruments to probe the mysteries of space.

In the late 1950s, the president and Congress moved to restore national confidence. Eisenhower appointed James R. Killian, president of the Massachusetts Institute of Technology (MIT), as his special assistant for science and technology and to oversee a crash program in missile development. The House and Senate followed by creating the National Aeronautics and Space Administration (NASA) in 1958. Congress appropriated vast sums to allow the agency to compete with the Russians in the space race. Soon a new group of heroes, the astronauts, began the training that led to suborbital flights and eventually to John Glenn's five-hour flight around the globe in 1962.

Congress also sought to match the Soviet educational advances by passing the National Defense Education Act (NDEA). This legislation authorized federal financing of scientific and foreign language programs in the nation's schools and colleges. Soon American students were hard at work mastering the "new physics" and the "new math."

The belief persisted, however, that the faults lay deeper, that in the midst of affluence and abundance Americans had lost their competitive edge. Economists pointed to the higher rate of Soviet economic growth, and social critics bemoaned a supermarket culture that stressed consumption over production, comfort over hard work.

FAREWELL TO REFORM

It is not surprising that the spirit of reform underlying the New Deal failed to flourish in the postwar years. Growing affluence took away the sense of grievance and the cry for change that was so strong in the 1930s. Eager to enjoy the new prosperity after years of want and sacrifice, the American people turned away from federal regulation and welfare programs.

TRUMAN AND THE FAIR DEAL

Harry Truman tried to capitalize on his upset victory in 1948 to offer a broad program of reform to the nation on January 5, 1949. Venturing beyond earlier proposals by FDR to increase the minimum wage and broaden Social Security coverage, he called for a "Fair Deal," a reform package that comprised a new program of national medical insurance, federal aid to education, enactment of a Fair Employment Practices Commission (FEPC) to prevent economic discrimination against blacks, and an overhaul of the farm subsidy program.

The Fair Deal was never enacted. Except for raising the minimum wage to 75 cents an hour and broadening Social Security to cover ten million more Americans, Congress refused to pass any of Truman's health, education, or civil rights measures. The nation's doctors waged an effective campaign against the president's health insurance plan, and southern senators blocked any action on the FEPC. Aid to education, repeal of Taft-Hartley, and the new farm program all failed to win congressional approval. Despite the Democratic victory in 1948, Congress remained under the control of a bipartisan conservative coalition of northern Republicans and southern Democrats, the same alignment that had halted Roosevelt's reforms after 1938.

Although his legislative failure became certain in 1950, when war once again subordinated domestic issues to foreign policy, President Truman deserves credit for maintaining and consolidating the New Deal. His spirited leadership prevented any Republican effort to repeal the gains of the 1930s. Moreover, even though he failed to get any new measures enacted, he broadened the reform agenda and laid the groundwork for future advances in health care, aid to education, and civil rights.

EISENHOWER'S MODERN REPUBLICANISM

The American people found that moderation was the keynote of the Eisenhower presidency. His major goal from the outset was to restore calm and tranquility to a badly divided nation. Unlike FDR and Truman, Eisenhower had no commitment to social change or economic reform. Ike was a fiscal conservative who was intent on balancing the budget. Yet unlike some Republicans of the extreme right wing, he had no plans to dismantle the social programs of the New Deal. He sought instead to keep military spending in check, to encourage as much private initiative as possible, and to reduce federal activities to the bare minimum. Defining his position as "Modern Republicanism," he claimed that he was "conservative when it comes to money and liberal when it comes to human beings."

On domestic issues, Eisenhower preferred to delegate authority and to play a passive role. He concentrated his own efforts on the Cold War abroad. The men he chose to run the nation reflected his preference for successful corporation executives. Thus George Humphrey, an Ohio industrialist, carried out a policy of fiscal stringency as secretary of the treasury, while Charles E. Wilson (the former head of General Motors) sought to keep the Pentagon budget under control as secretary of defense. Neither man was wholly successful, and both were guilty of tactless public statements. Humphrey warned that unless Congress showed budgetary restraint, "we're gonna have a depression which will curl your hair," and Wilson gained notoriety by proclaiming that "what was good for our country was good for General Motors, and vice versa."

Eisenhower was equally reluctant to play an active role in dealing with Congress. A fervent believer in the separation of powers, Ike did not want to engage in intensive lobbying. He left congressional relations to aides such as Sherman Adams, a former New Hampshire governor who served as White House chief of staff. Adams's skill at resolving problems at lower levels insulated Eisenhower from many of the nation's pressing domestic problems.

Republican losses in the midterm election of 1954 weakened Eisenhower's relations with Congress. The Democrats regained control of both houses and kept it throughout the 1950s. The president had to rely on two Texas Democrats, Senate Majority Leader Lyndon B. Johnson and Speaker of the House Sam Rayburn, for legislative action; at best, it was an awkward and uneasy relationship.

The result was a very modest legislative record. Eisenhower did continue the basic social measures of the New Deal. In 1954, he signed bills extending Social Security benefits to more than seven million Americans, raising the minimum wage to $1 an hour, and adding four million workers to those eligible for unemployment benefits. He consolidated the administration of welfare programs by creating the Department of Health, Education, and Welfare in 1953. But Ike steadfastly opposed Democratic plans for compulsory health insurance—which he condemned as the "socialization of medicine"—and comprehensive federal aid to education, preferring to leave everything except school construction in the hands of local and state authorities. This lack of presidential support and the continuing grip of the conservative coalition in Congress blocked any further reform in the 1950s.

The one significant legislative achievement of the Eisenhower years came with the passage of the Highway Act of 1956. After a twelve-year delay, Congress appropriated funds for a 41,000-mile interstate highway system consisting of multilane divided expressways that would connect the nation's major cities. Justified on grounds of national defense, the 1956 act pleased a variety of highway users: the trucking industry, automobile clubs, organized labor (eager for construction jobs), farmers (needing to speed their crops to market), and state highway officials (anxious for the 90 percent funding contributed by the federal

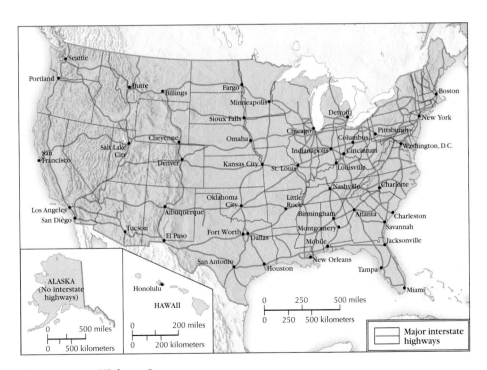

The Interstate Highway System

The 1956 plan to create an interstate highway system drastically changed America's landscape and culture. Today, the system covers about forty-five thousand miles, only a few thousand more miles than called for in the original plan.

THE ELECTION OF 1956

CANDIDATE	PARTY	POPULAR VOTE	ELECTORAL VOTE
Eisenhower	Republican	35,585,245	457
Stevenson	Democratic	26,030,172	73

government). Built over the next twenty years, the interstate highway system had a profound influence on American life. It stimulated the economy and shortened travel time dramatically, while at the same time intensifying the nation's dependence on the automobile and distorting metropolitan growth patterns into long strips paralleling the new expressways.

Overall, the Eisenhower years marked an era of political moderation. The American people, enjoying the abundance of the 1950s, seemed quite content with legislative inaction. The president was sensitive to the nation's economic health; when recessions developed in 1953 and again in 1957 after his landslide reelection victory, he quickly abandoned his goal of a balanced budget in favor of a policy advocating government spending to restore prosperity. These steps, along with modest increases in New Deal welfare programs, led to a steady growth in the federal budget from $29.5 billion in 1950 to $76.5 billion in 1960. Eisenhower was able to balance the budget in only three of his eight years in office, and the $12 billion deficit in 1959 was larger than any ever before recorded in peacetime. In this manner, Eisenhower was able to maintain the New Deal legacy of federal responsibility for social welfare and the state of the economy while at the same time successfully resisting demands for more extensive government involvement in American life.

THE STRUGGLE OVER CIVIL RIGHTS

Despite President Eisenhower's reluctance to champion the cause of reform, powerful pressures for change forced long-overdue action in one area of American life—the denial of basic rights to the nation's black minority. In the midst of the Cold War, the contradiction between the denunciation of the Soviet Union for its human-rights violations and the second-class status of African Americans began to arouse the national conscience. Fighting for freedom against communist tyranny abroad, Americans had to face the reality of the continued denial of freedom to a submerged minority at home.

African Americans had benefited economically from World War II, but they were still a seriously disadvantaged group. Those who had left the South for better opportunities in northern and western cities were concentrated in blighted and segregated neighborhoods, working at low-paying jobs, suffering economic and social discrimination, and failing to share fully in the postwar prosperity.

In the South, conditions were much worse. State laws forced blacks to live almost totally segregated from white society. Not only did African Americans attend separate (and almost always inferior) schools, but they also were rigidly segregated in all public facilities. "Segregation was enforced at all places of public entertainment, including libraries, auditoriums, and circuses," Chief Justice Earl Warren noted. "There was segregation in the hospitals, prisons, mental institutions, and nursing homes. Even ambulance service was segregated."

CIVIL RIGHTS AS A POLITICAL ISSUE

Truman was the first president to attempt to alter the historic pattern of racial discrimination in the United States. In 1946, he appointed a presidential commission on civil rights. A year later, in a sweeping report titled "To Secure These Rights," the commission recommended the reinstatement of the wartime Fair Employment Practices Committee (FEPC), the establishment of a permanent civil rights commission, and the denial of federal aid to any state that condoned segregation in schools and public facilities. But southern resistance blocked any action by Congress, and the inclusion of a strong civil rights plank in the 1948 Democratic platform led to the walkout of some southern delegations and a separate States' Rights (Dixiecrat) ticket in several states of the South that fall.

African American voters in the North overwhelmingly backed Truman over Dewey in the 1948 election. The African American vote in key cities—Los Angeles, Cleveland, and Chicago—ensured the Democratic victory in California, Ohio, and Illinois. Truman responded by including civil rights legislation in his Fair Deal program in 1949. Once again, however, determined southern opposition blocked congressional action.

Even though President Truman was unable to secure any significant legislation, he did succeed in adding civil rights to the liberal agenda. From this time forward, it would be an integral part of the Democratic reform program. Also, Truman used his executive power to assist African Americans, most notably in 1948 when he issued an order calling for the desegregation of the armed forces. The navy and the air force quickly complied, but the army resisted until the personnel needs of the Korean War finally overcame the military's objections. By the end of the 1950s, the armed forces had become far more integrated than American society at large.

DESEGREGATING THE SCHOOLS

The nation's schools soon became the primary target of civil rights advocates. The NAACP concentrated first on universities, successfully waging an intensive legal battle to win admission for qualified African Americans to graduate and professional schools. Led by Thurgood Marshall, NAACP lawyers then took on the broader issue of segregation in the country's public schools. Challenging the 1896 Supreme Court decision (*Plessy* v. *Ferguson*) that upheld the constitutionality of separate but equal public facilities, Marshall argued that even substantially equal but separate schools did profound psychological damage to African American children and thus violated the Fourteenth Amendment.

The Supreme Court was unanimous in its 1954 decision in the case of *Brown* v. *Board of Education of Topeka*. Chief Justice Earl Warren, recently appointed by President Eisenhower, wrote the landmark opinion flatly declaring that "separate educational facilities are inherently unequal." To divide grade school children "solely because of their race," Warren argued, "generates a feeling of inferiority as to their status in the community that may affect their hearts and minds in a way unlikely ever to be undone." Despite this sweeping language, Warren realized it would be difficult to change historic patterns of segregation quickly. Accordingly, in 1955 the Court ruled that desegregation of the schools should proceed "with all deliberate speed" and left the details to the lower federal courts.

Linda Brown (left). Her parents were the plaintiffs in the Brown *v.* Board of Education of Topeka *landmark Supreme Court case. Thurgood Marshall (right), a leading African American civil rights lawyer, was chief counsel for the Browns.*

"All deliberate speed" proved to be agonizingly slow. Officials in the border states quickly complied with the Court's ruling, but states deeper in the South responded with a policy of massive resistance. Local white citizens' councils organized to fight for retention of racial separation; 101 representatives and senators signed a Southern Manifesto in 1956 that denounced the *Brown* decision as "a clear abuse of judicial power." School boards, encouraged by this show of defiance, found a variety of ways to evade the Court's ruling. These stalling tactics led to long disputes in the federal courts; by the end of the decade, fewer than 1 percent of the black children in the Deep South attended school with whites.

A conspicuous lack of presidential support further weakened the desegregation effort. Dwight Eisenhower was not a racist, but he believed that people's attitudes could not be altered by "cold lawmaking"—only "by appealing to reason, by prayer, and by constantly working at it through our own efforts" could change be enacted. Quietly and unobtrusively, he worked to achieve desegregation in federal facilities, particularly in veterans' hospitals, navy yards, and the District of Columbia school system. Yet he refrained from endorsing the *Brown* decision, which he told an aide he believed had "*set back* progress in the South *at least fifteen years.*"

Southern leaders mistook Ike's silence for tacit support of segregation. In 1957, Governor Orville Faubus of Arkansas called out the national guard to prevent the integration of Little Rock's Central High School on grounds of a threat to public order. After 270 armed troops turned back 9 young African American students, a federal judge ordered the guardsmen removed; but when the black

Angry whites taunt one of the African American students trying to pass through the lines of Arkansas National Guardsmen to enroll in Little Rock's Central High School in 1957.

students entered the school, a mob of 500 jeering whites surrounded the building. Eisenhower, who had told Faubus that "the Federal Constitution will be upheld by me by every legal means at my command," sent in 1000 paratroopers to ensure the rights of the Little Rock Nine to attend Central High. The students finished the school year under armed guard. Then Little Rock authorities closed Central High School for the next two years; when it reopened, there were only three African Americans in attendance.

Despite the snail's pace of school desegregation, the *Brown* decision led to other advances. In 1957, the Eisenhower administration proposed the first general civil rights legislation since Reconstruction. Despite congressional compromises, the final act did create a permanent Commission for Civil Rights, one of Truman's original goals. It also provided for federal efforts aimed at "securing and protecting the right to vote." A second civil rights act in 1960 slightly strengthened the voting rights section.

Like the desegregation effort, the attempt to ensure African American voting rights in the South was still largely symbolic. Southern registrars used a variety of devices, ranging from intimidation to unfair tests, to deny African Americans suffrage. Yet the actions of Congress and the Supreme Court marked a vital turning point in national policy toward racial justice.

THE BEGINNINGS OF BLACK ACTIVISM

The most dynamic force for change came from African Americans themselves. The shift from legal struggles in the courts to protest in the streets began with an incident in Montgomery, Alabama. On December 1, 1955, Rosa Parks—a black seamstress who had been active in the local NAACP chapter—violated a city ordinance by refusing to give up her seat to a white person on a local bus. Her action, often viewed as spontaneous, grew out of a long tradition of black protest against the rigid segregation of the races in the South. Rosa Parks herself had been ejected from a bus a decade earlier for refusing to obey the driver's command, "Niggers move back."

Rosa Parks' arrest sparked a massive protest movement in Montgomery. Black women played a particularly important role in the protest, printing and handing out 50,000 leaflets to rally the African American community behind Parks. The movement also led to the emergence of Martin Luther King, Jr., as an eloquent new spokesman for African Americans.

King agreed to lead the subsequent bus boycott. The son of a famous Atlanta preacher, he had recently taken his first church in Montgomery after years of studying theology while earning a Ph.D. at Boston University. Now he would be able to combine his wide learning with his charismatic appeal in behalf of a prac-

Rosa Parks, whose refusal to
give up her seat to a white
man ignited the boycott, is
fingerprinted in February
1956 after her arrest under
an antiboycott law.

tical goal—fair treatment for the African Americans who made up the bulk of the
riders on the city's buses.

The Montgomery bus boycott started out with a modest goal. Instead of
challenging the legality of segregated seating, King simply asked that seats be
taken on a first-come, first-served basis, with African Americans being seated
from the back and the whites from the front of each bus. An effective system of
car pools enabled the protesters to avoid using the city buses. Soon they were insisting on a complete end to segregated seating as they sang their new song of
protest:

> Ain't gonna ride them buses no more
> Ain't gonna ride no more
> Why in the hell don't the white folk know
> That I ain't gonna ride no more.

The boycott ended in victory a year later when the Supreme Court ruled the
Alabama segregated seating law unconstitutional. King had won far more than
this limited dent in the wall of segregation, however. He had emerged as the
charismatic leader of a new civil rights movement—a man who won acclaim not
only at home but around the world. He led a triumphant Prayer Pilgrimage to
Washington in 1957 on the third anniversary of the *Brown* decision, stirring the
crowd of thirty thousand with his ringing demand for the right to vote. His cry
"Give us the ballot" boomed in salvos that civil rights historian Taylor Branch

likened to "cannon bursts in a diplomatic salute." His remarkable voice became familiar to the entire nation. Unlike many African American preachers, he never shouted, yet he captured his audience by presenting his ideas with both passion and a compelling cadence.

Even more important, he had a strategy and message that fitted perfectly with the plight of his followers. King came out of the bus boycott with the concept of passive resistance. "If cursed," he had told protesters in Montgomery, "do not curse back. If struck, do not strike back, but evidence love and goodwill at all times." The essence of his strategy was to use the apparent weakness of southern blacks—their lack of power—and turn it into a conquering weapon.

His ultimate goal was to unite the broken community through bonds of Christian love. He hoped to use nonviolence to appeal to middle-class white America, "to the conscience of the great decent majority who through blindness, fear, pride or irrationality have allowed their consciences to sleep." The result,

At a sit-in demonstration at a Woolworth's lunch counter on May 28, 1963, civil rights activists from Tougaloo College stoically bear the verbal and physical abuse of white hecklers. Sit-ins were one tactic activists used to draw national attention to racial injustice, to demand desegregation of public facilities, and to prompt the federal government to take a more active role to end segregation.

King prophesied, would be to enable future historians to say of the effort, "There lived a great people—a black people—who injected new meaning and dignity into the veins of civilization."

A year after the successful bus boycott, King founded the Southern Christian Leadership Conference (SCLC) to direct the crusade against segregation. Then in February 1960, another spontaneous event sparked a further advance for passive resistance. Four African American students from North Carolina Agricultural and Technical College sat down at a dime-store lunch counter in Greensboro, North Carolina, and refused to move after being denied service. Other students, both whites and blacks, joined in similar "sit-ins" across the South. By the end of the year, some fifty thousand young people had succeeded in desegregating public facilities in more than a hundred southern cities. Several thousand of the demonstrators were arrested and put in jail, but the movement gained strength, leading to the formation of the Student Nonviolent Coordinating Committee (SNCC) in April 1960. From this time on, the SCLC and SNCC, with their tactic of direct, though peaceful, confrontation, would replace the NAACP and its reliance on court action in the forefront of the civil rights movement. The change would eventually lead to dramatic success for the movement, but it also ushered in a period of heightened tension and social turmoil in the 1960s.

The 1950s ended with the national mood less troubled than when the decade began amid the turmoil of the second Red Scare and the Korean War, yet hardly as tranquil or confident as Eisenhower had hoped it would be. The American people felt reassured about the state of the economy, no longer fearing a return to the grim years of the Great Depression. At the same time, however, they were aware that abundance alone did not guarantee the quality of everyday life and realized that there was still a huge gap between American ideals and the reality of race relations, in the North as well as the South.

30

THE TURBULENT SIXTIES

O n Monday evening, September 26, 1960, John F. Kennedy and Richard M. Nixon faced each other in the nation's first televised debate between two presidential candidates. Kennedy, the relatively unknown Democratic challenger, had proposed the debates; Nixon, confident of his mastery of television, had accepted even though, as Eisenhower's vice president and the early front-runner in the election, he had more to lose and less to gain.

Richard Nixon arrived an hour early at the CBS studio in Chicago, looking tired and ill at ease. He was still recovering from a knee injury that had slowed his campaign and left him pale and weak as he pursued a hectic catch-up schedule. Makeup experts offered to hide Nixon's heavy beard and soften his prominent jowls, but the GOP candidate declined, preferring to let an aide apply a light coat of Max Factor's "Lazy Shave," a pancake cosmetic. John Kennedy, tanned from open-air campaigning in California and rested by a day spent nearly free of distracting activity, wore very light makeup.

At 8:30 P.M. central time, moderator Howard K. Smith welcomed a viewing audience estimated at seventy-seven million. Kennedy led off, echoing Abraham Lincoln by saying that the nation faced the question of "whether the world will exist half-slave and half-free." Although the ground rules limited the first debate to domestic issues, Kennedy argued that foreign and domestic policy were inseparable. He accused the Republicans of letting the country drift at home and abroad. "I think it's time America started moving again," he concluded. Nixon, caught off guard, seemed to agree with Kennedy's assessment of the nation's problems, but he contended that he had better solutions. "Our disagreement," the vice president pointed out, "is not about the goals for America but only about the means to reach those goals."

For the rest of the hour, the two candidates answered questions from a panel of journalists. Radiating confidence and self-assurance, Kennedy used a flow of statistics and details to create the image of a man deeply knowledgeable about all aspects of government. Nixon fought back with a defense of the Eisenhower record, but he seemed nervous and unsure of himself. The reaction shots of each candidate listening to the other's remarks showed Kennedy calm and serene, Nixon tense and uncomfortable.

Polls taken during the following few weeks revealed a sharp swing to Kennedy. Many Democrats and independents who had thought him too young or too inexperienced were impressed by his performance. Nixon suffered more from his unattractive image than from what he said; those who heard the debate on radio thought the Republican candidate more than held his own. In the three additional debates held during the campaign, Nixon improved his performance notably. But the damage had been done. A postelection poll revealed that of four million voters who were influenced by the debates, three million voted for Kennedy.

The televised debates were only one of many factors influencing the outcome of the 1960 election. In essence, Kennedy won because he took full advantage of all his opportunities. Lightly regarded by Democratic leaders, he won the nomination by appealing to the rank and file in the primaries, but then he astutely chose Lyndon Johnson of Texas as his running mate to blunt Nixon's southern strategy.

During the fall campaign, Kennedy exploited the national mood of frustration that had followed *Sputnik*. At home, he promised to stimulate the lagging economy and carry forward long-overdue reforms in education, health care, and civil rights under the banner of the "New Frontier." Abroad, he pledged a renewed commitment to the Cold War, vowing he would lead the nation to victory over the Soviet Union. He met the issue of his Catholicism head on, telling a group of Protestant ministers in Houston that as president he would always place country above religion. In the shrewdest move of all, he won over African American voters by helping to secure the release of Martin Luther King, Jr., from a Georgia jail where the civil rights leader was being held on a trumped-up charge.

The Democratic victory in 1960 was paper-thin. Kennedy's edge in the popular vote was only two-tenths of 1 percent, and his wide margin in the electoral college (303 to 219) was tainted by voting irregularities in several states—notably Illinois and Texas—which went Democratic by very slender majorities. Yet even though he had no mandate, Kennedy's triumph did mark a sharp political

THE ELECTION OF 1960

CANDIDATE	PARTY	POPULAR VOTE	ELECTORAL VOTE
Kennedy	Democratic	34,227,096	303
Byrd	States' Rights	—	15
Nixon	Republican	34,108,546	219
	Minor Parties	502,363	—

shift. In contrast to the aging Eisenhower, Kennedy symbolized youth, energy, and ambition. His mastery of the new medium of television reflected his sensitivity to the changes taking place in American life in the 1960s. He came to office promising reform at home and advances abroad. Over the next eight years, he and Lyndon Johnson achieved many of their goals. Yet the nation also became engulfed in angry protests, violent demonstrations, and sweeping social change in one of the stormiest decades in American history.

KENNEDY INTENSIFIES THE COLD WAR

John F. Kennedy was determined to succeed where he believed Eisenhower had failed. Critical of his predecessor for holding down defense spending and apparently allowing the Soviet Union to open up a dangerous lead in ICBMs, Kennedy sought to warn the nation of its peril and lead it to victory in the Cold War.

In his inaugural address, the young president sounded the alarm. Ignoring the domestic issues aired during the campaign, he dealt exclusively with the world. "Let every nation know, whether it wishes us well or ill, that we shall pay any price, bear any burden, meet any hardship, support any friend, oppose any foe," Kennedy declared, "to assure the survival and success of liberty. We will do all this and more."

From the day he took office, John F. Kennedy gave foreign policy top priority. In part, the decision reflected the perilous world situation, the immediate dangers ranging from the unresolved Berlin crisis, through a developing civil war in Vietnam, to the emergence of Fidel Castro as a Soviet ally in Cuba. But it also corresponded to Kennedy's personal priorities. As a congressman and senator, he had been an intense cold warrior. Bored by committee work and legislative details, he had focused on foreign policy in the Senate, gaining a seat on the Foreign

Relations Committee and publishing a book of speeches, *The Strategy of Peace,* in early 1960.

His appointments reflected his determination to win the Cold War. His choice of Dean Rusk, an experienced but unassertive diplomat, to head the State Department indicated that Kennedy planned to be his own secretary of state. He surrounded himself with young pragmatic advisers who prided themselves on toughness: McGeorge Bundy, dean of Harvard College, became national security adviser; Walt W. Rostow, an MIT economist, was Bundy's deputy; and Robert McNamara, the youthful president of the Ford Motor Company, took over as secretary of defense.

These New Frontiersmen, later dubbed "the best and the brightest" by journalist David Halberstam, all shared a hard-line view of the Soviet Union and the belief that American security depended on superior force and the willingness to use it.

FLEXIBLE RESPONSE

The first goal of the Kennedy administration was to build up the nation's armed forces. During the 1960 campaign, Kennedy had warned that the Soviets were opening a missile gap. In fact, due largely to Eisenhower's foresight, the United States had a significant lead in nuclear striking power by early 1961. Nevertheless, the new administration, intent on putting the Soviets on the defensive, authorized the construction of an awesome nuclear arsenal that included 1000 Minuteman solid-fuel ICBMs (five times the number Eisenhower had believed necessary) and 32 Polaris submarines carrying 656 missiles. The United States thus opened a missile gap in reverse, creating the possibility of a successful American first strike.

At the same time, the Kennedy administration augmented conventional military strength. Secretary of Defense McNamara developed plans to add five combat-ready army divisions, three tactical air wings, and a ten-division strategic reserve. These vast increases led to a $6 billion jump in the defense budget in 1961 alone. The president took a personal interest in counterinsurgency. He expanded the Special Forces unit at Fort Bragg, North Carolina, and insisted, over army objections, that it adopt a distinctive green beret as a symbol of its elite status.

The purpose of this buildup was to create an alternative to Eisenhower's policy of massive retaliation. Instead of responding to communist moves with nuclear threats, the United States could now call on a wide spectrum of force—ranging from ICBMs to Green Berets. Thus, as Robert McNamara explained, the new strategy of flexible response meant the United States could "choose among several operational plans." The danger was that such a powerful arsenal might tempt the new administration to test its strength against the Soviet Union.

CRISIS OVER BERLIN

The first confrontation came in Germany. Since 1958, Soviet Premier Khrushchev had been threatening to sign a peace treaty that would put access to the isolated western zones of Berlin under the control of East Germany. The steady flight of skilled workers to the West through the Berlin escape route weakened the East German regime dangerously, and the Soviets believed they had to resolve this issue quickly.

At a summit meeting in Vienna in June 1961, Kennedy and Khrushchev focused on Berlin as the key issue. The Russian leader called the current situation "intolerable" and announced the Soviet Union would proceed with an East German peace treaty. Kennedy was equally adamant, defending the American presence in Berlin. "I want peace," Khrushchev declared, "but, if you want war, that is your problem." "It is you, not I," the young president replied, "who wants to force a change." When the Soviet leader said he would sign a German peace treaty by December, Kennedy added, "It will be a cold winter."

The climax came sooner than either man expected. On July 25, Kennedy delivered an impassioned televised address to the American people in which he called the defense of Berlin "essential" to "the entire Free World." Announcing a series of arms increases, including $3 billion more in defense spending, the president took the unprecedented step of calling more than 150,000 reservists and national guardsmen to active duty.

Aware of superior American nuclear striking power, Khrushchev settled for a stalemate. On August 13, the Soviets sealed off their zone of the city. They began the construction of the Berlin Wall to stop the flow of brains and talent to the West. For a brief time, Russian and American tanks maneuvered within sight of each other at Checkpoint Charlie (where the American and Soviet zones met), but by fall, the tension gradually eased. Berlin—like Germany and, indeed, all of Europe—remained divided between the East and the West. Neither side could claim a victory, but Kennedy believed that at least he had proved to the world America's willingness to honor its commitments.

CONTAINMENT IN SOUTHEAST ASIA

Two weeks before Kennedy's inauguration, Khrushchev gave a speech in Moscow in which he declared Soviet support for "wars of national liberation." The Russian leader's words were actually aimed more at China than the United States; the two powerful communist nations were now rivals for influence in the Third World. But the new American president, ignoring the growing Sino-Soviet split, concluded the United States and Russia were locked in a struggle for the hearts and minds of the uncommitted in Asia, Africa, and Latin America.

East German soldiers repair a breach in the Berlin Wall made when an East German mechanic rammed an armored car into the wall while making his escape into West Berlin. On the other side of the wall, West Berliners observe the repair work.

Calling for a new policy of nation building, Kennedy advocated financial and technical assistance designed to help Third World nations achieve economic modernization and stable pro-Western governments. Measures ranging from the formation of the idealistic Peace Corps to the ambitious Alliance for Progress—a massive economic aid program for Latin America—were part of this effort. Unfortunately, Kennedy relied even more on counterinsurgency and the Green Berets to beat back the communist challenge in the Third World.

Southeast Asia offered the gravest test. Ngo Dinh Diem sought to establish a separate government in South Vietnam with large-scale American economic and military assistance. By the time Kennedy entered the White House, however, the communist government in North Vietnam, led by Ho Chi Minh, was directing the efforts of Vietcong rebels in the South. As the guerrilla war intensified in the fall of 1961, the president sent two trusted advisers, Walt Rostow and General Maxwell Taylor, to South Vietnam. They returned favoring the dispatch of eight thousand American combat troops. "As an area for the operation of U.S. troops," reported General Taylor, "SVN [South Vietnam] is not an excessively difficult or unpleasant place to operate."

The president decided against sending in combat troops in 1961, but he authorized substantial increases in economic aid to Diem and in the size of the military mission in Saigon. The number of American advisers in Vietnam grew from fewer than one thousand in 1961 to more than sixteen thousand by late 1963. American helicopters gave government forces mobility against the Vietcong, but by 1963, the situation had again become critical. Diem had failed to win the support of his own people; Buddhist monks set themselves aflame in public protests against him; and even Diem's own generals plotted his overthrow.

President Kennedy was in a quandary. He realized that the fate of South Vietnam would be determined not by America but by the Vietnamese. "In the final analysis," he said in September 1963, "it is their war. They are the ones who have to win it or lose it." But at the same time, Kennedy was not prepared to accept the possible loss of all Southeast Asia. Although aides later claimed he

Flames engulf Buddhist monk, the Reverend Quang Duc, who set himself afire at an intersection in Saigon, Vietnam, to protest persecution of Buddhists by Vietnam president Ngo Dinh Diem and his government. Other monks placed themselves in front of the wheels of nearby fire trucks to prevent them from reaching Duc.

planned to pull out after the 1964 election, Kennedy raised the stakes by tacitly approving a coup that led to Diem's overthrow and death on November 1, 1963. The resulting power vacuum in Saigon made further American involvement in Vietnam almost certain.

CONTAINING FIDEL CASTRO: THE BAY OF PIGS FIASCO

Kennedy's determination to check global communist expansion reached a peak of intensity in Cuba. In the 1960 campaign, pointing to the growing ties between the Soviet Union and Fidel Castro's regime, he had accused the Republicans of permitting a "communist satellite" to arise on "our very doorstep." Kennedy had even issued a statement backing "anti-Castro forces in exile," calling them "fighters for freedom" who held out hope for "overthrowing Castro."

In reality, the Eisenhower administration had been training a group of Cuban exiles in Guatemala since March 1960 as part of a CIA plan to topple the Castro regime. Many of the new president's advisers had doubts about the proposed invasion. The president, however, committed by his own campaign rhetoric and assured of success by the military, decided to proceed.

On April 17, 1961, fourteen hundred Cuban exiles moved ashore at the Bay of Pigs on the southern coast of Cuba. Even though the United States had masterminded the entire operation, Kennedy insisted on covert action, even canceling at the last minute a planned American air strike on the beachhead. With air superiority, Castro's well-trained forces had no difficulty in quashing the invasion. They killed nearly five hundred exiles and forced the rest to surrender within forty-eight hours.

Aghast at the swiftness of the defeat, President Kennedy took personal responsibility for the failure. In his address to the American people, however, he showed no remorse for arranging the violation of a neighboring country's sovereignty, only regret at the outcome. Above all, he expressed renewed defiance, warning the Soviets that "our restraint is not inexhaustible." For the remainder of his presidency, Kennedy continued to harass the Castro regime, imposing an economic blockade on Cuba, supporting a continuing series of raids by exile groups operating out of Florida, and failing to stop the CIA from experimenting with bizarre plots to assassinate Fidel Castro.

CONTAINING CASTRO: THE CUBAN MISSILE CRISIS

The climax of Kennedy's crusade came in October 1962 with the Cuban missile crisis. Throughout the summer and early fall, the Soviets engaged in a massive arms buildup in Cuba, ostensibly to protect Castro from an American invasion. In the United States, Republican candidates in the 1962 congressional elections called for a firm American response; Kennedy contented himself with a stern

warning against the introduction of any offensive weapons, believing their presence would directly threaten American security. Khrushchev publicly denied any
such intent, but secretly he took a daring gamble, building sites for twenty-four
medium-range (1000-mile) and eighteen intermediate-range (2000-mile) missiles in Cuba. Later he claimed his purpose was purely defensive, but most likely
he was responding to the pressures from his own military to close the enormous
strategic gap in nuclear striking power that Kennedy had opened.

On October 14, 1962, American U-2 planes finally discovered the missile
sites that were nearing completion. As soon as he learned of the Russian action,
Kennedy decided to seek a showdown with Khrushchev. Insisting on absolute secrecy, he convened a special group of advisers to consider the way to respond.

An initial preference for an immediate air strike gradually gave way to discussion of either a full-scale invasion or a naval blockade. The president and his
advisers ruled out diplomacy, rejecting a proposal to offer the withdrawal of ob-

*Aerial photographs taken by U-2 reconnaissance planes flying over Cuba revealed the presence of Russian
missile sites under construction on the island. Recently released information about the type and number of
Soviet nuclear warheads in Cuba reveals just how imminent was the threat of nuclear war had not the Soviets
capitulated to U.S. demands for removal of the missiles.*

solete American Jupiter missiles from Turkey in return for a similar Russian pull-out in Cuba. Kennedy finally agreed to a two-step procedure. He would proclaim a quarantine of Cuba to prevent the arrival of new missiles and threaten a nuclear confrontation to force the removal of those already there. If the Russians did not cooperate, then the United States would invade Cuba and dismantle the missiles by force.

On the evening of October 22, the president informed the nation of the existence of the Soviet missiles and his plans to remove them. He spared no words in blaming Khrushchev for "this clandestine, reckless, and provocative threat to world peace," and he made it clear that any missile attack from Cuba would lead to "a full retaliatory response upon the Soviet Union."

For the next six days, the world hovered on the brink of nuclear catastrophe. Khrushchev replied defiantly, accusing Kennedy of pushing mankind "to the abyss of a world nuclear-missile war." In the Atlantic, some sixteen Soviet ships continued on course toward Cuba, while the American navy was deployed to intercept them five hundred miles from the island.

The first break came at midweek when the Soviet ships suddenly halted to avert a confrontation at sea. "We're eyeball to eyeball," commented Secretary of State Dean Rusk, "and I think the other fellow just blinked." On Friday, Khrushchev sent Kennedy a long, rambling letter offering a face-saving way out—Russia would remove the missiles in return for an American promise never to invade Cuba. The president was ready to accept when a second Russian message raised the stakes by insisting that American Jupiter missiles be withdrawn from Turkey. Kennedy refused to bargain. Nevertheless, while the military went ahead with plans for the invasion of Cuba, the president, heeding his brother's advice, decided to make one last appeal for peace. Ignoring the second Russian message, he sent a cable to Khrushchev accepting his original offer.

On Saturday night, October 27, Robert Kennedy—the president's brother and most trusted adviser—met with Soviet ambassador Anatoly Dobrynin to make it clear this was the last chance to avert nuclear confrontation. "We had to have a commitment by tomorrow that those bases would be removed," Robert Kennedy recalled telling him. Then the president's brother calmly remarked that if Khrushchev did not back down, "there would be not only dead Americans but dead Russians as well."

In reality, John F. Kennedy was not quite so ready to risk nuclear war. He instructed his brother to assure Dobrynin that the Jupiter missiles would soon be removed from Turkey. The president preferred that the missile swap be done privately, but twenty-five years later, Secretary of State Dean Rusk revealed that JFK had instructed him to arrange a deal through the United Nations involving "the removal of both the Jupiters and the missiles in Cuba." In recently released transcripts of his meetings with his advisers, the president reaffirmed his intention of making a missile trade with Khrushchev publicly as a last resort to avoid nuclear war. "We can't very well invade Cuba with all its toil," he commented, "when we could have gotten them out by making a deal on the same missiles in Turkey."

President Kennedy never had to make this final concession. At nine the next morning, Khrushchev agreed to remove the missiles in return only for Kennedy's promise not to invade Cuba. The crisis was over.

The world, however, had come perilously close to a nuclear conflict. We now know the Soviets had nuclear warheads in Cuba, not only for twenty of the medium-range missiles, but also for short-range tactical launchers designed to be used against an American invading force. If Kennedy had approved the military's recommendations for an invasion of Cuba, the consequences might have been disastrous.

The peaceful resolution of the Cuban missile crisis became a personal and political triumph for John F. Kennedy. His party successfully overcame the Republican challenge in the November elections, and his own popularity reached new heights. The American people, on the defensive since *Sputnik,* suddenly felt that they had proved their superiority over the Russians.

The Cuban missile crisis had more substantial results as well. Shaken by their close call, Kennedy and Khrushchev agreed to install a "hot line" to speed direct communication between Washington and Moscow in an emergency. Long-stalled negotiations over the reduction of nuclear testing suddenly resumed, leading to the limited test ban treaty of 1963, which outlawed tests in the atmosphere while still permitting them underground. Above all, Kennedy displayed a new maturity as a result of the crisis. In a speech at American University in June 1963, he shifted from the rhetoric of confrontation to that of conciliation. Speaking of the Russians, he said, "Our most basic common link is the fact that we all inhabit this planet. We all breathe the same air. We all cherish our children's future. And we are all mortal."

Despite these hopeful words, the missile crisis also had an unfortunate consequence. Those who believed that the Russians understood only the language of force were confirmed in their penchant for a hard line. The Russian leaders drew similar conclusions. Aware the United States had a four-to-one advantage in nuclear striking power during the Cuban crisis, one Soviet official told his American counterpart, "Never will we be caught like this again." After 1962, the Soviets embarked on a crash program to build up their navy and to overtake the American lead in nuclear missiles. Within five years, they had the nucleus of a modern fleet and had surpassed the United States in ICBMs. Kennedy's fleeting moment of triumph thus ensured the escalation of the arms race. His legacy was a bittersweet one of short-term success and long-term anxiety.

THE NEW FRONTIER AT HOME

Kennedy hoped to change the course of history at home as well as abroad. His election marked the arrival of a new generation of leadership. For the first time, people born in the twentieth century who had entered political life after World War II were in charge of national affairs. Kennedy's inaugural call to get the nation moving again was particularly attractive to young people, who had shunned political involvement during the Eisenhower years.

The new administration reflected Kennedy's aura of youth and energy. Major cabinet appointments went to activists—notably Connecticut governor Abraham Ribicoff as secretary of health, education, and welfare; labor lawyer Arthur J. Goldberg as secretary of labor; and Arizona congressman Stuart Udall as secretary of the interior. The most controversial choice was Robert F. Kennedy, the president's brother, as attorney general. Critics scoffed at his lack of legal experience; in fact, the president prized his brother's loyalty and shrewd political advice.

Equally important were the members of the White House staff who handled domestic affairs. Like their counterparts in foreign policy, these New Frontiersmen prided themselves on being tough-minded and pragmatic. In contrast to Eisenhower, Kennedy relied heavily on academics and intellectuals to help him infuse the nation with energy and a new sense of direction.

Kennedy's greatest asset was his own personality. A cool, attractive, and intelligent man, he possessed a sense of style that endeared him to the American public. He invited artists and musicians as well as corporate executives to White House functions, and he sprinkled his speeches with references to Emerson and Shakespeare. He seemed to be a new Lancelot, bent on calling forth the best in national life; admirers likened his inner circle to King Arthur's court at Camelot.

THE CONGRESSIONAL OBSTACLE

Neither Kennedy's wit nor his charm proved strong enough to break the logjam in Congress. Since the late 1940s, a series of reform bills ranging from health care to federal aid to education had been stalled on Capitol Hill. Despite JFK's victory, the election of 1960 clouded the outlook for his New Frontier program. The Democrats had lost twenty seats in the House and two in the Senate; even though they retained majorities in both branches, a conservative coalition of northern Republicans and southern Democrats opposed all efforts at reform.

The situation was especially critical in the House, where 101 southern representatives held the balance of power between 160 northern Democrats and 174 Republicans. Aided by Speaker Sam Rayburn, Kennedy was able to enlarge the Rules Committee and overcome a traditional conservative roadblock, but the narrowness of the vote, 217 to 212, revealed how difficult it would be to enact reform measures. The president gave up the fight for health care in the Senate and settled instead for a modest increase in the minimum wage.

Kennedy had no more success in enacting his program in 1962 and 1963. The conservative coalition stood firmly against education and health-care proposals. Although the composition of Congress was his main obstacle, Kennedy's greater interest in foreign policy and his distaste for legislative infighting contributed to the outcome. JFK did not enjoy "blarneying with pompous congressmen and simply would not take the time to do it," one observer noted. As a result, the New Frontier languished in Congress.

ECONOMIC ADVANCE

Kennedy gave a higher priority to the sluggish American economy. During the last years of Eisenhower's administration, the rate of economic growth had slowed to just over 2 percent annually, while unemployment rose to new heights with each recession. JFK was determined to stimulate the economy to achieve a much higher rate of long-term growth. In part, he wanted to redeem his campaign pledge to get the nation moving again; he also believed the United States had to surpass the Soviet Union in economic vitality.

Kennedy received conflicting advice from the experts. Those who claimed the problem was essentially a technological one urged manpower training and area-redevelopment programs to modernize American industry. Others called for federal spending to rebuild the nation's public facilities. Kennedy sided with the first group, largely because Congress was opposed to massive spending on public works.

The actual stimulation of the economy, however, came not from social programs but from greatly increased appropriations for defense and space. A $6 billion increase in the arms budget in 1961 gave the economy a great lift, and Kennedy's decision to send an astronaut to the moon eventually cost $25 billion. By 1962, more than half the federal budget was devoted to space and defense; aircraft and computer companies in the South and West benefited, but unemployment remained uncomfortably high in the older industrial areas of the Northeast and Midwest.

The administration's desire to keep the inflation rate low led to a serious confrontation with the business community. Kennedy relied on informal wage and price guidelines to hold down the cost of living. But in April 1962, just after the president had persuaded the steelworkers' union to accept a new contract with no wage increases and only a few additional benefits, U.S. Steel head Roger Blough informed Kennedy that his company was raising steel prices by $6 a ton. Outraged, the president publicly called the increase "a wholly unjustifiable and irresponsible defiance of the public interest" and accused Blough of displaying "contempt for the interests of 185 million Americans."

Roger Blough soon gave way. The president's tongue-lashing, along with a cutoff in Pentagon steel orders and the threat of an antitrust suit, forced him to reconsider. When several smaller steel companies refused to raise their prices in hopes of expanding their share of the market, U.S. Steel rolled back its prices. The business community deeply resented the president's action.

Troubled by his strained relations with business and by the continued lag in economic growth, the president decided to adopt a more unorthodox approach in 1963. Walter Heller, chairman of the Council of Economic Advisers, had been arguing since 1961 for a major cut in taxes in the belief it would stimulate consumer spending and give the economy the jolt it needed. The idea of a tax cut and resulting deficits during a period of prosperity went against economic orthodoxy, but Kennedy finally gave his approval. In January 1963, the president proposed a tax reduction of $13.5 billion. When finally enacted by Congress in 1964, the massive tax cut led to sustained economic advance for the rest of the decade.

Kennedy's economic policy was far more successful than his legislative efforts. Although the rate of economic growth doubled to 4.5 percent by the end of 1963 and unemployment was reduced substantially, the cost of living rose only 1.3 percent a year. Personal income went up 13 percent in the early 1960s, but the greatest gains came in corporate profits—up 67 percent in the period. Despite the overall economic growth, the public sector continued to be neglected. "I am not sure what the advantage is," complained economist John Kenneth Galbraith, "in having a few more dollars to spend if the air is too dirty to breathe, the water too polluted to drink, the commuters are losing out in the struggle to get in and out of the cities, the streets are filthy, and the schools so bad that the young, perhaps wisely, stay away."

MOVING SLOWLY ON CIVIL RIGHTS

Kennedy faced a genuine dilemma over the issue of civil rights. Despite his own lack of a strong record while in the Senate, he had portrayed himself during the 1960 campaign as a crusader for African American rights. He had promised to launch an attack on segregation in the Deep South, but his fear of alienating the large bloc of southern Democrats forced him to downplay civil rights legislation.

The president's solution was to defer congressional action in favor of executive leadership in this area. He directed his brother, Attorney General Robert Kennedy, to continue and expand the Eisenhower administration's efforts to achieve voting rights for southern blacks. To register previously disfranchised citizens, the Justice Department worked with the civil rights movement—notably the Student Nonviolent Coordinating Committee (SNCC)—in the Deep South. In two years, the Kennedy administration increased the number of voting rights suits fivefold. Yet the attorney general could not force the FBI to provide protection for the civil rights volunteers who risked their lives by encouraging African Americans to register.

Kennedy did succeed in appointing a number of African Americans to high government positions: Robert Weaver became chief of the federal housing agency, and Thurgood Marshall, who pleaded the *Brown* v. *Topeka* school desegregation case before the Supreme Court, was named to the U.S. Circuit Court. On the other hand, among his judicial appointments, Kennedy included one Mississippi jurist who referred to African Americans in court as "niggers" and once compared them to "a bunch of chimpanzees."

The civil rights movement refused to accept Kennedy's indirect approach. In May 1961, the Congress of Racial Equality (CORE) sponsored a "freedom ride" in which a biracial group attempted to test a 1960 Supreme Court decision outlawing segregation in all bus and train stations used in interstate commerce. When they arrived in Birmingham, Alabama, the freedom riders were attacked by a mob of angry whites. The attorney general quickly dispatched several hundred federal marshals to protect the freedom riders, but the president, deeply involved in the Berlin crisis, was more upset at the distraction the protesters created. Kennedy directed one of his aides to get in touch with the leaders of CORE. "Tell them to call it off," he demanded. "Stop them."

In September, after the attorney general finally convinced the Interstate Commerce Commission to issue an order banning segregation in interstate terminals and buses, the freedom rides ended. The Kennedy administration then sought to prevent further confrontations by involving civil rights activists in its voting drive.

A pattern of belated reaction to southern racism marked the basic approach of the Kennedys. When James Meredith courageously sought admission to the all-white University of Mississippi in 1962, the president and the attorney general worked closely with Mississippi governor Ross Barnett to avoid violence. Despite Barnett's later promise of cooperation, the night before Meredith enrolled at the University of Mississippi, a mob attacked the federal marshals and national guard troops sent to protect him. The violence left 2 dead and 375 injured, including 166 marshals and 12 guardsmen, but Meredith attended the university and eventually graduated.

In 1963, Kennedy sent the deputy attorney general to face down Governor George C. Wallace, an avowed segregationist who had promised "to stand in the schoolhouse door" to prevent the integration of the University of Alabama. After a brief confrontation, Wallace yielded to federal authority, and two African American students peacefully desegregated the state university.

"I HAVE A DREAM"

Martin Luther King, Jr., finally forced Kennedy to abandon his cautious tactics and come out openly in behalf of racial justice. In the spring of 1963, King began a massive protest in Birmingham, one of the South's most segregated cities. Public marches and demonstrations aimed at integrating public facilities and opening up jobs for African Americans quickly led to police harassment and many arrests, including that of King himself. Police Commissioner Eugene "Bull" Connor was determined to crush the civil rights movement; King was equally determined to prevail.

Bull Connor played directly into King's hands. On May 3, as six thousand children marched in place of the jailed protesters, authorities broke up a demonstration with clubs, snarling police dogs, and high-pressure water hoses strong enough to take the bark off a tree. With a horrified nation watching scene after scene of this brutality on television, the Kennedy administration quickly intervened to

The attempts of African Americans to end discrimination and secure their civil rights met with violent resistance in Birmingham, Alabama, where police used snarling dogs, fire hoses, clubs, and electric cattle prods to turn back the unarmed demonstrators.

Reverend Martin Luther King, Jr., addresses the crowd at the March on Washington in August 1963. The largest single demonstration of the early 1960s, the march reflected the spirit and determination of many devoted to the cause of equality for African Americans. In his speech, King recounted the difficulties of blacks' struggle for freedom, then stirred the crowd with the description of his dream for America: "I have a dream that one day this nation will rise up and live out the true meaning of its creed—we hold these truths to be self-evident, that all men are created equal."

arrange a settlement with the Birmingham civic leaders that ended the violence and granted the protesters most of their demands.

More important, Kennedy finally ended his long hesitation and sounded the call for action. "We are confronted primarily with a moral issue," he told the nation on June 11. "It is as old as the Scriptures and is as clear as the American Constitution." Eight days later, the administration sponsored civil rights legislation providing equal access to all public accommodations as well as an extension of voting rights for African Americans.

Despite pleas from the government for an end to demonstrations and protests, civil rights leaders kept pressure on the administration. They scheduled a massive march on Washington for August 1963. On August 28, more than 200,000 marchers gathered for a daylong rally in front of the Lincoln Memorial where they listened to hymns, speeches, and prayers for racial justice. The climax of the event was Martin Luther King, Jr.'s eloquent description of his dream for America. It concluded:

When we let freedom ring, when we let it ring from every village and every hamlet, from every state and every city, we will be able to speed up that day when all God's children, black men and white men, Jews and Gentiles, Protestants and Catholics, will be able to join hands and sing, in the words of that old Negro spiritual, "Free at last! Free at last! Thank God almighty, we are free at last!"

By the time of Kennedy's death in November 1963, his civil rights legislation was well on its way to passage in Congress. Unlike Eisenhower, he had provided presidential leadership for the civil rights movement. His emphasis on executive action gradually paid off, especially in extending voting rights. By early 1964, 40 percent of southern blacks had the franchise, compared to only 28 percent in 1960. Moreover, Kennedy's sense of caution and restraint, painful and frustrating as it was to African American activists, had proved well founded. Avoiding an early, and possibly fatal, defeat in Congress, he had waited until a national consensus emerged and then had carefully channeled it behind effective legislation. Behaving very much the way Franklin Roosevelt did in guiding the nation into World War II, Kennedy chose to be a fox rather than a lion on civil rights.

THE SUPREME COURT AND REFORM

The most active impulse for social change in the early 1960s came from a surprising source: the usually staid and conservative Supreme Court. Under the leadership of Earl Warren, a pragmatic jurist more noted for his political astuteness than his legal scholarship, the Court ventured into new areas. A group of liberal judges argued for social reform, while advocates of judicial restraint led by Felix Frankfurter fought stubbornly against the new activism.

The resignation of Frankfurter in 1962 enabled President Kennedy to appoint Secretary of Labor Arthur Goldberg, a committed liberal, to the Supreme Court. With a clear majority now favoring judicial intervention, the Warren Court issued a series of landmark decisions designed to extend to state and local jurisdictions the traditional rights afforded the accused in federal courts. Thus in *Gideon* v. *Wainwright* (1963), *Escobedo* v. *Illinois* (1964), and *Miranda* v. *Arizona* (1966), the majority decreed that defendants had to be provided lawyers, had to be informed of their constitutional rights, and could not be interrogated or induced to confess to a crime without defense counsel being present. In effect, the Court extended to the poor and the ignorant those constitutional guarantees that had always been available to the rich and to the legally informed—notably hardened criminals.

The most far-reaching Warren Court decisions came in the area of legislative reapportionment. In 1962, the Court ruled in *Baker* v. *Carr* that Tennessee had to redistribute its legislative seats to give citizens in Memphis equal representation. Subsequent decisions reinforced the ban on rural overrepresentation as the Court proclaimed that places in all legislative bodies, including the House of Representatives, had to be allocated on the basis of "people, not land or trees or pastures." The principle of "one man, one vote" greatly increased the political power of cities at the expense of rural areas.

The activism of the Supreme Court stirred up a storm of criticism. The rulings that extended protection to criminals and those accused of subversive activity led some Americans to charge that the Court was encouraging crime and weakening national security. The 1962 *Engel* v. *Vitale* decision banning school prayer incensed many conservative Americans, who saw the Court as undermining moral values. Legal scholars worried more about the weakening of the Court's prestige as it became more directly involved in the political process. On balance, however, the Warren Court helped achieve greater social justice by protecting the rights of the underprivileged and by permitting dissent and free expression to flourish.

"LET US CONTINUE"

The New Frontier came to a sudden and violent end on November 22, 1963, when Lee Harvey Oswald assassinated John F. Kennedy as the president rode in a motorcade in downtown Dallas. The shock of losing the young president, who had become a symbol of hope and promise for a whole generation, stunned the entire world. The American people were bewildered by the rapid sequence of events: the brutal killing of their beloved president; the televised slaying of Oswald by Jack Ruby in the basement of the Dallas police station; the composure and dignity of Kennedy's widow, Jacqueline, at the ensuing state funeral; and the hurried Warren Commission report, which identified Oswald as the lone assassin. Afterward, critics would charge that Oswald had been part of a vast conspiracy, but at the time, the prevailing national reaction was a numbing sense of loss.

Vice President Lyndon B. Johnson moved quickly to fill the vacuum left by Kennedy's death. Sworn in on board Air Force One as he returned to Washington, Johnson soon met with a stream of world leaders to reassure them of American political stability. Five days after the tragedy in Dallas, Johnson spoke eloquently to a special joint session of Congress. Recalling JFK's inaugural summons, "Let us begin," the new president declared, "Today in the moment of new resolve, I would say to all my fellow Americans, 'Let us continue.'"

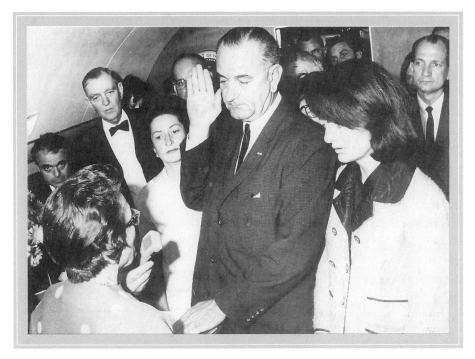

Aboard Air Force One on the return from Dallas to Washington, DC, Judge Sarah Hughes administers the presidential oath of office to a grim Lyndon Johnson.

JOHNSON IN ACTION

Lyndon Johnson suffered from the inevitable comparison with his young and stylish predecessor. LBJ was acutely aware of his own lack of polish; he sought to surround himself with Kennedy advisers and insiders, hoping their sophistication would rub off on him. Johnson's assets were very real—he possessed an intimate knowledge of Congress, an incredible energy and determination to succeed, and a fierce ego. When a young marine officer tried to direct him to the proper helicopter, saying, "This one is yours," Johnson replied, "Son, they are all my helicopters."

LBJ's height and intensity gave him a powerful presence; he dominated any room he entered, and he delighted in using his physical power of persuasion. One Texas politician explained why he had given in to Johnson: "Lyndon got me by the lapels and put his face on top of mine and he talked and talked and talked. I figured it was either getting drowned or joining."

Yet LBJ found it impossible to project his intelligence and vitality to large audiences. Unlike Kennedy, he wilted before the camera, turning his televised speeches into stilted and awkward performances. Trying to belie his reputation as

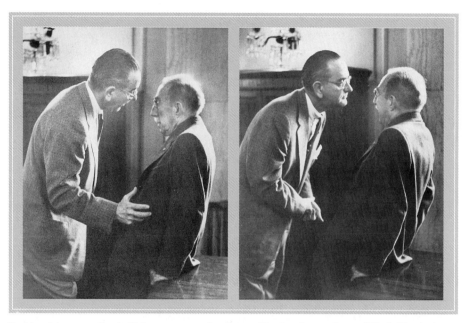

President Johnson applies the "Johnson treatment" to Senator Theodore Francis Green of Rhode Island. A shrewd politician and master of the legislative process, Johnson always knew which votes he could count on, those he couldn't, and where and how to apply pressure to swing votes his way.

a riverboat gambler, he came across like a foxy grandpa, clever, calculating, and not to be trusted.

Whatever his shortcomings in style, however, Johnson possessed far greater ability than Kennedy in dealing with Congress. He entered the White House with more than thirty years of experience in Washington as a legislative aide, congressman, and senator. His encyclopedic knowledge of the legislative process and his shrewd manipulation of individual senators had enabled him to become the most influential Senate majority leader in history. Famed for "the Johnson treatment," a legendary ability to use personal persuasion to reach his goals, Johnson in fact relied more on his close ties with the Senate's power brokers—or "whales," as he called them—than on his exploitation of the "minnows."

Above all, Johnson sought consensus. Indifferent to ideology, he had moved easily from New Deal liberalism to oil-and-gas conservatism as his career advanced. He had performed a balancing act on civil rights, working with the Eisenhower administration on behalf of the 1957 Voting Rights Act, yet carefully weakening it to avoid alienating southern Democrats. When Kennedy dashed Johnson's own intense presidential ambitions in 1960, LBJ had gracefully agreed to be his running mate and had endured the humiliation of the vice presidency loyally and silently. Suddenly thrust into power, Johnson used his gifts wisely.

Citing his favorite scriptural passage from Isaiah, "Come now, and let us reason together, saith the Lord," he concentrated on securing passage of Kennedy's tax and civil rights bills in 1964.

The tax cut came first. Aware of the power wielded by Senate Finance Committee Chairman Harry Byrd, a Virginia conservative, Johnson astutely lowered Kennedy's projected $101.5 billion budget for 1965 to $97.9 billion. Although Byrd voted against the tax cut, he let the measure out of his committee, telling Johnson, "I'll be working for you behind the scenes." In February, Congress reduced personal income taxes by more than $10 billion, touching off a sustained economic boom.

Johnson was even more influential in passing the Kennedy civil rights measure. Staying in the background, he encouraged liberal amendments that strengthened the bill in the House. Johnson refused all efforts at compromise, counting on growing public pressure to force northern Republicans to abandon their traditional alliance with southern Democrats. Everett M. Dirksen of Illinois, the GOP leader in the Senate, met repeatedly with Johnson at the White House. When LBJ refused to yield, Dirksen finally announced, "The time has come for equality of opportunity in sharing in government, in education, and in employment," and led a Republican vote to end a 57-day filibuster.

The 1964 Civil Rights Act, signed on July 2, made illegal the segregation of African Americans in public facilities, established an Equal Employment Opportunity Commission to lessen racial discrimination in employment, and protected the voting rights of African Americans. An amendment sponsored by segregationists in an effort to weaken the bill added gender to the prohibition of discrimination in Title VII of the act; in the future, women's groups would use the clause to secure government support for greater equality in employment and education.

THE ELECTION OF 1964

Passage of two key Kennedy measures within six months did not satisfy Johnson, who wanted now to win the presidency in his own right. Eager to surpass Kennedy's narrow victory in 1960, he hoped to win by a great landslide.

Searching for a cause of his own, LBJ found one in the issue of poverty. Beginning in the late 1950s, economists had warned that the prevailing affluence disguised a persistent and deep-seated problem of poverty. In 1962 Michael Harrington's book *The Other America* attracted national attention. Writing with passion and eloquence, Harrington claimed that nearly one-fifth of the nation, some thirty-five million Americans, lived in poverty.

Johnson quickly took over poverty proposals that Kennedy had been developing and made them his own. In his January 1964 State of the Union address

LBJ announced, "This administration, today, here and now, declares unconditional war on poverty in America." During the next eight months, Johnson fashioned a comprehensive poverty program under the direction of R. Sargent Shriver, Kennedy's brother-in-law. The president added $500 million to existing programs to come up with a $1 billion effort that Congress passed in August 1964.

The new Office of Economic Opportunity (OEO) set up a wide variety of programs, ranging from Head Start for preschoolers to the Job Corps for high school dropouts in need of vocational training. The level of funding was never high enough to meet the OEO's ambitious goals, and a controversial attempt to include representatives of the poor in the Community Action Program led to bitter political feuding with city and state officials. Nonetheless, the war on poverty, along with the economic growth provided by the tax cut, helped reduce the ranks of the poor by nearly ten million between 1964 and 1967.

The new program established Johnson's reputation as a reformer in an election year, but he still faced two challenges to his authority. The first was Robert F. Kennedy, the late president's brother, who continued as attorney general but who wanted to become vice president and Johnson's eventual successor in the White House. Desperate to prove his ability to succeed without Kennedy help, LBJ commented, "I don't need that little runt to win" and chose Hubert Humphrey as his running mate.

The second challenge was the Republican candidate, Senator Barry Goldwater, an outspoken conservative from Arizona. An attractive and articulate man, Goldwater advocated a rejection of the welfare state and a return to unregulated free enterprise. To Johnson's delight, Goldwater chose to place ideology ahead of political expediency. The senator spoke out boldly against the Tennessee Valley Authority, denounced Social Security, and advocated a hawkish foreign policy. "In Your Heart, You Know He's Right," read the Republican slogan, leading the Democrats to reply, "Yes, Far Right."

Johnson stuck carefully to the middle of the road, embracing the liberal reform program—which he now called the Great Society—while stressing his concern for balanced budgets and fiscal orthodoxy. The more Goldwater sagged in the polls, the harder Johnson campaigned, determined to achieve his treasured landslide. On election day, LBJ received 61.1 percent of the popular vote and an overwhelming majority in the electoral college. Equally important, the Democrats achieved huge gains in Congress, controlling the House by a margin of 295 to 140 and the Senate by 68 to 32. Kennedy's legacy and Goldwater's candor had enabled Johnson to break the conservative grip on Congress for the first time in a quarter century.

THE ELECTION OF 1964

CANDIDATE	PARTY	POPULAR VOTE	ELECTORAL VOTE
Johnson	Democratic	43,126,584	486
Goldwater	Republican	27,177,838	52

THE TRIUMPH OF REFORM

LBJ moved quickly to secure his legislative goals. Despite solid majorities in both Houses, including seventy first-term Democrats who had ridden into office on his coattails, Johnson knew he would have to enact the Great Society as swiftly as possible. "You've got to give it all you can, that first year," he told an aide. "Doesn't matter what kind of majority you come in with. You've got just one year when they treat you right, and before they start worrying about themselves."

Johnson gave two traditional Democratic reforms—health care and education—top priority. Aware of strong opposition to a comprehensive medical program, LBJ settled for Medicare, which mandated health insurance under the Social Security program for Americans over age 65, and a supplementary Medicaid program for the indigent. To symbolize the end of a long struggle, Johnson flew to Independence, Missouri, so Truman could witness the ceremonial signing of the Medicare law, which had its origins in Truman's 1949 health insurance proposal.

LBJ overcame the religious hurdle on education by supporting a child-benefit approach, allocating federal money to advance the education of students in parochial as well as public schools. The Elementary and Secondary Education Act of 1965 provided more than $1 billion in federal aid, the largest share going to school districts with the highest percentage of impoverished pupils.

Civil rights proved to be the most difficult test of Johnson's leadership. Martin Luther King, concerned that three million southern blacks were still denied the right to vote, in early 1965 chose Selma, Alabama, as the site for a test case. The white authorities in Selma, led by Sheriff James Clark, used cattle prods and bullwhips to break up the demonstrations. Johnson intervened in March, after TV cameras showed Sheriff Clark's deputies brutally halting a march from Selma to Montgomery. The president ordered the Alabama National Guard to federal duty to protect the demonstrators, had the Justice Department draw up a new voting rights bill, and personally addressed the Congress on civil rights. LBJ

AFRICAN AMERICAN VOTER REGISTRATION BEFORE AND AFTER THE 1965 VOTING RIGHTS ACT

STATE	1960	1966	INCREASE	PERCENTAGE OF INCREASE OVER 1960
Alabama	66,000	250,000	184,000	278.8
Arkansas	73,000	115,000	42,000	57.5
Florida	183,000	303,000	120,000	65.6
Georgia	180,000	300,000	120,000	66.7
Louisiana	159,000	243,000	84,000	52.8
Mississippi	22,000	175,000	153,000	695.4
North Carolina	210,000	282,000	72,000	34.3
South Carolina	58,000	191,000	133,000	229.3
Tennessee	185,000	225,000	40,000	21.6
Texas	227,000	400,000	173,000	76.2
Virginia	100,000	205,000	105,000	105.0

Compiled from U.S. Bureau of the Census, *Statistical Abstract of the United States.*

issued a compelling call to action. "Their cause must be our cause, too. Because it is not just Negroes, but really it is all of us who must overcome the crippling legacy of bigotry and injustice."

Five months later, Congress passed the Voting Rights Act of 1965. Once again Johnson had worked with Senate Republican leader Dirksen to break a southern filibuster and assure passage of a measure. The act banned literacy tests in states and counties in which less than half the population had voted in 1964 and provided for federal registrars in these areas to assure African Americans the franchise.

The results were dramatic. In less than a year, 166,000 African Americans were added to the voting rolls in Alabama; African American registration went up 400 percent in Mississippi. By the end of the decade, the percentage of eligible African American voters who had registered had risen from 40 to 65 percent. For the first time since Reconstruction, African Americans had become active participants in southern politics.

Before the 89th Congress ended its first session in the fall of 1965, it had passed eighty-nine bills. These included measures to create two new cabinet departments (Transportation, and Housing and Urban Affairs); acts to provide for highway safety and to ensure clean air and water; and large appropriations for higher education, public housing, and the continuing war on poverty. In nine months, Johnson had enacted the entire Democratic reform agenda.

The man responsible for this great leap forward, however, had failed to win the public adulation he so deeply desired. His legislative skills had made the most of the opportunities offered by the 1964 Democratic landslide, but the people did not respond to Johnson's leadership with the warmth and praise they had showered on Kennedy. Reporters continued to portray him as a crude wheeler-dealer; as a maniac who drove around Texas back roads at 90 miles an hour, one hand on the wheel and the other holding a can of beer. No one was more aware of this lack of affection than LBJ himself. His public support, he told an aide, is "like a Western river, broad but not deep."

Johnson's realization of the fleeting nature of his popularity was all too accurate. The dilemmas of the Cold War began to divert his attention from domestic concerns and eventually, in the case of Vietnam, would overwhelm him. Yet his legislative achievements were still remarkable. In one brief outburst of reform, he had accomplished more than any president since FDR.

Difficulties abroad would dim the luster of the Johnson presidency, but they could not diminish the lasting impact of the Great Society on American life. Federal aid to education, the enactment of Medicare and Medicaid, and, above all, the civil rights acts of 1964 and 1965 changed the nation irrevocably. The aged and the poor now were guaranteed access to medical care; communities saw an infusion of federal funds to improve local education; and African Americans could now begin to attend integrated schools, enjoy public facilities, and gain political power by exercising the right to vote. But even at this moment of triumph for liberal reform, new currents of dissent and rebellion were brewing.

JOHNSON ESCALATES THE VIETNAM WAR

Lyndon Johnson stressed continuity in foreign policy just as he had in enacting Kennedy's domestic reforms. He not only inherited the policy of containment from his fallen predecessor, but he shared the same Cold War assumptions and convictions. And, feeling less confident about dealing with international issues, he tended to rely heavily on Kennedy's advisers—notably Secretary of State Rusk, Secretary of Defense McNamara, and McGeorge Bundy, the national security adviser.

Johnson had broad exposure to national security affairs. He had served on the Naval Affairs Committee in the House before and during World War II, and as Senate majority leader he had been briefed and consulted regularly on the crises of the 1950s. A confirmed cold warrior, he had also seen in the 1940s the devastating political impact on the Democratic party of the communist triumph in

China. "I am not going to lose Vietnam," he told the American ambassador to Saigon just after taking office in 1963. "I am not going to be the president who saw Southeast Asia go the way China went."

Aware of the problem Castro had caused John Kennedy, LBJ moved firmly to contain communism in the Western Hemisphere. In 1965, to block the possible emergence of a Castro-type government, LBJ sent twenty thousand American troops to the Dominican Republic. Johnson's flimsy justifications—ranging from the need to protect American tourists to a dubious list of suspected communists among the rebel leaders—served only to alienate liberal critics in the United States, particularly Senate Foreign Relations Committee Chairman J. William Fulbright, a former Johnson favorite. The intervention ended in 1966 with the election of a conservative government. Senator Fulbright, however, continued his criticism of Johnson's foreign policy by publishing *The Arrogance of Power*, a biting analysis of the fallacies of containment. Fulbright's defection symbolized a growing gap between the president and liberal intellectuals; the more LBJ struggled to uphold the Cold War policies he had inherited from Kennedy, the more he found himself under attack from Congress, the media, and the universities.

THE VIETNAM DILEMMA

It was Vietnam rather than Latin America that became Lyndon Johnson's obsession and led ultimately to his political downfall. Inheriting an American commitment that dated back to Eisenhower to support an independent South Vietnam, the new president believed he had little choice but to continue Kennedy's policy in Vietnam. The crisis created by Diem's overthrow only three weeks before Kennedy's assassination led to a vacuum of power in Saigon that prevented Johnson from conducting a thorough review and reassessment of the strategic alternatives in Southeast Asia. In 1964, seven different governments ruled South Vietnam; power changed hands three times within one month.

Resisting pressure from the Joint Chiefs of Staff for direct American military involvement, LBJ continued Kennedy's policy of economic and technical assistance. He sent in seven thousand more military advisers and an additional $50 million in aid. While he insisted it was still up to the Vietnamese themselves to win the war, he expanded American support for covert operations, including amphibious raids on the North.

These undercover activities led directly to the Gulf of Tonkin affair. On August 2, 1964, North Vietnamese torpedo boats attacked the *Maddox,* an American destroyer engaged in electronic intelligence gathering in the Gulf of Tonkin. The attack was prompted by the belief the American ship had been involved in a South Vietnamese raid nearby. The *Maddox* escaped unscathed, but to show American resolve, the navy sent in another destroyer, the *C. Turner Joy.* On the evening of August 4, the two destroyers, responding to sonar and radar contacts, opened fire on North Vietnamese gunboats in the area. Johnson ordered retaliatory air strikes on North Vietnamese naval bases. Later investigation indicated that the North Vietnamese gunboats had not launched a second attack on the American ships.

The next day, the president asked Congress to pass a resolution authorizing him to take "all necessary measures to repel any armed attack against the forces of the United States and to prevent further aggression." Later, critics charged that LBJ wanted a blank check from Congress to carry out the future escalation of the Vietnam War, but such a motive is unlikely. He had already rejected immediate military intervention. In part, he wanted the Gulf of Tonkin Resolution to demonstrate to North Vietnam the American determination to defend South Vietnam at any cost. He also wanted to preempt the Vietnam issue from his Republican opponent, Barry Goldwater, who had been advocating a tougher policy. By taking a firm stand on the Gulf of Tonkin incident, Johnson could both impress the North Vietnamese and outmaneuver a political rival at home.

Congress responded with alacrity. The House acted unanimously, while only two senators voted against the Gulf of Tonkin Resolution. Johnson appeared to have won a spectacular victory. His standing in the Gallup poll shot up from 42 to 72 percent, and he had effectively blocked Goldwater from exploiting Vietnam as a campaign issue.

In the long run, however, this easy victory proved costly. Having used force once against North Vietnam, LBJ was more likely to do so in the future. And although he apparently had no intention of widening the conflict in August 1964, the congressional resolution was phrased broadly enough to enable him to use whatever level of force he wanted—including unlimited military intervention. Above all, when he did wage war in Vietnam, he left himself open to the charge of deliberately misleading Congress. Presidential credibility proved ultimately to be Johnson's Achilles' heel; his political downfall began with the Gulf of Tonkin Resolution.

ESCALATION

Full-scale American involvement in Vietnam began in 1965 in a series of steps designed primarily to prevent a North Vietnamese victory. With the political situation in Saigon growing more hopeless every day, the president's advisers urged the bombing of the North. American air attacks would serve several purposes: they would block North Vietnamese infiltration routes, make Hanoi pay a heavy price for its role, and lift the sagging morale of the South Vietnamese. But most important, as McGeorge Bundy reported after a visit to Pleiku (site of a Vietcong attack on an American base which took nine lives), "Without new U.S. action de-

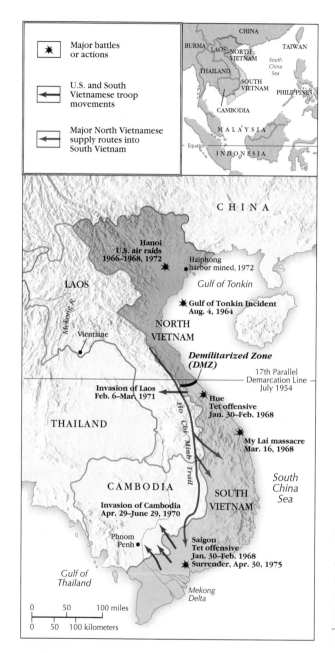

Southeast Asia and the Vietnam War

American combat forces in South Vietnam rose from sixteen thousand in 1963 to a half million in 1968, but a successful conclusion to the conflict was no closer.

feat appears inevitable—probably not in a matter of weeks or perhaps even months, but within the next year or so." In February 1965 Johnson cited the Pleiku attack in ordering a long-planned aerial bombardment of selected North Vietnamese targets.

The air strikes, aimed at impeding the communist supply line and damaging Hanoi's economy, proved ineffective. In April, Johnson authorized the use of American combat troops in South Vietnam, restricting them to defensive operations intended to protect American air bases. In mid-July, Secretary of Defense McNamara recommended sending a hundred thousand combat troops to Vietnam, more than doubling the American forces there. He believed this escalation would lead to a "favorable outcome," but he also told the president that an additional hundred thousand soldiers might be needed in 1966 and that American battle deaths could rise as high as five hundred a month (by early 1968, they hit a peak of more than five hundred a week).

At the same time, other advisers, most notably Undersecretary of State George Ball, spoke out against military escalation in favor of a political settlement. Warning that the United States was likely to suffer France's fate in Vietnam of "national humiliation," Ball told the president that he had "serious doubt that an army of westerners can successfully fight Orientals in an Asian jungle."

Lyndon Johnson was genuinely torn, asking his advisers at one point, "Are we starting something that in two to three years we simply can't finish?" But he finally decided he had no choice but to persevere in Vietnam. Although he insisted on paring down McNamara's troop request, LBJ settled on a steady military escalation designed to compel Hanoi to accept a diplomatic solution. In late July, the president permitted a gradual increase in the bombing of North Vietnam and allowed American ground commanders to conduct offensive operations in the South. Most ominously, he approved the immediate dispatch of fifty thousand troops to Vietnam and the future commitment of fifty thousand more.

These July decisions formed "an open-ended commitment to employ American military forces as the situation demanded," wrote historian George Herring, and they were "the closest thing to a formal decision for war in Vietnam." Convinced that withdrawal would destroy American credibility before the world and that an invasion of the North would lead to World War III, Johnson opted for large-scale but limited military intervention. Moreover, LBJ feared the domestic consequences of either extreme. A pullout could cause a massive political backlash at home, as conservatives condemned him for betraying South Vietnam to communism. All-out war, however, would mean the end of his social programs. Once Congress focused on the conflict, he explained to biographer Doris Kearns, "that bitch of a war" would destroy "the woman I really loved—the Great Society." So he settled for a limited war, committing a half million American troops to battle in Southeast Asia, all the while pretending it was a minor engagement and refusing to ask the American people for the support and sacrifice required for victory.

Lyndon Johnson was not solely responsible for the Vietnam War. He inherited both a policy that assumed Vietnam was a vital national interest and a deteriorating situation in Saigon that demanded a more active American role. Truman, Eisenhower, and Kennedy had taken the United States deep into the Vietnam maze; it was Johnson's fate to have to find a way out. But LBJ bears full responsibility for the way he tried to resolve his dilemma. The failure to confront the people with the stark choices the nation faced in Vietnam, the insistence on secrecy and deceit, the refusal to acknowledge that he had committed the United States to a dangerous military involvement—these were Johnson's sins in Vietnam. His lack of self-confidence in foreign policy and fear of domestic reaction led directly to his undoing.

STALEMATE

For the next three years, Americans waged an intensive war in Vietnam and succeeded only in preventing a communist victory. American bombing of the North proved ineffective. The rural, undeveloped nature of the North Vietnamese economy meant there were few industrial targets. Nor were the efforts to destroy supply lines any more successful. American planes pounded the Ho Chi Minh trail that ran down through Laos and Cambodia, but the North Vietnamese used the jungle canopy effectively to hide their shipments. In fact, the American air attacks, with their inadvertent civilian casualties, gave North Vietnam a powerful propaganda weapon, which it used to sway world opinion against the United States.

The war in the South went no better. Despite the steady increase in American ground forces, from 184,000 in late 1965 to more than 500,000 by early 1968, the Vietcong still controlled much of the countryside. The search-and-destroy tactics employed by the American commander, General William Westmoreland, proved ill suited to the situation. In a vain effort to destroy the enemy, Westmoreland used superior American firepower wantonly, devastating the countryside, causing many civilian casualties, and driving the peasantry into the arms of the guerrillas. Inevitably, these tactics led to the slaughter of innocent civilians, most notably at the hamlet of My Lai. In March 1968, an American company led by Lieutenant William Calley, Jr., killed more than two hundred unarmed villagers.

The main premise of Westmoreland's strategy was to wage a war of attrition that would finally reach a "crossover point" when communist losses each month would be greater than the number of new troops they could recruit. He hoped to lure the Vietcong and the North Vietnamese regulars into pitched battles in which American firepower would inflict heavy casualties. But soon it was the communists who were deciding where and when the fighting would take place, provoking American attacks in remote areas of South Vietnam that favored the defenders. By the end of 1967, the nearly half million American troops Johnson had sent to Vietnam had failed to defeat the enemy. At best, LBJ had only achieved a bloody stalemate that gradually turned the American people against a war they had once eagerly embraced.

YEARS OF TURMOIL

The Vietnam War became the focal point for a growing movement of youthful protest that made the 1960s the most turbulent decade of the twentieth century. Disenchantment with conventional middle-class values, a rapid increase in college enrollments as a result of the post–World War II baby boom, a reaction against the crass materialism of the affluent society—with its endless suburbs and shopping malls—all led American youth to embrace an alternative lifestyle based on the belief that people are "sensitive, searching, poetic, and capable of love." They were ready to create a counterculture.

The agitation of the 1960s was at its height between 1965 and 1968, the years that marked the escalation of the Vietnam War. Disturbances on college campuses reflected growing discontent in other parts of society, from the urban ghettos to the lettuce fields of the Southwest. All who felt disadvantaged—students, African Americans, Hispanics, Native Americans, women, hippies—took to the streets to give vent to their feelings.

THE STUDENT REVOLT

The first sign of student rebellion came in the fall of 1964 at the prestigious University of California at Berkeley. A small group of radical students resisted university efforts to deny them a place to solicit volunteers and funds for off-campus causes. Forming the Free Speech movement, they struck back by occupying administration buildings and blocking the arrest of a nonstudent protester. For the next two months, the campus was in turmoil until the protesters won the rights of free speech and association that they championed.

The Free Speech movement at Berkeley offered many insights into the causes of campus unrest. It was fueled in part by student suspicion of an older, Depression-born generation that viewed affluence as the answer to all problems. Unable to exert much influence on the power structure that directed the consumer society, the students turned on the university. They viewed higher education as the faithful servant of a corporate culture: the university trained hordes of technicians, harbored research laboratories that perfected dreadful weapons, and used IBM punch cards to regiment students.

Student protest found its full expression in the explosive growth of the Students for a Democratic Society (SDS). Founded in Port Huron, Michigan, in 1962, the radical organization wanted to rid American society of poverty, racism, and violence. Although the SDS embraced many traditional liberal reforms, its founders advocated a new approach called participatory democracy. In contrast to both liberalism and old-style socialism, the SDS sought salvation through the individual rather than the group. Personal control of one's life and destiny, not the creation of new bureaucracies, was the hallmark of the New Left.

In the next few years, the SDS grew phenomenally. Spurred on by the Vietnam War and massive campus unrest, the SDS could count more than a hundred thousand followers and was responsible for disruptions at nearly a thousand colleges in 1968. Yet its very emphasis on the individual and its fear of bureaucracy left it leaderless and subject to division and disunity. By 1970, a split between factions, some of which were given to violence, led to its complete demise.

The meteoric career of the SDS symbolized the turbulence of the 1960s. For a brief time, it seemed as though the nation's youth had gone berserk, indulging in a wave of experimentation with drugs, sex, and rock music. Older Americans believed that all the nation's traditional values, from the Puritan work ethic to the family, were under attack. Not all American youth joined in the cultural insurgency; the rebellion was generally limited to children of the upper middle class. But like the flappers of the 1920s, the protesters set the tone for an entire era and left a lasting impression on American society.

PROTESTING THE VIETNAM WAR

The most dramatic aspect of the youthful rebellion came in opposing the Vietnam War. The first student "teach-ins" began at the University of Michigan in March 1965; soon they spread to campuses across the nation. More than twenty thousand protesters, under SDS auspices, gathered in Washington in April to listen to entertainers Joan Baez and Judy Collins sing antiwar songs. "End the War in Vietnam Now, Stop the Killing" read the signs.

One of the great ironies of the Vietnam War was the system of student draft deferments, which enabled most of those enrolled in college to avoid military service. As a result, the children of the well-to-do, who were more likely to attend college, were able to escape the draft. Consequently, a sense of guilt led many college activists who were safe from Vietnam because of their student status to take the lead in denouncing an unjust war.

As the fighting in Southeast Asia intensified in 1966 and 1967, the protests grew larger and the slogans more extreme. "Hey, Hey, LBJ, how many kids did

Antiwar protesters came face-to-face with military police in the October 1967 March on the Pentagon. Leaders of the march announced that the demonstration marked the end of peaceful protest against the war and the beginning of a new stage of "active resistance." Borrowing techniques from the civil rights movement, some of the demonstrators staged a sit-down in the Pentagon parking lot.

you kill today?" chanted students as they proclaimed, "Hell, no, we won't go!" At the Pentagon in October 1967, more than a hundred thousand demonstrators confronted a cordon of military policemen guarding the heart of the nation's war machine.

The climax came in the spring of 1968. Driven by both opposition to the war and concern for social justice, the SDS and African American radicals at Columbia University joined forces in April. They seized five buildings, effectively paralyzing one of the country's leading colleges. After eight days of tension, the New York City police regained control. The brutal repression quickened the pace of protest elsewhere. Students held sit-ins and marches at more than one hundred colleges, from Cheyney State in Pennsylvania to Northwestern in Illinois.

The students failed to stop the war, but they did succeed in gaining a voice in their education. University administrations allowed undergraduates to sit on faculty curriculum-planning committees and gave up their once rigid control of dormitory and social life. But the students' greatest impact lay outside politics and the campus. They spawned a cultural uprising that transformed the manners and morals of America.

THE CULTURAL REVOLUTION

In contrast to the elitist political revolt of the SDS, the cultural rebellion by youth in the 1960s was pervasive. Led by college students, young people challenged the prevailing adult values in clothing, hairstyles, sexual conduct, work habits, and music. Blue jeans and love beads took the place of business suits and wrist-watches; long hair and unkempt beards for men, bare feet and bralessness for women became the new uniform of protest.

Music became the touchstone of the new departure. Folksingers such as Joan Baez and Bob Dylan, popular for their songs of social protest in the mid-1960s, gave way first to rock groups such as the Beatles, whose lyrics were often sugges-tive of drug use, and then to "acid rock" as symbolized by the Grateful Dead. The climactic event of the decade came at the Woodstock concert at Bethel in upstate New York when 400,000 young people indulged in a three-day festival of rock music, drug experimentation, and public sexual activity.

Former Harvard psychology professor Timothy Leary encouraged youth to join him in trying out the drug scene. Millions accepted his invitation to "tune in, turn on, drop out" literally, as they experimented with marijuana and with LSD, a new and dangerous chemical hallucinogen. The ultimate expression of insurgency was the Yippie movement, led by Jerry Rubin and Abbie Hoffman. Shrewd buf-foons who mocked the consumer culture, they delighted in capitalizing on the mood of social protest to win attention. Once, when testifying before a congres-sional committee investigating internal subversion, Rubin dressed as a Revolutionary War soldier; Hoffman appeared in the gallery of the New York Stock Exchange in 1967, raining money down on the cheering brokers below.

"BLACK POWER"

The civil rights movement, which had spawned the mood of protest in the 1960s, fell on hard times later in the decade. The legislative triumphs of 1964 and 1965 were relatively easy victories over southern bigotry; now the movement faced the far more complex problem of achieving economic equality in the cities of the North, where more than half of the nation's African Americans lived in poverty. The civil rights movement had raised the expectations of urban African Americans for improvement; frustration mounted as they failed to experience any significant economic gain.

The first sign of trouble came in the summer of 1964, when African American teenagers in Harlem and Rochester, New York, rioted. The next sum-mer, a massive outburst of rage and destruction swept over the Watts area of Los Angeles as the inhabitants burned buildings and looted stores. Riots in the sum-mer of 1966 were less destructive, but in 1967 the worst ones yet took place in Newark and in Detroit, where forty-three were killed and thousands were injured. The mobs attacked the shops and stores, expressing a burning grievance against a consumer society from which they were excluded by their poverty.

The civil rights coalition fell apart, a victim of both its legislative success and economic failure. Black militants took over the leadership of the Student Nonviolent Coordinating Committee (SNCC); they disdained white help and even reversed Martin Luther King's insistence on nonviolence. SNCC's new leader, Stokely Carmichael, told blacks they should seize power in those parts of the South where they outnumbered whites. Soon his calls for "black power" became a rallying cry for more militant blacks who advocated the need for African Americans to form "our own institutions, credit unions, co-ops, political parties" and even write "our own history."

King suffered the most from this extremism. His denunciation of the Vietnam War cost him the support of the Johnson administration and alienated him from the more conservative civil rights groups such as the NAACP and the Urban League. He finally seized on poverty as the proper enemy for attack, but before he could lead his Poor People's March on Washington in 1968, he was assassinated in Memphis in early April.

Both blacks and whites realized the nation had lost its most eloquent voice for racial harmony. His tragic death elevated King to the status of a martyr, but it also led to one last outbreak of urban violence. African Americans exploded in angry riots in 125 cities across the nation; the worst rioting took place in Washington, DC, where buildings were set on fire within a few blocks of the White House. "It was as if the city were being abandoned to an invading army," wrote a British journalist. "Clouds of smoke hung over the Potomac, evoking memories of the London blitz."

Yet there was a positive side to the emotions engendered by black nationalism. Leaders urged African Americans to take pride in their ethnic heritage, to embrace their blackness as a positive value. African Americans began to wear Afro hairstyles and dress in dashikis, stressing their African roots. Students began to demand new black studies programs in the colleges; the word *Negro*—identified with white supremacy of the past—virtually disappeared from usage overnight, replaced by the favored *Afro-American* or *black*. Singer James Brown best expressed the sense of racial identity: "Say It Loud—I'm Black and I'm Proud."

ETHNIC NATIONALISM

Other groups quickly emulated the African American phenomenon. Native Americans decried the callous use of their identity as football mascots; in response, universities such as Stanford changed their symbols. Puerto Ricans demanded their history be included in school and college texts. Polish, Italian, and

In March 1966, César Chávez, shown here speaking at the first United Farm Workers convention, led striking grape pickers on a 250-mile march from Delano, California, to the state capital at Sacramento to dramatize the plight of the migrant farmworkers. With the slogan "God is beside you on the picket line," the march took on the character of a religious pilgrimage.

Czech groups insisted on respect for their nationalities. Congress acknowledged these demands with passage of the Ethnic Heritage Studies Act of 1972.

Mexican Americans were in the forefront of the ethnic groups that became active in the 1970s. The primary impulse came from the efforts of César Chávez to organize the poorly paid grape pickers and lettuce workers in California into the National Farm Workers Association (NFWA). Chávez appealed to ethnic nationalism in mobilizing Mexican American field hands to strike against grape growers in the San Joaquin Valley in 1965. A national boycott of grapes by Mexican Americans and their sympathizers among the young people of the counterculture led to a series of hard-fought victories over the growers. The five-year struggle resulted in a union victory in 1970, but at an enormous cost—95 percent of the farmworkers involved had lost their homes and their cars. Nevertheless, Chávez succeeded in raising the hourly wage of farmworkers in California to $3.53 by 1977 (it had been $1.20 in 1965).

Chávez's efforts helped spark an outburst of ethnic consciousness among Mexican Americans that swept through the urban barrios of the Southwest. Mexican American leaders campaigned for bilingual programs and improved educational opportunities. Young activists began to call themselves Chicanos, which had previously been a derogatory term, and to take pride in their cultural heritage; in 1968, they succeeded in establishing the first Mexican American studies program at California State College at Los Angeles.

WOMEN'S LIBERATION

Active as they were in the civil rights and antiwar movements, women soon learned that the male leaders of these causes were little different from corporate executives—they expected women to fix the food and type the communiqués while the men made the decisions. Understandably, women soon realized that they could only achieve respect and equality by mounting their own protest.

In some ways, the position of women in American society was worse in the 1960s than it had been in the 1920s. After forty years, a lower percentage of women were enrolled in the nation's colleges and professional schools. Women were still relegated to stereotyped occupations such as nursing and teaching; there were few female lawyers and even fewer women doctors. And gender roles, as portrayed on television commercials, continued to call for the husband to be the breadwinner and the wife to be the homemaker.

Betty Friedan was one of the first to seize on the sense of grievance and discrimination that developed among white middle-class women in the 1960s. The beginning of the effort to raise women's consciousness was her 1963 book, *The Feminine Mystique*. Calling the American home "a comfortable concentration camp," she attacked the prevailing view that women were completely contented with their housekeeping and child-rearing tasks, claiming that housewives had no self-esteem and no sense of identity.

The 1964 Civil Rights Act helped women attack economic inequality head-on by making it illegal to discriminate in employment on the basis of sex. Women filed suit for equal wages, demanded that companies provide day care for their infants and preschool children, and entered politics to lobby against laws that—in the guise of protection of a weaker sex—were unfair to women. As the women's liberation movement grew, its advocates began to attack laws banning abortion and waged a campaign to toughen the enforcement of rape laws.

The women's movement met with many of the same obstacles as other protest groups in the 1960s. The moderate leadership of the National Organization for Women (NOW), founded by Betty Friedan in 1966, soon was challenged by those with more extreme views. Ti-Grace Atkinson and Susan Brownmiller attacked revered institutions—the family and the home—and denounced sexual intercourse with men, calling it a method of male domination. Many women were repelled by the harsh rhetoric of the extremists and expressed satisfaction with their lives. But despite these disagreements, most women supported the effort to achieve equal status with men, and in 1972, Congress responded by voting to send the Equal Rights Amendment to the state legislatures for ratification.

THE RETURN OF RICHARD NIXON

The turmoil of the 1960s reached a crescendo in 1968 as the American people responded to the two dominant events of the decade—the war in Vietnam and the cultural insurgency at home. In an election marked by a series of bizarre events, including riots and an assassination, Richard Nixon staged a remarkable comeback to win the post denied him in 1960.

VIETNAM UNDERMINES LYNDON JOHNSON

A controversial Vietcong offensive in early 1968 proved to be the decisive event in breaking the stalemate in Vietnam and driving Lyndon Johnson from office. Using deceptive tactics, the North Vietnamese began a prolonged siege of an American marine base at Khe Sanh, deep in the northern interior. Fearing another Dien Bien Phu, Westmoreland rushed in reinforcements, sending more than 40 percent of all American infantry and armor battalions into the two northernmost provinces of South Vietnam.

The Vietcong then used the traditional lull in the fighting at Tet, the lunar New Year, to launch a surprise attack in the heavily populated cities. Beginning on January 30, 1968, the VC struck at thirty-six of the forty-four provincial capitals. The most daring raid came at the American embassy compound in Saigon. Although the guerrillas were unable to penetrate the embassy proper, for six hours television cameras caught the dramatic battle that ensued in the courtyard before military police finally overcame the attackers.

Although caught off guard, American and South Vietnamese forces succeeded in repulsing the Tet offensive quickly everywhere except in Hue, the old imperial capital, which was retaken only after three weeks of heavy fighting that left this beautiful city, in the words of one observer, "a shattered, stinking hulk, its streets choked with rubble and rotting bodies."

Tet proved to be the turning point of the Vietnam War. Although the communists failed to win control of the cities and suffered heavy losses, they still held on to most of the rural areas and had scored an impressive political victory. CBS-TV newscaster Walter Cronkite took a quick trip to Saigon to find out what had hap-

President Johnson, alone in the Cabinet room, rests his head on his hand as he listens to a tape from his son-in-law Marine Captain Charles Robb recounting his combat experiences in Vietnam. Johnson stunned the nation with his announcement on March 31, 1968, that he would not seek reelection. Poor results in the March primaries and public opinion polls indicated that support for LBJ was eroding.

pened. Horrified at what he saw, he exclaimed to his guides, "What the hell is going on? I thought we were winning the war." He returned home to tell the American people, "It seems now more certain than ever that the bloody experience of Vietnam is to end in a stalemate."

President Johnson reluctantly came to the same conclusion after the Joint Chiefs of Staff requested an additional 205,000 troops to achieve victory in Vietnam following the Tet offensive. He began to listen to his new secretary of defense, Clark Clifford, who had replaced Robert McNamara in January 1968. In mid-March, the president decided to limit the bombing of North Vietnam in an effort to open up peace negotiations with Hanoi. In a speech to the nation on Sunday evening, March 31, 1968, Johnson outlined his plans for a new effort at ending the war peacefully and then concluded by saying, as proof of his sincerity, "I shall not seek, and I will not accept, the nomination of my party for another term as your president."

In the fourteen years since the siege of Dien Bien Phu, American policy had gone full cycle in Vietnam. Even though Eisenhower had decided against using force to rescue the French, his commitment to the Diem regime in Saigon had led eventually to American military involvement on a massive scale. Three years of inconclusive fighting and a steadily mounting loss of American lives had disillusioned the American people and finally cost Lyndon Johnson the presidency. And the full price the nation would have to pay for its folly in Southeast Asia was still unknown—the Vietnam experience would continue to cast a shadow over American life for years to come.

THE DEMOCRATS DIVIDE

Lyndon Johnson's withdrawal from the presidential race after the Tet offensive set the tone for the 1968 election. LBJ's decision had come in response to political as well as military realities. By 1966, the antiwar movement had spread from the college campuses to Capitol Hill. Chairman J. William Fulbright gave the protests a new respectability when his Senate Foreign Relations Committee held probing hearings on the war, broadcast on television to the entire country.

The essentially leaderless protest against the war took on a new quality on January 3, 1968, when Senator Eugene McCarthy, a Democrat from Minnesota, announced he was challenging LBJ for the party's presidential nomination. Intellectual, cool, aloof, and almost arrogant, McCarthy raised the banner of idealism, telling audiences, "Whatever is morally necessary must be made politically possible." College students flocked to his campaign, shaving their beards and cutting their hair to be "clean for Gene." In the New Hampshire primary in early March, the nation's earliest political test, McCarthy shocked the political experts by coming within a few thousand votes of defeating President Johnson.

McCarthy's strong showing in New Hampshire led Robert Kennedy, who had been weighing the risks in challenging Johnson, to enter the presidential race. Elected senator from New York in 1964, Bobby Kennedy had become an effective voice for the disadvantaged, as well as an increasingly severe critic of the Vietnam War. He attracted strong support among blue-collar workers, African Americans, Chicanos, and other minorities who formed the nucleus of the continuing New Deal coalition.

Lyndon Johnson's dramatic withdrawal caused an uproar in the Democratic party. With Johnson's tacit backing and strong support from party regulars and organized labor, Vice President Hubert H. Humphrey immediately declared his candidacy. Humphrey, aware that he was totally unacceptable to the antiwar movement, decided to avoid the primaries and work for the nomination within the framework of the party.

Kennedy and McCarthy, the two antiwar candidates, were thus left to compete in the spring primaries, requiring agonizing choices among those who desired change. Kennedy won everywhere except in Oregon, but his narrow victory in California ended in tragedy when a Palestinian immigrant, Sirhan Sirhan, assassinated him in a Los Angeles hotel.

With his strongest opponent struck down, Hubert Humphrey had little difficulty at the Chicago convention. The vice president relied on party leaders to defeat an antiwar resolution and win the nomination on the first ballot by a margin of more than two to one.

Humphrey's triumph was marred by violence outside the heavily guarded convention hall. Radical groups had urged their members to come to Chicago to agitate; the turnout was relatively small but included many who were ready to provoke the authorities in their despair over the convention's outcome. Epithets

While party factions quarreled inside the convention hall at the 1968 Democratic National Convention in Chicago, in the streets outside Chicago police clashed violently with antiwar demonstrators. Here, a Chicago policeman squirts Mace into the crowd of protestors gathered outside the Conrad Hilton hotel where Democratic candidate Hubert H. Humphrey had his convention headquarters.

and cries of "pigs" brought on a savage response from the police. "The cops had one thing on their mind," commented journalist Jimmy Breslin. "Club and then gas, club and then gas, club and then gas."

The bitter fumes of tear gas hung in the streets for days afterward; the battered heads and bodies of demonstrators and innocent bystanders alike flooded the city's hospital emergency rooms. What an official investigation later termed a "police riot" marred Humphrey's nomination and made a sad mockery out of his call for "the politics of joy." The Democratic party itself had become the next victim of the Vietnam War.

THE REPUBLICAN RESURGENCE

The primary beneficiary of the Democratic debacle was Richard Nixon. Written off as politically dead after his unsuccessful race for governor of California in 1962, Nixon had slowly rebuilt his place within the party by working loyally for Barry Goldwater in 1964 and for GOP congressional candidates two years later. At the GOP convention in Miami Beach, Nixon won an easy first-ballot nomination and chose Maryland governor Spiro Agnew as his running mate. Agnew, little known on the national scene, had won the support of conservatives by taking a strong stand against African American rioters.

In the fall campaign, Nixon opened up a wide lead by avoiding controversy and reaping the benefit of discontent with the Vietnam War. He played the peace issue shrewdly, appearing to advocate an end to the conflict without ever taking a definite stand. Above all, he chose the role of reconciler for a nation torn by emotion, a leader who promised to bring a divided country together again.

Humphrey, in contrast, found himself hounded by antiwar demonstrators who heckled him constantly. He walked a tightwire, desperate for the continued support of President Johnson but handicapped by LBJ's stubborn refusal to end all bombing of North Vietnam. Only when he broke with Johnson in late September by announcing that if elected he would "stop the bombing of North Vietnam as an acceptable risk for peace" did his campaign begin to gain momentum.

Unfortunately for Humphrey, a third-party candidate cut deeply into the normal Democratic majority. George Wallace had first gained national attention as the racist governor of Alabama whose motto was "Segregation now . . . segregation tomorrow . . . segregation forever." In 1964, he had shown surprising strength in Democratic primaries in northern states. By attacking both black leaders and their liberal white allies, Wallace appealed to the sense of powerlessness among the urban working classes. "Liberals, intellectuals, and longhairs have

THE ELECTION OF 1968

CANDIDATE	PARTY	POPULAR VOTE	ELECTORAL VOTE
Nixon	Republican	31,770,237	301
Humphrey	Democratic	31,270,533	191
Wallace	American Independent	9,906,141	46
	Minor Parties	239,908	—

run the country for too long," Wallace told his followers. "When I get to Washington," he promised, "I'll throw all these phonies and their briefcases into the Potomac."

Running on the ticket of the American Independent Party, Wallace was a close third in the September polls. But as the election neared, his following declined. Humphrey continued to gain, especially after Johnson agreed in late October to end all bombing of North Vietnam. By the first week in November, the outcome was too close for the experts to call.

Nixon won the election with the smallest share of the popular vote of any winning candidate since 1916. But he swept a broad band of states from Virginia and the Carolinas through the Midwest to the Pacific for a clear-cut victory in the electoral college. Humphrey held on to the urban Northeast; Wallace took just five states in the Deep South, but his heavy inroads into blue-collar districts in the North shattered the New Deal coalition.

The election marked a repudiation of the politics of protest and the cultural insurgency of the mid-1960s. The combined popular vote for Nixon and Wallace, 56.5 percent of the electorate, signified there was a silent majority that was fed up with violence and confrontation. A growing concern over psychedelic drugs, rock music, long hair, and sexual permissiveness had offset the usual Democratic advantage on economic issues and led to the election of a Republican president.

At the election of Richard Nixon, an era came to an end with the passing of two concepts that had guided American life since the 1930s. First, the liberal reform impulse, which reached its zenith with the Great Society legislation in 1965, had clearly run its course. Civil rights, Medicare, and federal aid to education would continue in place, but Nixon's triumph signaled a strong reaction against the growth of federal power. At the same time, the Vietnam fiasco spelled the end of activist foreign policy that had begun with American entry into World War II. Containment, so successful in protecting western Europe against the Soviet threat, had proved a disastrous failure when applied on a global scale. The last three decades of the twentieth century would witness a struggle to replace outmoded liberal internationalism with new policies at home and abroad.

31

A CRISIS IN CONFIDENCE, 1969–1980

O n the evening of June 17, 1972, five men broke into the headquarters of the Democratic National Committee in the Watergate complex. They wore surgical gloves and carried cans of Mace, lock-picking tools, camera equipment, and telephone bugging devices. Busy filming documents and checking on electronic bugs planted two weeks before, the burglars were caught by police after an alert security guard discovered they had carelessly left doors taped open.

The leader of the group, Gary McCord, a former CIA employee, was working for CREEP (the Committee to Re-Elect the President), and police quickly found the telephone number of White House aide E. Howard Hunt in his address book. Despite this obvious tie to the Nixon administration, presidential press secretary Ron Ziegler denied any White House involvement in the Watergate break-in, dismissing it as "a third-rate burglary attempt."

In fact, this criminal act was a direct outgrowth of the paranoia that characterized the Nixon presidency. Aware that he had won office by a very narrow margin in 1968, Nixon was determined to do everything possible to ensure his reelection in 1972. Concerned about leaks from the White House, he authorized wiretaps on the telephones of both reporters and key aides. After the *New York Times* and the *Washington Post* began publishing the Pentagon Papers, Nixon took drastic measures to plug any further leaks of secret documents. His aides created

Daniel Ellsberg after the opening session of his trial. Ellsberg was indicted for espionage, theft, and conspiracy, but the case was dismissed on the grounds of government misconduct.

a self-styled "plumbers" unit within the White House directed by G. Gordon Liddy, a former FBI agent, and E. Howard Hunt, a veteran of the CIA. Charged with preserving secrecy and discrediting those who spoke to the press, Hunt and Liddy set out to embarrass Daniel Ellsberg, the Defense Department official who had leaked the Pentagon Papers, going so far as to break into his psychiatrist's office in search of damning information.

Convinced that people throughout society were working for his defeat in 1972, Nixon ordered aides John Dean and Charles Colson to prepare an "enemies list." They eventually compiled a roster of several hundred prominent citizens, ranging from movie stars such as Jane Fonda and Paul Newman to twelve African American congressmen. The plan was to direct the IRS and other government agencies to target these "enemies" for audits and investigations, or, as John Dean put it, to use "the available federal machinery to screw our political enemies." Operating under a siege mentality, the Nixon White House was prepared to do anything necessary to defeat its opponents, who were thought to include the media, the intellectual community, and virtually all minority groups.

The president's greatest concern was guaranteeing his reelection. He appointed Attorney General John Mitchell to head CREEP and gave him access to extensive funds and the use of men similar to Liddy and Hunt. The bungled Watergate break-in, directed by Liddy and Hunt, was thus the culmination of abuses of power that grew directly out of Nixon's personal insecurity.

The president probably did not have any advance knowledge of the break-in, but he committed a criminal act by authorizing a far-reaching cover-up. On June 23, he ordered his aides to instruct the FBI to defer to the CIA in regard to the Watergate burglary, invoking nonexistent national security concerns to block an investigation that might expose White House involvement. Determined to contain the damage, Nixon told John Mitchell, "I want you to stonewall it, let them plead the Fifth Amendment, cover-up, or anything else." Putting John Dean in charge, Nixon successfully covered up the Watergate affair while winning reelection in 1972, only to have the whole matter later unravel and drive him from office.

Watergate was but the first of a series of shocks in the 1970s that shook the confidence of the American people. War in the Middle East led to a sharp increase in the price of oil and waves of inflation that devastated the economy. Revolutions in Nicaragua and Iran added to the dilemmas confronting the nation's leaders. By the end of the decade, the American people were beginning to question the validity of traditional American values and institutions as they tried to cope with difficult challenges at home and abroad.

NIXON IN POWER

Before Watergate cast its long shadow over his presidency, Nixon dealt ably with a wide range of issues at home and abroad. While his domestic policies had only limited success, he proved both skillful and effective in the international arena, achieving a significant, though temporary, reduction in Cold War tensions.

The man who took office as the thirty-sixth president of the United States on January 20, 1969, seemed to be a new Nixon. Gone were the fiery rhetoric and the penchant for making enemies. In their place, observers found an air of moderation and restraint. He appeared to have his emotions under firm control, but beneath the surface he remained bitter, hurt, and sensitive to criticism.

An innately shy man, Nixon hoped to enjoy the power of the presidency in splendid solitude. Described by Barry Goldwater as "the most complete loner I've ever known," Nixon assembled a powerful White House staff whose main task was to isolate him from Congress, the press, and even his own cabinet. Loyal subordinates such as H. R. Haldeman and John Ehrlichman took charge of domestic issues, often making decisions without even consulting Nixon. Foreign policy was Nixon's great passion, and here he relied heavily on Henry Kissinger, his national security adviser, to formulate policy.

The Nixon White House soon could be likened to a fortress under siege. Distrusting everyone, from the media to members of his own party, the president sought to rule the nation without help from either Congress or his cabinet. In his quest for privacy, the president cut himself off from the nation and thus sowed the seeds of his downfall.

RESHAPING THE GREAT SOCIETY

Nixon began his first term on a hopeful note, promising the nation peace and respite from the chaos of the 1960s. Rejecting the divisions that had split Americans apart, he promised in his inaugural address to "bring us together." "We cannot learn from one another until we stop shouting at one another—until we speak quietly enough so that our words can be heard as well as our voices."

Nixon's moderation promised a return to the politics of accommodation that had characterized the Eisenhower era. Faced with a Democratic Congress, Nixon, like Ike, appeared ready to accept the main outlines of the welfare state. Instead of any massive overthrow of the Great Society, he focused on making the federal bureaucracy function more efficiently.

Nixon was successful in shifting responsibility for social problems from Washington to state and local authorities. He developed the concept of revenue sharing, by which federal funds would be dispersed to state, county, and city agencies to meet local needs. In 1972, Congress finally approved a measure to share $30.1 billion with local governments over a five-year period.

In the area of civil rights, Nixon made a shrewd political move. Action by Congress and the outgoing Johnson administration had ensured that massive desegregation of southern schools, delayed for more than a decade by legal action, would finally begin just as Nixon took office. Nixon and his attorney general, John Mitchell, decided to shift the responsibility for this process to the courts. In the summer of 1969, the Justice Department asked a federal judge to delay the integration of thirty-three school districts in Mississippi. The Supreme Court quickly ruled against the Justice Department. Thus, in the minds of southern white voters, it was the hated Supreme Court, not Richard Nixon, who had forced them to integrate their schools.

Nixon used similar tactics in his attempt to reshape the Supreme Court along more conservative lines. His appointment of Warren Burger, an experienced federal judge with moderate views, to replace the retiring Earl Warren as Chief Justice met with little objection. But liberal Democrats succeeded in blocking

High school students in Woodville, Mississippi, board a school bus after their first day of class in a now all-black school. The school, which was formerly predominantly white, was one of thirty Mississippi schools under court order to speed desegregation.

the nomination first of Clement Haynesworth of South Carolina and then of G. Harrold Carswell of Florida. Nixon denounced his opponents for insulting "millions of Americans who live in the South" by turning down his two southern nominees. Once again, the president had used the Supreme Court to enhance his political appeal to Southerners.

Nixon finally filled the Court position with Harry Blackmun, a respected moderate from Minnesota, who easily won confirmation. Subsequently, the president appointed Lewis Powell, a distinguished Virginia lawyer, and William Rehnquist, a rigidly conservative Justice Department attorney from Arizona, to the Supreme Court. Surprisingly, the Burger Court, despite its more conservative makeup, did not engage in any massive overturn of the Warren Court's decisions.

The moderation of the Supreme Court and the legislative record of the Nixon administration indicated that the nation was not yet ready to abandon the reforms adopted in the 1960s. The pace of change slowed down, but the commitment to social justice was still clear.

NIXONOMICS

The economy posed a more severe test for Richard Nixon. He inherited growing inflation stemming from the Vietnam War. Although Lyndon Johnson finally secured a tax increase from Congress in 1968 which produced a balanced budget in 1969, the heavy expense of the fighting in Vietnam since 1965 had led to massive deficit spending. As a result, in 1968 the cost of living rose 5 percent. Strongly opposed to the idea of federal controls, Nixon at first opted for a reduction in government spending while encouraging the Federal Reserve Board to raise interest rates, thereby slowing the rate of business expansion.

The result was disastrous. Inflation continued, reaching nearly 6 percent by the end of 1970, the highest rate since the Korean War. At the same time, the economy underwent its first major recession since 1958. Unemployment rose to 6 percent by the end of 1970, and business failures jumped alarmingly. Democrats quickly coined a new word, *Nixonomics,* to describe the disaster.

Conditions seemed to worsen in 1971. Inflation continued unabated, and the nation's balance of trade became negative as imports exceeded exports by a substantial margin, leading to a weakening of the dollar abroad.

In mid-August, Nixon acted boldly to halt the economic decline. Abandoning his earlier resistance to controls, he announced a ninety-day freeze on wages and prices to be followed by federally imposed guidelines in both areas. The new secretary of the treasury, Democrat John Connally, carried out a devaluation of the dollar, which led to a greatly improved balance of trade. The sudden Nixon economic reversal quickly ended the recession, with industrial production increasing more than 5 percent in the first quarter of 1972.

BUILDING A REPUBLICAN MAJORITY

"The Great Nixon Turnaround," as historian Lloyd Gardner termed it, came too late to help the Republicans in the 1970 congressional elections. From the time he took office in 1969, the president was obsessed with the fact that he had received only 43 percent of the popular vote in 1968. The Republicans were still a minority party, and to be reelected in 1972, Nixon would need to win over southern whites and blue-collar workers who had voted for Wallace in 1968.

Attorney General John Mitchell, who had been Nixon's campaign manager in 1968, had devised a southern strategy to help achieve a Republican majority by 1972. The administration's well-publicized objection to school desegregation in the South and the attempt to put Haynesworth and Carswell on the Court were part of this design. Kevin Phillips, one of Mitchell's aides, urged the Nixon administration to direct its appeal to "middle Americans"—southern whites, Catholic ethnic groups, blue-collar workers, and, above all, the new suburbanites of the South and West, the emerging Sunbelt.

Nixon unleashed Vice President Spiro Agnew in an attempt to exploit the social issue in the 1970 election. Blaming all of society's problems—from drug abuse and sexual permissiveness to crime in the streets—on Democratic liberals and their allies in the media, Agnew delivered a series of scathing speeches. He denounced intellectuals as "an effete corps of impudent snobs" and damned the press as "nattering nabobs of negativism."

The Democrats struck back by changing their tactics. Their candidates were careful to stress economic issues, blaming the Republicans for both inflation and recession. On social issues, they joined in the chorus against crime, pornography, and drugs.

The outcome was a standoff. Agnew's attacks helped the GOP limit the usual off-year losses in the House to nine seats, while the Republicans gained two votes in the Senate. But the Democrats did well in state elections and proved once again that economic issues were crucial in American politics. Nixon and the Republicans still did not command a national majority.

IN SEARCH OF DÉTENTE

Richard Nixon gave foreign policy top priority, and he proved surprisingly adept at it. In Kissinger, he had a White House specialist who had devoted his life to the study of diplomacy. A refugee from Nazi Germany, Kissinger had become a professor of government at Harvard, the author of several influential books, and an acknowledged authority on international affairs. Nixon and Kissinger approached foreign policy from a similar realistic perspective. Instead of viewing the Cold War as an ideological struggle for survival with communism, they saw it as a traditional great-power rivalry, one to be managed and controlled rather than to be won.

Kissinger and Nixon had a grand design. Realizing that recent events, especially the Vietnam War and the rapid Soviet arms buildup of the 1960s, had eroded America's position of primacy in the world, they planned a strategic retreat. Russia had great military strength, but its economy was weak and it had a dangerous rival in China. Kissinger planned to use American trade to induce Soviet cooperation, while at the same time improving U.S. relations with China.

Nixon and Kissinger shrewdly played the China card as their first step toward achieving détente—that is, a relaxation of tension—with the Soviet Union. In February 1972, accompanied by a planeload of reporters and television camera crews, Nixon made a triumphal tour of China, ending more than two decades of Sino-American hostility. Nixon agreed to establish an American liaison mission in Beijing as a first step toward diplomatic recognition.

The Soviets, who viewed China as a dangerous adversary along a 2000-mile frontier in Asia, responded by agreeing to reach an arms control pact with the

United States. The Strategic Arms Limitation Talks (SALT) had been under way since 1969. During a visit to Moscow in May 1972, President Nixon signed two vital documents with Soviet leader Leonid Brezhnev. The first limited the two superpowers to two hundred antiballistic missiles (ABMs) apiece; the second froze the number of offensive ballistic missiles for a five-year period. SALT I recognized the existing Soviet lead in missiles, but the American deployment of multiple independently targeted reentry vehicles (MIRVs) ensured a continuing strategic advantage for the United States.

The SALT I agreements were most important as a symbolic first step toward control of the nuclear arms race. They signified that the United States and Russia were trying to achieve a settlement of their differences by peaceful means.

ENDING THE VIETNAM WAR

Vietnam remained the one foreign policy challenge that Nixon could not overcome. He had a three-part plan to end the conflict—gradual withdrawal of American troops and training of South Vietnamese forces to take over the combat role, renewed bombing, and a hard line in negotiations with Hanoi. The number of American soldiers in Vietnam fell from 543,000 in early 1969 to less than 30,000 by 1972.

Renewed bombing proved the most controversial part of the plan. In April 1970, Nixon ordered both air and ground strikes into neutral Cambodia, causing a massive outburst of antiwar protests at home. Tragedy struck at Kent State University in Ohio in early May. After rioters had firebombed an ROTC building, the governor sent in national guard troops who were taunted and harassed by irate students. The guardsmen then opened fire, killing four students and wounding eleven more. A week later, two African American student demonstrators were killed at Jackson State College in Mississippi; soon riots and protests raged on more than four hundred campuses across the country.

Nixon had little sympathy for the demonstrators, calling the students "bums" who were intent on "blowing up the campuses." The "silent majority" to whom he appealed seemed to agree; one poll showed that most Americans blamed the students, not the national guard, for the deaths at Kent State. Nixon's Cambodian invasion did little to shorten the Vietnam War, but the public reaction reinforced the president's resolve not to surrender.

The third tactic, negotiation with Hanoi, finally proved successful. In the summer and fall of 1972, the two sides were near agreement, but South Vietnamese objections blocked a settlement before the 1972 election. When the North Vietnamese tried to make last-minute changes, Nixon ordered a series of savage B-52 raids on Hanoi that finally led to the signing of a truce on January 27,

The renewed bombing of North Vietnam and invasion of Cambodia ordered by Nixon in hopes of ending the conflict precipitated student protests at many campuses. At Kent State University in Ohio, demonstrators and bystanders were shot by national guardsmen.

1973. In return for the release of all American prisoners of war, the United States agreed to remove its troops from South Vietnam within sixty days. The political clauses allowed the North Vietnamese to keep their troops in the South, thus virtually guaranteeing future control of all Vietnam by the communists.

The agreement was, in fact, a disguised surrender, but finally the American combat role in the Vietnam War was over. After eight years of fighting, the United States had emerged from the quagmire in Southeast Asia. Yet, known only to a few insiders around the president, the nation was already deeply enmeshed in another dilemma—what Gerald R. Ford termed "the long national nightmare" of Watergate.

THE CRISIS OF DEMOCRACY

The June 1, 1972, break-in at the Democratic National Committee offices came back to haunt Richard Nixon in 1973 and 1974. His determination to stonewall the press on any White House involvement in the burglary—including instructions to his aides to lie under oath—proved successful in the short run, but eventually the cover-up led to his downfall.

THE ELECTION OF 1972

CANDIDATE	PARTY	POPULAR VOTE	ELECTORAL VOTE
Richard Nixon	Republican	46,740,323	520
George McGovern	Democratic	28,901,598	17
John Hospers	Minor Parties	1,983,231	1

THE ELECTION OF 1972

The irony of the Watergate break-in was that by the time it occurred, Nixon's election was assured. Aided by Republican dirty tricks, the Democrats self-destructed. First, Edmund Muskie, the front-runner, replying in the New Hampshire primary to a letter accusing him of prejudice against French Canadians, lost his composure. Then a lone assassin, Arthur Bremer, shot and seriously wounded George Wallace. Paralyzed, Wallace was forced to drop out of the race, leaving Nixon with a complete monopoly over the political right.

Senator George McGovern of South Dakota finally emerged as the Democratic nominee. He ran on a platform that advocated a negotiated settlement in Vietnam, the right to abortion, and tolerance of diverse lifestyles. The South Dakota senator hoped to unite the New Left with traditional Democratic voters, but his strong stand against the Vietnam War greatly strengthened Nixon's appeal.

Instead of focusing on his own record in office, Richard Nixon shrewdly let McGovern's perceived extremism and New Left support become the main issue in the campaign. Nixon let others campaign for him, relying heavily on the recent improvement in the economy and his foreign policy triumphs with China and Russia to sway the nation's voters.

The result was a stunning victory. Nixon won a popular landslide with 60.8 percent of the vote—second only to Lyndon Johnson's record in 1964—and an even more decisive sweep of the electoral college. The very low turnout and Democratic control of both Houses of Congress suggests the election was primarily a repudiation of McGovern, rather than an endorsement of Richard Nixon. The voting patterns did suggest, however, the beginning of a major political realignment, as only blacks, Jews, and low-income voters continued to vote overwhelmingly Democratic, while the GOP made significant gains in the Sunbelt states of the South and West.

Senator Sam Ervin, chairman of the Senate Watergate Committee, swears in former Nixon White House aide John Dean. Dean's testimony before the Committee implicated Nixon in the Watergate scandal.

THE WATERGATE SCANDAL

Despite the best efforts of John Dean, the Watergate cover-up began to unravel in early 1973. Hunt and Liddy were convicted and went to prison without implicating anyone else in the Nixon administration; James McCord became the first to break the silence. Sentenced to a long jail term by Judge John Sirica, McCord asked for leniency, informing Sirica he had received money from the White House and had been promised a future pardon in return for his silence. By April 1973, Nixon was forced to fire John Dean and to allow Haldeman and Ehrlichman, who were deeply implicated, to resign. The Senate then appointed a special committee to investigate the Watergate episode. In a week of dramatic testimony, John Dean revealed the president's personal involvement in the cover-up. Still, it was basically a matter of whose word was to be believed, that of the president or that of a discredited aide, and Nixon hoped to weather the storm.

The existence of tapes of conversations in the Oval Office, recorded regularly since 1970, finally brought Nixon down. At first, the president tried to invoke executive privilege to withhold the tapes. Then Nixon tried to release only a few of the less damaging ones, but the Supreme Court ruled unanimously in June 1974 that the tapes had to be turned over to Judge Sirica.

By that time, the House Judiciary Committee had voted three articles of impeachment, charging Nixon with obstruction of justice, abuse of power, and contempt of Congress. Faced with the release of tapes that directly implicated him in the cover-up, the president finally chose to resign on August 9, 1974.

Nixon's resignation proved to be the culmination of the Watergate scandal. The entire episode revealed both the weaknesses and strengths of the American political system. Most regrettable was the abuse of presidential authority—a reflection both of the growing power of the modern presidency and of the fatal flaws in Richard Nixon's character. Realizing he had reached the White House almost by accident, Nixon did everything possible to retain his hold on his office. He used the plumbers to maintain executive secrecy, and he directed the Internal

An embattled Richard Nixon waves good-bye after resigning the presidency on August 9, 1974.

Revenue Service and the Justice Department to punish his enemies and reward his friends.

But Watergate also demonstrated the vitality of a democratic society. The press showed how investigative reporting could unlock even the most closely guarded executive secrets. Judge Sirica proved that an independent judiciary was still the best bulwark for individual freedom. And Congress rose to the occasion, both by carrying out a successful investigation of executive misconduct and by following a scrupulous and nonpartisan impeachment process that left Nixon with no chance to escape his fate.

The nation survived the shock of Watergate with its institutions intact. Attorney General John Mitchell and twenty-five presidential aides were sentenced to jail terms. Congress, in decline since Lyndon Johnson's exercise of executive dominance, was rejuvenated, with its members now intent on extending congressional authority into all areas of American life.

ENERGY AND THE ECONOMY

In the midst of Watergate, the outbreak of war in the Middle East threatened a vital national interest—the supply and price of the fuel on which the American way of life was based. In the course of the 1970s, the resulting energy crisis helped touch off an inflationary impulse that had a profound impact on the national economy.

THE OCTOBER WAR

On October 6, 1973, Egypt and Syria launched a surprise attack on Israel. The fighting caught American leaders completely off guard. President Nixon and Henry Kissinger, who had become secretary of state in September, expected Israel to repel the Arab invaders and display the same military dominance it had used to win the Six Day War in 1967. In that conflict, Israel had devastated its Arab neighbors, taking possession of the Golan Heights from Syria, the Sinai peninsula from Egypt, and Jerusalem and the West Bank from Jordan. Instead of increasing Israeli security, however, the conquests had only added to Middle East tensions. They unified the Arab countries, who now called for the return of their lands, and increased their dependence on the Soviet Union for arms and political support.

Henry Kissinger used the October War, which began on the Jewish holy day of Yom Kippur, as an opportunity to shift American policy from its traditional pro-Israeli position to a more neutral stance—as the honest broker between Israel and its Arab neighbors. When the Israelis quickly routed their opponents, the United States intervened diplomatically to prevent a victory for

As prices climbed and supplies dwindled, Americans found themselves waiting in long lines to fill their cars' gas tanks. Service stations reduced their operating hours and restricted the amount of gasoline consumers could buy, but many stations still ran out of fuel before they could accommodate all their customers.

Israel that would preclude American mediation. The fighting finally ended in late October; Israel had repulsed the Arab attack but had been stopped short of complete victory.

Kissinger's apparent diplomatic triumph, however, was offset by an unforeseen consequence of the Yom Kippur War. On October 17, the Arab members of the Organization of Petroleum Exporting Countries (OPEC) announced a 5 percent cut in oil production, with additional cuts of 5 percent each month until Israel gave up the lands it had taken in 1967. President Nixon announced a $2.2 billion aid package for Israel on October 19, and the next day Saudi Arabia cut off oil shipments to the United States and to the Netherlands, the European nation that had most strongly supported American policy in the Middle East.

The Arab oil embargo had a disastrous impact on the American economy. Arab countries cut production by 25 percent from the September 1973 level, leading to a 10 percent curtailment in the world supply. For the United States, which imported one-third of its daily consumption, this meant a loss of nearly

2 million barrels a day. Long lines formed at automobile service stations as motorists who feared running out of gas kept filling their tanks.

President Nixon responded with a series of temporary measures, including pleas to turn down thermostats in homes and offices and reduce automobile speed limits to 50 miles an hour. When the Arab oil embargo ended in March, after Kissinger negotiated an Israeli pullback in the Sinai, gasoline once again became plentiful; thermostats were raised, and people resumed their love affair with the automobile.

The energy crisis, however, did not end with the lifting of the embargo. The Arab action marked the beginning of a new era in American history. The United States, with only 6 percent of the world's population, had been responsible for nearly 40 percent of the earth's energy consumption. In 1970, domestic oil production began to decline; the embargo served only to highlight the fact that the nation was now dependent on other countries for its economic well-being. A nation that based its way of life on abundance and expansion suddenly was faced with the reality of limited resources and economic stagnation.

THE OIL SHOCKS

Cheap energy had been the underlying force behind the amazing growth of the American economy after World War II. The world price of oil had actually declined in the 1950s and 1960s as huge new fields in the Middle East and North Africa began to produce. The GNP had more than doubled between 1950 and 1973; the American people had come to base their way of life on gasoline prices that averaged about 35 cents a gallon. The huge gas-guzzling cars, the flight to the suburbs, the detached houses cooled by central air-conditioning represented a dependence on inexpensive energy that everyone took for granted.

The first great oil shock of the 1970s came with the October War and the resulting Arab oil embargo. In the ensuing shortfall, the OPEC nations quickly raised prices, first from $3 to more than $5 a barrel, then to $11.65. The effect on the American economy was devastating. Gasoline prices jumped from 35 to 65 cents a gallon; the cost of manufacturing went up proportionately, while utility rates rose sharply as a result of the higher cost of fuel oil and natural gas. Suddenly, Americans faced drastic and unexpected increases in such everyday expenses as driving to work and heating their homes.

The result was a sharp decline in consumer spending and the worst recession since World War II. The GNP dropped by 6 percent in 1974, and unemployment rose to more than 9 percent, the highest level since the Great Depression of the 1930s. Detroit was hit the hardest. Car sales declined by 20 percent, and by the fall of 1974, America's Big Three automakers had laid off more than 225,000 workers.

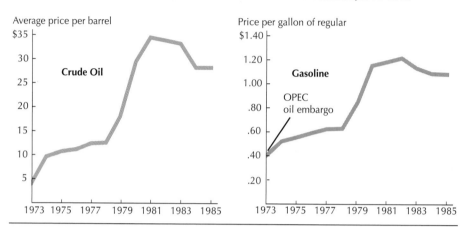

The Oil Shocks: Price Increases of Crude Oil and Gasoline, 1973–1985

President Gerald R. Ford, who followed Richard Nixon into the White House (see p. 1029), responded belatedly to the economic crisis by proposing a tax cut to stimulate consumer spending. Congress passed a $22.8 billion reduction in taxes in early 1975, which led to a gradual recovery by 1976. The resulting budget deficits, however, helped keep inflation above 5 percent and prevented a return to full economic health.

Jimmy Carter of Georgia, who succeeded Ford, had little more success in achieving a rapid rate of economic growth. In 1979, the outbreak of the Iranian Revolution and the overthrow of the shah touched off another oil shock. Although the cutoff of Iranian oil led to a shortfall of only 3 percent of the world's oil supply, the members of the OPEC cartel took advantage of the situation to double prices over the next eighteen months. Gasoline prices climbed to more than $1 a gallon at American service stations, leading to an even greater wave of inflation than in 1973.

The American people panicked. When lines began to form at gas stations in California and Florida in early May 1979, drivers started filling their tanks every day or two. The long lines frustrated American drivers, who took out their fury on the Carter administration. In June, the president's staff warned him of the danger in the "worsening short-term energy crisis." "Nothing else has so frustrated, confused, angered the American people," Carter was told, "or so targeted their distress at you personally."

By the fall of 1979, world supply had caught up with demand, and the oil scare ended. But the price of gasoline remained at more than $1 a gallon, and the inflation rate reached double-digit levels again. The twin oil shocks of the 1970s had left the economy battered and had undermined the average American's faith in the future.

THE SEARCH FOR AN ENERGY POLICY

The oil shocks of 1973 and 1979 were but two symptoms of a much deeper energy crisis. Put simply, the United States was running out of the fossil fuels on which it had relied for its economic growth in the past. Domestic oil production peaked in 1970 and declined every year thereafter; there were more ample reserves of natural gas, but both fuels were nonrenewable sources of energy that eventually would be exhausted. American political leaders had to devise a national policy to meet not only the temporary shortfalls of the 1970s but also the long-term energy problem inherent in past reliance on fossil fuels.

The success of the environmental movement in the late 1960s and early 1970s compounded the problem. Congress created the Environmental Protection Agency in 1970 to monitor industry and passed a Clean Air Act that encouraged public utilities to shift from using coal, which polluted the atmosphere, to clean-burning fuel oil and natural gas to generate electricity.

The energy crunch pitted the environmentalists against advocates of economic growth. Those who put ecology first lost out. By the end of the decade, groups such as the Sierra Club and Friends of the Earth had failed in their efforts to halt the gradual relaxation of environmental regulations that prohibited strip mining of coal and offshore drilling for oil.

The nation's leaders had a difficult time devising a coherent and workable long-term national energy policy. Gerald Ford favored expanding production to overcome the shortage. The Republicans advocated removing price controls on oil and natural gas to bring in new supplies of the fuels as well as greater production of coal and expanded nuclear power plants.

The Democrats, in contrast, were intent on shielding American consumers from the full brunt of the world price increase; Democratic leaders in Congress wanted to continue an elaborate system of price controls instituted by Nixon in 1973. They preferred standby plans for gas rationing to reliance on the marketplace to allocate scarce supplies.

The nation failed to adopt either the Republican or the Democratic energy plans; instead, Congress tried to muddle through with elements of both approaches. Thus, on the production front, it approved construction of the Alaskan pipeline. On the conservation side, Congress continued the price controls on domestic oil and mandated annual increases in automobile gasoline mileage that forced Detroit to produce more fuel-efficient cars.

The overall outcome, however, was a patchwork that fell far short of a coherent national strategy for solving the energy problem. Oil imports actually increased by 50 percent between 1973 and 1979, rising from 6 million to 9 million barrels a day, an amount nearly half of the nation's daily petroleum usage.

THE GREAT INFLATION

The gravest consequence of the oil shocks was inflation. The startling increase in price levels in the 1970s stemmed from many causes. The Vietnam War created budget deficits that grew from $63 billion for the entire decade of the 1960s to a total of $420 billion in the 1970s. A worldwide shortage of food triggered a 20 percent rise in American food prices in 1973 alone. But above all else, the primary source of the great inflation of the 1970s was the sixfold increase in petroleum prices.

The impact on consumers was staggering. The price of an automobile jumped 72 percent between 1973 and 1978. During the decade, the price of a hamburger doubled and the cost of a loaf of bread—the proverbial staff of life—rose from 24 to 89 cents. Corresponding wage increases failed to keep pace with inflation; in 1980, the real income of the average American family fell by 5.5 percent.

Curbing inflation proved to be beyond the power of the federal government. President Ford's early efforts to roll back prices by rhetoric were a casualty of the 1974 recession. President Carter proved equally powerless. Finally, in October 1979, the Federal Reserve Board, led by Carter appointee Paul Volcker, began a sustained effort to halt inflation by curtailing the supply of money in circulation. The new tight-money policy served only to heighten inflation in the short run by driving the prime interest rate to 20 percent in 1980.

THE SHIFTING AMERICAN ECONOMY

Inflation and the oil shocks helped bring about significant changes in American business and industry in the 1970s. The most obvious result was the slowing of the rate of economic growth. More important, American industry began to lose its position of primacy in world markets. In 1959, U.S. firms had been the leaders in eleven of thirteen major industrial sectors. By 1976, American companies led in only seven areas, and in all but one category—aerospace—U.S. corporations had declined in relation to Japanese and western European competitors.

The most serious losses came in the heavy industries in which the United States had once led the world. New steel producers in western Europe, Japan, and the Third World were producing steel far more efficiently than their American counterparts. As a result, by the end of the 1970s, American firms

Explosive charges felled four giant blast furnaces of the U.S. Steel plant in Youngstown, Ohio, in April 1982. The furnaces, which stood 12 stories high and weighed 3000 tons apiece, had been built in the early 1900s. The plant closed in early 1980.

were closing down their obsolete mills in the East and Midwest, idling thousands of workers.

Foreign competition did even more damage in the automobile industry. The oil shocks led to a consumer demand for small, efficient cars. German and Japanese automakers seized the opportunity to expand their once low volume of sales in the United States. By 1977, imported cars had captured 18.3 percent of the American market. In response, Detroit spent $70 billion retooling to produce a new fleet of smaller, lighter front-wheel-drive cars; but American manufacturers barely survived the foreign invasion. Only government-backed loans helped the Chrysler Corporation stave off bankruptcy.

In other areas, American corporations fared much better. The multinationals that had emerged in the boom years of the 1960s continued to thrive. IBM sold computers all over the globe. The growth of high-technology industries proved to be the most profitable new trend of the 1970s. Computer companies and electronics firms grew at a rapid rate, especially after the development of the silicon chip, a small, wafer-thin microprocessor capable of performing complex calculations almost instantly.

The result was a geographic shift of American industry from the East and Midwest to the Sunbelt. Electronics manufacturers flourished in California, Texas, and North Carolina, where they grew up around major universities. At the same time, the decline of the steel and auto industries was leading to massive unemployment and economic stagnation in the northern industrial heartland.

The overall pattern was one of an economy in transition. The oil shocks had caused serious problems of inflation, slower economic growth, and rising unemployment rates. But American business still displayed the enterprise and the ability to develop new technologies that gave promise of renewed economic vitality.

PRIVATE LIVES—PUBLIC ISSUES

Sweeping changes in the private lives of the American people began in the 1970s and continued for the rest of the century. The traditional American family, with the husband the wage earner and the wife the homemaker, gave way to much more diverse living arrangements. The number of working women, including wives and mothers, increased sharply; the wage gap between the sexes narrowed, but women still lagged noticeably behind men in earnings. Finally, the years since 1970 saw the emergence of an active gay rights movement as more and more homosexuals began to disclose their sexual identities and demand an end to discrimination.

THE CHANGING AMERICAN FAMILY

Family life underwent a number of significant shifts after 1970. The most notable was a decline in the number of families with two parents and one or more children under 18. By 1990, in only 21 percent of the two-parent families was the mother solely engaged in child rearing. A few fathers stayed at home with the children, but in the great majority of these families, both parents worked outside the home.

The number of married-couple households without children remained nearly constant at 30 percent, but there was a marked increase in the number of people living alone. The birthrate, however, after a steady fall in the 1970s and early 1980s, climbed again as the baby boom generation began to mature. There was a marked increase in the number of births to women over age 30, as well as a very high proportion of children born to single mothers—27 percent of all births, compared to just 11 percent twenty years earlier.

By the mid-1990s, as the baby boom generation matured, several changes in living patterns were apparent. The divorce rate, which had doubled between the mid-1960s and the late 1970s, leveled off in the 1980s and then dropped slightly between 1990 and 1995. There was a slight drop in the birthrate by the mid-

1990s, as baby boomers moved beyond the childbearing age and younger people postponed marriage until they were in their mid-twenties. Noting that married couples headed 78 percent of all American families, a conservative analyst concluded that "reports of the traditional family's death are greatly exaggerated."

Changes in modern American life have affected traditional family structure. A large number of people either never marry or postpone marriage until late in the childbearing period. The traditional family unit, with the working father and the mother rearing the children at home, is rapidly declining. Women without partners headed more than one-third of all impoverished families, and children made up 40 percent of the nation's poor. Although politicians, especially Republicans, refer to family values during campaigns, the fact remains that the American family underwent great stress due to social changes in the last third of the twentieth century, and children have suffered disproportionately.

GAINS AND SETBACKS FOR WOMEN

American women have experienced significant changes in their way of life and their place in society in the past quarter century. The prevailing theme is the increasing percentage of working women. There was a rapid movement of women into the labor force in the 1970s. The trend continued through the 1980s. Fully 61 percent of the nearly nineteen million new jobs created during the decade were filled by women; many of these new jobs, however, were entry-level or low-paying service positions.

Women scored some impressive breakthroughs. They began to enter corporation boardrooms and became presidents of major universities. Women entered blue-collar, professional, and small-business fields traditionally dominated by men. Reagan's appointment of Sandra Day O'Connor to the Supreme Court in 1981 marked a historic first; Clinton doubled the number of women on the Court with his selection of Ruth Bader Ginsburg.

Yet at the same time, women encountered a great deal of resistance. Most women continued to work in female-dominated fields—as nurses, secretaries, teachers, and waitresses. Those who entered such "male" areas as management and administration soon encountered the "glass ceiling." In 1990, only 4.3 percent of corporate officers were women. Most in business worked at the middle and lower rungs of management with staff jobs in personnel and public relations, not key operational positions in sales and marketing that would lead to the boardroom. The economic boom of the 1990s, however, led to a steady increase in the number of women executives; in 1998, there was an increase of 514,000.

Even with these gains, however, by 1999 women's wages still averaged only 73 percent of men's earnings. Younger women did best; those between 16 and 24 earned almost 90 cents for every dollar paid to a male in the same age group.

Older women, who often had no other source of support, fared poorly; those over the age of 50 earned only 64 percent as much as men their age. Feminists had once hoped to close the gender gap by the year 2000, but experts predicted women would not reach pay equity with men until 2018.

The most encouraging development for women came in business ownership. The number of female business owners increased 40 percent between 1987 and 1992, twice the national rate of business growth. A women's trade group estimated that in 1996, women owned almost eight million businesses, employing more than eighteen million workers—one out of four American workers.

Beyond economic opportunity, the women's movement had two goals in recent years. The first was ratification of the Equal Rights Amendment (ERA). Approved by Congress in 1972, the ERA stated simply, "Equality of rights under the law shall not be denied or abridged by the United States or any state on account of sex." Within a year, twenty-two states had approved the amendment, but the efforts gradually faltered just three states short of ratification. Right-wing activist Phyllis Schlafly led an organized effort to defeat the ERA, claiming the amendment would lead to unisex toilets, homosexual marriages, and the drafting of women. The National Organization for Women (NOW) fought back, persuading Congress to extend the time for ratification by three years and waging intense campaigns for approval in Florida and Illinois. But the deadline for ratification finally passed on June 30, 1982, with the ERA forces still three states short. NOW leader Eleanor Smeal vowed a continuing struggle: "The crusade is not over. We know that we are the wave of the future."

Voting on the Equal Rights Amendment
By the end of 1974, thirty-four states had ratified the ERA; Indiana finally approved the amendment in 1977, but the remaining fifteen states held out, leaving ratification three states short of the required three-fourths majority.

The women's movement focused even more of its energies in protecting a major victory it had won in 1973 in *Roe* v. *Wade,* affirming that women had the constitutional right to abortion. "Right-to-life" groups, consisting mainly of orthodox Catholics, fundamentalist Protestants, and conservatives, fought back. In 1978, with strong support from President Carter, Congress passed the Hyde amendment, which denied the use of federal funds to pay for abortions for poor women.

As Presidents Reagan and Bush appointed more conservative judges to the Court, prochoice groups began to fear the future overturn of *Roe* v. *Wade*. The Court avoided a direct challenge, contenting itself with lesser actions that upheld the rights of states to regulate abortion clinics and require the approval of one parent or a judge before a minor could have an abortion. Abortion became an issue in presidential contests, with the Republicans upholding a prolife position and the Democrats taking a prochoice stand. Even the exercise of the right to abortion proved difficult and sometimes dangerous in view of the often violent protests of prolife groups outside abortion clinics. For women, abortion was a hard-won right they still had to struggle to protect.

THE GAY LIBERATION MOVEMENT

On the evening of July 29, 1969, a squad of New York policemen raided the Stonewall Inn, a Greenwich Village bar frequented by "drag queens" and lesbians. As the patrons were being herded into vans, a crowd of gay onlookers began to jeer and taunt the police. A riot quickly broke out. "Beer cans and bottles were heaved at the windows and a rain of coins descended on the cops," reported the *Village Voice*. The next night, more than four hundred police officers battled two thousand gay demonstrators through the streets of Greenwich Village. The two-day Stonewall Riots marked the beginning of the modern gay liberation movement. Refusing to play the role of victims any longer, gays decided to affirm their sexual preference and demand an end to discrimination against homosexuals.

Within a few days, two new organizations were formed in New York, the Gay Liberation Front and the Gay Activist Alliance, with branches and offshoots quickly appearing in cities across the country. The basic theme of gay liberation was to urge all homosexuals to "come out of the closet" and affirm with pride their sexual identity. "Come out for freedom! Come out now!" proclaimed the Gay Liberation Front's newspaper. "Come out of the closet before the door is nailed shut!"

In the course of the 1970s, hundreds of thousands of gays and lesbians responded to this call. They formed more than a thousand local clubs and organizations and won a series of notable victories. In 1974, the American Psychiatric

Association stopped classifying homosexuality as a mental disorder. Gays fought hard in cities and states for laws forbidding discrimination against homosexuals in housing and employment, and in 1980, they finally succeeded in getting a gay rights plank in the Democratic National Platform.

In the 1980s, the onset of the AIDS epidemic forced the gay liberation movement on the defensive. Stung by the accusation that AIDS was a "gay disease," male homosexuals faced new public condemnation at a time when they were trying desperately to care for the growing number of victims of the disease within their ranks. The gay organizations formed in the 1970s to win new rights now were channeling their energies into caring for the ill, promoting safe sex practices, and fighting for more public funding to help conquer AIDS. In 1986, ACT UP (AIDS Coalition to Unleash Power) began a series of violent demonstrations in an effort to shock the nation into doing more about AIDS.

The movement also continued to stimulate gay consciousness in the 1980s. In 1987, an estimated 600,000 gays and lesbians took part in a march on Washington on behalf of gay rights. Every year afterward, gay groups held a National Coming Out Day in October to encourage homosexuals to proclaim proudly their sexual identity. In a more controversial move, some gay leaders encouraged "outing"—releasing the names of prominent homosexuals, primarily politicians and movie stars, in an effort to make the nation aware of how many Americans were gay or lesbian. Gay leaders claimed there were more than twenty million gays and lesbians in the nation. A sociological survey released in the spring of 1993 contradicted those numbers, finding only 1.1 percent of American males exclusively homosexual. Whatever the actual number, it was clear by the 1990s that gays and lesbians formed a significant minority that had succeeded in forcing the nation, however grudgingly, to respect its rights.

There was one battle, however, in which victory eluded the gay liberation movement. In the 1992 election, Democratic candidate Bill Clinton promised to end the ban on homosexuals in the military. In his first days in office, however, President Clinton stirred up great resistance in the Pentagon and Congress when he tried to issue an executive order forbidding such discrimination. The Joint Chiefs of Staff and many Democrats warned that acceptance of gays and lesbians would destroy morale and seriously weaken the armed forces. Clinton finally settled for the Pentagon's compromise "Don't ask, don't tell" policy that would permit homosexuals to continue serving in the military as they had in the past as long as they did not reveal their sexual preference and refrained from homosexual conduct. However disappointed gays and lesbians were in Clinton's retreat, their leaders understood that the real problem was the resistance of mainstream America to full acceptance of homosexuality.

Public attitudes toward gays and lesbians seemed to be changing in the 1990s, but the growing tolerance had definite limits. In a 1996 poll, 85 percent of those questioned believed that gays should be treated equally in the workplace, up from 76 percent in 1992. Violence against gays, however, continued, most notably in the 1998 fatal beating of Matthew Shepard, a 21-year-old gay college student, in Wyoming.

The issue of same-sex marriage came to a head at the end of the century. In 1996, President Clinton signed the Defense of Marriage Act, which decreed that states did not have to recognize same-sex marriages performed elsewhere. But in 2000, following a state supreme court ruling, the Vermont legislature legalized "civil unions" between individuals of the same sex, enabling gays and lesbians to receive all the legal benefits available to married couples. Overall, the American people appeared to be inclined to oppose discrimination against gays and lesbians, while they still refused to sanction the practice of homosexuality.

POLITICS AFTER WATERGATE

The energy crisis and the economic dislocations of the mid-1970s could not have come at a worse time. Watergate had a paralyzing impact on the American political system. An awareness that the Cold War had led to an imperial presidency created a growing demand to weaken the power of the president and strengthen congressional authority. The result was increasing tension between the White House and Capitol Hill, preventing the strong, effective leadership needed to meet the unprecedented problems of the 1970s.

THE FORD ADMINISTRATION

Gerald R. Ford had the distinction of being the first president who had not been elected to national office. Richard Nixon had appointed him to the vice presidency to succeed Spiro Agnew, who had been forced to resign in order to avoid prosecution for accepting bribes while he was governor of Maryland. Ford, an amiable and unpretentious Michigan congressman who had risen to the post of House minority leader, seemed ready to restore public confidence in the presidency when he replaced Nixon in August 1974.

Ford's honeymoon lasted only a month. On September 8, 1974, he shocked the nation by announcing he had granted Richard Nixon a full and unconditional pardon for all federal crimes he may have committed. Some critics charged darkly that Nixon and Ford had made a secret bargain; others pointed out how unfair it was for Nixon's aides to serve their prison terms while the chief criminal went free. Ford apparently acted in an effort to end the bitterness over

Watergate, but his attempt backfired, eroding public confidence in his leadership and linking him indelibly with the scandal.

Ford soon found himself fighting an equally difficult battle on behalf of the beleaguered CIA. The Watergate scandal and the Vietnam fiasco had eroded public confidence in the government and lent credibility to a startling series of disclosures about past covert actions. The president allowed the CIA to confirm some of the charges, and then he made things worse by blurting out to the press the juiciest item of all: the CIA had been involved in plots to assassinate foreign leaders. Senate and House select committees appointed to investigate the CIA now focused on the assassination issue, eventually charging that the agency had been involved in no less than eight separate attempts to kill Fidel Castro.

In late 1975, President Ford finally moved to limit the damage to the CIA. He appointed George Bush, then a respected former Republican congressman, as the agency's new director and gave him the authority both to reform the CIA and to strengthen its role in shaping national security policy. Most notably, Ford issued an executive order outlawing assassination as an instrument of American foreign policy.

Ford proved less successful in his dealings with Congress on other issues. Though he prided himself on his good relations with members of both houses, he opposed Democratic measures such as federal aid to education and control over strip mining. In a little more than a year, he vetoed thirty-nine separate bills. In fact, Ford, who as a congressman had opposed virtually every Great Society measure, proved far more conservative than Nixon in the White House.

THE 1976 CAMPAIGN

Ford's lackluster record and the legacy of Watergate made the Democratic nomination a prize worth fighting for in 1976. A large field of candidates entered the contest, but a virtual unknown, former Georgia governor James Earl Carter, quickly became the front-runner. Aware of the voters' disgust with politicians of both parties, Jimmy Carter ran as an outsider, portraying himself as a Southerner who had no experience in Washington and one who could thus give the nation fresh and untainted leadership.

Carter swept through the primaries and won the Democratic nomination easily, naming Senator Walter Mondale of Minnesota as his running mate. The polls gave Carter a 33-point lead when the campaign began, but he quickly lost ground as he began to hedge on the issues. President Ford counterattacked, but hurt his cause by misspeaking in a televised debate. Responding to a question about Iron Curtain countries, he declared, "There is no Soviet domination of eastern Europe."

THE ELECTION OF 1976

CANDIDATE	PARTY	POPULAR VOTE	ELECTORAL VOTE
Jimmy Carter	Democratic	40,830,763	297
Gerald Ford	Republican	39,147,793	240

Carter won an extremely narrow victory in 1976. Despite Watergate and Ford's weak record, the Democratic candidate took only 49.98 percent of the popular vote. Ford swept nearly the entire West, but Carter carried the South and key northern industrial states. The outcome turned on class and racial factors. "The affluent, the well-educated, the suburbanites largely went for Ford," commented one observer, "the socially and economically disadvantaged for Carter." The black vote clinched the victory for the Democrats. Carter received more than 90 percent of the votes of African Americans, and their ballots provided the margin of victory in Ohio, Pennsylvania, and seven southern states.

DISENCHANTMENT WITH CARTER

The new president, described by an associate as "superficially self-effacing but intensely shrewd," was an ambitious and intelligent politician. He had a rare gift for sensing what people wanted and appearing to give it to them. Liberals thought he clearly stood with them; conservatives were equally convinced he was on their side. He was especially adept at utilizing symbols. He emerged from airplanes carrying his own garment bag; after his inauguration, he walked up Pennsylvania Avenue hand in hand with his wife Rosalynn and daughter Amy. "Look," he seemed to be saying, "I am just an ordinary citizen who happens to be in the White House."

The substance, however, failed to match the style. He had no discernible political philosophy, no clear sense of direction. He sought the White House convinced that he was brighter and better than his competitors, but once there, he had no cause or mission to fulfill.

The makeup of his administration reflected the conflicting tendencies that would eventually prove destructive. In the White House, he surrounded himself with close associates from Georgia, fellow outsiders such as presidential adviser Hamilton Jordan and press secretary Jody Powell. Yet he picked established Democrats for key cabinet positions: Cyrus Vance, a New York lawyer, as secretary of state; and Joseph Califano, a former aide to Lyndon Johnson, to head Health, Education, and Welfare. In the lower ranks, however, he selected liberal activists, people who were intent on regulating business and preserving the environment. The result was bound to be tension and conflict, as the White House staff and the federal bureaucracy worked at cross-purposes, one group seeking change while the other attempted to protect the president.

Lacking both a clear set of priorities and a coherent political philosophy, the Carter administration had little chance to succeed. The president strove hard for a balanced budget but was forced to accept mounting deficits. Federal agencies fought to save the environment and help consumers but served only to anger industry.

In the crucial area of social services, Joseph Califano failed repeatedly in his efforts to carry out long-overdue reforms. His attempts to overhaul the nation's welfare program, which had become a $30 billion annual operation serving some thirty million Americans, won little support from the White House. Carter's unwillingness to take the political risks involved in revamping the overburdened Social Security system by reducing benefits and raising the retirement age blocked Califano's efforts.

Informed by his pollsters in 1979 that he was losing the nation's confidence, Carter sought desperately to redeem himself. He gave a speech in which he seemed to blame his failure on the American people, accusing them of creating "a crisis of confidence . . . that strikes at the very heart and soul and spirit of our national will." Then, a week after what his critics termed the "national malaise" speech, he requested the resignation of Califano and the secretary of the treasury. But neither the attempt to pin responsibility on the American people nor the firing of cabinet members could hide the fact that Carter, despite his good intentions and hard work, had failed to provide the bold leadership the nation needed.

FROM DÉTENTE TO RENEWED COLD WAR

America's political position in the world declined sharply in the 1970s. In part, the fault was internal. The Vietnam War left the American people convinced that the nation should never again intervene abroad, and Watergate discredited strong presidential leadership, shifting power over foreign policy to Congress. The new national consensus was symbolized by the War Powers Act, passed in 1973, which required the president to consult with Congress before sending American troops into action overseas. At the same time, external events and developments, notably the control over oil exercised by OPEC and the threats posed by revolutionary nationalism in the Middle East and Latin America, further weakened

American foreign policy. No longer able to dominate the international scene, the United States began to play the role of spectator, and at times even of victim.

RETREAT IN ASIA

It was Gerald Ford's fate to reap where Nixon had sown. In 1974, Congress cut in half the administration's request for $1.4 billion in military aid to South Vietnam. A year later, when a North Vietnamese offensive proved surprisingly successful, Ford was unable to get Congress to grant any additional aid. Bereft of American assistance, the South Vietnamese government was unable to stop the advance on Saigon in April 1975. American forces concentrated on evacuating 150,000 loyal South Vietnamese, but many more were left behind when the last helicopter left the roof of the embassy in Saigon. After a quarter century of futile effort, the United States finally had to admit defeat in the nation's longest and most humiliating foreign war.

Less than a month later, Ford had a chance to remind the world of American power. The Khmer Rouge government of Cambodia seized an American freighter, the *Mayaguez,* and imprisoned its crew. Ford authorized an armed attack on Cambodia by two thousand marines from bases in Thailand. By the time the

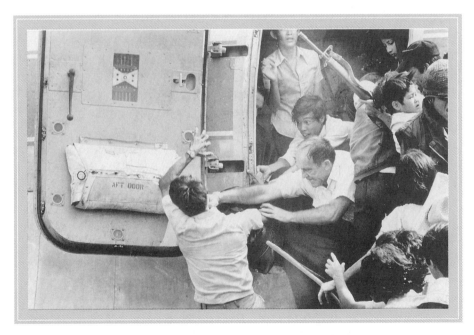

An American official punches a man trying to board a plane already overloaded with refugees during the chaotic evacuation of the city of Nha Trang in South Vietnam in the spring of 1975. Just after this plane left, communist troops took over the city.

American forces landed on a small offshore island, Cambodia had freed the crewmen. The nation took pride in the president's resort to force, but forty Americans paid for his decision with their lives.

ACCOMMODATION IN LATIN AMERICA

President Carter was more successful than Ford in adjusting to the growing nationalism in the world, particularly in Central America, where the United States had imposed order for most of the twentieth century by backing reactionary regimes.

The first test came in Panama. Resentment over American ownership of the Panama Canal had led Lyndon Johnson to enter into negotiations aimed at the eventual return of the waterway to Panama. Carter completed the long diplomatic process in 1977 by signing two treaties. One restored sovereignty in the 500-square-mile Canal Zone to Panama, while the other provided for gradual Panamanian responsibility for operating the canal, with appropriate safeguards for its use and defense by the United States. In negotiating the treaties, Carter was trying both to right an ancient wrong and to create stability in a highly volatile region.

The real struggle over the treaties took place in the Senate. Conservative Republicans expressed outrage over what they termed a "giveaway" of the Panama Canal. Intensive personal lobbying by President Carter, as well as bipartisan support from influential Republicans such as Gerald Ford and Henry Kissinger, finally led to Senate ratification with just one vote to spare, thus paving the way for the return of the canal to Panama by the year 2000.

Carter was less successful, however, in dealing with a growing problem of left-wing uprisings in Central America. In mid-1979, dictator Anastasio Somoza capitulated to the Sandinista forces in Nicaragua. Despite American attempts to moderate the Sandinista revolution, the new regime moved steadily to the left, developing close ties with Castro's Cuba. In neighboring El Salvador, a growing leftist insurgency against a repressive regime put the United States in an awkward position. Carter tried to use American economic aid to encourage the military junta in El Salvador to carry out democratic reforms. But after the guerrillas launched a major offensive in January 1981, he authorized large-scale military assistance to the government for its war against the insurgents, setting a precedent for the future.

THE QUEST FOR PEACE IN THE MIDDLE EAST

The inconclusive results of the 1973 October War gave Henry Kissinger the opportunity to play the role of peacemaker in the troubled Middle East. Shuttling back and forth between Cairo and Jerusalem, and then to Damascus, the secre-

A highlight of Carter's presidency was his role in helping negotiate the Camp David accords between Israeli Prime Minister Menachem Begin (right) and Egyptian President Anwar Sadat (left). The agreements set the stage for a peace treaty between Israel and Egypt.

tary of state finally succeeded in arranging a pullback of Israeli forces in both the Sinai and the Golan Heights. Although he failed to achieve his goal of an Arab-Israeli settlement, Kissinger had succeeded in demonstrating that the United States could play the role of neutral mediator between the Israelis and Arabs.

In November 1977, Egyptian president Anwar Sadat stunned the world by traveling to Jerusalem in an effort to reach agreement directly with Israel. The next year, President Carter invited both Sadat and Israeli prime minister Menachem Begin to negotiate under his guidance at Camp David. For thirteen days, Carter met with Sadat and Begin, finally emerging with the ambiguous Camp David accords. A framework for negotiations rather than an actual peace settlement, the Camp David agreements dealt gingerly with the problem of Palestinian autonomy in the West Bank and Gaza Strip areas. In 1979, Israel and Egypt signed a peace treaty that provided for the gradual return of the entire Sinai to Egypt but left the fate of the Palestine Arabs vague and unsettled.

Any sense of progress in the Middle East as a result of Camp David was quickly offset in 1979 with the outbreak of the Iranian Revolution. Under Nixon

Iranian demonstrators, atop the U.S. embassy in Teheran, burn an American flag. The violent actions and virulent anti-Americanism of the Iranians shocked U.S. citizens.

and Kissinger, the United States had come to depend heavily on the shah and his powerful army for defense of the vital Persian Gulf. Carter continued the close relationship with the shah, despite growing signs of domestic discontent with his leadership. By 1978, Iran was in chaos as the exiled Ayatollah Ruholla Khomeini led a fundamentalist Muslim revolt against the shah.

Unaware of the deep resentment most Iranians felt toward the shah, the Carter administration misjudged the nature of the Iranian Revolution. When the shah decided to leave the country in January 1979, Carter tried to work with a moderate regime rather than encourage an army coup. With Khomeini's return from exile, Muslim militants quickly came to power in Teheran. In October 1979, Carter permitted the exiled shah to enter the United States for medical treatment. Irate mobs in Iran denounced the United States, and on November 4, militants seized the U.S. embassy in Teheran and took fifty-eight Americans prisoner.

The prolonged hostage crisis revealed the extent to which American power had declined in the 1970s. Carter relied first on diplomacy and economic reprisals in a vain attempt to free the hostages. In his State of the Union message in January 1980, the president enunciated a new Carter doctrine, telling the world the United States would fight to protect the vital oil supplies of the Persian Gulf. "Twin threats to the flow of oil—from regional instability and now potentially from the Soviet Union—require that we firmly defend our vital interest when threatened."

Carter was unable to back up his brave words with meaningful action. In April 1980, the president authorized a desperate rescue mission that ended in failure when several helicopters broke down in the Iranian desert. The mission was aborted, an accident cost the lives of eight crewmen, and Secretary of State Cyrus Vance—who had opposed the rescue attempt—resigned in protest. The hostage crisis dragged on through the summer and fall of 1980, a symbol of American weakness that proved to be a powerful political handicap to Carter in the upcoming presidential election.

THE COLD WAR RESUMES

The policy of détente was already in trouble when Carter took office in 1977. Congressional refusal to relax trade restrictions on the Soviet Union had doomed Kissinger's attempts to win political concessions from the Soviets through economic incentives. The Kremlin's repression of the growing dissident movement and its harsh policy restricting the emigration of Soviet Jews had caused many Americans to doubt the wisdom of seeking accommodation with the Soviet Union.

President Carter's emphasis on human rights appeared to the Russians to be a direct repudiation of détente. In his inaugural address, Carter reaffirmed his concern over the mistreatment of human beings anywhere in the world, declaring that "our commitment to human rights must be absolute." It was easier said than done. Carter did withhold aid from authoritarian governments in Chile and Argentina, but equally repressive regimes in South Korea and the Philippines continued to receive generous American support. The Soviets, however, found even an inconsistent human rights policy to be threatening, particularly after Carter received Soviet exiles in the White House.

Zbigniew Brzezinski, Carter's national security adviser, worked from the outset to reverse the policy of détente. Commenting that he was "the first Pole in three hundred years in a position to really stick it to the Russians," he favored confrontation with the Kremlin. Although Carter signed a SALT II treaty with Russia in 1979, lowering the ceiling on nuclear delivery systems to 2250, growing opposition in the Senate played directly into Brzezinski's hands. He prevailed on the president to advocate adoption of a new MX missile to replace the existing Minuteman ICBMs, which some experts thought were now vulnerable to a Soviet first strike. This new weapons system ensured that regardless of SALT, the nuclear arms race would be speeded up in the 1980s.

Brzezinski also was successful in persuading the president to use China to outmaneuver the Soviets. On January 1, 1979, the United States and China exchanged ambassadors, thereby completing the reconciliation that Nixon had begun in 1971. The new relationship between Beijing and Washington presented the Soviet Union with the problem of a link between its two most powerful enemies.

The Cold War, in abeyance for nearly a decade, resumed with full fury in December 1979 when the Soviet Union invaded Afghanistan. Although this move was designed to ensure a regime friendly to the Soviet Union, it appeared to many like the beginning of a Soviet thrust toward the Indian Ocean and the Persian Gulf. Carter responded to this aggression with a series of symbolic acts: the United States banned the sale of high technology to Russia, embargoed the export of grain, and even boycotted the 1980 Moscow Olympics. These American moves did not halt the invasion of Afghanistan; instead, they put the United States and Russia back on a collision course.

The results doomed détente. Aware that he could not get a two-thirds vote in the Senate, Carter withdrew the SALT II treaty. The hopeful phrases of détente gave way to belligerent rhetoric. Jimmy Carter, who had come into office hoping to advance human rights and control the nuclear arms race, now found himself a victim of the renewed Cold War.

National frustration over the hostages in Iran and the Soviet invasion of Afghanistan, coupled with anxiety over the energy crunch and rampant inflation, eroded public confidence in the Carter administration. A leader who had benefited from Vietnam and Watergate had now been betrayed by events. Despite his substantial achievements—the Camp David agreements, the Panama Canal treaties—Carter had to take the blame for developments overseas that were beyond his control. By mid-1980, the president's overall approval rating had fallen to 23 percent in the Gallup poll. The American people, disillusioned by the failures of Nixon, Ford, and Carter, yearned for new political leadership to meet the challenges facing the nation at home and abroad.

32

THE REPUBLICAN RESURGENCE, 1980–1992

In October 1964, the Republican National Committee sponsored a televised address by Hollywood actor Ronald Reagan on behalf of Barry Goldwater's presidential candidacy. Reagan's speech had originally been aired on a Los Angeles station; the resulting outpouring of praise and campaign contributions led to its national rebroadcast.

In contrast to Goldwater's strident rhetoric, Reagan used relaxed, confident, and persuasive terms to put forth the case for a return to individual freedom. Instead of the usual choice between increased government activity and less government involvement, often couched in terms of the left and the right, Reagan presented the options of either going up or down—"up to the maximum of human freedom consistent with law and order, or down to the ant heap of totalitarianism." Then, borrowing a phrase from FDR, he told his audience: "You and I have a rendezvous with destiny. We can preserve for our children this the last best hope of man on earth, or we can sentence them to take the first step into a thousand years of darkness."

Although the speech did not rescue Goldwater's unpopular candidacy, it marked the beginning of Ronald Reagan's remarkable political career. A popular Hollywood actor whose movie career had begun to fade in the 1950s, Reagan had become an effective television performer as host of "The General Electric Theater." His political views, once liberal, moved steadily to the right as he became a spokesperson for a major American corporation. In 1965, a group of wealthy friends persuaded him, largely on the basis of the success of "the speech," to run for the California governorship.

Reagan proved to be an attractive candidate. His friendly, relaxed manner and his mastery of television enabled him to present his strongly conservative message without appearing to be a rigid ideologue of the right. He won handily by appealing effectively to rising middle-class suburban resentment over high taxes, expanding welfare programs, and bureaucratic regulation.

In two terms as governor, Reagan displayed natural ability as a political leader. Instead of insisting on implementing all of his conservative beliefs, he proved surprisingly flexible. Symbolic victories were his specialty; in one example he managed to confront campus radicals and fire Clark Kerr, chancellor of the University of California, while at the same time generously funding higher education.

By the time Reagan left the governor's office in 1974, many signs pointed to a growing conservative mood across the nation. In a popular rebellion against escalating property taxes in 1978, California's voters passed Proposition 13, which called for a 57 percent cut in taxes and resulted in a gradual reduction in social services. Religious leaders were especially outraged over the 1962 Supreme Court

Ronald Reagan appears with Rev. Jerry Falwell at a Moral Majority rally in Dallas, Texas, in 1980. Falwell's Moral Majority and other similar evangelical groups endorsed conservative positions on a variety of issues, including abortion and school prayer. In his two presidential election campaigns, Reagan vigorously sought the support of Falwell's followers.

ruling in *Engel* v. *Vitale* outlawing school prayer. In the South, where daily prayers were the customary way of beginning the school day, the reaction was intense. One Alabama congressman denounced the Supreme Court justices, proclaiming, "They put the Negroes in the schools and now they're driving God out."

Concern over school prayer, along with rising abortion and divorce rates, impelled religious groups to engage in political activity to defend what they viewed as traditional family values. Jerry Falwell, a successful Virginia radio and television evangelist, founded the Moral Majority, a fundamentalist group dedicated to preserving the "American way of life."

The population shift of the 1970s, especially the rapid growth of the Sunbelt region in the South and West, added momentum to the conservative upsurge. Those moving to the Sunbelt tended to be white, middle- and upper-class suburbanites who were attracted both by economic opportunity and by a political climate stressing low taxes, less government regulation, and more reliance on the marketplace. The political impact of population shifts from East to West and North to South during the 1970s was reflected in the congressional gains (seventeen seats) by Sunbelt and Far West states after the 1980 census.

Conservatives also succeeded, for the first time since World War II, in making their cause intellectually respectable. Scholars and academics on the right flourished in new "think tanks." Neoconservatism, led by Norman Podhoretz's magazine *Commentary*, became fashionable among many intellectuals who were former liberal stalwarts. They denounced liberals for being too soft on the communist threat abroad and too willing to compromise high standards at home in the face of demands for equality from African Americans, women, and the disadvantaged.

By the end of the 1970s, Ronald Reagan was recognized as the nation's most effective leader of the conservative resurgence. His personal charm softened the hard edges of his right-wing call to arms, and his conviction that America could regain its traditional self-confidence by reaffirming basic ideals had a broad appeal to a nation shaken by inflation at home and humiliation abroad. In 1976, Reagan had barely lost to Gerald Ford at the Republican convention; four years later, he overcame an early upset by George Bush in Iowa to win the GOP presidential nomination handily.

In his acceptance speech at the Republican convention in Detroit, he set forth the themes that endeared him to conservatives—less government, balanced budget, family values, and peace through increased military spending. Reagan offered reassurance and hope for the future. He spoke of restoring to the federal government "the capacity to do the people's work without dominating their lives." In Ronald Reagan, the Republicans had found the perfect candidate to exploit both the American people's frustration with the failures in domestic and foreign policy of the 1970s and the growing conservative mood of the nation.

California members of Reagan Youth finish a sign in support of their candidate to be used at the 1980 Republican National Convention in Detroit.

REAGAN IN POWER

The liberal Democratic political coalition, originally created by Franklin D. Roosevelt in the Great Depression, finally split apart by the end of the 1970s. The Watergate scandal gave the Democrats a brief reprieve, but by the end of the decade, the Republicans were using the conservative upsurge to make inroads among such traditionally Democratic groups of voters as Jews, Southerners, and blue-collar workers. Yet the continuing appeal of the New Deal legacy prevented a total political realignment.

THE REAGAN VICTORY

In 1980, Jimmy Carter, who had used the Watergate trauma to win the presidency, found himself in trouble. Inflation, touched off by the second oil shock of the 1970s, reached double-digit figures. The Federal Reserve Board's effort to tighten the money supply had led to a recession. What Ronald Reagan dubbed the "misery index," the combined rate of inflation and unemployment, hit 28 percent early in 1980 and stayed above 20 percent throughout the year.

Foreign policy proved almost as damaging to Carter. The Soviet invasion of Afghanistan eroded hopes for continued détente; the hostage crisis in Iran highlighted the nation's sense of helplessness. In the short run, Carter used that crisis to beat back the challenge to his renomination by Senator Edward Kennedy. The Democrats rallied behind Carter, although the delegates to the party's convention displayed a notable lack of enthusiasm in renominating him.

Ronald Reagan and his running mate, George Bush, hammered away at the state of the economy and the world. Reagan scored heavily among traditionally Democratic blue-collar groups by blaming Carter for inflation. Reagan also accused Carter of allowing the Soviets to outstrip the United States militarily and promised a massive buildup of American forces if he was elected. Although Republican strategists feared Carter might spring an "October surprise"—a negotiated release of the American hostages at the height of the campaign—the Iranian situation actually helped Reagan by accentuating U.S. weakness in the world.

The president struck back by claiming that Reagan was too reckless to conduct American foreign policy in the nuclear age. The attack backfired. In a televised debate arranged late in the campaign, Reagan assured the American people of his devotion to peace, leaving Carter with the onus of trying to land a low blow. At the end of the confrontation, Reagan scored impressively when he summed up the country's dire economic condition by suggesting that voters ask themselves simply, "Are you better off now than you were four years ago?"

On election day, the American people answered with a resounding "no." Reagan carried forty-four states and gained 51 percent of the popular vote. Carter won only six states and 41 percent of the popular vote. Reagan clearly benefited from the growing political power of the Sunbelt; he carried every state west of the Mississippi except Minnesota. In the South, Reagan lost only Georgia, Carter's home state. Even more impressive were Reagan's inroads into the old New Deal coalition. He received 50.5 percent of the blue-collar vote and 46 percent of the Jewish vote, the best showing by a Republican since 1928. Only one group remained loyal to Carter: African American voters gave him 85 percent of their ballots.

THE ELECTION OF 1980

CANDIDATE	PARTY	POPULAR VOTE	ELECTORAL VOTE
Reagan	Republican	43,899,248	489
Carter	Democratic	35,481,435	49
Anderson	Independent	5,719,437	—
	Minor Parties	921,299	—

Republican gains in Congress were even more surprising. For the first time since 1954, the GOP gained control of the Senate, 53 to 46, and the party picked up 33 seats in the House to narrow the Democratic margin from 114 to 50.

The meaning of the election was less clear than its outcome. Nearly all observers agreed that the voters had rendered an adverse judgment on the Carter administration. But most experts did not assess the outcome to be a major realignment in American politics equivalent to the Democratic victory of FDR in 1932. The fact that the Democrats still held a sizable majority in the House was seen as proof of their party's continuing strength. Political scientist Walter Dean Burnham termed the result "a conservative revitalization," but one that stopped short of making the GOP the dominant party.

Journalist Theodore White disagreed, viewing the outcome as a repudiation of the Democratic coalition that had dominated American politics since the days of Franklin D. Roosevelt and the New Deal. White had a strong case. In the eight presidential elections from 1952 to 1980, Republican candidates received 52.3 percent of the popular vote, compared to 47.7 percent for the Democrats; Republicans won four elections (1952, 1956, 1972, and 1980) comfortably, one (1968) narrowly, and lost two close races (1960 and 1976). Only in 1964 did the Republicans lose by a wide margin. Reagan's victory in 1980 thus marked the culmination of a Republican presidential realignment that ended a half-century of Democratic dominance.

CUTTING SPENDING AND TAXES

When Ronald Reagan took office in January 1981, the ravages of inflation had devastated the economy. Interest rates hovered near 20 percent, while the value of the dollar, compared to 1960, had dropped to just 36 cents. The new president blamed what he termed "the worst economic mess since the Great Depression" on high federal spending and excessive taxation. "Government is not the solution to our problems," Reagan announced in his inaugural address, "government is the problem."

The president embraced the concept of supply-side economics as the proper remedy for the nation's economic ills. Supply-side economists believed that the private sector, freed of the ever increasing burden of government spending, would shift its resources from tax shelters to productive investment, leading to an economic boom that would provide enough new income to offset the lost revenue. Although many other economists worried that the 30 percent cut in income taxes that Reagan favored would lead to staggering deficits, the president was confident that his program would both stimulate the economy and reduce the role of government.

In pursuing his economic goals, Reagan relied primarily on the director of the Office of Management and Budget, David Stockman. A former Michigan congressman who had become a convert to supply-side economics, Stockman was charged with carrying out Reagan's policies of cutting government spending and sharply reducing taxes. At the same time, Reagan supported the efforts of Paul Volcker, the banker Carter had appointed to head the Federal Reserve Board, to stem inflation by restricting the money supply, and even appointed him to a second four-year term in 1983.

The president and his budget director made spending the first target. Quickly deciding not to attack such popular middle-class entitlement programs as Social Security and Medicare, and sparing critical social services for the "truly deserving needy," they concentrated on slashing $41.4 billion from the budget by cutting heavily into other social programs. Reagan used his charm and powers of persuasion to woo conservative Democrats from the West and South. Reagan won a commanding 253 to 176 margin of victory for his budget in the House, and an even more lopsided vote of 78 to 20 in the Senate in May. A jubilant Reagan told a Los Angeles audience that he had achieved "the greatest reduction in government spending that has ever been attempted."

The president proved equally successful in reducing taxes. He advocated a cut of 10 percent in personal income taxes for three consecutive years. When the Democrats countered with a two-year plan that would reduce taxes by only 15 percent, Reagan compromised with a proposal to cut taxes by 5 percent the first year but insisted on the full 10 percent reduction for the second and third years. In July, both houses passed the tax cut by impressive margins. In securing reductions in spending and lowering taxes, Reagan had demonstrated beyond any doubt his ability to wield presidential power effectively. As *Time* magazine commented, no president since FDR had "done so much of such magnitude so quickly to change the economic direction of the country."

LIMITING THE ROLE OF GOVERNMENT

Reagan met with only mixed success in his other efforts to restrict government activity and reduce federal regulation of the economy. Cutting back on the scope of federal agencies and limiting their impact on American business was a central tenet of the president's political philosophy. To the outrage of environmentalists, Secretary of the Interior James Watt opened up federal land to coal and timber production and made more than a billion acres of land available for offshore oil drilling. Though Watt was eventually forced to resign, the Reagan administration continued its policy of reducing government intervention in business long after Watt's departure.

The Professional Air Traffic Controllers' Organization (PATCO) was one of the few unions to support Reagan in the 1980 campaign. But when PATCO struck in August 1981, Reagan unhesitatingly fired the striking air traffic controllers and refused to rehire them when the strike collapsed.

Transportation Secretary Drew Lewis proved to be the most effective cabinet member in the administration's first two years. He helped relieve the troubled American automobile industry of many of the regulations adopted in the 1970s to reduce air pollution and increase passenger safety. At the same time, he played a key role in the behind-the-scenes negotiations that led Japan to agree in the spring of 1981 to restrict its automobile exports to the United States for the next three years.

Lewis gained notoriety in opposing a strike by the air traffic controllers' union (PATCO) in the summer of 1981. The president fired the striking workers, decertified the union, and ordered Lewis to hire and train thousands of new air traffic controllers at a cost of $1.3 billion. For the Reagan administration, the price was worth paying to prove that no group of government employees had the right to defy the public interest.

The Reagan administration was less successful in trying to cut back on the entitlement programs that it viewed as the primary cause of the growing budget deficits. Social Security was the greatest offender. A 500 percent increase in Social Security benefits in the 1970s threatened to bankrupt the system's trust fund by the end of the century. Reagan met a sharp rebuff when he tried to make substantial cuts in future benefits. The president then appointed a bipartisan commission to recommend ways to protect the system's endangered trust fund. In March 1983, Congress approved a series of changes that guaranteed the solvency of Social Security by gradually raising the retirement age, delaying cost-of-living increases for six months, and taxing pensions paid to the well-to-do elderly.

The administration's record in dealing with women's concerns and civil rights proved clumsy and divisive. Although feminist groups were disappointed by the administration's strong rhetorical attacks on legalized abortion, the appointment of Sandra Day O'Connor to the Supreme Court pleased them. His appointments to the lower federal courts were a better indication of his administration's relatively low regard for women and minorities. Of the first seventy-two Reagan nominees to the federal judiciary, only three were women; just one of the sixty-nine men was African American.

Chief Justice Warren Burger swears in Sandra Day O'Connor, the first woman to serve on the U.S. Supreme Court, in September 1981.

The administration's civil rights record proved especially revealing. Aware of how few African Americans had supported the GOP in 1980, Reagan made no effort to reward this group with government jobs or favors. Instead, the Justice Department actively opposed affirmative action measures that resulted in minority hiring quotas. The Republicans also failed to take the lead in renewing the original Voting Rights Act of 1965. After opposing key amendments designed to strengthen the historic legislation that had finally enabled African Americans to participate fully in southern politics, Reagan belatedly endorsed and signed a measure to extend the Voting Rights Act for twenty-five years.

REAGANOMICS

The sweeping reductions in domestic spending and income taxes that Reagan achieved in 1981 gave rise to conflicting economic expectations. Supply-side economists believed that the tax relief granted investors would lead to rapid business growth, which would raise more than enough new revenue to offset the lower rates. The administration's critics, on the other hand, were sure that heavy defense spending coupled with tax reductions would create massive deficits and result in economic stagnation. Neither group proved to be right.

RECESSION AND RECOVERY

The supply-side theory became the first economic casualty of the 1980s. The naive belief that a combination of cuts in social spending and sharply reduced taxes could unleash an economic boom that would avoid huge deficits was the victim of both Reagan's insistence on huge increases in defense spending and the Federal Reserve Board's tight-money policy. It was the latter that touched off a recession that began in the fall of 1981 and grew steadily worse throughout 1982, with unemployment reaching a postwar high of 10.4 percent in October.

Still, Reagan refused to give up his income tax cuts. With the first 10 percent reduction due to come in July 1982, he claimed that his policies had not yet been given a chance. But he did prove flexible in other ways, slightly moderating the defense buildup, accepting fewer cuts in social programs than he proposed, and finally agreeing to a $98 billion increase in miscellaneous federal taxes. He refused, however, to cancel the final 10 percent cut in income taxes due in mid-1983. Instead, he declared that all signs pointed to "a strong recovery."

Whether by design or good luck, the president's optimism proved justified. In the second quarter of 1983, the economy came to life. The final 10 percent tax cut in July stimulated consumer spending. The long-depressed automobile industry began to boom. The American people went on a great buying spree with consumer installment debt increasing as much in the first six months of 1983 as in all of 1982.

Best of all, inflation remained under control as the economy expanded. The cost of living dropped to 3.8 percent in 1983; at the same time, interest rates fell to 10.5 percent, enabling consumers to buy goods and corporations to expand their inventories much more easily. A combination of long-term Federal Reserve policy, the impact of the recession, and a worldwide decline in energy and food prices enabled the Reagan administration to take credit for solving the problem that had proved fatal for Carter and the Democrats.

THE GROWING DEFICIT

A new problem emerged in the mid-1980s to cloud Reagan's claims of economic recovery—the growing federal budget deficit. As the economy weakened and unemployment increased, tax revenues fell below projections while government spending on unemployment insurance and other social programs climbed. The deficit reached $207.8 billion in 1983, nearly triple the pre-Reagan high of $70.5 billion in 1976.

Some economists were predicting that at current spending and tax rates, the deficit would rise to more than $300 billion a year by the end of the decade. The result, many feared, would be soaring interest rates. In fact, a slumping world economy led to a massive infusion of foreign investment, which kept the prime rate from rising above 11 percent.

When the deficit continued to climb during the economic recovery of the mid-1980s, Congress finally came forward with what appeared to be a drastic solution. Republican senators Phil Gramm of Texas and Warren Rudman of New Hampshire joined with Democrat Ernest Hollings of South Carolina to set a series of budgetary ceilings designed to eliminate the deficit entirely by 1991. After considerable revision, the Balanced Budget Act, known as Gramm-Rudman, succeeded in halting the deficit spiral. The president and Congress were able to lower the deficit from a peak of $221 billion in 1986 to a more manageable $155 billion by 1988.

In essence, Gramm-Rudman was a political compromise. The price Reagan had to pay for Democratic help in resolving his budgetary crisis was to stop the increase in defense spending. But at the same time, by agreeing to sizable budget deficits for the next few years, the Democrats who controlled Congress had to give up any hope of expanding existing social programs or enacting new ones, such as a comprehensive national health plan.

Another alarming deficit—in the balance of overseas trade—also became an important issue in the mid-1980s. American exports had been falling steadily since the 1970s as a result of the decline in traditional manufacturing indus-tries—iron and steel, electronics, and automobiles. The Japanese had been the biggest gainers as they dominated the American market in consumer goods such as television sets and VCRs.

A sharp rise in the value of the dollar, beginning in 1983, accentuated the problem by making American goods too expensive in foreign markets. The result was a trade deficit that grew from a modest $31 billion in 1981 to an alarming $171 billion by 1987. The only way the United States could equalize the balance of international payments was to import even more capital from abroad. Led by the Japanese, foreign investors poured large sums into the United States. As a re-sult, in 1985, the United States, a creditor nation since World War I, suddenly be-came a debtor, owing the rest of the world more each year than it received from previous foreign investments. In late 1985, the Reagan administration joined with the governments of Japan and western Europe to devalue the dollar. The re-sulting decline in the dollar stimulated American exports and helped reduce the trade deficit to more manageable proportions by 1989.

In the 1980s, the American people had begun living beyond their means. Just as the government incurred large deficits rather than raising taxes to pay for the huge defense buildup, so consumers had cut back on personal saving in order to buy imported cars, television sets, and VCRs, encouraging further foreign invest-ment. By 1988, foreigners held $400 billion in U.S. Treasury securities, had in-vested another $300 billion in American industry, and owned 21 percent of the nation's banking assets. At the end of the decade, the American people were sending $60 billion a year overseas just to pay the interest on the public and pri-vate obligations. Reaganomics had succeeded in continuing America's traditional high standard of living, but at a very high price—massive borrowing that mort-gaged the nation's future.

THE RICH GROW RICHER

There were both gains and losses in the Reagan years. Inflation fell from double-digit levels by 1982 and averaged about 4 percent for the rest of the decade. A sharp drop in the world price of oil in late 1985 helped lower the trade deficit and brought inflation down to less than 2 percent.

After the end of the 1982 recession, employment grew steadily; by 1990, there were nearly nineteen million more Americans working than in 1980. There were losers as well, however. Blue-collar jobs declined as American industry, no-tably steel and autos, streamlined operations by closing obsolete plants and farm-ing out manufacturing to foreign producers with far lower labor costs. Companies that specialized in labor-intensive consumer products, such as Eastman Kodak and General Electric, virtually stopped all manufacturing in the

United States, concentrating instead on marketing and distributing goods made abroad to their specifications.

At the same time, however, the service sector expanded rapidly, especially the financial, transportation, and health-care industries. Accountants, lawyers, and technicians flourished, with women especially benefiting from the change from blue- to white-collar jobs. By 1990, nearly one in three workers was an executive, technician, or professional; only one in five worked in factories. Labor unions were especially hard hit; union membership dropped from 23 percent of the workforce in 1980 to 15.5 percent by 1992.

The most striking change in the decade was the growing inequality of wealth in America. In the five income categories used by the Census Bureau, the poorest 20 percent of Americans fared badly, dropping 6 percent in pretax income in the 1980s. The three middle groups gained about 5 percent. The top fifth did far better, increasing their incomes by 20 percent over the decade. The top 1 percent, the truly rich, did best of all, doubling their after-tax income in ten years.

The income disparity was the product of both economic restructuring and Republican tax policy. The decline in manufacturing meant that many assembly-line workers lost their jobs and were working for little more than the minimum wage in the service sector. At the same time, income tax cuts and adjustments reduced the top tax rate from 70 percent to 31 percent. A parallel increase in Social Security payroll taxes meant that by the end of the decade, the tax burden for a middle-class family was 37.3 cents of every dollar earned, compared to 35 cents for the wealthy.

The economic inequities of the 1980s were most clearly reflected in the transfer of actual wealth—housing, property, stocks, savings, and retirement accounts. Between 1983 and 1989, 55 percent of the gain in family wealth went to the top 0.5 percent of the population. The poor and the lower middle class actually lost $256 billion in assets during this boom period. By the end of the decade, the top fifth of the population owned 80 percent of the nation's entire household wealth.

REAGAN AFFIRMED

"Are you better off now than you were four years ago?" Reagan had asked voters at the end of his 1980 debate with Jimmy Carter. By the mid-1980s, he appeared to have delivered on his implicit promise to stem inflation and revive the stagnant American economy.

Despite the growing gap between the rich and the poor, Reagan could boast of impressive economic gains after weathering the 1982 recession. The recovery led to 16 million new jobs as the unemployment rate dropped back under 6 percent. Inflation remained low and median family income moved steadily upward.

The economic boom that began in 1983 came at just the right time for the Republican party. By early 1984, with personal income rising at an annual rate of 10.3 percent from January to June and unemployment shrinking rapidly, Democratic prospects dimmed for the presidential election. After a long, bruising primary battle, Walter Mondale, former Minnesota senator and Carter's vice president, won the Democratic nomination. In a bold break with tradition, he chose a woman as a running mate, Congresswoman Geraldine Ferraro of New York.

When the Republicans renominated Reagan and Bush, the campaign quickly came down to one issue: leadership. The GOP claimed that Reagan had overcome the problems that overwhelmed Carter, notably inflation at home and disrespect abroad. The president told voters they should reelect him: "You ain't seen nothin' yet."

Mondale and Ferraro, in contrast, accused Reagan of helping the rich at the expense of the poor, saddling future generations with huge deficits. In a surprise move, the Democratic candidate announced he intended to raise taxes to curb the deficit and then accused Reagan of harboring a "secret plan" to increase taxes himself.

These tactics failed to gain support; the outcome was a far greater Reagan victory than in 1980. With a solid base in the South and West, the president cut deeply into the normally Democratic states of the Northeast and the swing states of the Midwest to take the electoral votes of all but Minnesota and the District of Columbia. Exit surveys revealed that economic issues were uppermost in the minds of voters; in the midst of a strong economic recovery, Reagan won a majority among all voters earning more than $12,500 a year. More than two-thirds of the white male voters in the nation stood behind Reagan, who won even a majority of the blue-collar and women's votes. Of all the traditional Democratic groups, only African Americans proved loyal to the party, giving Mondale 90 percent of their votes.

The 1984 election was far more of a triumph for Reagan than for his party. In Congress, the GOP gained only fourteen seats, leaving the Democrats firmly in control of the House; in the Senate, the Republicans lost two places, narrowing

The Election of 1984

Candidate	Party	Popular Vote	Electoral Vote
Reagan	Republican	54,451,521	525
Mondale	Democratic	37,565,334	13

their majority to 54 to 46. Republicans were encouraged by a strong showing among the young, with Reagan taking 56 percent of the vote of the baby boomers (those aged 25 to 34) and 60 percent of the postboomers (those aged 18 to 24). The nation seemed to be dividing politically along economic lines, with the wealthy and affluent supporting the president while a growing underclass of African Americans, Hispanics, and the working poor were voting solidly Democratic. Middle-class Americans who held the balance revealed their mixed feelings by backing a Republican for president and Democratic candidates for the House and Senate.

REAGAN AND THE WORLD

Ronald Reagan was even more determined to reverse the course of American policy abroad than at home. He believed that under Carter, American prestige and standing in the world had dropped to an all-time low. Intent on restoring traditional American pride and self-respect, Reagan's mission was to strengthen America's defenses and recapture world supremacy from the Soviet Union.

In reality, the new president was simply continuing the hard line that Carter had begun to take after the invasion of Afghanistan. The Democrats had begun a massive military buildup in 1979 that included plans for cruise missiles in Europe, a rapid deployment force in the Middle East, and a 5 percent increase in the defense budget.

Under Reagan, the Pentagon flourished. Secretary of Defense Caspar Weinberger presented a plan that would more than double defense spending. The emphasis was on new weapons, ranging from the B-1 bomber to the expansion of the navy from 456 to 600 ships. Despite growing opposition in Congress, by 1985 the defense budget grew to more than $300 billion at the very time the administration was cutting back on domestic spending.

After some initial difficulty, Reagan proved more successful than Jimmy Carter in bringing harmony and order to the conduct of American foreign policy. His first secretary of state was Alexander Haig, a former general and White House chief of staff under Nixon. Haig, outspoken and assertive, tried to establish his primacy over the policymaking process, only to alienate the entire White House staff. Finally, in mid-1982, Reagan replaced Haig as secretary of state with George Shultz, a professional economist with extensive government experience, whose low-key and relaxed style brought an air of calm reassurance to the conduct of American foreign policy.

Despite the steady increase in defense spending and the formation of a smoothly functioning foreign policy team, Reagan soon found his diplomatic goals were more difficult to achieve than the budgetary and tax measures he had pushed through Congress so speedily. Yet in the long run, he could claim credit for a goal that had eluded his predecessors in the White House—the end of the Cold War.

CHALLENGING THE "EVIL EMPIRE"

The belief that the Soviet Union was a deadly enemy that threatened the well-being and security of the United States was the central tenet of Reagan's approach to foreign policy. He saw the Russians as bent on world revolution, ready "to commit any crime, to lie, to cheat" to advance their cause. Citing what he called a "record of tyranny," Reagan denounced the Russians before the UN in 1982.

Given this view of Russia as "the focus of evil in the modern world," it is not surprising that the new president continued the hard line that Carter had adopted after the invasion of Afghanistan. Abandoning détente, Reagan proceeded to implement a 1979 decision to place 572 Pershing II and cruise missiles in western Europe within range of Moscow to match Soviet deployment of medium-range missiles aimed at NATO countries. Despite strong protests from the Soviet Union, as well as growing uneasiness in Europe and an increasingly vocal nuclear freeze movement at home, the United States began putting the weapons in bases in Great Britain and Germany in November 1983. The Soviets, claiming the move gave them only ten minutes of warning time in case of an American attack, responded by breaking off disarmament negotiations in Geneva.

The nuclear arms race had now reached a more dangerous level than ever before. The United States stepped up research and development of the Strategic Defense Initiative (SDI), an antimissile system based on the use of lasers and particle beams to destroy incoming missiles in outer space. SDI was quickly dubbed "star wars" by the media. Critics doubted that SDI could be perfected, but they warned that even if it were, the result would be to escalate the arms race by forcing the Russians to build more offensive missiles in order to overcome the American defense system. The Reagan administration, however, defended star wars as a legitimate attempt to free the United States from the deadly trap of deterrence, with its reliance on the threat of nuclear retaliation to keep the peace.

TURMOIL IN THE MIDDLE EAST

Reagan tried to continue Carter's basic policy in the turbulent Middle East. In April 1982, the Israelis honored a Camp David pledge by making their final withdrawal from the Sinai. Reagan hoped to achieve the other Camp David objective of providing a homeland for the Palestinian Arabs on the West Bank, but Israel instead continued to extend Jewish settlements into the disputed area. The threat of the Palestine Liberation Organization (PLO), based in southern Lebanon and frequently raiding across the border into Israel, seemed to be the major obstacle to further progress.

On June 6, 1982, with tacit American encouragement, Israel invaded southern Lebanon in order to secure its northern border and destroy the PLO. The Reagan administration made no effort to halt the offensive but did join with France and Italy in sending a multinational force to permit the PLO to evacuate to Tunisia. Unfortunately, the United States soon became enmeshed in the Lebanese civil war, which had been raging since 1975. American marines, sent to Lebanon as part of the multinational force to restore order, were caught up in the renewed hostilities between Muslim and Christian militia.

In the face of growing congressional demands for the withdrawal of the marines, Reagan declared they were there to protect Lebanon from the designs of Soviet-backed Syria. But finally, after terrorists drove a truck loaded with explosives into the American barracks, killing 239 marines, the president had no choice but to pull out. The last American unit left Beirut in late February 1984. Despite his good intentions, Reagan had experienced a humiliation similar to Carter's in Iran—one that left Lebanon in shambles and the Arab-Israeli situation worse than ever.

CONFRONTATION IN CENTRAL AMERICA

Reagan faced a difficult situation in Central America. In an area marked by great extremes of wealth, with a small landowning elite and a mass of peasants mired in dire poverty, the United States sought moderate middle-class regimes to support. Washington usually ended up backing repressive right-wing dictatorships rather than the more leftist groups who raised the radical issues of land reform and redistribution of wealth. Yet it was often oppression by U.S.-supported regimes that drove those seeking political change to embrace revolutionary tactics.

This is precisely what happened in Nicaragua, where the Sandinista coalition finally succeeded in overthrowing the repressive Somoza regime in 1979. In an effort to strengthen the many middle-class elements in the original Sandinista government and to avoid forcing Nicaragua into the Cuban and Soviet orbit, Carter extended American economic aid.

The Reagan administration quickly reversed this policy. Alexander Haig cut off all aid to Nicaragua in the spring of 1981, accusing the Sandinistas of driving out the moderates and welcoming Cuban advisers and Soviet military assistance. The criticism became a self-fulfilling prophecy as Nicaragua became even more dependent on Cuba and the Soviet Union.

The United States and Nicaragua were soon on a collision course. In April 1983, President Reagan asked Congress for the money and authority to oust the

Sandinistas. When Congress, fearful of repeating the Vietnam fiasco, refused, Reagan opted for covert action. The CIA began supplying the Contras, exiles fighting against the Sandinistas from bases in Honduras and Costa Rica. The U.S.-backed rebels tried to disrupt the Nicaraguan economy, raiding villages, blowing up oil tanks, and even mining harbors. Then, in 1984, Congress passed the Boland Amendment prohibiting any U.S. agency from spending money in Central America. The withdrawal of U.S. financial backing left the Contras in a precarious position.

The situation proved little better in El Salvador where left-wing groups had been waging a guerrilla war against a reactionary regime dominated by wealthy landowners since the 1970s. Reagan stepped up support for a government headed by middle-of-the-roader José Napoleon Duarte. In 1984, Duarte was able to win a decisive election victory over the extreme right and began modest reforms in an effort to undercut the appeal of the guerrillas.

Reagan's only clear-cut triumph in the hemisphere came in the Caribbean. In October 1983, a military coup led to the death of the leftist prime minister of Grenada, who was subsequently replaced by an even more radical regime. The Reagan administration, already upset by Grenada's close ties to Cuba, decided to intervene to prevent the communists from acquiring a strategic military base.

Nearly two thousand U.S. marines invaded Grenada on October 25, 1983. After brief but spirited resistance from eight hundred Cuban workers and troops on the island, the American forces claimed a victory that cost eighteen lives. The administration proudly displayed pictures of captured Soviet arms to justify the resort to force; American medical students, shown on television kissing the ground as they returned to the United States, enabled the administration to label the operation a "rescue mission."

Aside from Grenada, however, the Reagan administration had little to show for its massive military buildup. In the Middle East, its well-intentioned use of marines had ended in disaster; its determined opposition to left-wing groups in Central America had at best achieved a stalemate. Relations with the Soviet Union had fallen into one of the deepest chills of the entire Cold War with the nuclear arms race more intense than ever.

TRADING ARMS FOR HOSTAGES

The Reagan administration's policies in the Middle East and Central America reached a tragic convergence in the Iran-Contra affair. In mid-1985, Robert McFarlane, a retired marine officer who had become national security adviser a year earlier, began a new initiative designed to restore American influence in the troubled Middle East. Concerned over the fate of six Americans held hostage in Lebanon by groups thought to be loyal to Iran's Ayatollah Khomeini, McFarlane

Despite Oliver North's questionable conduct, the public elevated him to near hero status during the televised Iran-Contra hearings. The bemedaled marine testified that he believed his deeds were justified as a defense of democracy.

proposed trading American antitank missiles to Iran in return for the hostages' release. The Iranians, desperate for weapons in the war they had been waging against Iraq since 1980, seemed willing to comply.

McFarlane soon found himself in over his head. He relied heavily on a young marine lieutenant colonel assigned to the National Security Council (NSC), Oliver North, and North in turn sought the assistance of CIA director William Casey. Casey saw the Iran initiative as an opportunity to use the NSC to mount the kind of covert operation denied the CIA under the post-1975 congressional oversight policy. By early 1986, when John Poindexter, a naval officer with little political experience, replaced a burned-out McFarlane as national security adviser, Casey was able to persuade the president, over the strenuous objections of both Secretary of State Shultz and Secretary of Defense Weinberger, to go ahead with shipments of TOW antitank missiles and HAWK antiaircraft missiles to Iran.

The concept of trading arms for hostages was fatally flawed. Although one hostage had been released after an initial shipment of antitank missiles to Iran by way of Israel, the shipments of additional TOWs directly from the United States, as well as HAWKs, had led to the release of only two more hostages. Meanwhile, terrorist groups in Iran had seized several more Americans; by

1987, nine Americans were being held hostage in Lebanon. As one observer commented, "As soon as Iran realized how highly we valued getting those hostages back, they apparently kept a good supply of hostages to ensure that we would do their bidding."

The arms deal with Iran was bad policy, but what came next was criminal. Ever since the Boland Amendment in late 1984 had cut off congressional funding, the Reagan administration had been searching for ways to supply the Contras in Nicaragua. In early 1986, Oliver North had what he later described as a "neat idea"—he could use the enormous profits from the sale of weapons to Iran to finance the Contras. North's ploy was clearly not only illegal but unconstitutional, since it meant usurping the congressional power of the purse.

Unlike the policy of trading arms for hostages, the diversion of the profits to the Contras was a closely held secret. Apparently, only North, Casey, and Poindexter were aware of the illegal activity until November 1986, when the press finally learned of the Iranian arms sales. North then hurriedly destroyed most of the incriminating documents, but he overlooked one key memo that revealed the Contra diversion.

The political fallout was very heavy. The administration, having learned from the Watergate cover-up, tried to control the damage by breaking the bad news itself. Every effort was made to protect President Reagan; Attorney General Edwin Meese blamed Poindexter and North, who both were dropped from the NSC. Despite these efforts to spare the president's reputation, a CBS–*New York Times* poll taken in December 1986 revealed that Reagan's popularity had dropped from 67 percent to 46 percent in just a month, the steepest decline ever recorded.

The vital question of whether Ronald Reagan had approved of the Contra diversion was never answered satisfactorily. A protracted congressional hearing in the summer of 1987 did little to clear up the confusion. Oliver North used his televised appearances to win public sympathy if not approval. Poindexter insisted under oath that he had never informed the president he and North had used the profits from arms sales to Iran to fund the Contras in defiance of Congress. The only other man who knew what had actually happened was William Casey; his death from a brain tumor in mid-1987 left the mystery unsolved.

While Reagan escaped the Iran-Contra affair without being held fully responsible for it, his presidency was in serious trouble. In Congress, the Democrats, who gained control of the Senate as well as the House in the 1986 elections, began to override his vetoes, reject his nominees, and bring a total halt to even humanitarian aid to the Contras. Ronald Reagan was still in the White House, but his reliance on others to conduct the affairs of state had robbed him of his power to lead the nation.

REAGAN THE PEACEMAKER

By the end of 1987, the president had made a remarkable recovery. Stepping into the foreign affairs arena, Reagan, with strong pressure from his wife, Nancy, shed his image as a hawk and set out to reverse the course of Soviet-American relations.

A momentous change in leadership in the Soviet Union proved fortunate. The illness and death of Leonid Brezhnev in 1982, followed in rapid succession by the deaths of two aged successors, led finally to the selection of Mikhail Gorbachev, a younger and more dynamic Soviet leader. Gorbachev was intent on improving relations with the United States as part of his new policy of *perestroika* (restructuring the Soviet economy) and *glasnost* (political openness). Soviet economic performance had been deteriorating steadily and the war in Afghanistan had become a major liability. Gorbachev needed a breathing spell in the arms

Reagan and Gorbachev in Red Square. During the summits between the two leaders, the American public grew to admire the Soviet premier for his policies of perestroika *("restructuring")* and glasnost *("openness").*

race and a reduction in Cold War tensions in order to carry out his sweeping changes at home.

The first meeting between Reagan and Gorbachev, at Geneva in 1985, went well, but it did not lead to any significant agreements. A hurried summit at Reykjavik, Iceland, in October 1986, just before the Iran-Contra affair had become public, nearly led to a historic breakthrough. Only Soviet insistence that Reagan cancel SDI blocked agreement on an ambitious proposal to abolish all nuclear weapons within a decade.

The apparent failure at Reykjavik, however, did not halt the new momentum toward peace; both leaders needed a foreign policy triumph too much not to continue the dialogue. Throughout 1987, experts worked out the details of an Intermediate Nuclear Forces agreement that promised to become the most significant disarmament achievement since SALT I in 1972. Meeting in Washington in December 1987, Reagan and Gorbachev agreed to remove and destroy all intermediate-range missiles and to permit on-site inspection to verify the process.

A fourth Reagan-Gorbachev summit in Moscow in mid-1988 did not achieve any further progress toward the goal of reducing the nuclear arsenals, but the pictures of Reagan and Gorbachev strolling amiably about Red Square in front of Lenin's tomb, saluting tourists, and taking turns kissing babies, gave rise to the hope that an end to the Cold War was finally in sight.

When Reagan returned home, his popularity soared to 70 percent, higher than it had been before the Iran-Contra affair. He had not only succeeded in making a major breakthrough in the nuclear arms race, but he could also claim that his policies had led to a moderation in Soviet behavior when Gorbachev moved to end the war in Afghanistan. The first Soviet units pulled out in April 1988, with the final evacuation due to be completed early the next year. By the time Reagan left office in January 1989, he had scored a series of foreign policy triumphs that offset the Iran-Contra fiasco and thus helped redeem his presidency.

SOCIAL DILEMMAS

Two complex social issues arose in the 1980s that stood in sharp contrast to the prevailing sense of well-being. A massive viral epidemic and a new drug crisis threatened the social fabric of the United States, yet President Reagan failed to respond promptly or effectively to either one; his successors in the White House, George Bush and Bill Clinton, would find the problems equally frustrating.

THE AIDS EPIDEMIC

The outbreak of AIDS (acquired immune deficiency syndrome) in the early 1980s took most Americans by surprise. Even health experts had difficulty grasping the nature and extent of the new public health threat. Doctors first noticed a few cases of a rare form of pneumonia and an unusual type of skin cancer in male patients in New York City and San Francisco in 1981. The Centers for Disease Control noted the phenomenon in a June 1981 bulletin, but it was several years before researchers finally identified it as a hitherto unknown human immunodeficiency virus (HIV). HIV apparently originated in Central Africa and spread to the United States, where it found its first victims primarily among gay men.

Initially, AIDS was perceived as a threat only to gay men. With a growing sense of urgency as the death toll mounted, gay men began to practice safer sex. It soon became clear, however, that AIDS could not be so easily contained. It began to appear among intravenous (IV) drug users who shared the same needles and eventually among hemophiliacs and others receiving frequent blood transfusions. The threat of a contaminated national blood supply terrified middle-class America.

Scientists tried to reassure the public by explaining that the virus could be spread only by the exchange of bodily fluids, primarily blood and semen, and not by casual contact. Controversy soon developed over proposals for mandatory blood tests for suspected HIV carriers and for the quarantine of AIDS victims. The integrity of hospital blood supplies caused the most realistic concern; in 1985, a new test finally gave reassurance that transfusions could be performed safely.

The Reagan administration proved slow and halting in its approach to the AIDS epidemic. The lack of sympathy for gays and a need to reduce the deficit worked against any large increase in health spending; what little money was devoted to AIDS went almost entirely for research rather than for educational measures to slow its spread.

While the administration dallied, the grim toll mounted. Because the average time between the initial HIV infection and the first symptoms of AIDS was five years and the delay could be as long as fourteen years, efforts at prevention had little immediate impact. In November 1983, there were 2803 known cases and 1416 deaths; by mid-1985, more than 12,000 cases and more than 6000 deaths had been reported.

Growing public concern finally led to action. In 1987, Ronald Reagan appointed a special presidential commission headed by Admiral James Watkins to study the AIDS epidemic. The Watkins report in 1988 criticized the administration's AIDS efforts as "inconsistent" and recommended a new effort that included antidiscrimination legislation and explicit prevention education. In the fall, Congress voted to spend $1.3 billion to fight AIDS, with much of the money going for confidential testing and counseling and home care for victims.

Despite the new efforts, the epidemic continued to grow. The U.S. Centers for Disease Control in Atlanta reported more than 200,000 cases at the end of

1991; the total had increased to more than 500,000 by mid-1996. By then, 345,000 AIDS victims had died, making it the leading cause of death for Americans aged 25 to 44.

The number of those infected with HIV appeared to be stabilizing by the mid-1990s at between 650,000 and 900,000. Yet what was once known as the "gay disease" had spread far beyond that one group in society by the end of the century. Minorities and the young were at greatest risk. African American youths made up two-thirds of the new HIV cases among people under 25.

The most encouraging development was a drop in the death rate from AIDS that began in the mid-1990s. Health officials attributed the decline to heavier spending on treatment and prevention and, above all, to powerful new drug combinations. The decline in deaths began to slow by the end of the decade, however, falling from 42 percent in 1997 to just 20 percent in 1998. The so-called AIDS cocktail was very expensive and did not work for everyone. "Too many people are still dying," warned one official, "and too many people are still getting infected." And even the possibility that the most deadly disease in history might be contained in the United States was offset by a growing realization that AIDS was threatening to decimate the population of Third World countries, especially in sub-Sahara Africa.

THE WAR ON DRUGS

The 1980s witnessed the rapid spread of cocaine use in America, leading to a growing sense of social crisis by the end of the decade. Cocaine had long been viewed as a relatively harmless recreational drug used by only a few people—rock musicians, Hollywood producers, and the very wealthy. By the end of the 1970s, the snorting of the pure white powder, distilled from the leaves of coca plants grown in the foothills of the Andes, had spread throughout the upper middle class. Bankers, lawyers, and doctors began to use it occasionally to achieve a moment of ecstasy. The costs, however, were very high—$100 for a few snorts and the danger of dying from an overdose or literally blowing one's mind. "Chronic cocaine use," warned one expert, "is the same as putting one's car in neutral with the brakes on and pressing the accelerator to the floor for hours—eventually, the engine will burn out." Nevertheless, the number of users reached more than four million by 1982.

In the mid-1980s, cocaine suddenly was perceived as a danger to American society. Moat ominous was the emergence of "crack," a cheap cocaine derivative that could be smoked in a pipe to give a very intense high. Dealers sold this new form of cocaine for as little as $10 a dose, opening up a vast new market among the poor in the urban ghettos. By 1986, an estimated 5.8 million people were using cocaine at least once a month, and more than 600,000 were confirmed addicts.

Despite its relatively low cost, crack led to an explosion of urban crime. The brief but intense high lasted only a few minutes, leading users to keep smoking more and forcing them to use ever larger amounts to achieve the by now indispensable euphoria. Needing as much as $1000 worth of crack each day to sustain their habits, users turned to crime to gain the necessary funds.

The Reagan administration tried several approaches to the problem posed by cocaine. In 1982, First Lady Nancy Reagan chose drug education as her special project. Using the slogan "Just say no," she urged schools, churches, and civic groups to inform young people about the dangers of cocaine. Her program helped educate the middle class but had little impact on crack smokers in the ghetto.

In the mid-1980s, the administration began to place greater emphasis on interdiction, using agents of the Drug Enforcement Agency, the Customs Bureau, and the Coast Guard to try to seal off the nation's borders. An international cartel of drug dealers, led by a group of Colombians, overcame this effort by saturating the nation with cocaine. In reality, the Reagan administration was unwilling to devote the personnel and resources that truly effective interdiction would require; with one eye on the deficit, Washington was content with a few highly publicized skirmishes in what it termed the war on drugs.

The very nature of the cocaine industry frustrated a third, and potentially most promising, countermeasure—wiping out the coca fields and processing plants in South America. The administration relied on diplomatic efforts in cooperation with the governments of Colombia, Bolivia, and Peru to curb the trade in cocaine, but with little success. South American farmers could make five times as much money growing coca leaves as food crops; it was estimated that Bolivia received $600 million a year in hard currency from the drug trade, compared to profits of only $400 million from tin and other legal exports.

By the time Ronald Reagan left office, the problem remained as serious as ever. Latin America was producing nearly 400 tons of cocaine a year, five times the amount consumed in the United States; the wholesale price of a kilogram of the white powder in Miami and Los Angeles had dropped from $50,000 to less than $15,000 between 1982 and 1987. A government report in mid-1989 claimed that overall use of drugs, including heroin and marijuana, had declined 25 percent since 1985, while the number of people using cocaine at least once a week had risen from 647,000 to 862,000.

Only one thing had changed dramatically—public awareness. A Gallup poll taken in the summer of 1989 showed that for the first time in recent history, the American people regarded illegal drugs as their greatest concern. Twenty-seven percent of those polled placed drugs highest on the national agenda, a result George Gallup found "virtually unprecedented."

Despite this new awareness, the efforts of the Bush administration proved no more successful than the Reagan program. An ambitious "Andean Strategy," funded at more than $2 billion, pledged American support for antidrug programs in Colombia, Bolivia, and Peru. Yet by 1992, coca leaf production had reached a record level of 336,300 tons, nearly three times as high as in 1984.

The Clinton administration proved equally unsuccessful in its two-part approach to the drug problem. One aspect of the new Democratic strategy was to focus primarily on trying to curtail drug use in the United States. But a reduced budget and the inherent difficulty in attacking the causes of drug addiction blocked any progress. By 1996, the number of Americans engaging in illicit drug use, primarily marijuana, had dropped to twelve million, but the number of heroin and cocaine users remained stable at about three million. More alarming was the dramatic increase in drug use among teenagers, climbing 80 percent between 1992 and 1996.

The other Clinton administration approach to the drug war was to focus its overseas efforts primarily on eradicating the source of cocaine in Colombia, Bolivia, and Peru. A presidential directive issued in November 1993 targeted foreign drug cartels as a "national security threat." The flow of drugs into the United States, however, continued unabated, with Mexico becoming the new pipeline, funneling an estimated 210 tons of cocaine to the United States in 1995. In 2000, the Clinton administration unveiled a plan to spend $1.3 billion on a massive effort to destroy drug cultivation in southern Colombia. The funds were to be used to supply Blackhawk helicopters to three battalions of American-trained Colombian drug-fighting troops and to cover the cost of relocating an estimated 10,000 plantation workers. By the turn of the century, it was clear that there was no end in sight to the war on drugs.

PASSING THE TORCH

Reagan's triumphal reelection in 1984 raised Republican hopes that they had achieved a major political realignment in 1980. The economic boom that had begun after the 1982 recession, along with the promise of the end of the Cold War, reinforced this trend and enabled George Bush to replace Ronald Reagan in the White House.

THE CHANGING PALACE GUARD

Ronald Reagan had always been unusually dependent on aides and assistants. He saw his own role as one above the heat of bureaucratic battle—providing the nation with a set of goals and a vision for the future. As the great communicator, he would build the public consensus and let others manage the more mundane task of turning his dreams into reality.

His initial success depended heavily on the very effective White House team of James Baker, Edwin Meese, and Michael Deaver. Baker, a Texan with extensive Washington experience, became the chief of staff, managing the White House and directing legislative strategy. Shrewd and pragmatic, he outmaneuvered Californian Meese, who accepted the role of counselor to the president, advising Reagan on policy but having little to do with its implementation. Assistant to the President Deaver, the final member of the trio, had the full confidence of Nancy Reagan and devoted himself to the goal of enhancing her husband's public image.

Ronald Reagan's laid-back style was misleading. Although it is true he preferred to be presented with solutions rather than problems, it was Reagan's personal commitment to cutting taxes, reducing domestic spending, and rebuilding America's defenses that gave shape and coherence to his administration's policies. In the Oval Office, he thrived on the interplay among Baker, Meese, and Deaver, letting them present various alternatives and then instinctively suggesting compromises.

An abrupt change in the White House staff in 1985 nearly proved disastrous for Reagan. Tired of the constant infighting, Baker agreed to Secretary of the Treasury Donald Regan's suggestion that the two men swap jobs. A self-made Wall Street operator, Regan possessed a confident, abrasive manner and a determination to assert his authority as White House chief of staff. When Meese became attorney general and Deaver left the government later in 1985, Regan extended his own control and thus ended the give-and-take in the Oval Office that had allowed Reagan to shape the final policy choices during his first term.

At first, Regan and Baker were able to score a major victory. Intent on lowering taxes still more on the wealthy while capitalizing on growing congressional demands for a simpler and fairer revenue system, the two men pressed for a major overhaul of the income tax. Making the necessary compromises with leaders in Congress, they shaped the 1986 Tax Reform Act, which cut the top rate from 50 to 28 percent while sharply reducing unproductive tax shelters. The new rates exempted six million people at the lower end from paying taxes while an alternative minimum tax prevented the rich from escaping their fair share.

The administration had only partial success in another area—appointing conservative federal judges who would simply follow the law and leave policy issues to Congress and state legislatures. In 1986, after a brief skirmish with the Senate, Reagan succeeded in replacing outgoing Chief Justice Warren Burger with the Supreme Court's strongest conservative, William Rehnquist. Equally conservative appeals court judge Antonin Scalia joined the Supreme Court at the same time. But in 1987, when the president nominated Robert Bork, an outspoken opponent of judicial activism, to fill the next vacancy, Democrats drew the line. Opposition from labor and civil rights groups finally led the Senate to reject Bork's nomination by a vote of 58 to 42. It was a bittersweet victory, however, as Reagan responded by appointing the moderately conservative, but far more diplomatic, Anthony Kennedy to the Court.

The Bork defeat was especially hard on Attorney General Meese, who by then had become an embarrassment to Reagan. Charges of loose financial dealings and unethical conduct in office led to the appointment of a special prosecutor. Although he found no evidence that the attorney general had broken the law, the prosecutor admitted that some of Meese's dealings had the "appearance" of impropriety. The Meese affair, along with the conviction of Deaver for lying to Congress, Pentagon procurement scandals, and serious irregularities in the Department of Housing and Urban Development, left the Reagan administration with the appearance of tolerating corruption. Coupled with the far more serious Iran-Contra affair, the scandals indicated that Reagan's habit of delegating authority to his subordinates had greatly weakened his presidency.

THE ELECTION OF 1988

The Democrats approached the 1988 election with growing optimism. They had regained control of the Senate in 1986, Reagan no longer would be on the Republican ticket, and Iran-Contra and the vast increase in the national debt since 1980 all appeared to place the GOP on the defensive. Michael Dukakis, the successful governor of Massachusetts, emerged from the grueling primary contests as the clear-cut winner. With the selection of moderate Texas senator Lloyd Bentsen as his vice presidential running mate, Dukakis left the convention at Atlanta confident of victory, with polls showing him ahead by 17 points.

The Republican nominee, Vice President George Bush, proved to be a much stronger candidate than anyone had expected. Despite the controversial choice of Indiana senator Dan Quayle as his running mate, Bush quickly regained the lead. The Republicans waged a ruthless attack on Dukakis, portraying him as soft on crime and defense. Above all, the GOP candidate repeatedly promised not to raise taxes, reiterating his favorite line: "Read my lips—no new taxes."

The outcome confirmed the pollsters' projections. Bush won overwhelmingly in the South, carried most of the West, and defeated Dukakis in such key industrial states as Michigan and Pennsylvania. His victory reflected the natural advantage of an incumbent at a time when the economy was healthy and the world at relative peace. Yet Dukakis could take some comfort in blocking a Republican landslide. Although the voters elected a Republican president, they also increased the Democratic margins in both the House and Senate. Bush would be the first

THE ELECTION OF 1988

CANDIDATE	PARTY	POPULAR VOTE	ELECTORAL VOTE
Bush	Republican	48,886,097	426
Dukakis	Democratic	41,809,074	112

new president since John F. Kennedy to enter the White House while his party lost ground in Congress.

The election of 1988 indicated that, at least on the presidential level, a significant change had taken place in American politics in 1980. Bush consolidated the GOP's grip on the electoral college, winning in the Sunbelt states of the South and West. At the same time, racial polarization in politics continued, with Dukakis getting 88 percent of the African American vote and 69 percent of the Hispanic ballots. The Democrats, despite their success in Congress, faced the challenge of trying to regain the support of white middle-class voters for their presidential candidates.

DEFAULTS AND DEFICITS

Many people expected the Bush administration to reflect the reputation of the new president—bland and cautious, lacking in vision but safely predictable. At home, he lived up to his reputation, sponsoring few initiatives in education, health care, and environmental protection while continuing the Reagan theme of limiting federal interference in the everyday lives of American citizens. The one exception was the Americans with Disabilities Act (ADA), passed by Congress in 1991, which prohibited discrimination against the disabled in hiring, transportation, and public accommodations. Beginning in July 1992, ADA called for all public buildings, restaurants, and stores to be made accessible to those with physical handicaps and required that businesses with twenty-five or more workers hire new employees without regard to disability.

Most of Bush's time was taken up with two pressing domestic problems. First, the nation's savings and loan industry, based on U.S. government–insured deposits, was in grave trouble as a result of lax regulation and unwise loan policies. After record losses of $13.4 billion in 1988, more than 250 savings and loans had been forced to close. The continuing budget deficit provided an even greater challenge. Despite Gramm-Rudman, the nation continued to spend beyond its means, with deficits still running over $150 billion a year.

The president and Congress finally reached agreement on both issues. In August 1989, Congress passed an administration bill to close or merge more than seven hundred ailing savings and loans at a cost of $157 billion over a ten-year period. A new federal agency, the Resolution Trust Corporation, closed more than five hundred savings and loans, primarily in the Sunbelt states. It took over the properties on which developers had secured loans many times their actual value and gradually sold them off at discount prices. By the time the Resolution Trust Corporation expired in 1992, the initial cost to the government was more than $150 billion, and the eventual bill for the savings and loan cleanup, including interest, was estimated at between $500 and $700 billion.

Action on the budget proved even more difficult. Facing a Gramm-Rudman goal of $110 billion for the 1991 budget, Bush persuaded Congress to accept a deficit of $105 billion in late 1989. In the fall of 1990, Bush finally agreed to break his "no new taxes" pledge and support a budget that included new taxes on the wealthy along with substantial spending cuts. The resulting agreement projected a savings of $500 billion over five years, half from reduced spending and half from new revenue generated by increasing the top tax rate from 28 percent to 31 percent and raising taxes on gasoline, luxury goods, and beer and wine.

Unfortunately for the president, the budget deal coincided with the beginning of a slow but painful recession that ended the Republican prosperity of the 1980s. Not only did Bush face recriminations from voters for breaking his "Read my lips" pledge, but the economic decline led to greatly reduced government revenues. As a result, the deficit continued to soar, rising to just under $300 billion in 1992. Despite the 1990 budget agreement, the national debt increased by more than $1 trillion during Bush's presidency.

THE END OF THE COLD WAR

Abroad, the Bush administration faced an unprecedented year of change that appeared to mark the end of the post–World War II era. In country after country, communism gave way to freedom as the Cold War faded away more quickly than anyone had expected.

The first attempt at internal liberation proved tragically abortive. In May 1989, students in China began a monthlong demonstration for freedom in Beijing's Tiananmen Square that attracted worldwide attention. Americans were fascinated to see the Chinese students call for democracy with a hunger strike and a handcrafted replica of the Statue of Liberty. But on the evening of June 4, the Chinese leaders sent tanks and troops to Tiananmen Square to crush the student demonstration. By the next day, full-scale repression swept over China; several hundred protesters were killed, and thousands were injured. Chinese leaders

Fed up with government corruption, Chinese students demonstrated for democracy. Their nonviolent protest in Peking's Tiananmen Square was crushed when tanks, armored personnel carriers, and trucks cleared the square after firing randomly on the unarmed students.

imposed martial law to quell the dissent and shatter American hopes for a democratic China.

President Bush responded cautiously. While he did suspend sales of military equipment to China and stopped all government-to-government trade, he neither imposed stiffer sanctions nor engaged in harsh rhetoric. Bush wanted to preserve American influence with the Chinese government.

A far more promising trend toward freedom began in Europe in mid-1989. In June, Lech Walesa and his Solidarity movement came to power in free elections in Poland. Soon the winds of change were sweeping over the former Iron Curtain countries. A new regime in Hungary opened its borders to the West in September, allowing thousands of East German tourists in Hungary to flee to freedom. One by one, the repressive governments of eastern Europe fell. The most heartening scene of all took place in East Germany in early November when the new communist leaders suddenly announced the opening of the Berlin Wall. Workers quickly demolished a 12-foot-high section of this despised physical symbol of the Cold War, joyously singing a German version of "For He's a Jolly Good Fellow."

For three decades the Berlin Wall stood as the most visible symbol of the division between East and West in the Cold War. Dismantling of the Wall in November 1989 marked the beginning of the end of the Cold War.

Most people realized it was Mikhail Gorbachev who was responsible for the liberation of eastern Europe. In late 1988, he signaled the spread of his reforms to the Soviet satellites by renouncing the Brezhnev doctrine, which called for Soviet control of eastern Europe. It was Gorbachev's refusal to use armed force to keep repressive regimes in power that permitted the long-delayed liberation of the captive peoples of eastern Europe.

Yet by the end of 1991, both Gorbachev and the Soviet Union had become victims of the demise of communism. On August 19, 1991, eight right-wing plotters placed Gorbachev under arrest while he was vacationing in the Crimea and attempted to seize control of the government in Moscow. But Boris Yeltsin, the newly elected president of the Russian Republic, broke up the coup by mounting a tank in Moscow and demanding Gorbachev's release. The Red Army rallied to Yeltsin's side. The coup failed and Gorbachev was released, only to resign in December 1991 after the fifteen republics dissolved the Soviet Union. Yeltsin then disbanded the Communist party and continued

The following legend accompanies the map:

1. **Poland.** Solidarity Party sweeps elections, June 1989.

2. **Czechoslovakia.** Communist leadership ousted, Nov. 1989; country divided into Czech Republic and Slovakia, Jan. 1, 1993.

3. **Germany.** Berlin Wall breached, Nov. 1989; East and West Germany reunited, Oct. 1990.

4. **Yugoslavia.** Country disintegrates, 1991–92; civil war begins in Bosnia and Herzegovina, 1992.

5. **Romania.** Communist dictator Ceausescu overthrown and executed, Dec. 1989; Salvation Front led by dissident former Communists wins elections, May 1990.

6. **Lithuania** declares independence, Mar. 1990.

7. **Latvia and Estonia** begin process of separation from Soviet Union, Apr. 1990.

8. **Hungary.** Free election sweeps non-Communists into power, Apr. 1990.

9. **Bulgaria.** Government pledges free elections and new constitution in 1990; free elections sweep non-Communists into power.

10. **Albania.** Free elections sweep non-Communists into power.

11. **Soviet Union.** Dissolved, Dec. 1991; Russia and 10 former Soviet republics form Commonwealth of Independent States.

The End of the Cold War

Free elections in Poland in June 1989 triggered the domino effect in the fall of communism in eastern Europe and the former Soviet Union. Changes in policy came quickly, but the restructuring of social and economic institutions continues to take time.

the reforms begun by Gorbachev to establish democracy and a free market system in Russia.

The Bush administration, although criticized for its cautious approach, welcomed the demise of communism and offered economic assistance to Russia and the other former Soviet republics. The most important steps came in the critical area of nuclear weapons. In 1991, Bush and Gorbachev signed START I, agreeing to reduce nuclear warheads to less than ten thousand apiece; in late 1992, Bush and Yeltsin agreed on the terms of START II, which would reduce the number of nuclear weapons on each side to just over three thousand, a level not seen since the mid-1960s. Although several of the republics, notably Ukraine, had not yet agreed even to START I, Bush could claim that by the time he left office in January 1993, the Cold War was over.

WAGING PEACE

The end of the Cold War, however, did not bring about a world free of violence. In December 1989, twenty-seven thousand American troops invaded Panama and quickly installed a new government friendly to the United States in the largest American military operation since the Vietnam War. Despite the death of twenty-three Americans and several hundred Panamanians, this action won approval from the people of both countries when it resulted in the capture of drug-trafficking General Manuel Noriega. By taking such bold and decisive action in Panama, Bush was able to shake his reputation for caution. But critics noted that the president had waged war without consulting Congress.

Eight months later, Bush suddenly faced a much graver challenge. On August 2, 1990, Saddam Hussein, the dictatorial ruler of Iraq, stunned the world by invading defenseless Kuwait and threatening Saudi Arabia and the oil-rich Persian Gulf region. The president responded firmly, despite an earlier balance-of-power policy of supporting Iraq against Iran. He accused Saddam of naked aggression and carefully built up a UN coalition to uphold what he termed "a new world order." Equally important, he quickly persuaded Saudi Arabia to accept a huge American troop buildup, dubbed Desert Shield. With the United States once again importing nearly half the oil used each day by the American people, control of the Persian Gulf was clearly a vital national interest.

Debate raged, however, on the best way to meet the Iraqi threat. Many Democrats in Congress supported Bush's efforts to place international economic sanctions on Iraq but opposed the use of force. Bush had clearly opted for a different solution by November, massing far more troops in the Persian Gulf area than were needed to defend Saudi Arabia—Operation Desert Shield was giving way to Desert Storm. After securing UN support, Bush narrowly persuaded Congress to approve the use of force to liberate Kuwait.

Antiaircraft fire lights up the sky over Baghdad, Iraq, during the Persian Gulf War. A month of strikes on Iraqi targets was followed by a ground offensive that lasted only one hundred hours before Iraqi troops began to surrender and President Bush ordered a cease-fire. Critics of Bush's decision argued that stopping the advance allowed an unvanquished Saddam Hussein to remain in power in Iraq.

On January 17, 1991, the president unleashed a devastating aerial assault on Iraq. F-117A stealth fighters and Tomahawk cruise missiles hit key targets in Baghdad. The air attack, virtually unchallenged by the Iraqis, wiped out command and control centers and enabled the coalition bombers to demoralize the beleaguered enemy troops. After five weeks, Bush gave his approval for the long-awaited ground assault. Led by General H. Norman Schwarzkopf, the allied armored units swept across the desert in a great flanking operation while a combined force of U.S. marines and Saudi troops drove directly into Kuwait City. In just one hundred hours, the American-led offensive liberated Kuwait and sent Saddam Hussein's vaunted Republican Guard fleeing back into Iraq.

In a controversial decision, President Bush, acting on the advice of General Colin Powell, chairman of the Joint Chiefs, halted the advance and agreed to an armistice with Iraq. Critics claimed that with just a few more days of fighting American forces could have encircled the Republican Guard and ended Saddam's cruel regime. But the president, fearful of disrupting the allied coalition and of having American troops mired down in a guerrilla war, stopped when he had achieved his announced goal of liberating Kuwait.

Desert Storm brought mixed blessings. It was a great personal victory for George Bush, who saw his approval rating climb to an unprecedented level— nearly 90 percent. American military leaders believed they had finally atoned for Vietnam, a sentiment widely shared by a euphoric public. The United States had deployed more than 500,000 troops, as many as were in Vietnam in 1968, and had lost just 146 lives in inflicting a stinging defeat on a dangerous bully. Best of all, the price of oil, which had climbed to nearly $40 a barrel in October, fell back to less than $20, allowing Americans to fill the gas tanks of their cars for just over $1 a gallon.

At the same time, however, Saddam Hussein continued to rule in Baghdad, persecuting Kurds in northern Iraq and Shi'ite Muslims in the south. He survived several attempts on his life and frustrated U.S. efforts to uncover and destroy his chemical, biological, and nuclear weapons facilities. And over the next few years, American veterans began to complain of debilitating symptoms of what came to be known as Gulf War syndrome.

In the long run, the Persian Gulf War may have damaged George Bush more than it helped him politically. It was his concentration on the Gulf crisis that led him to enter into the budget deal with congressional Democrats in the fall of 1990—a deal that alienated conservative Republicans and left him open to the charge of violating his 1988 campaign pledge not to raise taxes. Most damaging of all for Bush, the Gulf War had halted a slow recovery from the lingering recession and revived fears over America's economic health in the post–Cold War era. For twelve years, the Republicans had relied on a robust economy to enact their programs and consolidate their power—now the Democrats finally had a chance to accuse the GOP of endangering the nation's economic health.

33

AMERICA IN FLUX
The Anxious Nineties

O
n June 27, 1991, Thurgood Marshall, the first African American to sit on the Supreme Court, informed President Bush he was retiring due to ill health. A month later, Bush announced the nomination of Clarence Thomas, a black judge on the Court of Appeals in Washington, to take Marshall's place.

The contrast between the two justices was startling. Marshall had gained national fame for arguing the case for the *Brown* decision in 1954 that desegregated the nation's schools. A firm believer in affirmative action, he had been the Court's most liberal member. Thomas, on the other hand, was a conservative who believed in black self-help. Born in poverty in Georgia, he took to heart the admonition of the grandfather who raised him: "Anything you got you got by the sweat of your brow." After graduating from Holy Cross College and Yale Law School, Thomas eventually headed the Equal Employment Opportunity Commission (EEOC) during the Reagan years. Dismissing affirmative action as "social engineering" that creates a "narcotic of dependency," Thomas opposed racial quotas.

Despite his color, black organizations such as the NAACP opposed the confirmation of a judge who had once said that civil rights leaders did nothing but "bitch, bitch, bitch, moan, and whine." At the Senate Judiciary Committee hearings on his nomination, Thomas refused to reveal his views on sensitive issues such as abortion, but he did retreat from some of his earlier conservative opinions, even acknowledging that his own career had benefited from affirmative action programs.

George Bush's controversial nomination of Clarence Thomas to the U.S. Supreme Court culminated in three days of televised hearings when Anita Hill, a law professor at the University of Oklahoma, accused Thomas of sexual harassment. Despite the charges, the Senate confirmed Thomas's appointment by a 52 to 48 margin. Although Hill's charges failed to block Thomas's confirmation, they did help to create a new concern for the treatment of women in the workplace.

Although the Judiciary Committee deadlocked 7 to 7 on his nomination, observers expected the full Senate to confirm his appointment by a wide margin when it voted on October 8. Just before the vote, however, sensational charges of sexual harassment led to three days of new hearings before the Judiciary Committee that were televised to the entire nation. Anita Hill, a black law professor at the University of Oklahoma, testified that while working for Thomas at both the Justice Department and the EEOC, she had turned down his attempts to date her. She then accused Thomas of sexual harassment, recalling in vivid detail the way Thomas described to her scenes of bestiality, rape, and group sex from pornographic movies he had seen and then boasted of his own sexual prowess. Despite his unwelcome advances, Hill admitted, she had followed Thomas from the Justice Department to the EEOC and had called on him on occasion in later years for advice and career assistance.

Thomas categorically denied all the charges. He accused the Judiciary Committee of conducting "a high-tech lynching of an uppity black who in any way deigns to think for himself." His lawyers brought forth four women who had worked with him in the 1980s who all testified his conduct was above reproach, with one suggesting Anita Hill had had a crush on Thomas that he discouraged.

It came down to who people believed was telling the truth. Four witnesses recalled Anita Hill telling them about Thomas's advances; at her own request, she took and passed a lie detector test. But a public opinion poll taken at the close of the televised hearings indicated that 58 percent of the American people believed Thomas while only 24 percent believed Hill. A bare majority of the senators apparently agreed. On October 15, the Senate confirmed Thomas by a vote of 52 to 48, the narrowest margin ever for a Supreme Court appointment.

The Clarence Thomas–Anita Hill confrontation raised issues that did not end with Thomas's confirmation. The extent to which the nation should extend affirmative action to help offset past discrimination continued to be a matter of concern and debate in regard to university admissions and employment opportunities. The issue of sexual harassment, a traditional feminist grievance, took on new importance. American women in particular resented the way the all-male Judiciary Committee had treated the polite and composed Anita Hill. Republican members, notably Senator Arlen Specter of Pennsylvania, had cross-examined her ruthlessly, suggesting she was either a disappointed suitor or mentally unstable.

Most of all, the televised hearings of the Thomas nomination were indicative of the social unrest that characterized American life at the end of the twentieth century. The place of women in society, the continuing racial tension, changes in family structure, and the constantly shifting nature of the American population created a feeling of uneasiness. Despite a sustained economic boom and a welcome federal surplus by the end of the decade, the decline of manufacturing, the drop in defense spending with the end of the Cold War, and the trend toward greater inequality in income all contributed to a sense of disruption. People could rejoice in escaping the fear of nuclear annihilation, but they missed the old certainties of the Cold War era and were unsure of what the future held for them.

The Changing American Population

From the *Mayflower* to the covered wagon, movement has always characterized the American people. The 1970s and 1980s witnessed two significant shifts in the American population: movement internally to the Sunbelt region of the South and West and a remarkable influx of immigrants from developing nations. These changes led to increased urbanization, greater ethnic diversity, and growing social unrest.

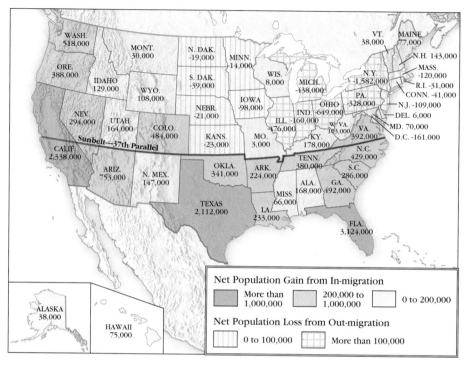

Migration to the Sunbelt, 1970–1981

Florida, California, and Texas gained the most people in the 1970s; New York, Ohio, and Illinois recorded the greatest losses.

A PEOPLE ON THE MOVE

The most striking finding in the 1980 census was that for the first time in American history, more than half the people lived in the South and West; the Sunbelt had boomed. The Sunbelt, best defined as a broad band running across the country below the 37th parallel from the Carolinas to Southern California, had begun to flourish with the buildup of military bases and defense plants during World War II. Rapid population growth continued with the stimulus of heavy Cold War defense spending and accelerated in the 1970s when both new high-technology firms and more established industries were attracted by lower labor costs and the favorable climate of the Sunbelt states. Florida, Texas, and California led the way, each gaining more than two million new residents in the 1970s.

In the next decade and a half, the flow continued, but at a slower rate. The Northeast and Midwest continued to lose population to the South and West. By the late 1980s, however, with the slowing of defense spending, rising real estate prices, and growing congestion, states such as Texas and California no longer attracted as many new residents. With the aging of the baby boom generation and the growth of two-income families, fewer people were pulling up roots by the 1990s. In 1998, 16 percent of the population changed residences, but most stayed in the same county; less than 3 percent moved to another state.

Despite the drop in migration, the South, particularly Florida, continued to boom, and cities throughout the Sunbelt thrived. Eight of the nation's cities now had more than one million residents; four were in the Sunbelt, and of the rest, only New York gained in population in the 1980s.

The increasing urbanization of America had both positive and negative aspects. People living in the large metropolitan areas were both more affluent and better educated than their rural counterparts. Family income among people living in the bigger cities and their suburbs ran $9000 a year more, and three-fourths of the urban population had graduated from high school, compared to two-thirds of other Americans. Yet these advantages were offset by rising urban crime rates, longer commuting time in heavy traffic, and higher living costs. Nevertheless, the big cities and their suburbs continued to thrive, accounting for 75.2 percent of all Americans by 1990.

Another striking population trend was the nationwide rise in the number of the elderly. At the beginning of the century, only 4.1 percent of the population was aged 65 or older; by 1997, those over 65 made up 13 percent of the population, with the nearly four million over 85 the fastest growing group of all. The Census Bureau projected a slower rate of increase to 2010 and then a big jump as the baby boomers reach 65.

Six of every ten older Americans were women, and they tended to have a higher rate of chronic disease and to be worse off economically than men the same age. Many of the oldest old, those over 85, lived in nursing homes and accounted for one-third of all Medicaid payments. Yet only 12.4 percent of the elderly lived below the poverty line; the annual cost-of-living increases in Social Security payments spared them the worst ravages of inflation. Most impressive of all was their political power: two-thirds of those over 65 voted regularly, compared to just under half of the entire population. The American Association of Retired Persons (AARP), with more than thirty million members, proved very effective in Washington in protecting the interests of the elderly, particularly in regard to Medicare.

THE REVIVAL OF IMMIGRATION

The flow of immigrants into the United States reached record proportions in the 1990s as a result of new policies adopted in 1965 replacing the national origins quota system. With an estimated one million newcomers arriving each year, by 2000 nearly one in ten Americans was foreign-born.

The new wave of immigrants came mainly from Latin America and Asia. In the 1980s, Mexico supplied the largest number of immigrants, 1.6 million, followed by the Philippines with more than 500,000. The new immigrants tended to settle in urban areas. In California, the influx of immigrants from Asia and Mexico created growing pressure on public services, especially during the recession of the early 1990s.

The arrival of more than 26 million immigrants in three decades was bound to lead to controversy over whether immigrants were a benefit or a liability to American society. A study by the National Academy of Sciences in 1997 reported that, in the long run, immigrants and their families more than paid their way. In regard to employment, immigrants tended to help consumers and employers by working for relatively low wages in restaurants, the textile industry, and farming, but they hurt low-skilled U.S. workers by keeping wages low. Economist George J. Borjas, himself a refugee from Cuba, claimed that immigrants from developing countries lacked the education and job skills needed to achieve the level of prosperity attained by newcomers in the past; instead of entering the mainstream of American life, they were likely to remain a permanent underclass.

In regard to the often-expressed concern that immigrants are slow to learn English and assimilate, a study covering Southern California in the 1980s offered some reassurance. The number of Hispanic immigrants who spoke English rose from one-third to nearly three-fourths during the decade, while the poverty rate among Asian men fell from one-third to less than one-tenth. "The speed of immigrants' upward mobility is striking," commented demographer Dowell Myers.

Public attitudes began to shift toward the end of the century. A 1997 poll showed that the number of people who believed immigrants were bad for the nation had dropped from 60 percent in 1993 to 42 percent, with 43 percent affirming the benefits of immigration for the country. The booming economy, with resulting low unemployment, made newcomers willing to do the hard jobs shunned by the native-born appear to be a blessing rather than a threat.

ADVANCE AND RETREAT FOR AFRICAN AMERICANS

African Americans formed the largest of the nation's ethnic groups. In 1999, there were 34.8 million blacks in the United States, nearly 13 percent of the population. Although there had been some movement of African Americans back to the South, the great majority lived in the crowded ghettos of cities of the Northeast, Midwest, and Pacific Coast.

Middle-class African Americans had made some gains during the 1970s and 1980s. By 1976, one-third of all black workers held white-collar jobs—double the rate of 1960. Education proved the key to African American advances. Black graduates of the nation's colleges and universities had relatively easy entry into higher-paying jobs in banks, corporations, and government agencies. Black college enrollment increased by 43 percent between 1970 and 2000, giving more African Americans the opportunity for a middle-class lifestyle.

Many well-educated and affluent African Americans tended to behave like whites in similar circumstances. Some joined the flight to the suburbs, leaving the central city in even larger proportions than whites. By the 1980s, many young African Americans, trained as doctors, lawyers, or business executives, returned to cities in the South to pursue their careers. The trend continued in the 1990s. By the end of the century, Atlanta led all metropolitan areas with a gain of 159,830 new black residents in the decade. In fact, the South had become the most thoroughly integrated of all the nation's regions.

Yet despite these gains, there were setbacks as well for African Americans. In the *Bakke* decision, the Supreme Court ruled against racial quotas for blacks at a University of California medical school, although the ruling did permit universities to consider race as "simply one element" in efforts to select diverse student bodies. In subsequent decisions, the Court upheld an affirmative action program designed by Kaiser Aluminum to help advance minority workers and ordered

Supporters of affirmative action protested the decision of the U.S. Supreme Court in the Bakke *case. The Court ruled against the use of racial quota systems to achieve racial balance. However, the Court did uphold the principle of affirmative action by ruling that race could be one of several factors used in making hiring or admissions decisions.*

American Telephone and Telegraph to hire more African Americans and women to make up for past discrimination.

A series of Supreme Court decisions in 1989 sharply narrowed the scope of affirmative action programs. In one case involving setting aside 30 percent of all city contracts in Richmond, Virginia, for minority contractors, the Court ruled against such rigid racial quotas. In 1991, the president and Congress compromised on a new civil rights act that restored in large measure the rights of both blacks and women to sue businesses for acts of racial discrimination and sexual harassment.

Affirmative action yielded only mixed results for blacks. For those able to gain university admission, such programs proved helpful, but even blacks who graduated from college did not do as well economically as their white counterparts. The Census Bureau reported in 1991 that African American college graduates received only 77 percent as much as white graduates employed in executive and administrative positions. For black males with a high school degree, the gap was even larger; they earned only $60 for every $100 paid to white men with a comparable education.

For blacks without education, the situation was much worse. Even in the boom years of the 1980s, unemployment rates for African Americans remained over 10 percent, more than double that for whites, and among black teenagers, the level was a staggering 40 percent. In the recession of 1990–1991, black workers lost 59,579 jobs. Blue-collar African American workers were especially hard hit, losing one-third of the 180,210 blue-collar jobs lost during the recession.

Nor did blacks share equally in the economic recovery of the 1990s. In 1998, the median family income for African Americans was just $25,351, compared to more than $40,000 for white, non-Hispanic households. More than two million black families were living below the poverty line in 1998; the poverty rate for blacks was nearly double that for white Americans.

Rodney King became a symbol of black frustration in the United States. In March 1991, a bystander videotaped four Los Angeles policemen brutally beating King, who had been stopped for a traffic violation. The pictures of the rain of blows on King shocked the nation. Nearly a year later, when an all-white jury acquitted the four officers of charges of police brutality, rioting erupted in South Central Los Angeles that for a time threatened the entire city when the police failed to respond promptly. Looting stores at will and setting businesses on fire, the rioters focused the nation's attention on the plight of urban blacks. In the aftermath of the riot, government and state agencies promised new efforts to help the ghetto dwellers. Urban blacks, however, saw little hope for improvement. A

A bystander recorded on videotape the police beating of motorist Rodney King, whom police had stopped for speeding and drunken driving. The acquittal of four police officers on charges of police brutality touched off the worst incidence of urban violence in the twentieth century. More than fifty people died in the rioting and property damage exceeded $1 billion.

poll taken in April 1992 revealed that 51 percent of African Americans believed life had "gotten worse" during the past ten years, up from 35 percent in mid-1991. For black youths in Los Angeles, surrounded by gang warfare and drive-by shootings, their only aspiration was simply to stay alive.

THE SURGING HISPANICS

People with Spanish surnames, labeled Hispanics by the Census Bureau, formed the nation's second-largest ethnic group. The rapidly growing Hispanic population had climbed to more than 35 million by 2000. Both a high birthrate and heavy immigration from Western Hemisphere countries helped Hispanics account for 12.5 percent of the nation's population, and demographers predicted Hispanics would replace African Americans as the nation's largest minority group by the year 2005.

The Census Bureau identified four major Hispanic categories in 1990. Mexican Americans, the largest group at more than 20 million, were concentrated in the Southwest. There were 3 million Puerto Ricans, mainly living in or near New York City. Cuban Americans, located primarily in South Florida, numbered almost 1.5 million. Finally, there were 6.5 million in the Census Bureau category "other Hispanics."

The Hispanic groups had several features in common. All were relatively youthful, with a median age of 22 and a high fertility rate. They tended to be relatively poor, with one-fourth falling below the poverty line. Although the position of Hispanics had improved considerably in the boom years of the 1980s and 1990s, they still lagged behind mainstream America. The poverty rate among Hispanics was twice the national average, higher even than for blacks; family median income in 1998 was $28,330, only two-thirds of the level for other Americans.

Lack of education was a key factor in preventing economic progress for Hispanics. The American Council on Education released a report in 1991 that found Hispanics "are grossly under-represented at every rung of the educational ladder." Fewer Hispanics graduated from high school than other minorities and their school dropout rate was the nation's highest at more than 50 percent. As a result, in 1999 more than a quarter of Hispanic adults had only a grade-school education, compared to less than 5 percent of non-Hispanic whites.

The entry of several million illegal immigrants from Mexico, once derisively called "wetbacks" and now known as "undocumented aliens," created a substantial social problem for the nation and especially for the Southwest. Critics argued that the aliens took jobs away from U.S. citizens, kept wages artificially low, and received extensive welfare and medical benefits that strained budgets in states such as Texas and California.

Defenders of the undocumented aliens contended that the nation gained from the abundant supply of workers who were willing to work at backbreaking jobs shunned by most Americans. Moreover, defenders stated, illegal entrants usually paid sales and withholding taxes but rarely used government services for fear of being deported. Whichever view was correct, by the mid-1980s, an exploited class of illegal aliens was living on the edge of poverty. The *Wall Street Journal* summed it up best by observing, "The people who benefit the most from this situation are certainly the employers, who have access to an underground market of cheap, productive labor."

Concern about economic competition from an estimated four million Mexican "illegals" led Congress to pass a major immigration reform bill in 1986. The legislation imposed fines and possible prison sentences on those who knowingly employed illegal immigrants. Mexican American leaders feared the sanctions would discourage businesses from hiring anyone of Mexican descent, but they approved of an amnesty provision that enabled aliens who could prove they were living in the United States before January 1, 1982, to become legal residents.

The 1986 law failed to stem the problem of illegal immigration. Authorities noted a decline in the number of illegal entrants a year in the late 1980s, but by the early 1990s there was a new surge from Mexico, Central America, and China. In 1993, Lawrence H. Fuchs, acting chair of the U.S. Commission on

Immigration Reform, estimated the numbers of illegals to be as high as 500,000 a year. In 1997, however, an official study jointly conducted by U.S. and Mexican scholars used census data to arrive at a much lower figure. Whatever the actual yearly addition, the Immigration and Naturalization Service estimated in 1997 that 5 million foreigners, mainly from Mexico and Central America, were living illegally in the United States—2 million in California alone. Thus the projections for the Hispanic population, 24.5 percent of the total by the middle of the next century, may well prove to be too low.

ASIAN AMERICANS ON THE RISE

Asian Americans were the fastest-growing minority group at the end of the century. In 1999, there were nearly 11 million Americans of Asian or Pacific Island descent. Although they represented only 3.9 percent of the total population, they were increasing at seven times the national rate, and future projections indicated that by 2050 one in ten Americans would be of Asian ancestry.

The Chinese formed the largest single group of Asian Americans, followed by Filipinos, Japanese, Indians, Koreans, and Vietnamese. Immigration was the primary reason for the rapid growth of all these groups except the Japanese.

Compared to other minorities, Asian Americans are relatively well educated and affluent. Three out of four Asian youths graduate from high school, compared to less than one out of two for blacks and Hispanics. Asian Americans also have the highest percentage of college graduates and recipients of doctoral degrees of any minority group. Many Asians have entered professional fields, and as a result, the median income for Asian American families is more than $4000 higher than the 1998 national level.

Not all Asian Americans have fared well, however. Refugees from Southeast Asia have experienced both economic hardship and persecution. The median family income for Vietnamese Americans in the mid-1980s was $8000 below that for whites. Vietnamese fishermen who settled on the Gulf Coast experienced repeated attacks on their livelihood in Texas and Louisiana. In the Los Angeles riots in 1992, Korean stores and shops became a main target for looting and firebombing.

But the overall experience of Asian Americans has been a positive one. They came to America seeking economic opportunity, or as many put it, "to climb the mountain of gold." "People are looking for a better life," a Chinese spokeswoman explained. "It's as simple as that, and we will continue to come here."

Jay Kwan, a Korean greengrocer, reflects the economic rewards Asian immigrants were able to achieve by long hours of hard toil. Kwan worked as a janitor on arriving in New York City in the 1970s, saving enough in three years to buy a produce store in Brooklyn. Alongside his wife and brother, he worked 15 hours a day. Despite being robbed several times, he formed good relations with his neighbors and was able to make a modest profit. Yet his goal was always more than simply earning a living. "I am first generation," he told a reporter. "I am not working for myself. I am working for the second generation."

Such dedication has helped Asian Americans to make remarkable progress. Nearly 11 percent of Harvard's entering class in 1985 was of Asian ancestry. Asian Americans, according to sociologist Peter I. Rose, are part of "the most upwardly mobile group in the country. They have caught up to and are even surpassing the Joneses and the Smiths, as well as the Cohens and the Levines."

MELTING POT OR MULTIETHNIC DIVERSITY?

"Cultural diversity probably accelerated more in the 1980s than any other decade," noted demographer Carl Haub. The influx of people from all around the world, not just from Europe, had profound implications for American culture. Traditionally, the favorite American self-image was the melting pot, the title of Israel Zangwill's play written in 1908, at the height of European immigration into the nation. "America is God's crucible, the great Melting-Pot where all the races of Europe are melting and re-forming," one of his characters proclaimed.

The melting pot image carried with it the concept of stripping newcomers of their culture and national traits and casting them into an Anglo-Saxon mold. Dubious for European immigration, this analogy has seemed irrelevant to the Third World migration to America in recent times. Instead of recasting immigrants into an American type, immigration could better be seen as broadening the diversity that always has characterized the United States. Now, instead of the usual division between blacks and whites, America is composed of Asians as well as Europeans, Hispanics as well as African Americans. Sociologist Amitai Etzioni suggests replacing the melting pot image with a "mosaic" portraying a nation in which ethnic groups proudly retain their own identities "while recognizing that they are integral parts of a more encompassing whole."

The new awareness of ethnic diversity manifested itself in many ways. In public education, blacks led a crusade against Eurocentric curriculum and demanded a new emphasis on the influence of African culture; on college campuses, the call for multicultural courses and separate departments for African American, Asian American, and Hispanic studies created controversy. Citing the forecasts of a declining Anglo dominance and the rise of minority groups in the next century, ethnic leaders advocated cultural pluralism. Raul Yzaguirre, president of the National Council of La Raza, an Hispanic advocacy group, argued that

America has never had a real melting pot in which all races contributed to the mix. "What we've had is a pressure cooker, where everybody has had to come in and become Anglophiles."

Many Americans found themselves perplexed and uncertain of their cultural identity by the end of the twentieth century. A Census Bureau survey, asking people to state their ancestry, revealed that fully one-fourth of Americans listed Germany first, with Ireland and England a distant second and third. Some Hispanics found the census racial classifications—black, Asian–Pacific Islander, white, or American Indian—meaningless. "I don't really consider myself Caucasian," objected Jose Arroyo of San Jose, California. "My roots go down into the Indians of Mexico."

In the 1990s, people of mixed racial parentage demanded that the census for 2000 include a box labeled "multiracial" rather than just the meaningless "other." Susan Graham, a white Georgian mother of two multiracial children, founded a group called Project RACE (Reclassify All Children Equally), which argued that the four million children of more than a million interracial marriages deserved their own census category. Civil rights groups, however, objected, fearing cuts in government benefits to minorities based on the census figures. The Census Bureau compromised in 2000 by adding four new dual-race categories—American Indian–white, American Indian–black, Asian-white, and black-white. The government, however, would continue to classify multiracial individuals by the minority portion of their heritage.

Horace Kallen, one of the early critics of Zangwill's melting pot analogy, offered the most appealing image of the nation's diverse heritage. He likened the United States to a symphony orchestra, in which each nationality and ethnic group contributed its "own specific timbre and tonality" to create "a multiplicity in a unity, an orchestration of mankind." As Americans wrestle with the continuing dilemma embodied in the national motto, *E pluribus unum,* the image of a great symphony in which all groups blend harmoniously offers a way to balance the pride individuals find in ethnic identity with the need for national unity.

ECONOMIC CROSSCURRENTS

The strains that first hit the American economy in the lean years of the 1970s continued to erode the confidence of the American people. Despite a seven-year boom in the 1980s, recessions in 1982 and 1990 and the abrupt drop in defense spending with the end of the Cold War led to heavy unemployment. At the same time, changes in the economy tended to hurt blue-collar workers and benefit upper-income groups the most.

RECESSION AND STAGNATION

In July 1990, the American economy, which had been steadily expanding for seven years, suddenly plunged into a recession. Although mild by postwar standards, the 1990 recession proved unusually stubborn. The recovery proved slow and uneven, stalling twice before leading to renewed growth in mid-1992. Unemployment remained flat eighteen months after the recession ended, and the gross domestic product (GDP) rose just 2.9 percent in the same period, only one-third of the average growth following other postwar recessions.

The political impact was devastating for the Bush administration. By June 1992, nearly ten million Americans were unemployed. Unlike the 1982 recession, which had hit hardest in the industrial heartland, the 1990 downturn was experienced most strongly in New England and California, the boom areas of the 1980s. And in contrast to previous recessions, in which blue-collar workers had fared the worst, many white-collar employees and college graduates lost their jobs. The poverty rate, which had remained steady throughout the 1980s, climbed nearly a full point to 14.2 percent.

The sluggish recovery was primarily the result of the massive restructuring of the American economy brought on by the end of the Cold War. The fall of the Berlin Wall had resulted in annual reductions of more than 5 percent in defense spending in the early 1990s. Between 1990 and 1992, defense contractors dismissed 225,000 workers, accounting for more than 15 percent of the almost 1.5 million jobs lost during the recession.

It was George Bush's misfortune that the long-sought end of the Cold War coincided with the 1990 recession. For more than three decades, heavy military spending had kept the nation prosperous while masking a growing lack of U.S. competitiveness in the global economy. The sudden cutback in defense spending, coupled with the surging economic performance of nations such as Japan and Germany, put the United States in a difficult position. The average American worker, whose paycheck dropped from $454 a week in 1988 to $440 by 1992, was ready to look beyond the Republican party for relief.

THE PLIGHT OF THE MIDDLE CLASS

No economic issue had more political impact by 1992 than the widespread belief in the decline of the American middle class. While Democrats blamed Reaganomics for favoring the wealthy at the expense of the average American, the woes of the middle class since the early 1970s transcended partisan explanation.

The actual fate of middle-class Americans since the early 1970s reveals a more complicated pattern. The most frequently cited measure of economic well-being is median family income. Between 1947 and 1973, family income doubled.

The economic inequities of the 1980s, with the growing disparity in income between rich and poor and tax policies that favored the rich over the poor and middle class, came to a head in the recession of the early 1990s. Drawing by Dana Fradon; copyright © 1992. The New Yorker Magazine, Inc.

But after 1973, median family income failed to advance. Inflation caused it to drop in the late 1970s, and the recession of 1982 led to a second decline. Family income rose steadily in the boom years of the 1980s, only to fall back with the 1990 recession. Middle-class Americans suddenly realized that for twenty years their economic position had remained stagnant.

Economists offered conflicting views of the plight of the middle class. A report by the New York City Department of Consumer Affairs claimed that most Americans had to work longer just to keep even. Working wives became a necessity; it took two incomes and many more hours of work in the 1980s for the average family with children to maintain a decent standard of living. As a result, the middle class declined from 71.2 percent of the population in 1969 to 63.3 percent by 1989.

A Congressional Budget Office report in 1993, however, indicated that baby boomers were better off than their parents were. The older half, those between

35 and 44, fared best, but even the young boomers who entered the workforce in the 1980s enjoyed higher incomes than their parents. The rise in disposable personal income reflected the same trend. The amount that individuals had left to save or spend after taxes increased from $11,013 in 1973 to $14,154 in 1990.

More important than the numbers was the growing belief of middle-class Americans that the next generation would not fare as well as their parents had. The feeling of diminished expectations was the product of many factors. The rapid expansion and affluence of the 1950s and 1960s was a happy accident unlikely to occur again. The inflation in real estate by the 1980s added greatly to the net worth of an older generation. The resurgence of Japan and Germany and the relative decline of American industry ensured a much lower rate of national economic growth. Above all, the baby boom generation took the affluence of postwar America for granted and expected to continue to enjoy all the blessings of an abundant society.

The reality of two decades of stagnation in median family income and successive recessions that held back long-term economic growth raised serious questions for a generation that had never known the deprivations of the Great Depression and World War II. Even though they continued to enjoy a standard of living that was the envy of most of the world, they began to wonder if their children would be denied the American dream. It is not surprising, then, that the American people were prepared to listen to new political voices that promised to revitalize not just the economy but the American way of life itself.

DEMOCRATIC REVIVAL

The Democrats, victims of the runaway inflation of the 1970s, became the beneficiaries of the lingering recession of the early 1990s. Moving away from its traditional liberal reliance on big government, the party regained strength by choosing moderate candidates and tailoring its programs to appeal to the hard-pressed middle class. These new tactics enabled the Democrats to regain the White House in 1992 and retain it in 1996, despite a Republican sweep of Congress in 1994. The key figure in this political shift was Bill Clinton, who overcame some early setbacks to reap the rewards of a sustained economic boom.

THE ELECTION OF 1992

The persistence of the recession that had begun two years earlier became the dominant political reality of 1992. As Bush's popularity plummeted, two men sought to capitalize on the dismal state of the U.S. economy. First, Arkansas governor Bill Clinton defeated a field of five other challengers for the Democratic nomination by becoming the champion of economic renewal. Clinton stressed the need for investment in the nation's future—rebuilding roads and bridges, training workers for high-tech jobs, and solving the growing national health care crisis.

Despite his victories in the Democratic primaries, however, Clinton faced a new rival in H. Ross Perot. An eccentric Texas billionaire, Perot singled out the deficit as the nation's gravest problem and agreed to run as an independent candidate in response to a grassroots movement (which he financed) to place his name on the November ballot.

When Clinton and his running mate, Senator Albert Gore, Jr., of Tennessee, succeeded in unifying the Democratic party and gaining agreement on a moderate platform promising economic change, Perot stunned his supporters by suddenly dropping out of the race in July. Clinton immediately became the front-runner, rising from 30 percent to more than 50 percent in the polls, leaving Bush far behind. With unemployment continuing unabated and the economy faltering, the American people turned their backs on George Bush and the Reagan revolution.

A relentless Democratic attack on the administration's lackluster economic performance overcame all the president's efforts to remind the nation of Reagan prosperity and Bush triumphs abroad. Even GOP assaults on Clinton's character, notably his evasion of the draft during the Vietnam War, failed to halt the Democratic momentum. The message that Clinton's political advisers tacked up at the Democratic candidate's headquarters in Little Rock—"The economy, stupid"—provided the key to victory in November. Clinton wound up with 43 percent of the popular vote but with a commanding lead in the electoral college, 370 to 168 for Bush. Perot, who had reentered the race, won 19 percent of the popular vote but failed to carry a single state.

THE ELECTION OF 1992

CANDIDATE	PARTY	POPULAR VOTE	ELECTORAL VOTE
Clinton	Democratic	44,908,232	370
Bush	Republican	39,102,282	168
Perot	Independent	19,725,433	—
	Minor Parties	773,161	—

For political scientists, 1992 was a clear case of a negative referendum. Voters had decisively rejected the Reagan-Bush programs. Clinton maintained the Democratic grip on ethnic minorities, winning 83 percent support from African Americans and 62 percent from Hispanics, and cut deeply into the crucial middle class by doing better than Bush among those earning between $30,000 and $75,000 a year.

Most important, Clinton had broken the GOP's grip on the South and West—only Texas and the interior western states had remained Republican strongholds. Yet while there was no doubt about the rejection of Bush, there remained a question of precisely what change the electorate wanted most—responsible budgetary policies to reduce the deficit or federal spending programs to achieve jobs and economic growth.

ECONOMIC RECOVERY

In the White House, Bill Clinton proved to be the most adept politician since Franklin Roosevelt. Born William Jefferson Clinton in Hope, Arkansas, in 1946, he weathered a difficult childhood by developing skills at dealing with people and using personal charm to achieve his goals. His intelligence and ambition helped him gain a strong education as an undergraduate at Georgetown University and a law student at Yale, with a two-year stint in between as a Rhodes scholar at Oxford. Entering politics, he won election first as Arkansas attorney general and then as governor. Defeated after his first term in 1980, Clinton won the nickname "Comeback Kid" by regaining the governor's office in 1982, using it to earn a reputation as one of the nation's most successful young political leaders during the following ten years.

Bill Clinton's political gifts centered on the easy way in which he was able to reconcile what biographer Martin Walker called "the ambivalence between the bubba and the brains, between the redneck and [the] Rhodes scholar." Raised by women, he had a sensitivity to human suffering and an understanding of the tribulations of daily life that gave him a broad political appeal. Empathy, charm, and understanding, combined with a genuine desire to serve, made him a formidable political leader.

Unfortunately, serious flaws marred his political gifts. His eagerness to please undercut his devotion to principle. Despite his apparently sincere devotion to causes such as civil rights and equality for women, even those who voted for Clinton had doubts about his personal integrity. One writer summed up his contradictory nature by describing him as "a man who loves the fruits of compromise but treasures the idea of his own unbending goodness."

What often saved Clinton from his own worst faults was his loyal wife, Hillary Rodham Clinton. An accomplished attorney, she rescued his candidacy in 1992 by defending him against charges of adultery. But more important, from the outset she was his political partner, sharing in the strategic planning that won him the presidency. They made a formidable political team, with her idealism offsetting his pragmatism.

In his first months in office, Bill Clinton's political skills appeared to evaporate. His inept handling of the "gays in the military" issue, made worse by his own draft evasion during the Vietnam War and several botched cabinet appointments, robbed him of the usual honeymoon period new presidents enjoy. He reacted with bitter indignation to the ensuing media criticism, refusing to hold a White House press conference during his first two months in office.

In appointing his cabinet, Clinton did try to live up to his pledges of ethnic and gender diversity. Hazel O'Leary, a black woman, served as secretary of energy, while Janet Reno, a political unknown, became attorney general. The cabinet included two Hispanics, Henry Cisneros and Federico Peña, and two African Americans, Mike Espy and Ronald Brown.

Diversity ended there, however. Fourteen of the eighteen cabinet members were lawyers, and most were wealthy. Secretary of Labor Robert Reich, a Harvard professor, was one of the few advocates for working-class Americans. Beyond the cabinet, two-thirds of the Clinton administration appointees were white men; minorities made up just 14 percent of the Clinton team, barely higher than the 13 percent under Bush.

Clinton's most important appointments came in the economic realm. In a series of meetings held in Little Rock shortly after the 1992 election, the president-elect learned that the economic dilemmas facing the nation were bleaker than he had realized. During the campaign, he had promised middle-class tax cuts and a spending program to both stimulate the economy and provide a new focus for government activity. But now his advisers warned him that the mounting national budget deficit made such measures impossible. The interest on the debt was running at nearly $300 billion a year; with most of the federal budget tied up in entitlement programs such as Social Security and Medicare, there was no room for additional discretionary spending, much less tax cuts.

Of all the economic advisers who made the pilgrimage to Little Rock, the one whom Clinton found most persuasive was a Republican—Alan Greenspan, the chairman of the Federal Reserve Board. Stressing the need to reduce the deficit, projected to reach nearly $400 billion by 1997, Greenspan argued for a comprehensive deficit reduction plan that would lead to lower interest rates on long-term bonds, thus reducing the government's debt payments and stimulating business growth. In other words, by biting the fiscal bullet now, Clinton could enjoy the best of both worlds—he could gain credit for reducing the deficit while "growing the economy," as he had pledged during the campaign.

The announcement of Clinton's economic team signaled his acceptance of the Greenspan approach. Senator Lloyd Bentsen, a fiscal conservative, became secretary of the treasury, with Robert Rubin, a Wall Street bond trader, serving as special assistant for economic policy. By choosing such a conservative team to guide economic policy, Clinton was risking the fate of his administration on the single issue of deficit reduction.

The president made this crucial decision public in a nationally televised budget speech to both houses of Congress on February 17, 1993. With Alan Greenspan seated next to Hillary Clinton in the gallery, the president boldly outlined a plan to cut the deficit by $500 billion.

The applause for Clinton's economic plan reverberated far beyond the halls of Congress. Polls showed his approval rating rising from 51 to 63 percent in two weeks as the public approved of his willingness to give the deficit his highest priority. More important, in late February, interest rates on 30-year bonds dropped below 7 percent for the first time ever. Greenspan had been right, and Clinton had won his biggest gamble.

The president still had to wage a long and determined fight to complete his economic program. It took all-out arm-twisting from the White House to get Congress to approve the final budget terms—$241 billion in new taxes and $255 billion in spending cuts, for a total reduction of $496 billion over four years. In late August, the House approved the budget by just two votes, and in the Senate, Vice President Gore cast his vote to break a 50 to 50 deadlock.

Despite the narrow margin, it was a major achievement. Clinton stood firm on deficit reduction, compromising on details but insisting on a program that promised to cut the deficit in half within four years. Moreover, he succeeded in increasing income tax rates on the wealthy from 33 to 39.6 percent. At the same time, he secured passage of the earned income tax credit for the working poor, providing as much as $3500 a year to keep a low-income family above the poverty line. And best of all, lower interest rates created by action of the Federal Reserve Board led to a steadily expanding economy that made Clinton's deficit reduction goals realistic. Unlike George Bush in 1990, who sealed his political doom by reneging on his promise not to raise taxes, a healthier economy enabled Clinton both to raise taxes and to win respect by standing on principle. He did, however, risk the same fate as Bush since Republicans were quick to call the budget deal "the biggest tax increase in the history of the world."

PRESIDENT VERSUS CONGRESS

Deficit reduction marked only the beginning of Bill Clinton's struggles with Congress. For the next four years, he engaged in a series of confrontations, winning some and losing some with first Democratic and then Republican majorities in the two houses.

His most important triumph came when Congress approved the North American Free Trade Agreement (NAFTA) in the fall of 1993. NAFTA, initiated and nearly completed by Bush, was a free trade plan that combined 250 million Americans with 90 million Mexicans and 27 million Canadians into a common market without tariff barriers. Clinton saw it as the first step in creating similar free-trade associations with Asia and Europe that would enable the United States to dominate global markets. Calling NAFTA "a defining moment" for the nation, he proclaimed, "This country is now the most productive country in the world."

Critics of NAFTA did not share Clinton's optimism. Representing both ends of the political spectrum, they warned that free trade would undermine small American companies and send millions of American jobs to exploited and underpaid workers in Third World countries. The issue of free trade divided the Democratic party, with many liberals and labor union members strongly opposed. Ross Perot, the defeated 1992 third-party candidate, became the best known critic, especially with his vivid claim about the loud "sucking sound" that would signal the flushing of American jobs down the drain.

As he had done with deficit reduction, Clinton appealed shrewdly to moderates of both parties. He pointed to the increased opportunity for American exports. To allay the objections of environmentalists and organized labor, he negotiated "sidebar" agreements dealing with pollution and workplace standards in Mexico and Canada.

The toughest fight came in the House, but 102 Democrats finally joined with 132 Republicans to approve NAFTA by a 34-vote margin, giving Clinton a solid victory there. The Senate added its consent by a vote of 61 to 38. Thus Clinton triumphed over key elements within his own party to achieve a significant goal.

During the next four years, NAFTA failed to justify either the hopes of its supporters or the fears of its detractors. The true impact of NAFTA will become apparent only in the twenty-first century. If it leads to Clinton's vision of a common market for the entire Western Hemisphere, it may well prove to be his most lasting achievement.

At the height of the debate over NAFTA, President Clinton allowed his wife to make public his administration's massive plan for health reform in an unprecedented appearance before the House Ways and Means Committee. When he first took office, the president had signaled the importance of the health care issue by appointing Hillary Clinton to head a task force to find a comprehensive solution to the nation's health care problem. The Clintons had two primary objectives. The first was an all-embracing health care system that would include the thirty-seven million Americans who lacked health insurance. At the same time, they were committed to reduce the skyrocketing cost of health care—13 percent of the GDP, nearly twice the cost of health care in other industrial nations. The trick would be to devise a system that would reduce costs while extending medical insurance to everyone in the nation, without raising taxes or adding to the deficit. The only possible solution involved rationing health care by having someone in authority place limits on the medical services each American could receive—a strategy that was political dynamite.

The plan that Hillary Clinton presented to the House Ways and Means Committee in October 1993 had two key features. First, it required large companies to offer a generous health care package to all workers, with employers paying 80 percent of the estimated $4200 annual cost per family. The second feature dealt with small businesses, which were required to form large health alliances so that they could purchase equally generous benefit packages from insurance companies. The task force believed that these mandatory health alliances would have enough clout to bargain for competitive rates, thereby sharply reducing health costs.

The initial public reception was favorable. According to a CNN poll, 61 percent of the American people said they were ready to pay higher taxes for a truly comprehensive health care system. When Congress began studying the details, however, attitudes started to change. The complex bill was referred to ten separate committees, inviting legislative chaos. And then opponents, primarily Republicans and representatives of small business, counterattacked. Spending nearly $60 million to fight the Clinton program, its critics claimed that it would deprive Americans of the right to choose their own doctors.

The administration's health care plan was soon in deep trouble. By midsummer, only 39 percent of the American people expressed confidence in the administration's health proposal. When Democrats were unable to round up sixty votes to break a Republican filibuster on procedural issues in late August 1994, the Senate dropped the issue, effectively killing the Clinton health plan.

In retrospect, it seems evident that the incompatible goals of reducing costs while striving for universal coverage had doomed the plan from the outset. Shrewder political maneuvering by the Clintons might have enabled them to salvage a scaled-down health reform.

Clinton's failure to deliver on his health care promise helped fuel a dramatic Republican resurgence. A young maverick congressman from Georgia, Newton

Leroy "Newt" Gingrich, had been leading a Republican attack against the House Democratic leadership. Using a well-funded political action committee, GOPAC, Gingrich supported other young, conservative Republicans who waged constant guerrilla war against the Democratic leadership. Gingrich believed that a vulnerable Clinton made 1994 the right year for an all-out effort to capture control of both houses of Congress.

In an attempt to transform 435 separate races into one national contest, Gingrich asked all GOP candidates to sign a ten-point Contract with America. The Contract consisted of familiar conservative goals, including a balanced budget amendment to the Constitution and term limits for members of Congress. For the first time in recent political history, a party sought to win Congress on ideological issues rather than relying on individual personalities.

A series of embarrassing disclosures involving Bill Clinton's character made this tactic particularly effective in 1994. During the 1992 campaign, the *New York Times* had raised questions about a bankrupt Arkansas land development called Whitewater in which the Clintons had lost a modest investment. In late 1993, the Resolution Trust Corporation began exploring Hillary Clinton's relationship with Madison Guaranty, a failed financial institution that had loaned the Clintons money for their Whitewater investment. Republicans were quick to charge that, in effect, American taxpayers were left holding the bill for a corrupt Arkansas bank that had close ties to the Clintons. Although there was no evidence of illegal acts, at the president's request, Attorney General Janet Reno appointed a special prosecutor to investigate the Whitewater affair.

Additional scandals cropped up over activities that had taken place after Clinton was elected president. Then in early 1994, Paula Jones, a former Arkansas state employee, charged that in 1991, then-Governor Clinton had exposed himself to her in a Little Rock hotel room and asked for oral sex.

While there was no clear-cut evidence to substantiate any of the charges against the president or his wife, Republicans used these episodes to revive earlier questions about Bill Clinton's character. More important, they were able to make more substantial attacks on the president, pointing to his failure to enact health care reform and, above all, reminding voters that in 1993 Clinton had enacted "the biggest tax increase" of all time.

The outcome of the November 1994 vote stunned political observers. The Republicans won both houses, gaining 9 seats in the Senate for a 53 to 47 edge and an astonishing 53 in the House to take control for the first time in forty years, 230 to 204.

There were two ways to view the remarkable about-face. Claiming that voters endorsed their Contract with America, the GOP hailed the outcome as a mandate to dismantle the welfare state in favor of free market economics. Clinton and some of his advisers, however, noted that the 1994 election was hardly representative of the country as a whole. The turnout was low—less than 40 percent, compared to 56 percent when Clinton won the presidency just two years before. Nationally, barely more than half of those voting supported Republicans, so that in effect just 20 percent of the electorate had determined the outcome.

The most striking statistic lay in the gender breakdown. Women voted for Democratic candidates by a margin of 53 to 47, while men went Republican by a much bigger differential, 57 to 43. In effect, an outpouring of "angry white males" who believed that Clinton was unfit to be president determined the outcome. The lesson for Clinton was clear. If he could win back the women and minorities who had voted for him in 1992 but stayed home in 1994, he had a chance to play the part of Comeback Kid once more.

THE CLINTON REBOUND

The Clinton campaign's 1992 slogan—"The economy, stupid"—proved even more apt four years later. The candidate who had accused his opponent of ignoring the economic suffering accompanying the recession of 1990–1991 now became the beneficiary of the recovery that had actually begun before the 1992 election.

The scope of the prosperity that spread throughout America in the 1990s was astonishing. Leaner American corporations, benefiting from downsizing, now found they could compete on favorable terms with Japanese and German rivals. Productivity shot up, keeping labor costs down. By 1996, Clinton could boast that nine million new jobs had been created since he took office and that the United States now led all other nations in the export of manufactured goods.

Clinton not only could claim credit for this remarkable resurgence, but he had the political skill to assuage the heavy human costs involved. He criticized corporations for dismissing so many employees in their quest for competitive advantages in the global marketplace, and he expressed concern over the growing inequality of wealth that benefited the educated and penalized the unskilled. In persuading Congress to pass the Family and Medical Leave Act in 1993 and increasing the minimum wage in 1996, the president was able to present himself as a caring leader concerned about the welfare of all Americans, not just the rich and powerful.

The Republicans, fresh from their sweeping victory in Congress, ironically became the vehicle for Clinton's political rehabilitation. In 1995, despite ma-

Consumers were the losers in the battle over the balanced budget waged by President Clinton and the Republican Congress when the failure to provide monies for operating expenses forced the shutdown of government services and facilities, like the Smithsonian Institution.

jorities in both houses, the GOP enacted only four minor parts of the Contract with America. Although the House of Representatives passed all but one item, the more cautious Senate refused to go along with such measures as term limits for members of Congress and a constitutional amendment requiring a balanced budget.

The president found Gingrich and his followers a perfect foil. When they demanded a balanced budget by early in the next century, Clinton agreed in principle, but then refused to accept GOP plans to slash programs such as Medicare and Medicaid. Portraying himself as the defender of the downtrodden, Clinton claimed that the Republican cuts in education, college loans, and health care would hurt children, ambitious young people, and the elderly.

The GOP leadership in Congress then made a gross miscalculation by threatening to close down the government to force Clinton to give way. The president stood firm, aware that Gingrich's negative ratings were higher than his own. Twice the Republicans shut down all but the most vital of federal services. The public outcry, however, directed almost entirely against Gingrich and the GOP, finally forced the Republicans to relent. They accepted a compromise in early 1996 that optimistically promised a balanced budget in seven years.

Once he had regained the initiative, Clinton pressed his advantage. The president pursued a policy of "triangulation," in which he distanced himself from both conservative Republicans and liberal Democrats to take the political high ground—the center. He signed a welfare reform bill, slightly more acceptable than the two he had vetoed before, to fulfill his earlier promise "to end welfare as we know it." The new legislation turned the welfare program over to the states, funded by scaled-down federal grants, and required recipients to find work within two years or lose their benefits.

While Republican hopefuls fought each other in a series of grueling and expensive party primaries, Clinton began raising huge sums to conduct a massive television campaign. Throughout the spring and summer, the airwaves were filled with 30-second commercials picturing the Republicans as trying to weaken Medicare and deny social services to those in need. By the time the GOP nominated Bob Dole, the respected but dour Senate majority leader from Kansas, the contest was all but over. Having used up nearly all his federal matching funds in the primaries, Dole was unable to counter Clinton's television blitz. By the traditional Labor Day starting date for the presidential campaign, Clinton had established a double-digit lead in the polls.

The ensuing fall campaign turned out to be anticlimactic. Everything Dole tried proved ineffective. His proposal of a 15 percent across-the-board tax cut found little acceptance. The GOP candidate began raising questions about Clinton's integrity, but an electorate that had grown bored with the unsubstantiated Whitewater charges failed to respond.

On election day, the president won his expected victory. A low turnout (10 million fewer voters than in 1992) and the third-party candidacy of Ross Perot (only a nuisance factor in 1996) prevented Clinton from winning a clear majority of the popular vote. But he carried 31 states with 379 electoral votes, for a deci-

THE ELECTION OF 1996

CANDIDATE	PARTY	POPULAR VOTE	ELECTORAL VOTE
Clinton	Democratic	47,401,185	379
Dole	Republican	39,197,469	159
Perot	Independent	8,085,294	—

sive victory over Dole, who won just 19 states with 159 electoral votes. Clinton's strategy of winning back the vote of women and minorities with his stress on education, health care, and providing opportunities for the young paid off handsomely. The gender gap was evident—men split evenly between Dole and Clinton, but 54 percent of female voters backed the president and only 38 percent voted for his GOP challenger. And, in contrast to 1994, women outnumbered men at the polls by a margin of 52 to 48.

In winning a second term, Clinton was both skillful and lucky. He benefited from the powerful economic growth that surpassed even his own expectations. But Clinton was also fortunate in the men who opposed him. Gingrich and Dole were experienced and able congressional leaders, but neither possessed the charisma or the public sensitivity that enabled Clinton to connect with the voter.

Yet it took both political skill and daring to weather the rejection Clinton experienced in 1994 and to adapt to the changing mood of the American people. Clinton won the gamble that he could turn the Republican shutdown of government into a political victory. And even though the president probably had little to do with the underlying causes of the economic boom, his willingness to adopt Greenspan's fiscal strategy and stake everything on deficit reduction gave him a reasonable claim to some of the credit. Most important, Clinton won in large measure because, unlike his opponents in 1992 and 1996, he seemed to embody, in the words of a British observer, "all the characteristics of his generation, distilled to an intensity that matched his ambition."

AFTER THE COLD WAR

American foreign policy underwent notable changes in the 1990s. Unlike his predecessor, Bill Clinton gave top priority to domestic issues rather than international affairs. And where Bush had viewed the world largely in geopolitical terms, stressing American strategic interests, Clinton gave economics top consideration, seeking markets abroad to stimulate the dormant American economy. Yet there was one similarity—under Clinton, as under Bush, American foreign policy continued to drift, lacking direction in the confusing post–Cold War world.

CLINTON AND THE WORLD

In choosing his foreign policy team, Clinton wisely went with experienced professionals to whom he could delegate foreign policy while he carried out his domestic agenda. Secretary of State Warren M. Christopher, who had served under Jimmy Carter, pursued a cautious, lawyerly approach to world problems. Christopher and his second-term replacement, Madeleine Albright, worked

The lack of any clear principle or philosophy guiding Clinton's foreign policy hampered the effort to define the proper role for and responsibilities of the United States, the only remaining super-power, in the post–Cold War era.

skillfully on the international issues confronting the nation, but they were hampered by the lack of any overarching principle to guide them.

Clinton's greatest challenge was in dealing with America's old Cold War rivals, Russia and China. Inheriting the chaos left by the breakup of the Soviet Union, the president concentrated on two issues. First, he followed Bush's lead in backing Russian President Boris Yeltsin to the hilt. In 1993, Clinton persuaded Congress to provide a $2.5 billion aid package to help Yeltsin carry out his free market reforms of the devastated Russian economy. The Clinton administration strongly supported Yeltsin and his successor, Vladimir V. Putin, despite Russia's continuing brutal war with Chechnya, and succeeded in maintaining good relations with Russia.

Clinton was even more successful on the second issue—preventing the proliferation of nuclear weapons among the former republics of the Soviet Union. With patient diplomacy, Christopher and his aides won agreements from Belarus and Kazakhstan to scrap their deadly ICBMs. Ukraine proved more difficult, but in 1994, Clinton persuaded President Leonid D. Kuchma to surrender his country's entire nuclear stockpile. Clinton's effort on behalf of nuclear nonproliferation in the former Soviet Union was perhaps his most important, if least heralded, achievement.

The president's policy toward China was more questionable. Clinton ignored China's dismal human rights record and continued Bush's policy of extending most favored nation status to Beijing annually. The growing importance of trade with China led Clinton to overlook the memory of the Tiananmen Square massacre and the continued persecution of dissidents in China. As trade with China began to rival that with Japan, the president announced a policy of "constructive engagement." It was better, he and his spokespeople declared, to keep talking and trading with China than to harden Chinese resentment against the West by harping on moral issues. In 2000, Clinton won a notable victory for free trade when the House voted to give China permanent most favored nation status.

The Chinese, however, proved to be less than cooperative. China ignored U.S. protests over its exports of missiles to Iran and continued to stifle dissent at home. The administration did send aircraft carriers to signify its support for Taiwan when China conducted provocative missile tests near the island on the eve of an election.

In the Middle East the administration continued the efforts to broker a peace between Israel and the Palestinian Arabs. Despite a promising beginning at a meeting between Yasir Arafat and Yitzhak Rabin in Washington in 1993, Clinton was unable to overcome the implacable ethnic and religious tensions that blocked the path to peace in the Middle East. Clinton's final attempt, a meeting between Arafat and Israeli Prime Minister Ehud Barak at Camp David in July 2000, proved futile.

In Iraq, Clinton met the continued defiance of Saddam Hussein by twice ordering American cruise missile attacks on Iraqi military targets. U.S. relations with Iran failed to improve, even with the election of a more moderate prime minister in 1997. Saudi Arabia remained a staunch ally, despite strains from a terrorist attack that killed nineteen American air force personnel in 1996. More worrisome was the increasingly heavy U.S. reliance on Persian Gulf oil as a result of Americans' love affair with gas-guzzling vans, pickup trucks, and sport utility vehicles. A sharp increase in the price of oil in early 2000 brought howls of protest from angry motorists and highlighted the risk of continuing American dependence on foreign oil.

INTERVENING IN SOMALIA AND HAITI

The most difficult foreign policy decisions for the Clinton administration came over the question of whether to use American troops to intervene abroad. The end of the Cold War made it much more difficult for the president and his advisers to decide when the national interest required sending American men and women into harm's way. Between 1993 and 1999, Clinton opted for foreign intervention in four areas—Somalia, Haiti, Bosnia, and Kosovo—with decidedly mixed results.

Clinton inherited the Somalian venture. In December 1992, George Bush had sent twenty-five thousand American troops to that starving country on a humanitarian mission. Under Clinton, however, the original aim of using troops to protect the flow of food supplies gradually shifted to supporting a UN effort at nation building. Tragedy struck in October 1993 when eighteen American soldiers died in a botched attempt to capture a local warlord. When television cameras recorded the naked corpse of a U.S. helicopter pilot being dragged through the streets of Somalia's capital, an angry Congress demanded a quick end to the intervention. Secretary of Defense Les Aspin resigned his office, after accepting responsibility for refusing to provide the U.S. commander with the tanks and aerial gunships he had requested. American forces left Somalia by the end of March 1994 in what was unquestionably the low point of Clinton's foreign policy.

The lack of clear criteria governing intervention that had brought on the disaster in Somalia almost led to another fiasco in Haiti. Seeking to halt the flow into Florida of thousands of Haitians fleeing both poverty and tyranny, Clinton worked to compel the military rulers of Haiti to abdicate in favor of the man they had overthrown in 1991, Jean-Bertrand Aristide.

After nearly a year of trade sanctions and increasing diplomatic pressure, the president prepared to use force to remove the generals. At the last minute, a three-member peace mission worked out a compromise that allowed U.S. troops to land unopposed in late September 1994. Aristide returned to Haiti to take power in mid-October, but he could do little either to restore democracy or achieve economic progress in view of his country's bankrupt treasury, devastated economy, and deep political divisions. By the time Aristide turned over the presidency to his elected successor in 1996, Haiti remained mired in hopeless poverty.

HALTING CIVIL WAR IN BOSNIA

Bosnia provided an even sterner test for the president's foreign policy. The breakup of Yugoslavia in 1991 led the Muslim president of Bosnia to ask the European Community to recognize the independence of Bosnia-Herzegovina. Bosnia's ethnic and religious makeup—44 percent Muslim, 31 percent Serb, and 17 percent Croat—quickly led to civil war by the spring of 1992. The Bosnian Serbs used the guns and heavy weaponry of the former Yugoslavian army to seize more than 70 percent of Bosnian territory. The Muslim and Croatian forces, hampered by an international arms embargo, were unable to mount effective resistance as the Serbs began a policy of "ethnic cleansing," driving Muslims and Croats from their ancestral homes and farms and beginning a lethal bombardment of the capital, Sarajevo.

Although Clinton had criticized Bush's failure to stop the fighting in Bosnia, the new president followed an equally cautious policy at first. When the Serbs rejected a proposal to divide Bosnia along ethnic lines in the spring of 1993, the president fell back on using American air power to patrol no-fly zones over Bosnia designed to protect UN peacekeeping efforts. Meanwhile, Serb artillery continued to pour a withering fire on the civilian population of Sarajevo, and journalists reported a series of brutal atrocities in which Serb troops slaughtered thousands of Muslim men.

After two years of passively watching Bosnian suffering, Clinton finally unleashed American air power. In the summer of 1995, American planes under NATO auspices began a series of air strikes on the Serb forces shelling Sarajevo from the surrounding mountains.

The air campaign, which lasted for two weeks, along with a major counteroffensive by Croatian and Muslim forces, finally led to a cease-fire in mid-October 1995. The three warring factions sent delegations to discuss a settlement at Wright-Patterson Air Force Base in Dayton, Ohio. After three weeks of talks, U.S. mediator Richard Holbrooke secured their agreement to create a weak central government for all Bosnia at Sarajevo and to divide the rest of the country into two parts—a Muslim-Croatian federation with 51 percent of the territory and a Serbian enclave with 49 percent. The Dayton plan called for free elections, the return of refugees to their former homes, and a NATO force to oversee the peace process.

Clinton took a calculated risk in sponsoring the Dayton settlement. The division of Bosnia into two competing halves meant only a temporary halt to the fighting rather than an end to the struggle for control of the country. But in halting the fighting at least temporarily, and especially in lifting the siege of Sarajevo, Clinton could take credit for a major humanitarian achievement. He displayed uncharacteristic political courage in agreeing to commit twenty thousand American troops to the International Force (IFOR) that would undertake the dangerous task of supervising the implementation of the Dayton accords.

The American troops, originally scheduled to leave by late 1996, stayed on in reduced numbers when the original departure date was postponed indefinitely. Few refugees were able to return to their original farms and villages. British, French, and U.S. members of IFOR faced tense confrontations with angry Serb mobs. Yet, the net result was an uneasy truce without fighting and without peacekeeping casualties. Clinton had not only been brave; he had been lucky as well.

SAVING KOSOVO

President Clinton faced an even more serious challenge in another Balkan troublespot—Kosovo. Serbian leader Slobodan Milosevic had ended the province's autonomy within Yugoslavia and imposed Serbian rule in 1989, even though 90 percent of the population was ethnic Albanian. When these people, who called themselves Kosovars, resisted by waging guerrilla war against the Serbian police, Milosevic responded with a campaign of repression and ethnic cleansing that outraged world opinion. After diplomatic efforts failed in 1998 and early 1999, the United States and NATO began an aerial assault on Serbia on March 24, 1999, in an effort to end the persecution of the Kosovars.

At first it appeared that Clinton and his outspoken secretary of state, Madeleine Albright, had miscalculated. The initial air attacks, largely directed at remote military bases, failed to persuade Milosevic to seek peace. Instead, he stepped up the ethnic cleansing in Kosovo, forcing hundreds of thousands of Kosovars to flee to neighboring Albania and Macedonia. NATO pilots, restricted to flying above 15,000 feet to avoid antiaircraft fire, were unable to hit the elusive Serbian forces in Kosovo. Other members of NATO ruled out the use of ground forces, the only realistic way to stop the Serbian repression.

Clinton, despite his reputation as an opportunist, stayed the course in Kosovo. He took the high ground, explaining to the American people his devo-

Refugees from Kosovo seeking to escape the physical danger of Serbian leader Slobodan Milosevic's campaign of repression and ethnic cleansing also had to cope with the psychological trauma of terror and fear as they were forced to leave their homes and homeland.

tion to a humanitarian cause. "It is perhaps the first conflict ever fought where no one wanted any land, or money, or geopolitical advantage," he declared. "We just wanted to stop and reverse ethnic cleansing."

His perseverance paid off. Unable to strike effectively at the Serbian army in Kosovo, NATO planes concentrated on the infrastructure of Serbia, targeting bridges, oil refineries, and, most important of all, power stations. By the end of May, Serbia had lost 60 percent of its electrical capacity and the domestic pressure on Milosevic began to mount. Milosevic finally agreed to end his attempts to purge Kosovo of its Albanian inhabitants. An agreement signed on June 10, 1999, called for the withdrawal of all Serb forces and placed Kosovo under UN supervision, with NATO troops acting as peacekeepers.

The conflict over Kosovo revealed both the strengths and weaknesses of the United States in the turbulent post–Cold War world. American military power, while great, was limited by the need to work with allies and by a strong desire to avoid risking American lives. Clinton could boast of an amazing result—NATO had waged a 12-week air campaign without the loss of a single pilot. Yet the United States had been unable to prevent Milosevic from uprooting and terrorizing nearly one million Kosovars.

The Clinton record abroad highlights the dilemma facing the United States in the post–Cold War world. Lacking the central focus of rivalry with another super power, the United States must decide when and where to bring its great power to bear without exhausting itself in endless adventures overseas. Clinton failed in Somalia, achieved only limited success in Haiti, but he could claim credit for ending a bloody civil war in Bosnia and for rescuing the Kosovars from Milosevic's ethnic cleansing. Like his predecessor, however, Clinton was unable to define a clear international mission for post–Cold War America. As a result, instead of setting the global agenda, the United States remained the prisoner of events abroad.

THE END OF THE CENTURY

It was the best of times; it was the worst of times. The nineties witnessed an un-paralleled burst of economic growth that clearly established the United States as the world's richest nation. Yet in the same decade, violence in the form of angry protests from both the extreme right and the extreme left, as well as a series of senseless school shootings, shocked the nation. Waco, Oklahoma City, Seattle, Littleton—these sites of violence and devastation revealed deep flaws in American society. Even the man who claimed credit for the prosperity, Bill Clinton, nearly lost the presidency over a sexual affair with a White House intern.

FROM DEFICIT TO SURPLUS

In early 2000, the boom of the 1990s officially became the longest sustained period of economic growth in American history. Since March 1991, the economy
had expanded by an incredible 64 percent, creating 20 million new jobs.
Unemployment dropped below 5 percent in 1997. Best of all, inflation remained
low, averaging just over 2 percent a year and thus enabling family income to surpass the previous all-time high of the early 1970s. The wealthy continued to make
the greatest gains, but prosperity reached every level, with those at the bottom
making real, if modest, advances.

Economists had difficulty explaining the happy situation. The primary factor
appeared to be continued increases in productivity, which allowed the economy
to expand without creating inflationary pressures. Businesses invested heavily in
new technology—especially computers and sophisticated software—that enabled workers to increase their output steadily. While the growth in exports that
Clinton fought for acted as a stimulus, it was the American consumer who was
the real hero. Foreign trade accounted for only about 10 percent of the output;
the rest came from constantly increasing domestic purchases of cars, computers,
household goods, and the myriad items that made up the largest consumer market in the world.

The wise and mysterious policies of Federal Reserve Chairman Alan
Greenspan helped sustain the boom by keeping inflation in check. He shrewdly
lowered interest rates in late 1997 to stimulate the economy during the Asian
turmoil. Then he began to raise them in 1999 and 2000 to the highest level of the
decade to slow down the economy and prevent surging world oil prices from
leading to a repetition of the great inflation of the 1970s.

The greatest benefit of the remarkable economic boom was the transformation of the federal budget. The worrisome deficits of the early 1990s disappeared, replaced with surpluses, at first modest, but then substantial. By 2000,
the surplus was more than $100 billion. The future promised to be even brighter,
with the Congressional Budget Office predicting a $2.2 trillion windfall in the
first decade of the new century.

The two parties could not agree on how to spend the unexpected bonanza.
Republicans called for across-the-board tax reductions, while Democrats wanted
to shore up the faltering Social Security and Medicare programs. Clinton's veto
of congressional tax cuts led to a deadlock that actually seemed to accomplish
what most Americans preferred—paying off the national debt that had grown so
large from past deficits.

The optimistic forecasts all depended on sustaining an unprecedented economic expansion. A recession, the normal pattern in the business cycle of the

past, would make the debate over whether to reduce taxes or shore up social programs irrelevant. Those who won control of the White House and Congress in 2000, therefore, would face the challenge not only of spending the surplus wisely, but also of ensuring its very existence.

VIOLENCE IN THE 1990S

Amid the unprecedented prosperity, a series of violent episodes disturbed the nation in the last decade of the century. Across the political spectrum, those who feared the loss of personal freedom resorted to force to express their discontent.

On the right, the militia movement accelerated after a shoot-out at Ruby Ridge, Idaho, in August 1992. Trying to arrest Christian survivalist Randy Weaver for illegal arms sales, federal agents shot and killed Weaver's wife and son during an eleven-day siege. Ruby Ridge became the rallying cry for right-wing activists who expressed their hatred for blacks, homosexuals, abortionists, and above all, the federal government.

A second tragic incident—the siege and destruction of the Branch Davidian compound in Waco, Texas, in 1993—intensified the militia impulse. What began in January as an attempt to arrest charismatic leader David Koresh on gun-dealing charges finally ended in April with the death of 75 Branch Davidians. As a stunned nation tried to understand what had happened at Waco, many dissidents had a ready explanation: An evil government, part of an international conspiracy to create a new world order at the expense of traditional American liberties, was responsible.

On April 19, 1995, the second anniversary of the Waco tragedy, Timothy McVeigh set off a powerful bomb in a rented Ryder truck in the street next to the federal building in Oklahoma City. McVeigh would eventually be sentenced to die for his crime. Yet he showed no remorse, reflecting the views expressed by the bomber in a novel McVeigh sold at gun shows around the country: "There is no way we can destroy the System without hurting many thousands of innocent people—no way."

The hatred of corporate America was as strong on the far left as on the far right. Its most dramatic expression came from the Unabomber—an unknown enemy of the global economy who sent sixteen bombs through the mail to corporation executives and university professors between 1978 and 1995, killing three people and injuring twenty-three others. In 1995, the *Washington Post* published his "manifesto," a 35,000-word polemic in which he blamed modern technology for all of humanity's ills.

Nearly a year later, in April 1996, federal agents arrested Theodore J. Kaczynski at a remote cabin in Montana. Theodore Kaczynski had earned a doc-

An aerial view of the destroyed Alfred P. Murrah Federal Building in Oklahoma City suggests the extent of the physical damage caused by the bomb blast on April 19, 1995, but cannot come close to expressing the human tragedy of the loss of 169 lives and the hundreds of injuries suffered.

torate in mathematics at Harvard and held a tenure-track teaching position at the University of California in Berkeley, but in 1969 he resigned in order to live in seclusion without modern conveniences. Kaczynski pled guilty to thirteen federal charges and was sentenced to prison for life without the possibility of parole. While few condoned his violent acts, some sympathized with Kaczynski's resentment over the degree to which technology encroached on individual privacy and curtailed personal freedom.

The clearest expression of unhappiness with the global economy of the 1990s came at the World Trade Organization (WTO) meeting in Seattle in late 1999. More than forty thousand protesters gathered to denounce the secret and autocratic way that the WTO encouraged the exploitation of both low-paid workers and natural resources in developing countries. At first, orderly marches led by organized labor and environmental groups drew large crowds and sent an important message of dissent. But then more violent demonstrators, notably black-clad anarchists from Eugene, Oregon, began smashing windows and trashing stores. The police overreacted, using tear gas, nightsticks, and rubber bullets to clear the streets and arrest more than 500 demonstrators. Despite the violence, the protesters succeeded not only in interrupting the WTO meeting, which adjourned without reaching any new trade agreements, but also in gaining worldwide attention for their grievances. Many Americans began to wonder whether the stunning advances in technology and world trade were compromising the traditional values and personal freedom they had always prized.

Even more perplexing were the series of senseless school shootings that occurred in the late 1990s. They began in Pearl, Mississippi, on October 1, 1997, when a 16-year-old boy stabbed his mother to death and then fatally shot two girls and wounded seven other high school students. Similar outbursts at West Paducah, Kentucky; Jonesboro, Arkansas; and Springfield, Oregon, in the 1997–1998 school year saw angry teenagers kill nine of their classmates and three adults. The culmination came at Columbine High School in Littleton, Colorado, in April 1999. Eric Harris and Dylan Klebold used automatic weapons to slaughter twelve fellow students and a teacher in the worst incident of school violence in American history.

The youthful killers had much in common. They all were white, above average in intelligence, attended nonurban schools, came from middle-class families, and were deeply alienated. All appeared to hold grudges against classmates they believed had ostracized them. Harris and Klebold considered themselves outcasts at Columbine and responded by wearing long black coats with swastikas and greeting each other in public with "Heil Hitler" salutes.

Explanations for their violent behavior ranged from easy access to guns to the violence of pop culture. In all five cases it was clear afterward that those who committed the crimes gave ample warning that something was very wrong. At Columbine, the two killers focused their psychology class project on mass murderer Jeffrey Dahmer and prepared a video for another class showing them pretending to shoot their archenemies, the school athletes.

Critics called for tighter gun controls, greater parental supervision of teenagers, and restrictions on the extreme lyrics of popular music and the violent nature of video games. "When you look at the overall pattern," commented one expert, "it's a pretty serious wake-up call." If nothing else, the school shootings revealed that beneath the veneer of prosperity there were deep flaws in both family structure and popular culture at the end of the century.

SHADOW ON THE WHITE HOUSE

"CLINTON ACCUSED OF URGING AIDE TO LIE," read the headline in the *Washington Post* on the morning of January 21, 1998. For the first time, the

American people learned that Kenneth Starr, the special prosecutor appointed in 1994 to probe the Whitewater affair, was now investigating charges that President Clinton had conducted a clandestine affair with a White House intern, Monica Lewinsky. For the next year, the Lewinsky scandal dominated national attention as Bill Clinton fought hard to save his presidency.

Clinton's relationship with Lewinsky began in November 1995 during one of the governmental shutdowns caused by the budget deadlock between the Republican Congress and the White House. With many of the staff temporarily laid off, the 22-year-old intern was able to achieve her goal of meeting privately with the president. For the next few months they had a sexual relationship without engaging in intercourse. Worried aides tried to break off the affair by transferring Lewinsky to a Pentagon job, but Clinton and Lewinsky met twice in early 1997, before the president terminated the relationship in April.

Two developments led to the public disclosure of the relationship. First, lawyers in the Paula Jones case sought to depose Monica Lewinsky in preparation for asking Bill Clinton under oath whether or not he had engaged in a sexual relationship with her. The president telephoned Lewinsky in December 1997 to urge her to file an affidavit denying the affair; in his own deposition on January 17, 1998, the president flatly stated, "I have never had sexual relations with Monica Lewinsky."

Unfortunately for Clinton, Linda Tripp, one of Monica Lewinsky's coworkers at the Pentagon, had recorded twenty hours of telephone conversations in which Lewinsky had described her sexual encounters with the president. On January 12, Tripp informed Starr's office of the tapes, thereby providing evidence, which Starr used to get the authority to investigate the Lewinsky relationship.

Clinton, caught off guard, was slow to respond to the public outcry. At first, he had the White House issue a blanket denial. Five days after the story broke, Bill Clinton finally spoke directly to the nation. At the end of a televised statement on after-school care, he turned to the cameras, wagged his finger, and said, "I want to say one thing to the American people . . . I did not have sexual relations with that woman, Miss Lewinsky."

For the next six months, the president stoutly maintained his innocence, aided greatly by Hillary Clinton who stood by her husband and charged that Starr's investigation was part of a "vast right-wing conspiracy" designed to drive him from the White House. Impressed with her wifely devotion, many Americans withheld judgment. Indeed, with the economy booming, Clinton's approval rate in the polls went from the low 60s to more than 70 percent. Starr's inability to

Members of the House Judiciary Committee listen to Clinton's testimony during the hearings on the president's impeachment in December 1998. The Committee sent four articles of impeachment to the full House, and the House adopted two—one count of perjury and one of obstruction of justice. The Senate could not muster the two-thirds majority required for conviction, and so Clinton was acquitted of both articles.

work out an immunity agreement with Monica Lewinsky allowed the matter to drift for months.

Matters finally came to a head in August when Lewinsky reached agreement with Starr's office. She gave a detailed account of her ten sexual encounters with the president and provided crucial physical evidence implicating Clinton. At the same time, she cast doubt on obstruction of justice charges against Clinton and his associates by denying that they had tried to buy her silence with job offers.

Realizing that he could no longer deny the affair, the president sought to limit the damage. On August 17 he admitted having "inappropriate intimate contact" with Lewinsky to Starr's grand jury, but insisted that he had not engaged in a sexual relationship. That evening Clinton spoke briefly to the nation. The president for the first time admitted to a relationship with Lewinsky that was "not appropriate" and "wrong." He said he regretted misleading the people and especially his wife, but he refused to apologize for his behavior or his false denials.

Clinton's fate hung in the balance. For the first time, some Democrats began to speak out. But just when Clinton was most vulnerable, the special prosecutor rescued him. In early September, Starr sent a 452-page report to Congress outlining eleven possible impeachment charges against Clinton. The key one was perjury, and Starr believed he had to go into excruciating detail on all ten sexual encounters between Clinton and Lewinsky to prove that the president had lied when he denied engaging in sexual relations with the intern.

Many Americans responded by condemning Starr rather than the president. Shocked by the sordid details, they blamed the prosecutor for exposing families to distasteful sexual practices on the evening news. When Hillary Clinton continued to support her husband, a majority of the public seemed to conclude that however bad the president's conduct, it was a private matter, one to be settled between a husband and a wife, not in the public arena.

Republican leaders ignored public sentiment and pressed ahead with impeachment proceedings. The clearest warning sign came in November, when the Democrats surprised the nation by gaining five seats in the House of Representatives and narrowed the GOP margin to six votes. In December, the House voted on four articles of impeachment, rejecting two, but approving two others—perjury and obstruction of justice—by small margins in nearly straight party-line votes.

The final showdown in the Senate was anticlimatic. With a two-thirds vote required to find the president guilty and remove him from office, there was no chance of conviction in the highly charged partisan mood that prevailed. The evidence against Clinton was strongest on the perjury charge, but on February 12, 1999, the GOP was unable to muster even a majority, with 45 in favor and 55 opposed. After a second, closer vote, 50 to 50, on obstruction of justice, the presiding officer, Chief Justice William Rehnquist, declared, "Acquitted of the charges."

Clinton had survived the Monica Lewinsky affair because once again he proved to be a far more skillful politician than his Republican opponents. With his wife's unflagging support, he was able to persuade the American people that his political opponents were waging a vendetta against him.

Yet Bill Clinton emerged from the ordeal with his presidency badly damaged. People forgave him his personal failings during an era of unrivaled prosperity, but they no longer held him in high esteem. His final two years in office would be devoted to a concerted effort to restore his damaged reputation. Desperate for a legacy to mark his White House years, Clinton failed to realize that he had already created an enduring one—he would always be remembered as the president who dishonored his office by his unseemly affair with a young intern.

A NATION DIVIDED

Two dominant trends shaped the election of 2000. The first, which favored the Democrats, was the economic boom that had erased the budget deficit and brought prosperity to nearly all Americans in the 1990s. At the same time, however, many voters felt a sense of disappointment and even betrayal because of Clinton's personal failings. The conflict between material abundance and moral values resulted in the closest election in more than a century.

The two candidates, Governor George W. Bush of Texas and Vice President Al Gore of Tennessee, had little in common. Gore had spent eighteen years in Washington as a congressman, senator, and vice president. Somewhat stiff and aloof in manner, he had mastered the intricacies of all the major policy issues and had the experience and knowledge to lead the nation. Bush, in contrast, had pursued a business career before winning the governorship of Texas in 1994. Personable and outgoing, Bush had the temperament for leadership but lacked not only experience but a full grasp of national issues. Journalists were quick to seize on the weaknesses of both men, accusing Gore of frequent and misleading exaggeration and Bush of mangling words and speaking only in generalities.

Both Bush and Gore were able to win their party's nominations after brief contests. The vice president, the acknowledged heir to Clinton, defeated former New Jersey Senator Bill Bradley with relative ease. The governor had more difficulty in turning back the challenge of Arizona Senator John McCain, who attracted support from independents and Democrats by championing campaign finance reform. But both candidates were hurt by the primaries. Bush was forced to move sharply to the right, jeopardizing his claim to stand for "compassionate conservatism," while Gore's aggressive tactics led Bradley to ask the embarrassing question, "How can we trust what you say as president if you don't tell the truth as a candidate."

The conventional political wisdom pointed to an easy win for Al Gore in the November election, but two factors reduced his chances. In the past, the candidate of a party in power during prosperous times had a clear advantage. A perceived need to separate himself from Clinton's scandals, however, led Gore to run as his own man and fail to capitalize on the president's glowing economic record. The decision of consumer advocate Ralph Nader to run for president on the Green Party ticket further complicated Gore's campaign and forced him to move to the left, enabling Bush to appeal more effectively to moderate independents.

In the fall campaign, the candidates presented American voters with a clear choice. Bush called for limiting the role of government and relying instead on the free market. The centerpiece of his campaign was a proposed across-the-board tax cut that would be of greatest benefit to the wealthy. He also favored partial privatization of Social Security and placed greater weight on the private sector in his prescription drug plan and other reform proposals. Gore became the advocate of government action, calling for an expanded federal role in education and health care. Delivering a fervent populist attack on big business Gore repeatedly charged that Bush's tax cut would not benefit the average American but only help "the wealthiest one percent."

The race for the White House, to the delight of the media, proved to be close and exciting. Bush led in the polls until Gore moved ahead after the Democratic convention in August. His vice presidential choice of Connecticut Senator Joe Lieberman, a moderate and a Jew, proved popular, while Bush's running mate, former defense secretary Dick Cheney, failed to excite the electorate. But the vice president's surprisingly uneven performance in three televised debates allowed Bush to regain a narrow lead in the polls in October until Gore began to draw even in the final week of the campaign.

The early returns on election night proved that the polls were right in stressing the closeness of the presidential race. Gore seemed the likely winner when the networks mistakenly predicted a Democratic victory in Florida. When the TV analysts put Florida back in the undecided column Bush began to forge ahead, sweeping the rest of the south. After midnight, when the networks again mistakenly called Florida, this time for Bush, the vice president telephoned the governor to concede, only to recant an hour later when it became clear that the Bush margin in Florida was paper thin.

For the next five weeks, all eyes were on the outcome in Florida. Gore had a lead of more than 200,000 nationwide in the popular vote and 267 electoral votes, yet Bush, with 246 votes in the Electoral College, could win the presidency with Florida's 25. Both sides sent phalanxes of lawyers to Florida. Bush's team sought to certify the results that showed the governor with a lead of 930 votes out of nearly six million cast. Citing many voting problems disclosed by the

THE ELECTION OF 2000

CANDIDATE	PARTY	POPULAR VOTE	ELECTORAL VOTE
Bush	Republican	50,456,167	271
Gore	Democratic	50,996,064	266*
Nader	Green	2,864,810	—

*One District of Columbia Gore elector abstained.

media, Gore asked for a recount in three heavily Democratic counties in south Florida. All three used antiquated punch card machines that resulted in some ballots not being clearly marked for any presidential candidate. For weeks the results in Florida, and hence of the entire election, appeared to depend on how one divined the intent of a voter based on hanging, dimpled, or pregnant chads.

The decision finally came in the courts. Democrats appealed the initial attempt to certify Bush as the victor to the Florida Supreme Court, where the majority of judges had been appointed by Democratic governors. The Florida court twice ordered recounts, but Bush's lawyers appealed to the United States Supreme Court. On December 12, five weeks after the election, the Court overruled the state court's call for a recount in a 5 to 4 decision that reflected a longstanding ideological divide among the nine justices. The next day, Gore gracefully conceded, and Bush finally became president-elect.

Although the rule of law prevailed, neither the winner nor the loser could take much pride in their party's behavior. The Republicans displayed an unseemly haste to have Bush declared the victor in Florida despite obvious voting irregularities. And the Democrats, while championing the principle of counting every vote, damaged their case from the outset by asking for recounts in just the three counties they believed would help their cause. The courts proved equally susceptible to partisan rather than legal considerations, issuing rulings that mirrored their political makeup.

When the Electoral College finally voted on December 18, there were 271 votes cast for Bush and 266 for Gore (one District of Columbia Gore elector abstained). Nearly complete election totals showed that Gore had received more than 500,000 more popular votes than Bush.

Bush's narrow victory revealed deep divisions in American life at the end of the twentieth century. The rural West and South went for Bush, along with a few key Midwest and border states, while Gore won the urban states along both coasts. There was an equally strong divide along economic lines, with the poor voting for Gore, the rich for Bush, and the middle class dividing evenly between the two candidates. Gore continued to benefit from the gender gap, winning 54 percent of the women's vote, and he won an even larger share of the black vote, 90 percent, than Clinton in 1996. The two candidates split the suburban vote evenly, and Bush succeeded in recapturing the lead among Catholic voters.

Nader proved to be less successful than early polls predicted, winning less than 3 percent of the national vote. Gore carried the states of the Pacific Northwest and the upper Midwest where Nader had the most support, but Nader's 96,837 votes in Florida probably cost Gore that crucial state.

Exit polls confirmed the underlying split in the electorate. More than 60 per-cent of voters surveyed said issues were more important than personality. Yet Bush was the overwhelming choice of those who placed primary emphasis on character and values. It was clear that Bush, who ended every campaign speech with a promise to restore dignity and honor to the White House, had used Clinton's foibles to counter Democratic claims of achieving prosperity. By the narrowest of margins, the American people appeared to have placed values ahead of material well-being in the election of 2000.

APPENDIX

The Declaration of Independence

In Congress, July 4, 1776

The Unanimous Declaration
of the Thirteen United States of America,

When, in the course of human events, it becomes necessary for one people to dissolve the political bonds which have connected them with another, and to assume, among the powers of the earth, the separate and equal station to which the laws of nature and of nature's God entitle them, a decent respect to the opinions of mankind requires that they should declare the causes which impel them to the separation.

We hold these truths to be self-evident: That all men are created equal; that they are endowed by their Creator with certain unalienable rights; that among these are life, liberty, and the pursuit of happiness; that, to secure these rights, governments are instituted among men, deriving their just powers from the consent of the governed; that whenever any form of government becomes destructive of these ends, it is the right of the people to alter or to abolish it, and to institute new government, laying its foundation on such principles, and organizing its powers in such form, as to them shall seem most likely to effect their safety and happiness. Prudence, indeed, will dictate that governments long established should not be changed for light and transient causes; and accordingly all experience hath shown that mankind are more disposed to suffer, while evils are sufferable, than to right themselves by abolishing the forms to which they are accustomed. But when a long train of abuses and usurpations, pursuing invariably the same object, evinces a design to reduce them under absolute despotism, it is their right, it is their duty, to throw off such government, and to provide new guards for their future security. Such has been the patient sufferance of these colonies; and such is now the necessity which constrains them to alter their former systems of government. The history of the present King of Great Britain is a history of repeated injuries and usurpations, all having in direct object the establishment of an absolute tyranny over these states. To prove this, let facts be submitted to a candid world.

He has refused his assent to laws, the most wholesome and necessary for the public good.

He has forbidden his governors to pass laws of immediate and pressing importance, unless suspended in their operation till his assent should be obtained; and, when so suspended, he has utterly neglected to attend to them.

He has refused to pass other laws for the accommodation of large districts of people, unless those people would relinquish the right of representation in the legislature, a right inestimable to them, and formidable to tyrants only.

He has called together legislative bodies at places unusual, uncomfortable, and distant from the depository of their public records, for the sole purpose of fatiguing them into compliance with his measures.

He has dissolved representative houses repeatedly, for opposing, with manly firmness, his invasions on the rights of the people.

He has refused for a long time, after such dissolutions, to cause others to be elected; whereby the legislative powers, incapable of annihilation, have returned to the people at large for their exercise; the state remaining, in the mean time, exposed to all the dangers of invasions from without and convulsions within.

He has endeavored to prevent the population of these states; for that purpose obstructing the laws for naturalization of foreigners; refusing to pass others to encourage their migration hither, and raising the conditions of new appropriations of lands.

He has obstructed the administration of justice, by refusing his assent to laws for establishing judiciary powers.

He has made judges dependent on his will alone, for the tenure of their offices, and the amount and payment of their salaries.

He has erected a multitude of new offices, and sent hither swarms of officers to harass our people and eat out their substance.

He has kept among us, in times of peace, standing armies, without the consent of our legislatures.

He has affected to render the military independent of, and superior to, the civil power.

He has combined with others to subject us to a jurisdiction foreign to our constitution, and unacknowledged by our laws, giving his assent to their acts of pretended legislation:

For quartering large bodies of armed troops among us;

For protecting them, by a mock trial, from punishment for any murder which they should commit on the inhabitants of these states;

For cutting off our trade with all parts of the world;

For imposing taxes on us without our consent;

For depriving us, in many cases, of the benefits of trial by jury;

For transporting us beyond seas, to be tried for pretended offenses;

For abolishing the free system of English laws in a neighboring province, establishing therein an arbitrary government, and enlarging its boundaries, so as to render it at once an example and fit instrument for introducing the same absolute rule into these colonies;

For taking away our charters, abolishing our most valuable laws, and altering fundamentally the forms of our governments;

For suspending our own legislatures, and declaring themselves invested with power to legislate for us in all cases whatsoever.

He has abdicated government here, by declaring us out of his protection and waging war against us.

He has plundered our seas, ravaged our coasts, burned our towns, and destroyed the lives of our people.

He is at this time transporting large armies of foreign mercenaries to complete the works of death, desolation, and tyranny already begun with circumstances of cruelty and perfidy scarcely paralleled in the most barbarous ages, and totally unworthy the head of a civilized nation.

He has constrained our fellow-citizens, taken captive on the high seas, to bear arms against their country, to become the executioners of their friends and brethren, or to fall themselves by their hands.

He has excited domestic insurrection among us, and has endeavored to bring on the inhabitants of our frontiers the merciless Indian savages, whose known rule of warfare is an undistinguished destruction of all ages, sexes, and conditions.

In every stage of these oppressions we have petitioned for redress in the most humble terms; our repeated petitions have been answered only by repeated injury. A prince, whose character is thus marked by every act which may define a tyrant, is unfit to be the ruler of a free people.

Nor have we been wanting in our attentions to our British brethren. We have warned them, from time to time, of attempts by their legislature to extend an unwarrantable jurisdiction over us. We have reminded them of the circumstances of our emigration and settlement here. We have appealed to their native justice and magnanimity; and we have conjured them, by the ties of our common kindred, to disavow these usurpations, which would inevitably interrupt our connections and correspondence. They, too, have been deaf to the voice of justice and of consanguinity. We must, therefore, acquiesce in the necessity which denounces our separation, and hold them, as we hold the rest of mankind, enemies in war, in peace friends.

We, therefore, the representatives of the United States of America, in General Congress assembled, appealing to the Supreme Judge of the world for the rectitude of our intentions, do, in the name and by the authority of the good people of these colonies, solemnly publish and declare, that these United Colonies are, and of right ought to be, FREE AND INDEPENDENT STATES; that they are absolved from all allegiance to the British crown, and that all political connection between them and the state of Great Britain is, and ought to be, totally dissolved; and that, as free and independent states, they have full power to levy war, conclude peace, contract alliances, establish commerce, and do all other acts and things which independent states may of right do. And for the support of this declaration, with a firm reliance on the protection of Divine Providence, we mutually pledge to each other our lives, our fortunes, and our sacred honor.

JOHN HANCOCK

BUTTON GWINNETT
LYMAN HALL
GEO. WALTON
WM. HOOPER
JOSEPH HEWES
JOHN PENN
EDWARD RUTLEDGE
THOS. HEYWARD, JUNR.
THOMAS LYNCH, JUNR.
ARTHUR MIDDLETON
SAMUEL CHASE
WM. PACA
THOS. STONE
CHARLES CARROLL OF
    CARROLLTON
GEORGE WYTHE
RICHARD HENRY LEE
TH. JEFFERSON
BENJ. HARRISON

THOS. NELSON, JR.
FRANCIS LIGHTFOOT LEE
CARTER BRAXTON
ROBT. MORRIS
BENJAMIN RUSH
BENJA. FRANKLIN
JOHN MORTON
GEO. CLYMER
JAS. SMITH
GEO. TAYLOR
JAMES WILSON
GEO. ROSS
CAESAR RODNEY
GEO. READ
THO. M'KEAN
WM. FLOYD
PHIL. LIVINGSTON
FRANS. LEWIS
LEWIS MORRIS

RICHD. STOCKTON
JNO. WITHERSPOON
FRAS. HOPKINSON
JOHN HART
ABRA. CLARK
JOSIAH BARTLETT
WM. WHIPPLE
SAML. ADAMS
JOHN ADAMS
ROBT. TREAT PAINE
ELBRIDGE GERRY
STEP. HOPKINS
WILLIAM ELLERY
ROGER SHERMAN
SAM'EL HUNTINGTON
WM. WILLIAMS
OLIVER WOLCOTT
MATTHEW THORNTON

The Constitution of the United States of America

PREAMBLE

We the People of the United States, in Order to form a more perfect Union, establish Justice, insure domestic Tranquility, provide for the common defence, promote the general Welfare, and secure the Blessings of Liberty to ourselves and our Posterity, do ordain and establish this Constitution for the United States of America.

ARTICLE I

Section 1

All legislative Powers herein granted shall be vested in a Congress of the United States, which shall consist of a Senate and House of Representatives.

Section 2

The House of Representatives shall be composed of Members chosen every second Year by the People of the several States, and the Electors in each State shall have the Qualifications requisite for Electors of the most numerous Branch of the State Legislature.

No Person shall be a Representative who shall not have attained to the Age of twenty five Years, and been seven Years a Citizen of the United States, and who shall not, when elected, be an inhabitant of that State in which he shall be chosen.

Representatives and direct Taxes shall be apportioned among the several States which may be included within this Union, according to their respective Numbers, *which shall be determined by adding to the whole Number of free Persons, including those bound to Service for a Term of Years, and excluding Indians not taxed, three fifths of all other Persons.* * The actual Enumeration shall be made within three Years after the first Meeting of the Congress of the United States, and within every subsequent Term of ten Years, in such Manner as they shall by Law direct. The Number of Representatives shall not exceed one for every thirty Thousand, but each State shall have at Least one Representative; *and until such enumeration shall be made, the State of New Hampshire shall be entitled to chuse three, Massachusetts eight, Rhode-Island and Providence Plantations one, Connecticut five, New York six, New Jersey four, Pennsylvania eight, Delaware one, Maryland six, Virginia ten, North Carolina five, South Carolina five, and Georgia three.*

When vacancies happen in the Representation from any State, the Executive Authority thereof shall issue Writs of Election to fill such Vacancies.

The House of Representatives shall chuse their Speaker and other Officers; and shall have the sole Power of Impeachment.

Section 3

The Senate of the United States shall be composed of two Senators from each State, *chosen by the Legislature thereof,* for six Years; and each Senator shall have one Vote.

---

* *Passages no longer in effect are printed in italic type.*

Immediately after they shall be assembled in Consequence of the first Election, they shall be divided as equally as may be into three Classes. The Seats of the Senators of the first Class shall be vacated at the Expiration of the second Year, of the second Class at the Expiration of the fourth Year, and of the third Class at the Expiration of the sixth Year so that one third may be chosen every second Year; and if Vacancies happen by Resignation, or otherwise, during the Recess of the Legislature of any state, the Executive thereof may make temporary Appointments until the next Meeting of the Legislature, which shall then fill such Vacancies.

No Person shall be a Senator who shall not have attained to the Age of thirty Years, and been nine Years a Citizen of the United States, and who shall not, when elected, be an Inhabitant of that State for which he shall be chosen.

The Vice President of the United States shall be President of the Senate, but shall have no Vote, unless they be equally divided.

The Senate shall chuse their other Officers, and also a President *pro tempore,* in the Absence of the Vice President, or when he shall exercise the Office of President of the United States.

The Senate shall have the sole Power to try all Impeachments. When sitting for that Purpose, they shall be on Oath or Affirmation. When the President of the United States is tried the Chief Justice shall preside: And no Person shall be convicted without the Concurrence of two thirds of the Members present.

Judgment in Cases of Impeachment shall not extend further than to removal from Office, and disqualification to hold and enjoy any Office of honor, Trust or Profit under the United States: but the Party convicted shall nevertheless be liable and subject to Indictment, Trial, Judgment and Punishment, according to Law.

Section 4

The Times, Places and Manner of holding Elections for Senators and Representatives, shall be prescribed in each State by the Legislature thereof; but the Congress may at any time by Law make or alter such Regulations, except as to the Places of chusing Senators.

The Congress shall assemble at least once in every Year, *and such Meeting shall be on the first Monday in December, unless they shall by Law appoint a different Day.*

Section 5

Each House shall be the Judge of the Elections, Returns and Qualifications of its own Members, and a Majority of each shall constitute a Quorum to do Business; but a smaller Number may adjourn from day to day, and may be authorized to compel the Attendance of absent Members, in such Manner, and under such Penalties as each House may provide.

Each House may determine the Rules of its Proceedings, punish its Members for disorderly Behaviour, and, with the Concurrence of two thirds, expel a Member.

Each House shall keep a Journal of its Proceedings, and from time to time publish the same, excepting such Parts as may in their Judgment require Secrecy; and the Yeas and Nays of the Members of either House on any question shall, at the Desire of one fifth of those Present, be entered on the Journal.

Neither House, during the Session of Congress, shall, without the Consent of the other, adjourn for more than three days, nor to any other Place than that in which the two Houses shall be sitting.

Section 6

The Senators and Representatives shall receive a Compensation for their Services, to be ascertained by Law, and paid out of the Treasury of the United States. They shall in all Cases, except

Treason, Felony and Breach of the Peace, be privileged from Arrest during their Attendance at the Session of their respective Houses, and in going to and returning from the same; and for any Speech or Debate in either House, they shall not be questioned in any other Place.

No Senator or Representative shall, during the Time for which he was elected, be appointed to any civil Office under the Authority of the United States, which shall have been created, or the Emoluments whereof shall have been encreased during such time, and no Person holding any Office under the United States, shall be a Member of either House during his Continuance in Office.

Section 7

All Bills for raising Revenue shall originate in the House of Representatives; but the Senate may propose or concur with Amendments as on other Bills.

Every Bill which shall have passed the House of Representatives and the Senate, shall, before it become a Law, be presented to the President of the United States; If he approve he shall sign it, but if not he shall return it, with his Objections to the House in which it shall have originated, who shall enter the Objections at large on their Journal, and proceed to reconsider it. If after such Reconsideration two thirds of that House shall agree to pass the Bill, it shall be sent, together with the Objections, to the other House, by which it shall likewise be reconsidered, and if approved by two thirds of that House, it shall become a Law. But in all such Cases the Votes of both Houses shall be determined by yeas and Nays, and the Names of the Persons voting for and against the Bill shall be entered on the Journal of each House respectively. If any Bill shall not be returned by the President within ten Days (Sundays excepted) after it shall have been presented to him, the Same shall be a Law, in like Manner as if he had signed it, unless the Congress by their Adjournment prevent its Return, in which Case it shall not be a Law.

Every Order, Resolution, or Vote to which the Concurrence of the Senate and House of Representatives may be necessary (except on a question of Adjournment) shall be presented to the President of the United States; and before the Same shall take Effect, shall be approved by him, or being disapproved by him, shall be repassed by two thirds of the Senate and House of Representatives, according to the Rules and Limitations prescribed in the Case of a Bill.

Section 8

The Congress shall have Power To lay and collect Taxes, Duties, Imposts and Excises, to pay the Debts and provide for the common Defence and general Welfare of the United States; but all Duties, Imposts and Excises shall be uniform throughout the United States;

To borrow Money on the credit of the United States;

To regulate Commerce with foreign Nations, and among the several States, and with the Indian Tribes;

To establish an uniform Rule of Naturalization, and uniform Laws on the subject of Bankruptcies throughout the United States;

To coin Money, regulate the Value thereof, and of foreign Coin, and fix the Standard of Weights and Measures;

To provide for the Punishment of counterfeiting the Securities and current Coin of the United States;

To establish Post Offices and post Roads;

To promote the Progress of Science and useful Arts, by securing for limited Times to Authors and Inventors the exclusive Right to their respective Writings and Discoveries;

To constitute Tribunals inferior to the supreme Court;

To define and punish Piracies and Felonies committed on the high Seas, and Offences against the Law of Nations;

To declare War, grant Letters of Marque and Reprisal, and make Rules concerning Captures on Land and Water;

To raise and support Armies, but no Appropriation of Money to that Use shall be for a longer Term than two Years;

To provide and maintain a Navy;

To make Rules for the Government and Regulation of the land and naval Forces;

To provide for calling forth the Militia to execute the Laws of the Union, suppress Insurrections and repel Invasions;

To provide for organizing, arming, and disciplining, the Militia, and for governing such Part of them as may be employed in the Service of the United States, reserving to the States respectively, the Appointment of the Officers, and the Authority of training the Militia according to the discipline prescribed by Congress;

To exercise exclusive Legislation in all Cases whatsoever, over such District (not exceeding ten Miles square) as may, by Cession of particular States, and the Acceptance of Congress, become the Seat of the Government of the United States, and to exercise like Authority over all Places purchased by the Consent of the Legislature of the State in which the Same shall be, for the Erection of Forts, Magazines, Arsenals, dock-Yards, and other needful Buildings;— And

To make all Laws which shall be necessary and proper for carrying into Execution the foregoing Powers, and all other Powers vested by this Constitution in the Government of the United States, or in any Department of Officer thereof.

Section 9

The Migration or Importation of such Persons as any of the States now existing shall think proper to admit, shall not be prohibited by the Congress prior to the Year one thousand eight hundred and eight, but a Tax or duty may be imposed on such Importation, not exceeding ten dollars for each Person.

The Privilege of the Writ of Habeas Corpus shall not be suspended, unless when in Cases of Rebellion or Invasion the public Safety may require it.

No Bill of Attainder or ex post facto Law shall be passed.

No Capitation, or other direct, Tax shall be laid, unless in Proportion to the Census or Enumeration herein before directed to be taken.

No Tax or Duty shall be laid on Articles exported from any State.

No Preference shall be given by any Regulation of Commerce or Revenue to the Ports of one State over those of another: nor shall Vessels bound to, or from, one State, be obliged to enter, clear, or pay Duties in another.

No Money shall be drawn from the Treasury, but in Consequence of Appropriations made by Law; and a regular Statement and Account of the Receipts and Expenditures of all public Money shall be published from time to time.

No Title of Nobility shall be granted by the United States: And no Person holding any Office of Profit or Trust under them, shall, without the Consent of the Congress, accept of any present, Emolument, Office, or Title, of any kind whatever, from any King, Prince, or foreign State.

Section 10

No State shall enter into any Treaty, Alliance, or Confederation; grant Letters of Marque and Reprisal; coin Money; emit Bills of Credit; make any Thing but gold and silver Coin a Tender in Payment of Debts; pass any Bill of Attainder, ex post facto Law, or Law impairing the obligation of Contracts, or grant any Title of Nobility.

No State shall, without the Consent of the Congress, lay any Imposts or Duties on Imports or Exports, except what may be absolutely necessary for executing its inspection Laws: and the net Produce of all Duties and Imposts, laid by any State on Imports or Exports, shall be for the Use of the Treasury of the United States; and all such Laws shall be subject to the Revision and Controul of the Congress.

No State shall, without the Consent of Congress, lay any Duty of Tonnage, keep Troops, or Ships of War in time of Peace, enter into any Agreement or Compact with another State, or with a foreign Power, or engage in War, unless actually invaded, or in such imminent Danger as will not admit of delay.

ARTICLE II
Section 1

The executive Power shall be vested in a President of the United States of America. He shall hold his Office during the Term of four Years, and, together with the Vice President, chosen for the same Term, be elected, as follows:

Each State shall appoint, in such Manner as the Legislature thereof may direct, a Number of Electors, equal to the whole Number of Senators and Representatives to which the State may be entitled in the Congress: but no Senator or Representative, or Person holding an Office of Trust or Profit under the United States, shall be appointed an Elector.

The Electors shall meet in their respective States, and vote by Ballot for two Persons, of whom one at least shall not be an Inhabitant of the same State with themselves. And they shall make a List of all the Persons voted for, and of the Number of Votes for each; which List they shall sign and certify, and transmit sealed to the Seat of the Government of the United States, directed to the President of the Senate. The President of the Senate shall, in the Presence of the Senate and House of Representatives, open all the Certificates, and the Votes shall then be counted. The Person having the greatest Number of Votes shall be the President, if such Number be a Majority of the whole number of Electors appointed; and if there be more than one who have such Majority, and have an equal Number of Votes, then the House of Representatives shall immediately chuse by Ballot one of them for President; and if no Person have a Majority, then from the five highest on the List the said House shall in like Manner chuse the President. But in chusing the President, the Votes shall be taken by States, the Representation from each State having one Vote; A quorum for this Purpose shall consist of a Member or Members from two thirds of the States, and a Majority of all the States shall be necessary to a Choice. In every Case, after the Choice of the President, the Person having the greatest Number of Votes of the Electors shall be the Vice President. But if there should remain two or more who have equal Votes, the Senate shall chuse from them by Ballot the Vice President.

The Congress may determine the time of chusing the Electors, and the Day on which they shall give their Votes; which Day shall be the same throughout the United States.

No person except a natural born Citizen, *or a Citizen of the United States, at the time of the Adoption of this Constitution,* shall be eligible to the Office of President; neither shall any Person be eligible to that Office who shall not have attained to the Age of thirty five Years, and been fourteen Years a Resident within the United States.

In Case of the Removal of the President from Office, or of his Death, Resignation, or Inability to discharge the Powers and Duties of the said Office, the Same shall devolve on the Vice President, and the Congress may by Law provide for the Case of Removal, Death, Resignation or Inability, both of the President and Vice President, declaring what Officer shall then act as President, and such Officer shall act accordingly, until the Disability be removed, or a President shall be elected.

The President shall, at stated Times, receive for his Services, a Compensation, which shall neither be encreased nor diminished during the Period for which he shall have been elected, and he shall not receive within that period any other Emolument from the United States, or any of them.

Before he enter on the Execution of his Office, he shall take the following Oath or Affirmation:—"I do solemnly swear (or affirm) that I will faithfully execute the Office of President of the United States, and will to the best of my Ability, preserve, protect and defend the Constitution of the United States."

Section 2

The President shall be Commander in Chief of the Army and Navy of the United States, and of the Militia of the several States, when called into the actual Service of the United States; he may require the Opinion, in writing, of the principal Officer in each of the executive Departments, upon any Subject relating to the Duties of their respective Offices, and he shall have Power to grant Reprieves and Pardons for Offences against the United States, except in Cases of Impeachment.

He shall have Power, by and with the Advice and Consent of the Senate, to make Treaties, provided two thirds of the Senators present concur; and he shall nominate, and by and with the Advice and Consent of the Senate, shall appoint Ambassadors, other public Ministers and Consuls, Judges of the supreme Court, and all other Officers of the United States, whose Appointments are not herein otherwise provided for, and which shall be established by Law: but the Congress may by Law vest the Appointment of such inferior Officers, as they think proper in the President alone, in the Courts of Law, or in the Heads of Departments.

The President shall have Power to fill up all Vacancies that may happen during the Recess of the Senate, by granting Commissions which shall expire at the End of their next Session.

Section 3

He shall from time to time give to the Congress Information of the State of the Union, and recommend to their Consideration such Measures as he shall judge necessary and expedient; he may, on extraordinary Occasions, convene both Houses, or either of them, and in Case of disagreement between them, with Respect to the Time of Adjournment, he may adjourn them to such Time as he shall think proper; he shall receive Ambassadors and other public Ministers; he shall take Care that the Laws be faithfully executed, and shall Commission all the officers of the United States.

Section 4

The President, Vice President and all civil Officers of the United States, shall be removed from Office on Impeachment for, and Conviction of, Treason, Bribery or other high Crimes and Misdemeanors.

ARTICLE III

Section 1

The judicial Power of the United States, shall be vested in one supreme Court, and in such inferior Courts as the Congress may from time to time ordain and establish. The Judges, both of the supreme and inferior Courts, shall hold their offices during good Behaviour, and shall, at stated Times, receive for their Services, a Compensation, which shall not be diminished during their Continuance in Office.

Section 2

The judicial Power shall extend to all Cases, in Law and Equity, arising under this Constitution, the Laws of the United States, and Treaties made, or which shall be made, under their Authority;—to all Cases affecting Ambassadors, other public Ministers and Consuls;—to all Cases of admiralty and maritime Jurisdiction;—to Controversies to which the United States shall be a Party;—to Controversies between two or more States;—*between a State and Citizens of another State;*—between Citizens of different States;—between Citizens of the same State claiming Lands under Grants of different States, and between a State, or the Citizens thereof, and foreign States, Citizens or Subjects.

In all Cases affecting Ambassadors, other public Ministers and Consuls, and those in which a State shall be Party, the supreme Court shall have original Jurisdiction. In all the other Cases before mentioned, the supreme Court shall have appellate Jurisdiction, both as to Law and Fact, with such Exceptions, and under such Regulations as the Congress shall make.

The Trial of all Crimes, except in Cases of Impeachment, shall be by Jury; and such Trial shall be held in the State where the said Crimes shall have been committed, but when not committed within any State, the Trial shall be at such Place or Places as the Congress may by Law have directed.

Section 3

Treason against the United States, shall consist only in levying War against them, or in adhering to their Enemies, giving them Aid and Comfort. No person shall be convicted of Treason unless on the Testimony of two Witnesses to the same overt Act, or on Confession in open Court.

The Congress shall have Power to declare the Punishment of Treason, but no Attainder of Treason shall work Corruption of Blood, or Forfeiture except during the Life of the Person attainted.

ARTICLE IV

Section 1

Full Faith and Credit shall be given in each State to the public Acts, Records, and judicial Proceedings of every other State. And the Congress may by general Laws prescribe the Manner in which such Acts, Records and Proceedings shall be proved, and the Effect thereof.

Section 2

The Citizens of each State shall be entitled to all Privileges and Immunities of Citizens in the several States.

A Person charged in any State with Treason, Felony, or other Crime, who shall flee from Justice, and be found in another State, shall on Demand of the executive Authority of the State from which he fled, be delivered up, to be removed to the State having Jurisdiction of the Crime.

No Person held to Service or Labour in one State, under the Laws thereof, escaping into another, shall, in Consequence of any Law or Regulation therein, be discharged from such Service or Labour, but shall be delivered up on Claim of the Party to whom such Service or Labour may be due.

Section 3

New States may be admitted by the Congress into this Union; but no new State shall be formed or erected within the Jurisdiction of any other State; nor any State be formed by the Junction of two or more States, or Parts of States, without the Consent of the Legislatures of the States concerned as well as of the Congress.

The Congress shall have Power to dispose of and make all needful Rules and Regulations respecting the Territory or other Property belonging to the United States; and nothing in this Constitution shall be so construed as to Prejudice any Claims of the United States, or of any particular States.

Section 4

The United States shall guarantee to every State in this Union a Republican Form of Government, and shall protect each of them against Invasion; and on Application of the Legislature, or of the Executive (when the Legislature cannot be convened) against domestic violence.

ARTICLE V

The Congress, whenever two thirds of both Houses shall deem it necessary, shall propose Amendments to this Constitution, or, on the Application of the Legislatures of two thirds of the several States, shall call a Convention for proposing Amendments, which, in either Case, shall be valid to all Intents and Purposes, as Part of this Constitution, when ratified by the Legislatures of three fourths of the several States, or by Conventions in three fourths thereof, as the one or the other Mode of Ratification may be proposed by the Congress; Provided *that no Amendment which may be made prior to the Year One thousand eight hundred and eight shall in any Manner affect the first and fourth Clauses in the Ninth Section of the first Article;* and that no State, without its Consent, shall be deprived of its equal Suffrage in the Senate.

ARTICLE VI

All Debts contracted and Engagements entered into, before the Adoption of this Constitution, shall be as valid against the United States under this Constitution, as under the Confederation.

This Constitution, and Laws of the United States which shall be made in Pursuance thereof; and all Treaties made, or which shall be made, under the Authority of the United States, shall be the supreme Law of the Land; and the Judges in every State shall be bound thereby, any Thing in the Constitution or Laws of any State to the Contrary notwithstanding.

The Senators and Representatives before mentioned, and the Members of the several State Legislatures, and all executive and Judicial Officers, both of the United States and of the several States, shall be bound by Oath or Affirmation, to support this Constitution; but no religious Test shall ever be required as a Qualification to any Office of public Trust under the United States.

ARTICLE VII

The Ratification of the Conventions of nine States, shall be sufficient for the Establishment of this Constitution between the States so ratifying the Same.

Done in Convention by the Unanimous Consent of the States present the Seventeenth Day of September in the Year of our Lord one thousand seven hundred and Eighty seven and of the Independence of the United States of America the Twelfth* IN WITNESS whereof We have hereunto subscribed our Names,

GEORGE WASHINGTON
President and Deputy from Virginia

Delaware
GEORGE READ
GUNNING BEDFORD, JR.
JOHN DICKINSON
RICHARD BASSETT
JACOB BROOM

Maryland
JAMES MCHENRY
DANIEL OF ST. THOMAS JENIFER
DANIEL CARROLL

Virginia
JOHN BLAIR
JAMES MADISON, JR.

North Carolina
WILLIAM BLOUNT
RICHARD DOBBS SPRAIGHT
HUGH WILLIAMSON

South Carolina
JOHN RUTLEDGE
CHARLES COTESWORTH PINCKNEY
CHARLES PINCKNEY
PIERCE BUTLER

Georgia
WILLIAM FEW
ABRAHAM BALDWIN

New Hampshire
JOHN LANGDON
NICHOLAS GILMAN

Massachusetts
NATHANIEL GORHAM
RUFUS KING

Connecticut
WILLIAM SAMUEL JOHNSON
ROGER SHERMAN

New York
ALEXANDER HAMILTON

New Jersey
WILLIAM LIVINGSTON
DAVID BREARLEY
WILLIAM PATERSON
JONATHAN DAYTON

Pennsylvania
BENJAMIN FRANKLIN
THOMAS MIFFLIN
ROBERT MORRIS
GEORGE CLYMER
THOMAS FITZSIMONS
JARED INGERSOLL
JAMES WILSON
GOUVERNEUR MORRIS

---

*The Constitution was submitted on September 17, 1787, by the Constitutional Convention, was ratified by the Convention of several states at various dates up to May 29, 1790, and became effective on March 4, 1789.

Amendments to the Constitution

AMENDMENT I

Congress shall make no law respecting an establishment of religion, or prohibiting the free exercise thereof; or abridging the freedom of speech, or of the press; or the right of the people peaceably to assemble, and to petition the Government for a redress of grievances.

AMENDMENT II

A well regulated Militia being necessary to the security of a free State, the right of the people to keep and bear Arms, shall not be infringed.

AMENDMENT III

No Soldier shall, in time of peace be quartered in any house, without the consent of the Owner, nor in time of war, but in a manner to be prescribed by law.

AMENDMENT IV

The right of the people to be secure in their persons, houses, papers, and effects, against unreasonable searches and seizures, shall not be violated, and no Warrants shall issue, but upon probable cause, supported by Oath or affirmation, and particularly describing the place to be searched, and the persons or things to be seized.

AMENDMENT V

No person shall be held to answer for a capital, or otherwise infamous crime, unless on a presentment or indictment of a Grand Jury, except in cases arising in the land or naval forces, or in the Militia, when in actual service in time of War or public danger; nor shall any person be subject for the same offense to be twice put in jeopardy of life or limb; nor shall be compelled in any criminal case to be a witness against himself, nor be deprived of life, liberty, or property, without due process of law; nor shall private property be taken for public use, without just compensation.

AMENDMENT VI

In all criminal prosecutions, the accused shall enjoy the right to a speedy and public trial, by an impartial jury of the State and district wherein the crime shall have been committed, which district shall have been previously ascertained by law, and to be informed of the nature and cause of the accusation; to be confronted with the witnesses against him; to have compulsory process for obtaining witnesses in his favor, and to have the Assistance of Counsel for his defence.

AMENDMENT VII

In Suits at common law, where the value in controversy shall exceed twenty dollars, the right of trial by jury shall be preserved, and no fact tried by a jury, shall be otherwise re-examined in any Court of the United States, than according to the rules of the common law.

AMENDMENT VIII

Excessive bail shall not be required, nor excessive fines imposed, nor cruel and unusual punishments inflicted.

AMENDMENT IX

The enumeration in the Constitution, of certain rights, shall not be construed to deny or disparage others retained by the people.

AMENDMENT X*

The powers not delegated to the United States by the Constitution, nor prohibited by it to the States, are reserved to the States respectively, or to the people.

AMENDMENT XI
[ADOPTED 1798]

The Judicial power of the United States shall not be construed to extend to any suit in law or equity, commenced or prosecuted against one of the United States by Citizens of another State, or by Citizens or Subjects of any Foreign State.

AMENDMENT XII
[ADOPTED 1804]

The Electors shall meet in their respective states, and vote by ballot for President and Vice President, one of whom, at least, shall not be an inhabitant of the same state with themselves; they shall name in their ballots the person voted for as President, and in distinct ballots the person voted for as Vice President, and they shall make distinct lists of all persons voted for as President, and of all persons voted for as Vice President, and of the number of votes for each, which lists they shall sign and certify, and transmit sealed to the seat of the government of the United States, directed to the President of the Senate;—The President of the Senate shall, in the presence of the Senate and House of Representatives, open all the certificates and the votes shall then be counted;—The person having the greatest number of votes for President, shall be the President, if such number be a majority of the whole number of Electors appointed; and if no person have such majority, then from the persons having the highest numbers not exceeding three on the list of those voted for as President, the House of Representatives shall choose immediately, by ballot, the President. But in choosing the President, the votes shall be taken by states, the representation from each state having one vote; a quorum for this purpose shall consist of a member or members from two-thirds of the states, and a majority of all the states shall be necessary to a choice. And if the House of Representatives shall not choose a President whenever the right of choice shall devolve upon them, before *the fourth day of March* next following, then the Vice President shall act as President, as in the case of the death or other constitutional disability of the President.—The person having the greatest number of votes as Vice President, shall be the Vice President, if such number be a majority of the whole number of Electors appointed, and if no person have a majority, then from the two highest numbers on the list, the Senate shall choose the Vice President; a quorum for the purpose shall consist of two-thirds of the whole number of Senators, and a majority of the whole number shall be necessary to a choice. But no person con-

*The first ten amendments (the Bill of Rights) were ratified, and their adoption was certified, on December 15, 1791.

stitutionally ineligible to the office of President shall be eligible to that of Vice President of the United States.

AMENDMENT XIII
[ADOPTED 1865]

Section 1

Neither slavery nor involuntary servitude, except as a punishment for crime whereof the party shall have been duly convicted, shall exist within the United States, or any place subject to their jurisdiction.

Section 2

Congress shall have power to enforce this article by appropriate legislation.

AMENDMENT XIV
[ADOPTED 1868]

Section 1

All persons born or naturalized in the United States, and subject to the jurisdiction thereof, are citizens of the United States and of the State wherein they reside. No State shall make or enforce any law which shall abridge the privileges or immunities of citizens of the United States; nor shall any State deprive any person of life, liberty, or property, without due process of law; nor deny to any person within its jurisdiction the equal protection of the laws.

Section 2

Representatives shall be apportioned among the several States according to their respective numbers, counting the whole number of persons in each State, excluding Indians not taxed. But when the right to vote at any election for the choice of electors for President and Vice President of the United States, Representatives in Congress, the Executive and Judicial officers of a State, or the members of the Legislature thereof, is denied to any of the male inhabitants of such State, being twenty-one years of age, and citizens of the United States, or in any way abridged, except for participation in rebellion, or other crime, the basis of representation therein shall be reduced in the proportion which the number of such male citizens shall bear to the whole number of male citizens twenty-one years of age in such State.

Section 3

No person shall be a Senator or Representative in Congress, or elector of President and Vice President, or hold any office, civil or military, under the United States, or under any State, who, having previously taken an oath, as a member of Congress, or as an officer of the United States, or as a member of any State legislature, or as an executive or judicial officer of any State, to support the Constitution of the United States, shall have engaged in insurrection or rebellion against the same, or given aid or comfort to the enemies thereof. But Congress may by a vote of two-thirds of each House, remove such disability.

Section 4

The validity of the public debt of the United States, authorized by law, including debts incurred for payment of pensions and bounties for services in suppressing insurrection or rebellion, shall not be questioned. But neither the United States nor any State shall assume or pay any debt or obligation incurred in aid of insurrection or rebellion against the United States, or any claim for the loss or emancipation of any slave; but all such debts, obligations and claims shall be held illegal and void.

Section 5

The Congress shall have power to enforce, by appropriate legislation, the provisions of this article.

AMENDMENT XV
[ADOPTED 1870]

Section 1

The right of citizens of the United States to vote shall not be denied or abridged by the United States or by any State on account of race, color, or previous condition of servitude.

Section 2

The Congress shall have power to enforce this article by appropriate legislation.

AMENDMENT XVI
[ADOPTED 1913]

The Congress shall have power to lay and collect taxes on incomes, from whatever source derived, without apportionment among the several States, and without regard to any census or enumeration.

AMENDMENT XVII
[ADOPTED 1913]

The Senate of the United States shall be composed of two Senators from each State, elected by the people thereof, for six years; and each Senator shall have one vote. The electors in each State shall have the qualifications requisite for electors of the most numerous branch of the State legislatures.

When vacancies happen in the representation of any State in the Senate, the executive authority of such State shall issue writs of election to fill such vacancies: *Provided,* That the legislature of any State may empower the executive thereof to make temporary appointments until the people fill the vacancies by election as the legislature may direct.

This amendment shall not be so construed as to affect the election or term of any Senator chosen before it becomes valid as part of the Constitution.

AMENDMENT XVIII
[ADOPTED 1919, REPEALED 1933]

Section 1

After one year from the ratification of this article the manufacture, sale, or transportation of intoxicating liquors within, the importation thereof into, or the exportation thereof from the United States and all territory subject to the jurisdiction thereof for beverage purposes is hereby prohibited.

Section 2

The Congress and the several States shall have concurrent power to enforce this article by appropriate legislation.

Section 3

This article shall be inoperative unless it shall have been ratified as an amendment to the Constitution by the legislatures of the several States, as provided in the Constitution, within seven years from the date of the submission hereof to the States by the Congress.

AMENDMENT XIX
[ADOPTED 1920]

The right of citizens of the United States to vote shall not be denied or abridged by the United States or by any State on account of sex.

Congress shall have power to enforce this article by appropriate legislation.

AMENDMENT XX
[ADOPTED 1933]

Section 1

The terms of the President and Vice President shall end at noon on the 20th day of January, and the terms of Senators and Representatives at noon on the 3d day of January, of the years in which such terms would have ended if this article had not been ratified and the terms of their successors shall then begin.

Section 2

The Congress shall assemble at least once in every year, and such meeting shall begin at noon on the 3d day of January, unless they shall by law appoint a different day.

Section 3

If, at the time fixed for the beginning of the term of the President, the President elect shall have died, the Vice President elect shall become President. If a President shall not have been chosen before the time fixed for the beginning of his term, or if the President elect shall have failed to qualify, then the Vice President elect shall act as President until a President shall have qualified; and the Congress may by law provide for the case wherein neither a President elect nor a Vice President elect shall have qualified, declaring who shall then act as President, or the manner in which one who is to act shall be selected, and such person shall act accordingly until a President or Vice President shall have qualified.

Section 4

The Congress may by law provide for the case of the death of any of the persons from whom the House of Representatives may choose a President whenever the right of choice shall have devolved upon them, and for the case of the death of any of the persons from whom the Senate may choose a Vice President whenever the right of choice shall have devolved upon them.

Section 5

Sections 1 and 2 shall take effect on the 15th day of October following the ratification of this article.

Section 6

This article shall be inoperative unless it shall have been ratified as an amendment to the Constitution by the legislatures of three fourths of the several States within seven years from the date of its submission.

Amendment XXI
[Adopted 1933]

Section 1

The eighteenth article of amendment to the Constitution of the United States is hereby repealed.

Section 2

The transportation or importation into any State, Territory, or possession of the United States for delivery or use therein of intoxicating liquors in violation of the laws thereof, is hereby prohibited.

Section 3

This article shall be inoperative unless it shall have been ratified as an amendment to the Constitution by conventions in the several States, as provided in the Constitution, within seven years from the date of the submission hereof to the States by the Congress.

Amendment XXII
[Adopted 1951]

Section 1

No person shall be elected to the office of the President more than twice, and no person who has held the office of President, or acted as President, for more than two years of a term to which some other person was elected President shall be elected to the office of the President more than once. But this Article shall not apply to any person holding the office of President when this Article was proposed by the Congress, and shall not prevent any person who may be holding the office of President, or acting as President, during the term within which this Article becomes operative from holding the office of President or acting as President during the remainder of such term.

Section 2

This article shall be inoperative unless it shall have been ratified as an amendment to the Constitution by the legislatures of three-fourths of the several States within seven years from the date of its submission to the States by the Congress.

Amendment XXIII
[Adopted 1961]

Section 1

The District constituting the seat of Government of the United States shall appoint in such manner as the Congress shall direct:

A number of electors of President and Vice President equal to the whole number of Senators and Representatives in Congress to which the District would be entitled if it were a State, but in no event more than the least populous State; they shall be in addition to those appointed by the States, but they shall be considered, for the purposes of the election of President and Vice President, to be electors appointed by a State; and they shall meet in the District and perform such duties as provided by the twelfth article of amendment.

Section 2

The Congress shall have power to enforce this article by appropriate legislation.

AMENDMENT XXIV
[ADOPTED 1964]

Section 1

The right of citizens of the United States to vote in any primary or other election for President or Vice President, for electors for President or Vice President, or for Senator or Representative in Congress, shall not be denied or abridged by the United States or any state by reason of failure to pay any poll tax or other tax.

Section 2

The Congress shall have the power to enforce this article by appropriate legislation.

AMENDMENT XXV
[ADOPTED 1967]

Section 1

In case of the removal of the President from office or his death or resignation, the Vice President shall become President.

Section 2

Whenever there is a vacancy in the office of the Vice President, the President shall nominate a Vice President who shall take the office upon confirmation by a majority vote of both houses of Congress.

Section 3

Whenever the President transmits to the President pro tempore of the Senate and the Speaker of the House of Representatives his written declaration that he is unable to discharge the powers and duties of his office, and until he transmits to them a written declaration to the contrary, such powers and duties shall be discharged by the Vice President as Acting President.

Section 4

Whenever the Vice President and a majority of either the principal officers of the executive departments or of such other body as Congress may by law provide, transmit to the President pro tempore of the Senate and the Speaker of the House of Representatives their written declaration that the President is unable to discharge the powers and duties of his office, the Vice President shall immediately assume the powers and duties of the office as Acting President.

Thereafter, when the President transmits to the President pro tempore of the Senate and the Speaker of the House of Representatives his written declaration that no inability exists, he shall resume the powers and duties of his office unless the Vice President and a majority of either the principal officers of the executive department or of such other body as Congress may by law provide, transmit within four days to the President pro tempore of the Senate and the Speaker of the House of Representatives their written declaration that the President is unable to discharge the powers and duties of his office. Thereupon Congress shall decide the issue, assembling within 48 hours for that purpose if not in session. If the Congress, within 21 days after receipt of the latter written declaration, or, if Congress is not in session, within 21 days after Congress is required to assemble, determines by two-thirds vote of both houses that the President is unable to discharge the powers and duties of his office, the Vice President shall continue to discharge the same as Acting President; otherwise, the President shall resume the powers and duties of his office.

AMENDMENT XXVI
[ADOPTED 1971]

Section 1

The right of citizens of the United States, who are 18 years of age or older, to vote shall not be denied or abridged by the United States or any state on account of age.

Section 2

The Congress shall have the power to enforce this article by appropriate legislation.

AMENDMENT XXVII
[ADOPTED 1992]

No law, varying the compensation for the services of the Senators and Representatives shall take effect, until an election of Representatives shall have intervened.

Recommended Reading

CHAPTER 1 | NEW WORLD ENCOUNTERS

The histories of three different peoples coming together for the first time in the New World has generated provocative interdisciplinary scholarship. Two excellent studies of encounters between Native Americans and Europeans—works that attempt to recapture the Indians' side of the story—are Inga Clendinnen, *Aztecs: An Interpretation* (1991), and James Axtell's pioneering ethnography, *The Invasion Within: The Contest of Cultures in Colonial North America* (1986). Other innovative books explore how early European invaders imagined the New World: Stephen Greenblatt, *Marvelous Possessions: The Wonder of the New World* (1991), and Anthony Pagden, *European Encounters with the New World: From Renaissance to Romanticism* (1992). For a readable introduction to the heated controversy over Columbus's proper standing in history, consider Kirkpatrick Sale, *The Conquest of Paradise: Christopher Columbus and the Columbian Legacy* (1990). For a good investigation of Indian culture in New Spain after the conquest, see Stuart B. Schwartz, *Victors and the Vanquished: Spanish and Nahua Views of the Conquest of Mexico* (1999).

CHAPTER 2 | ENGLAND'S COLONIAL EXPERIMENTS: THE SEVENTEENTH CENTURY

For a good survey of the political and economic development of England's thirteen mainland colonies, examine Milton Klein and Jacob Cooke, eds., *A History of the American Colonies in Thirteen Volumes* (1973–1986). Another useful overview of the field is Jack Greene and J. R. Pole, eds., *Colonial British America: Essays in the New History of the Early Modern Era* (1984).

Some of the most readable histories of early colonial settlement were written by actual participants. Two of seventeenth-century New England's celebrated leaders produced splendid accounts. See especially Bradford's *Of Plymouth Plantation,* edited by Samuel E. Morison (1952), and Winthrop's *Journal,* edited by Richard S. Dunn et al. (1996). For a tough-minded account of the ordeal of the first Jamestown colonists, turn to Captain John Smith, *A Selected Edition of His Writings,* edited by Karen O. Kupperman (1988).

CHAPTER 3 | PUTTING DOWN ROOTS: FAMILIES IN AN ATLANTIC EMPIRE

The most innovative research on topics covered in this chapter explores the history of New World slavery during the period before the American Revolution. Much of this literature is boldly interdisciplinary, providing not only a fresh comparative interpretation of the creation and development of African American cultures, but also a splendid insight into how imaginative scholars reconstruct the pasts of peoples who for a very long time have been denied a voice in mainstream histories. Among the most impressive recent works are Ira Berlin, *Many Thousands Gone: The First Two Centuries of Slavery in North America* (2000); Philip Morgan, *Slave Counterpoint: Black Culture in the Eighteenth-Century Chesapeake and Lowcountry* (1998); and Robin Blackburn, *The Making of New*

World Slavery, 1492–1800 (1997). These books owe a lot to several path-breaking studies that deserve careful attention: Winthrop D. Jordan, *White Over Black: American Attitudes Toward the Negro, 1550–1812* (1968), and Edmund S. Morgan, *American Slavery, American Freedom: The Ordeal of Colonial Virginia* (1975).

CHAPTER 4 | FRONTIERS OF EMPIRE: EIGHTEENTH-CENTURY AMERICA

Jon Butler provides a general introduction to the topics addressed in this chapter in *Becoming America: Revolution Before 1776* (2000). But one should not ignore Richard Hofstadter's brilliant, often disturbing discussion of class and race: *America at 1750: A Social Portrait* (1971). An analysis of European migration to British America can be found in Bernard Bailyn, *The Peopling of British North America: An Introduction* (1988). Commercial growth and population expansion are covered thoroughly in John J. McCusker and Russell R. Menard, *The Economy of British America, 1607–1789* (1985). The book that has redefined how we think about eighteenth-century Native American history is Richard White, *The Middle Ground: Indians, Empires, and Republics in the Great Lakes Region* (1991). Fred Anderson offers the most complete treatment of war and empire in *Crucible of War: The Seven Years' War and the Fate of Empire in British North America, 1754–1766* (2000).

CHAPTER 5 | THE AMERICAN REVOLUTION: FROM GENTRY PROTEST TO POPULAR REVOLT, 1763–1783

The American Revolution has generated a rich historiography. No sooner had the fighting ceased than the participants, Loyalists as well as Patriots, began to interpret the events leading to the creating of an independent republic. The most insightful book is David Ramsay's *The History of the American Revolution*, originally published in 1789 and recently reprinted in volumes edited by Lester H. Cohen (1990). A general guide to the period is provided by Jack P. Greene and J. R. Pole, eds., *The Blackwell Encyclopedia of the American Revolution* (1991); and John M. Faragher, ed., *The Encyclopedia of Colonial and Revolutionary America* (1996). Two reliable surveys are Merrill Jensen, *The Founding of a Nation: A History of the American Revolution, 1763–1776* (1968), and Edmund S. Morgan, *Birth of the Republic, 1763–1789*, rev. ed. (1992). Two books that transformed how an entire generation interpreted the Revolution are Edmund S. Morgan and Helen M. Morgan, *The Stamp Act Crisis: Prologue to Revolution* (1953), and Bernard Bailyn, *The Ideological Origins of the American Revolution* (1967).

CHAPTER 6 | THE REPUBLICAN EXPERIMENT

The drafting and ratification of the Constitution has generated many highly partisan interpretations by historians as well as legal scholars. The best way to comprehend the major issues debated at the Philadelphia Convention and then later at the separate state ratifying conventions is to examine the key documents of the period. One could do no better than reading James Madison, *Journal of the Federal Constitution* (reprinted in many modern editions), a detailed account of what actually occurred at the Convention, and Bernard Bailyn, ed., *The Debate on the Constitution: Federalists and Antifederalists Speeches, Articles, and Letters During the Struggle Over Ratification* (1993). Gordon S. Wood analyzed late-eighteenth-century republican political thought in his masterful *The Creation of the American Republic, 1776–1787* (1969), a work now supplemented by his provocative *Radicalism of the American Revolution* (1992). Three recent titles have helped define how we think about the political experience of the 1780s: Jack N. Rakove, *The Beginnings of*

National Politics: An Interpretive History of the Continental Congress (1979); Rakove, *Original Meanings: Politics and Ideas in the Making of the Constitution* (1996); and Peter Onuf, *Statehood and Union: A History of the Northwest Ordinance* (1987).

CHAPTER 7 | DEMOCRACY IN DISTRESS: THE VIOLENCE OF PARTY POLITICS, 1788–1800

Stanley Elkins and Eric McKitrick provides a detailed survey of the major political events of this period in *The Age of Federalism: The Early American Republic* (1993). More than any of the major political figures, Thomas Jefferson has generated interpretive scholarship. Merrill D. Peterson offers an encyclopedic account of Jefferson's day-to-day political activities in *Thomas Jefferson and the New Nation: A Biography* (1970). More recently, Joseph Ellis has attempted to explain the complex character of Jefferson's political thought: *American Sphinx: The Character of Thomas Jefferson* (1997). For thoughtful explorations of the ideological issues that divided Federalists and Republicans, one should look at Gordon Wood, *Radicalism of the American Revolution* (1993); Joyce Appleby, *Liberalism and Republicanism in Historical Imagination* (1992); and Drew McCoy, *The Elusive Republic: The Political Economy in Jeffersonian America* (1980). Still valuable for its imaginative treatment of the development of party politics during the 1790s is Richard Hofstadter, *The Idea of a Party System: The Rise of Legitimate Opposition in the United States, 1780–1840* (1969).

CHAPTER 8 | JEFFERSONIAN ASCENDANCY: THEORY AND PRACTICE OF GOVERNMENT

The best written and in many ways the fullest account of the first two decades of the nineteenth century remains Henry Adams's classic *History of the United States During the Administration of Jefferson and Madison,* 9 vols. (1889–1891). Anyone interested in the problems that Jefferson faced as president should start with Merrill D. Peterson, *Thomas Jefferson and the New Nation: A Biography* (1970), and Peter S. Onuf, *Jeffersonian America* (2001). A fine legal history can be found in Jean Edward Smith, *John Marshall: Definer of a Nation* (1996). A brilliant exploration of the evolution of republican ideas after the retirement of Madison is Drew R. McCoy, *The Last of the Founding Fathers: James Madison and the Republican Legacy* (1989). Nathan O. Hatch provides an excellent account of popular religion in *The Democratization of American Christianity* (1989). Laurel Ulrich has written a splendid study of a remarkable woman in the age of Jefferson: *A Midwife's Tale: The Life of Martha Balland, Based on Her Diary, 1785–1812* (1990). A fine account of the Lewis and Clark Expedition is Stephen Ambrose, *Undaunted Courage: Meriwether Lewis, Thomas Jefferson, and the Opening of the American West* (1996).

CHAPTER 9 | NATION BUILDING AND NATIONALISM

The standard surveys of the period between the War of 1812 and the age of Jackson are two works by George Dangerfield: *The Era of Good Feelings* (1952) and *Awakening of American Nationalism, 1815–1828* (1965); but see also the early chapters of Charles Sellers, *The Market Revolution: Jacksonian America, 1815–1846* (1991). For a positive account of the venturesome, entrepreneurial spirit of the age, see Joyce Appleby, *Inheriting the Revolution: The First Generations of Americans* (2000). Malcolm J. Rohrbough, *The Trans-Appalachian Frontier* (1978), is more comprehensive and authoritative. Outstanding studies of economic transformation and the rise of a market economy are George R. Taylor, *The Transportation Revolution, 1815–1860* (1951); Paul W. Gates, *The Farmer's Age: Agriculture, 1815–1860* (1960); Stuart Bruchey, *Growth of the Modern*

American Economy (1975); and Douglas C. North, *The Economic Growth of the United States, 1790–1860* (1961). The Marshall Court and legal and constitutional developments are covered in Robert K. Faulkner, *The Jurisprudence of John Marshall* (1968), and G. Edward White, *The Marshall Court and Cultural Change, 1815–1835* (1991). Samuel F. Bemis, *John Quincy Adams and the Foundations of American Policy* (1949), provides the classic account of the statesmanship that led to the Monroe Doctrine. But see also Ernest May, *The Making of the Monroe Doctrine* (1976), for a persuasive newer interpretation of how the doctrine originated.

CHAPTER 10 | THE TRIUMPH OF WHITE MEN'S DEMOCRACY

Arthur M. Schlesinger, Jr., *The Age of Jackson* (1945), sees Jacksonian democracy as a progressive protest against big business and stresses the participation of urban workers. Marvin Meyers, *The Jacksonian Persuasion: Politics and Belief* (1960), argues that Jacksonians appealed to nostalgia for an older America—"an idealized ancestral way" they believed was threatened by commercialization. Lee Benson, *The Concept of Jacksonian Democracy: New York as a Test Case* (1964), finds an ethnocultural basis for democratic allegiance. A sharply critical view of Jacksonian leadership—one that stresses opportunism, greed, and demagoguery—can be found in Edward Pessen, *Jacksonian America: Society, Personality, and Politics,* rev. ed. (1979). An excellent recent survey of Jacksonian politics is Harry L. Watson, *Liberty and Power* (1990), which stresses the crisis of "republicanism" at a time of "market revolution." Daniel Feller, *Jacksonian Promise: America, 1815–1840* (1995), focuses on the optimism that marked all sides of the political conflict and points to the similarities between the political parties. Development of the view that Jacksonianism was a negative reaction to the rise of market capitalism can be found in Charles Sellers, *The Market Revolution* (1991).

The classic study of the new party system is Richard P. McCormick, *The Second Party System: Party Formation in the Jacksonian Era* (1966). On who the anti-Jacksonians were, what they stood for, and what they accomplished, see Michael Holt's magisterial, *The Rise and Fall of the American Whig Party* (1999). James C. Curtis, *Andrew Jackson and the Search for Vindication* (1976), provides a good introduction to Jackson's career and personality. On Jackson's popular image, see John William Ward, *Andrew Jackson: Symbol for an Age* (1955). On the other towering political figures of the period, see Merrill D. Peterson, *The Great Triumvirate: Webster, Clay, and Calhoun* (1987). The culture of the period is well surveyed in Russel B. Nye, *Society and Culture in America, 1830–1860* (1960). Alexis de Tocqueville, *Democracy in America,* 2 vols. (1945), is a foreign visitor's wise and insightful analysis of American life in the 1830s.

CHAPTER 11 | THE PURSUIT OF PERFECTION

Alice Felt Tyler, *Freedom's Ferment: Phases of American Social History from the Colonial Period to the Outbreak of the Civil War* (1944), gives a lively overview of the varieties of pre–Civil War reform activity. Ronald G. Walters, *American Reformers, 1815–1860,* rev. ed. (1997), provides a modern interpretation of these movements. Steven Mintz, *Moralists and Modernizers: America's Pre–Civil War Reformers* (1995), provides another good overview of the reform activities during this period. A particularly useful collection of documents on reform movements and other aspects of antebellum culture is David Brion Davis, *Antebellum American Culture: An Interpretive Anthology* (1979). The best general work on the revivalism of the Second Great Awakening is William G. McLoughlin, *Modern Revivalism* (1959). A general survey of the religious ferment of this period is Nathan O. Hatch, *The Democratization of American Christianity* (1989). Paul E. Johnson,

A Shopkeeper's Millennium: Society and Revivals in Rochester, New York, 1815–1837 (1978), incisively describes the impact of the revival on a single community. The connection between religion and reform is described in Robert H. Abzug, *Cosmos Crumbling: American Reform and the Religious Imagination* (1994). A good introduction to the changing roles of women and the family in nineteenth-century America is Carl N. Degler, *At Odds: Women and the Family in America from the Revolution to the Present* (1980). On the rise of the domestic ideology, see Nancy F. Cott, *The Bonds of Womanhood: "Woman's Sphere"in New England, 1780–1835* (1977). The condition of working-class women is incisively treated in Christine Stansell, *City of Women: Sex and Class in New York, 1789–1860* (1986).

David J. Rothman, *The Discovery of the Asylum: Social Order and Disorder in the New Republic* (1971), provides a penetrating analysis of the movement for institutional reform. On the foremost institutional reformer of the era, see Thomas J. Brown, *Dorothea Dix: New England Reformer* (1998). For good surveys of abolitionism, see James Brewer Stewart, *Holy Warriors: The Abolitionists and American Slavery* (1976), and Julie Roy Jeffrey, *The Great Silent Army of Abolitionism: Ordinary Women in the Antislavery Movement* (1998).

CHAPTER 12 | AN AGE OF EXPANSIONISM

An overview of expansion to the Pacific is Ray A. Billington, *The Far Western Frontier, 1830–1860* (1956). The impulse behind Manifest Destiny has been variously interpreted. Albert K. Weinberg's classic *Manifest Destiny: A Study of National Expansionism in American History* (1935) describes and stresses the ideological rationale. Frederick Merk, *Manifest Destiny and Mission in American History* (1963), analyzes public opinion and shows how divided it was on the question of territorial acquisitions. Norman A. Graebner, *Empire on the Pacific: A Study in American Continental Expansionism* (1956), highlights the desire for Pacific harbors as a motive for adding new territory. The most complete and authoritative account of the diplomatic side of expansionism in this period is David M. Pletcher, *The Diplomacy of Annexation: Texas, Oregon, and the Mexican War* (1973). Charles G. Sellers, *James K. Polk: Continentalist, 1843–1846* (1966), is the definitive work on Polk's election and the expansionist policies of his administration. A very good account of the Mexican-American War is John S. D. Eisenhower, *So Far from God: The U.S. War with Mexico* (1989). On the California gold rush, see Malcolm J. Rohrbough, *Days of Gold: The California Gold Rush and the American Nation* (1997).

Economic developments of the 1840s and 1850s are well covered in George R. Taylor, *The Transportation Revolution, 1815–1960* (1952), and Albert Fishlow, *American Railroads and the Transformation of the Ante-Bellum Economy* (1965). For an overview of immigration in this period, see the early chapters of Roger Daniels, *Coming to America: Immigration and Ethnicity in American Life* (1990). On the Irish, see Kerby A. Miller, *Emigrants and Exiles: Ireland and the Irish Exodus to America* (1985). Oscar Handlin, *Boston Immigrants: A Study in Acculturation*, rev. ed. (1959), is a classic study of immigration to one city. A standard work on the antebellum working class is Sean Wilentz, *Chants Democratic: New York City and the Rise of the American Working Class, 1788–1850* (1984); for the new approach to labor history that emphasizes working-class culture, see Herbert G. Gutman, *Work, Culture, and Society in Industrializing America* (1976). For the rich public life of antebellum cities, see Mary P. Ryan, *Civic Wars: Democracy and Public Life in the American City During the Nineteenth Century* (1997). A pathbreaking and insightful study of workers in the textile industry is Thomas Dublin, *Women at Work: The Transformation of Work and Community in Lowell, Massachusetts, 1826–1860* (1979).

CHAPTER 13 | MASTERS AND SLAVES

Major works that take a broad view of slavery are Kenneth M. Stampp, *The Peculiar Institution: Slavery in the Antebellum South* (1956), which stresses its coercive features; John W. Blassingame, *The Slave Community: Plantation Life in the Antebellum South* (1972), which focuses on slave culture and psychology; and Eugene D. Genovese, *Roll, Jordan, Roll: The World the Slaves Made* (1974), which probes the paternalistic character of the institution and the way in which slaves made a world for themselves within its bounds. For an overview of the history of slavery, see Peter Kolchin, *American Slavery, 1619–1877* (1993).

On the economics of slavery, see Gavin Wright, *The Political Economy of the Cotton South: Households, Markets, and Wealth in the Nineteenth Century* (1978). Clement Eaton, *The Growth of Southern Civilization, 1790–1860* (1961), provides a good introduction to life in the Old South. A more recent and insightful interpretation of antebellum southern society is James Oakes, *Slavery and Freedom: An Interpretation of the Old South* (1990). On the effect of slavery and the plantation on women, see Elizabeth Fox-Genovese, *Within the Plantation Household: Black and White Women of the Old South* (1988), and Deborah Gray White, *Ar'n't I a Woman: Female Slaves in the Plantation South* (1985). On the slave trade, see two excellent studies: Michael Tadman, *Speculators and Slaves: Masters, Traders, and Slaves in the Old South* (1989), and Walter Johnson, *Soul by Soul: Life Inside the Antebellum Slave Market* (1999).

Black resistance to slavery is described in Vincent Harding, *There Is a River: The Black Struggle for Freedom in America* (1981). Slave culture is examined in Albert J. Raboteau, *Slave Religion: The "Invisible Institution" in the Antebellum South* (1978); Herbert G. Gutman, *The Black Family in Slavery and Freedom, 1750–1925* (1976); Lawrence W. Levine, *Black Culture and Consciousness: Afro-American Folk Thought from Slavery to Freedom* (1977); and Sterling Stuckey, *Slave Culture: Nationalist Theory and the Foundations of Black America* (1987). A work that enriches the previously accepted conception of the black family under slavery is Brenda Stevenson, *Life in Black and White: Family and Community in the Slave South* (1996).

CHAPTER 14 | THE SECTIONAL CRISIS

The best general account of the politics of the sectional crisis is David M. Potter, *The Impending Crisis, 1848–1861* (1976). This well-written and authoritative work combines a vivid and detailed narrative of events with a shrewd and detailed interpretation of them. On the demise of the Whigs, see Michael F. Holt, *The Rise and Fall of the American Whig Party* (1999). The most important studies of northern political sectionalism are Eric Foner, *Free Soil, Free Labor, Free Men: The Ideology of the Republican Party Before the Civil War* (1970), and William E. Gienapp, *The Origins of the Republican Party, 1852–1856* (1987), on the Republican party generally; and Don E. Fehrenbacher, *Prelude to Greatness: Lincoln in the 1850s* (1962), on Lincoln's rise to prominence. On the background of southern separatism, see William W. Freehling, *The Road to Disunion: Secessionists at Bay, 1776–1854* (1990), and William L. Barney, *The Road to Secession: A New Perspective on the Old South* (1972).

CHAPTER 15 | SECESSION AND THE CIVIL WAR

The best one-volume history of the Civil War is James M. McPherson, *Battle Cry of Freedom: The Civil War Era* (1988). Other valuable surveys of the war and its aftermath are J. G. Randall and David Herbert Donald, *The Civil War and Reconstruction*, 2nd ed. (1969), and James M. McPherson, *Ordeal by Fire: The Civil War and Reconstruction* (1981). An excellent shorter account is

David Herbert Donald, *Liberty and Union* (1978). The Confederate experience is covered in Clement Eaton, *A History of the Southern Confederacy* (1954), and Emory M. Thomas, *The Confederate Nation, 1861–1865* (1979). Eaton stresses internal problems and weaknesses; Thomas highlights achievements under adversity. Gary W. Gallagher, *The Confederate War* (1997), argues, contrary to a common view, that the South lost the war simply because it was overpowered and not because of low morale or lack of a will to win. On the North's war effort, see Phillip Paludan, *A People's Contest: The Union and the Civil War, 1861–1865* (1988). The best one-volume introduction to the military side of the conflict is still Bruce Catton, *This Hallowed Ground: The Story of the Union Side of the Civil War* (1956).

Lincoln's career and wartime leadership are well treated in David Herbert Donald, *Lincoln* (1995). Another competent biography is Stephen B. Oates, *With Malice Toward None: The Life of Abraham Lincoln* (1977). A penetrating analysis of events immediately preceding the fighting is Kenneth M. Stampp, *And the War Came: The North and the Sectional Crisis* (1950). John Hope Franklin, *The Emancipation Proclamation* (1963), is a good short account of the North's decision to free the slaves. An incisive account of the transition from slavery to freedom is Barbara Jeanne Fields, *Slavery and Freedom on the Middle Ground: Maryland in the Nineteenth Century* (1985). The circumstances and activities of southern women during the war are covered in Drew Faust, *Mothers of Invention: Women of the Slaveholding States in the American Civil War* (1996). The experiences of northern women are described in Elizabeth D. Leonard, *Yankee Women: Gender Battles in the Civil War* (1994). Five leading historians offer conflicting interpretations in their attempts to explain the South's defeat in *Why the North Won the Civil War*, edited by David Donald (1960). A brilliant study of the writings of those who experienced the war is Edmund Wilson, *Patriotic Gore: Studies in the Literature of the American Civil War* (1962). On the intellectual impact of the war, see George M. Fredrickson, *The Inner Civil War: Northern Intellectuals and the Crisis of the Union*, 2nd ed. (1993).

CHAPTER 16 | THE AGONY OF RECONSTRUCTION

The best one-volume account of Reconstruction is Eric Foner, *Reconstruction: America's Unfinished Revolution* (1988). Two excellent short surveys are Kenneth M. Stampp, *The Era of Reconstruction, 1865–1877* (1965), and John Hope Franklin, *Reconstruction: After the Civil War* (1961). Both were early efforts to synthesize modern "revisionist" interpretations. W. E. B. DuBois, *Black Reconstruction in America, 1860–1880* (1935), remains brilliant and provocative. Reconsiderations of Reconstruction issues can be found in J. Morgan Kousser and James M. McPherson, eds., *Region, Race, and Reconstruction: Essays in Honor of C. Vann Woodward* (1982), and Eric Foner, *Nothing But Freedom: Emancipation and Its Legacy* (1983). Morton Keller, *Affairs of State: Public Life in Late Nineteenth Century America* (1977), provides an insightful analysis of American government and politics during Reconstruction and afterward. A perspective on the corruption of the period is provided by Mark Wahlgren Summers in *The Era of Good Stealings* (1993).

Formulation and implementation of northern policies on Reconstruction are covered in Eric L. McKitrick, *Andrew Johnson and Reconstruction, 1865–1867* (1960); William R. Brock, *An American Crisis: Congress and Reconstruction, 1865–1867* (1963); and William Gillette, *Retreat from Reconstruction, 1869–1879* (1979). Leon F. Litwack, *Been in the Storm So Long: The Aftermath of Slavery* (1979), provides a moving portrayal of the black experience of emancipation. On what freedom meant in economic terms, see Gerald David Jaynes, *Branches Without Roots: Genesis of the Black Working Class in the American South, 1862–1882* (1986). A work that focuses on ex-slaves' attempts to create their own economic order is Julie Saville, *The Work of Reconstruction: Free Slave to Wage Laborer in South Carolina, 1860–1870* (1994). The best overview of the postwar southern economy is Gavin Wright, *Old South, New South* (1986). The best introduction to the Grant era is William S. McFeeley, *Grant: A Biography* (1981). On the end of Reconstruction and the character of the post-Reconstruction South, see two classic works by C. Vann Woodward: *Reunion and Reaction*, rev. ed. (1956), and *Origins of the New South, 1877–1913* (1951). A good recent survey of the South after Reconstruction is Edward Ayers, *The Promise of the New South* (1992).

CHAPTER 17 | THE WEST: EXPLOITING AN EMPIRE

The best traditional account of the movement west is Ray Allen Billington, *Westward Expansion* (1967), which also has a first-rate bibliography. Walter Prescott Webb, *The Great Plains* (1931), offers a fascinating analysis of development on the Plains.

For examples of the work of "new Western historians," see Donald Worster, *Rivers of Empire* (1985), a powerful study of the "hydraulic" society, and his *Under Western Skies: Nature and History in the American West* (1992); William Cronon, *Nature's Metropolis: Chicago and the Great West* (1991), a provocative analysis of the relationship of Chicago and the West; Patricia Nelson Limerick, *The Legacy of Conquest* (1987); and Richard White, *"It's Your Misfortune and None of My Own": A History of the American West* (1991).

More recent authors have taken fresh and stimulating looks at older or ignored questions. Robert R. Dykstra, *The Cattle Towns* (1968), examines five Kansas cattle towns, with interesting results. Elliott West discusses childhood in *Growing Up with the Country: Childhood on the Far Western Frontier* (1989), and the Plains, in *The Contested Plains: Indians, Goldseekers, and the Rush to Colorado* (1998). Julie Roy Jeffrey, *Frontier Women: The Trans-Mississippi West* (1979); Joanna L. Stratton, *Pioneer Women: Voices from the Kansas Frontier* (1981); and Deena J. González, *Refusing the Favor: The Spanish-Mexican Women of Santa Fe, 1820–1880* (1999), are perceptive works on a neglected topic. John Mack Faragher, *Women and Men on the Overland Trail* (1979), and John Phillip Reid, *Law for the Elephant* (1980), examine relationships on the trails west.

CHAPTER 18 | THE INDUSTRIAL SOCIETY

Samuel P. Hays, *The Response to Industrialism: 1885–1914* (1957), is an influential interpretation of the period. Douglass C. North, *Growth and Welfare in the American Past: A New Economic History* (1966), is stimulating. David Montgomery, *The Fall of the House of Labor* (1987), is an outstanding study of labor in the period.

Alfred D. Chandler, *The Visible Hand: The Managerial Revolution in American Business* (1978); Olivier Zunz, *Making America Corporate, 1870–1920* (1990); and JoAnne Yates, *Control Through Communication: The Rise of System in American Management* (1989), are perceptive. The railroad empire is treated in John R. Stilgoe, *Metropolitan Corridor: Railroads and the American Scene* (1983); John Hoyt Williams, *A Great and Shining Road: The Epic Story of the Transcontinental Railroad* (1988); and John F. Stover, *American Railroads* (1961). On the steel industry, see Peter Temin, *Iron and Steel in Nineteenth-Century America* (1964).

Two superb books by Sam Bass Warner, Jr., *Streetcar Suburbs: The Process of Growth in Boston, 1870–1900* (1962), and *The Urban Wilderness: A History of the American City* (1973), examine technology and city development. The wage earner is examined in Herbert G. Gutman, *Work, Culture, and Society in Industrializing America* (1976). Two books by Stephan Thernstrom, *Poverty and Progress: Social Mobility in the Nineteenth-Century City* (1964) and *The Other Bostonians: Poverty and Progress in the American Metropolis, 1880–1970* (1973), examine mobility. Philip S. Foner, *Women and the American Labor Movement*, 2 vols. (1979); Susan E. Kennedy, *If All We Did Was to Weep at Home* (1979); Barbara Mayer Wertheimer, *We Were There: The Story of Working Women in America* (1977); and Alice Kessler-Harris, *Out to Work: A History of Wage-Earning Women in the United States* (1982), are excellent on the subject of women in the workplace.

CHAPTER 19 | TOWARD AN URBAN SOCIETY, 1877–1900

On urban America, see Sam Bass Warner, Jr., *Streetcar Suburbs* (1962) and *The Urban Wilderness* (1972). William R. Taylor, *In Pursuit of Gotham: Culture and Commerce in New York* (1992); Eric H. Monkkonen, *America Becomes Urban* (1988); and David Schuyler, *The New Urban Landscape* (1986), are also valuable. See also two books by Jon C. Teaford: *The Unheralded Triumph: City Government in America, 1870–1900* (1984) and *City and Suburb: The Political Fragmentation of Metropolitan America, 1850–1970* (1979).

For family life, see Joseph Kett, *Rites of Passage: Adolescence in America* (1977); Elaine Tyler May, *Great Expectations: Marriage and Divorce in Post-Victorian America* (1980); Steven Mintz, *A Prison of Expectations: The Family in Victorian Culture* (1983); Stephen M. Frank, *Life With Father: Parenthood and Masculinity in the Nineteenth-Century American North* (1998); and Norma Basch, *In the Eyes of the Law: Women, Marriage, and Property in Nineteenth-Century New York* (1982). Karen Lystra, *Searching the Heart: Women, Men, and Romantic Love in Nineteenth-Century America* (1989), is valuable.

Urban reform is examined in Judith Ann Trolander, *Professionalism and Social Change: From the Settlement House Movement to Neighborhood Centers, 1886 to the Present* (1987), and Allen F. Davis, *Spearheads for Reform: The Social Settlements and the Progressive Movement, 1890–1914* (1967), and *American Heroine: The Life and Legend of Jane Addams* (1973).

CHAPTER 20 | POLITICAL REALIGNMENTS IN THE 1890s

The best study of the 1890s depression is Charles Hoffman, *The Depression of the Nineties: An Economic History* (1970). H. Wayne Morgan, *From Hayes to McKinley: National Party Politics, 1877–1896* (1969), and Richard J. Jensen, *The Winning of the Midwest* (1971), are good on politics. David P. Thelen, *The New Citizenship: Origins of Progressivism in Wisconsin, 1885–1900* (1972), stresses the impact of the depression on ideas and attitudes. C. Vann Woodward examines the South in *Origins of the New South, 1877–1913* (1951). Studies of politics in the late nineteenth century include Glenn C. Altschuler and Stuart M. Blumin, *Rude Republic: Americans and Their Politics in the Nineteenth Century* (2000); Steven P. Reti, *Silver and Gold: The Political Economy of International Monetary Conferences, 1867–1892* (1998); Stephen Kantrowitz, *Ben Tillman and the Reconstruction of White Supremacy* (2000).

On Populism, see John D. Hicks, *The Populist Revolt* (1931), and Lawrence Goodwyn, *Democratic Promise: The Populist Moment in America* (1976). See also Victoria Saker Woeste, *The Farmer's Benevolent Trust: Law and Agricultural Cooperation in Industrial America, 1865–1945* (2000); Elizabeth Sanders, *Roots of Reform: Farmers, Workers, and the American State, 1877–1917* (1999); Marion K. Barthelme, (ed.), *Women in the Texas Populist Movement* (1997); and O. Gene Clanton, *Populism: The Humane Preference in America* (1991) and *Congressional Populism and the Crisis of the 1890's* (1999).

Social and labor unrest is covered in Almont Lindsey, *The Pullman Strike* (1942); Stanley Buder, *Pullman* (1967); Nick Salvatore, *Eugene V. Debs* (1982); and Shelton Stromquist, *A Generation of Boomers: The Pattern of Railroad Labor Conflict in Nineteenth-Century America* (1987).

CHAPTER 21 | TOWARD EMPIRE

The best general account of the development of American foreign policy during the last part of the nineteenth century is Walter LaFeber, *The New Empire: An Interpretation of American Expansion, 1860–1898* (1963). William Appleman Williams, *The Tragedy of American Diplomacy* (1959), examines the economic motives for expansion. See also Paul Wolman, *Most Favored Nation: The Republican Revisionists and U.S. Tariff Policy, 1897–1912* (1992). Lewis L. Gould persuasively reassesses McKinley's diplomacy and wartime leadership in *The Presidency of William McKinley* (1980).

Graham A. Cosmas presents a detailed account of military organization and strategy in *An Army for Empire: The United States Army in the Spanish-American War* (1971); Willard B. Gatewood, Jr., offers a fascinating glimpse of the thoughts of some black soldiers in the war in *"Smoked Yankees"and the Struggle for Empire: Letters from Negro Soldiers, 1898–1902* (1971). Gerald F. Linderman relates the war to the home front in *The Mirror of War: American Society and the Spanish-American War* (1974).

CHAPTER 22 | THE PROGRESSIVE ERA

There are several important analyses of the progressive era, including Robert H. Wiebe, *The Search for Order, 1877–1920* (1967); Richard Hofstadter, *The Age of Reform* (1955); Samuel P. Hays, *The Response to Industrialism* (1957); and Gabriel Kolko, *The Triumph of Conservatism* (1963). C. Vann Woodward, *Origins of the New South, 1877–1913* (1951), is a superb account of developments in the South, along with William A. Link, *The Paradox of Southern Progressivism, 1880–1930* (1992).

James T. Kloppenberg, *Uncertain Victory: Social Democracy and Progressivism in European and American Thought, 1870–1920* (1986), examines progressivism at home and abroad. C. Vann Woodward, *The Strange Career of Jim Crow* (1955), traces the civil rights setbacks of the Progressive Era.

Studies of youth, age, and family life include Joseph Kett, *Rites of Passage* (1977); Elizabeth J. Clapp, *Mothers of All Children: Women Reformers and the Rise of Juvenile Courts in Progressive Era America* (1998); Katrina Irving, *Immigrant Mothers: Narratives of Race and Maternity, 1890–1925* (2000); and Tamara K. Hareven, *Transitions: The Family and Life Course in Historical Perspective* (1978). See also Eleanor Flexner, *Century of Struggle: The Women's Rights Movement in the United States* (1959); Nan Enstad, *Ladies of Labor, Girls of Adventure: Working Women, Popular Culture, and Labor Politics at the Turn of the Twentieth Century* (1999); Gayle Gullett, *Becoming Citizens: The Emergence and Development of the California Women's Movement, 1880–1911* (1999); and Rosalyn Terborg-Penn, *African American Women in the Struggle for the Vote, 1850–1920* (1998).

CHAPTER 23 | FROM ROOSEVELT TO WILSON IN THE AGE OF PROGRESSIVISM

George Mowry, *The Era of Theodore Roosevelt* (1958), and Arthur S. Link, *Woodrow Wilson and the Progressive Era* (1954), trace the social and economic conditions of the period. See also Henry F. Pringle's *Theodore Roosevelt* (1931) and John M. Blum's perceptive and brief *The Republican Roosevelt* (1954). The definitive biography of Wilson is Arthur S. Link, *Wilson*, 5 vols. (1947–1965).

Samuel P. Hays offers an influential interpretation of progressivism in *Conservation and the Gospel of Efficiency* (1959). Albro Martin, *Enterprise Denied: Origins of the Decline of American Railroads, 1897–1917* (1971), argues persuasively that reformers damaged as well as regulated. Samuel Haber, *The Quest for Authority and Honor in the American Professions, 1750–1900* (1991), examines the changing nature of the professions.

CHAPTER 24 | THE NATION AT WAR

American foreign policy between 1901 and 1921 has been the subject of considerable study. Richard W. Leopold, *The Growth of American Foreign Policy* (1962), is balanced and informed. Robert E. Osgood, *Ideals and Self-Interest in America's Foreign Relations* (1953), and William Appleman Williams, *Roots of the Modern American Empire* (1969), explore the forces underlying American foreign policy.

For American policy toward Latin America, see Dana G. Munro's detailed account, *Intervention and Dollar Diplomacy in the Caribbean, 1900–1920* (1964). Arthur S. Link examines Wilson's foreign policy in his exceptional five-volume biography, *Wilson* (1947–1965), and in *Woodrow Wilson: Revolution, War, and Peace* (1979).

Studies of events at home during the war include David M. Kennedy, *Over Here* (1980); Robert D. Cuff, *The War Industries Board* (1973); and Maurine W. Greenwald, *Women, War, and Work* (1980). Arthur Walworth, *America's Moment, 1918: American Diplomacy at the End of World War I* (1977), examines Wilson's attempt to create a peaceful world order.

CHAPTER 25 | TRANSITION TO MODERN AMERICA

William Leuchtenburg provides the best overview of the 1920s in *The Perils of Prosperity, 1914–1932* (1958). He stresses the theme of rural-urban conflict and claims that the achievements of the decade were more significant than its failures. The essays in John Braeman, Robert H. Bremner, and David Brody, eds., *Change and Continuity in Twentieth-Century America: The 1920s* (1968), illuminate important aspects of the period.

A fully detailed account of economic developments in the decade is George Soule, *Prosperity Decade* (1947). Two classic studies, Frederick Lewis Allen, *Only Yesterday* (1931), and Helen Lynd and Robert Lynd, *Middletown* (1929), offer valuable insights into social and cultural trends. The most recent overview of the decade is David J. Goldberg, *Discontented America* (1999).

The spirit of rural discontent with the new urban society is captured best in Lawrence Levine, *Defender of the Faith* (1965), an account of the last ten years of William Jennings Bryan's life. For changing political alignments of the 1920s, see David Burner, *The Politics of Provincialism* (1968).

CHAPTER 26 | FRANKLIN D. ROOSEVELT AND THE NEW DEAL

The best overall account of political developments in the 1930s is William Leuchtenburg, *Franklin D. Roosevelt and the New Deal* (1963). Leuchtenburg offers a balanced treatment but concludes by defending Roosevelt's record. For a more critical view, see James MacGregor Burns, *Roosevelt: The Lion and the Fox* (1956), which portrays FDR as an overly cautious political leader; and Robert A. McElvaine, *The Great Depression: America, 1929–1941* (1984), which laments the New Deal's failure to make more sweeping changes in American life.

David M. Kennedy provides a comprehensive portrait of American life during both the Great Depression and World War II in *Freedom from Fear* (1999). For a sympathetic examination of the New Deal through 1936, see Arthur M. Schlesinger, Jr., *The Age of Roosevelt*, 3 vols. (1957–1960); Paul Conkin offers a brief but provocative critique of Roosevelt's policies in *The New Deal* (1967). George McJimsy, *The Presidency of Franklin Delano Roosevelt* (2000), is the most recent and best-balanced account.

CHAPTER 27 | AMERICA AND THE WORLD, 1921-1945

The best general account of American attitudes toward the world in the 1920s can be found in Warren I. Cohen, *Empire Without Tears* (1987). Robert Dallek provides a thorough account of FDR's diplomacy in *Franklin D. Roosevelt and American Foreign Policy, 1932–1945* (1979). For a more critical view, see Robert A. Divine, *Roosevelt and World War II* (1969).

Two good books on the continuing controversy over Pearl Harbor are Roberta Wohlstetter, *Pearl Harbor: Warning and Decision* (1962), and Gordon W. Prange, *At Dawn We Slept* (1981). Both authors deny the charge that Roosevelt deliberately exposed the naval base to attack.

In his brief overview of wartime diplomacy, *American Diplomacy During the Second World War,* 2nd ed. (1985), Gaddis Smith stresses the tensions within the victorious coalition. The best accounts of the home front are Richard Polenberg, *War and Society* (1972); John W. Blum, *V Was for Victory* (1976); and Doris Kearns Goodwin, *No Ordinary Time* (1995).

CHAPTER 28 | THE ONSET OF THE COLD WAR

The Cold War spawned a vast array of books, some enduring in nature and many that are already outdated. The best general guide to American diplomacy since World War II is Walter LaFeber, *America, Russia and the Cold War, 1945–1992,* 8th ed. (1997). On the much debated question of the origins of the Cold War, the most balanced account is Daniel Yergin, *Shattered Peace* (1977). John Lewis Gaddis, *We Now Know* (1997), integrates new disclosures from Soviet and Chinese archives to provide the best rounded account of the Cold War through the early 1960s.

The classic account of containment is still the lucid recollection of its chief architect, George Kennan, *Memoirs, 1925–1950* (1967). John Lewis Gaddis uses Kennan's ideas as a point of departure for his account of the changing nature of American Cold War policy in *Strategies of Containment* (1982). Melvyn P. Leffler offers a full account of the development of containment in *A Preponderance of Power* (1992). For developments in the Far East, consult the perceptive book by Akira Iriye, *The Cold War in Asia* (1974).

The best book on the Truman period is Alonzo L. Hamby, *Man of the People* (1995), which provides a balanced portrait of a controversial leader. Richard M. Fried offers a perceptive overview of the postwar anticommunist crusade in *Nightmare in Red: The McCarthy Era in Perspective* (1990).

Stephen A. Ambrose evaluates Dwight D. Eisenhower positively in the second volume of his biography, *Eisenhower: The President* (1985). For an equally favorable analysis, see Robert A. Divine, *Eisenhower and the Cold War* (1981).

CHAPTER 29 | AFFLUENCE AND ANXIETY

Two excellent books survey the social, cultural, and political trends in the United States during the postwar period. In *One Nation Divisible* (1980), Richard Polenberg analyzes class, ethnic, and racial changes; James T. Patterson offers a perceptive overview of American life from the end of World War II through the mid-1970s in *Grand Expectations* (1996).

Richard Pells provides a sweeping survey of the American intellectual community's response to the Cold War in *The Liberal Mind in a Conservative Age* (1985). The broadest account of American life during the decade is David Halberstam, *The Fifties* (1993).

Charles Alexander provides a balanced view of the Eisenhower years in *Holding the Line* (1975), portraying the Republican president as an able chief executive who was well suited to the times. Taylor Branch gives a comprehensive account of the genesis of the civil rights movement in

Parting the Waters: America in the King Years, 1954–1963 (1988). Three fine biographies—David L. Lewis's *King* (1970), Stephen B. Oates's *Let the Trumpet Sound* (1982), and David Garrow's *Bearing the Cross* (1986)—present perceptive portraits of Martin Luther King, Jr., the movement's most influential leader.

CHAPTER 30 | THE TURBULENT SIXTIES

The best general account of the 1960s is Jim F. Heath, *Decade of Disillusionment* (1975), which stresses the continuity in policy between the Kennedy and Johnson administrations. Richard Reeves offers a full account of Kennedy's White House years in *President Kennedy* (1993); the best study of Kennedy's foreign policy is Michael R. Beschloss, *The Crisis Years: Kennedy and Khrushchev, 1960–1963* (1991).

Robert Dallek offers a balanced view of Johnson's presidential years in *Flawed Giant* (1998); for LBJ's foreign policy, see H. W. Brands, *The Wages of Globalism* (1995). The best introduction to the Vietnam War is the balanced survey by George Herring, *America's Longest War,* 3rd ed. (1995). For contrasting views of Johnson's responsibility for the Vietnam conflict, see Fredrik Logevall, *Choosing War* (1999), highly critical, and Lloyd Gardner, *Pay Any Price* (1995), more understanding.

The most comprehensive account of the student protests is Terry Anderson, *The Movement and the Sixties* (1995). In *The Sixties* (1987), Todd Gitlin, a sociologist and former SDS leader, offers a sympathetic analysis of the motives and aspirations of the youthful protesters.

Garry Wills provides the most revealing portrait of Richard Nixon's character and prepresidential career in *Nixon Agonistes* (1970). The best account of the 1968 election is Lewis L. Gould, *1968: The Election That Changed America* (1993).

CHAPTER 31 | A CRISIS IN CONFIDENCE, 1969–1980

The most comprehensive account of Nixon's political career and presidency is the three-volume biography by Stephen E. Ambrose, *Nixon* (1987–1992). Melvin Small offers a balanced assessment of Nixon's White House years in *The Presidency of Richard Nixon* (1999).

Stanley Kutler provides a thorough account of the scandal that drove Nixon from office in *The Wars of Watergate* (1990). For foreign policy under Nixon, see William P. Bundy, *A Tangled Web* (1998), and Jeffrey Kimball, *Nixon's Vietnam War* (1998).

In *The Prize* (1991), Daniel Yergin puts the energy crisis of the 1970s in historical perspective. David Frum gives a lively overview of popular culture in *How We Got Here: The 70's* (2000). The best history of the Carter administration is Burton I. Kaufman, *The Presidency of Jimmy Carter* (1993).

CHAPTER 32 | THE REPUBLICAN RESURGENCE, 1980–1992

A British observer, Godfey Hodgson, gives a perceptive and balanced analysis of the conservative movement that led to Reagan's election in *The World Turned Right Side Up* (1996). The most detailed account of the Reagan presidency is the second volume of journalist Lou Cannon's biography, *President Reagan* (1991). Bob Schieffer and Gary Paul Gates offer a critical overview of the Reagan administration in *The Acting President* (1989), which focuses on Reagan's detached style of leadership.

The most revealing accounts by insiders are Martin Anderson, *Revolution* (1988), one of the few to give a positive view of the Reagan presidency, and George Shultz, *Turmoil and Triumph* (1992), the complete treatment of Reagan's foreign policy. John Robert Greene provides a balanced view of the Bush administration in *The Presidency of George Bush* (2000). For foreign policy, see George Bush and Brent Scowcroft, *A World Transformed* (1998).

CHAPTER 33 | AMERICA IN FLUX: THE ANXIOUS NINETIES

The best account of recent immigration into the United States from developing countries is David Reimers, *Still the Golden Door,* 2nd ed. (1992). Steven F. Lawson, *Running for Freedom* (1991), traces the growth of black participation in American politics since World War II, with special emphasis on the South.

British journalist Martin Walker gives a balanced account of Clinton's first term in *The President We Deserve* (1996). For the Lewinsky scandal and the impeachment proceedings, see Michael Isikoff, *Uncovering Clinton* (2000), and Richard A. Posner, *An Affair of State* (1999).

Suggested Web Sites

CHAPTER 1 | NEW WORLD ENCOUNTERS

Vikings in the New World
http://www.anthro.mankato.msus.
edu/prehistory/vikings/vikhome.html
This site explores the history of some of the
earliest European visitors to America.

Sir Francis Drake
http://www.mcn.org/2/oseeler/
drake.htm
This comprehensive site covers much of
Drake's life and voyages.

Ancient Mesoamerican Civilizations
http://www.angelfire.com/ca/
humanorigins/index.html
Kevin L. Callahan of the University of
Minnesota Department of Anthropology
maintains this page that supplies information
regarding Mesoamerican civilizations with
well-organized essays and photos.

National Museum of the American Indian
http://www.si.edu/nmai
The Smithsonian Institution maintains this
site, providing information about the
museum. The museum is dedicated to
everything about Native Americans.

1492: An Ongoing Voyage
http://metalab.unc.edu/expo/1492.
exhibit/Intro.html
An exhibit of the Library of Congress,
Washington, D.C. With brief essays and images about early civilizations and contact in the
Americas.

The Computerized Information Retrieval System on Columbus and the Age of Discovery
http://muweb.millersv.edu/
~columbus/
The History Department and Academic
Computing Services of Millersville University,
Pennsylvania, provide this text retrieval system containing more than 1000 text articles
from various magazines, journals, newspapers,
speeches, official calendars, and other sources
relating to various encounter themes

Cahokia Mounds
http://medicine.wustl.edu/
~mckinney/cahokia/cahokia.html
The Cahokia Mounds State Historical Site
gives information about a fascinating pre-
Columbian culture in North America.

Mexico Pre-Columbian History
http://www.mexonline.com/
precolum.htm
This site "provides information on the Aztecs,
Maya, Mexica, Olmecs, Toltec, Zapotecs and
other pre-European cultures, as well as information on museums, archeology, language,
and education."

White Oak Fur Post
http://www.whiteoak.org/
This site documents an eighteenth-century fur
trading post among the Indians in what would
become Minnesota.

The Search for La Salle's Ship La Belle
http://www.thc.state.tx.us/Belle/index.html
Texas Historical Commission site about the archaeological dig to recover the ship of one of America's famous early explorers.

The Discoverers' Web
http://www.win.tue.nl/cs/fm/engels/discovery/
Andre Engels maintains this complete collection of information on the various efforts at exploration.

CHAPTER 2 | ENGLAND'S COLONIAL EXPERIMENTS: THE SEVENTEENTH CENTURY

The Plymouth Colony Archive Project at the University of Virginia
http://www.people.virginia.edu/~jfd3a/
This site contains comprehensive and fairly extensive information about late seventeenth-century Plymouth Colony.

Jamestown Rediscovery
http://www.apva.org
This site mounted by the Association for the Preservation of Virginia Antiquity has excellent material on archaeological excavations at Jamestown.

Georgia Before Oglethorpe
http://members.aol.com/jeworth/gboindex.htm

This resources guide informs about Native American Georgia in the seventeenth century.

William Penn, Visionary Proprietor
http://xroads.virginia.edu/~CAP/PENN/pnhome.html
William Penn had an interesting life, and this site is a good introduction to the man and some of his achievements.

LVA Colonial Records Project— Index of digital facsimiles of documents on early Virginia
http://eagle.vsla.edu/colonial/
This site contains numerous early documents, but it is unguided and a little difficult to use.

CHAPTER 3 | PUTTING DOWN ROOTS: FAMILIES IN AN ATLANTIC EMPIRE

DPLS Archive: Slave Movement During the 18th and 19th Centuries (Wisconsin)
http://dpls.dacc.wisc.edu/slavedata/index.html
This site explores the slave ships and the slave trade that carried thousands of Africans to the New World.

Excerpts from Slave Narratives
http://vi.uh.edu/pages/mintz/primary.htm
Accounts of slavery from the seventeenth through nineteenth centuries speak volumes about the many impacts of slavery.

Witchcraft in Salem Village
http://etext.virginia.edu/salem/witchcraft/
Extensive archive of the 1692 trials and life in late seventeenth-century Massachusetts.

Salem Witchcraft Trials (1692)
http://www.law.umkc.edu/faculty/projects/ftrials/salem/salem.htm
Images chronology, court, and official documents by Dr. Doug Linder at University of Missouri–Kansas City Law School.

Colonial Documents
http://www.yale.edu/lawweb/avalon/18th.htm

The key documents of the Colonial Era are reproduced here, as are some important documents from earlier and later periods in American history.

LVA Colonial Records Project—Index of digital facsimiles of documents on early Virginia
http://eagle.vsla.edu/colonial/

This site contains numerous early documents, but it is unguided and a little difficult to use.

CHAPTER 4 | FRONTIERS OF EMPIRE: EIGHTEENTH-CENTURY AMERICA

History Buff's Reference Library
http://www.discovery.com/guides/history/historybuff.html

Brief journalistic essays on newspaper coverage of sixteenth- to eighteenth-century American history.

Benjamin Franklin Documentary History Web Site
http://www.english.udel.edu/lemay/franklin/

University of Delaware professor J. A. Leo LeMay tells the story of Franklin's varied life in seven parts on this intriguing site.

Jonathan Edwards
http://www.jonathanedwards.com/

Speeches by this famous preacher of the Great Awakening are on this site.

Religion and the Founding of the American Republic
http://lcweb.loc.gov/exhibits/religion/religion.html

This Library of Congress site is an on-line exhibit about religion and the creation of the United States.

Smithsonian Institution
http://www.americanhistory.si.edu/hohr/springer

Part of the Smithsonian's on-line museum, this exhibit enables students to examine artifacts from the home of New Castle, Delaware, residents Thomas and Elizabeth Springer and interpret the lives of a late eighteenth-century American family.

National Museum of the American Indian
http://www.si.edu/nmai

The Smithsonian Institution maintains this site, providing information about the museum. The museum is dedicated to everything about Native Americans.

The French and Indian War
http://digitalhistory.org

Digital History LTD provides extensive archives in this site not intended for an exclusively academic audience.

The French and Indian War
http://web.syr.edu/~laroux/

This site is about French soldiers who came to New France between 1755 and 1760 to fight in the French and Indian War.

DoHistory, Harvard University Film Study Center
http://www.dohistory.org/

Focusing on the life of Martha Ballard, a late eighteenth-century New England woman, this site employs selections from her diary, excerpts from a book and film of her life, and other primary documents to enable students to conduct their own historical investigation.

CHAPTER 5 | THE AMERICAN REVOLUTION: FROM GENTRY PROTEST TO POPULAR REVOLT, 1763–1783

Canada History
http://www.civilization.ca/
index1e.html
Canada and the United States shared a colonial past but developed differently in the long run. This site is a part of the virtual museum of the Canadian Museum of Civilization Corporation.

Georgia's Rare Map Collection
http://scarlett.libs.uga.edu/darchive/
hargrett/maps/colamer.html
http://scarlett.libs.uga.edu/darchive/
hargrett/maps/revamer.html
These two sites contain maps for Colonial and Revolutionary America.

Maryland Loyalists and the American Revolution
http://www.erols.com/candidus/
index.htm
This look at Maryland's loyalists promotes the author's book, but the site has good information about an underappreciated phenomenon, including loyalist songs and poems.

The American Revolution
http://revolution.h-net.msu.edu/
This site accompanies the PBS series *Revolution* with essays and resource links.

CHAPTER 6 | THE REPUBLICAN EXPERIMENT

The Leslie Brock Center for the Study of Colonial Currency
http://www.virginia.edu/~econ/
brock.html
This site includes both useful primary and secondary documents on early American currency.

Northwest Territory Alliance
http://www.nwta.com/main.html
This Revolutionary Era reenactment organization site contains several links and is an interesting look at historical reenactment.

Independence Hall National Historical Park
http://www.nps.gov/inde/visit.html
This site includes images and historical accounts of Independence Hall and other Philadelphia buildings closely associated with the nation's founding.

Biographies of the Founding Fathers
http://www.colonialhall.com/
This site provides interesting information about the men who signed the Declaration of Independence and includes a trivia section.

The Federalist Papers
http://www.law.emory.edu/
FEDERAL/federalist/
This site is a collection of the most important Federalist Papers, a series of documents designed to convince people to support the new Constitution and the Federalist party.

The Constitution and the Amendments
http://www.law.emory.edu/
FEDERAL/usconst.html
This is a searchable site to the Constitution, especially useful for its information about the Bill of Rights and other constitutional amendments.

Documents from the Continental Congress and the Constitutional Convention, 1774–1789

http://memory.loc.gov/ammem/
bdsds/bdsdhome.html

The Continental Congress Broadside Collection (253 titles) and the Constitutional Convention Broadside Collection (21 titles) contain 274 documents relating to the work of Congress and the drafting and ratification of the Constitution. Items include extracts of the journals of Congress, resolutions, proclamations, committee reports, treaties, and early printed versions of the United States Constitution and the Declaration of Independence. Most broadsides are one page long; others range from one to twenty-eight pages.

CHAPTER 7 | DEMOCRACY IN DISTRESS: THE VIOLENCE OF PARTY POLITICS, 1788–1800

Temple of Liberty—Building the Capitol for a New Nation

http://www.lcweb.loc.gov/exhibits/
us.capitol/s0.html

Compiled from holdings in the Library of Congress, this site contains detailed information on the design and early construction of the Capitol building in Washington, DC.

The Electoral College

http://www.nara.gov/fedreg/elctcoll/
index.html

This National Archives and Records Administration site explains how the electoral college works.

George Washington Papers

http://www.virginia.edu/gwpapers/

Information on the publishing project, with selected documents, essays, and an index of the published volumes.

George Washington at Home

http://www.mountvernon.org/

Pictures and documents of Mount Vernon, the home of the first president, George Washington.

George Washington Papers at the Library of Congress, 1741–1799

http://memory.loc.gov/ammem/
gwhtml/gwhome.html

This site is "the complete George Washington Papers from the Manuscript Division at the Library of Congress consists of approximately 65,000 documents. This is the largest collection of original Washington documents in the world."

Archiving Early America

http://earlyamerica.com/

Old newspapers are excellent windows into the issues of the past. This site includes the Keigwin and Matthews collection of historic newspapers.

John Adams

http://www.whitehouse.gov/WH/
glimpse/presidents/html/ja2.html

This site contains biographical information about the second president, his inaugural address, and links to his more quotable phrases.

CHAPTER 8 | JEFFERSONIAN ASCENDANCY: THEORY AND PRACTICE OF GOVERNMENT

Thomas Jefferson

http://www.pbs.org/jefferson/

A companion site to the Public Broadcasting Service series on Jefferson, especially important because it contains a fine collection of other people's views of Jefferson.

Some Writings of Thomas Jefferson

http://www.geocities.com/Athens/
Forum/9061/USA/early/jeff.html

This site features many of Jefferson's noted writings as well as some that are less well known.

White House Historical Association

http://www.whitehousehistory.org/whha/default.asp

This site contains a timeline of the history of the White House and several interesting photos and links.

Thomas Jefferson on Politics and Government

http://etext.virginia.edu/jefferson/quotations/

Selected quotations from Jefferson that reveal a strong libertarian bent make up this topical Web site.

Thomas Jefferson On-line Resources at the University of Virginia

http://etext.virginia.edu/jefferson/

Mr. Jefferson's University—the University of Virginia—houses this site with numerous online resources about Jefferson and his times.

The Jefferson Bibliography Database

http://etext.virginia.edu/jefferson/bibliog/

This invaluable site compiles and annotates a bibliography of works on Jefferson from 1826 to 1990.

Exploring the West from Monticello: An Exhibition of Maps and Navigational Instruments

http://www.lib.virginia.edu/exhibits/lewis_clark/home.html

Maps and charts reveal knowledge and conceptions about the known and the unknown. This site includes a number of eighteenth-century maps.

Lewis and Clark PBS Web site from PBS

http://www.pbs.org/lewisandclark/

This is a companion site to Ken Burns' containing a timeline of the expedition, a collection of related links, a bibliography, and more than 800 minutes of unedited, full-length RealPlayer interviews with seven experts featured in the film.

The War of 1812

http://members.tripod.com/~war1812/index.html

In-depth and varied information about the War of 1812.

CHAPTER 9 | NATION BUILDING AND NATIONALISM

The Era of the Mountain Men

http://www.xmission.com/~drudy/amm.html

Private letters can speak volumes about the concerns and environment of the writers and recipients. Letters from early settlers west of the Mississippi River are offered on this site.

Prairietown, Indiana

http://www.indianapolis.in.us/cp/stories.html

This fictional model of a town and its inhabitants on the early frontier says much about America's movement westward and the everyday lives of Americans.

The Seminole Indians of Florida

http://www.seminoletribe.com/

Before he was president, Andrew Jackson began a war against the Seminole Indians.

Erie Canal On-line

http://www.syracuse.com/features/eriecanal

This site, built around the diary of a fourteen-year-old girl who traveled from Amsterdam to Syracuse, New York, in the early nineteenth century, explores the construction and importance of the Erie Canal.

Whole Cloth: Discovering Science and Technology Through American Textile History
http://www.si.edu/lemelson/centerpieces/whole_cloth/
The Jerome and Dorothy Lemelson Center for the Study of Invention and Innovation/Society for the History of Technology put together this site, which includes excellent activities and sources concerning early American manufacturing and industry.

The National Road
http://www.connerprairie.org/ntlroad.html
The National Road was a hot political topic in the Early Republic and was part of the beginning of the development of America's infrastructure.

CHAPTER 10 | THE TRIUMPH OF WHITE MEN'S DEMOCRACY

Indian Affairs: Laws and Treaties, compiled and edited by Charles J. Kappler (1904)
http://www.library.okstate.edu/kappler
This digitized text at Oklahoma State University includes preremoval treaties with the Five Civilized Tribes and other tribes.

Jacksonian Era Medicine and Life
http://www.indianapolis.in.us/cp/jmed.html
Survival was far from certain in the Jacksonian Era. This site discusses some of the reasons and some of the possible cures of the times.

The University of Pennsylvania In 1830
http://www.upenn.edu/1830/
This "virtual tour" shows what a fairly typical campus looked like and what student life was like at one of the larger universities in the Antebellum Era.

19th Century Scientific American On-line
http://www.history.rochester.edu/Scientific_American/
Magazines and journals are windows through which we can view society. This site provides on-line editions of one of the more interesting nineteenth-century journals.

National Museum of the American Indian
http://www.si.edu/nmai
The Smithsonian Institution maintains this site, providing information about the museum, which is dedicated to everything about Native Americans.

The Alexis de Tocqueville Tour: Exploring Democracy in America
http://www.tocqueville.org/
Text, images, and teaching suggestions are a part of this companion site to C-SPAN's recent programming on de Tocqueville.

CHAPTER 11 | THE PURSUIT OF PERFECTION

America's First Look into the Camera: Daguerreotype Portraits and Views, 1839–1862
http://memory.loc.gov/ammem/daghtml/daghome.html
The Library of Congress's daguerreotype collection consists of more than 650 photographs dating from 1839 to 1864. Portraits, architectural views, and some street scenes make up most of the collection.

1830s Clothing
http://www.connerprairie.org/clothing.html
See how clothing worn in the Early Republic was quite different from what people wear today.

Votes for Women: Selections from the National American Woman Suffrage Association Collection, 1848–1921
http://memory.loc.gov/ammem/naw/nawshome.html

This Library of Congress site contains 167 books, pamphlets, and other artifacts documenting the suffrage campaign.

History of the Suffrage Movement
http://www.rochester.edu/SBA

This site includes a chronology, important texts relating to women's suffrage, and biographical information about Susan B. Anthony and Elizabeth Cady Stanton.

By Popular Demand: "Votes for Women" Suffrage Pictures, 1850–1920
http://memory.loc.gov/ammem/vfwhtml/vfwhome.html

Portraits, suffrage parades, picketing suffragists, an antisuffrage display, and cartoons commenting on the movement make up this Library of Congress site.

Women in America, 1820 to 1842
http://xroads.virginia.edu/~HYPER/DETOC/FEM/home.htm

This University of Virginia site takes a look at women in antebellum America.

Godey's Lady's Book On-line
http://www.history.rochester.edu/godeys/

Here is on-line text of this interesting nineteenth-century journal.

Important Black Abolitionists
http://www.loc.gov/exhibits/african/influ.html

An exhibit site from the Library of Congress, with pictures and text, which discusses some key African American abolitionists and their efforts to end slavery.

CHAPTER 12 | AN AGE OF EXPANSIONISM

Pioneering the Upper Midwest: Books from Michigan, Minnesota, and Wisconsin, ca. 1820–1910
http://memory.loc.gov/ammem/umhtml/umhome.html

This Library of Congress site looks at first-person accounts, biographies, promotional literature, local histories, ethnographic and antiquarian texts, colonial archival documents, and other works from the seventeenth to the early twentieth century. It covers many topics and issues that affected Americans in the settlement and development of the Upper Midwest.

The Mexican-American War Memorial Homepage
http://sunsite.dcaa.unam.mx/revistas/1847/

Images and text explain the causes, courses, and outcomes of the Mexican-American War.

On the Trail in Kansas
http://www.ukans.edu/carrie/kancoll/galtrl.htm

This Kansas Collection site holds several good primary sources with images concerning the Oregon trail and America's early movement westward.

The Era of the Mountain Men
http://www.xmission.com/~drudy/amm.html

Private letters can speak volumes about the concerns and environment of the writers and recipients. Letters from early settlers west of the Mississippi River are offered on this site.

Chapter 13 | Masters and Slaves

"Been Here So Long": Selections from the WPA American Slave Narratives
http://newdeal.feri.org/asn/index.htm
Slave narratives are some of the more interesting primary sources about slavery.

Exploring Amistad
http://amistad.mysticseaport.org/main/welcome.html
Mystic Seaport runs this site that includes extensive collections of historical resources relating to the revolt and subsequent trial of enslaved Africans.

Africans in America: America's Journey Through Slavery
http://www.pbs.org/wgbh/aia/home.html
This PBS site contains images and documents recounting the slavery in America.

Amistad Trials (1839–1840)
http://www.law.umkc.edu/faculty/projects/ftrials/amistad/AMISTD.HTM
Images, chronology, and court and official documents comprise this site by Dr. Doug Linder at University of Missouri–Kansas City Law School.

Slave Narratives
http://docsouth.unc.edu/neh/neh.html
This site presents the telling narratives of several slaves housed at the Documents of the American South collection and the University of North Carolina.

The Settlement of African Americans in Liberia
http://www.loc.gov/exhibits/african/perstor.html
This site contains images and text relating to the colonization movement to return African Americans to Africa.

Images of African Americans from the Nineteenth Century
http://digital.nypl.org/schomburg/images_aa19/
The New York Public Library–Schomburg Center for Research in Black Culture site contains numerous visuals.

Chapter 14 | The Sectional Crisis

Secession Era Editorials Project
http://history.furman.edu/~benson/docs/
Furman University is digitizing editorials about the secession crisis and already includes scores of them on this site.

John Brown Trial Links
http://www.law.umkc.edu/faculty/projects/ftrials/Brown.html
For information about the trial of John Brown, this site provides a list of excellent links.

Abraham Lincoln and Slavery
http://odur.let.rug.nl/~usa/H/1990/ch5_p6.htm
This site discusses Lincoln's views and actions concerning slavery, especially the Lincoln-Douglas debate.

Bleeding Kansas
http://www.ukans.edu/carrie/kancoll/galbks.htm
Contemporary and later accounts of America's rehearsal for the Civil War comprise this University of Kansas site.

The Compromise of 1850 and the Fugitive Slave Act
http://www.pbs.org/wgbh/aia/part4
From the series on Africans in America, an analysis of the Compromise of 1850 and of the effects of the Fugitive Slave Act on black Americans.

The 1850s: An Increasingly Divided Union
http://nac.gmu.edu/mmts/50proto.html
A tutorial skills development site focusing on the events in the 1850s leading to the Civil War; from MMTS, the Multi-Media Thinking Skills project.

Words and Deeds in American History
http://lcweb2.loc.gov/ammem/mcchtml/corhome.html
A Library of Congress site containing links to Frederick Douglass; the Compromise of 1850; speeches by John C. Calhoun, Daniel Webster, and Henry Clay; and other topics from the Civil War era.

CHAPTER 15 | SECESSION AND THE CIVIL WAR

The American Civil War Homepage
http://sunsite.utk.edu/civil-war/warweb.html
This site has a great collection of hypertext links to the most useful identified electronic files about the American Civil War.

The Valley of the Shadow: Living the Civil War in Pennsylvania and Virginia
http://jefferson.village.virginia.edu/vshadow/vshadow.html
This project tells the histories of two communities on either side of the Mason-Dixon line during the Civil War. It includes narrative and an electronic archive of sources.

Civil War @ Charleston
http://www.awod.com/gallery/probono/cwchas/cwlayout.html
This site covers the history of the Civil War in and around Charleston, South Carolina.

Abraham Lincoln Association
http://www.alincolnassoc.com/
This site allows the search of digital versions of Lincoln's papers.

Crisis at Fort Sumter
http://www.tulane.edu/~latner/CrisisMain.html
This well-crafted use of hypermedia with assignments or problems explains and explores the events in and around the start of the Civil War.

U.S. Civil War Center
http://www.cwc.lsu.edu/
This is a site whose mission is to "locate, index, and / or make available all appropriate private and public data regarding the Civil War and to promote the study of the Civil War from the perspectives of all professions, occupations, and academic disciplines."

The Papers of Jefferson Davis Home Page
http://www.ruf.rice.edu/~pjdavis/jdp.htm
This site tells about the collection of Jefferson Davis Papers and includes a chronology of his life, a family genealogy, some key Davis documents on-line, and a collection of related links.

History of African Americans in the Civil War

http://www.itd.nps.gov/cwss/
history/aa_history.htm

This National Park Service site explores the history of the United States Colored Troops.

Civil War Women

http://scriptorium.lib.duke.edu/
collections/civil-war-women.html

This site includes original documents, links, and biographical information about several women and their lives during the Civil War.

Assassination of President Abraham Lincoln

http://memory.loc.gov/ammem/
alhtml/alrintr.html

Part of the American Memory series with introduction, timeline, and gallery.

Selected Civil War Photographs

http://lcweb2.loc.gov/ammem/
cwphome.html

Library of Congress site with more than 1,000 photographs, many from Matthew Brady.

A Timeline of the Civil War

http://www.historyplace.com/
civilwar/index.html

A complete timeline of the Civil War, well illustrated with photographs.

National Civil War Association

http://www.ncwa.org/info.html

One of the many Civil War Reenactment organizations in the United States.

CHAPTER 16 | THE AGONY OF RECONSTRUCTION

Diary and Letters of Rutherford B. Hayes

http://www.ohiohistory.org/
onlinedoc/hayes/index.cfm

The Rutherford B. Hayes Presidential Center in Fremont, Ohio, maintains this searchable database of Hayes's writings.

Images of African Americans from the 19th Century

http://digital.nypl.org/schomburg/
images_aa19/

The New York Public Library–Schomburg Center for Research in Black Culture site contains numerous visuals.

Freedmen and Southern Society Project (University of Maryland, College Park)

http://www.inform.umd.edu/ARHU/
Depts/History/Freedman/home.html

This site contains a chronology and sample documents from several print collections or primary sources about emancipation and freedom in the 1860s.

Andrew Johnson

http://www.whitehouse.gov/WH/
glimpse/presidents/html/aj17.html

White House history of Johnson.

Ulysses S. Grant

http://www.whitehouse.gov/WH/
glimpse/presidents/html/ug18.html

White House history of Grant.

History of the Suffrage Movement

http://www.rochester.edu/SBA

This site includes a chronology, important texts relating to woman suffrage, and biographical information about Susan B. Anthony and Elizabeth Cady Stanton.

CHAPTER 17 | THE WEST: EXPLOITING AN EMPIRE

Indian Affairs: Laws and Treaties, compiled and edited by Charles J. Kappler (1904)

http://www.library.okstate.edu/kappler

This digitized text at Oklahoma State University includes preremoval treaties with the Five Civilized Tribes and other tribes.

Native American Documents Project

http://www.csusm.edu/projects/nadp/nadp.htm

California State University at San Marcos has several digital documents relating to Native Americans on this site.

Geronimo

http://odur.let.rug.nl/~usa/B/geronimo/geronixx.htm

This site contains biographical and autobiographical information about the famous Native American who resisted European American domination.

National Museum of the American Indian

http://www.si.edu/nmai

The Smithsonian Institution maintains this site, providing information about the museum. The museum is dedicated to everything about Native Americans.

The Northern Great Plains, 1880–1920: Photographs from the Fred Hultstrand and F. A. Pazandak Photograph Collections

http://memory.loc.gov/ammem/award97/ndfahtml/ngphome.html

This American Memory site from the Library of Congress contains "two collections from the Institute for Regional Studies at North Dakota State University" with "900 photographs of rural and small town life at the turn of the century." Included are "images of sod homes and the people who built them; images of farms and the machinery that made them prosper; and images of one-room schools and the children that were educated in them."

On the Trail in Kansas

http://www.ukans.edu/carrie/kancoll/galtrl.htm

This Kansas Collection site holds several good primary sources with images concerning the Oregon trail and America's early movement westward.

"California as I Saw It": First-Person Narratives of California's Early Years, 1849–1900

http://memory.loc.gov/ammem/cbhtml/cbhome.html

This site is a part of the American Memory series and contains "full texts and illustrations of 190 works documenting the formative era of California's history through eyewitness accounts." It covers the Gold Rush, the interaction of various groups, and the settling of the region.

Home on the Range/Cowboy Heritage

http://history.cc.ukans.edu/heritage/old_west/cowboy.html

This site tells the history of the cattle trails and towns such as Dodge City, with useful text, links, documents, and maps.

The Evolution of the Conservation Movement, 1850–1920

http://memory.loc.gov/ammem/amrvhtml/conshome.html

This American Memory site brings together scores of primary sources and photographs about "the historical formation and cultural foundations of the movement to conserve and protect America's natural heritage."

Heroes and Villains in Kansas

http://www.ukans.edu/carrie/kancoll/galhero.htm

The Kansas Collection Gallery of both famous and little-known people who made up the history of the state.

CHAPTER 18 | THE INDUSTRIAL SOCIETY

Alexander Graham Bell Family Papers at the Library of Congress
http://memory.loc.gov/ammem/bellhtml/bellhome.html
This site contains papers from 1862 to 1939, but includes a chronology, images, selected documents, and interpretive essays about Bell.

The Richest Man in the World: Andrew Carnegie
http://www.pbs.org/wgbh/amex/carnegie/
This American Experience/PBS site provides images and text about Carnegie's life and activities.

Anarchist Archive at Pitzer University
http://dwardmac.pitzer.edu/Anarchist_Archives/archivehome.html
This archive includes classic anarchist texts, especially information about and graphics of the Haymarket Riot.

John D. Rockefeller and the Standard Oil Company
http://www.micheloud.com/FXM/SO/
This study with accompanying images by François Micheloud tells of the rise of Rockefeller and his mammoth company.

National Refinery Company
http://www.enarco.com/
This positive history of the company reflects the industrial changes of late-nineteenth-century America.

A Short History of American Labor
http://www.unionweb.org/history.htm
This brief essay is adapted from AFL-CIO *American Federationist*, March 1981.

American Labor History
http://www.geocities.com/CollegePark/Quad/6460/AmLabHist/index.html
This site takes a general look at the history of labor in America.

Labor-Management Conflict in American History
http://www.history.ohio-state.edu/projects/laborconflict/
This Ohio State University site includes primary accounts of some of the major events in the history of labor-management conflict in the late nineteenth and early twentieth centuries.

Samuel Gompers Papers at the University of Maryland
http://www.inform.umd.edu/HIST/Gompers/web1.html
This site includes information about the papers project but also has a photo gallery, selected documents, and a brief history of the first president of the American Federation of Labor.

CHAPTER 19 | TOWARD AN URBAN SOCIETY, 1877–1900

The American Experience: America 1900
http://www.pbs.org/wgbh/amex/1900/
Companion to the PBS documentary, this site includes audio clips of respected historians on the economics, politics, and culture of 1900, a primary source database, a timeline of the year, downloadable software to compile a family tree, and other materials.

Touring Turn-of-the-Century America: Photographs from the Detroit Publishing Company, 1880–1920
http://memory.loc.gov/ammem/detroit/dethome.html

This Library of Congress collection has thousands of photographs from turn-of-the-century America.

World's Columbian Exposition: Idea, Experience, Aftermath
http://xroads.virginia.edu/~MA96/WCE/title.html
This site has a virtual tour of the fair, along with contemporary reactions and modern analysis.

United States History: The Gilded Age (1890) to World War I
http://www.emayzine.com/lectures/Gilded~1.htm
This site consists of a good overview essay of the era.

The Gilded Page
http://www.em.edu/~srnels/gilded.html

This site has links to scores of Gilded Age and Progressive Era documents.

Chapter Three: American Socialists and Reformers
http://www.vineyard.net/vineyard/history/pdgech3.htm
This site includes a fine essay about Edward Bellamy and some of the movements and ideas he inspired.

African American Perspectives: Pamphlets from the Daniel A. P. Murray Collection, 1818–1907
http://memory.loc.gov/ammem/aap/aaphome.html
This collection includes writings of famous African Americans, including Frederick Douglass, Booker T. Washington, Ida B. Wells-Barnett, Benjamin W. Arnett, Alexander Crummel, and Emanuel Love.

CHAPTER 20 | POLITICAL REALIGNMENTS IN THE 1890S

World's Columbian Exposition: Idea, Experience, Aftermath
http://xroads.virginia.edu/~MA96/WCE/title.html
This site has a virtual tour of the fair, along with contemporary reactions and modern analysis.

Election of 1896
http://jefferson.village.virginia.edu/seminar
This University of Virginia site contains biographical information, images, cartoons, and related links about the pivotal 1896 election.

The Era of William McKinley
http://www.history.ohio-state.edu/projects/mckinley/default.htm
This site contains numerous images from various stages of William McKinley's career along with a brief biographical essay. This Ohio State University site also has a section with an excellent collection of cartoons from the era.

CHAPTER 21 | TOWARD EMPIRE

William McKinley and the Spanish-American War
http://www.history.ohio-state.edu/projects/mckinley/SpanAmWar.htm
Part of Ohio State University's site about William McKinley, this part highlights the Spanish-American War with an essay and photos.

Sentenaryo/Centennial: The Philippine Revolution and Philippine-American War
http://www.boondocksnet.com/centennial/index.html
Jim Zwick organizes primary documents, images, and essays focusing on the Philippines and American involvement.

Anti-Imperialism in the United States, 1898–1935

http://www.boondocksnet.com/ail98-35.html

Jim Zwick edits this extensive site, collating a large number of primary documents about anti-imperialism in America.

Photos of the Philippine-American War

http://www.msstate.edu/Archives/History/USA/filipino/filipino.html

The Philippine-American War is one of the least discussed military engagements in American history. Many tactics employed then were later used in the Vietnam war.

Imperialism Web Page

http://www.smplanet.com/imperialism/toc.html

Focusing on the period around the turn of the century, this site puts much information about American imperialism in one place.

Images from the Philippine-United States War

http://www.geocities.com/djmabry/USA/twenty/filipino.html

The Philippine-American War is one of the least discussed military engagements in American history. Many tactics employed then were later used in the Vietnam War. This site is an archive of historical texts.

Theodore Roosevelt Association

http://www.theodoreroosevelt.org/

This site contains much biographical and research information about this famous American.

CHAPTER 22 | THE PROGRESSIVE ERA

NAACP Online

http://www.naacp.org/about/history.html

The National Association for the Advancement of Colored People official Web site explains its mission and includes a primary document explaining the start of the NAACP.

The Evolution of the Conservation Movement, 1850–1920

http://memory.loc.gov/ammem/amrvhtml/conshome.html

This American Memory site brings together scores of primary sources and photographs about "the historical formation and cultural foundations of the movement to conserve and protect America's natural heritage."

The Triangle Shirtwaist Factory Fire, March 25, 1911

http://www.ilr.cornell.edu/trianglefire/

The Kheel Center for Labor-Management Documentation and Archives at Cornell University put together this excellent site

composed of oral histories, cartoons, images, and essays.

Labor-Management Conflict in American History

http://www.history.ohio-state.edu/projects/laborconflict/

This site at Ohio State University includes primary accounts of some of the major events in the history of labor-management conflict in the late nineteenth and early twentieth centuries.

Inside an American Factory: The Westinghouse Works, 1904

http://lcweb2.loc.gov/ammem/papr/west/westhome.html

Part of the American Memory Project at the Library of Congress, this site provides a glimpse inside a turn-of-the-century factory.

African American Women Writers of the Nineteenth Century

http://digital.nypl.org/schomburg/writers_aa19/

The New York Public Library's Schomburg Center for Research in Black Culture maintains this site that contains a large number of digital texts by African American women of the nineteenth century.

Touring Turn-of-the-Century America: Photographs from the Detroit Publishing Company, 1880–1920
http://memory.loc.gov/ammem/detroit/dethome.html
This Library of Congress collection has thousands of photographs from turn-of-the-century America.

Bill Haywood Trial (1907)
http://www.law.umkc.edu/faculty/projects/ftrials/haywood/haywood.htm

This site contains images, chronology, and court and official documents maintained by Dr. Doug Linder at University of Missouri–Kansas City Law School.

Margaret Sanger Papers Project
http://www.nyu.edu/projects/sanger/
This site at New York University contains information about Margaret Sanger and digital versions of several of her works.

National Arts and Crafts Archives
http://arts-crafts.com/index.html
This site serves as a guide to materials on the Arts and Crafts movement, which lasted roughly from 1890 to 1929.

CHAPTER 23 | FROM ROOSEVELT TO WILSON IN THE AGE OF PROGRESSIVISM

Theodore Roosevelt Association
http://www.theodoreroosevelt.org/
This site contains much biographical and research information about Theodore Roosevelt.

Woodrow Wilson
http://www.ipl.org/ref/POTUS/wwilson.html
This page contains basic factual data about

Wilson's election and presidency, speeches, and on-line biographies.

History of the Suffrage Movement
http://www.rochester.edu/SBA
This site includes a chronology, important texts relating to woman suffrage, and biographical information about Susan B. Anthony and Elizabeth Cady Stanton.

CHAPTER 24 | THE NATION AT WAR

Woodrow Wilson
http://www.ipl.org/ref/POTUS/wwilson.html
This page contains basic factual data about Wilson's election and presidency, speeches, and on-line biographies.

World War 1 Document Archive
http://www.lib.byu.edu/~rdh/wwi/
This archive contains sources about World War I in general, not just America's involvement.

World War One: Trenches on the Web
http://www.worldwar1.com/index.html
This site provides a mass of data concerning the prosecution of the world's first global war.

The Great Migration in Chicago
http://lcweb.loc.gov/exhibits/african/afam011.html
This site looks at the black experience in the Great Migration at one prominent destination.

The American Experience: Influenza
http://www.pbs.org/wgbh/pages/amex/influenza

This PBS site reveals the impact of the great flu epidemic of 1918.

CHAPTER 25 | TRANSITION TO MODERN AMERICA

Automotive History at the Michigan Electronic Library
http://mel.org/business/autos-history.html

This page has several links to sites about automotive history in America.

Harlem 1900–1940: An African American Community
http://www.si.umich.edu/CHICO/Harlem/

The New York Public Library's Schomburg Center for Research in Black Culture hosts this site that includes a database, a timeline, and an exhibit.

William P. Gottlieb Photographs of the Golden Age of Jazz
http://memory.loc.gov/ammem/wghtml/wghome.html

The Music Division of the Library of Congress has numerous images, audio, and scanned articles from the 1940s.

The Scopes Trial
http://xroads.virginia.edu/~UG97/inherit/1925home.html

This site gives a general description of the trial and the issues surrounding it.

American Temperance and Prohibition
http://www.cohums.ohio-state.edu/history/projects/prohibition

This site looks at the temperance movement over time and contains many informative links.

National Arts and Crafts Archives
http://arts-crafts.com/index.html

This site serves as a guide to materials on the Arts and Crafts movement, which lasted roughly from 1890 to 1929.

The Flapper
http://www.pandorasbox.com/flapper.html

This site contains many links to information about the popular culture of the 1920s with special reference to the flapper.

The Calvin Coolidge Experience
http://www.geocities.com/CapitolHill/4921/

This site is an unusual look at one of America's less colorful presidents.

CHAPTER 26 | FRANKLIN D. ROOSEVELT AND THE NEW DEAL

Voices from the Dust Bowl: the Charles L. Todd and Robert Sonkin Migrant Worker Collection, 1940–1941
http://memory.loc.gov/ammem/afctshtml/tshome.html

Farm Security Administration (FSA) studies of migrant work camps in central California in 1940 and 1941 are the bulk of this site. The collection includes audio recordings, photographs, manuscript materials, and publications.

New Deal Network
http://newdeal.feri.org/

This database includes photographs, political cartoons, and texts—including speeches, letters, and other historic documents—from the New Deal period.

Franklin Delano Roosevelt

http://www.ipl.org/ref/POTUS/
fdroosevelt.html

This site provides information about FDR, the only president to serve more than two terms.

Picture Archive: Photographs of the Great Depression, 1935–1942

http://www.corbis.com/fdr/fsa/
map.html

These photographs reveal the real impact of the Great Depression on American life.

Newspaper Events Not Big in History

http://www.ybi.com/brink/author/
1933/index.html

This site lists dozens of events that were front-page news in 1933 but failed to make the history books.

A New Deal for the Arts

http://www.nara.gov/exhall/newdeal/
newdeal.html

Artwork, documents, and photographs recount the federal government's efforts to fund artists in the 1930s in the National Archives site.

America from the Great Depression to World War II: Photographs from the FSA and OWI, ca. 1935–1945

http://memory.loc.gov/ammem/
fsowhome.html

These images in the Farm Security Administration–Office of War Information Collection show Americans from all over the nation experiencing everything from despair to triumph in the 1930s and 1940s.

CHAPTER 27 | AMERICA AND THE WORLD, 1921–1945

A People at War

http://www.nara.gov/exhall/people/
people.html

This National Archives exhibit takes a close look at the contributions millions of Americans made to the war effort.

Powers of Persuasion—Poster Art of World War II

http://www.nara.gov/education/
teaching/posters/poster.html

These powerful posters at the National Archives were part of the battle for the hearts and minds of the American people.

America from the Great Depression to World War II: Photographs from the FSA and OWI, ca. 1935–1945

http://memory.loc.gov/ammem/
fsowhome.html

These images in the Farm Security Administration–Office of War Information Collection show Americans from all over the nation experiencing everything from despair

to triumph in the 1930s and 1940s.

A-Bomb WWW Museum

http://www.csi.ad.jp/ABOMB/

This site offers information about the impact of the first atomic bomb as well as the background and context of weapons of total destruction.

The United States Holocaust Memorial Museum

http://www.ushmm.org/index.html

This is the official Web site of the Holocaust Museum in Washington, DC.

World War II Pictures

http://www.corbis.com/FDR/
ww2.html

This Corbis site houses many pictures about the second world war and American involvement in the conflict.

Tuskegee Airmen

http://www.wpafb.af.mil/museum/
history/prewwii/ta.htm

The Air Force Museum at Wright-Patterson

Air Force Base maintains this site about the African American pilots of World War II.

Abraham Lincoln Brigade Archives
http://www.alba-valb.org
This Brandeis University site has posters and photographs from the Spanish civil war and the unit of American volunteers who fought in it.

World War II Resources: Primary Source Materials on the Web
http://www.ibiblio.org/pha/index.html
This site has a large number of searchable primary texts from all aspects of World War II.

CHAPTER 28 | THE ONSET OF THE COLD WAR

Harry S Truman
http://www.ipl.org/ref/POTUS/hstruman.html
This page contains basic factual data about Truman's election and presidency, speeches, and on-line biographies.

Cold War
http://cnn.com/SPECIALS/cold.war/
This is the companion site to the CNN Perspectives series on the Cold War. It contains information including interactive timelines and a quiz.

Beyond the Playing Field: Jackie Robinson, Civil Rights Advocate
http://www.nara.gov/education/teaching/robinson/robmain.html
This National Archives and Records Administration teaching materials site contains images, essays, and documents about Robinson and Civil Rights.

Negro Leagues Baseball On-line Archive
http://www.negroleaguebaseball.com/
Essays about desegregation, baseball, and Jim Crow as well as images of teams and players comprise much of this site.

Korean War Project
http://www.koreanwar.org
This site has information about the Korean War and is a guide to resources on the struggle.

NATO at 50
http:www.cnn.com/SPECIALS/1999/nato/
This site from CNN has an excellent timeline and images telling the history of the North Atlantic Treaty Organization.

Senator Joe McCarthy—A Multimedia Celebration
http://webcorp.com/mccarthy/
This webcorp site includes audio and visual clips of McCarthy's speeches.

Harry S Truman Library and Museum
http://www.trumanlibrary.org
This presidential library site has numerous photos and various important primary documents relating to Truman.

CHAPTER 29 | AFFLUENCE AND ANXIETY

Fifties Website Home Page
http://www.fiftiesweb.com/
This entertaining site tells about and samples music and television from the 1950s. It also includes a related links page.

1950s America
http://dept.english.upenn.edu/~afilreis/50/home.html
This site by Professor Al Filreis of the University of Pennsylvania contains a large

array of 1950s literature and images in an alphabetical index.

Levittown: Documents of an Ideal American Suburb
http://www.uic.edu/~pbhales/Levittown/

The postwar boom in housing made suburban living the cultural norm in America and shaped a generation. The story of the classic suburb, Levittown, is told on this site in pictures and text.

Dwight David Eisenhower
http://www.ipl.org/ref/POTUS/ddeisenhower.html

This site contains basic factual data about Eisenhower's election and presidency, including speeches and other materials.

The Dwight D. Eisenhower Library and Museum
http://www.eisenhower.utexas.edu/

This site contains mainly photos of the presidents.

CHAPTER 30 | THE TURBULENT SIXTIES

Fourteen Days in October: The Cuban Missile Crisis
http://library.advanced.org/11046/

This creative site allows the viewer to explore the Cuban missile crisis.

John Fitzgerald Kennedy
http://www.ipl.org/ref/POTUS/jfkennedy.html

This site contains basic factual data about Kennedy's election and presidency, speeches, and on-line biographies.

The Kennedy Assassination
http://mcadams.posc.mu.edu/home.htm

This well-organized site has images, essays, and photos on the assassination.

Lyndon B. Johnson
http://www.ipl.org/ref/POTUS/lbjohnson.html

This page contains basic factual data about Johnson's election and presidency, speeches, and on-line biographies.

Lyndon B. Johnson Library and Museum
http://www.lbjlib.utexas.edu/

This presidential library contains images and on-line exhibits.

National Aeronautics and Space Administration
http://www.hq.nasa.gov/office/pao/History/histsub.htm

NASA's Office of Policy and Plans History Office maintains this site about NASA and its history.

Investigating the Vietnam War
http://www.spartacus.schoolnet.co.uk/vietintro.htm

This site from Spartacus Educational Publishing, U.K., has an excellent list of annotated links to the best Vietnam-related sites.

Vietnam War Bibliography
http://hubcap.clemson.edu/~eemoise/bibliography.html

Edwin Moise of Clemson University maintains this extensive bibliography of print works about Vietnam and the Vietnam War.

Vietnam On-line
http://www.pbs.org/wgbh/pages/amex/vietnam/index.html

From PBS and the American Experience, this site contains a detailed, interactive timeline of the war, interpretive essays, and autobiographical reflections.

My Lai Court-Martial (1970)
http://www.law.umkc.edu/faculty/
projects/ftrials/mylai/mylai.htm
This site contains images, chronology, and court and official documents maintained by Dr. Doug Linder at University of Missouri–Kansas City Law School.

JFK Assassination Web Page
http://ourworld.compuserve.com/
homepages/MGriffith_2/jfk.htm
This is a personal but thorough page that is a guide to the best Internet resources for the assassination.

Martin Luther King, Jr. Papers Project
http://www.stanford.edu/group/King/
This site at Stanford University has links and selected digital documents by and concerning Martin Luther King, Jr.

National Civil Rights Museum
http://www.mecca.org/~crights/
nc2.html
This site allows a virtual tour of the museum with its interpretive exhibits.

The Digger Archives
http://www.diggers.org/
This site provides information about The San Francisco Diggers, which became one of the legendary groups in the Haight-Ashbury from 1966 to 1968.

Free Speech Movement: Student Protest—U.C. Berkeley, 1964–65
http://www.lib.berkeley.edu/BANC/
FSM/
The Bancroft Library at U.C. Berkeley houses this exhibit with oral histories, a chronology, and documents.

Voices of the Civil Rights Era
http://www.webcorp.com/
civilrights/index.htm
Webcorp provides audio clips from prominent figures of the Civil Rights era including Martin Luther King, Jr., and Malcolm X.

Martin Luther King, Jr.
http://www.seattletimes.com/mlk/
This site from the *Seattle Times* has several articles about King and the Civil Rights Movement.

The Sixties Project
http://lists.village.virginia.edu/sixties/
This University of Virginia site has extensive exhibits, documents, and personal narratives from the 1960s.

Civil Rights Oral History Bibliography
http://www-dept.usm.edu/~mcrohb/
This University of Southern Mississippi site includes complete transcripts of the selected oral resources.

1969 Woodstock Festival and Concert
http://www.woodstock69.com/index.
htm
This site provides pictures and lists of songs from the famous rock festival.

National Civil Rights Museum in Memphis, Tennessee
http://www.midsouth.rr.com/
civilrights/
This site houses images with annotation from the museum.

United States vs. Cecil Price et al. (The "Mississippi Burning" Trial), 1967
http://www.law.umkc.edu/faculty/
projects/ftrials/price&bowers/
price&bowers.htm
This site contains images, chronology, and court and official documents maintained by Dr. Doug Linder at University of Missouri–Kansas City Law School.

CHAPTER 31 | A CRISIS IN CONFIDENCE, 1969–1980

May 4, 1970: Twenty-five Years of Remembrance
http://www.library.kent.edu/exhibits/
4may95/index.html
This site commemorates the twenty-fifth anniversary of the shootings at Kent State
University with a detailed chronology and
other information.

Documents from the Women's Liberation Movement
http://scriptorium.lib.duke.edu/wlm/
Primary documents on-line from the Special
Collections Library at Duke University provide firsthand information about the women's
liberation movement.

Constitutional Issues: Watergate and the Constitution
http://www.nara.gov/education/
teaching/watergate/watergat.html
From the National Archives' teaching materials, this site has a good chronology of
Watergate and a 1974 memorandum from the
Watergate Special Prosecution Force weighing
the pros and cons of seeking an indictment
against former President Richard Nixon.

CNN 1970s Interactive Timeline
http://cnn.com/SPECIALS/1999/
century/episodes/08/
CNN has a series of interactive timelines with
several interesting sites. This one covers the
years from 1970 to 1979.

Richard Milhous Nixon
http://www.ipl.org/ref/POTUS/
rmnixon.html

This site contains basic factual data about
Nixon's election and presidency, speeches, and
on-line biographies.

Watergate 25
http://www.washingtonpost.com/
wp-srv/national/longterm/watergate/
front.htm
This site features a chronology, images,
searchable articles, and a good deal of background information about the burglary and its
consequences.

Gerald Rudolph Ford
http://www.ipl.org/ref/POTUS/
grford.html
This site contains basic factual data about
Ford's election and presidency, speeches, and
on-line biographies.

James Earl Carter, Jr.
http://www.ipl.org/ref/POTUS/
jecarter.html
This site contains basic factual data about
Carter's election and presidency, speeches,
and on-line biographies.

Giant Leap
http://cnn.com/TECH/specials/
apollo/
This CNN site commemorates the thirtieth
anniversary of the 1969 moonwalk and tells
the story of NASA and the ongoing space program.

Chapter 32 | The Republican Resurgence, 1980–1992

The 80s Server
http://www.80s.com/
This site has a variety of sources of information about the 1980s, but the best parts are open to members only.

The Gulf War
http://www.pbs.org/pages/frontline/gulf/index.html
This Frontline and PBS site combines personal accounts with a chronology and general information about the war.

Ronald Wilson Reagan
http://www.ipl.org/ref/POTUS/rwreagan.html
This site contains basic factual data about Reagan's election and presidency, speeches, and on-line biographies.

George Herbert Walker Bush
http://www.ipl.org/ref/POTUS/ghwbush.html
This site contains basic factual data about Bush's election and presidency, speeches, and on-line biographies.

Chapter 33 | America in Flux: The Anxious Nineties

American Identities
http://xroads.virginia.edu/~YP/ethnic.html
This site suggests resources for studying America's multiple ethnic identities.

William Jefferson Clinton
http://www.ipl.org/ref/POTUS/wjclinton.html
This site contains basic factual data about Clinton's election and presidency, speeches, and on-line biographies.

Investigating the President: The Trial
http://www.cnn.com/ALLPOLITICS/resources/1998/lewinsky
This site from CNN provides information and documents about the scandals surrounding President Clinton and his impeachment.

Special Report: U.S. v. Microsoft
http://www.policy.com/reports/dojvsms/
This site provides background information and documents on the antitrust case.

Virtual Museum of Computing
http://vmoc.i.am/
This site relates the history of computing through a series of on-line exhibits.

A Brief History of the Internet, Version 3.1
http://www.isoc.org/internet-history/
The Internet Society puts out this site that explores the development and impact of the Internet.

Virtual Museum of Computing
http://www.cs.reading.ac.uk/museum/vlmp/computing.html
This University of Reading site says it is "an eclectic collection of World Wide Web hyperlinks connected with the history of computing and on-line computer-based exhibits."

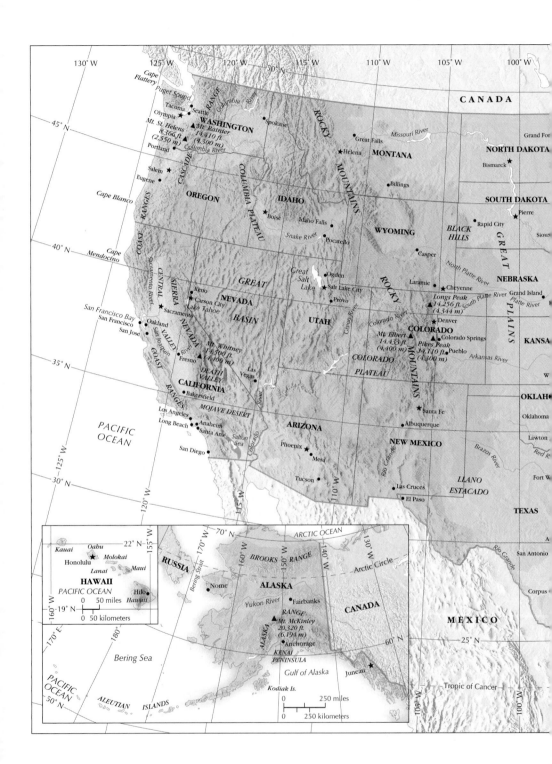

130° W 125° W 120° W 50° N 115° W 110° W 105° W 100° W

CANADA

Cape Flattery
Puget Sound
Tacoma • Seattle
Olympia ★
Mt. St. Helens
8,366 ft.
(2,550 m)
Portland •

Columbia River
WASHINGTON
Mt. Rainier
14,410 ft.
(4,300 m)
Columbia River

Spokane •

45° N

ROCKY

Great Falls •
Missouri River

• Helena

MONTANA

Grand For

NORTH DAKOTA
Bismarck ★

Salem ★
Eugene •

OREGON

MOUNTAINS

Billings •

40° N

Cape Blanco

CASCADE

COLUMBIA

Boise •

Idaho Falls •

IDAHO

Snake River • Pocatello

WYOMING

Casper •

BLACK
HILLS

Rapid City •

Pierre ★

Sioux

SOUTH DAKOTA

RANGES

COAST

Cape Mendocino

PLATEAU

Great
Salt
Lake

• Ogden
Salt Lake City •
• Provo

Laramie •
Cheyenne •

North Platte River

Grand Island
South Platte River

GREAT

NEBRASKA

Sacramento River

CENTRAL

SIERRA

Reno •
Carson City ★
Lake Tahoe
Sacramento ★

GREAT

NEVADA

BASIN

UTAH

ROCKY

Colorado River

Longs Peak
14,256 ft.
(4,344 m)

Denver •

Platte River

35° N

San Francisco Bay
San Francisco •
San Jose •

Oakland •
San Jose

VALLEY

NEVADA

COAST

Mt. Whitney
14,500 ft.
(4,400 m)
Fresno •

San Joaquin River

DEATH
VALLEY

Las
Vegas

Green River

COLORADO
PLATEAU

MOUNTAINS

COLORADO

Mt. Elbert
14,433 ft.
(4,400 m)

Pikes Peak
14,110 ft.
(4,300 m)

Colorado Springs •
• Pueblo

Arkansas River

KANSAS

W

CALIFORNIA

Bakersfield •

MOJAVE DESERT

RANGES

Los Angeles •
Long Beach •
• Santa Ana
Anaheim

Colorado River

Salton
Sea

ARIZONA

Santa Fe •

Albuquerque •

OKLAH

Oklahoma

Lawton

PACIFIC
OCEAN

San Diego •

Phoenix ★
• Mesa

NEW MEXICO

Brazos River

Red R

125° W

30° N

Tucson •

Rio Grande

Las Cruces •
• El Paso

LLANO
ESTACADO

Fort W

TEXAS

120° W

115° W

101° W

Kauai
22° N
Oahu ★ Molokai
Honolulu Lanai • Maui
HAWAII
PACIFIC OCEAN
0   50 miles
0   50 kilometers
Hilo •
Hawaii
19° N

70° N

RUSSIA

Bering Strait

Nome •

Yukon River

ARCTIC OCEAN

BROOKS' RANGE

160° W

150° W

140° W

130° W

Arctic Circle

Arctic Circle

ALASKA

Fairbanks •

RANGE
Mt. McKinley
20,320 ft.
(6,194 m)
• Anchorage
KENAI
PENINSULA

CANADA

60° N

25° N

San Antonio

Corpus

MEXICO

170° E

180°

Bering Sea

PACIFIC
OCEAN

50° N

ALEUTIAN ISLANDS

Gulf of Alaska

Kodiak Is.

Juneau ★

0   250 miles
0   250 kilometers

Tropic of Cancer

105° W

100° W

Political and Physical Map of the United States

Land Elevation

Feet		Meters
10,000		3,000
7,000		2,000
3,000		1,000
700		200
(Sea Level) 0		0 (Sea Level)
Below Sea Level		Below Sea Level

International boundaries
State boundaries
⊛ National capital
★ State capital

ATLANTIC OCEAN

PUERTO RICO (U.S.)
San Juan

0   100 miles
0   100 kilometers

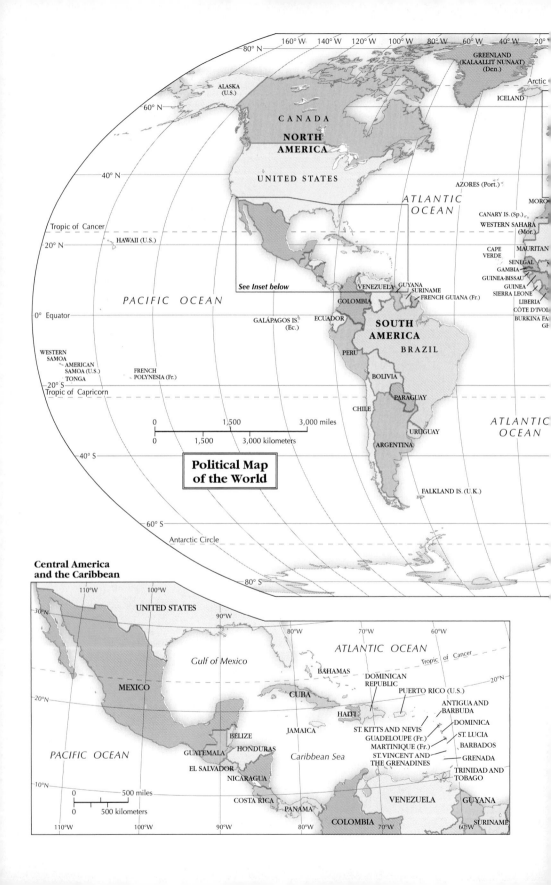

Political Map of the World

80° N
60° N
40° N
Tropic of Cancer
20° N
0° Equator
20° S
Tropic of Capricorn
40° S
60° S
Antarctic Circle
80° S

160° W 140° W 120° W 100° W 80° W 60° W 40° W 20°

GREENLAND
(KALAALLIT NUNAAT)
(Den.)

Arctic
ICELAND

ALASKA
(U.S.)

C A N A D A

NORTH
AMERICA

UNITED STATES

AZORES (Port.)

ATLANTIC
OCEAN

MORO

CANARY IS. (Sp.)
WESTERN SAHARA
(Mor.)

HAWAII (U.S.)

CAPE   MAURITAN
VERDE
SENEGAL
GAMBIA
GUINEA-BISSAU
GUINEA
SIERRA LEONE
LIBERIA
CÔTE D'IVOI
BURKINA FA
GH

See Inset below

VENEZUELA GUYANA
SURINAME
FRENCH GUIANA (Fr.)
COLOMBIA

PACIFIC OCEAN

GALÁPAGOS IS
(Ec.)

ECUADOR

SOUTH
AMERICA

PERU

BRAZIL

WESTERN
SAMOA
AMERICAN
SAMOA (U.S.)
TONGA

FRENCH
POLYNESIA (Fr.)

BOLIVIA

PARAGUAY

CHILE

ATLANTIC
OCEAN

0   1,500   3,000 miles
0   1,500   3,000 kilometers

URUGUAY

ARGENTINA

FALKLAND IS. (U.K.)

Central America and the Caribbean

110°W   100°W

UNITED STATES

90°W
80°W

ATLANTIC OCEAN

70°W
60°W

Tropic of Cancer

30°N

Gulf of Mexico

BAHAMAS

DOMINICAN
REPUBLIC

20°N

PUERTO RICO (U.S.)

MEXICO

CUBA

ANTIGUA AND
BARBUDA

20°N

HAITI

DOMINICA

JAMAICA

ST. KITTS AND NEVIS
GUADELOUPE (Fr.)
MARTINIQUE (Fr.)
ST. VINCENT AND
THE GRENADINES

ST. LUCIA
BARBADOS
GRENADA

BELIZE

GUATEMALA HONDURAS

Caribbean Sea

PACIFIC OCEAN

EL SALVADOR

NICARAGUA

TRINIDAD AND
TOBAGO

10°N

0   500 miles
0   500 kilometers

COSTA RICA

PANAMA

VENEZUELA

GUYANA

COLOMBIA

70°W

SURINAME

110°W   100°W   90°W   80°W   60°W

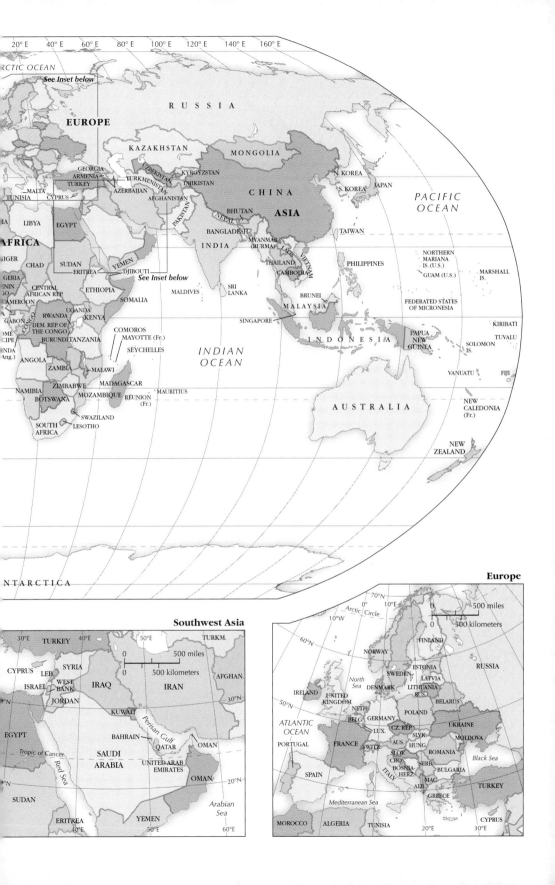

CREDITS

Unless otherwise credited, all photographs are the property of Addison Wesley Educational Publishers, Inc. Page abbreviations are as follows: **T** top, **C** center, **B** bottom, **L** left, **R** right.

CHAPTER 16

503-506 The Library of Congress **508** Chicago Historical Society [(none)-00434] **512** National Archives **514** Stock Montage, Inc. **517** © Collection of The New-York Historical Society [50475] **519** Valentine Museum, Richmond, Virginia **525L** Culver Pictures **525R** Corbis-Bettmann **526** Rutherford B. Hayes Presidential Center, Fremont, Ohio **533** Corbis **535** Yale Joel/LIFE MAGAZINE © Time Inc.

CHAPTER 17

544 From *A Pictographic History of the Oglala Sioux* by Amos Bad Heart Bull, text by Helen Blish, University of Nebraska Press **545** Smithsonian Institution **546L** Arizona Historical Society/Tucson [19831] **546R** Arizona Historical Society/Tucson [19830] **551** Denver Public Library, Western History Collection **553** Baker Library, Harvard Business School **556** © The New-York Historical Society [16212] **558** Denver Public Library, Western History Department **564** From *The Black West* by William Loren Katz **566** Haynes Foundation Collection/Montana Historical Society, Helena

CHAPTER 18

577 Union Pacific Historical Collection **581** © Bettmann/Corbis **585** Courtesy George Eastman House **586** Edison National Historic Site/U.S. Department of the Interior, National Park Service **589** The Museum of the City of New York **591** Brown Brothers **593** Courtesy, Metropolitan Life Insurance Company **595** The Library of Congress **598** The Granger Collection, NY **599** © Bettmann/Corbis

CHAPTER 19

606 Photograph by Byron, The Byron Collection, Museum of the City of New York **607** The Library of Congress **609** New York Public Library, Astor, Lenox and Tilden Foundations **619-621** Brown Brothers **624** Michigan Historical Collections, Bentley Historical Library, University of Michigan **626** The Library of Congress **632L** Brown Brothers **632R** Jane Addams Memorial Collection, Special Collections, University Library, University of Illinois at Chicago

CHAPTER 20

637 The Library of Congress **644** Corbis-Bettmann **647** North Carolina Division of Archives & History **649** The Kansas State Historical Society, Topeka **652** © Minnesota Historical Society/Corbis **658L** Valentine Museum **658R** © Bettmann/Corbis **660** Corbis-Bettmann **662** Culver Pictures

CHAPTER 21

670 The Library of Congress **672** © The New-York Historical Society **677** Hawaii State Archives **681** *Harper's Weekly* **683** *New York Journal,* February 17, 1898 **686T** Chicago Historical Society [ICHi-08425] **686B** Courtesy of USMA Archives, West Point, NY **690** New York Public Library, Astor, Lenox and Tilden Foundations **693-697** Culver Pictures

CHAPTER 22

700L The Lawrence Lee Pelletier Library, Allegheny College **700R** Culver Pictures **704** New York Public Library, Astor, Lenox and Tilden Foundations **707L-R** Brown Brothers **710L** U.S. Dept. of Labor **710R** Courtesy George Eastman House **711** Culver Pictures **712** Corbis-Bettmann **717** National Archives **721** Brown Brothers **723** Manchester, N.H., Historic Association

CHAPTER 23

733-739 Culver Pictures **743** Rare Book, Manuscript, & Special Collections Library, Duke University **746** Cleveland Picture Collection, Cleveland Public Library **748** State Historical Society of Wisconsin Visual Archives [WHi (X3) 13031] **753** Courtesy, The Lilly Library, Indiana University, Bloomington, Indiana **754** Warsaw Collection, Smithsonian Institution **763** Brown Brothers **767T** National Archives **767B** The Archives of Labor and Urban Affairs, Wayne State University

CHAPTER 24

770 © FPG International Corp. **771** *New York Tribune*, May 8, 1915 **782** Dokumentations- und Informationszentrum Munchen GmbH, Bilderdienst **783** *Des Moines Register and Leader*, July 1915 **788** National Archives **792** Brown Brothers **795** Corbis-Bettmann **797** National Archives **802** Corbis-Bettmann

CHAPTER 25

807-812 From the collections of the Henry Ford Museum & Greenfield Village **813** *Frank Leslie's Illustrated Newspaper*, September 11, 1920 **818TL** Brown Brothers **822** Culver Pictures **824** Archive Photos/Getty Images **827** Corbis-Bettmann **828** *Life*, 1922. TimePix

CHAPTER 26

838T AP/Wide World **838B** Corbis-Bettmann **843** Brown Brothers **847** AP/Wide World Photos **848** Culver Pictures **849** Archive Photos/Getty Images **852** The Library of Congress **856** UPI/Corbis-Bettmann **857** AP/Wide World Photos **859** The Franklin D. Roosevelt Library, Hyde Park, NY

CHAPTER 27

867 Brown Brothers **873** AP/Wide World Photos **876** UPI/Corbis-Bettmann **881** Official U.S. Navy Photograph **887** Photo by Vernon T. Manion. Courtesy Boeing Aircraft Corporation. **889** The Library of Congress **891** National Archives **895** Courtesy of the World Federation of Bergen-Belsen Associations **897** Ed Clark/LIFE MAGAZINE © Time Inc. **899** Underwood & Underwood/Corbis-Bettmann

CHAPTER 28

910 The Fotomas Index **911** UPI/Corbis-Bettmann **917** Carl Mydens, LIFE MAGAZINE © Time Inc. **921-923** UPI/Corbis-Bettmann **924** Hank Walker, LIFE MAGAZINE © Time Inc. **928** From Herblock's *Special for Today* (Simon & Schuster, 1958). Originally appeared in *The Washington Post*. **929** AP/Wide World Photos **933** Express Newspapers/Archive Photos/Getty Images **935** From *Cartoons and Lampoons*, © 1982 Samuel A. Tower **936** UPI/Corbis-Bettmann

CHAPTER 29

939L Magnum Photos **945** National Archives **947** © Allen Ginsberg Trust **948** Copyright © 1957 by The New York Times Co. Reprinted by permission. **954L** Carl Iwasaki/TimePix **954R** © Eve Arnold/Magnum **955** UPI/Corbis-Bettmann **957** AP Photo/Gene Herrick **958** AP/Wide World Photos

CHAPTER 30

965 UPI/Corbis-Bettman **966** AP/Wide World Photos **968** Archive Photos/Getty Images **975** Charles Moore/Black Star **976** AP/Wide World Photos **979** UPI/Corbis-Bettmann **980L-R** George Tames/NYT Pictures **993** Paul Conklin/TimePix **996** Bob Fitch/Black Star **999** Lyndon Baines Johnson Library **1001** AP/Wide World Photos

CHAPTER 31

1006-1009 UPI/Corbis-Bettmann **1013** Kent State University Archives **1015** AP/Wide World Photos **1016** Roland Freeman/Magnum Photos **1018** Tony Korody/Corbis-Sygma **1023-1033** UPI/Corbis-Bettmann **1035** Bill Fitz-Patrick/The White House **1036** © Philippe Ledru/Sygma

CHAPTER 32

1040 © John Bryson/Sygma **1042** AP/Wide World Photos **1046** UPI/Corbis-Bettmann **1047** Michael Evans/The White House **1057** Fred Ward/Black Star **1060** Corbis-Bettmann **1069** Black Star **1070** © R. Bossu/Sygma/Corbis **1073** Sygma/Corbis

CHAPTER 33

1076L-R Markel/Gamma-Liaison/Getty Images **1081** Martin Levick/Black Star **1083** © KTLA/Sygma/Corbis **1089** © The New Yorker Collection 1992 Dana Fradon from cartoonbank.com. All Rights Reserved. **1099** © Tom Horan/Sygma/Corbis **1102** King Features Syndicate **1106** Albert Facelly/Sipa Press **1110** © Paul Kregger/Sygma/Corbis **1113** © R. Trippett/Sipa Press

INDEX

ADDITIONAL TITLES
OF INTEREST

Note to Instructors: Any of these Penguin-Putnam, Inc., titles can be packaged with this book at a special discount. Contact your local Longman sales representative for details on how to create a Penguin-Putnam, Inc., Value Package.

Horatio Alger, Jr., *Ragged Dick & Struggling Upward*

Louis Auchincloss, *Woodrow Wilson*

Edward Bellamy, *Looking Backward*

Willa Cather, *O Pioneers!*

Alexis De Tocqueville, *Democracy in America*

Frederick Douglass, *Narrative of the Life of Frederick Douglass*

Gordon Hutner, *Immigrant Voices*

Martin Luther King, Jr., *Why We Can't Wait*

L. Jesse Lemisch (Editor), *Benjamin Franklin: The Autobiography & Other Writings*

Sinclair Lewis, *Babbitt*

Wendy Martin (Editor), *Colonial American Travel Narratives*

Toni Morrison, *Beloved*

Thomas Paine, *Common Sense*

Clinton Rossiter (Editor), *The Federalist Papers*

Upton Sinclair, *The Jungle*

Harriet Beecher Stowe, *Uncle Tom's Cabin*

Mark Twain, *Adventures of Huckleberry Finn*